Financial Accounting

A Business Process Approach

Second Edition

Jane L. Reimers

Rollins College, Crummer Graduate School of Business

PEARSON

Prentice Hall

Upper Saddle River, New Jersey 07458

Library of Congress Cataloging-in-Publication Data

Reimers, Jane L.
    Financial accounting : a business process approach / Jane L. Reimers. — 2nd ed.
        p. cm.
    Includes bibliographical references and index.
    ISBN 978-0-13-147386-7
    1. Accounting. 2. Financial statements. I. Title.
    HF5636.R45 2008
    657--dc22

                                                                2007014501

AVP/Executive Editor: Steve Sartori
Product Development Manager: Ashley Santora
Assistant Editor: Susan Abraham
Media Project Manager: Ashley Lulling
Senior Marketing Manager: Jodi Bassett
Marketing Assistant: Ian Gold
Associate Director, Production Editorial: Judy Leale
Senior Managing Editor: Cynthia Zonneveld
Senior Production Editor: Carol Samet
Permissions Coordinator: Charles Morris
Manufacturing Buyer: Michelle Klein
Design/Composition Manager: Christy Mahon
Composition Liaison: Suzanne Duda
Designer: Steven Frim
Interior Design: Judy Allen
Cover Design: Steven Frim
Cover Illustration/Photo: Fotosearch.com
Director, Image Resource Center: Melinda Patelli
Manager, Rights and Permissions: Zina Arabia
Manager, Visual Research: Beth Brenzel
Manager, Cover Visual Research & Permissions: Karen Sanatar
Image Permission Coordinator: Craig A. Jones
Composition: Carlisle Publishers Services
Full-Service Project Management: Carlisle Publishers Services
Printer/Binder: Courier/Kendallville
Typeface: 10/12 Times

Credits and acknowledgments borrowed from other sources and reproduced, with permission, in this textbook appear on appropriate page.

Credits: p. 216 Reprint Courtesy of International Business Machines Corporation, © copyright 2006; p. 241 Reprinted by permission of Barnes & Noble; pp. 352, 353 Used with permission from McDonald's Corporation; Used by permission of Wendy's; p. 385 Reprinted by permission of Linens N Things, Inc.; pp. 389, 401 Reprinted by permission of Papa Johns; p. 484 © Google Inc. Used with permission; pp. 485, 486 Used by permission of J&J Snack Foods Corp.; p. 541 Reprinted with permission of Staples; On-Line Appendix Reprinted with permission of Office Depot

Pearson Education LTD.
Pearson Education Singapore, Pte. Ltd.
Pearson Education Canada, Ltd.
Pearson Education—Japan

Pearson Education Australia PTY, Limited
Pearson Education North Asia Ltd.
Pearson Educación de Mexico, S. A. de C. V.
Pearson Education Malaysia, Pte. Ltd.

10 9 8 7 6 5 4 3 2 1
ISBN-13:   978-0-13-147386-7
ISBN-10:   0-13-147386-7

For my son

Brief Contents

Contents

Chapter 4   Acquisition and Use of Long-Term Operational Assets   153

Chapter 5   The Purchase and Sale of Inventory   209

Preface

Connecting Accounting to Business

One of the biggest challenges we face as accounting professors is motivating our students to learn accounting. There's no doubt that accounting is important to business, and the current events of the past few years have provided compelling examples. My approach to the first course in accounting is based on emphasizing the relationship between business and accounting.

Organized for Students

The topics are organized to match the way a business works. After introducing the basic accounting concepts using a small start-up company in Chapters 1–3, the book covers the traditional accounting topics—long-term assets, inventory, cash and accounts receivable, debt, and equity—in an order that matches how business works. Rather than relying on the balance sheet order, which makes no sense to students who are just learning about the balance sheet, this approach presents a business topic and then shows how we account for it. This is a subtle but important difference. The approach makes sense to students, so it provides an underlying motivation for students to learn about accounting. And it works!

Accounting Is for ALL Business Majors (and even many non-business majors)

With a focus on what a business does and less focus on bookkeeping, this approach helps all majors understand financial statements. It's not just for accounting majors! Although the mechanics of debits and credits are included in an appendix for professors who want to use this tool, the fundamental accounting equation and the path from business transactions to financial statements are at the heart of this approach. To be good users of financial statements, students must understand how the statements are prepared. Nothing teaches this as well as actually preparing the statements. Using a new color-coded accounting equation, students will be able to see exactly how business transactions are summarized and presented on each of the four basic financial statements.

> Review the inside front cover to see the color-coded accounting equation. This has proven to be extremely popular with students in the introductory course.

All of our students—both accounting and non-accounting majors—need to understand the basic relationship between business transactions and the financial statements. This approach provides a strong foundation for accounting majors while keeping the content relevant for all majors.

What's New in This Edition?

- **Color-coded accounting equations** throughout the book makes it easy for students to see how transactions flow into the financial statements.
- **Increased use of real-world companies** and their financial statements helps students see how accounting information is actually presented, preparing them for what they will encounter in the future.

- **Focus on Ethics** opens each chapter with a current relevant example of how important ethics is to accounting and business.
- **Ethics** has been added to each chapter's section on business risk and control (new section is Business Risk, Control, and Ethics).
- **Chapter summary points** are included at the end of each chapter.
- **Tom's Wear example, a continuing case, is integrated** into the chapters throughout the book.
- **A new summary problem** is included in each chapter.
- **A second set of exercises** is included in each chapter, and a new section on **Financial Statement Analysis** is included in the end-of-chapter material.

Supplements

Instructor's Manual

Each chapter of this comprehensive resource consists of a list of the student learning objectives, a narrative overview of main topics, an outline with teaching tips, a 10-problem multiple-choice quiz cross-referenced to the outline and arranged for easy copying, suggested readings, examples of ways to integrate supplements, and transparency masters. The Instructor's Manual is also available to adopters on the Instructor's Resource CD-ROM and online at **www.prenhall.com/reimers**.

Solutions Manual

Included are detailed solutions to all the end-of-chapter exercises, problems, and cases. This manual provides suggestions for alternative chapter sequences, a categorization of assignment material and check figures. The Solutions Manual is also available to adopters on the Instructor's Resource CD-ROM and online at **www.prenhall.com/reimers**.

Test Item File and TestGen

The printed **Test Item File** includes over 1,000 questions, including conceptual and quantitative multiple-choice exercises, true/false responses, critical thinking problems, and exercises. Each question will identify the difficulty level and the corresponding learning objective. **TestGen** testing software is an easy-to-use computerized testing program. It can create exams, evaluate, and track student results. All Test Item File questions are available in the TestGen format.

PowerPoint Slides

PowerPoint presentations are available for each chapter of the text. Instructors have the flexibility to add slides and/or modify the existing slides to meet course needs. The PowerPoint slides are also available to adopters on the Instructor's Resource CD-ROM and online at **www.prenhall.com/reimers**.

Instructor's Resource CD-ROM

The **Instructor CD** contains supplements on a single CD-ROM that include the Instructor's Resource Manual, Test Item File, TestGen, and PowerPoint slides. Enjoy the freedom to transport the entire package from office, to home, to classroom. The CD-ROM enables you to customize any of the ancillaries, print only the chapters or materials you wish to use, or access any item from the package within the classroom!

Instructor's Resource Center (http://www.prenhall.com/reimers)

This password-protected site is accessible from the catalog page for *Financial Accounting: A Business Process Approach, 2e* and hosts the same resources as the IRCD. For your convenience, they can be downloaded to your computer.

Companion Web Site (http://www.prenhall.com/reimers)

Our Web site offers an expansive array of internet-based support. Available to both students and instructors are: chapter objectives, online "Study Guide," Internet exercises, and "In the News," as well as other student resources.

Student Study Guide

This chapter-by-chapter learning aid systematically and effectively helps students study financial accounting and get the maximum benefit from their study time. Each chapter provides a chapter overview and a chapter review and review questions/exercises with solutions that best test the student's understanding of the material.

Acknowledgments

Instructors from colleges and universities across the country helped with the revision of *Financial Accounting: A Business Approach*. Their suggestions and comments were invaluable. All of the Prentice Hall people who worked on this edition also deserve special thanks. I am grateful to all of the following people for their help.

Loren Wenzel, Marshall University
Diane Tanner, University of North Florida
Joseph Morris, Southeastern Louisiana University
Cal Christian, East Carolina University
Donna Ulmer, St. Louis Community College at Meramec
Mary Ann Reynolds, Western Washington University
James Lukawitz, University of Memphis
Sharon Ford, Delta State University
Sheila Handy, Lafayette College
Patricia Lopez, Valencia Community College
Mary Ann Prater, Clemson University
Nancy Lynch, West Virginia University
Janice Mardon, Green River Community College

To the loyal users of the first edition of my book, your support of this book has made this revision possible. You have inspired me with your dedication to finding the best ways to teach introductory financial accounting. Special thanks to Nancy Lynch and Nancy Ruhe from the University of West Virginia who have given me extraordinary support with this book. I am also grateful to Carolyn Streuly, who has worked tirelessly on checking the accuracy of the book and the solutions, for her unbelievable attention to the details that are so important in an accounting text.

To my family and friends, including all of my colleagues at Rollins, thank you for all of the opportunities and support you have given me. I am grateful to a handful of special friends who have gone above and beyond anything I could expect from friends. You know who you are. Thank you.

Finally, to my son, thank you for all you have given me for over 30 years. I am so proud of the person you have grown to be. This book is for you.

Jane L. Reimers
Professor, Crummer Graduate School of Business
Rollins College

About the Author

In 2003, Jane Reimers joined the Crummer Graduate School of Business at Rollins College following 14 years at Florida State University, where she held the KPMG Professorship in Accounting. During her tenure there, she served as both department chair and as an associate dean for graduate programs. Before joining the FSU faculty, she taught in the MBA program at Duke University's Fuqua School of Business.

Professor Reimers grew up in the Orlando area, earning her bachelor's degree at the University of Florida and her master's degree at the University of Central Florida. She worked as a high school math teacher and as an auditor with a national accounting firm in Orlando before going on to the University of Michigan, where she earned a Ph.D. in accounting. At FSU, she won a University Teaching Award and has published research in the Journal of Accounting Research, The Accounting Review, Auditing: A Journal of Practice and Theory, Accounting Horizons, Decision Sciences, and Accounting, Organizations and Society.

Business: What's It All About?

When you finish studying Chapter 1, you should understand what a business does and how the financial statements reflect information about business transactions.

Learning Objectives

When you are finished studying this chapter, you should be able to:

1. Describe what a business does and the various ways a business can be organized.

2. Classify business transactions as operating, investing, or financing activities.

3. Describe who uses accounting information and why accounting information is important to them.

4. Identify the elements and explain the purpose of the four basic financial statements and be able use basic transaction analysis to prepare each statement—the income statement, the statement of changes in shareholders' equity, the balance sheet, and the statement of cash flows.

5. Identify the elements of a real company's financial statements.

6. Describe the risks associated with being in business and the part that ethics plays in business.

Ethics Matters

When you are asked to do something you believe may be unethical, ask yourself the following questions: (1) Is it legal? (2) Will it harm anyone? (3) Would you mind reading about your decision in the morning newspaper?

In 2005, a documentary called "The Smartest Guys in the Room" was nominated for an Academy Award. It is the story of the rise and fall of Enron, the energy giant that filed for bankruptcy in 2001. Although the symptoms of the scandal were fraudulent financial statements and accounting failures, at the heart of Enron's failure was a lack of ethics. The unethical decisions and actions of some of Enron's managers and executives paved the way for one of the largest bankruptcies in U.S. history. In May 2006, Enron's founder, Ken Lay, and CEO Jeffrey Skilling were both found guilty of conspiring to defraud shareholders. In July 2006, Ken Lay died before he could be sentenced. In October 2006, Jeff Skilling was sentenced to 24 years in prison.

Photo of Bernie Ebbers
testifying before Congress . . . . .

Have you ever heard of Enron? WorldCom? Sarbanes-Oxley? Much of the business press in the past few years has focused on the Sarbanes-Oxley Act of 2002. The law was motivated by the financial scandals and business failures—such as Enron and WorldCom—in the early part of the decade. The U.S. Congress felt the need to pass new business regulations to help restore confidence in the capital markets. No respectable businessperson can remain ignorant about this law and its relationship to accounting. In the investigation and trial of Bernard Ebbers, the former CEO of WorldCom, Ebbers was quoted as saying that he did not know finance and he did not know accounting. His conviction and long prison sentence tell us that this is no longer acceptable. Everyone in business must know something about accounting.

Do you think accounting is important? Anyone who has a television or reads a newspaper is reminded almost every day of the importance of accounting. Now more than ever, it is crucial for people in business to understand basic accounting. In this chapter, you will start with a simple business to learn the basic ideas of how a business works and why the financial reporting for a business is so important to its success. As you learn about accounting, you will understand more and more about what has been happening in companies such as Enron, Xerox, Tyco, HealthSouth, Adelphia, and others that have been caught "cooking the books." Before you can understand how and why these companies are cooking the books, you must learn about the "books"—a company's accounting records—and about financial statements. But even before that, you must understand what business is all about.

L.O. 1
Describe what a business does and the various ways a business can be organized.

Purpose and Organization of a Business

Tom Phillips loved to play basketball. He also wanted to start his own business. One day he had an inspiration that put both ideas together—T-shirts for casual players like himself, not for players on a team. Tom polled the friends he played with regularly; they all liked the idea, agreeing that they would buy such a T-shirt, perhaps with a "no-look" pass on it, if it were available. Six years after Tom had this idea, he is president of a successful company, Tom's Wear, with sales last year of $15 million.

How does a business get started and, once started, how does it succeed? Generally, a business is formed to provide goods or services for the purpose of making a profit for its owner or owners. It begins by obtaining financial resources—and that means money. Tom's Wear began as a business with $5,000 of Tom's own money and a $500 loan from his mother. The financial resources to start a business—called **capital**—come from the owners of the business (like Tom), who are investors, or from creditors (like Tom's mom), who are lenders.

Capital is the name for the resources used to start and run a business.

Why buy a T-shirt from Tom rather than from the manufacturer of plain T-shirts? It's all about value. We order clothes from Lands' End because the company provides added value to us. Instead of going to the mall to buy our clothes, we may prefer the convenience of mail-order delivery. Lands' End customers find value in this service. What all businesses have in common is that they provide their customers with something of value. A business may start from scratch and create something of value or it may simply add value to an existing product or service. For some customers, the value that Lands' End adds to the product may be its easy order and delivery procedures. For other customers, the added value may be in the monogram the company will put on shirts or towels to personalize them. Businesses create or add value to earn money for the owners.

An enterprise—another name for a business organization—with this goal is called a **for-profit firm**. In contrast, a firm that provides goods or services for the sole purpose of helping people instead of making a profit is called a **not-for-profit organization**. A not-for-profit organization is more likely to be called an organization or agency than a business. Even though it is called not-for-profit, this type of organization does not mind making a profit. The difference is that a not-for-profit organization uses any profit to provide more goods and services to the people it serves rather than distributing profits to its owners. Both for-profit organizations and not-for-profit organizations provide value. Throughout this book, we will be dealing primarily with for-profit organizations—businesses.

To be a viable business, Tom's Wear needed to provide customers with something of value. Tom purchased T-shirts with his special logo and then provided them to his customers.

> A **for-profit firm** has the goal of making a profit for its owners.

> A **not-for-profit firm** has the goal of providing goods or services to its clients.

What Is Business All About?

A simple model of the firm is shown in Exhibit 1.1. The inputs in a firm include capital, equipment, inventory, supplies, and labor. The firm acquires goods and services and pays for them. The firm then takes these inputs and converts them into outputs by adding value. The outputs of a firm are its products or services. As the firm carries out these activities—acquiring inputs, converting them to outputs, and providing those outputs to customers—information about these activities is recorded in the company's information system. Both insiders—the owners and the firm's employees—and outsiders—the creditors, governmental agencies, and potential investors—use the information.

A business must successfully plan, control, and evaluate its activities. If it does these activities well, the business will survive. If it does them very well, it will make a profit. Profit is the difference between the revenue—the amount a business earns for the goods it sells or the services it provides—and the expenses of selling those goods or providing those services. The complexity of a company's planning, control, and evaluation processes depends on the type, size, and structure of the business. You will see this as we look at businesses in two ways: the nature of their operations and who owns them.

The Nature of Business Operations

The operation of a business depends on what the business has been formed to do. From that perspective, there are four types of businesses: service, merchandising, manufacturing, and financial services. Although most businesses can be classified as one of these four types, many large businesses are a combination of two or more.

A **service company** provides a service—it does something for you, rather than sells something to you. Services range from activities you cannot see, such as the advice provided by lawyers or tax consultants, to activities you can see, such as house cleaning or car washing. During the past two decades, our economy has been producing more services than goods. Google is an example of a service firm.

> A **service company** does something for its customers;

INPUTS		OUTPUTS
Capital, Financing Property, Plant, Equipment Raw Materials Labor Inventory Goods & Services	Value-added conversion →	Product or Service

EXHIBIT 1.1

The Firm
A firm takes inputs, adds value, and provides the output to its customers.

Target is an example of a retail firm. It buys goods and sells them to the final consumer.

A **merchandising** company sells a product to its customers.

A **merchandising** company buys goods, adds value to them, and then sells them with the added value. It does not make the goods, and it does not buy them to use. Instead, a merchandising business buys the goods for the purpose of adding its own particular value to them and, after adding value, sells them to another company or person.

There are two types of merchandising companies:

- a wholesale company, which buys goods, adds value, and sells them to other companies
- a retail company, which buys goods, adds value, and sells them to customers who consume them—which is why you will see these customers referred to as "final consumers"

Both wholesale and retail merchandising companies add value to the goods they buy. Wholesale companies are not familiar to us because we do not buy things from them. Prentice Hall, the publisher of this text, for example, sells textbooks to your school's bookstore. When you need a book, you go to the bookstore—a retail business—to buy it. You do not go to the wholesale company, Prentice Hall. You do not care what business transactions take place to get the book from the factory, where it is printed and the covers are put on, to the bookstore. At the bookstore, the books are provided along with thousands of others, but in a way that you can immediately and conveniently purchase the one or two books you need. The bookstore is an example of a retailer. Retail store is widely used to describe the companies we find in every shopping mall.

A **manufacturing** company makes the goods it sells.

A **manufacturing** company makes the products it sells. Manufacturing companies vary in size and complexity. Making clay pots and vases in a space not larger than a garage is a manufacturing business. Automobile giants such as Ford and General Motors, owned by many thousands of people and employing hundreds of thousands of workers at all levels in enormous factories all over the world, are large, complex, manufacturing businesses.

Financial services companies deal in services related to money.

Financial services companies do not make tangible products, and they do not sell products made by another company. They deal in services related to money. Banks are one kind of financial services company; they lend money to borrowers to pay for cars, houses, and furniture. Another type of financial services company is an insurance company, which provides some financial protection in the case of loss of life or property.

Your Turn 1-1
Your Turn
Your Turn

1. **What is the main purpose of a business?**
2. **Describe the four general types of businesses and what each does.**

Ownership Structure of a Business

No matter what type of product or service it provides, a business must have an owner or owners. The government owns some businesses, but in the United States, an individual or a group of individuals owns most businesses. Business ownership generally takes one of three general forms: a sole proprietorship, a partnership, or a corporation.

UNDERSTANDING **Business**

Starting A New Business: The Business Plan

Have you ever considered starting your own business? According to the Small Business Administration (SBA), "Small Business by the Numbers," June 2004, small businesses—those with fewer than 100 employees—

- represent more than 99.7% of all employers
- employ half of all private-sector workers and 39% of workers in high-tech jobs
- provide 60% to 80% of the net new jobs annually

The SBA was established by Congress in 1953 to assist small businesses. In addition to the many contributions SBA makes to ongoing businesses, the SBA provides information and guidance for starting a business. It all starts with a business plan. The SBA describes four sections to be included in the body of the business plan: the business description, the financial management plan, the management plan, and a marketing plan.

The business description is the foundation for the rest of the business plan. It should give the form of your business enterprise—a sole proprietorship, a partnership, or a corporation. The business description should also describe the nature of your business—manufacturing, merchandising, or service. Then, more specific details should be explained—goals and objectives, operating procedures, location, personnel, marketing, licenses and insurance, and financing plans.

Once the business description is completed, the focus shifts to specific items for the next three sections.

A financial management plan, including a start-up budget and an operating budget, must be prepared in detail. The financial statements are prepared based on the budgets. The financial statements are a significant part of a business plan.

The management plan addresses the functioning of business operations. Strengths and weaknesses of the personnel and the business as a whole should be assessed. Once identified, potential problems can be addressed and solved. To succeed as a business, management's goal should be to keep the employees and customers happy.

Finally, the marketing plan must be created. The marketing plan is designed to attract and keep customers. By identifying and getting to know the sector of the market you want to serve, you can appeal to its wants and needs. Such characteristics as age, sex, income, and educational levels of potential customers can help you prepare a marketing plan to develop a customer base.

A good business plan is essential for starting a successful company. For more information on the SBA and creating a business plan, visit the SBA Web site at www.sbaonline.sba.gov/.

Sole Proprietorships. If a single person owns a business, like the clay pot maker in his garage, it is a **sole proprietorship**. A new business often starts as a sole proprietorship. In the course of running the business, a sole proprietorship accumulates financial information—such as the cost of materials, equipment, rent, electricity, and income from sales—but is not required by law to make any of that financial information available to the public. That means the average person is not privy to this information. Naturally, the Department of Revenue in the states where the company operates will receive some of this information from the company's sales tax return.

> A **sole proprietorship** is a company with a single owner.

A business in the form of a sole proprietorship is not separate from its owner in terms of responsibility and liability—the owner is personally responsible for all the decisions made for the business. For example, the income from the business is included as income on the owner's individual income tax return. The business does not have its own tax return.

Also, as a sole proprietor, you are responsible for your company's debts. Your company's bills are your bills; if there is not enough money in your company's "pockets" to pay its bills, then you must pay the bills from your pockets. Moreover, you own the company's assets, and your personal assets are the company's assets—even if those personal assets are the only way of paying your company's bills.

Even though the financial records of a business—the company's books—should always be kept separate from the owner's personal financial records, there is no separation of the sole proprietorship's books and its owner's books for tax and legal purposes. For example, your business checking account should be separate from your personal checking account, but the income you earn from your business and the income you earn from other sources must both be included on your individual, personal tax return.

You will see in Exhibit 1.2 that there are more sole proprietorships in the United States than any other form of business. Notice, however, that profits for sole proprietorships do not come close to the enormous profits earned by corporations.

Partnerships.   A business **partnership** is owned by two or more people, although it is similar to a sole proprietorship in the sense that the income both partners earn (or lose) from the business partnership is included on their own personal tax returns. When two or more people form a business as partners, they usually hire an attorney to help them define the specific terms of their business relationship. Details regarding how much work each will do and how they will divide the profits from the business are specified in a document called a partnership agreement. Like a sole proprietorship, the owners—each of the partners—are responsible for everything the company does. For example, if the company is sued for violating an employee's civil rights, then the partners are legally liable. The company's assets are the partners' assets, and the company's debts are the partners' debts. Even so, as with a

> A **partnership** is a company owned by two or more individuals.

EXHIBIT 1.2

Types of Firms and Their Profits

Although over two-thirds of U.S. firms are sole proprietorships, more than two-thirds of firm profits are made by corporations.
Source: Internal Revenue Service Web site (www.irs.gov)

Types of Firms

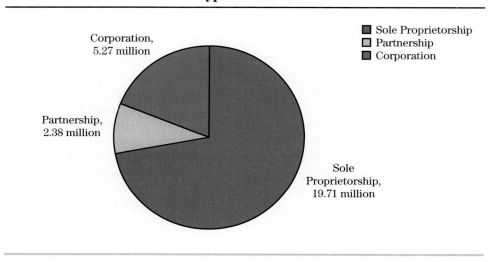

Corporation, 5.27 million

Partnership, 2.38 million

Sole Proprietorship, 19.71 million

- Sole Proprietorship
- Partnership
- Corporation

Profits by Type of Firm

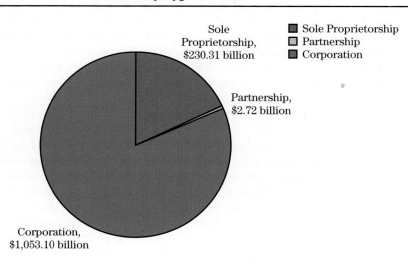

Sole Proprietorship, $230.31 billion

Partnership, $2.72 billion

Corporation, $1,053.10 billion

- Sole Proprietorship
- Partnership
- Corporation

sole proprietorship, the financial records of a partnership should be separate from the partners' personal financial records.

Corporations. A **corporation** is legally separate and financially separate from its owners. Individual states control the rules for forming corporations within their boundaries. A company must have a corporate charter that describes the business, how the business plans to acquire financing, and how many owners it will be allowed to have. Ownership in a corporation is divided into units called **shares of common stock**, each representing ownership in a fraction of the corporation. An owner of shares of stock in a corporation is called a **stockholder** or a **shareholder**. Most corporations have many shareholders, although there is no minimum number of owners required. A corporation whose shares of stock are owned by a very small number of people is called a closely held corporation.

> A **corporation** is a special legal form for a business in which the business is a legal entity separate from the owners. A corporation may have a single owner or a large number of owners.

As legal entities, corporations may enter into contracts just like individuals. A corporation pays taxes on its earnings. A corporation's owners do not include the corporation's income in their personal tax returns—unlike the owner of a sole proprietorship or the partners in a partnership. Each individual corporation owner does not have individual legal responsibility for the corporation's actions, as is true for the owners of a sole proprietorship or partnership. For example, a shareholder cannot be sued for the illegal actions of the corporation. The managers are held responsible for the actions of the corporation, and only the corporation's assets are at risk.

> **Shares of common stock** are the units of ownership in a corporation.

> **Stockholders** or **shareholders** are the owners of the corporation.

Dell Inc. is one of America's best-known corporations. Dell was founded in 1984 by Michael Dell, currently the computer industry's longest-tenured chief executive officer, on this simple concept: By selling computers directly to customers, Dell could get a clear picture of its customers' needs and then efficiently provide the most effective products to meet those needs. The company has offered new shares of stock to anyone who is able and willing to invest in the company by making them available for sale on a stock exchange. A **stock exchange** is a marketplace for buying and selling shares of a publicly traded corporation.

> A **stock exchange** —also called the **stock market** —is a marketplace where buyers and sellers exchange their shares of stock. Buying and selling shares of stock can also be done on the Internet.

After the shares are issued—sold for the first time to the public—investors who want to become owners of a corporation may purchase the shares from people who want to sell the same shares. The buyers and sellers get together, usually through a stockbroker, by using a stock exchange. Stockbrokers represent people who want to buy shares and the people who want to sell shares of a corporation. Stockbrokers work for firms such as Merrill Lynch and Charles Schwab. There are several stock exchanges—known collectively as the **stock market**—in the United States; the New York Stock Exchange is the largest. If you wanted to be one of the owners of Dell Corporation, you could purchase shares by contacting a stockbroker.

Another way to buy or sell shares of stock—also known as trading—is to use the Internet. Many companies now provide a way for investors to buy and sell stock without a stockbroker. As Internet usage continues to grow at an incredible pace, more and more people are taking advantage of electronic trading in shares of stock.

Regulation Shareholders usually hire people who are not owners of the corporation to manage the business of the corporation. This separation of ownership and management can create problems. For example, there may be a large number of owners, and they may be far away from the location of the business. How can the owners be sure that the managers are running the corporation the way the owners want it to be run? How do the owners monitor the managers to be sure they are not taking advantage of the power of being a manager of a large company, for example, buying expensive items like country club memberships and luxury cars for the business?

To protect the owners with respect to issues like these, the government created the **Securities and Exchange Commission (SEC)** to monitor the activities and financial reporting of corporations that sell shares of ownership on the stock exchanges. The SEC sets the rules for stock exchanges and for the financial reporting of publicly traded corporations for the entire United States. The degree of regulation for corporations depends on the size and nature of the business. A business that provides an essential product or service, such as electric power generating companies, has more rules to follow than a business that provides something not essential, but discretionary, such as toys. Large companies have more rules than smaller companies because large companies provide more opportunities for managers to take advantage of the owners.

> The **Securities and Exchange Commission (SEC)** is the governmental agency that monitors the stock market and the financial reporting of the firms that trade in the market.

Advantages of a Corporation Advantages of the corporate structure of a business organization include:

■ Investors can diversify their financial risk. Being able to buy a small share in a variety of corporations means that persons are able to balance the risks they are taking as business owners. For example, an investor may own shares in a soft drink company and also own shares in a coffee company. If coffee companies have a bad year due to a shortage of coffee beans, people will be likely to buy more soft drinks. By owning a little of each type of company, an investor reduces overall risk.

■ Owners have limited liability. Individual owners risk only the amount of money they have invested in the company. That is the amount they paid for the shares of stock. If the corporation is found legally responsible for injury to an employee or customer, or if the business fails, only the corporation's assets are at risk—not the owner's personal property. (In contrast, there is no limit to the legal liability of a sole proprietor or a partner. Both the assets of the business and the personal assets of the owner or owners are at risk.)

Disadvantages of a Corporation Disadvantages of the corporate structure of a business organization include:

■ Separation of management and ownership creates a difference in knowledge about the operations of the business. Suppose you own 100 shares of Dell Corporation stock. The managers of Dell will know many details of the business that you do not know. For example, the managers are aware of all possible investment options for the company's extra cash. They may select the option that minimizes clerical work, whereas an owner might prefer an option that involves more work but would secure a higher return.

There are literally thousands of such details that owners do not know, many of which they do not even want to know. However, the owners want some assurance that managers are acting in the best interests of the shareholders. Owners need information about how well the business is doing to assess how the actions and decisions of the managers are affecting the business. The owners need some assurance that managers are providing complete and accurate information about the business. Both the individual states and the SEC at the federal level set rules for the financial reporting of corporations. A corporation's type of busi-

WHAT IS A LIMITED LIABILITY PARTNERSHIP (LLP)?

WHAT IS A LIMITED LIABILITY CORPORATION (LLC)?

In the past 10 years, some new business forms with characteristics of a partnership and characteristics of a corporation have become commonplace. Both LLPs and LLCs have the tax advantages of a partnership and the legal liability advantages of a corporation.

An LLP is a business form mostly of interest to partners in professions such as law, medicine, and accounting. An LLP's owners—who are the partners—are not personally liable for the malpractice of the other partners. They are personally liable for many types of obligations owed to the LLP's creditors, lenders, and landlords. Owners of an LLP report their share of profit or loss on their personal tax returns. The LLP form of business organization is not available in all states, and it is often limited to a short list of professions—usually attorneys and accountants. You will notice that the four largest international accounting firms have all taken this organizational form. The letters LLP will appear after the firm's name.

An LLC is a corporation that has characteristics of a partnership. It has the advantage of limited liability like a regular corporation with the tax advantage of a partnership. It generally requires less paperwork and documentation than a regular corporation.

ness and its size determine how extensive its reporting requirements are. We will come back to this subject many times throughout our discussions of financial accounting.

■ Corporate income is taxed twice. Unlike a sole proprietorship or partnership, a corporation pays income taxes on its net income. After that net income (or at least a part of it) is divided by the number of shareholders of the corporation and distributed among shareholders as **dividends**, the shareholders must include the dividend income on their personal tax returns. This amounts to double taxation on the same income. The income of the corporation—which is owned by shareholders—is taxed as corporation income, and then the amount passed on to owners as dividend income is again taxed, as personal income. (Current tax laws do allow some exemption for dividend income to the shareholder, so this disadvantage can be reduced by a change in the tax law.)

> **Dividends** are the earnings of a corporation distributed to the owners of the corporation.

---

1. **What are the different forms of business ownership?**
2. **From the owners' point of view, what are the advantages and disadvantages of each form of ownership?**

Your Turn 1-2
Your Turn
Your Turn

Business Activities and the Flow of Goods and Services

> **L.O. 2**
> Classify business transactions as operating, investing, or financing activities.

A person who takes the risk of starting a business is often called an entrepreneur. Our entrepreneur, Tom, started a T-shirt business. Exhibit 1.3 shows the events for Tom's Wear that followed. Identifying those events and analyzing the transactions are the first steps in understanding how a business works.

We can classify each step in the process of developing a business in terms of exchanges—who gets what and who gives what in return. One of the important functions of accounting is to provide information about these economic exchanges, also known as business transactions. In accounting, we often classify transactions as operating activities, investing activities, or financing activities. Operating activities are transactions related to the general operations of a firm—what the firm is in business to do. Investing activities are transactions related to buying and selling items that the firm will use for longer than a year. Financing activities are those that deal with how a business gets it funding—how it obtains the capital needed to finance the business.

The first exchange starts the business—Tom invests his own $5,000 in the business. From the perspective of the business, this is called a contribution. It is often called **contributed capital**. As with all transactions, we look at this from the point of view of the business entity. This transaction is the exchange of cash for ownership in the business. Because this transaction deals with the way Tom's Wear is financed, it is classified as a financing transaction.

> **Contributed capital** is an owner's investment in a company.

You may need to think about it to see the *give* part of this exchange—it is the business giving ownership to Tom. Because Tom has chosen to organize his business firm as a corporation, this share of ownership is called stock. For a sole proprietorship or a partnership, the ownership has no special name. Tom has chosen the corporate form of organization because of the limited legal liability of a corporation. The *get* part of the exchange is the business getting the $5,000 cash. Because Tom is the only shareholder, he owns 100% of the stock.

EXHIBIT 1.3

How a Business Works

These business transactions show Tom's Wear's first month of business.

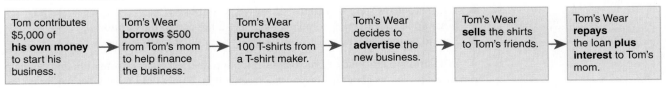

The second transaction is between Tom's Wear and Tom's mother. The business borrows $500 from her. Tom's Wear gets an economic resource—cash—and in exchange Tom's Wear gives an I-owe-you (IOU). From the perspective of Tom's Wear, this transaction involves a cash receipt. Borrowing money to finance a business is the get side of the exchange. The give side is the IOU to Mom. Technically, it is not really the give side until Tom repays the loan with cash. The IOU is useful for describing the timing difference between the time of the get and give sides of the exchange. We will see a lot of examples of this type of timing difference in accounting for business events. Again, this transaction is a financing activity.

The next transaction is the company's purchase of 100 T-shirts with a unique logo on them. The get part of the exchange is when Tom's Wear gets the shirts for the inventory. The give part of the exchange is when Tom's Wear gives cash to the T-shirt manufacturer. Remember, the exchange is seen through the eyes of Tom's Wear. The transaction would look different if we took the perspective of the T-shirt manufacturer. In business problems, we take one point of view throughout a problem or an analysis. This transaction is an operating activity.

The next transaction is the acquisition of a service. The economic resources exchanged in this transaction are advertising and cash. The get part is the acquisition or purchase of advertising. The give part is a cash disbursement transaction. Again, this is an operating activity.

Tom's Wear now sells the T-shirts, exchanging T-shirts for cash. Once again, the activity is an operating activity, precisely what Tom's Wear is in business to do—sell T-shirts.

Finally, Tom's Wear repays the $500 loan from Tom's mother plus interest. The company gives the economic resource of cash (amount of the loan, called the **principal**, plus **interest**, a cost of borrowing the money) to Tom's mom. Recall that the actual get part of this exchange occurred near the beginning of our story. The second transaction was when Tom's Wear took the cash, as a loan, from his mom. The IOU was a sort of marker, indicating that there would be a timing difference in the get and give parts of this transaction. Repayment of the principal of a loan is a financing activity. Repayment of interest, on the other hand, is considered an operating activity.

> The **principal** of a loan is the amount of money borrowed.

> The **interest** is the cost of borrowing that money—using someone else's money.

Your Turn 1-3
Your Turn
Your Turn

1. **What are the two sources of financing for a business, both used by Tom's Wear?**
2. **What do you call the cost of using someone else's money?**

L.O. 3
Describe who uses accounting information and why accounting information is important to them.

Information Needs for Decision Making in Business

To start a new business, Tom had many decisions to make. First, how would he finance it? What organizational form should it take? How many T-shirts should he buy? From whom should he buy them? How much should he pay for advertising? How much should he charge for the shirts?

After the first complete operating cycle, shown in Exhibit 1.4—beginning with cash, converting cash to inventory, selling the inventory, and turning inventory sales back into cash—Tom has more decisions to make. Should he buy T-shirts and do the whole thing again? If so, should he buy more T-shirts than he bought the first time and from the same vendor? To make these decisions, Tom must have information. The kind of information usually provided by accountants will provide the basis for getting a good picture of the performance of his business.

> **Revenue** is the amount the company has earned from providing goods or services to customers.

> **Expenses** are the costs incurred to generate revenue.

- What was **revenue** from sales during the accounting period? An accounting period is any length of time that a company uses to evaluate its operating performance. It can be a month, a quarter, or a year.
- What **expenses** were incurred so those sales could be made?
- What goods does Tom's company have left at the end of the period?
- Should he increase the price of the T-shirts he sells or lower the price?

In addition to this kind of financial information, there is other information that can help Tom make decisions about his business. For example, Tom would want information on the

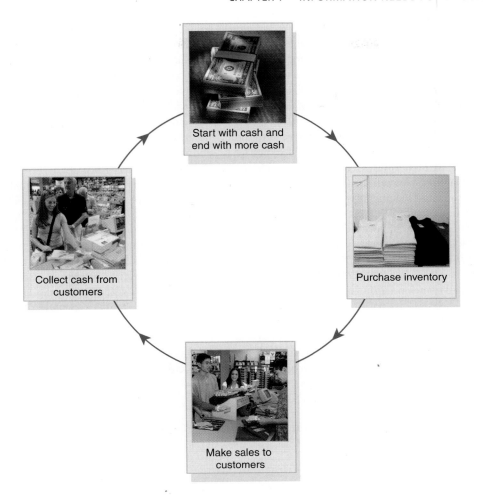

EXHIBIT 1.4

The Operating Cycle
The operating cycle shows how a firm starts with cash and, after providing goods to its customers, ends up with more cash.

reliability of different vendors and the quality of their merchandise to decide which vendor to use next time. Before the advances in computer technology that have enabled us to collect, organize, and report huge quantities of information besides financial information, a company had only the basic financial information to help make its business decisions. Today, financial information is just a part of a firm's information system.

A modern supermarket is a great example of a business that collects a tremendous amount of information. With a simple, swift swipe of the grocery item bar code past the checkout scanner, the store information system collects product data, recording and tracking information about vendors, product shelf life, customer preferences and buying habits, and the usual, typical financial information such as price and quantity of each item sold. As we look at business processes and the information needed to run a business, we will pay attention to the information reflected in the basic financial statements—the income statement, the balance sheet, the statement of changes in shareholders' equity, and the statement of cash flows. You will learn more about each of these statements soon.

1. **What are revenues and expenses?**
2. **What are the four basic financial statements?**

Your Turn 1-4
Your Turn
Your Turn

Who Needs Information About Transactions of the Business?

No part of any business can operate without information. The functions of the management of a company are to plan, to control, and to evaluate the operation of the business. To perform these functions effectively, management must have information about what the business has done, about what it is currently doing, and about where it looks like it is going or should be going. Traditionally, the accounting information system has provided only very general data about the past transactions of a business firm. A business firm used to keep two sets of records, each for specific purposes: one set for financial reporting and one set for internal decision making. Now, with modern computers and software that can organize information in a variety of ways with a few simple commands, one information system can accumulate and organize all data of a company. The managers of each business area—usually referred to as a department—can obtain and use whatever information is relevant to the decisions they make. Accountants, too, can obtain the information they need for preparing the basic financial statements.

The financial statements are based on a set of guidelines called **generally accepted accounting principles (GAAP)**. These guidelines are not exact rules. As you learn more about accounting, you will see that the amounts on the financial statements are not exact. To make the financial statements useful, we need to understand the guidelines and the choices used to construct them. Who sets the guidelines for financial reporting? As shown in Exhibit 1.5, at the top of the authority chain is the Securities and Exchange Commission (SEC). In the 1930s, Congress established the SEC to set the rules for corporations that trade on the public stock exchanges. The SEC has delegated much of the responsibility for setting financial standards to an independent group called the **Financial Accounting Standards Board (FASB)**. This is a group of professional business people, accountants, and accounting scholars who have the responsibility of setting current accounting standards. Accounting standards dictate the way business events are reported, so it makes sense that businesses are very interested in what the FASB does. The newest player in the rule-setting game is a group called the **Public Company Accounting Oversight Board (PCAOB)**. Mandated by the Sarbanes-Oxley Act in 2002, this independent board was created to oversee the auditing profession and public company audits.

Generally accepted accounting principles (GAAP) are the guidelines for financial reporting.

The **Financial Accounting Standards Board (FASB)** is the group that sets accounting standards. It gets its authority from the SEC.

The **Public Company Accounting Oversight Board (PCAOB)** is a group formed to oversee the auditing profession and the audits of public companies. Its creation was mandated by the Sarbanes-Oxley Act of 2002.

EXHIBIT 1.5

Who Sets the Guidelines for Financial Reporting?

The U.S. Congress established the Securities and Exchange Commission (SEC) in 1934. Auditing standards are set by the Public Company Oversight Board (PCAOB), and accounting standards (GAAP) are set by the Financial Accounting Standards Board (FASB).

Securities and Exchange Commission (SEC)

Public Company Accounting Oversight Board (PCAOB)

In response to the 2001–2002 discovery of accounting scandals, the SEC created the PCAOB to oversee the auditing profession and the audit of public companies.

Financial Accounting Standards Board (FASB)

The SEC has delegated much of the standards-setting responsibility to the FASB. The SEC retains and sometimes exercises the right to set accounting standards.

In many industries, there are regulatory agencies that require specific information from companies, particularly corporations. For example, the SEC requires corporations that trade on the stock exchanges to file many different kinds of reports about the company's transactions. We will come back to this topic near the end of the chapter when we turn our attention to real company financial statements.

For all businesses, payroll taxes and sales taxes must be reported and paid to state revenue agencies. The **Internal Revenue Service (IRS)** requires information from businesses concerning income and expenses, even if the income from the business flows through to the owners as it does for sole proprietorships and partnerships.

When a company wants to borrow money, creditors—the people and firms who lend money—require information about the company before they will lend money. Banks want to be sure that the loans they make will be repaid. The creditworthiness—a term indicating that a borrower has in the past made loan payments when due (or failed to make them when due)—of a business must be supported with information about the business. This information is usually very specific and very detailed.

Who else needs information about the business? Potential investors are information consumers. Suppose Tom wanted to find additional owners for his T-shirt business. That means he would be looking for someone who wanted to invest money in his T-shirt business in return for a portion of ownership in the company. A potential owner would want some reliable information about the business before making a financial investment. Publicly traded corporations—whose shares are traded on the stock exchanges—invite anyone willing and financially able to become an owner by offering for sale shares of stock in the corporation. Buying the stock of a corporation is investing in that corporation. Investors want information about a company before they will buy that company's stock. The SEC requires that the information provided by companies whose stock is publicly traded be accurate and reliable. That means the information in their financial statements must be audited. Audited information means it has been examined by professional accountants, called **certified public accountants (CPAs)**. We will talk more about that when we turn our attention to real company financial statements.

Finally, current and potential vendors, customers, and employees also need useful information about the company. They need to evaluate a company's financial condition to make decisions about working for, or doing business with, the company.

Accounting Information: A Part of the Firm's Information System

Have you ever filed an address change with a company only to find later that one department uses your new address while another department of that same company continues to use your old address? Even with such common data as customer names and addresses, the information is often gathered and maintained in several different places within the same organization. As computers and databases become more common, central data information systems are replacing departmental systems and eliminating their inefficiencies.

Because accountants have traditionally been the recorders and maintainers of financial information, it makes sense that they have expanded their role as the keepers of business information systems to include more than financial information. The cost of obtaining business information has decreased rapidly in the past few years. The financial accounting information a company reports is now just a part of the total available business information. The accounting information is provided in four basic financial statements and supporting notes.

Overview of the Financial Statements

There are four financial statements a company uses to report its financial condition and operations for a period of time.

1. Balance sheet
2. Income statement
3. Statement of changes in shareholders' equity
4. Statement of cash flows

The **Internal Revenue Service (IRS)** is the federal agency responsible for federal income tax collection.

A **certified public accountant (CPA)** is someone who has met specific education and exam requirements set up by individual states to make sure that only individuals with the appropriate qualifications can perform audits. To sign an audit report, an accountant must be a CPA.

L.O. 4
Identify the elements and explain the purpose of the four basic financial statements, and be able to prepare each statement—the income statement, the statement of changes in shareholders' equity, the balance sheet, and the statement of cash flows.

Notes to the financial statements are information provided with the four basic statements that describes the company's major accounting policies and provide other disclosures to help external users better understand the financial statements.

The balance sheet shows the accounting equation in detail. The statement shows:

Assets —economic resources owned or controlled by the business.

Liabilities —obligations of the business to creditors.

Shareholders' equity —the owner's claims to the assets of the company. There are two types: contributed capital and retained earnings.

A company's set of financial statements includes these four basic statements as well as an important section called **notes to the financial statements**. These notes, sometimes referred to as *footnotes*, are an integral part of the set of financial statements. The notes describe the company's major accounting policies and provide other disclosures to help external users better understand the financial statements. As you learn about the four statements, remember that you will be able to find additional information about each in the notes.

In this chapter, we will look at each financial statement briefly. Later chapters will go into each in detail.

Balance Sheet

A **balance sheet** describes the financial situation of a company at a specific point in time. It is a snapshot that captures the items of value the business possesses at a particular moment and how the company has financed them. A balance sheet has three parts:

- assets
- liabilities
- shareholders' equity

Assets are things of value owned or controlled by a business. Cash and equipment are common assets. When a business has an asset, someone has the rights to, that is, a claim to, that asset. There is a claim on every asset in a business. There are two groups who might have claims to a company's assets—creditors and owners.

The claims of creditors are called liabilities. **Liabilities** are amounts the business owes to others outside the business, those who have loaned money to the company and have not yet been fully repaid. For example, the amount of a loan—like your car loan—is a liability.

The claims of the owner are called **shareholders' equity**. Stockholders' equity and owners' equity are other names for the claims of the owners. Shareholders' equity is also called net assets because it is the amount left over after the amount of the liabilities is subtracted from the amount of the assets, or liabilities are netted out of assets.

There are two ways for the owners to increase their claims to the assets of the business. One is by making contributions, and the other is by earning it. When the business is successful, the equity that results from doing business and is kept in the company is called **retained earnings**. We will see the difference between contributed capital and retained earnings more clearly when we go through the first month of business for Tom's Wear.

Together, assets, liabilities, and shareholders' equity make up the balance sheet, one of the four basic financial statements. The following relationship, called the accounting equation, is the basis for the balance sheet:

$$\text{Assets} = \overbrace{\text{Claims}}$$
$$\text{Assets} = \text{Liabilities} + \text{Shareholders' equity}$$

Each transaction that takes place in a business can be recorded in the accounting equation, which is the basis of the balance sheet. In other words, every transaction is changing the balance sheet; but the balance sheet must stay in balance. Look at the transactions for Tom's Wear for January and see how each one changes the balance sheet.

Date	Transaction
January 1	Tom contributes $5,000 of his own money to start the business in exchange for common stock.
January 1	Tom's Wear borrows $500 from Tom's mom for the business.
January 5	Tom's Wear buys 100 T-shirts for $400 cash.
January 10	Tom's Wear pays a public relations firm $50 cash for advertising.
January 20	Tom's Wear sells 90 of the T-shirts to Tom's friends for $10 each (cash).
January 30	Tom's Wear repays Tom's mom the $500 plus $5 interest.
January 31	Tom's Wear declares and pays a $100 dividend.

Before the first transaction, there are no assets, no liabilities, and no equity. So the balance sheet equation is:

Assets	=	Liabilities	+	Shareholder's equity
0		0		0

Tom starts his company as a corporation. That means the owner's equity will be called shareholder's equity, and his initial contribution will be classified as common stock. We will discuss the details of equity in Chapter 9. This is how the first transaction affects the accounting equation:

Assets	=	Liabilities	+	Shareholder's equity
5,000 cash		0	+	$5,000 common stock

Also on January 1, Tom's Wear borrows $500. This is how the second transaction affects the accounting equation:

Assets	=	Liabilities	+	Shareholder's equity
500 cash		$500 notes payable		

A balance sheet can be prepared at any point in time to show the assets, liabilities, and equity for the company. If Tom's Wear prepared a balance sheet on January 2, these two transactions would be reflected in the amounts on the statement. Exhibit 1.6 shows the balance sheet at that time. With every subsequent transaction the balance sheet will change.

There are several characteristics of the balance sheet that you should notice in Exhibit 1.6. First, the heading on every financial statement specifies three things:

■ the name of the company
■ the name of the financial statement
■ the date

The date on the balance sheet is one specific date. If the business year for Tom's Wear, also known as its **fiscal year**, is from January 1 to December 31, the balance sheet at the beginning of the first year of business is empty. Until there is a transaction, there are no assets, no liabilities, and no equity.

> A **fiscal year** is a year in the life of a business. It may or may not coincide with the calendar year.

The balance sheet in Exhibit 1.6 for Tom's Wear is dated January 2. Tom's Wear has been in business for only 2 days. Even though a business would be unlikely to prepare a balance sheet just 2 days after starting the business, this is what the balance sheet for Tom's Wear would look like on January 2. The balance sheet shows the financial condition—assets, liabilities, and shareholder's equity—at the close of business on January 2. At this time, Tom's Wear had received $5,000 from the owner, Tom, and had borrowed $500 from Tom's mom. The total cash—$5,500—is shown as an asset, and the liability of $500 plus the shareholders' equity of $5,000 together show who has claim to the company's assets.

Because the balance sheet gives the financial position of a company at a specific point in time, a new, updated balance sheet could be produced after every transaction. However, no company would want that much information! When a company presents its revenues and

---

EXHIBIT 1.6

Balance Sheet for Tom's Wear at January 2

This shows a balance sheet after just two days of business for Tom's Wear. Notice that the accounting equation is in balance: assets = liabilities + shareholder's equity.

tom's wear

Tom's Wear, Inc.
Balance Sheet
At January 2, 2006

Assets		Liabilities and Shareholder's Equity	
Cash	$5,500	Note payable	$ 500
		Common stock	5,000
		Retained earnings	0
		Total liabilities and	
Total assets	$5,500	Shareholder's equity	$5,500

expenses for an accounting period, the information makes up the income statement. The company must show the balance sheet at the beginning of that period and the balance sheet at the end of that period. Those two balance sheets are called **comparative balance sheets**. For Tom's Wear, the first balance sheet for the fiscal year is empty. That is, at the beginning of the day on January 1, the accounting equation was $0 = 0 + 0$. Before we look at the balance sheet at January 31, we need to see the income statement for the month of January. We need the information on the income statement to see what happened during the time between the two balance sheets.

> **Comparative balance sheets** are the balance sheets from consecutive fiscal years for a single company.

Your Turn 1-5
Your Turn
Your Turn

1. What are the two parts of shareholder's equity?

2. What is a fiscal year?

Before we prepare an income statement for January for Tom's Wear or a balance sheet at January 31, we will look at each transaction that took place in January and see how each affects the accounting equation. This analysis is shown in Exhibit 1.7.

When a business is started, it begins with an empty balance sheet. For Tom's Wear, there are no assets, and therefore no claims, at the start of business on January 1. The first two transactions that started the business, Tom's contribution of $5,000 and the loan from Tom's mom for $500, occurred on January 1. First, Tom's contribution increases assets by $5,000 and shareholder's equity by $5,000, because the owner, Tom, has claim to the new asset. Then, Mom's loan increases assets by $500 and liabilities by $500. The company receives an asset—cash—and a creditor—Tom's mom—has claim to it. Following these two beginning transactions, the operations of the business begin. Each transaction that takes place during the month is shown as it affects the balance sheet. Study each transaction in Exhibit 1.7 as you read the following description of each.

■ On January 5, cash is decreased by $400 and inventory is increased by $400. This is called an asset exchange, because the company is simply exchanging one asset—cash—for another asset—inventory. Notice the entire effect of this exchange on the accounting equation is on one side of the equation. That is perfectly acceptable. Also notice an asset exchange has no effect on shareholder's equity. Tom still has claim to the same dollar amount of assets.

■ On January 10, Tom pays $50 for advertising. This is a cost Tom's Wear has incurred to generate revenue. Assets are decreased, and retained earnings, a component of shareholder's equity, is decreased. Why is retained earnings decreased? Because when assets are decreased by $50, someone's claim must be reduced. In this case, the owner's claims are reduced when assets are decreased. Retained earnings is the part of shareholder's equity that reflects the amount of equity the business has earned. (Throughout this book, as you study the transactions that take place in a business, you will see that all revenues increase retained earnings and all expenses decrease retained earnings.)

■ On January 20, Tom's Wear sells 90 T-shirts for $10 each. This sale increases assets—cash—by $900. Who has claim to this asset? The owner has this claim. Revenues increase retained earnings. At the time of the sale, an asset is reduced. The company no longer has 90 of the original 100 T-shirts in the inventory. Because each shirt cost $4 (and we recorded the T-shirts at their original cost), the firm now must reduce the asset inventory by $360. That reduction in assets is an expense and so shareholder's claims—via retained earnings—are reduced by the amount of that expense.

■ On January 30, Tom's Wear pays off the $500 loan with $5 interest. The repayment of the $500 principal reduces cash and eliminates the obligation that had been recorded as a liability. In other words, that liability is settled. The $500 reduction in assets is balanced in the accounting equation with a $500 reduction in the claims of creditors. However, the interest represents the cost of borrowing money. For a business, that is called interest expense. Like all expenses, it reduces the shareholder's claims by reducing retained earnings.

■ On January 31, Tom's Wear pays a $100 dividend. That reduction in cash reduces the shareholder's claims to the assets of the firm, shown by the decrease in retained earnings. The $100, after it is distributed, is now part of Tom's personal financial assets, which are entirely separate from the business.

EXHIBIT 1.7

Accounting Equation Worksheet for Tom's Wear for January

All of a firm's transactions can be shown in the accounting equation worksheet. The income statement, indicated by the red box, provides the details of revenues earned and expenses incurred. The transactions are then condensed into one number—net income—which becomes part of the statement of changes in shareholder's equity, indicated by the yellow box. Then, the information from the statement of changes in shareholder's equity is summarized as part of the balance sheet, shown in blue. All of the transactions have, either directly or indirectly, affected the balance sheet. The statement of cash flows shows how the company got its cash and how it spent its cash during the accounting period.

	Assets			=	Liabilities	+	Shareholder's Equity			
							Contributed Capital	Retained Earnings		
	Cash	+	Inventory	=	Notes Payable	+	Common Stock	+	Revenue and Expenses	Dividends
Balances at 1/1/06	0	+	0	=	0	+	0	+	0	
1/1/2006 Company receives $5,000 contribution from Tom.	5,000						5,000			
1/1/2006 Company borrows $500 from Tom's mom.	500				500					
1/5/2006 Company buys 100 shirts for $4 each.	(400)		400							
1/10/2006 Company purchases advertising for $50 cash.	(50)								(50) advertising expense	
1/20/2006 Company sells 90 T-shirts for $10 each. (inventory goes down)	900		(360)						900 sales revenue (360) cost of goods sold	
1/30/2006 Company pays off $500 loan plus $5 interest.	(505)				(500)				(5) interest expense	
1/31/2006 Company pays $100 dividend.	(100)									(100)
Balances 1/31/2006	$ 5,345	+	$ 40	=	0	+	$ 5,000	+	$ 485	$(100)

━ Income Statement   ━ Statement of Changes in Shareholder's Equity   ━ Balance Sheet   ━ Statement of Cash Flows

EXHIBIT 1.8

The Accounting Equation

This shows how the accounting equation forms the foundation for the statements.

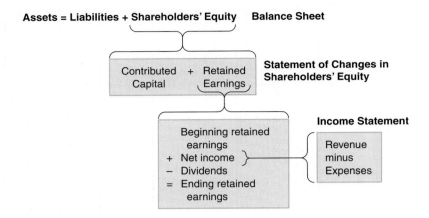

Using the accounting equation to keep track of the transactions of a business is a useful way to see how the financial statements are put together. Exhibit 1.8 shows how the statements are related to the basic accounting equation. The actual way a company keeps track of its financial transactions and its records—commonly called its **books**—can vary from a simple manual record-keeping system to a complex computerized system. No matter how a company keeps its records, the financial statements will look the same. The accounting equation is the basis for accumulating accounting information and communicating that information to decision makers. A company starts the year with a balance sheet (empty only at the start of the business firm), engages in business transactions during the year, and ends the year with a new, updated balance sheet. After a year of operations, the first statement a firm prepares is the income statement.

> The **books** are a company's accounting records.

Income Statement

> The **income statement** shows all revenues minus all expenses for an accounting period—a month, a quarter, or a year.

The most well-known financial statement is the **income statement**, also known as the statement of earnings, or the statement of operations, or the profit and loss statement (P&L). The income statement is a summary of all the revenues (from sales or services) a company earns minus all the expenses (costs incurred in the earning process) associated with earning that revenue. It describes the performance of a company during a specific period, which is called a fiscal period. Most often, fiscal period is used to describe the business year, which may or may not coincide with the calendar year. A fiscal year (not physical year) for a company may, for example, begin on July 1. That means the fiscal year of the business runs from July 1 of one year to June 30 of the next calendar year. Sometimes a company will end a fiscal year at a specific point in time that may result in slightly different dates for its year-end from year to year. For example, Dell Computers defines its fiscal year as the 52- or 53-week period ending on the Sunday nearest January 31.

Recall, the balance sheet gives the amount of assets, the amount of liabilities, and the amount of shareholder's equity of a business at a specific date. However, the first statement a firm prepares after completing an accounting period is the income statement. The income statement describes the operating performance of a company during a period. Look at the income statement for Tom's Wear in Exhibit 1.9. It shows the amount of sales the company made during the month, from January 1, 2006, through January 31, 2006. The expenses

News Flash

In the first quarter of 2006, JetBlue, a six-year-old discount airline increased revenue by $349 million, a whopping 31%. Still, the company posted its second consecutive quarterly loss. It takes more than strong revenue to make a profit. If costs are greater than revenue, a firm will have a net loss rather than a net income. Check out JetBlue's profits for the first quarter of 2007, following the delays due to a major winter storm.

Tom's Wear, Inc.
Income Statement
For the Month Ended January 31, 2006

Revenue		
Sales		$ 900
Expenses		
Cost of goods sold	$ 360	
Advertising	50	
Interest	5	
Total expenses		415
Net income		$ 485

EXHIBIT 1.9

Income Statement for Tom's Wear
The income statement for the month of January shows all of the revenue and all of the expenses for the month.

tom's wear

shown are also for the same period. The difference between the revenues and expenses is called **net income**, or net earnings.

Notice several things about the income statement:

■ First, only the cost of the T-shirts that were sold is included as an expense—cost of goods sold, also called cost of sales. The cost of the T-shirts that were not sold is shown as an asset called inventory on the balance sheet.

■ Second, the repayment of the loan from Tom's mom is not shown as an expense. The only expense related to borrowing money is the interest owed to the lender. The repayment of principal is not an expense.

Also notice that dividends, a corporation's distribution to owners, are excluded from the income statement. Tom could have paid himself a salary for running the business. That salary would have been an expense, but he decided not to do that. Instead, he decided to take cash out of the business as a dividend. Dividends are not a component of earnings; they are a distribution of earnings.

> Net income equals all revenues minus all expenses for a specific period of time.

The Difference between the Balance Sheet and the Income Statement

You should get a better idea of the difference between the balance sheet and the income statement by thinking about your own personal finances. If you were asked to prepare a personal balance sheet, you would list all your assets, such as your cash on hand (no matter how little) and the cost of your car, clothes, computer, and CD collection. Then, you would list all the people to whom you owe money and how much money you owe to each. This might include some credit card companies and perhaps a bank for a car loan. All these assets and liabilities are measured in dollars. The specific point of time associated with a balance sheet must be given. For example, if you were listing your assets and liabilities on the last day of 2007, your balance sheet date would be December 31, 2007. Remember the accounting equation:

$$Assets \quad = \quad Liabilities \quad + \quad Shareholders' \ equity$$

If you subtract the amount of your liabilities—what you owe to others—from your assets, the difference is your equity. Shareholders' equity is sometimes called the residual, indicating that it is the amount left over after the claims of creditors are deducted from a company's assets.

In contrast, if you constructed a personal income statement, it would cover a period of time. For example, what was your net income total during the year 2007? You would list all revenue you received during the year and then subtract all your expenses during the same year. The difference would be your net income for the year. There is no equation to balance. The income statement lists all of your sources of revenue and subtracts the related expenses, leaving a difference, hopefully positive, called net income. If the subtraction of expenses from revenues results in a negative number, that amount is called a net loss.

Your Turn 1-6
Your Turn
Your Turn

1. **What is gross profit?**
2. **Describe the difference in the time periods captured by the income statement and the balance sheet.**

Statement of Changes in Shareholders' Equity

As its name suggests, the statement of changes in shareholders' equity shows the changes that have taken place in the amount of shareholders' equity during a period. For a corporation, the statement is called the **statement of changes in shareholders' equity** because the owners are known as shareholders. (When there is only one owner, use the singular "shareholder's equity." When there are two or more owners, use the plural "shareholders' equity." If you don't know the number of owners, using the plural is the accepted practice.) The statement starts with the amount of contributed capital on a given balance sheet date and summarizes the additions and subtractions from that amount during a specific period, usually a year. In this course, we will not see deductions from contributed capital. Contributed capital is reduced in only very special circumstances, and those will be studied in more advanced accounting courses. The second part of the statement starts with the beginning balance in **retained earnings** and then shows the additions—net income is the most common—and the deductions—dividends are the most common. Contributed capital and retained earnings are then added to show the total amount of shareholder's equity at the end of the accounting period. For demonstration purposes, we will look at monthly financial statements for Tom's Wear Inc. throughout this book.

The statement of changes in shareholder's equity for Tom's first month of business is shown in Exhibit 1.10. The statement starts with the shareholder's equity—also called stockholder's or owner's equity—at the beginning of the month. Tom's Wear has nothing on the first day of the month, because the company is just getting started. Then, capital contributions—owner's contributions to the business—made during the month are listed. Tom contributed $5,000 to the business. In a corporation, contributions take the form of shares of stock. Next, the statement shows beginning retained earnings, the equity that owners have as a result of the business earning income, rather than from contributions. The beginning retained earnings balance is zero because January was the company's first month of doing business. Net income for the period—$485—is shown as an increase to retained earnings. The dividends of $100 are shown as a decrease to retained earnings. The amount of retained earnings at the end of the period is then added to contributed capital at the end of the period to give the total shareholder's equity at the end of the period.

After preparing the income statement for the month and the statement of changes in shareholder's equity for the same month, you will be able to prepare the end-of-the-month balance sheet. If you set up the balance sheet horizontally in the accounting equation format as shown in Exhibit 1.7, you can view the changes in assets, liabilities, and shareholder's equity from the

---

The **statement of changes in shareholder's equity** starts with the beginning amount of contributed capital and shows all changes during the accounting period. Then the statement shows the beginning balance in retained earnings with its changes. The usual changes to retained earnings are the increase from net income and the decrease from dividends paid to shareholders.

Retained earnings is the total of all net income amounts minus all dividends paid in the life of the company. It is descriptively named—it is the earnings that have been kept (retained) in the company. The amount of retained earnings represents the part of the owner's claims that the company has earned (i.e., not contributed). Retained earnings is *not* the same as cash.

EXHIBIT 1.10

Statement of Changes in Shareholder's Equity for Tom's Wear

This statement shows all of the changes to shareholder's equity that occurred during the period.

tom's wear

Tom's Wear, Inc.
Statement of Changes in Shareholder's Equity
For the Month Ended January 31, 2006

Beginning contributed capital	$ 0	
Stock issued during the month	5,000	
Ending contributed capital		$ 5,000
Beginning retained earnings	$ 0	
Net income for the month	485	
Dividends	(100)	
Ending retained earnings		385
Total shareholders' equity		$ 5,385

Tom's Wear, Inc.
Balance Sheet
At January 31, 2006

Assets		Liabilities and Shareholder's equity	
Cash	$5,345	Notes payable	$ 0
Inventory	40		
		Common stock	5,000
		Retained earnings	385
	———	Total liabilities and	
Total assets	$5,385	Shareholder's equity	$5,385

beginning to the end of the month, with each transaction keeping the accounting equation in balance. The balance sheet for Tom's Wear Inc. at January 31 is shown in Exhibit 1.11.

Statement of Cash Flows

The **statement of cash flows** is needed to form a complete picture of the financial position of a company. This statement is, in theory, the easiest to understand; and many people consider it the most important. It is a list of all the cash that has come into a business—its cash receipts—and all the cash that has gone out of the business—its cash disbursements—during a specific period. In other words, it shows all the cash inflows and all the cash outflows for a fiscal period. Compare the cash inflows and cash outflows for a specific period with the revenues and expenses for the same specific period on the income statement. Accountants measure revenue as what the company has earned during the period, even if it is not equal to the amount of cash actually collected. Accountants measure expenses as the costs incurred to generate those revenues, even if they are not the same as the amounts actually paid in cash. Because this way of measuring revenues and expenses may not have an exact correspondence to the amount of cash collected and disbursed, the statement of cash flows is necessary to get a complete picture of the business transactions for the period.

The statement of cash flows is divided into three sections:

- cash from operating activities
- cash from investing activities
- cash from financing activities

These represent the three general types of business activities. Exhibit 1.12 shows some common transactions and how they fit into these classifications. Remember that the transactions must be cash transactions to be shown on the statement of cash flows.

Cash inflows and outflows from operating activities pertain to the general operating activities of the business. For Tom's Wear, purchasing T-shirts is an operating activity. Look at the other cash flows from operations on the statement of cash flows in Exhibit 1.13.

Cash inflows and outflows from investing activities are the cash flows related to the purchase and sale of assets that a firm uses for more than a year. If Tom decided to purchase a piece of equipment to silk-screen his own shirts, that purchase would be an investing activity—not an operating activity—because Tom's Wear is not in the business of buying and selling equipment. The purchase and sale of assets that last longer than a year—often called long-term assets—are investing activities.

Financing activities are related to a company's sources of capital. The two sources of capital, usually in the form of cash, for financing a business are contributions from owners and loans from creditors. Any cash inflows related to these transactions are classified as cash inflows from financing activities. Financing outflows include repayment of the principal of loans and distributions to owners. Tom's repayment of the $500 loan is an example of a financing cash outflow.

EXHIBIT 1.11

Balance Sheet for Tom's Wear at January 31

After a month of transactions, this is the balance sheet for Tom's Wear. Notice how all the information from the income statement and statement of changes in shareholder's equity is incorporated in the totals shown on the balance sheet.

tom's wear

The **statement of cash flows** shows all the cash collected and all the cash disbursed during the period. Each cash amount is classified as one of three types:

1. **Cash from operating activities**—cash transactions that relate to the everyday, routine transactions needed to run a business
2. **Cash from investing activities**—transactions involving the sale and purchase of long-term assets used in the business
3. **Cash from financing activities**—transactions related to how a business is financed. Examples: contributions from owners and amounts borrowed as long-term loans.

EXHIBIT 1.12

Types of Cash Flows

All transactions can be classified as one of these three types. When the transactions are cash, they appear on the statement of cash flows.

	Operating Activities	Investing Activities	Financing Activities
Cash inflows...	From customers who purchase products. From interest or dividend income earned from bank deposits.	From sale of property and equipment.	From issuing long-term debt. From issuing stock.
Cash outflows...	To suppliers for the purchase of inventory. To employees in the form of salaries.	To purchase plant and equipment. To purchase investments in other firms.	To repay long-term debt principal. To pay dividends to owners.

EXHIBIT 1.13

Statement of Cash Flows for Tom's Wear

The statement of cash flows shows all of the cash inflows and outflows during the period. At the end of the statement, the beginning cash balance is added to the change in cash to give the ending cash balance.

tom's wear

Tom's Wear, Inc.
Statement of Cash Flows
For the Month Ended January 31, 2006

Cash from operating activities:
Cash collected from customers .... $ 900
Cash paid to vendors .... (400)
Cash paid for advertising .... (50)
Cash paid for interest .... (5) .... $ 445

Cash from investing activities: 0

Cash from financing activities:
Contributions from owners $5,000
Cash from loan 500
Cash to repay loan .... (500)
Cash paid for dividends .... (100) 4,900
Increase in cash $5,345
Add beginning cash balance 0
Ending cash balance $5,345

You should begin to see the relationship between the four financial statements. Study Exhibit 1.14, where all of the statements for Tom's Wear for January are shown with arrows indicating the relationships between the statements. All four financial statements will be discussed in detail in the chapters to follow. By the time you are finished, you will be able to read and understand what is on most financial statements. You will also be able to analyze business transactions and understand how they affect the financial statements of a business.

EXHIBIT 1.14

Summary of Tom's Wear's Financial Statements and Their Relationships
This shows how the four financial statements are related.

tom's wear

Tom's Wear, Inc.
Income Statement
For the Month Ended January 31, 2006

Revenue		
Sales		$ 900
Expenses		
Cost of goods sold		(360)
Advertising expense		(50)
Interest expense		(5)
Net income		
		$ 485

Tom's Wear, Inc.
Statement of Changes in Shareholder's Equity
For the Month Ended January 31, 2006

Contributed capital	
Beginning balance	$ –
Contributions during the month	5,000
Ending balance	5,000
Retained earnings	
Beginning balance	$ –
+ Net income	485
– Dividends	(100)
Ending balance	385
Total shareholders' equity	$ 5,385

Tom's Wear, Inc.
Statement of Cash Flows
For the Month Ended January 31, 2006

Cash from operating activities:			
Cash collected from customers	$ 900		
Cash paid to vendors	(400)		
Cash paid for advertising	(50)		
Cash paid for interest	(5)	$ 445	
Cash from investing activities:		–	
Cash from financing activities:			
Contributions from owners	$ 5,000		
Cash from loan	500		
Cash to repay loan	(500)		
Cash paid for dividends	(100)	4,900	
Increase in cash		$5,345	
Add beginning cash balance		0	
Ending cash balance		$5,345	

Tom's Wear, Inc.
Balance Sheet
At January 31, 2006

Assets	
Cash	$5,345
Inventory	40
Total assets	$5,385
Liabilities & Shareholder's Equity	
Liabilities	
Note payable	–
Shareholder's Equity	
Contributed capital	5,000
Retained earnings	385
Total Liabilities and Shareholder's equity	$5,385

Your Turn 1-7
Your Turn
Your Turn

1. **Refer to Exhibit 1.14. How is the income statement related to the balance sheet? In other words, how does the amount of net income affect the balance sheet?**
2. **Why is it necessary to have both an income statement and a statement of cash flows? Look at the statements for Tom's Wear and explain why they are different.**

Flow of Information and the Financial Statements

A company records and uses a large amount of information about its transactions. The amount of data and the way the information is collected and stored vary widely from company to company. The information contained in the four financial statements is a specific, well-defined part of the information available from a company's overall information system. The purpose of these four financial statements is to provide the financial information needed to represent and evaluate the transactions of the business. Investors, regulators, vendors, customers, and creditors rely on financial accounting information for decision making.

L.O. 5
Identify the elements of a real firm's financial statements.

Real Company Financial Statements

All publicly traded corporations—ones that sell their stock in the public stock exchanges such as the New York Stock Exchange (NYSE)—must prepare the four basic financial statements every year. Even though these statements are much more complicated than those of Tom's Wear, you will see all of the basic financial statement elements that were on the statements for Tom's Wear.

The SEC requires these companies to regularly supply information about what is happening in their firms. Check out the SEC's Web site at www.sec.gov. Explore the links to see if you can find some recent corporate filings. One of the most important filings a company must make is the 10-K, an important report that companies file with the SEC. It provides a comprehensive overview of the registrant's business. An important part of a 10-K is a company's audited financial statements, without the company's sales pitch and story found in its glossy annual report. The 10-K report includes information you simply will not find in most annual reports, such as insider stock holdings and brief biographies of the management team. The report must be filed within 90 days after the end of the company's fiscal year.

Look at Dell Inc.'s, formerly called the Dell Computer Corporation, comparative balance sheets (see Exhibit 1.15). Notice the similarities between the real world of Dell and the fictitious world of Tom's Wear—the balance sheets for both actually balance. Both companies list assets first, then liabilities and stockholders' equity. Both companies have used dollars to measure their balance sheet items. There are differences between the balance sheets of the real-world example and our not-so-real-world example, which we will discuss in later chapters.

A **single-step income statement** groups all revenues together and shows all expenses deducted from total revenue.

A **multistep income statement** starts with sales and subtracts cost of goods sold to get a subtotal called gross profit on sales, also known as gross margin. Then, other operating revenues are added and other operating expenses are deducted. A subtotal for operating income is shown before deductions related to nonoperating items and taxes are deducted. Then, income taxes are subtracted, leaving net income.

Dell's income statement (consolidated statements of income in Exhibit 1.16) does not look exactly like the Tom's Wear income statement (Exhibit 1.9). First, Dell provides three years of comparative income statements. Both Dell and Tom's Wear have revenues and expenses, but the two companies have presented the data in a different order. Tom's Wear lists revenue first and then groups all the expenses together. This is called a **single-step income statement**. Dell lists its largest revenue first and then subtracts the largest expense related to the revenue, *cost of revenue*—also known as *cost of goods sold*, which gives a subtotal called gross margin. This is called a **multistep income statement**. If we were to recast Tom's income statement into a multistep income statement, we would subtract the cost of goods sold of $360 from the sales revenue of $900 to get a subtotal of $540 for Tom's gross margin. Although Dell and Tom's Wear have arranged their revenues and expenses differently, net income for each company is still the difference between all revenues and all expenses. That is what net income always is, no matter how the revenues and expenses are grouped on the statement.

EXHIBIT 1.15

Comparative Balance Sheets for Dell

This is Dell's balance sheet, taken from its annual report.

Dell, Inc.
Consolidated Statements of Financial Position
(in millions)

> Statement of Financial Position is just another name for the balance sheet.

> Assets are shown first on the balance sheet.

Assets	February 3, 2006	January 28, 2005
Current assets:		
Cash and cash equivalents	$ 7,042	$ 4,747
Short-term investments	2,016	5,060
Accounts receivable, net	4,089	3,563
Financing receivables, net	1,363	985
Inventories	576	459
Other	2,620	2,083
Total current assets	17,706	16,897
Property, plant, and equipment, net	2,005	1,691
Investments	2,691	4,294
Long-term financing receivables, net	325	199
Other non-current assets	382	134
Total assets	$ 23,109	$ 23,215

> Liabilities and Stockholders' Equity are shown together.

> Notice that the balance sheet actually balances.

Liabilities and Stockholders' Equity		
Current liabilities:		
Accounts payable	$ 9,840	$ 8,895
Accrued and other	6,087	5,241
Total current liabilities	15,927	14,136
Long-term debt	504	505
Other non-current liabilities	2,549	2,089
Total liabilities	18,980	16,730
Commitments and contingent liabilities (Note 8)	–	–
Stockholders' equity:		
Preferred stock and capital in excess of $.01 par value; shares issued and outstanding: none	–	–
Common stock and capital in excess of $.01 par value; shares authorized: 7,000; shares issued 2,818 and 2,769, respectively	9,540	8,195
Treasury stock, at cost; 488 and 284 shares, respectively	(18,007)	(10,758)
Retained earnings	12,746	9,174
Other comprehensive loss	(103)	(82)
Other	(47)	(44)
Total stockholders' equity	4,129	6,485
Total liabilities and stockholders' equity	$ 23,109	$ 23,215

The accompanying notes are an integral part of these consolidated financial statements

A company's set of financial statements include the four basic statements—balance sheet, income statement, statement of changes in shareholders' equity, and the statement of cash flows—as well as an important section called Notes to the Financial Statements. These notes, sometimes referred to as footnotes, are an integral part of the set of financial statements. The notes describe the company's major accounting policies and provide other disclosures required by the accounting standards and the SEC. Accompanying every public company's annual financial statements is an audit opinion. Exhibit 1.17 shows the audit opinion from the most recent financial statements of Dell Corporation. Read it and think about whether or not it makes you feel confident in the reliability of the financial statements.

EXHIBIT 1.16

Dell's Income Statements

This shows the income statements for Dell for three consecutive years.

Dell, Inc.
Consolidated Statements of Income
(in millions, except per share amounts)

	Fiscal Year Ended		
	February 3, 2006	January 28, 2005	January 30, 2004
Net revenue	$ 55,908	$ 49,205	$ 41,444
Cost of revenue	45,958	40,190	33,892
Gross margin	9,950	9,015	7,552
Operating expenses:			
Selling, general, and administrative	5,140	4,298	3,544
Research, development, and engineering	463	463	464
Total operating expenses	5,603	4,761	4,008
Operating income	4,347	4,254	3,544
Investment and other income, net	227	191	180
Income before income taxes	4,574	4,445	3,724
Income tax provision	1,002	1,402	1,079
Net income	$ 3,572	$ 3,043	$ 2,645

EXHIBIT 1.17

Report of the Independent Auditor

Every public company is required to have an audit. Only part of the audit report is shown here.

Report of Independent Registered Public Accounting Firm

To the Board of Directors and Shareholders of Dell Inc.

We have completed integrated audits of the 2006 and 2005 consolidated financial statements of Dell Inc. (the "Company") and of its internal control over financial reporting as of February 3, 2006 and an audit of its 2004 consolidated financial statements in accordance with the standards of the Public Company Accounting Oversight Board (United States). Our opinions based on our audits, are presented below.

Consolidated Financial Statements and Financial Statement Schedule

In our opinion, the consolidated financial statements listed in the accompanying index present fairly, in all material respects, the financial position of Dell Inc. and its subsidiaries at February 3, 2006 and January 28, 2005, and the results of their operations and their cash flows for each of the three years in the period ended February 3, 2006 in conformity with accounting principles generally accepted in the United States of America. In addition, in our opinion, the financial statement schedule listed in the accompanying index presents fairly, in all material respects, the information set forth therein when read in conjunction with the related financial statements. These financial statements and financial statement schedule are the responsibility of the Company's management. Our responsibility is to express an opinion on these financial statements and financial statement schedule based on our audits. We conducted our audits of these statements in accordance with the standards of the Public Company Accounting Oversight Board (United States). Those standards require that we plan and perform the audit to obtain reasonable assurance about whether the financial statements are free of material misstatement. An audit of financial statements includes examining, on a test basis, evidence supporting the amounts and disclosures in the financial statements, assessing the accounting principles used and significant estimates made by management, and evaluating the overall financial statement presentation. We believe that our audits provide a reasonable basis for our opinion.

PricewaterhouseCoopers LLP
Austin, Texas
March 15, 2006

Consolidated means that any firms controlled by Dell are included in Dell's financial statements.

What do you think it means for the statements to "present fairly"?

What is a reasonable basis for an opinion?

Business Risk, Control, and Ethics

Starting a business is more than having a good idea about what it should be and obtaining the financing to get it going. Both are a good beginning, but they must be followed with sound business planning for acquiring goods and services and selling the company's products or services. Part of that planning is identifying the risks involved. Before we discuss the details of the business activities in the chapters to follow, we consider the risks of being in business and how we can minimize the negative consequences of those risks.

A **risk** may be generally defined as anything that exposes us to potential injury or loss. In business, risks can turn into significant losses, scandals, or total company failure. There are hundreds of risks that any business faces. Some examples are

- the risk of product failure that might result in the death of consumers
- the risk that someone will steal assets from the company
- the risk that poor-quality inventory will be purchased and sold

What losses could result? For a serious product failure, such as the Firestone tires on the Ford Explorers in the early 2000s, the financial losses to the business could amount to millions of dollars in lawsuit settlements. For employee theft, the potential losses range from significant financial losses to the loss of a company secret that could cause a business to fail. Poor-quality inventory could result in the loss of customers and reputation.

Risks relate to all aspects of the business, including:

- general strategic risks—for example, should we market our cigarettes to teenagers?
- operating risks—for example, should we operate without a backup power supply?
- financial risks—for example, should we borrow the money from the bank or get it from our shareholders?
- information risks—for example, should we use a manual accounting system?

The potential losses from taking on business risks may be the loss of reputation, loss of customers, loss of needed information, or loss of assets. All the losses translate into monetary losses that can put the company at risk for total failure.

It is difficult to think of business risk without considering the relationship of risks to ethics. When the risks of business result in losses or legal exposure, a firm's managers want to minimize the damage to the firm. In such cases, the ethical standards of the firm and its managers become paramount. A manager must always put good ethical behavior above putting a good face on the firm's financial position or performance. Failure to do this has resulted in huge losses for employees and investors. Enron, WorldCom, and HealthSouth are just a few examples to consider. See how many of the faces you recognize in Exhibit 1.18.

L.O. 6
Describe the risks associated with being in business and the part that ethics plays in business.

A **risk** is a danger—something that exposes a business to a potential injury or loss.

BUSINESS RISK AND ETHICS

In 1996, Betty Vinson, pictured here, joined the accounting department of a small long-distance company that would later become WorldCom. In 2003, Vinson faced 15 years in federal prison for her part in WorldCom's $11 billion fraud: Asked by her bosses to make false accounting entries, Vinson balked—and then caved. At the end of 18 months, she had helped falsify at least $3.7 billion in profits. When Vinson and some colleagues threatened to quit, CFO Scott Sullivan told them to "Think of [the company] as an aircraft carrier. We have planes in the air. Let's get the planes landed. Once they are landed, if you still want to leave, then leave." Vinson cooperated with authorities during WorldCom's trial and in August of 2005 was sentenced to 5 months in jail and 5 months of house arrest.

How did investors, board members, and auditors all miss the signs of WorldCom's fraud? By the time you have finished this accounting course, you may be able to answer that question. At the very least, you will have a better understanding of how WorldCom was able to mislead its investors.

EXHIBIT 1.18

Examples of Business Failures, 2001–2005

Company	What Happened	The Outcome of the Trials
Enron, an energy company	Filed for bankruptcy protection in December 2001. At the time, Enron was the seventh-largest company in the United States based on revenue.	Guilty: Andrew Fastow, the former CFO, was sentenced to 10 years in prison in 2004 after pleading guilty to securities and wire fraud. Kenneth Lay (pictured here), former CEO, and Jeff Skilling, former CEO and President, were both found guilty of fraud and conspiracy charges in May 2006. Lay died in July 2006 before sentencing. In October 2006, Skilling was sentenced to 24 years in prison.
Adelphia, a cable company	Filed for bankruptcy protection in June 2002. At the time, Adelphia was the sixth-largest cable company in the United States. John Rigas, founder and CEO, charged with conspiracy, bank fraud, and securities fraud in July 2004.	Guilty: John Rigas, founder, and Timothy Rigas, the former CFO, were found guilty in July 2004 of taking more than $2 billion from the company for their own personal use and lying to the public about Adelphia's financial condition. John Rigas was sentenced to 15 years and Timothy Rigas was sentenced to 20 years in prison.
Arthur Andersen, an accounting firm	One of the five largest accounting firms in the world, Andersen surrendered its state licenses in August 2002 to practice before the SEC. Andersen served as the auditors of Enron and WorldCom.	Guilty Verdict Overturned: Andersen was initially found guilty in 2004 of obstructing justice in the Enron case. This marked the end of one of the five largest accounting firms in the world, which had been founded in 1914 and employed nearly 28,000 people at the time of its demise. In 2005, the Supreme Court overturned Andersen's conviction. Although the ruling came too late to save Andersen, it restored some respect for the accounting firm that was once considered the best in the world.
WorldCom, a telecommunications company	Filed for bankruptcy protection July 2002 after disclosing it overstated profits by $3.8 billion.	Guilty: CEO Bernard Ebbers (left), a former milkman who became the CEO of WorldCom, was convicted in March 2005 on all nine counts for his role in an $11 billion accounting scandal—the largest in U.S. history. Ebbers was sentenced to 25 years in prison in July 2005.
Tyco, a developer of electronics, fire and security products, healthcare products, and plastic and engineering products	Executives Dennis Kozlowski and Mark Swartz indicted in September 2002 for allegedly stealing more than $600 million from the firm.	Guilty: Kozlowski and Swartz were convicted in June 2005, and each was sentenced to 25 years in prison.
Computer Associates, a computer company	Former chief executive Sanjay Kumar indicted in April 2004 for fraudulent accounting of over $2 billion and obstruction of justice.	Guilty: Kumar pleaded guilty to the charges in May 2006 and was sentenced to 12 years in prison in November 2006.

Why do people take risks? Every risk brings a potential reward. The reward is why we are in business. An entrepreneur like Tom has put his money and his reputation at risk to start a business. Why? For the potential of developing a successful business. To deal with the risks and increase the chances to reap the rewards, a firm must establish and maintain control over its operations, assets, and information system. A control is an activity performed to minimize or eliminate a risk. As we study the business processes that Tom will be engaged in during his first year in business, we will look at how he can control the risk involved in each process.

Chapter Summary Points

- A business is started when investors are willing to risk their money to start a business—to provide something of value for customers and to make a profit. The investors may be owners or creditors.
- Investors, vendors, customers, and governmental agencies require financial information about businesses. There are four basic financial statements that provide the information: the income statement, the balance sheet, the statement of changes in shareholders' equity, and the statement of cash flows.
- The financial statements are based on a set of guidelines called generally accepted accounting principles (GAAP). The SEC and the FASB are currently the important players in the rule-setting game.
- The accounting equation, assets = liabilities + shareholder's equity, is the basis of the balance sheet. It is a snapshot of the business at a specific point in time.
- The income statement shows all revenues and expenses for a period of time, resulting in net income.
- The statement of changes in shareholders' (owners') equity shows the changes in shareholders' equity—both contributed capital and retained earnings—for a period of time.
- The statement of cash flows presents all the cash inflows and outflows for a period of time. It accounts for the difference between the balances in cash on the balance sheets at the end of two consecutive accounting periods.
- Notes to the financial statements are an important part of the financial information provided with a firm's four financial statements.

Chapter Summary Problems

Suppose the following transactions occurred during Lexar Computer Inc.'s first month of business.

1. Two friends together contributed $50,000 from their savings to start Lexar Computer Inc. In return, the corporation issued 100 shares of common stock to each of them.
2. The company paid $20,000 cash for parts for new computers that it planned to make during the next few months.
3. The company rented office space for the month for $350 cash.
4. The company hired and paid employees for work done during the month for a total of $1,500.
5. The company sold computers for $40,000 cash. (These computers were made from the parts the company purchased in item 2.)
6. The company paid $400 in dividends to its shareholders.
7. On the last day of the month, the company purchased $12,000 worth of office furniture and equipment on credit. (Lexar signed a 60-day note—i.e., borrowed the money—from the furniture company.)

Instructions

a. For each transaction, tell whether the related accounting information will be shown on the income statement, the balance sheet, or both.

b. For each transaction, tell whether it is an operating, investing, or financing activity.

c. For each transaction, identify an asset or a liability that is affected by the transaction, and tell whether it is an increase or a decrease to the asset or liability you named.

Solution

Transaction	Which financial statements are affected?	Which activity?	Which asset or liability is affected?
1. Two friends together contributed $50,000 cash to start Lexar Computer Inc. In return, the corporation issued 100 shares of common stock to each of them.	Balance sheet	Financing	Asset: Cash—increased
2. The company paid $20,000 cash for parts for new computers that it planned to make during the next few months.	Balance sheet	Operating	Assets: Inventory—increased; Cash—decreased
3. The company rented office space for the month for $350 cash.	Balance sheet and income statement	Operating	Asset: Cash—decreased
4. The company hired and paid employees for work done during the month for a total of $1,500.	Balance sheet and income statement	Operating	Asset: Cash—decreased
5. The company sold computers for $40,000 cash. (These computers were made from the parts the company purchased in item 2.)	Balance sheet and income statement	Operating	Asset: Cash—increased
6. The company paid $400 in dividends to its shareholders.	Balance sheet	Financing	Asset: Cash—decreased
7. The company purchased $12,000 worth of office furniture and equipment on credit. (Lexar signed a 60-day note with the furniture company.)	Balance sheet	Investing	Asset: Equipment—increased; Liability: Notes payable—increased

Key Terms for Chapter 1

Assets (p. 14)
Balance sheet (p. 14)
Books (p. 18)
Capital (p. 2)
Cash from financing activities (p. 21)
Cash from investing activities (p. 21)
Cash from operating activities (p. 21)

Certified public accountant (CPA) (p. 13)
Comparative balance sheets (p. 16)
Contributed capital (p. 9)
Corporation (p. 7)
Dividends (p. 9)
Expenses (p. 10)
Financial Accounting Standards Board (FASB) (p. 12)

Financial services company (p. 4)
Fiscal year (p. 15)
For-profit firm (p. 3)
Generally accepted accounting principles (GAAP) (p. 12)
Income statement (p. 18)
Interest (p. 10)
Internal Revenue Service (IRS) (p. 13)

Liabilities (p. 14)
Manufacturing
   company (p. 4)
Merchandising
   company (p. 4)
Multistep income
   statement (p. 24)
Net income (p. 19)
Not-for-profit firm (p. 3)
Notes to the financial
   statements (p. 14)
Partnership (p. 6)
Principal (p. 10)

Public Company
   Accounting Oversight
   Board (PCAOB) (p. 12)
Retained earnings (p. 20)
Revenue (p. 10)
Risk (p. 27)
Securities and Exchange
   Commission
   (SEC) (p. 7)
Service company (p. 3)
Shareholder (stockholder)
   (p. 7)
Shareholders' equity (p. 14)

Shares of common
   stock (p. 7)
Single-step income
   statement (p. 24)
Sole proprietorship (p. 5)
Statement of cash
   flows (p. 21)
Statement of changes
   in shareholder's
   equity (p. 20)
Stock exchange (stock
   market) (p. 7)

Answers to YOUR TURN Questions

Your Turn 1-1

1. The main purpose of a business is to make a profit, increasing the value of the company for the owners.
2. The four general types of businesses are:
    a. Service company: provides a service—it does something for its customers rather than selling them a tangible product.
    b. Merchandising company: buys goods, adds value to them, and then sells them with the added value.
    c. Manufacturing company: makes products and sells them to other companies and sometimes to the final consumers.
    d. Financial services company: provides services related to money—insurance, banking, etc.

Your Turn 1-2

1. The three general forms of business ownership are: 1- sole proprietorships (single owner); 2- partnerships (multiple owners); 3- corporations (potential for widespread ownership often with separation of ownership and management).
2. Some advantages and disadvantages of each business form are:

	Sole Proprietorship	Partnership	Corporation
Advantages:	Owner control Taxes flow to proprietor's income	Owners control Taxes flow to partners' income	Limited liability for owners Often easier to raise capital For owners, they may diversify their investments across many different companies, often for a very small investment
Disadvantages:	Owner is liable for all business decisions	Partners are liable for all business decisions	Often, management and owners are separate, creating a conflict of interests
	Often difficult to raise capital	Often difficult to raise capital	Corporation pays taxes and then owners pay taxes again on the dividends they receive (unless the tax law makes dividends exempt from tax)

Your Turn 1-3

1. The two sources of financing for a business are investments by owners (contributed capital) and loans from outsiders (liabilities).
2. Interest is the cost of using someone else's money.

Your Turn 1-4

1. Revenues are the amounts a company earns from providing goods or services to its customers. Expenses are the costs to earn those revenues.
2. The four statements are: income statement, balance sheet, statement of changes in owner's equity, and statement of cash flows.

Your Turn 1-5

1. The two parts of shareholders' equity are contributed capital and retained earnings (earned capital).
2. A fiscal year is a year in the life of a business for financial reporting purposes. It may begin at any time and ends a year later.

Your Turn 1-6

1. Gross profit is equal to sales minus cost of goods sold. It is also called gross margin.
2. The time period captured by the income statement is an accounting period, often a fiscal year. The statement covers a period of time. On the other hand, the balance sheet describes the financial position of a company at a given point in time.

Your Turn 1-7

1. The income statement gives the revenues and expenses for the period. The net amount, net income, is added to retained earnings. So the income statement number becomes part of the retained earnings total on the year-end balance sheet.
2. The income statement shows all revenues and expenses for a period of time—all the revenues that have been earned and expenses incurred to earn those revenues. The statement of cash flows simply lists the cash inflows and outflows during the period. The income statement and the statement of cash flows for Tom's Wear are different because Tom's Wear paid cash for some inventory that was not sold, so the cost of that inventory is not included in the income statement's cost of goods sold. Also, any transactions with owners (contributions and dividends) are not included on the income statement.

Questions

1. What is the purpose of a business?
2. Is the goal of all organizations to make a profit?
3. Name the three types of activities that make up most business transactions.
4. What are the possible ownership structures for a business?
5. What are the advantages of the corporate form of ownership?
6. What are the disadvantages of the corporate form of ownership?
7. Who are some of the people in need of business information and for what purposes?
8. What is the relationship between the information available to a business and the information provided in financial statements?
9. What are the basic financial statements? Describe the information that each provides.
10. What makes the income statement different from the statement of cash flows?

Multiple-Choice Questions

1. What type of activities relate to what the firm is in business to do?
   a. Investing activities
   b. Operating activities
   c. Financing activities
   d. Protection activities
2. Which financial statement is similar to the accounting equation?
   a. The income statement
   b. The balance sheet
   c. The statement of changes in shareholders' equity
   d. The statement of cash flows

3. The Pets Plus Superstore Inc. acquires 50 doggie beds from a supplier for $500 in cash. What is the give portion of this transaction?
   a. Pets Plus giving the doggie beds to customers in return for cash
   b. The supplier giving the doggie beds to Pets Plus
   c. Pets Plus giving $500 in cash to the supplier
   d. The supplier giving $500 to Pets Plus

4. The two parts of shareholders' equity are
   a. Assets and liabilities
   b. Net income and common stock
   c. Contributed capital and retained earnings
   d. Revenues and expenses

5. Which financial statement is a snapshot of the financial position of a company at a specific point in time?
   a. Income statement
   b. Balance sheet
   c. Statement of changes in shareholders' equity
   d. Statement of cash flows

6. Online Pharmacy Company borrowed $5,000 cash from the National Bank. As a result of this transaction,
   a. Assets would decrease by $5,000
   b. Liabilities would increase by $5,000
   c. Equity would increase by $5,000
   d. Revenue would increase by $5,000

7. Accounting information is
   a. Useful in profitable businesses only
   b. Considered the most important part of a company's information system by all managers
   c. An integral part of business
   d. Used only by CPAs

8. During its first year of business, West Company earned service revenues of $2,000. If the company collected $700 related to those sales, how much revenue would be shown on West's income statement for the year?
   a. $2,000
   b. $700
   c. $1,300
   d. Cannot be determined with the given information

9. Interest is the cost of
   a. Purchasing inventory
   b. Making a sale
   c. Being in business
   d. Using someone else's money

10. The balance sheet of United Studios at December 31 showed assets of $30,000 and shareholders' equity of $20,000. What were the liabilities at December 31?
    a. $30,000
    b. $10,000
    c. $20,000
    d. $50,000

Short Exercises

SE1-1. *Classify business transactions. For each of the following cash transactions, identify whether it is better described as an operating, financing, or investing activity.* (LO 2)
   a. An entrepreneur contributes his own money to start a new business.
   b. The business buys a building.
   c. The business purchases inventory.
   d. The business sells inventory to customers.
   e. The business repays a loan.

SE1-2. *Identify balance sheet items.* Classify the items listed (1 to 6) under the balance sheet headings of: (LO 4)
  a. Assets
  b. Liabilities
  c. Shareholders' equity
       1. _____Cash
       2. _____Contributions from owners
       3. _____Equipment
       4. _____Notes payable
       5. _____Retained earnings
       6. _____Accounts receivable

SE1-3. *Calculate owner's equity.* Donkey Doughnut Company shows $125,000 worth of assets on its December 31, 2009, balance sheet. If the company's total liabilities are $35,750, what is the amount of owners' equity? (LO 4)

SE1-4. *Calculate inventory.* Given the following items and amounts on Wedding Supplies Inc.'s December 31, 2010, balance sheet, how much inventory did Wedding Supplies have on hand on December 31, 2010? (LO 4)

Cash	$150
Inventory	???
Equipment	$400
Liabilities	$400
Owner's equity	$700

SE1-5. *Calculate liability.* Given the following items on Tiffany Restoration Company's June 30, 2009, balance sheet, how much did the company owe its creditors on June 30, 2009? (LO 4)

Cash	$ 1,725	Liabilities	???
Inventory	205		
Equipment	10,636	Contributed capital	$8,600
Other assets	8,135	Retained earnings	7,450
Total	$20,701		

SE1-6. *Income statement analysis.* For each of the following, calculate the missing amount: (LO 4)
  a. Revenues $560; Expenses $350; Net Income = _____
  b. Net Income $500; Expenses $475; Revenues = _____
  c. Expenses $600; Revenues $940; Net Income = _____
  d. Revenues $1,240; Net Income $670; Expenses = _____
  e. Net Income $6,450; Expenses $2,500; Revenues = _____

SE1-7. *Calculate owners' equity.* Jenna & Yvonne Enterprises has $40,000 in cash, $20,000 in inventory, $17,000 balance due to creditors, and $18,000 balance due from customers. What is the amount of owners' equity? (LO 4)

SE1-8. *Calculate owner's equity.* Given the amounts for the balance sheet on June 30, 2011, how much owner's equity did College Bookstore have on June 30, 2011? (LO 4)

Cash	$300
Inventory	$450
Other assets	$350
Accounts payable	$ 75
Notes payable	$ 50
Salaries payable	$125
Owner's equity	????

SE1-9. *Calculate retained earnings.* After one year of business, Holt's Computer Repair Inc. had $6,000 in assets, $3,500 in liabilities, and $1,000 in contributed capital. What is the amount of retained earnings at the end of the corporation's first year of business? (LO 4)

SE1-10. *Calculate retained earnings.* Joe's Repair Shop had a retained earnings balance of $1,000 on December 31, 2008. For year 2009, sales were $12,000 and expenses were $8,500. Cash dividends of $2,000 were distributed on December 31, 2009. What was the amount of retained earnings on December 31, 2009? (LO 4)

SE1-11. *Identify and classify financial statement items.* Shelby Pet Boutiques Inc. sells products for the pampered pet. These items were shown on Shelby's financial statements presented in the company's 2008 annual report. For each item, give the type of financial statement item (asset, liability, shareholder's equity, revenue, expense) and the financial statement on which it appears. (LO 4)

a. Interest expense
b. Accounts payable
c. Equipment
d. Common stock
e. Sales revenue

SE1-12. *Identify business risks.* Give three risks of being in business and what you might do to minimize those risks. (LO 6)

Exercises—Set A

E1-1A. *Business exchanges. Identify the transactions from the following story. For each, identify the give and get portion. Who would be interested in this information?* (LO 1, 3)
Latasha Jones decided to go into business for herself. As a talented Web designer, she decided to open a small consulting firm with $5,000 of her own money, for which she received common stock. Latasha borrowed $500 from her best friend to help get the business started, and in exchange she gave her friend an I-owe-you (IOU). The company bought a state-of-the-art desktop computer, complete with the accessories and software needed to get the business off the ground, at a total cost of $6,000. The business required a separate phone line, which cost $450. Then, the company put an advertisement in the local newspaper, at a cost of $45 per month for weekly ads. The company was ready to go. All of the payments were cash.

E1-2A. *Analyze business transactions using the accounting equation.* Jamie Bailey opened a hair salon and spa named "Brazwells at Bradford Inc." The following transactions occurred during its first month of business. Enter each transaction below into the accounting equation and identify an increase or decrease to assets, liabilities, shareholder's equity, revenues, or expenses. (LO 4)

1. Jamie contributed $8,000 of personal savings in exchange for stock, and the salon borrowed $6,000 from the bank to start the business.
2. The salon bought $5,000 of inventory from a manufacturer in the Caribbean.
3. Brazwells bought two salon chairs equipped with hair dryers at a cost of $2,500 each.
4. The salon paid rent expense of $375 the first month.
5. Brazwells earned service revenue of $4,000 and sold the entire $5,000 of inventory it had purchased to customers for $7,500 cash.

All the transactions were for cash. Use the following format:

					Shareholder's equity		
	Total assets	=	Total liabilities	+	Contributed capital	+	Retained earnings
Transaction 1:	________		________		________		________

E1-3A. *Classify business transactions.* For each of the transactions in E1-2A, tell whether the transaction was an operating, investing, or financing activity. (LO 2)

E1-4A. *Analyze the balance sheet.* Use the balance sheet for Rainy Day Umbrellas & Rain-coats Inc. at June 30, 2009, to answer the following questions: (LO 3, 4)

Balance Sheet
Rainy Day Umbrellas & Raincoats Inc.

At June 30, 2009	Assets	Liabilities and Shareholders' Equity	
Cash	$ 4,500	Accounts payable	$ 2,500
Short-term investments	350	Notes payable (equipment)	10,250
Accounts receivable	385		
Inventory	250	Contributed capital	3,450
Prepaid insurance	200	Retained earnings	2,485
Prepaid rent	500		
Equipment (net)	12,500		
	$18,685		$18,685

a. List the assets the company had on June 30, 2009. Who has claim to these assets?
b. List the liabilities the company had on June 30, 2009.
c. Who are the potential users of this financial information?

E1-5A. *Analyze business transactions using the accounting equation.* Enter each transaction below into the accounting equation. Then, calculate the (1) amount of assets owned by Jasmine's Sushi Bar Inc. at the end of its first month of business, and (2) the amount of net income for the month. All these transactions took place during the first 30 days of business. (LO 4)

a. Jasmine started the sushi bar by contributing $12,000 in exchange for common stock, and the business borrowed $10,000 from the bank.
b. Jasmine's Sushi Bar purchased $2,000 worth of sushi and other items (its inventory) for cash.
c. The sushi bar hired a sushi expert to help train Jasmine and help run the new company. For this service, Jasmine's paid $50 each day.
d. The bar was popular and Jasmine's sold three-fourths of its inventory for total cash revenues of $6,000.
e. Jasmine's paid rent expense of $345 the first month.
f. Jasmine's repaid $500 of the bank loan along with $20 of interest for the first month.

E1-6A. *Classify business transactions.* Classify each of the transactions in E1-5A as an operating, investing, or financing activity. (LO 2)

E1-7A. *Business transactions effects on shareholders' equity.* For each of the transactions given, tell whether it increases, decreases, or has no effect on shareholders' equity. Consider both shareholders' equity components—contributed capital and retained earnings. (LO 4)

a. Two friends get together, each contributing $6,500 to start the Sweet Tooth Candy Corporation, in exchange for common stock.
b. Sweet Tooth purchases equipment for $3,500 cash.
c. Sweet Tooth purchases $4,500 worth of inventory for cash.
d. Sweet Tooth pays expenses of $1,500 for electricity and phone for the month.
e. Sweet Tooth makes cash sales to customers of $5,725 during the month.
f. Sweet Tooth pays employees $175 for hours worked during the month.
g. Sweet Tooth declares and distributes $250 dividends to each of its owners at the end of the month.

E1-8A. *Classify cash flows.* Classify each transaction as an operating, investing, or financing activity. Assume all transactions are for cash. (LO 2, 4)

a. Jackie Benefield makes a contribution of $95,000 to start the Horse Trails & Stables from her personal funds.
b. The company purchases three horses and some equipment for $25,000 in cash.

c. The company purchases $5,000 worth of advertising with the local newspaper.

d. The company pays rent of $15,000 for barn and pasture space as well as use of 50 acres of land for riding trails.

e. The company hires several people to clean stables at a cost of $600 for the month.

f. The first customers pay Horse Trails & Stables $4,225 for 6 months' worth of riding lessons.

E1-9A. *Analyze business transactions using the accounting equation.* Enter each transaction into the accounting equation and identify its increase or decrease to assets, liabilities, shareholder's equity, revenues, or expenses of Green Trees & Lawn Corp. (LO 4)

a. Green Trees & Lawn earned and collected the cash for $15,000 in service revenues.

b. The business paid $2,000 cash for supplies.

c. Green Trees & Lawn paid $1,500 of a $4,000 note payable to creditors.

d. The company paid $1,100 for rent expense.

e. The company's owner provided $7,500 in additional financing in exchange for common stock.

f. The business paid $2,100 in dividends.

g. Green Trees & Lawn loaned $2,225 cash to another company.

Use the following format:

				Shareholder's equity	
Total assets	=	Total liabilities	+	Contributed capital	+ Retained earnings
Transaction a:					

E1-10A. *Changes in net income.* For each of the following transactions, determine if there is an increase, decrease, or no change on net income for Fun Movie Productions Inc. (LO 4)

a. Fun Movie earned $10,000 in monthly sales.

b. The firm recorded a decrease in inventory of $6,000 due to the monthly sales.

c. The company paid current month's rent of $1,500.

d. The company paid employees $2,500 for work done in the current month.

e. The company purchased land for $7,500.

f. Fun Movie invested $4,000 in another company's stock.

g. The firm paid $1,000 in cash dividends.

E1-11A. *Relationship between income statement and balance sheet.* Fill in the amounts for X, Y, and Z in the table shown below. (The company started business on January 1, 2009.) (LO 4)

	Dec. 31 2009	Dec. 31 2010
Assets	$1,000	$2,500
Liabilities	X	$1,000
Contributed capital	$ 300	$ 300
Retained earnings	Y	Z
Revenue	$300	$2,500
Expenses	$100	$1,500

E1-12A. *Revenues and the statement of cash flows.* Joan started a catering business on the first day of July. She catered 10 parties in July and earned $300 for each party. Most of her customers paid her at the time she provided her services, but one customer, George Smith, asked Joan to send him a bill and he would then send her a check. She sent George an invoice but had not received his payment by the end of July. When Joan prepares her first monthly income statement, how much will the statement show for revenue for the month? How much will be shown on the statement of cash flows as cash collected from customers for the first month? (LO 4)

E1-13A. *Expenses and the statement of cash flows.* Naida decided to open a candle shop. During her first month of business, she purchased candles from the supplier for a total of $500 and paid in cash. She sold half of those candles during the month. On the income statement for the month, what amount would appear for the cost of goods sold expense? On the statement of cash flows, what amount would appear as the cash paid to suppliers? Classify each of these activities as operating, financing, or investing. (LO 4)

E1-14A. *Retained earnings and cash.* The Flower Shop Inc. started business on January 1, 2009, with $5,000 cash contribution from its owners in exchange for common stock. The company used $3,000 of the cash for equipment for the new shop and $1,500 for flowers for its inventory. During the month, the company earned $3,000 revenue from the sale of the entire inventory. On January 31, the owners then spent $2,500 for more flowers for the inventory. What is the retained earnings balance on January 31? How much cash does the company have on hand on January 31? Explain what retained earnings are and why this amount is not cash. *Use the accounting equation to help answer the questions.* (LO 4)

E1-15A. *Classify cash flows.* For E1-14A, what amounts would The Flower Shop show on its statement of cash flows for the month of January 2006? Classify each as an operating, investing, or financing cash flow. (LO 2, 4)

Exercises—Set B

E1-1B. *Business exchanges. Identify the transactions from the following story. For each, identify the give and get portion. Who would be interested in this information? (LO 1, 3)*
Bonnie Lawhon decided to start a business for herself breeding AKC miniature dachshunds. As a talented breeder who gave puppies to her friends and family, she decided to open a small kennel with $6,500 of her own money. She received common stock in exchange. The business had concrete poured and fences installed to give the dogs and puppies shelter at a cost of $3,250, paid in cash. Then, Bonnie's business hired a consultant to design and maintain a Web page for the company at a cost of $200 for the original design and $25 a month maintenance. She paid for the design and one month's maintenance fee. The business required a separate mobile phone to be purchased at a cost of $169 cash. Then, the business put an advertisement in the local newspaper, at a cost of $20 per month for weekly ads. The business paid cash for one month's advertising. The business was ready to go.

E1-2B. *Analyze business transactions using the accounting equation.* Chris Evans opened a fishing supply store named Evans Bait & Tackle Inc. The following transactions occurred during its first month. Enter each transaction into the accounting equation and identify an increase or decrease to assets, liabilities, shareholder's equity, revenues, or expenses. (LO 4)

1. Chris Evans used $115,000 of personal savings in exchange for common stock, and the business borrowed $20,000 from the bank to start the business.
2. The business purchased a small building for $55,000.
3. The business ordered $6,500 worth of inventory.
4. The business paid operating expenses of $315 the first month.
5. Evans Bait & Tackle Inc. sold $2,500 of inventory to customers for $5,215.

All the transactions were for cash. Use the following format:

	Total assets	=	Total liabilities	+	Shareholder's equity Contributed capital	+	Retained earnings
Transaction 1:	_____		_____		_____		_____

E1-3B. *Classify business transactions.* For each of the transactions in E1-2B, tell whether the transaction was an operating, investing, or financing activity. (LO 2)

E1-4B. *Analyze the balance sheet.* Use the balance sheet for Pet Specialty Supplies Inc. at December 31, 2009, to answer the following questions. (LO 3, 4)

Balance Sheet
Pet Specialty Supplies Inc.
At December 31, 2009

Assets		Liabilities and Shareholder's Equity	
Cash	$ 3,000	Accounts payable	$ 1,500
Short-term investments	30	Notes payable (van)	12,500
Accounts receivable	465		
Inventory	725	Paid-in capital	2,000
Prepaid insurance	500	Retained earnings	4,020
Prepaid rent	300		
Mobile grooming van (net)	15,000		
	$20,020		$20,020

    a. List the assets the company had on December 31, 2009. Who has claim to these assets?
    b. List the liabilities the company had on December 31, 2009.
    c. Who are the potential users of this financial information?

E1-5B. *Analyze business transactions using the accounting equation.* Enter each transaction into the accounting equation. Then, calculate the (1) amount of assets owned by Barry's Barrels of Ice Cream Inc. at the end of its first month of business and (2) the amount of net income for the month. All transactions took place during the first month; Barry's was open for 25 days. (LO 4)
    a, Barry started the business by contributing $8,500 in exchange for common stock, and the firm borrowed $2,500 from the bank.
    b. Barry's Barrels of Ice Cream purchased an ice cream delivery truck for $3,500 cash.
    c. The business purchased $1,500 worth of ice cream and other items (its inventory) for cash.
    d. Barry hired a delivery driver to work 2 days a week for a total of 8 days the first month to help deliver ice cream for the new company. For this service, Barry's paid $25 each day worked.
    e. The ice cream delivery service was popular and Barry's sold two-thirds of its inventory for total cash revenues of $4,500.
    f. Barry's paid operating expenses of $115 the first month.
    g. Barry's repaid $100 of the bank loan along with $5 of interest for the first month.

E1-6B. *Classify business transactions.* For each of the transactions in E1-5B, tell whether the transaction was an operating, investing, or financing activity. (LO 2)

E1-7B. *Business transactions effects on shareholders' equity.* For each of the transactions given next, tell whether it (1) increases, (2) decreases, or (3) has no effect on shareholders' equity. Consider both shareholders' equity components—contributed capital and retained earnings. (LO 4)
    a. Two friends get together, each contributing $23,250 to start the Spotless Cleaning Corporation in exchange for common stock.
    b. Spotless Cleaning purchases a company van for $30,000 cash.
    c. Spotless Cleaning purchases $2,250 worth of inventory for cash.
    d. Spotless Cleaning pays expenses of $2,150 for gas and auto insurance.
    e. Spotless Cleaning earns service revenue from customers of $8,150 during the month and received payment in cash.
    f. Spotless Cleaning pays employees $465 for hours worked during the month.
    g. Spotless Cleaning declares and distributes $360 dividends to each of its owners at the end of the month.

E1-8B. *Classify cash flows.* Classify each cash transaction for the statement of cash flows as an operating, investing, or financing activity. (LO 2, 4)

    a. William makes a contribution of $75,000 from his personal funds to start the Cookie Dough & More Ice Cream Co. and received common stock in exchange.

    b. The company purchases a building and some equipment for $45,000 in cash.

    c. The company purchases $5,500 worth of advertising time on a local television station for cash.

    d. The company pays electricity and insurance expenses of $1,500 for the month.

    e. The company hires several people to help make ice cream at a cost of $350 for the month and pays them in cash.

    f. The National Bank pays $2,500 for ice cream and catering services for its grand opening.

E1-9B. *Analyze business transactions using the accounting equation.* Enter each transaction into the accounting equation and identify an increase or decrease to assets, liabilities, shareholders' equity, revenues, or expenses of Captured Memories Photography Inc. (LO 4)

    a. Captured Memories earned $16,150 in sales revenues.

    b. The firm paid $1,500 cash for supplies.

    c. Captured Memories paid $1,000 of a $3,000 note payable to creditors.

    d. The company paid $1,750 for operating expenses.

    e. The company's owner provided $6,500 in additional financing in exchange for common stock.

    f. The firm paid $1,020 in dividends.

    g. Captured Memories loaned $1,000 cash to another company.

Use the following format:

				Shareholder's equity		
Total assets	=	Total liabilities	+	Contributed capital	+	Retained earnings
Transaction a:						

E1-10B. *Changes in net income.* For each of the following transactions, determine if there is an increase, decrease, or no change on net income for Wisteria Lane Productions Inc. (LO 4)

    a. Wisteria Lane earned $12,000 in monthly sales.

    b. The firm recorded a decrease in inventory of $7,500 due to the monthly sales.

    c. Supplies were purchased for $50, and all of them were used.

    d. The company paid employees $1,715 for current work done.

    e. The company purchased land for $26,500.

    f. Wisteria Lane paid rent of $2,500 for the current month.

    g. The firm paid $1,000 in cash dividends.

E1-11B. *Relationship between income statement and balance sheet.* Fill in the amounts for X, Y, and Z in the table. The company started business on July 1, 2008. (LO 4)

	June 30 2009	June 30 2010
Assets	$2,000	$4,250
Liabilities	X	$2,500
Contributed capital	$ 500	$ 700
Retained earnings	Y	Z
Revenue	$ 800	$7,200
Expenses	$ 250	$6,700

E1-12B. *Revenues and the statement of cash flows.* Lynda Watson started a consulting business on the first day of April. She provided consulting services for 30 hours in April and earned $140 per hour. Most of her clients paid her at the time she provided her services, but one customer, Ray Linch, asked Lynda to send him a bill for the 5 hours she worked for him and he would then send her a check. She sent Ray an invoice but had not received his payment by the end of April. When Lynda prepares her first monthly income statement, how much will the statement show for revenue for the month? How much will be shown on the statement of cash flows for the month as cash collected from customers? (LO 4)

E1-13B. *Expenses and the statement of cash flows.* Naida owns a candle shop. During her third month of business, she paid $50 to principal and $5 to interest on a loan from the bank. On the income statement for the month, what amount would appear as an expense? On the statement of cash flows, what amount would appear as the loan payment to principal? Would each of these activities be classified as operating, financing, or investing? (LO 4)

E1-14B. *Retained earnings and cash.* Cookies & Pastries Inc. started business on July 1, 2010, with $16,000 cash contribution from its owners in exchange for common stock. The company used $7,500 of the cash for equipment for the new shop and $3,500 for cookies and pastries for its inventory. During the month, the company earned $7,000 cash revenue from the sale of the entire inventory. On July 31, the owners spent $5,000 for more cookies and pastries for the inventory. What is the retained earnings balance on July 31? How much cash does the company have on hand on July 31? Explain what retained earnings are and why this amount is not cash. *Use the accounting equation to help answer the questions.* (LO 4)

E1-15B. *Classify cash flows.* For E1-14B, what amounts would Cookies & Pastries Inc. show on its statement of cash flows for the month of July 2010? Classify each as an operating, investing, or financing activity. (LO 2, 4)

Problems—Set A

P1-1A. *Analyze income statement and balance sheet. A set of financial statements for Seminole Company follows.* (LO 4)

Excel Template
www.prenhall.com/reimers

Seminole Company
Income Statement
For the year ended 12/31/07

Sales	$600,000
Cost of goods sold	?
Gross profit on sales	375,000
Administrative expenses	54,000
Operating income	?
Interest expense	6,000
Income tax expense	94,500
Net income	?

Seminole Company
Balance Sheet
At 12/31/07

Cash	$?	Accounts payable	$ 13,350
Accounts receivable	13,024	Notes payable	9,830
Inventory	43,271		
Equipment	972,684	Contributed capital	605,000
		Retained earnings	?
Total	$1,129,780	Total	?

Required

Fill in the missing amounts (indicated with question marks).

P1-2A. *Analyze business transactions using the accounting equation.* The following transactions apply to Jenna & Frith's Maid Service during April 2008. (LO 3, 4)

1. Jenna started the business by depositing $5,000 in a business checking account on April 1 in exchange for common stock.
2. The company provided services to clients and received $4,215 in cash.
3. The company borrowed $1,200 from the bank for the business by signing a note.
4. The company paid $1,125 of operating expenses.
5. The company purchased a new computer for $3,000 cash to use to keep track of its customers, starting next month.
6. The company distributed $1,050 to the owner.

Required

    a. Enter the transactions into the accounting equation.
    b. What are the total assets of the company at the end of April 2008?
    c. Prepare a statement of cash flows for April 2008.
    d. What was net income for April 2008?
    e. Who might find the information on Jenna & Frith's Maid Service financial statements useful?

P1-3A. *Analyze business transactions and the effect on the financial statements.* The following business transactions occurred during Gator's Antiques Inc.'s first month of business. (LO 2, 4)

1. Philip Gator began his antique business by depositing $15,000 into the business checking account. He received common stock in exchange.
2. Gator's Antiques provided services to customers for $25,000.
3. The company paid travel expenses in the amount of $700.
4. Gator's Antiques borrowed $1,000 from the bank for operating capital.
5. The company purchased $150 worth of office supplies (for future use) from Office Market for cash.
6. During the month, Gator's paid $3,500 for operating expenses.
7. The company paid monthly rent on the retail space in the amount of $500.
8. The company paid the staff $1,200.
9. The company paid a dividend of $100 to the owner, Philip Gator.
10. On the last day of the month, Gator's purchased equipment costing $7,500 by signing a note payable with the bank.

Required

For each transaction (items 1–10), do the following:
    a. Identify whether it is an operating, investing, or financing transaction.
    b. Determine whether there is an increase, decrease, or no effect on the total assets of the business.
    c. Determine whether there is an increase, decrease, or no effect on net income.
    d. Indicate on which financial statement each amount would appear: the income statement (IS), the balance sheet (BS), the statement of changes in shareholder's equity (OE), or the statement of cash flows (CF). (Some will be shown on more than one statement.)

P1-4A. *Analyze business transactions and the effect on the financial statements.* Using transactions 1–10 in P1-3A, answer the following questions: (LO 4)

Required

    a. What is the cash balance at the end of Gator's first month of business?
    b. Does Gator's Antiques have any liabilities at the end of the first month of business? If so, how much?
    c. Which assets will appear on the balance sheet at the end of Gator's first month of business?
    d. Did Gator's Antiques generate net income or net loss for its first month of business? How much?

P1-5A. *Analyze effect of transactions on accounting equation.* What will be the effects (increase, decrease, or no effect) on total assets, total liabilities, and total stockholder's equity in each of the following situations? When shareholder's equity changes, note whether it is contributed capital or retained earnings that changes. Identify whether each transaction is an operating, investing, or financing transaction. (LO 2, 4)

	Total assets	=	Total liabilities	+	Shareholder's equity	
					Contributed capital +	Retained earnings
1. Received cash and issued shares of common stock	_____		_____		_____	_____
2. Purchased equipment with cash	_____		_____		_____	_____
3. Received cash from customers for services rendered	_____		_____		_____	_____
4. Borrowed money from the bank	_____		_____		_____	_____
5. Received a utility bill and paid cash for it	_____		_____		_____	_____

P1-6A. *Analyze business transactions and prepare the financial statements.* The following cash transactions took place during April 2009, the first month of business for Fast Food Supplies Inc. (LO 4)

1. Kristin Adams started a business, Fast Food Supplies Inc. by contributing $6,000. She received common stock in exchange.
2. The company earned and received cash of $900 in revenue.
3. The company paid expenses of $650 in cash.
4. Company paid dividends of $25.
5. On April 30, the company borrowed $3,000 from the local bank by signing a 3-year note.

Required

    a. Show how each transaction affects the accounting equation.
    b. Prepare the four basic financial statements for the month of April. (Balance Sheet at April 30, 2009)

P1-7A. *Retained earnings portion of the statement of changes in shareholder's equity.* The following information is for Pete's Pet Shop. (LO 4)

1. Retained earnings on January 1, 2010, were $100,000.
2. In January, revenues were $50,000 and expenses were $60,000.
3. In February, revenues were $70,000 and expenses were $65,000.
4. In March, revenues were $90,000 and expenses were $55,000.
5. The only dividends paid were in March for $3,000.

Excel Template
www.prenhall.com/reimers

Required

Prepare the retained earnings portion of the statement of changes in shareholder's equity for the three months ended March 31, 2010, for Pete's Pet Shop.

Problems—Set B

P1-1B. *Analyze income statement and balance sheet. A set of financial statements for Shelby's Music Inc. follows.* (LO 4)

Excel Template
www.prenhall.com/reimers

Shelby's Music Inc.
Income Statement
For the year ended June 30, 2008

Sales	x
Cost of goods sold	375,000
Gross profit on sales	525,000
Administrative expenses	x
Operating income	419,000
Interest expense	x
Income taxes	142,450
Net income	264,550

Shelby's Music Inc.
Balance Sheet
At June 30, 2008

Cash	$158,592	Accounts payable	$ 14,070
Accounts receivable	18,621	Notes payable	12,520
Inventory	x		
Equipment	895,895	Contributed capital	x
		Retained earnings	425,000
Total	x	Total	$1,231,000

Required

Fill in the missing amounts.

P1-2B. *Analyze business transactions using the accounting equation.* The following transactions apply to Xavier Bostic's Auto Detail Service during November 2008. (LO 3, 4)

1. Xavier started the business by depositing $3,350 in a business checking account on November 1 in exchange for common stock.
2. The company purchased a vacuum cleaner for $1,145 cash.
3. The company borrowed $1,575 from the bank for the business by signing a note.
4. The company provided services to clients and received $5,705 in cash.
5. The company paid $535 of operating expenses.
6. The company made a distribution of $200 to the owner.

Required

a. Enter the transactions into the accounting equation.
b. What are the total assets of the company at the end of November 2008?
c. Prepare a statement of cash flows for November 2008.
d. What was net income for November 2008?
e. Who might find the information on Xavier Bostic's Auto Detail Service financial statements useful?

P1-3B. *Analyze business transactions and the effect on the financial statements.* The following business transactions occurred during Dolphin's Dinghies Inc.'s first month of business. (LO 2, 4)

1. Douglas Dolphin began his dinghy business by depositing $40,000 into the business checking account in exchange for common stock.
2. The company paid travel expenses in the amount of $250.
3. Dolphin's Dinghies borrowed $5,000 from the bank for operating capital.
4. The company purchased $350 worth of office supplies (for future use) from Office Supermarket for cash.
5. During the month, Dolphin's repaired customers' dinghies for $8,900 cash.
6. The company paid the monthly rent on the retail space in the amount of $1,200.

7. The company paid the staff $3,000.
8. Other operating expenses for the month were $1,500, which were paid in cash.
9. On the last day of the month, the company purchased equipment costing $17,000 by signing a note payable with the bank.
10. The company paid a dividend of $175 to the owner, Douglas Dolphin.

Required

For each transaction (items 1–10), do the following:
   a. Identify whether it is an operating, investing, or financing transaction.
   b. Determine whether there is an increase, decrease, or no effect on the total assets of the business.
   c. Determine whether there is an increase, decrease, or no effect on net income.
   d. Indicate on which financial statement each amount would appear: the income statement (IS), the balance sheet (BS), the statement of changes in stockholder's equity (SE), or the statement of cash flows (CF). (Some will be shown on more than one statement.)

P1-4B. *Analyze business transactions and the effect on the financial statements.* Using transactions 1–10 in P1-3B, answer the following questions. (LO 4)

Required

   a. What is the cash balance at the end of Dolphin's first month of business?
   b. Does Dolphin's Dinghies have any liabilities? If so, how much?
   c. Which assets will appear on the balance sheet at the end of Dolphin's first month of business?
   d. Did Dolphin's Dinghies generate net income or net loss for its first month of business? How much?

P1-5B. *Analyze effect of transactions on accounting equation.* What will be the effects (increase, decrease, or no effect) on total assets, total liabilities, and total shareholder's equity in each of the following situations? When shareholder's equity changes, note whether it is contributed capital or retained earnings that changes. Identify whether each transaction is an operating, investing, or financing transaction. (LO 2, 4)

	Total assets	=	Total liabilities	+	Contributed capital	+	Retained earnings
					Shareholder's equity		
1. Purchased land with cash	_____		_____		_____		_____
2. Performed services and received cash from customers	_____		_____		_____		_____
3. Received cash from the issue of shares of common stock	_____		_____		_____		_____
4. Paid cash for inventory	_____		_____		_____		_____
5. Sold inventory for cash	_____		_____		_____		_____

P1-6B. *Analyze business transactions and prepare the financial statements.* The following cash transactions took place during January 2007, the first month of business for Auto Detail Unlimited, a corporation. (LO 4)

1. Dustin Soper started Auto Detail Unlimited by contributing $24,000 cash and received common stock in exchange.
2. The company earned and received $3,100 cash in service revenue.

3. The company paid employees $985 cash.
4. Miscellaneous expenses paid amounted to $650 cash.
5. The company paid cash dividends of $500.
6. On January 31, the company borrowed $8,000 from the local bank, to be repaid at the end of December 2007.

Required

a. Show how each transaction affects the accounting equation.
b. Prepare the four basic financial statements for the month of January. (Balance sheet at January 31, 2007.)

Excel Template
www.prenhall.com/reimers

P1-7B. *Retained earnings portion of the statement of changes in shareholder's equity.* The following information is for Pete's Pet Shop. (LO 4)

1. Retained earnings on April 1, 2008 were $127,000.
2. In April, revenues were $85,000 and expenses were $72,000.
3. In May, revenues were $16,582 and expenses were $37,000.
4. In June, revenues were $82,000 and expenses were $18,582.
5. The company paid dividends in April of $8,000 and in June of $19,500.

Required

Prepare the retained earnings portion of the statement of changes in shareholder's equity for the quarter (3 months) ended June 30, 2008, for Pete's Pet Shop.

Financial Statement Analysis

FSA 1-1. Use Apple Computer Inc.'s balance sheets given here to answer the questions. (LO 5)

Apple Computer Inc.
Condensed Balance Sheets
(in millions)

Assets:	At 9/24/05	9/25/04
Cash and cash equivalents	$ 3,491	$ 2,969
Short-term investments	4,770	2,495
Accounts receivable (net)	895	774
Inventories	165	101
Other current assets	979	716
Total current assets	10,300	7,055
Property, plant, and equipment (net)	817	707
Goodwill	69	80
Other assets	365	208
Total assets	$ 11,551	$ 8,050

Liabilities and Shareholders' Equity:

	At 9/24/05	9/25/04
Accounts payable	$ 1,779	$ 1,451
Accrued expenses	1,705	1,200
Total current liabilities	3,484	2,651
Other noncurrent liabilities	601	323
Total liabilities	4,085	2,974
Common stock	3,521	2,514
Retained earnings	4,005	2,670
Other equity accounts	(60)	(108)
Total shareholders' equity	7,466	5,076
Total liabilities and shareholders' equity	$ 11,551	$ 8,050

Required

a. What date marks the end of Apple's most recent fiscal year?

b. Did Apple earn a net income or net loss during the year? How can you tell?

c. Did the owners of Apple make any capital contributions during the year (or did Apple get some new owners)?

d. Did Apple buy or sell any property, plant, or equipment during the year? How can you tell?

e. On the last day of the fiscal year, did Apple have any debts? If so, what was the total amount?

FSA 1-2. The statement of cash flows for Apple Computer Inc. for the year ended September 24, 2005, is shown below. Use it to answer the following questions. (LO 5)

Apple Computer Inc.
Adapted Statement of Cash Flows
For the year ended September 24, 2005

(in millions)	
Cash and cash equivalents, beginning of the year	$2,969
Operating Activities:	
Net income (loss)	1,335
Adjustments to reconcile net income to cash generated by operating activities:	1,200
Cash generated by operating activities	2,535
Investing Activities:	
Purchase of short-term investments	(11,470)
Proceeds from maturities of short-term investments	8,609
Proceeds from sales of short-term investments	586
Purchase of property, plant, and equipment	(260)
Other	(21)
Cash generated by (used for) investing activities	(2,556)
Financing Activities:	
Proceeds from issuance of common stock	543
Cash generated by (used for) financing activities	543
Increase (decrease) in cash and cash equivalents	522
Cash and cash equivalents, end of the year	$3,491

Required

a. Did Apple purchase any property, plant, or equipment during the year?

b. If you were to examine Apple's balance sheet at September 24, 2005, what amount would be shown for cash and cash equivalents?

c. Was cash generated from operations or used by operations? By what amount?

d. Did Apple receive any new contributions from owners during the year? How can you tell?

e. What was the primary source of cash for Apple for the year ended September 24, 2005? What does this say to you about Apple's operations for this year?

FSA 1-3. Use the annual report from **Office Depot** found on this book's website to answer these questions. (LO 2, 3, 5)

Required

a. What type of business is Office Depot and how is it organized?

b. Suppose you inherited $10,000 when your great-uncle passed away and you want to invest in a promising company. Would you invest in Office Depot? What information in the annual report would be useful in your decision? Be specific. Is there any information that is not provided in the annual report that you would want to have before making your decision?

c. What is your opinion of the information in the annual report? For example, do you think it is accurate? Useful? Interesting? Informative? Why or why not?

Critical Thinking Problems

Risks and Controls

Being in business is risky. Imagine that you are starting a business. What type of business would you start? What are the most significant risks you face with your business? What controls would you put into effect to minimize those risks?

Group Problem

Look at the four basic financial statements for Staples, found in the book's appendix. Find the total assets, liabilities, and shareholders' equity for the two most recent years. As a group, discuss the change in the company's financial position without looking at the income statement. Jot down your opinions. Then, study the income statement for the most recent year. Do the results support your opinions about the balance sheet changes? What information do these statements provide for your analysis? What additional information would be useful? After answering these questions as a group, look at the notes to the financial statements. Do the notes help answer any of your questions?

Make a list of 10 questions you have about the financial statements. Try to answer them and discuss why you would like answers to these questions. Save the list so you can check to see how many of the questions you are able to answer at the end of the course.

Ethics

Does your school have an honor code? If it does, it very likely addresses the issue of cheating on assignments or exams. Have you ever cheated on an exam? Have you ever "borrowed" a friend's assignment and used it to help you complete yours? Have you ever been a witness to a violation of the honor code by your peers? Compare Target's code of ethics (called Business Conduct Guide and found at *www.targetcorp.com/targetcorp_group/ investor-relations/investor-relations.jhtml*) to your school's honor code. How are they similar in purpose and scope? How are they different? If you compare your behavior to that of some of the executives of Enron, WorldCom, or Tyco, how do you stack up?

Internet Exercise: Disney Corporation

The Walt Disney Company is a diversified worldwide entertainment company with interests in ABC TV, ESPN, film production, theme parks, publishing, a cruise line, Infoseek, and the NHL Mighty Ducks. By using the Disney Web site, you can explore vacation options and get Disney's latest financial information.
Please go to the Disney Web site at http://corporate.disney.go.com/investors/

IE1-1. What is the Walt Disney Company's key objective?
Go to Financial Information and click on the most recent annual report.

a. What are the key businesses of the Walt Disney Company? Identify whether you think the primary business activity is manufacturing, merchandising, or service for each key business segment.

b. Use the Site Map to find Financial Highlights. Identify the amount of total revenues and operating income for the most recent year. On which financial statement will you find these amounts reported? Is the Walt Disney Company a proprietorship, a partnership, or a corporation? How can you tell?

c. Use the Site Map to find Financial Review. What key business segment earns the greatest proportion of revenues? Identify the proportion of revenues earned by each key business segment, listing them in the order of greatest proportion to least proportion. Does this order surprise you? Explain why or why not?

Please note: Internet Web sites are constantly being updated. Therefore, if the information is not found where indicated, please explore the annual report further to find the information.

Qualities of Accounting Information

Here's Where You've Been . . .

In Chapter 1, you learned that a business adds value to make a profit. You learned that business transactions can be classified as operating, investing, or financing. The four basic financial statements—the income statement, the statement of changes in shareholders' equity, the balance sheet, and the statement of cash flows—provide information about these business processes.

Here's Where You're Going . . .

When you are finished with Chapter 2, you should understand the qualities of the information in the financial statements. You should be able to recognize and explain the difference between accrual basis accounting and cash basis accounting.

Learning Objectives

When you are finished studying this chapter, you should be able to:

1. Define generally accepted accounting principles and explain why they are necessary.

2. Explain the objective of financial reporting and the qualities necessary to achieve this objective.

3. Identify the elements of the financial statements and describe their characteristics.

4. Define accrual accounting, explain how it differs from cash basis accounting, and identify examples of accrual accounting on actual financial statements.

5. Compute and explain the meaning of the current ratio.

6. Identify the risks and potential frauds related to financial accounting records, and explain the controls needed to ensure their accuracy.

Ethics Matters

In April 2006, with just two weeks until the start of his trial, Computer Associates International's former CEO, Sanjay Kumar, pleaded guilty to securities fraud and obstruction of justice. Not only did Kumar engage in a conspiracy to inflate the firm's 2000 and 2001 sales revenue, he also authorized a $3.7 million payment to buy the silence of potential witnesses. In November 2006, he was sentenced to 12 years in prison and fined $8 million for his part in the $2.2 billion fraud.

Why would a smart and wealthy man falsify accounting records, taking the risk of a long prison sentence? Sometimes people in power begin to feel invincible. It is important for every individual to have a strong sense of ethical behavior and to apply high moral standards to every business decision, no matter how small. Too often a number of seemingly small decisions can add up to one big crime.

L.O.1

Define generally accepted accounting principles and explain why they are necessary.

Net profit equals all revenues minus all expenses.

Information for Decision Making

After Tom sold his first batch of T-shirts, he had some decisions to make. The biggest one was whether or not to continue in business. What he needed to know to evaluate that decision was whether or not the company made a profit in January. **Net profit** is the amount left after all expenses are deducted from all revenues.

For Tom's Wear, the accounting period is the first month of doing business, January 1 through January 31. Information about the month's operations is summarized on the income statement—one of the four basic financial statements. The revenues for the period amounted to $900; that is the total amount the company earned when it sold 90 shirts. The expenses were the cost of the T-shirts sold, the cost of the advertising, and the interest paid on the loan from Tom's mom. The cost of the 90 T-shirts sold was $360, advertising expense was $50, and the cost of borrowing the money—interest expense—was $5. When those expenses, totaling $415, are deducted from the sales revenue of $900, the remaining $485 is net profit. Tom's Wear added value by ordering shirts with the special logo and providing them to Tom's friends at a convenient time and place. And Tom's Wear achieved its goal—to make a profit.

On the income statement in Exhibit 2.1, you will see $485 shown as net income, another name for profit. The term profit can be applied to a single sale, a group of sales, or all the transactions for a period of time of business activity, whereas net income is a more specific term for describing a company's entire profit for a specific time period. The company made a gross profit of $540 on the sale of 90 t-shirts, and Tom's Wear's net income for his first month of business activity was $485.

Financial reporting provides information for decision making. An income statement, like the one shown for Tom's Wear, is one source of information. When the second month of business activity is complete, Tom will prepare another income statement and will be able to compare the two statements. To make such a comparison meaningful, Tom needs to use the same rules for preparing the two statements. If Tom wanted to compare his company's performance to the performance of another T-shirt company, he would need to be sure that the other company was using the same rules to prepare its income statement. For financial information to be useful for evaluating the performance of a business across time or for comparing two different companies, the same rules must be used consistently.

As you learned in Chapter 1, there is a set of guidelines called generally accepted accounting principles (GAAP) that a company must follow when preparing its financial statements, which help ensure consistency. These guidelines—usually known as accounting principles— were historically developed through common usage. A principle was acceptable if it was used and acknowledged by most accountants. Today the process of establishing GAAP is more formal, with the SEC and the FASB responsible for setting accounting standards.

EXHIBIT 2.1

Income Statement for Tom's Wear for January

This is a simple income statement for one month of business.

Tom's Wear, Inc.
Income Statement
For the Month Ended January 31, 2006

Revenue		
Sales		$ 900
Expenses		
Cost of goods sold	$ 360	
Advertising expense	50	
Interest expense	5	
Total expenses		415
Net income		$ 485

tom's wear

1. **What does GAAP stand for?**
2. **Why are guidelines needed for financial reporting?**

Your Turn 2-1
Your Turn
Your Turn

L.O.2
Explain the objective of financial reporting and the qualities necessary to achieve this objective.

Characteristics of Accounting Information

What Makes Information Useful?

The most general and the most important objective of financial reporting is to provide useful information for making decisions. What makes information useful? According to the FASB, the information must be relevant, reliable, comparable, and consistent.

Relevant. For information to be *relevant*, it needs to be significant enough to influence business decisions. The information should help confirm or correct the users' expectations. No matter how significant the information is, however, it must be timely to be relevant. For example, the price of fuel is extremely important information to an airline such as Southwest or JetBlue, and a manager needs this information to make decisions about ticket prices. However, if the firm reports fuel prices only monthly, the information will not be timely enough to be relevant. To be relevant, information must be useful in predicting the future. Currently, the SEC requires firms to submit their financial information within 60 days of the end of the firm's fiscal year.

Reliable. When information is *reliable*, you can depend on it and you can verify its accuracy. The information is completely independent of the person reporting it. To be reliable, the information in the financial statements must be a faithful representation of what it intends to convey. For example, Borders Group Inc. reported $4.04 billion in sales for its fiscal year ended January 28, 2006. This amount must be true and verifiable; otherwise, the information could be misleading to investors. As you learned in Chapter 1, it is part of the auditors' job to make sure Borders has the documentation to confirm the accuracy of its sales amount. Anyone who examines Borders' sales records should come up with the same amount.

Comparable. In addition to being relevant and reliable, useful information possesses *comparability*. This means investors will be able to compare corresponding financial information between two similar companies—how one company's net income compares with another company's net income. In putting together financial statements, accountants must allow for meaningful comparisons. Because there are often alternative ways to account for the same transaction within GAAP, companies must disclose the methods they select. This disclosure allows educated investors to adjust the reported amounts to make them comparable. For example, Sears may account for its inventories by averaging the cost of its purchases, whereas Wal-Mart may use a method that assumes the first items purchased are the

EXHIBIT 2.2

Qualitative Characteristics of Accounting Information

  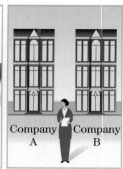 

Relevance: Information that will provide a basis for forecasts of future firm performance by the CEO and CFO, among others. What's ahead for this company?

Reliability: Information that is neutral and verifiable. Is the information independent of the specific person who prepared it?

Comparability: Different companies use the same set of accounting rules. Does the information allow meaningful comparisons of two different companies?

Consistency: A company uses the same rules from year to year. Does the information allow meaningful comparisons of a company's performance at different points in time?

first items sold. As a requirement of GAAP, Sears and Wal-Mart will disclose these choices in the notes to their financial statements so that investors can compare the inventory information of the companies.

Consistent. To be useful, accounting information must be consistent. *Consistency* is the characteristic that makes it possible to track a company's performance or financial condition from one year to the next. Only if a company uses the same accounting methods from period to period are we able to make meaningful comparisons. For example, total revenues for Target were $51.3 billion for the fiscal year ended January 28, 2006, and $46.7 billion for the fiscal year ended January 29, 2005. Only when these two numbers are based on the same set of accounting methods can investors determine why sales increased. If the increase was caused partly or solely by the change in the way the company measured sales, then investors would be misled about the company's actual performance. Financial statement users want to rely on the firm's consistent application of accounting standards. Exhibit 2.2 summarizes the desired qualitative characteristics accounting information must have to be considered useful by the FASB.

Your Turn 2-2
Your Turn
Your Turn

1. **What is the purpose of financial statements?**
2. **What four characteristics explain what the FASB means by "useful" information?**

Assumptions and Principles Underlying Financial Reporting

Financial information pertains to only the firm, not to any other parties such as the firm's owners. This distinction between the financial information of the firm and the financial information of other firms or people is called the **separate-entity assumption**. It means that the financial statements of a business do not include any information about the finances of individual owners or other companies. Look at the income statement in Exhibit 2.1, which summarizes the company's revenues and expenses. You will notice that the items on the financial statements are expressed in amounts of money. This is called the **monetary-unit assumption**. When you observe that Tom's Wear had expenses of $415 during January 2006, you know that the amount includes only company expenses. Suppose Tom took a vacation to Hawaii at a cost of $3,000. No part of that transaction would be part of Tom's Wear's financial reports because of the separate-entity assumption.

The **separate-entity assumption** means that the firm's financial records and financial statements are completely separate from those of the firm's owners.

The **monetary-unit assumption** means that the items on the financial statements are measured in monetary units (dollar in the U.S.).

At a minimum, firms prepare new financial statements every year. For internal use, financial statements are prepared more frequently. The SEC requires publicly traded firms to prepare a new set of financial statements each quarter, which enables users to compare the company's performance from one quarter (every three months) to the next. Accountants divide the life of a business into time periods so they can prepare reports about the company's performance during those time periods. This creation of time periods is called the **time-period assumption**. Although most companies report financial information every three months, only the annual financial information is audited. Most companies use the calendar year as their fiscal year.

The **time-period assumption** means that the life of a business can be divided into meaningful time periods for financial reporting.

Assets are recorded at their original cost to the company. This is known as the **historical-cost principle**. Accountants use cost because the cost of an asset is a reliable amount—it is unbiased and verifiable. Accountants assume a company will continue to remain in business for the foreseeable future, unless they have clear evidence it will either close or go bankrupt. This is called the **going-concern assumption**. With this assumption, financial statement values are meaningful. Would the bank lend money to a firm if the firm were not going to continue operating in the foreseeable future? If the firm expects to liquidate, the values on the financial statements lose their meaning. If a company is not a going concern, the values on the financial statements would need to be liquidation values to be useful.

The **historical-cost principle** means that transactions are recorded at actual cost.

The **going-concern assumption** means that, unless there is obvious evidence to the contrary, a firm is expected to continue operating in the foreseeable future.

As you have read about the four financial statements and the notes to the statements, you have learned about the qualities of financial information and the assumptions and principles that provide the foundation of financial reporting. Without these assumptions and principles, managers, investors, and analysts could not rely on the information to make decisions.

To complete the foundation for financial reporting and to enable you to gain a full understanding of the information contained in the financial statements, you will need to know about two constraints that apply to the preparation of the statements. A *constraint* in financial accounting is a limit or control imposed by GAAP. There are two constraints: materiality and conservatism.

Materiality refers to the size or significance of an item or transaction in relation to the company's overall financial performance or financial position. An item is material if it is large enough to influence investors' decisions. For example, the cost of fuel, the amounts paid to employees, and the cost of buying or leasing airplanes are all material items for JetBlue or Southwest Airlines. In contrast, an item is considered immaterial if it is too small to influence investors. GAAP does not have to be strictly applied to immaterial items (measured in total). For example, suppose JetBlue Airlines made an isolated error and failed to record the revenue from your $350 ticket purchased and used in 2005. Because JetBlue's total revenue was over $1.6 billion for its fiscal year ended December 31, 2005, the company would not need to correct this single error. The item is considered immaterial. (However, if there were lots of these errors, the total amount could be material.)

Conservatism refers to the choices accountants make when preparing the financial statements. When there is any question about how to account for a transaction, the accountant should select the treatment that will be least likely to overstate income or overstate assets. Accountants believe it is better to understate income or assets than it is to overstate either. For example, JetBlue's December 31, 2005, balance sheet shows total property and equipment of over $2.9 billion. GAAP requires JetBlue to evaluate these assets to make sure they are not overstated with respect to their future revenue-generating potential.

Elements of the Financial Statements

As you learned in Chapter 1, a complete set of financial statements includes the:

1. Income statement
2. Balance sheet (sometimes called the statement of financial position)
3. Statement of changes in shareholders' equity (also called the statement of changes in owners' equity)
4. Statement of cash flows
5. Notes to the financial statements

L.O.3
Identify the elements of the financial statements and describe their characteristics.

GAAP describe the individual items that are included in the financial statements. To learn what is shown on each financial statement, we will look at the second month of business for

Tom's Wear. We will take the second month's transactions and see how they affect the accounting equation and the financial statements. Then, we will relate the statements to the qualitative characteristics described by GAAP.

At the beginning of the second month, on February 1, 2006, Tom's Wear has a balance sheet that is identical to the balance sheet dated January 31, 2006. Recall that the company's assets, liabilities, and shareholder's equity balances roll forward when the new period starts.

Transactions for the Second Month of Business

The transactions for Tom's Wear's second month of business are shown in Exhibit 2.3. The first transaction in February is the purchase of 200 T-shirts, costing $4 each. Last month, Tom's Wear paid cash for the purchase of the T-shirts. This month, the company buys them on credit, also known as **on account**. This means Tom's Wear will pay for them later. The purchase increases the company's assets—$800 worth of T-shirts—and the $800 claim belongs to the vendor. When a company owes a vendor, **accounts payable** are the amounts the company owes. This is the first transaction shown in Exhibit 2.4, where the transactions are presented in the accounting equation worksheet.

Next, Tom hires a company to advertise his business immediately. This cost is $150 for a service. Tom's Wear pays $100 when the service is provided, so the company still owes $50. Like the first transaction, this one also postpones payment. However, in this transaction, Tom's Wear has incurred an expense. In the first transaction—when the inventory was purchased—Tom's Wear gained an asset. The cost of the shirts will become an expense when the shirts are sold. In contrast, the work done related to the advertising is complete, and that signals an expense. (The timing of recognizing expenses can be tricky; the next chapter will discuss timing in detail.) The $150 expense, like all expenses, reduces the owner's claims to the assets of the firm. Assets decrease by $100, the cash paid for the advertising; and the remaining $50 increases creditors' claims—liabilities—because it will be paid later. It is shown as other payables because accounts payable is generally reserved for amounts a firm owes its vendors. This is the second transaction shown in Exhibit 2.4. Notice that the expense is recorded even though all of the cash has not yet been paid.

As his business grows, Tom decides his company needs some insurance. Tom's Wear pays $150 for 3 months' worth of coverage, beginning February 14. When a company pays for something in advance, the item purchased is something of future value to the company. Because such an item provides future value, it is classified as an asset. Items purchased in advance may seem like unusual assets, and often have the word *prepaid* with them to provide information about what sort of assets they are. Common prepaid items are insurance, rent, and supplies. In this case, Tom's Wear has purchased an asset called **prepaid insurance**. Cash is decreased by $150, and the new asset—prepaid insurance—is increased by $150. Notice that insurance expense has not been recorded. Until some of the insurance is used up—and it can be used up only from one point in time to a subsequent point in time—there is no expense. This is another case of the cash flow being different than the expense.

On account means *on credit*. The expression applies to either buying or selling on credit.

Accounts payable are amounts that a company owes its vendors. They are liabilities and are shown on the balance sheet.

Prepaid insurance is the name for insurance a business has purchased but not yet used. It is an asset.

EXHIBIT 2.3

Transactions for Tom's Wear for February

Date	Transaction
February 1	Tom's Wear purchases 200 T-shirts at $4 each. They are purchased on credit.
February 5	Tom's Wear buys advertising for $150, paying $100 in cash and the remainder on account. The ad runs immediately.
February 14	Tom's Wear purchases 3 months' worth of insurance for $150 cash, with the policy beginning on the date of purchase.
February 23	Tom's Wear sells 185 T-shirts for $10 each. 170 of these are sold for cash and the remainder on account.
February 28	Tom's Wear declares and pays a dividend of $100.

EXHIBIT 2.4

Transactions for Tom's Wear for February in the Accounting Equation Worksheet

The income statement is prepared first. Then, the net income can be used on the Statement of Changes in Shareholder's Equity. The total contributed capital and retained earnings from that statement are then used on the balance sheet. Finally, the cash transactions are reorganized for the statement of cash flows.

	Assets				=	Liabilities		+	Shareholder's Equity			
									Contributed Capital	Retained Earnings		
												Beginning RE 385
	Cash	Accounts Receivable	Inventory	Prepaid Insurance		Accounts Payable	Other Payables		Common Stock	Revenues	Expenses	Dividends
Beginning Balances	$ 5,345		40						5,000			
Feb 1			800			800						
Feb 5	(100)						50				(150)	
Feb 14	(150)			150								
Feb 23	1,700	150								1,850		
			(740)								(740)	
Feb 28	(100)											(100)
Subtotals	$ 6,695	150	100	150	=	0	50		5,000	1,850	(890)	(100)
Adjustment				(25)							(25)	
Ending Balances	$ 6,695	150	100	125	=	800	50		5,000	1,850	(915)	(100)
												385

— Income Statement   — Statement of Changes in Shareholder's Equity   — Balance Sheet   — Statement of Cash Flows

Accounts receivable are amounts customers owe a company for goods or services purchased on credit.

The company's success continues with the sale of 185 more T-shirts at $10 each. Although Transaction 4 shows these sales as a single transaction, they could have been individual sales. They are grouped together here to make the presentation simple. Of the 185 shirts sold, 170 were sold for cash of $1,700 (170 shirts at $10 each) and 15 were sold on credit for $150 (15 shirts at $10 each). When a sale is made on credit, **accounts receivable** are the amounts owed to the firm by customers. Accounts receivable are assets—things of value to a business. This is the fourth transaction shown in Exhibit 2.4. Notice that the rest of this transaction includes the decrease in inventory of $740 (185 shirts at $4 each) with a corresponding expense—cost of goods sold of $740—which decreases retained earnings by $740.

At the end of the second month of business, Tom's Wear pays a dividend of $100 to its only stockholder, Tom. This transaction reduces assets—cash—by $100, and it reduces retained earnings by $100. This is the fifth transaction shown in Exhibit 2.4.

The financial statements for February can be prepared with the information from these transactions. However, there is still one more step before accurate financial statements can be prepared. This step is called **adjusting the books**. You need to review the amount that has been recorded for each asset and each claim to make sure every amount correctly reflects the financial situation of the company on the specific date of the balance sheet—the last day of the fiscal period (month, quarter, or year). After reviewing the transactions for Tom's Wear during the month, can you identify any amount that seems incorrect to you? Start at the beginning of the accounting equation worksheet in Exhibit 2.4 and look at each item that has been recorded. The assets are cash, $6,695; accounts receivable, $150; inventory, $100; and prepaid insurance, $150. Are these amounts accurate at February 28, 2006, the end of the second month of Tom's Wear? Is any asset likely to communicate incorrect information?

Adjusting the books means to make changes in the accounting records, at the end of the period, just before the financial statements are prepared, to make sure the amounts reflect the financial condition of the company at that date.

Yes—prepaid insurance, as it currently appears in the company's records, will not express what it should. Because the balance sheet will have the date February 28, 2006, Tom's Wear wants the amount of prepaid insurance to be accurate at that date. What is the amount of the asset—insurance that is still unused—at the date of the balance sheet? The $150, paid on February 14, applied to 3 months. On February 28, half a month's worth has passed. So, approximately one-sixth (half a month's worth) of the prepaid insurance has been used. An adjustment must be made to make sure the correct amount of prepaid insurance is shown on the balance sheet. Like routine transactions, adjustments must keep the accounting equation in balance. To record this adjustment in the accounting equation, subtract $25 (1/6 × $150) from the prepaid insurance column, reducing the amount of prepaid insurance, and then reduce owner's claims by the same $25 amount. This reduction in the owner's claims is an expense—insurance expense—so it will be shown in the red-boxed area in the accounting equation worksheet. This adjustment is shown as A1 on the worksheet in Exhibit 2.4. The correct amount of the asset—the unused portion—will be shown on the balance sheet at February 28, 2006, as $125.

A review of the other items on the balance sheet does not reveal any other needed adjustments on this particular balance sheet date. In the next chapter, you will learn about other situations requiring adjustments before the financial statements can be prepared. For now, this adjustment makes the accounting records ready for the preparation of the financial statements at the end of February.

The income statement, prepared first, lists the revenues and expenses for the period; you can find those in the red-boxed area in Exhibit 2.4. All revenues increase retained earnings; all expenses decrease retained earnings. The only item that we regularly find under retained earnings that is *not* included on the income statement is a distribution to the owners, *dividends* in a corporation. GAAP says that distributions are not expenses.

All of the items for the income statement are in the red-boxed area of the worksheet. We can simply take the amounts in the red box in the retained earnings columns and group the transactions into revenues and expenses to form an income statement. The sales revenue, often simply called *sales*, is $1,850.

There are three types of expenses listed. One is the cost of goods sold—also known as cost of sales. Recall, this is the expense associated with selling something purchased from someone else. Tom's Wear has cost of goods sold of $740. The other two expenses are $150 for the advertising and $25 for insurance. Be sure you see and understand that the insurance expense is not the amount Tom's Wear actually paid to the insurance company. Instead, it

Tom's Wear, Inc.
Income Statement
For the Month Ended February 28, 2006

Revenue			
Sales			$ 1,850
Expenses			
Cost of goods sold		$ 740	
Advertising expense		150	
Insurance expense		25	
Total expenses			915
Net income			$ 935

EXHIBIT 2.5

Income Statement for Tom's Wear

This is the income statement for the second month of business for Tom's Wear.

is the cost of the insurance that was used during the period. The amount that has not been used as of February 28 remains on the balance sheet as an asset.

The net income for the period is $935—revenues of $1,850 minus expenses of $915. Check it out in Exhibit 2.5, the income statement for Tom's Wear for the month of February.

The statement of changes in shareholder's equity is prepared next (shown in Exhibit 2.6). This statement provides the details of the changes in shareholder's equity during the year. The information for this statement is found in the shareholder's equity columns of the worksheet in Exhibit 2.4, shown in the yellow-boxed area. Tom's Wear began the month with $5,000 in contributed capital. No new stock was issued during the month. That means no new contributions were made during the month. Retained earnings began the month with a balance of $385. Net income of $935 increases retained earnings, and the dividend of $100 decreases retained earnings. Because we have already prepared the income statement to summarize what happened in the red-boxed area in the retained earnings column, we do not need to list all of the individual items again. We just need to add net income as a single amount. The amount of retained earnings at the end of the period is $1,220 ($385 + 935 − 100).

Next, Tom's Wear prepares the balance sheet. The balance sheet was really prepared as the transactions were put in the accounting equation worksheet—but not in a way to communicate the information most effectively. The transactions need to be summarized and organized to communicate the information clearly and effectively. Each asset owned at February 28 is listed, along with the claims to those assets. Notice the similarity between the list of transactions on the worksheet in Exhibit 2.4 and the balance sheet in Exhibit 2.7.

Tom's Wear, Inc.
Statement of Changes in Shareholder's Equity
For the Month Ended February 28, 2006

Beginning common stock		$ 5,000	
Common stock issued during the month		0	
Ending common stock			$ 5,000
Beginning retained earnings		$ 385	
Net income for the month		935	
Dividends declared		(100)	
Ending retained earnings			1,220
Total shareholder's equity			$ 6,220

EXHIBIT 2.6

Statement of Changes in Shareholder's Equity for Tom's Wear for February

The Statement of Changes in Shareholder's Equity shows how all of the equity accounts have changed during the month.

EXHIBIT 2.7

Balance Sheet for Tom's Wear at February 28

The balance sheet at February 28 has incorporated the new retained earnings balance.

tom's wear

Tom's Wear, Inc.
Balance Sheet
At February 28, 2006

Assets		Liabilities and Shareholder's Equity	
Cash	$ 6,695	Accounts payable	$ 800
Accounts receivable	150	Other payables	50
Inventory	100		
Prepaid insurance	125	Common stock	5,000
		Retained earnings	1,220
		Total liabilities and	
Total assets	$ 7,070	shareholder's equity	$ 7,070

The assets are listed at their amounts on February 28, 2006. There is $6,695 cash. (The details of how this number was calculated will be shown on the statement of cash flows.) Tom's Wear also has accounts receivable of $150—the amount customers still owe the company for T-shirts purchased during the month but the cash has not been collected yet. There are 25 shirts left in the inventory, each having cost $4, for a total of $100.

The last asset is prepaid insurance, and the amount shown is $125—the unused portion at February 28. The adjustment reduced prepaid insurance by $25 for the amount used up during the last half of February.

There are two liabilities at February 28, 2006—accounts payable of $800 and other payables of $50. These amounts are still owed by Tom's Wear to creditors.

The last item is the amount of shareholder's equity. Because we have already prepared the statement of changes in shareholder's equity, we know that $5,000 is the total contributed capital—in the form of stock—and $1,220 is the amount of retained earnings. Together, the liabilities plus shareholder's equity add up to $7,070—the same amount as the total assets.

The statement of cash flows (shown in Exhibit 2.8) shows every cash collection and every cash disbursement for the month. Each cash transaction is classified as one of three types: operating, investing, or financing. To prepare this statement, you need to use the items from the transactions in the cash column of the worksheet in Exhibit 2.4, shown boxed in green. For each cash amount, ask yourself if it pertains to operating activities, investing activities, or financing activities.

The first cash amount in Exhibit 2.4 is the payment of $100 in cash for advertising; that was the second transaction. This $100 is an operating cash flow because it is a cash expense related to routine business activities.

The next cash transaction is the $150 paid to the insurance company. The purchase of insurance is an operating cash flow. Notice the statement of cash flows shows the cash paid—with no regard for when the insurance is used.

Transaction 4 involves cash inflows, for a total of $1,700. This transaction was a sale, which is an operating cash flow. Notice the cash in Transaction 4 is $1,700, representing 170 T-shirts sold for cash. Although 185 were actually sold, the cash for 15 of them has not been collected yet. In the statement of cash flows, every item must be cash only.

The final cash transaction is the distribution of $100 to the owner as dividends. This is classified as a financing cash flow because it relates to how the business is financed.

Be sure you see that the statement of cash flows includes every cash inflow and every cash outflow shown on the accounting equation worksheet. Also notice nothing else is included on this financial statement. The net amount is the change in the amount of cash during the period. The bottom of the statement of cash flows adds the beginning cash balance of $5,345 to the increase of $1,350 to get the ending cash balance of $6,695, shown on the February 28, 2006, balance sheet.

Notes to the financial statements are not included here for Tom's Wear, but you should never forget that they are a crucial part of the financial statements. There is an accounting principle called the **full-disclosure principle**, which means that companies should disclose

The **full-disclosure principle** means that the firm must disclose any circumstances and events that would make a difference to the users of the financial statements.

Tom's Wear, Inc.
Statement of Cash Flows
For the Month Ended February 28, 2006

Cash from operating activities
    Cash collected from customers .... $ 1,700
    Cash paid to advertising .... (100)
    Cash paid for insurance .... (150)

Net cash from operations .... $ 1,450

Cash from investing activities   0

Cash from financing activities
    Cash paid for dividends .... $ (100)
Net cash from financing .... (100)

Net increase in cash .... $ 1,350
Add beginning cash balance 5,345
Ending cash balance .... $ 6,695

EXHIBIT 2.8

Statement of Cash Flows for Tom's Wear for February

The Statement of Cash Flows provides details about the changes to cash during the period.

any circumstances and events that would make a difference to the users of the financial statements. Look at the notes in the financial statements of Staples in the appendix of the book. The notes are longer than the statements! As you gain an understanding of the complexity of the choices accountants make in preparing financial statements, you will see the need for notes to give the financial statement users information about those choices.

Is prepaid insurance an expense or an asset? Explain.

Assets

Looking at the balance sheet at February 28, 2006, for Tom's Wear, Exhibit 2.7, you see on the left the company's assets, also referred to as economic resources. According to GAAP, **assets** are those items of value that belong to or are controlled by the company. They are on the balance sheet as a result of past transactions, but they do have value, which they will provide in the future when they will be used to help the business produce revenue.

    The first asset on Tom's Wear's balance sheet is cash. The amount has been determined by past transactions, and the money has value because of what it can buy in the future. Other common assets include accounts receivable (amounts owed to the company by customers) and inventory (items purchased for sale). The last asset shown is prepaid insurance. This is the unused portion of the insurance—it still has value on February 28.

    Assets are listed on the balance sheet in order of **liquidity**. Liquidity refers to how easily an asset can be converted into cash. The assets that are expected to be used within a year are called **current assets**. The assets that will not be used within a year are called **noncurrent assets**, or **long-term assets**. So far, Tom's Wear has only current assets. Look at the balance sheet of Home Depot Inc. in Exhibit 2.9. The asset section of the balance sheet shows both current and long-term assets.

    Assets are one of three classifications of items on the balance sheet. The other two classifications tell who—creditors or owners—has claim to these assets. Recall, the balance sheet is essentially the accounting equation:

$$\text{Assets} = \text{Liabilities} + \text{Shareholders' equity}$$

Your Turn 2-3
Your Turn
Your Turn

Assets are the economic resources owned or controlled by a company, resulting from past transactions.

Liquidity is a measure of how easily an asset can be converted to cash. The more liquid an asset is, the more easily it can be turned into cash.

Current assets are the assets the company plans to turn into cash or use to generate revenue in the next fiscal year.

Noncurrent assets, or **long-term assets**, are assets that will last for more than a year.

EXHIBIT 2.9

Comparative Balance Sheets for The Home Depot

This is a recent balance sheet taken from the Home Depot's annual report.

The Home Depot, Inc. and Subsidiaries
Consolidated Balance Sheets

amounts in millions, except per share data	January 29, 2006	January 30, 2005
Assets		
Current assets:		
Cash and cash equivalents	$ 793	$ 506
Short-term investments	14	1,659
Receivables, net	2,396	1,499
Merchandise inventories	11,401	10,076
Other current assets	742	533
Total current assets	15,346	14,273
Property and equipment, at cost:		
Land	7,924	6,932
Buildings	14,056	12,325
Furniture, fixtures, and equipment	7,073	6,195
Leasehold improvements	1,207	1,191
Construction in progress	843	1,404
Capital leases	427	390
	31,530	28,437
Less accumulated depreciation and amortization	6,629	5,711
Net property and equipment	24,901	22,726
Notes receivable	348	369
Cost in excess of the fair value of net assets acquired	3,286	1,394
Other assets	601	258
Total assets	$ 44,482	$ 39,020
Liabilities and Stockholder's Equity		
Current liabilities:		
Short-term debt	$ 900	$ —
Accounts payable	6,032	5,766
Accrued salaries and related expenses	1,176	1,055
Sales taxes payable	488	412
Deferred revenue	1,757	1,546
Income taxes payable	388	161
Current installments of long-term debt	513	11
Other accrued expenses	1,647	1,504
Total current liabilities	12,901	10,455
Long-term debt, excluding current installments	2,672	2,148
Other long-term liabilities	977	871
Deferred income taxes	1,023	1,388
Stockholder's Equity		
Common stock, par value $0.05; authorized: 10,000 shares; issued 2,401 shares at January 29, 2006 and 2,385 shares at January 30, 2005; outstanding 2,124 shares at January 29, 2006 and 2,185 shares at January 30, 2005	120	119
Paid-in capital	7,287	6,650
Retained earnings	28,943	23,962
Accumulated other comprehensive income	409	227
Unearned compensation	(138)	(108)
Treasury stock, at cost, 277 shares at January 29, 2006 and 200 shares at January 30, 2005	(9,712)	(6,692)
Total stockholder's equity	26,909	24,158
Total liabilities and stockholder's equity	$ 44,482	$ 39,020

See accompanying Notes to Consolidated Financial Statements.

Liabilities

The January 2, 2006, balance sheet, shown in Exhibit 1.6, indicated that Tom's Wear owed $500 to Tom's mom. On February 28, 2006, that is no longer the case. The debt was paid off in January. On February 28, 2006, the only liabilities Tom's Wear has are accounts payable and other payables. **Liabilities** are amounts that the business owes. They are the claims of creditors. Usually, these claims will be paid to creditors in cash. Liabilities, like assets, are the result of past transactions or events. For example, a purchase of inventory items on credit creates a liability called accounts payable. The balance sheet on February 28, 2006 was prepared after the purchase of the shirts but before Tom paid for them, so the balance sheet shows the cost of the shirts as accounts payable. Once incurred, a liability continues as an obligation of the company until the company pays for it. The accounts payable amount for the T-shirts remains on the balance sheet until Tom pays the bill for the shirts. Often, liabilities involve interest—payment of an additional amount for the right to delay payment. When Tom's Wear repaid Tom's mom in January, he paid $5 interest for the use of her money.

> **Liabilities** are obligations the company has incurred to obtain the assets it has acquired.

Liabilities can also be current or noncurrent. If a liability will be settled with a current asset, it is called a **current liability**. For practical purposes, you can think about a current liability as a liability that will be paid off in the next year. **Noncurrent liabilities**, or **long-term liabilities**, will be paid off over a period longer than one year. Most balance sheets show a subtotal for current assets and a subtotal for current liabilities. That format is called a **classified balance sheet**. Look at the balance sheet for Home Depot, shown in Exhibit 2.9. See if you can find the subtotals for current assets and current liabilities. This is a classified balance sheet because it has two classifications of assets and liabilities—short term and long term.

> **Current liabilities** are liabilities the company will settle—pay off—in the next fiscal year.

> **Noncurrent liabilities**, or **long-term liabilities**, are liabilities that will take longer than a year to settle.

> A **classified balance sheet** shows a subtotal for many items, including current assets and current liabilities.

---

1. **What is the difference between a current asset and a long-term asset?**
2. **What is a classified balance sheet?**

Your Turn 2-4
Your Turn
Your Turn

Shareholders' Equity

Shareholders' equity, sometimes called net assets, is the owners' claims to the assets of the company. There are two ways owners can create equity in a company. The first way is by making capital contributions—**contributed capital**. Usually, the capital is cash, but it could be equipment or other items of value. When Tom started his T-shirt business, he invested $5,000 of his own money. Sometimes this is called the owner's investment in the company. The term investment may be confused with investments that the company itself makes with its extra cash. For example, General Motors may invest some of its extra cash in the stock of Google, which General Motors would call an investment. To avoid that confusion, we will refer to owners' investments in the firm as capital contributions.

> **Shareholders' equity** is the name for owners' claims to the assets of the firm. It includes both contributed capital and retained earnings.

> **Contributed capital**, sometimes called **paid-in capital**, is the amount the owners have put into the business.

The second way to create equity in a business is to make a profit. (That is the preferred way.) When Tom's Wear sells a shirt, the profit from that shirt increases Tom's equity in the company. Revenues increase shareholders' equity; expenses reduce shareholders' equity; and dividends, when declared, reduce shareholders' equity.

In corporations, the two types of equity are separated on the balance sheet. The first is **contributed capital,** also known as **paid-in capital**; the second is **retained earnings**. In a sole proprietorship or partnership, both types of equity are together called **capital**. Separating these amounts for corporations provides information for potential investors about how much the owners have actually invested in the corporation.

> **Retained earnings** is capital the company has earned and has not been distributed as dividends.

> **Capital** is the combined contributed capital and earned capital—retained earnings—of a sole proprietorship or partnership.

Measurement and Recognition in Financial Statements

We will now take a closer look at some of the features of the balance sheet and income statement. Recall, the balance sheet is simply the accounting equation: **Assets = Liabilities + Shareholders' equity**. The three elements are major categories, each divided into subcategories.

Measuring Assets. We will start with assets. The most well-known asset is cash. It is listed first on the balance sheet. As you will notice on Home Depot's balance sheet, all other assets are listed in order of their liquidity—how easily they can be converted to cash. A monetary value is computed for each asset. Cash, for example, is the total amount of money in checking and savings accounts. The next asset could be short-term investments, ones the company can easily sell for cash at any time. The next asset on the balance sheet is usually accounts receivable—the total amount that customers owe the company for credit sales. Inventory is another asset, measured at its cost. We saw that Tom's Wear's balance sheet included the cost of the T-shirts still in the inventory on the balance sheet date.

Earlier you learned two characteristics of the way things are measured for the financial statements. First, they are measured in monetary units. For us, that means dollars. For example, the actual number of T-shirts in the inventory is not shown on the balance sheet; only the cost of the inventory is shown. Second, the items on the financial statements are recorded at historical cost—what the company paid for them. They are not recorded at the amount the company hopes to sell them for. Some assets continue to be shown at cost on the balance sheet, and others are revalued to a more current amount for each balance sheet. You will learn the details of which assets are revalued and which assets are not revalued in the chapters to come.

Recognizing Revenue and Expenses. When should revenue be included on an income statement? GAAP says when it is earned, that is when revenue is **recognized**—meaning that is when revenue is included on the income statement. When Tom delivers a shirt to a customer, Tom's Wear has earned the revenue. This is called the **revenue-recognition principle**. When one of Tom's friends says he is going to buy a T-shirt next week, no revenue is recognized. When an exchange actually takes place, or when the earnings process is complete or "virtually complete," that is the time for revenue recognition. When Tom's Wear and a customer exchange the cash and the T-shirt, there is no doubt the transaction is complete. However, even when Tom's Wear only delivers the T-shirt and the customer agrees to pay for it later (the sale is on credit), the company will consider the earnings process virtually complete. Tom's Wear has done its part, so the sale is included on the income statement.

What about expenses? When an expense is recognized depends on when the revenue that results from that expense is recognized. Expenses are recognized—included on the income statement—when the revenue they were incurred to generate is recognized. This is called the **matching principle**, and it is the basis of the income statement. Expenses are matched with the revenue they helped to generate. An example is the cost of goods sold. Only the cost of the T-shirts *sold* is recognized—included as an expense on the income statement. The expense is matched with the revenue from the sale of those shirts. The cost of the unsold T-shirts is not an expense—and will not be an expense—until those shirts are sold. An expense is a cost that has been used to generate revenue. If a cost has been incurred but it has not been used up, it is classified as an asset until it is used. Prepaid insurance is an example of a cost that is classified as an asset until it is used; and when it is used, it becomes insurance expense.

Must the customer actually pay the company in cash before a sale can be counted as revenue? No. Notice that the sales of all the shirts are included in the sales total, even though 15 of the shirts have not been paid for yet. When a customer purchases an item on credit, the earnings process is considered virtually complete, even though the cash has not been collected. Similarly, a cost incurred in the generation of revenue need not be paid to be included on the income statement. In calculating the revenue and expenses for an income

Recognized revenue is revenue that has been recorded so that it will show up on the income statement.

The **revenue-recognition principle** says that revenue should be recognized when it is earned and collection is reasonably assured.

The **matching principle** says that expenses should be recognized—shown on the income statement—in the same period as the revenue they helped generate.

 News Flash

Accounting information really matters! Mills Corporation, a shopping-mall real-estate investment trust, disclosed that the SEC was investigating its accounting practices, including the way the firm recognizes revenue. An analyst for Banc of Americas Securities downgraded Mills shares to "sell" status because the announcement suggested the firm overbooked revenue and may have understated expenses. What happened? The firm's share price dropped by 12%.

statement, accountants do not follow the cash. Instead, they use the time when the "economic substance" of the transaction is complete.

Accountants use the expressions *virtually complete* and *economic substance* to describe the same idea—that a transaction does not need to be technically complete to recognize the resulting revenue. If the transaction is substantially complete, the revenue is recognized. When Tom's Wear sells the T-shirts, delivering them and receiving the customers' promise to pay is considered the economic substance of that transaction. Cash may come before the transaction is complete or it may come afterward. This way of accounting for revenues and expenses—using the economic substance of the transaction to determine when to include it on the income statement instead of using the exchange of cash—is called **accrual accounting**.

When to recognize revenue is easy for some businesses and extremely difficult for others. There is a lot of disagreement among accountants about the timing of revenue recognition. They agree that revenue should be recognized when the revenue has actually been earned and it is reasonable to assume the customer will pay. That is, the transaction is virtually complete. But they often cannot agree on exactly when that has happened. This is an important topic that is regularly debated in the financial community. Unfortunately, improper revenue recognition has caused serious problems for many companies. Many of the accounting scandals with the earnings reported by major corporations in the last few years are related to revenue recognition.

Exhibit 2.10 summarizes the assumptions, principles, and constraints of accounting information.

> **Accrual accounting** refers to the way we recognize revenues and expenses. Accountants do not rely on the exchange of cash to determine the timing of revenue recognition. Firms recognize revenue when it is earned and expenses when they are incurred—no matter when the cash is received or disbursed. Accrual accounting follows the matching principle.

EXHIBIT 2.10

Assumptions, Principles, and Constraints of Financial Reporting

Assumptions:	Time-period assumption	The life of a business can be divided into artificial time periods for financial reporting.
	Separate-entity assumption	Financial statements of a firm contain financial information about only that firm.
	Monetary-unit assumption	Only items that can be measured in monetary units are included in the financial statements.
	Going-concern assumption	A company will remain in business for the foreseeable future.
Principles:	Historical-cost principle	Assets are recorded at cost.
	Revenue-recognition principle	Revenue is recognized when it is earned and collection is reasonably assured.
	Matching principle	Expenses are recognized in the same period as the revenue they helped generate.
	Full-disclosure principle	A company should provide information about any circumstances and events that would make a difference to the users of the financial statements.
Constraints:	Materiality	Materiality refers to the size or significance of an item or transaction on the company's financial statements.
	Conservatism	When there is any question about how to account for a transaction, the accountant should select the treatment that will be least likely to overstate income or overstate assets.

REVENUE RECOGNITION

When to recognize revenue—record it so that it appears on the period's income statement—is one of the most difficult judgments a company must make. A 2005 study of 400 business leaders by RevenueRecognition.com and International Data Corporation found that more than half of all public companies have changed their revenue recognition policies as a result of Sarbanes-Oxley. But it is changing business models that account for more changes in revenue recognition policies than any other single factor. New business models can be quite complex, involving bundled products and services delivered over long periods of time. When to recognize revenue can be difficult to determine.

Your Turn 2-5
Your Turn
Your Turn

L.O.4
Define accrual accounting, explain how it differs from cash basis accounting, and identify examples of accrual accounting on actual financial statements.

An **accrual transaction** is one in which the revenue is earned or the expense is incurred before the exchange of cash.

A **deferral transaction** is one in which the exchange of cash takes place before the revenue is earned or the expense incurred.

Give an example of the matching principle from the income statement for Tom's Wear for February.

Accruals and Deferrals

Accrual Basis Accounting

The term *accrual basis accounting* includes two kinds of transactions in which the exchange of cash does not coincide with the economic substance of the transaction. The revenues and expenses are recognized at a time other than the time when the cash is collected or paid.

One kind of accrual basis transaction is an **accrual** and the other is a **deferral**. The meaning of each kind of accrual basis transaction is shown in Exhibit 2.11.

When the action comes before the cash, it is an *accrual*. When Tom's Wear made a credit sale, it was an accrual transaction. To accrue means to "build up" or "accumulate." In accounting, we are building up our sales or our expenses even though the cash has not been exchanged. The sale is completed first—merchandise is delivered to the customer—and the cash payment will come later. Instead of receiving the asset *cash* from the purchaser, the company records an asset called *accounts receivable*—meaning *cash* due from the purchaser. Accounts receivable is the amount owed to the company by customers. Because GAAP is based on accrual accounting, the necessary part of the transaction for recording the revenue is the actual sale of goods or services, not the cash receipt from the customers.

When the dollars come before the action, it is called a *deferral*. When Tom's Wear paid for the insurance, it was an advance purchase—as we all pay insurance premiums up front, not after the expiration date of the policy. But the amount paid for the insurance was not considered an expense until it was actually used. To defer something, in common language, means to put it off—to delay or postpone it. In the language of accounting, a deferral means that the company will postpone recognizing the expense until the insurance is actually used. When Tom's Wear paid the cash in advance of the period covered by the insurance, the company recorded the cash disbursement. In other words, Tom's Wear recorded it in the business records as cash that had been spent. However, the expense was not recognized when the cash was paid. It will be recognized—and remember, that means included on the income statement—when the cost is actually used.

EXHIBIT 2.11

Accrual Accounting

Accrual accounting involves both accruals and deferrals.

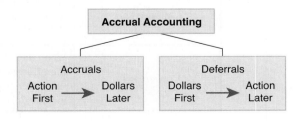

Cash Basis Versus Accrual Basis Accounting

There is another type of accounting called **cash basis accounting**—revenue is recognized only when the cash is collected, and expenses are recorded only when the cash is paid. This is *not* a generally accepted method of accounting according to the FASB and the SEC. Using the exchange of cash as the signal for recognizing revenue and expense does not communicate the performance of the business in a way that allows us to evaluate its achievements. The cash flows are important, but alone they do not provide enough information for decision makers. This does not stop some businesses from using it as the basis of their own accounting records. Remember, some businesses are not required to follow GAAP. For example, doctors who are sole proprietors may use cash basis accounting in their businesses. This means they recognize only the cash they receive as revenue. If they provide services to someone who has not yet paid for those services at the time an income statement is prepared, they would not include the fee not yet received as revenue for that income statement. That is not GAAP. If the doctors were following GAAP, they would count it as revenue and as a receivable (accounts receivable).

> **Cash basis accounting** is a system based on the exchange of cash. In this system, revenue is recognized only when cash is collected, and an expense is recognized only when cash is disbursed. This is not an acceptable method of accounting under GAAP.

Accounting Periods and Cutoff Issues

Why does it matter—for accounting purposes—if there is a difference between the time when the goods or services are exchanged—the economic substance of the transaction—and the time when the cash related to that transaction is received or disbursed? If a company makes a sale on credit and the cash is collected later, why does it matter when the sale is recognized—included as revenue on the income statement? Studying Tom's Wear will help you see the answers to these questions.

When Tom began his business in 2006, he chose the calendar year as his company's fiscal year. Each of his annual income statements will cover the period from January 1 to December 31 of a specific year. It is important that what appears on the income statement for a specific year is only the revenue earned during those 12 months and only the expenses incurred to generate that revenue. What is included as a sale during the period? Accountants have decided to use the exchange of goods and services, not the cash exchange, to define when a sale has taken place. Expenses are matched with revenues, also without regard to when the cash is exchanged. This makes the financial statements of all companies that follow GAAP consistent and comparable.

Exhibit 2.12 shows the relationship between the balance sheet and the income statement and the time periods involved. Recall, the balance sheet is a snapshot view of the assets, liabilities, and shareholders' equity on a specific date. For a company with a fiscal year-end on December 31, that is the date of the balance sheet. Remember, the end-of-the-year balance sheet for one year becomes the beginning-of-the-year balance sheet for the next year. When you are out celebrating New Year's Eve, nothing is happening to the balance sheet. When Tom goes to sleep on December 31, 2006, the cash on the December 31, 2006, balance sheet of Tom's Wear is exactly the amount of cash that the company will have on January 1, 2007. So the final balance sheet for one year simply rolls forward to the next year.

Then, transactions start happening—exchanges take place. The revenues and expenses for the period of time are shown on the income statement. The income statement covers a

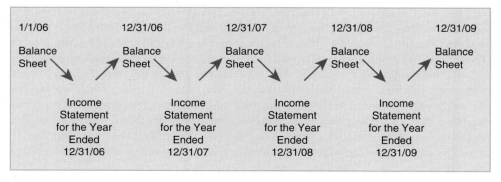

EXHIBIT 2.12

The Balance Sheet and Income Statement

Every balance sheet presents the assets, liabilities, and shareholders' equity of a business firm at a moment in time. The income statement describes what happened between two balance sheet dates.

period of time. A company may construct weekly, monthly, quarterly, or annual financial statements. Many companies prepare monthly and quarterly financial statements; all companies prepare annual financial statements. The income statement for a specific year gives the revenues and expenses for that year. It gives information about how the balance sheet has changed between the beginning of the year and the end of the year. The revenues increase owners' claims; expenses reduce owners' claims. If the difference between revenues and expenses is positive—if revenues are greater than expenses—the company has a net income. If the expenses are greater than revenues, the company has a net loss. The net income or net loss is sometimes called the *bottom line*.

Your Turn 2-6
Your Turn
Your Turn

What is the difference between cash basis and accrual basis accounting?

Financial statements provide information about the risk related to investing in a company. Will you get a good return on your investment? How long will it take?

How Investors—Owners and Creditors— Use Accrual Accounting Information

Owners and creditors are both considered investors in a business. Both invest their money to make money, and they both take a risk in investing their money in the business. In this context, you can think of risk as the uncertainty associated with the amount of future returns and the timing of future returns. Some investments are riskier than others are. For example, when a bank makes a loan to a company, the banker evaluates the ability of the company to repay the loan amount—the principal—plus interest—the cost of borrowing the money. If the bank makes a loan to a company that does not do well enough to repay the debt, the company may need to sell noncash assets to raise cash to pay off the loan plus interest due. When lending money, the bank must compare the risk with the expected return.

Most often, the risk and return of an investment change value in the same direction— we say they are positively correlated. *Positively correlated* means they move in the same direction—higher risk means higher expected return for taking the higher risk; lower risk means lower expected returns. For higher investment risk, the potential for a higher return is needed to attract investors.

Investing in a company as an owner is riskier than investing as a creditor. A creditor's claim to the assets of a company has priority over an owner's claim. (Creditors have first claim to the assets.) If a company has just enough money either to pay its creditors or to make a distribution to its owner or owners, the creditors must be paid, and *they always must be paid* before anything—if there is anything left—is distributed to the owners. That translates into less risk for a creditor. The owner's risk is that the company will go out of business.

However, the owner, who takes more risk, has the right to share the profit. So the risk for the owner is accompanied by the potential for a higher return. A creditor, on the other hand, will never receive more than the amount of the loan, plus the amount of interest that is agreed on when the loan is made.

Financial information is useful for someone deciding whether or not to invest in a company. Suppose Tom's Wear wanted to borrow money to expand. A bank would want to examine Tom's Wear's income statement, balance sheet, and the statement of cash flows. The reason is to evaluate potential risk—the company's ability to make the required principal and interest payments.

The balance sheet shows a company's assets and who has claim to them. A bank loan officer would use the information on the balance sheet to evaluate Tom's Wear's ability to repay the loan. He would want to be sure that the company did not have too many debts. The more debt a company has, the more cash it must generate to make the loan payments.

The information on the balance sheet would not be enough to assure the bank loan officer that Tom's Wear would be able to repay the loan. Because a loan is repaid over several months or years, information about the future earning potential of the business is important. Studying the past performance of a business helps predict its future performance. That makes the profit the company earned during the past year relevant to the banker. Details about the sales revenue and expenses incurred to generate that revenue would help the bank evaluate the company's potential to generate enough cash to repay a loan.

Still, the information on these two financial statements, no matter how relevant to the bank's evaluation, would not be enough. Another piece of the puzzle is the way the company manages its cash. A company may have little debt and lots of earning potential. However, if the company does not have enough cash, the loan payments cannot be made. Because cash collection is the bank's primary concern, the statement of cash flows provides additional information for the bank.

An Example to Illustrate the Information Financial Statements Provide

We will compare two companies, each starting its fiscal year with identical balance sheets. Then, during the first month of the year, they have very similar transactions. We will look at only a few of the transactions, and we will see that their income statements for the first month are the same. As you study the example, try to figure out why their income statements are the same. Their ending balance sheets and statements of cash flows are not the same. Where do the differences show up in the financial statements?

The two companies are Clean Sweep and Maids-R-Us. Both are cleaning businesses and both are sole proprietorships. Judy Jones owns Clean Sweep, and Betty Brown owns Maids-R-Us. On January 1, 2007, the two companies have identical balance sheets. Look at each item on the balance sheet in Exhibit 2.13 and be sure you know what it means. Do this before you go on.

Study each transaction and look at its effect on the accounting equation. Follow along using Exhibits 2.14 and 2.15.

Transaction 1: Each company earns $750 worth of revenue. Clean Sweep collects the cash, but Maids-R-Us extends credit to its customers. Clean Sweep records the asset cash, whereas Maids-R-Us records the asset *accounts receivable*. Both companies

EXHIBIT 2.13

Beginning Balance Sheet for Clean Sweep and Maids-R-Us

At the beginning of the month, both companies have the same balance sheet.

Clean Sweep or Maids-R-Us
Balance Sheet
At January 1, 2007

Assets
Cash .... $ 900
Supplies 200
Total assets .... $ 1,100
Liabilities
Notes payable .... $ 400
Owner's equity
Owner, Capital 700
Total liabilities and owner's equity .... $ 1,100

EXHIBIT 2.14

Transactions for January 2007 for Clean Sweep and Maids-R-Us

Be sure to study how the transactions are different for the two companies.

Both Clean Sweep and Maids-R-Us	Clean Sweep	Maids-R-Us
1. Clean 10 houses for a fee of $75 per house.	Collects the fees in cash at the time the services are rendered.	Agrees to extend credit to the customers. Fees will be collected after 30 days.
2. Make a loan payment plus interest.	Pays off the entire loan plus $40 interest.	Pays only $100 of the loan plus $40 interest.
3. Count the supplies on January 31 and find $25 worth left on hand.	Both will make an adjustment to show $175 worth of supplies used.	

EXHIBIT 2.15

Transactions for Clean Sweep and Maids-R-Us

The differences in the transactions between the two companies are reflected in the accounting equation worksheet.

Panel A: Clean Sweep

	Assets			= Liabilities +		Owner's Equity			
	Cash	Accounts Receivable	Supplies	Notes Payable	Beginning Capital	Revenues	Expenses	Dividends	
Beginning Balances	$ 900		200	400	700				
1.	750					750			
2.	(440)			(400)			(40)		
3.			(175)				(175)		
Ending Balances	$ 1,210	–	25 =	–	700	750	(215)		

━ Income Statement ━ Statement of Changes in Owner's Equity ━ Balance Sheet ━ Statement of Cash Flows

Panel B: Maids-R-Us

	Assets			= Liabilities +		Owner's Equity			
	Cash	Accounts Receivable	Supplies	Notes Payable	Beginning Capital	Revenues	Expenses	Dividends	
Beginning Balances	$ 900		200	400	700				
1.		750				750			
2.	(140)			(100)			(40)		
3.			(175)				(175)		
Ending Balances	$ 760	750	25 =	300	700	750	(215)		

have earned the same amount of revenue, so each will show $750 revenue on its income statement for the month.

Transaction 2: Each company makes a loan payment. Clean Sweep pays the entire amount of the note payable, $400, plus interest of $40. Maids-R-Us pays only $100 of principal on the note payable, plus interest of $40. The only expense in this transaction is the interest expense of $40. Both companies have incurred the same amount of interest expense, so each will show $40 interest expense on its income statement. The repayment of the principal of a loan does not affect the income statement.

Clean Sweep or Maids-R-Us
Income Statement
For the Month Ended
January 31, 2007

Revenue			
Cleaning fees			$ 750
Expenses			
Supplies		$ 175	
Interest		40	
Total expenses			215
Net income			$ 535

EXHIBIT 2.16

Income Statement for Clean Sweep and Maids-R-Us for January

Look back at Exhibit 2.15 to the accounting equation worksheet, where you will see the transactions in the red boxed area are the same for both companies. That means their income statements are identical.

Adjustment: At the end of the period, each company will record supplies expense of $175, leaving $25 as supplies on hand on the January 31 balance sheet. Both income statements will show supplies expense of $175.

We can construct an income statement for each company from the numbers in the red-boxed area in Exhibit 2.15. Revenues for the month of January amounted to $750; expenses were $215; so net income was $535. This is the case for both companies, as shown in Exhibit 2.16. Even though one company extended credit to its customers and the other collected cash for its services, the income statements are identical. The income statement is only concerned with revenues earned and expenses incurred, not with the timing of the related cash flows.

The balance sheet at January 31 for each company can be constructed by simply organizing the details of the ending balances of the accounting equation for each company in Exhibit 2.15. For a sole proprietorship, all owner's equity—contributed and earned—is added together and called *owner's capital.* The two balance sheets are shown in Exhibit 2.17. Notice the differences. Assets and liabilities are different for the two companies, but the owner's equity amounts are the same.

EXHIBIT 2.17

Balance Sheet for Clean Sweep and Maids-R-Us at January 31, 2007

The balance sheets are not the same. The total assets are different because Clean Sweep paid $300 more than Maids-R-Us on the note payable. They have different assets also. Maids-R-Us has accounts receivable of $750, revenue it earned but did not collect in January.

Clean Sweep
Balance Sheet
At January 31, 2007

Assets		Liabilities and Owner's Equity	
Cash	$ 1,210		
Supplies	25	Capital, Jones	$ 1,235
Total assets	$ 1,235	Total liabilities and owner's equity	$ 1,235

Maids-R-Us
Balance Sheet
At January 31, 2007

Assets		Liabilities and Owner's Equity	
Cash	$ 760	Notes payable	$ 300
Accounts receivable	750		
Supplies	25	Capital, Brown	$ 1,235
Total assets	$ 1,535	Total liabilities and owner's equity	$ 1,535

EXHIBIT 2.18

Statements of Cash Flow for Clean Sweep and Maids-R-Us

The differences in the cash transactions result in differences in the statements of cash flow.

Clean Sweep Statement of Cash Flows For the Month Ended January 31, 2007	Maids-R-Us Statement of Cash Flows For the Month Ended January 31, 2007

Clean Sweep

Cash from operating activities		
Cash collected from customers ...	$ 750	
Cash paid for interest	(40)	
Net cash from operations		$ 710
Cash from investing activities		0
Cash from financing activities		
Repayment of loan	(400)	
Net cash from financing		(400)
Net increase in cash		$ 310

Maids-R-Us

Cash from operating activities		
Cash paid for interest	$ (40)	
Net cash from operations		$ (40)
Cash from investing activities		0
Cash from financing activities		
Repayment of loan	(100)	
Net cash from financing		(100)
Net increase (decrease) in cash		$ (140)

It is important to understand why both companies have the same amount of owner's equity. Both had beginning equity of $700 plus net income for the month of $535, for a total of $1,235. That is the number you find on the January 31 balance sheet for owner's equity. The timing of cash receipts and disbursements does not affect owner's equity.

Finally, look at the statement of cash flows. As you have seen, the cash receipts and disbursements for the two companies were not the same. This shows up clearly on the statement of cash flows. The cash flow statement for each company shows all the cash received and all the cash disbursed for the month. The cash flow statements are shown in Exhibit 2.18.

Your Turn 2-7
Your Turn
Your Turn

1. Explain how the revenues recognized on the income statement differ from the revenues shown on the statement of cash flows.

2. Suppose a company earns $50,000 in sales revenue, 20% of which is provided on account. How much revenue will be shown on the period's income statement? How much will be shown on the period's statement of cash flows? How much revenue will be included in the retained earnings total on the end-of-the-period balance sheet?

Putting It All Together—the Objectives of Financial Statements

Financial information should be useful. What makes it useful is the way the transactions of the business are organized into the four basic financial statements:

1. The income statement
2. The statement of changes in owner's equity
3. The balance sheet
4. The statement of cash flows

UNDERSTANDING **Business**

Accounting Is Accrual but Cash Is King

In this chapter, you have learned that financial statements are prepared on an *accrual* basis, but that does not mean **cash** is not important. Here is what The Motley Fool said about cash in a June 2006 article, "The Next Enron":

> Cash is king. Despite what some business execs want you to believe, cash pays the bills—accounting earnings do not.

As a matter of fact, cash budgeting is one of the most important activities a company performs. The starting point for avoiding a cash crisis is to develop a comprehensive cash flow budget. If you read about the fall of Enron, you will learn that the company did not have a cash flow budget. Enron simply ran out of cash, and its problems with the SEC dried up their lines of credits with their banks.

Smart business owners develop annual or even multiyear cash flow projections to make sure they can meet ongoing business needs. Business owners also prepare and use *historical* cash flow statements to gain an understanding about where all of the cash came from and where all the cash went.

By estimating your cash inflows and outflows, you can

- Make sure you have enough cash to purchase sufficient inventory for planned sales.
- Take advantage of purchase discounts and special offers.
- Plan equipment purchases, repairs, and replacements.
- Be prepared for any financing you may need in periods of cash shortages—short-term credit lines, small loans, or long-term debt.

For a new or growing business, accurate cash flow projections can make the difference between success and failure. For an ongoing business, good cash budgeting can make the difference between moving forward and standing still.

How do you prepare a cash flow projection? According to the Women's Business Center, preparing a cash projection is like preparing a budget and balancing your checkbook at the same time. First, you estimate your cash inflows. Cash is generated primarily by sales. But in many businesses, some of the sales are *on account* (charge accounts, term payments, layaway, and trade credit). So you must estimate when those credit sales will turn into actual cash inflows. Then, you estimate all the cash disbursements you need to make and when you need to make them.

The goal of cash budgeting is to always have enough cash to keep your business running smoothly. If it turns out that you have more cash than you need, then you must figure out how best to use that extra cash—how to invest it. That is a cash flow problem that you definitely want!

The ongoing life of a business is broken into discrete periods so that performance can be evaluated for a specific period. For our cleaning business examples, the period is a month.

Income is measured in a way that captures the economic substance of earning revenue and incurring expenses; it is not based on cash collections and cash disbursements. Notice, the net incomes for Maids-R-Us and Clean Sweep for January are exactly the same, in spite of the differences in when the cash is collected and disbursed. Those timing differences are reflected on the balance sheet by the differences in cash and both receivables and payables; and differences are also shown on the statement of cash flows—the statement that provides the details of the timing of cash receipts and disbursements. The four statements have been designed to be relevant, reliable, consistent, and comparable.

In addition to these qualities, accounting information relies on the basic assumptions and principles we discussed earlier, shown in Exhibit 2.10. We can relate each of the assumptions and principles to the financial statements of Maids-R-Us.

- The separate-entity assumption means that only the business transactions of Maids-R-Us are shown in the financial statements—none of the owner's personal transactions are included.
- The going-concern assumption means we may assume that Maids-R-Us is an ongoing, viable business. According to GAAP, if it were not ongoing, the company would need to have all its assets appraised and listed at liquidation value.
- The monetary-unit assumption means everything shown on the financial statements is measured in monetary units, here dollars.
- The historical-cost principle means the items on the financial statements are valued at cost. For example, the supplies on the balance sheet are not valued at what they might be worth if resold or at the current cost, which might be higher than the amount that Maids-R-Us paid for them. They are valued at the price Maids-R-Us paid when they were purchased.
- The revenue-recognition principle means the revenue on the income statement has been earned. The related cash may not have been collected, but the work of earning it has been completed and collection of the receivables is reasonably assured.
- The matching principle means related revenues and expenses should be on the same income statement. Only the supplies that are used to earn the revenue during the period are counted as supplies expense. The unused supplies are reported on the balance sheet until they are actually used.

Accrual accounting is an accounting system in which the measurement of income is not based on cash receipts and cash disbursements. Instead, revenue is included in the calculation of income when it is earned, and expenses are included as they are matched to revenue. Timing differences between the economic substance of a transaction and the related cash flows do not affect income. That is why both companies have the same net income even though the timing of the cash flows is different.

Real Company Financial Statements

Even though Tom's Wear is a small, start-up company, its financial statements include the same types of financial statement items as large, well-established corporations. When Tom's Wear sold shirts to customers on credit, the balance sheet showed accounts receivable. Look at the balance sheet of Polo Ralph Lauren Corporation, shown in Exhibit 2.19. In the asset section, Polo Ralph Lauren Corporation's balance sheet shows accounts receivable of $455,682,000 at April 2, 2005, its fiscal year-end. Customers owe Polo Ralph Lauren Corporation this amount for products and services the company provided to its customers on credit.

Can you find another asset on the balance sheet that reflects the use of accrual, rather than cash basis, accounting? In the current asset section, the balance sheet lists prepaid expenses of $102,693,000. Although the details of Polo Ralph Lauren Corporation's prepaid expenses are not shown, the included items will be similar to prepaid insurance or prepaid rent—items the company has paid for but has not used yet. On the other side of the balance sheet, Polo Ralph Lauren Corporation has accounts payable of $184,394,000. This represents what the firm owes to vendors for inventory items the company has purchased but has not yet paid for.

Check out the other things you learned in this and the previous chapter about the balance sheet. First, it balances—assets = liabilities + shareholders' equity. Polo Ralph Lauren Corporation has a classified balance sheet. Current assets are shown first, with a subtotal; and current liabilities are also shown with a subtotal. Look at the stockholders' equity section. There is common stock and additional paid-in capital—both contributed capital amounts. Then, the balance sheet shows retained earnings, the amount of equity the shareholders have earned (less dividends) by Polo Ralph Lauren Corporation's operations.

EXHIBIT 2.19

Balance Sheet of Polo Ralph Lauren Corporation

Compare the balance sheet of Polo to that of Tom's Wear. See how many similarities you can find.

Polo Ralph Lauren
Consolidated Balance Sheets

(Dollars in thousands, except share data)	April 2, 2005	April 3, 2004 (As restated, see Note 2)
Assets		
Current assets:		
Cash and cash equivalents	$ 350,485	$ 352,335
Accounts receivable, net of allowances of $111,042 and $97,292	455,682	441,724
Inventories	430,082	373,170
Deferred tax assets	74,821	21,565
Prepaid expenses and other	102,693	98,357
Total current assets	1,413,763	1,287,151
Property and equipment, net	487,894	408,741
Deferred tax assets	35,973	65,542
Goodwill, net	558,858	341,603
Intangibles, net	46,991	17,640
Other assets	183,190	176,875
Total assets	$ 2,726,669	$ 2,297,552
Liabilities and Stockholders' Equity		
Current liabilities:		
Accounts payable	$ 184,394	$ 188,919
Income tax payable	72,148	77,736
Deferred tax liabilities	–	1,821
Accrued expenses and other	365,868	236,724
Total current liabilities	622,410	505,200
Long-term debt	290,960	277,345
Other noncurrent liabilities	137,591	99,560
Commitments and contingencies (Note 14)		
Stockholders' Equity		
Common stock		
Class A, par value $0.01 per share; 500,000,000 shares authorized: 64,016,034 and 61,498,183 shares issued and outstanding	652	620
Class B, par value $0.01 per share; 100,000,000 shares authorized: 43,280,021 shares issued and outstanding	433	433
Additional paid-in-capital	664,279	563,457
Retained earnings	1,090,310	921,602
Treasury stock, Class A, at cost (4,177,600 and 4,145,800 shares)	(80,027)	(78,975)
Accumulated other comprehensive income	29,973	23,104
Unearned compensation	(29,912)	(14,794)
Total stockholders' equity	1,675,708	1,415,447
Total liabilities and stockholders' equity	$ 2,726,669	$ 2,297,552

See accompanying Notes to Consolidated Financial Statements.

Also, there are two balance sheets shown, which you will recall are called *comparative balance sheets*. Take notice of the dates of the balance sheets. This financial statement shows the financial position of the company at a single point in time. For Polo Ralph Lauren Corporation, the last day of the fiscal year is the Saturday nearest to March 31, information disclosed in the notes to the financial statements.

L.O.5
Compute and explain the meaning of the current ratio.

Current ratio is a liquidity ratio that measures a firm's ability to meet its short-term obligations.

Applying Your Knowledge: Ratio Analysis

Every business must pay its bills. Suppliers, in particular, want to evaluate a company's ability to meet its current obligations. Simply looking at how much cash a company has does not provide enough information. Using ratios often provides additional insights. A financial ratio is a comparison of different amounts on the financial statements. Several ratios measure the short-term liquidity of a company. The most common is the **current ratio**, which accountants compute by dividing the total amount of current assets by the total amount of current liabilities. The ratio gives information about a company's ability to fund its current operations in the short run.

Using the current ratio, investors can compare the liquidity of one company to that of other companies of different types and sizes. Recall that liquidity is a measure of how easily a company can turn its current assets into cash to pay its debts as they come due. This information would be important to a supplier considering extending credit to a company. The current ratio also provides information about the liquidity of a company over time.

Look at the balance sheet for Home Depot in Exhibit 2.9. The current ratio at January 29, 2006, was

$$\$15,346 \text{ million} \div \$12,901 \text{ million} = 1.19$$

The current assets at January 30, 2005, totaled $14,273 million, and the current liabilities were $10,455 million. So the current ratio at January 30, 2005, was

$$\$14,273 \text{ million} \div \$10,455 \text{ million} = 1.37$$

Another way to think about the current ratio is to say that Home Depot had, at January 30, 2005, $1.37 of current assets with which to pay off each $1.00 of its current liabilities. Can you see why companies often strive to have a current ratio of 1 or greater? That would mean a firm has enough current assets to pay off its current liabilities. When using ratio analysis, it is often interesting to compare a firm's ratios to those of a competitor in the same industry. Lowe's, for example, had a current ratio of 1.34 at February 3, 2006, and 1.22 at January 28, 2005. The firm's current ratio has increased slightly while Home Depot's has decreased. However, for both companies, the current ratio has been above 1 for the past two years.

Looking at the current ratio for two consecutive years gives some information about Home Depot or Lowe's, but you would need much more information to reach any conclusions. As you learn more about financial statements, you will learn additional ratios and several ways to analyze a company's financial statements.

You might be surprised to know that some firms actually try to keep their current ratio *below* 1. If a firm generates a great deal of cash, it may know that it will generate sufficient cash to pay its current liabilities as they come due. Darden Restaurants, owners of Olive Garden, Red Lobster, and Smokey Bones, had a current ratio of 0.39 at May 29, 2005. Here's what Darden's management had to say about the current ratio in the firm's annual report:

> Cash flows generated from operating activities provide us with a significant source of liquidity, which we use to finance the purchases of land, buildings and equipment and to repurchase shares of our common stock. Since substantially all our sales are for cash and cash equivalents and accounts payable are generally due in five to 30 days, we are able to carry current liabilities in excess of current assets.

L.O.6
Identify the risks and potential frauds related to financial accounting records, and explain the controls needed to ensure their accuracy.

Business Risk, Control, and Ethics

Now that we have discussed the general characteristics of accounting information and the information shown on the four basic financial statements, we will take a look at how companies make sure the information in those statements is reliable.

Internal Controls—Definition and Objectives

Internal controls are the policies and procedures the managers of a firm use to protect the firm's assets and to ensure the accuracy and reliability of the firm's accounting records. Internal controls are a company's rules to help it keep its assets safe and to make sure its financial records are accurate. By adhering to those rules, a firm minimizes the risks of being in business. These rules are called internal controls because they are put in place and controlled within the company. Controls imposed from outside the firm—laws and regulations, for example—are not internal controls because they are not rules that originated within the company.

> **Internal controls** are a company's policies and procedures to protect the assets of the firm and to ensure the accuracy and reliability of the accounting records.

Special Internal Control Issues Related to Financial Statements

Accountants are particularly concerned with the financial statements. Whether you are involved in preparing them or using them to make decisions, you must have confidence that the information in them is accurate and reliable. When you see cash on a company's balance sheet, you should be confident this is actually the amount of cash the company had on the balance sheet date. The sales shown on the income statement should be sales that have been completed—goods delivered to the customers.

Inaccurate information creates enormous problems. The SEC has been especially concerned with the information contained in financial statements. For example, recently the SEC filed charges against Computron for improperly recording more than $9 million in revenue on its financial statements contained in its reports to the SEC. Improperly recorded revenue was the focus of a recent SEC investigation of the Mexican unit of Xerox Corp. Xerox officials in Mexico failed to set up appropriate allowances for bad debts and improperly classified sales, leases, and rentals, violating GAAP. The causes cited were (1) failure (of the Mexican executives) to adhere to Xerox's corporate policies and procedures, and (2) inadequate internal controls.

Exhibit 2.20 summarizes three types of controls a company can use to minimize the risk of errors in the accounting system: preventive controls, detective controls, and corrective controls.

Preventive Controls. These types of controls help prevent errors in an accounting system. When you order something from Amazon.com, the company gives you more than one chance to review and confirm your order. The computer program is designed to automatically insert the price of each item you order. These are controls that Amazon has put in place to help prevent errors from entering its accounting system.

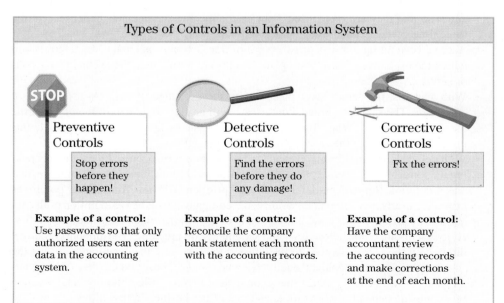

Types of Controls in an Information System

Preventive Controls
Stop errors before they happen!
Example of a control: Use passwords so that only authorized users can enter data in the accounting system.

Detective Controls
Find the errors before they do any damage!
Example of a control: Reconcile the company bank statement each month with the accounting records.

Corrective Controls
Fix the errors!
Example of a control: Have the company accountant review the accounting records and make corrections at the end of each month.

EXHIBIT 2.20

Types of Internal Controls

A company's accounting information system consists of three major types of controls: ones that prevent errors, ones that detect errors, and ones that correct errors.

News Flash

CA (previously known as Computer Associates International Inc.) has been in the news for several years. A recent development was former CEO Sanjay Kumar's guilty plea for fraud and obstruction of justice in 2006. Unfortunately for CA, there is more. New financial accounting woes, according to *The Wall Street Journal* (June 8, 2006), are the result of "holes in internal controls." The firm's accounting system allegedly allowed multiple people to get a commission from a single sale.

Detective Controls. Detective controls are those that help a company find errors. For example, at the end of every work day, a cashier at Target will count the money, ATM receipts, and credit card receipts in his or her drawer and compare the total to the total sales entered in the computer. This control will help Target find errors in its sales and receipts. Once the errors are found, they must be corrected.

Corrective Controls. Corrective controls are policies and procedures that correct any errors that have been discovered. Target has a policy for handling cash shortages—perhaps the cashier must make up any shortage.

As you learn more about accounting, you will see examples of preventive, detective, and corrective controls. Keep in mind that to be effective, a system of internal control must rely on the people who perform the duties assigned to them. An internal control system is only as effective as the people who execute it. Human error, collusion—two or more people working together to circumvent a policy or procedure—and changing conditions can all weaken a system of internal control.

Chapter Summary Points

- To make the financial statements useful, we need to understand the rules and the choices used to construct them. These rules are called Generally Accepted Accounting Principles (GAAP).
- Accounting according to GAAP is accrual based. That means that revenues are recognized when they are earned, not when the cash is collected. Costs are matched to revenues so that they are recognized—put on the income statement as expenses—at the same time as the revenues they helped generate.
- Accrual accounting consists of two types of transactions—accruals and deferrals—in which the exchange of cash takes place at a different time than the exchange of goods or services.
- With accruals, the action takes place before the exchange of cash. An example is a credit sale. The sale is recorded, but the cash will be collected later. Remember, accrue means to "build up." When Tom's Wear makes a sale on account, the company builds up sales, even though the cash has not been collected yet.
- With deferrals, the dollars are exchanged before the action occurs. An example is paying for something in advance. When Tom's Wear paid for the insurance in advance, that was a deferral. Remember, defer means to "postpone." When Tom's Wear purchases insurance in advance, prepaid insurance, the company postpones recognition of the expense. The action, in this case, is the passing of the time to which the insurance applies.
- Adjustments are made before financial statements are prepared. The amounts recorded throughout the year may need to be adjusted to make sure they accurately reflect the assets, liabilities, shareholders' equity, revenues, and expenses on the date of the statements. How we actually adjust the amounts to correctly reflect the financial position of a company depends on how we keep track of our business transactions.

Chapter Summary Problems

The following transactions took place during the first year of business for SW2 Company. (Dollars given are in millions. Use the numbers as shown, but make a note on your statements that the dollars are in millions.) The firm's year end is June 30.

1. Issued SW2 stock (received contributions from owners) in the amount of $250
2. Borrowed $850 from a local bank with a 6-year note (ignore interest expense)
3. Purchased land for $650 cash
4. Paid $25 for operating expenses
5. Purchased new equipment for cash of $300
6. Collected $800 from customers for services provided
7. Paid salaries to employees of $480
8. Purchased supplies for $20 on account, to be used in the coming year
9. Paid dividends to new shareholders of $5

Instructions

1. Set up an accounting equation worksheet like the one in Exhibit 2.4 and record each transaction on the worksheet. (Record the equipment purchase as an asset and ignore the fact that the equipment was probably used during the year. We will get to that topic in a later chapter. Also, ignore interest expense on the bank note.)
2. Prepare the four basic financial statements from the worksheet.

Solution (dollars in millions)

		Assets		=	Liabilities	+	Contributed Capital	Retained Earnings		
	Cash	Property, Plant, & Equipment	Supplies	Accounts Payable	Notes Payable		Common Stock	Revenues	Expenses	Dividends
1	250						250			
2	850				850					
3	(650)	650								
4	(25)								(25)	
5	(300)	300								
6	800							800		
7	(480)								(480)	
8			20	20						
9	(5)									(5)
	440	950	20	20	850		250	800	(505)	(5)

Check: Assets = $1,410   Liabilities + SH Equity = $1,410

From the accounting equation worksheet, you can prepare the financial statements. Start with the income statement. The red square indicates the revenues and expenses. In this case, it is a very condensed income statement. That is, the company would have many types of revenue accounts and many more expense accounts in its internal recordkeeping:

SW2 Company
Income Statement
For the Period Ended June 30
(in millions)

Revenue	$ 800
Expenses	505
Net income	$ 295

The next statement you prepare is the statement of changes in shareholders' equity. Notice how net income is used in this statement:

SW2 Company
Statement of Changes in Shareholders' Equity
For the Period Ended June 30
(in millions)

Contributed Capital:	
Beginning balance, common stock	$ –
Common stock issued	250
Ending balance, common stock	250
Retained Earnings:	
Beginning balance	$ –
+ Net income	**295**
– Dividends	(5)
Ending balance	290
Total Shareholders' Equity	$ 540

> These amounts will go to the equity section of the balance sheet.

The balance sheet is the next statement that you prepare. Notice that revenues, expenses, and dividends are *not* shown on the balance sheet. Those amounts have been folded into the retained earnings balance.

SW2 Company
Balance Sheet
At June 30
(in millions)

Assets	
Cash	$ 440
Supplies	20
Property, plant, & equipment	950
Total assets	$ 1,410
Liabilities & Shareholders' Equity	
Liabilities	
Accounts payable	20
Note payable	850
Shareholders' equity	
Contributed capital	250
Retained earnings	290
Total liabilities and shareholders' equity	$ 1,410

> The change in cash from the beginning of the year (0 in this example) to the amount on the year-end balance sheet ($440) will be explained by the statement of cash flows.

> These amounts came from the statement of changes in shareholders' equity.

Finally, you prepare the statement of cash flows. To do this, go down the list of transactions in the cash column of the worksheet and identify each as cash from operating activities, cash from investing activities, or cash from financing activities.

- All cash collected from customers and all cash paid for the expenses to run the day-to-day operations of the firm are cash flows from operations. For SW2, these are (4) cash paid for operating expenses, (6) cash collected from customers, and (7) cash paid to employees for salaries.
- All cash paid for land and equipment (assets that last longer than a year) are cash flows from investing activities. For SW2, these are (3) purchase of land and (5) purchase of equipment.
- All cash used to finance the business—from owners and long-term creditors—are cash flows from financing activities. For SW2, these are (1) issue of stock, (2) receipt of proceeds from loan, and (9) payment of dividends to shareholders.

Notice that Transaction 8, purchase supplies on account, does not affect the statement of cash flows. Why not? No cash is involved in the transaction. When the cash is paid in the next year, it will be an operating cash flow.

SW2 Company
Statement of Cash Flows
For the Period Ended June 30
(in millions)

Cash from operating activities:
Cash collected from customers .... $ 800
Cash paid for operating expenses .... (25)
Cash paid to employees .... (480) $ 295
Cash from investing activities:
Cash paid for land .... (650)
Cash paid for equipment .... (300)   (950)
Cash from financing activities:
Cash from common stock issued 250
Cash proceeds from loan 850
Cash paid for dividends .... (5)   1,095

Increase in cash 440
Add beginning cash balance 0
Ending cash balance .... $ 440

This is the cash balance found on the balance sheet.

Key Terms for Chapter 2

Accounts payable (p. 54)
Accounts receivable (p. 56)
Accrual (p. 64)
Accrual accounting (p. 63)
Adjusting the books (p. 56)
Assets (p. 59)
Capital (p. 61)
Cash basis accounting
 (p. 65)
Classified balance sheet
 (p. 61)
Contributed capital(p. 61)
Current assets (p. 59)
Current liabilities (p. 61)
Current ratio (p. 74)
Deferral (p. 64)

Equity (p. 61)
Full-disclosure principle
 (p. 58)
Going-concern assumption
 (p. 53)
Historical-cost principle
 (p. 53)
Internal controls (p. 75)
Liabilities (p. 61)
Liquidity (p. 59)
Long-term assets (p. 59)
Long-term liabilities (p. 61)
Matching principle (p. 62)
Monetary-unit assumption
 (p. 52)

Net profit (p. 50)
Noncurrent assets (p. 59)
Noncurrent liabilities
 (p. 61)
On account (p. 54)
Paid-in capital (p. 61)
Prepaid insurance (p. 54)
Recognized revenue (p. 62)
Retained earnings (p. 61)
Revenue-recognition
 principle (p. 62)
Separate-entity assumption
 (p. 52)
Time-period assumption
 (p. 53)

Answers to YOUR TURN Questions

Chapter 2

Your Turn 2-1

1. GAAP stands for generally accepted accounting principles.
2. Guidelines are needed to ensure the usefulness of the information so that a firm's performance can be compared from period to period and compared to other firms' performances.

Your Turn 2-2

1. The purpose of financial statements is to provide information useful for decision making.
2. Useful information is relevant, reliable, comparable, and consistent.

Your Turn 2-3

Prepaid insurance is an asset until the time to which the policy applies has expired. Then, it becomes an expense.

Your Turn 2-4

1. A current asset is one that is expected to be converted to cash or used in the next year. A long-term asset is one that is expected to last longer than a year.
2. A classified balance sheet is one that has subtotals for both current assets and current liabilities.

Your Turn 2-5

An example of the matching principle is cost of goods sold with sales. The cost of the T-shirts sold is put on the same income statement as the sales revenue from the sale of those shirts.

Your Turn 2-6

The difference between cash basis and accrual basis accounting is the timing of recognizing revenues and expenses. Cash basis accounting recognizes revenue when the cash is collected and expenses when cash is disbursed. In accrual accounting, revenues are recognized in the period in which they are earned (by the completion of the work) and expenses are matched to the revenues they help create.

Your Turn 2-7

1. On the income statement, the revenues earned are shown. (That is called *recognizing* the revenue.) On the statement of cash flows, only the amount of cash collected from customers is included.

2. If a company earns $50,000 worth of revenue, then all of that will be recognized—included on the income statement. The amount of cash collected is given as 80%, so $40,000 would be shown on the statement of cash flows as cash collected from customers. The entire amount, $50,000, will be in the retained earnings balance because the retained earnings increase is the amount that is on the income statement.

Questions

1. What is GAAP?
2. Name the four characteristics that help make accounting information useful.
3. What is the separate-entity assumption?
4. Why would the going-concern assumption be important to a bank giving a business a loan?
5. Explain materiality and give an example of both a material and an immaterial item.
6. What are the four basic financial statements?
7. Which financial statement pertains to a single moment in time?
8. What is a current asset? What is a current liability?
9. What are the two ways that equity is generated in a business?
10. What does the income statement report about a firm? Name the types of accounts that appear on the income statement.
11. What is the purpose of the statement of cash flows? How are the cash flows categorized? What is the significance of classifying cash flows into these categories?
12. What is the full-disclosure principle?
13. What does *recognize revenue* mean in accounting?
14. What is the matching principle?
15. What is an accrual? What is a deferral?
16. Must a company collect the money from a sale before the sale can be recognized?
17. What is the cost of goods sold?
18. Explain the difference between cash basis accounting and accrual basis accounting.
19. How is the current ratio computed? What does it tell us about a company?
20. Define internal control and explain why it is important.

Multiple-Choice Questions

1. If revenue exceeds expenses for a given period,
   a. Total assets for the period will decrease.
   b. Cash for the period will increase.
   c. The income statement will report net income.
   d. Liabilities for the period will decrease.
2. The matching principle is best described as the process of
   a. Matching assets to liabilities and owners' equity.
   b. Recognizing a cost as an expense in the period in which it is used to generate revenue.
   c. Matching cash collections to revenue.
   d. Matching income to owners' equity.
3. Which of the following would never appear on a company's income statement?
   a. Prepaid insurance
   b. Cost of goods sold
   c. Interest expense
   d. Sales revenue
4. Which of the following statements is consistent with accrual basis accounting?
   a. Revenues are recorded when cash is received.
   b. Expenses are recorded when cash is paid.
   c. Expenses are recorded in a different period than the related revenue.
   d. Revenues are recorded when earned and expenses are matched with the revenues.
5. Sales revenue is most often recognized in the period in which
   a. The customer agrees to purchase the merchandise.
   b. The seller agrees to sell the merchandise to the customer at a specified price.
   c. The seller collects cash from the customer.
   d. The seller delivers the merchandise to the customer.

6. Which of the following is an example of a financing cash outflow?
    a. Borrowing money from a bank by signing a long-term note payable
    b. Financing the purchase of a new factory by issuing new shares of stock
    c. Paying a cash dividend to stockholders
    d. Purchasing a new delivery truck
7. How are financial assets reported in the balance sheet?
    a. Chronologically
    b. Alphabetically
    c. In the order of their liquidity
    d. In the order of their relative values
8. Which of the following financial statement elements are found on the balance sheet?
    a. Insurance expense
    b. Retained earnings
    c. Sales revenue
    d. All of the above
9. A company's current ratio is 1.85. You can safely conclude that
    a. The company is a good investment.
    b. The company will have no trouble paying its current obligations.
    c. The company has a short-term problem related to paying its bills.
    d. The company has a long-term problem related to meetings its obligations.
10. Which of the following is not a type of internal control?
    a. Preventive
    b. Corrective
    c. Collusion
    d. Detective

Short Exercises

SE2-1. *Qualitative characteristics.* Give the accounting principle, assumption, constraint, or qualitative characteristic that is most applicable to each of the following: (LO 1, 2)
    a. Airlines check fuel prices daily to make decisions about ticket pricing.
    b. Personal transactions of the owner are separate from business transactions.
    c. The firm uses the same depreciation method from period to period.

SE2-2. *Basic accounting principles and assumptions.* Give the accounting principle, assumption, constraint, or qualitative characteristic that is most applicable to each of the following: (LO 1, 2, 3)
    a. Equipment is recorded as an asset and expensed over the periods in which it is used.
    b. The company prepares financial statements quarterly.
    c. When rent is purchased in advance, it is recorded as an asset.
    d. Assets such as inventory are valued in dollars, not units, for the financial statements.

SE2-3. *Basic accounting principles.* For each of the following, give the accounting principle or assumption that is best described: (LO 1, 2, 3)
    a. Carlene's Sweet Shop reports revenue when it is earned instead of when the cash is collected.
    b. The land on the balance sheet of Tia's Cotton Fabrics Inc. is valued at what it cost, even though it is worth much more.
    c. Designer Flowers recognizes depreciation expense for a delivery van over 7 years, the period in which the van is used to help generate revenue for the company.
    d. The owner of Munoz Plumbing thought that it would help the company's balance sheet to include as an asset some land she and her husband personally own. The accountant rejected this idea.

SE2-4. *Qualitative characteristics.* For each of the following items, explain what it means. Why are these characteristics important? (LO 2)
    a. Relevant
    b. Reliable

c. Comparable
d. Consistent

SE2-5. *Elements of the financial statements.* For each item that follows, tell whether it is an asset, a liability, or a shareholders' equity item. (LO 3)
   a. Computer
   b. Prepaid rent
   c. Retained earnings
   d. Notes payable
   e. Accounts receivable
   f. Common stock
   g. Accounts payable
   h. Cash
   i. Inventory

SE2-6. *Elements of the financial statements.* For each of the following items, give the financial statement on which it would appear. (*Hint:* some items will appear on more than one financial statement.) (LO 3)

Cash	Common stock
Sales revenue	Accounts receivable
Cost of goods sold	Net cash from operations
Equipment	Retained earnings
Long-term debt	Net income

SE2-7. *Revenue recognition.* Suppose Motor Trend Analysis Inc. performed services for a client on account on February 09, 2008. Motor Trend charged the client $3,050. The client paid for half of the services on February 29, 2008. The remaining balance was paid on March 5, 2008. How did these transactions affect Motor Trend's financial statements for the month of February and for the balance sheet ended February 29, 2008? (LO 3, 4)

SE2-8. *Accrual accounting versus cash basis accounting.* Hazel & Euglenia Grocery Inc. purchased inventory in June 2008 for $100,000 cash to sell in June and July. The company sold merchandise that cost $60,000 in June and the remainder in July. What is the cost of goods sold for June and for July 2008 if Hazel & Euglenia uses GAAP? What is the cost of goods sold for June and for July 2008 if Hazel & Euglenia uses cash basis accounting? (LO 4)

SE2-9. *Cash versus credit sales.* Suppose two companies are identical except for their credit policy. One company allows cash sales only, whereas the other sells for cash or credit. Suppose the two companies have the same sales revenue and expenses for the year. The only difference between the two is that the first company has no outstanding accounts (receivable), whereas the second has quite a few still outstanding at year-end. Of the four basic financial statements, which one or ones will be different between these two companies? Explain how and why they are different. (LO 3, 4)

SE2-10. *Compute and explain current ratio.* Given the following information, compute the current ratio for the two years shown. Explain the trend in the ratio for both years and what you think it means. (LO 5)

From balance sheet at	06/30/2008	06/30/2009
Current assets	$150,000	$180,000
Current liabilities	$100,000	$175,000

SE2-11. *Identify business risks and controls.* For each of the controls given, tell whether it is primarily a preventive control, a detective control, or a corrective control. (LO 6)

Retro Clothing Inc. has an online purchase system that automatically inserts the total price of each item a customer orders.

The teller double-checks the account number on the loan payment before applying payment.

External auditors are hired to audit the year-end financial statements.

Exercises—Set A

E2-1A. *GAAP and the income statement.* One of your friends started a business in 2008. At the end of the first year, December 31, 2008, he prepared the following income statement. Give three examples from the statement that indicate the statement was not prepared according to GAAP. (LO 1, 3)

Sales	$2,700
Inventory purchases	(1,500)
Rent for 2008 and 2009	(975)
Cash on hand	8,650
Due from customers	1,400
Net income	$10,275

E2-2A. *Relevance and reliability.* Your car has broken down, so you have decided to look for a replacement. You find an advertisement on the Internet for a used Lexus. When you contact the owner, this is what you find: (LO 2)

1. The car is a 2005 model.
2. The owner says he used the car only for driving to and from work.
3. The odometer reading is 68,759 miles.
4. The owner says that he had the oil changed every 3,000 to 5,000 miles since he bought the car new.
5. The owner says this is the best car he has ever owned.
6. The owner will provide a maintenance record prepared by a licensed mechanic.

Evaluate each item from the preceding list in terms of its relevance to the decision about whether to buy this car. Then, evaluate each item with respect to its reliability. What additional documentation or supporting evidence would you want for your decision?

E2-3A. *Elements of the financial statements.* The following accounts and balances were taken from the financial statements of Brand Names at a Discount Inc. For each item, identify the financial statement(s) on which the item would appear. Then, identify each balance sheet item as an asset, a liability, or a shareholders' equity account. (LO 3)

Van	$50,000
Interest receivable	32,500
Cash	78,000
Short-term notes payable	15,875
Net cash from operating activities	28,000
Building	31,853
Common stock	75,000
Retained earnings	100,000
Net cash from investing activities	40,000
Interest payable	650
Long-term mortgage payable	85,000
Salaries payable	1,315
Net cash from financing activities	10,000

E2-4A. *Net income and retained earnings.* Marge's Seafood Market Inc. reported the following (incomplete) information in its records for 2007: (LO 3)

Net income	$ 15,000
Sales	105,000
Beginning balance—retained earnings	30,000
Cost of goods sold	60,000
Dividends paid	2,000

a. If the sales revenue given is the only revenue for the year, what were the expenses for the year other than cost of goods sold?

b. What does the beginning balance of $30,000 for retained earnings mean? Is this useful information for potential investors?

c. What is the balance of retained earnings at the end of 2007?

E2-5A. *Elements of the financial statements.* Listed are elements of the financial statements discussed in this chapter. Match each element with the descriptions (use each as many times as necessary). (LO 3)

a. Assets
b. Liabilities
c. Shareholders' equity
d. Revenues
e. Expenses

1. _____ Debts of the company
2. _____ Economic resources with future benefit
3. _____ Inflows of assets from delivering or producing goods or services
4. _____ Things of value a company owns
5. _____ The residual interest in the assets of an entity that remains after deducting its liabilities
6. _____ The difference between what the company has and what the company owes
7. _____ The owner's interest in the company
8. _____ Outflows or using up of assets from delivering or producing goods and services
9. _____ Costs that have no future value
10. _____ The amount the company owes
11. _____ Sales

E2-6A. *Balance sheet and income statement transactions.* Unisource Company started the year with $2,000 in cash and common stock. During 2010, the Unisource Company earned $4,600 of revenue on account. The company collected $4,200 cash from accounts receivable and paid $2,850 cash for operating expenses. Enter the transactions into the accounting equation. (LO 3, 4)

a. What happened to total assets (increase or decrease and by how much)?
b. What is the cash balance on December 31, 2010?
c. What is the total shareholders' equity on December 31, 2010?
d. What is net income for the year?

E2-7A. *Income statement preparation.* Use the following to prepare an income statement for Crenshaw Consultants Inc. for the year ended June 30, 2010. (LO 3)

Service revenues	$54,000
Rent expense	1,000
Salary expense	6,000
Other operating expenses	24,000
Administrative expenses	8,500

E2-8A. *Classified balance sheet preparation.* The following items were taken from the December 31, 2011, financial statements of Health Trainers Inc. (All dollars are in millions.) Prepare a classified balance sheet as of December 31, 2011. (LO 3)

Property and equipment	$4,776	Accounts payable	1,560
Common stock	1,980	Other noncurrent liabilities	1,200
Long-term investments	3,218	Retained earnings	10,348
Short-term investments	1,689	Other current assets	554
Cash	1,240	Other noncurrent assets	2,487
Accounts receivable	1,200	Current portion of long-term debt	340
Inventories	1,134	Long-term debt	870

E2-9A. *Current ratio.* Use the balance sheet you prepared in E2-8A to compute Health Trainers' current ratio at December 31, 2011. What does it indicate? (LO 5)

E2-10A. *Current ratio.* The following data was taken from the 2008 and 2007 financial statements of Fancy Fish Stores Inc. Calculate the current ratio for each year. What happened to the company's liquidity from 2007 to 2008? (LO 5)

	2008	2007
Current assets	256,485	265,960
Total assets	433,202	406,974
Current liabilities	104,196	101,929
Total liabilities	180,466	182,093
Total shareholders' equity	252,736	224,881

E2-11A. *Identify business risks and controls.* Give two examples of controls that you believe would minimize the risk of errors in the accounting records of Sears Inc. (LO 6)

Exercises—Set B

E2-1B. *GAAP and the balance sheet.* One of your friends started a business in 2008. At the end of the first year, December 31, 2008, he prepared the following balance sheet. Give three examples from the statement that indicate the statement was not prepared according to GAAP. (LO 1, 3)

Assets		Liabilities	
Cash	$ 2,000	Notes payable	$ 1,000
Revenues	1,000	Expenses	1,000
Total assets	$ 3,000	Total liabilities	2,000
		Common stock	1,500
		Total liabilities & shareholders' equity	$ 3,500

E2-2B. *Relevance and reliability.* You have decided to open a restaurant, so you look around in your area to see if an established restaurant is for sale. You find an advertisement in the newspaper for a local sandwich shop for sale. When you contact the owner, this is what you find: (LO 2)

1. The restaurant has been open for 10 years.
2. The owner says owning the sandwich shop is a lot of fun.
3. The sandwich shop has increased profits each year, and the owner can provide financial records.
4. The sandwich shop location is downtown.
5. The owner says the building housing the restaurant has been remodeled and brought into compliance with all codes and regulations in the past year, and he can provide documentation.
6. The owner says the red carpet is the most beautiful carpet ever made.

Evaluate each item from the preceding list in terms of its relevance to the decision about whether to buy this restaurant. Then, evaluate each item with respect to its reliability. What additional documentation or supporting evidence would you want for your decision?

E2-3B. *Elements of the financial statements.* The following accounts and balances were taken from the financial statements of Quality Products Inc. For each item, identify the financial statement(s) on which the item would appear. Then, identify each balance sheet item as an asset, a liability, or a shareholders' equity account. (LO 3)

Equipment	$231,300
Accounts receivable	52,300
Cash	57,890
Short-term notes payable	23,200

Net cash from investing activities	89,300
Land	45,200
Common stock	100,000
Retained earnings	75,000
Net cash from financing activities	45,980
Accounts payable	32,100
Long-term mortgage payable	54,000
Interest payable	2,500
Net cash from operating activities	34,350

E2-4B. *Net income and retained earnings.* Manny's Cuban Bistro Inc. reported the following (incomplete) information in its records for 2009: (LO 3)

Net income	$ 17,850
Sales	75,000
Beginning balance—retained earnings	20,000
Cost of goods sold	40,000
Dividends paid	3,500

    a. If the sales revenue given is the only revenue for the year, what were the expenses for the year other than cost of goods sold?
    b. What does the beginning balance of $20,000 for retained earnings mean? Is this useful information for potential investors?
    c. What is the balance of retained earnings at the end of 2009?

E2-5B. *Elements of the financial statements.* Listed are elements of the financial statements discussed in this chapter. Match each element with the descriptions (use each as many times as necessary). (LO 3)
    a. Assets
    b. Liabilities
    c. Shareholders' equity
    d. Revenues
    e. Expenses
    f. Retained earnings
    g. Common stock

1. _____ Note signed with a bank
2. _____ Rent paid a year in advance
3. _____ Items that make up net income that appear on the income statement
4. _____ Items that appear on the balance sheet
5. _____ A share of ownership in a corporation
6. _____ Equity that results from doing business and is kept in the company rather than paid out to stockholders
7. _____ Shareholders' interest in the company
8. _____ Costs of the daily operations of a business
9. _____ Salaries owed to employees
10. _____ Cost of inventory when it is sold
11. _____ Revenue received for services not yet provided
12. _____ Interest received on notes receivable

E2-6B. *Balance sheet and income statement transactions.* Pet Caterers Inc. started the year with $3,500 in cash and common stock. During 2012, the Pet Caterers earned $6,500 of revenue on account. The company collected $5,900 cash from accounts receivable and paid $3,115 cash for operating expenses. Enter the transactions into the accounting equation. (LO 3, 4)
    a. What happened to total assets (increase or decrease and by how much)?
    b. What is the cash balance on December 31, 2012?
    c. What is the total shareholders' equity on December 31, 2012?
    d. What is net income for the year?

E2-7B. *Income statement preparation.* Use the following to prepare an income statement for Michael & Trina's Dazzling Landscape Service Inc. for the year ended June 30, 2009. (LO 3)

Service revenue	$22,500
Rent expense	1,500
Salary expense	1,225
Other operating expenses	9,850
Insurance expense	2,500

Excel Template
www.prenhall.com/reimers

E2-8B. *Classified balance sheet preparation.* The following items were taken from the December 31, 2012, financial statements of Calorie Counter Food Stores Inc. (All dollars are in thousands.) Prepare a classified balance sheet as of December 31, 2012. (LO 3)

Land and building	$5,800	Accounts payable	5,073
Common stock	2,104	Other noncurrent liabilities	1,311
Long-term investments	2,200	Retained earnings	6,450
Short-term investments	1,370	Other current assets	656
Cash	1,300	Other noncurrent assets	2,300
Accounts receivable	1,140	Current portion of long-term debt	203
Inventories	1,195	Long-term debt	820

E2-9B. *Current ratio.* Use the balance sheet you prepared in E2-8B to compute Calorie Counter Food Stores' current ratio at December 31, 2012. What does it indicate? (LO 5)

E2-10B. *Current ratio.* The following data was taken from the 2010 and 2009 financial statements of Kitten Caboodle Inc. Calculate the current ratio for each year. What happened to the company's liquidity from 2009 to 2010? (LO 5)

	2010	2009
Current assets	230,875	256,294
Total assets	386,182	363,170
Current liabilities	110,850	107,895
Total liabilities	165,432	167,670
Total shareholders' equity	220,750	195,500

E2-11B. *Identify business risks and controls.* Give two examples of controls that you believe would minimize the risk of errors in the accounting records of Home Depot Inc. (LO 6)

Problems—Set A

P2-1A. *Relationships between financial statement items.* Use the following information for USA Movers Inc. for the year ended June 30, 2009, to answer the following questions. Assume that the shareholders made no new contributions to the company during the year. (LO 3)

1. Revenues for the year ended June 30, 2009 = $350
2. Net income for the year ended June 30, 2009 = $110
3. Beginning balance (June 30, 2008, balance) in retained earnings = $140
4. Ending balance (June 30, 2009, balance) in retained earnings = $200
5. Total liabilities and shareholders' equity at June 30, 2009 = $600
6. Total liabilities at June 30, 2008 = $60
7. Total liabilities at June 30, 2009 = $50

Required

    a. What were the USA Movers' total expenses during the year ended June 30, 2009?

    b. What was the amount of the dividends declared during the year ended June 30, 2009?

    c. What is the total that owners invested in the USA Movers as of June 30, 2009?

    d. What were total assets on the company's June 30, 2008, balance sheet?

P2-2A. *Analyzing transactions.* Results Advertising Inc. entered into the following transactions during 2008: (LO 3)

1. Results Advertising Inc. started as a corporation with a $6,500 cash contribution from the owners in exchange for common stock.
2. Sales on account amounted to $4,100.
3. Cash collections of accounts receivable amounted to $3,900.
4. On October 1, 2008, the company paid $1,800 in advance for an insurance policy. The policy does not go into effect until 2009.

Required

Put each of the transactions in an accounting equation worksheet. Then, answer the following questions:

a. What is the amount of cash flow from operating activities for 2008?
b. What amount of total liabilities would appear on the Results Advertising December 31, 2008, balance sheet?
c. What is the amount of contributed capital as of December 31, 2008?
d. What amount of net income would appear on the income statement for the year ended December 31, 2008?

P2-3A. *Identify errors using GAAP; prepare a classified balance sheet; and calculate the current ratio.* An inexperienced accountant has put together a balance sheet for Wings and Things Inc. The balances shown are at June 30, 2011. (LO 1, 3, 5)

Assets		Liabilities and Equity	
Current Assets:		Current Liabilities:	
Cash	$ 27,000	Prepaid insurance	$ 2,000
Accounts receivable	6,000	Interest receivable	5,000
Land	30,000	Salaries payable	8,000
Supplies	5,000	Intangible assets	39,000
Operating expenses	2,000	Accounts payable	3,000
Total Current Assets	70,000	Total Current Liabilities	57,000
Salaries payable	46,000	Shareholder's Equity	
Buildings	36,000	Retained earnings	40,000
Equipment	13,000	Common stock	62,000
Intangible assets	6,000	Short-term note	10,000
Total Noncurrent assets	101,000	Total Shareholders' Equity	112,000
Total Assets	$ 171,000	Total Liabilities and Equity	$ 169,000

Required

a. Identify the errors in the balance sheet.
b. Using good form, prepare a corrected, classified balance sheet.
c. Calculate the current ratio using the corrected amounts from the balance sheet prepared in b. What does this ratio measure? Discuss the implications of Wings and Things' current ratio.
d. Explain why it is important to properly follow GAAP when preparing financial statements.

P2-4A. *Analyzing transactions and preparing financial statements.* Given the following transactions, (LO 3)

1. Aniseh Maximous opened Fresh Pastry Bakery by contributing $15,000 on April 1, 2008, in exchange for common stock.
2. Fresh Pastry borrowed $10,500 from the bank on April 1. The note is a 1-year, 12% note, with both principal and interest to be repaid on March 31, 2009.
3. Aniseh paid $1,500 cash to rent equipment for the shop for the first month.

4. Aniseh paid $655 cash for the utility bill for the first month.
5. Fresh Pastry was a hit and earned $7,500 in revenue the first month, all cash.
6. Aniseh hired a friend to be the customer service specialist for the pastry shop and paid $475 cash in salary expense for the first month.
7. The business paid distributions to owners in the amount of $1,000 for the first month.
8. At the end of the month, $105 of interest payable is due on the note from #2.

Required

a. Show how each transaction affects the accounting equation.
b. Prepare the four basic financial statements for the month of April. (The balance sheet *at* April 30.)
c. Give one additional piece of information related to the transactions that could be recorded in an information system for a purpose other than the financial statements.

P2-5A. *Analyze transactions from the accounting equation; prepare the four financial statements; and calculate the current ratio.* The following accounting equation worksheet shows the transactions for Blairstone Consulting & Advising Inc. for the first month of business, April 2009. (LO 3, 5)

| | Assets | | | = | Liabilities | | + | Shareholders' Equity | |
	Cash	Accounts receivable	Supplies		Accounts payable	Notes payable (5-year)		Contributed capital	Retained earnings
1	$3,000							$3,000 Common stock	
2	11,000					11,000			
3			15,000		15,000				
4		2,500							2,500 Revenue
5	10,000								10,000 Revenue
6	(8,000)		8,000						
7	1,200	(1,200)							
8	(3,400)				(3,400)				
9	(3,100)								(3,100) Expense
10	(500)								(500) Dividends

Required

a. Analyze each transaction in the accounting equation worksheet and describe the underlying exchange that resulted in each entry.
b. Has the company been profitable this month? Explain.
c. Prepare an income statement for the month ended April 30, 2009.
d. Prepare a statement of shareholders' equity for the month ended April 30, 2009.
e. Prepare a statement of cash flows for the month ended April 30, 2009.
f. Prepare a balance sheet at April 30, 2009.
g. Calculate the current ratio at April 30. What does this ratio measure?

P2-6A. *Analyzing transactions and preparing financial statements.* Kristin and Jenny Harrison graduated from the Aveda Institute at the end of June in 2010. They decided to withdraw $80,000 each from their trust fund to open a day spa, "A Day In Your Dreams"

Inc. in exchange for 5,000 shares of common stock. The firm signed a note with Uncle Damien for an additional $65,000. Kristin and Jenny formed A Day In Your Dreams Inc. on July 1, 2010. The business used available funds to purchase some land with a newly remodeled building for $215,000 and spa equipment for $20,000. The business also bought a computer system on account from DELL Inc. for $40,000, with payment due at the beginning of the following year. (LO 3, 5)

- During the first year of business, A Day In Your Dreams earned $150,000 in service revenue, but collected only $125,000; the remaining $25,000 was due early the next year.
- Salary expenses for the year were $35,000, of which $30,000 was paid in cash during the year; the remaining $5,000 was due the first day of the next year.
- The company paid operating expenses of $30,000 in cash during the year.
- The company sent a check during the last month of the year for $6,500 for interest expense due on the loan from Uncle Damien.
- The company invested $15,000 of cash in short-term investments at the end of the year.
- A Day In Your Dreams declared and paid dividends of $3,500 during the year.

Required

    a. Show how each transaction affects the accounting equation.

    b. Prepare the four basic financial statements for the year ended June 30, 2011. (The balance sheet *at* June 30, 2011.)

    c. Calculate the current ratio at June 30, 2011. What does this ratio measure? Discuss the implications of A Day In Your Dreams' current ratio.

Problems—Set B

P2-1B. *Relationships between financial statement items.* Use the following information for Multicultural Travel Inc. for the year ended December 31, 2010, to answer the questions. Assume that the shareholders made no new contributions to the company during the year. (LO 3)

1. Revenues for the year ended December 31, 2010 = $850
2. Net income for the year ended December 31, 2010 = $370
3. Beginning balance (December 31, 2009, balance) in retained earnings = $280
4. Ending balance (December 31, 2010, balance) in retained earnings = $360
5. Total liabilities and shareholders' equity at December 31, 2010 = $725
6. Total liabilities at December 31, 2009 = $80
7. Total liabilities at December 31, 2010 = $40

Required

    a. What were Multicultural Travel's total expenses during the year ended December 31, 2010?

    b. What was paid to shareholders during the year ended December 31, 2010?

    c. What is the total that owners invested in the Multicultural Travel as of December 31, 2010?

    d. What were total assets on Multicultural Travel's December 31, 2009, balance sheet?

P2-2B. *Analyzing transactions.* International News Herald Inc. entered into the following transactions during 2010: (LO 3)

1. International News Herald Inc. started as a corporation with a $7,250 cash contribution from the owners in exchange for common stock.
2. Newspaper sales, all on account, amounted to $8,900.
3. Cash collections of accounts receivable amounted to $4,750.
4. On November 1, 2010, the company paid $3,000 in advance for an insurance policy that does not go into effect until 2011.
5. The company paid dividends of $400.

Required

Put each of the transactions in an accounting equation worksheet. Then, answer the following questions:

    a. What is the amount of net cash from financing activities for the year ended December 31, 2010?

    b. What amount of total assets would appear on the December 31, 2010, balance sheet?

    c. What amount of net income would appear on the income statement for the year ended December 31, 2010?

    d. What is the amount of retained earnings as of December 31, 2010?

P2-3B. *Identify errors using GAAP; prepare a classified balance sheet; and calculate the current ratio.* An inexperienced accountant has put together a balance sheet for Art Objects Inc. The balances shown are at September 30, 2009. (LO 1, 3, 5)

Assets		Liabilities and Equity	
Current Assets:		Current Liabilities:	
Prepaid insurance	$ 30,000	Accounts receivable	$ 2,000
Cash	6,000	Other long-term assets	5,000
Land	28,000	Salaries payable	8,000
Other current assets	5,000	Intangible assets	35,000
Interest receivable	2,000	Accounts payable	4,000
Total current assets	71,000	Total current liabilities	54,000
Accounts payable	42,000	Shareholder's Equity	
Buildings	36,000	Retained earnings	52,000
Equipment	18,000	Common stock	47,000
Intangible assets	6,000	Short-term note	20,000
Total noncurrent assets	102,000	Total shareholders' equity	119,000
Total Assets	$ 173,000	Total Liabilities and Equity	$ 173,000

Required

    a. Identify the errors in the balance sheet.

    b. Using good form, prepare a corrected, classified balance sheet.

    c. Calculate the current ratio using the corrected amounts from the balance sheet prepared in b. What does this ratio measure? Discuss the implications of Art Objects' current ratio.

    d. Explain why it is important to properly follow GAAP when preparing financial statements.

Excel Template
www.prenhall.com/reimers

P2-4B. *Analyzing transactions and preparing financial statements.* Given the following transactions, (LO 3)

1. Leticia Shettle started a business, Exotic Travel Planners, by contributing $5,000 on July 1, 2010, in exchange for common stock.
2. The company borrowed $3,000 from the bank in July. The note is a 1-year, 10% note, with both principal and interest to be repaid on June 30, 2011.
3. The company earned $1,085 in cash revenue during July.
4. The company paid operating expenses of $725 for the month of July.
5. The company made distributions to owners in the amount of $55 in July.
6. At the end of July, $25 of interest payable is due on the note from #2.

Required

    a. Show how each transaction affects the accounting equation.

    b. Prepare the four basic financial statements for the month of July (balance sheet at July 31).

    c. Give one additional piece of information related to the transactions that could be recorded in an information system for a purpose other than the financial statements.

P2-5B. *Analyze transactions from the accounting equation; prepare the four financial statements; and calculate the current ratio.* The following accounting equation worksheet shows the transactions for Jackie Knight's Furniture Repairs, a corporation, for the first month of business November 2007. (LO 4, 5, 7)

		Assets			=	Liabilities		+	Shareholders' Equity	
	Cash	Accounts receivable	Supplies			Accounts payable	Long-term notes payable		Common stock	Retained earnings
1	$2,000								$2,000 Common stock	
2	4,000						4,000			
3	(5,000)									(5,000) Operating expenses
4	1,500									1,500 Service revenue
5		8,000								8,000 Service revenue
6			4,000			4,000				
7	6,000	(6,000)								
8	(400)					(400)				
9	(3,100)									(3,100) Salary expense
10	(200)									(200) Dividends

Required

    a. Analyze each transaction in the accounting equation worksheet and describe the underlying exchange that resulted in each entry.

    b. Has the company been profitable this month? Explain.

    c. Prepare an income statement for the month ended November 30, 2007.

    d. Prepare a statement of shareholders' equity for the month ended November 30, 2007.

    e. Prepare a statement of cash flows for the month ended November 30, 2007.

    f. Prepare a balance sheet at November 30, 2007.

    g. Calculate the current ratio at November 30, 2007. What does this ratio measure?

P2-6B. *Analyzing transactions and preparing financial statements.* Jackie, Chris, and Cindy started their own consulting firm. They contributed $30,000 each in exchange for 3,000 shares of common stock and borrowed another $60,000 by signing a 10-year note with Tallahassee Capital City Bank. They formed We Do It All Consulting Inc. on January 1, 2009. The business used available funds to purchase some land with an office building for $105,000 and office equipment and furniture for $25,000. The business also bought a computer system on account from Gateway Inc. for $21,500; payment was due at the beginning of the following year. (LO 3, 5)

• During the first year of business, We Do It All Consulting earned $185,000 in service revenue but had collected only $163,000; the remaining $22,000 was due early the next year.

• Salary expenses for the year were $55,000, of which the company paid $45,000 in cash during the year; the remaining $10,000 was due the first day of the next year.

- The company paid operating expenses of $27,500 in cash during the year.
- Interest expense for the year was $3,500 but was not due until the note matured.
- The company invested $18,000 of cash in a certificate of deposit at the end of the year.
- We Do It All Consulting declared and paid dividends of $4,800 during the year.

Required

a. Show how each transaction affects the accounting equation.
b. Prepare the four basic financial statements for the year ended December 31, 2009. (The balance sheet *at* December 31, 2009.)
c. Calculate the current ratio at December 31, 2009. What does this ratio measure? Discuss the implications of We Do It All Consulting's current ratio.

Financial Statement Analysis

FSA2-1. The balance sheets for Tootsie Roll Industries Inc. are shown here. (LO 3, 5)

	31-Dec-05	31-Dec-04
Assets	(in thousands)	
Cash	$ 91,336	$ 56,989
Investments	54,892	32,369
Receivables	33,624	37,457
Inventory	55,032	58,777
Other current assets	11,712	7,101
Net property plant & equipment	178,760	178,750
Other noncurrent assets	388,340	440,310
Total assets	$ 813,696	$ 811,753
Liabilities		
Bank loan (short-term)	32,001	6,333
Accounts payable	17,482	19,315
Dividends payable	4,263	3,659
Accrued liabilities	44,969	44,722
Income taxes payable	14,941	8,288
Total current liabilities	113,656	82,317
Noncurrent liabilities	82,635	159,257
Total liabilities	196,291	241,574
Contributed capital	463,108	434,047
Retained earnings	164,236	149,055
Other shareholders' equity accounts, net*	(9,939)	(12,923)
	617,405	570,179
Total liabilities and shareholders' equity	$ 813,696	$ 811,753

*This is an item you will learn about in a later chapter.

Required

a. What were the total current assets at December 31, 2004? 2005?
b. How are the assets ordered on the balance sheet?
c. What were the total current liabilities at December 31, 2004? 2005?
d. Calculate the current ratio at December 31, 2004 and December 31, 2005. What information do these numbers provide?

FSA2-2. Selected information from the comparative balance sheets for Sears Holdings Corporation are presented here. Although some accounts are not listed, all of the current assets and current liabilities are given. (LO 3, 4, 9)

	at January 28, 2006	at January 26, 2005
	(dollars in millions)	
Cash	$ 4,440	$3,435
Accounts receivable	811	646
Inventory	9,068	3,281
Other current assets	888	179
Property, plant, and equipment	9,823	315
Accounts payable	3,458	927
Other current liabilities	6,892	1,154
Long-term debt	8,612	2,101
Total shareholders' equity	11,611	4,469

Required

a. Provide the following values at the end of each given fiscal year.
    1. Current assets
    2. Current liabilities
    3. Current ratio
b. Based on your answers in part a, discuss the change in liquidity between the two years.

FSA2-3. A condensed statement of cash flows for Apple Computer Inc. for the year ended September 24, 2005, is shown here. Use it to answer the questions given after the statement. (LO 5)

Apple Computer Inc.
Statement of Cash Flows
For the year ended September 24, 2005

	(in millions)
Cash and cash equivalents, beginning of the year	$ 2,969
Cash generated by operating activities	2,535
Investing cash flows:	
Purchase of short-term investments	(11,470)
Proceeds from maturities of short-term investments	8,609
Proceeds from sales of short-term investments	586
Purchase of property, plant, and equipment	(260)
Other	(21)
Cash generated by (used for) investing activities	(2,556)
Financing cash flows:	
Proceeds from issuance of common stock	543
Cash generated by (used for) financing activities	543
Increase (decrease) in cash and cash equivalents	522
Cash and cash equivalents, end of the year	$ 3,491

Required

a. Did Apple purchase any property, plant, or equipment during the year?
b. If you were to examine Apple's balance sheet at September 24, 2005, what would be the amount for cash and cash equivalents?
c. Was cash generated from operations or used by operations? By what amount?
d. Did Apple receive any new contributions from owners during the year? How can you tell?

Critical Thinking Problems

Risk and Controls

Look at the information in the Staples annual report in appendix in addition to the financial statements. What kinds of risks does Staples face? Use the information in the annual report and your own experience to answer this question.

Ethics

Ken Jones wants to start a small business and has asked his uncle to lend him $10,000. He has prepared a business plan and some financial statements that indicate the business could be very profitable. Ken is afraid his uncle will want some ownership in the company for his investment, but Ken does not want to share what he believes will be a hugely successful company. What are the ethical issues Ken must face as he prepares to present his business plan to his uncle? Do you think he should try to *emphasize* the risks of ownership to his uncle to convince him it would be preferable to be a creditor? Why or why not?

Group Assignment

Look at the four basic financial statements for Tom's Wear in Exhibits 2.5, 2.6, 2.7, and 2.8. Work together to find numbers that show the links between the various financial statements. Then, write a brief explanation of how the statements relate to each other.

Internet Exercise: MSN Money and Merck

MSN Money offers information about companies, industries, people, and related news items. For researching a company, this Web site is a good place to start gathering basic information.

Please go to the www.prenhall.com/reimers Web site. Go to Chapter 2 and use the Internet Exercise company link. Or try http://moneycentral.msn.com.

IE 2-1. In the *Symbol* box, enter MRK for Merck and Co. Inc.
   a. What type of company is Merck?
   b. List three products manufactured by Merck.

IE 2-2. Click on Financial Statements.
   a. For the most recent year list the amounts reported for sales, cost of goods sold, and total net income. Does the amount reported for revenue represent cash received from customers during the year? If not, what does it represent? What does the amount reported for cost of goods sold represent? Is Merck a profitable company? How can you tell?
   b. For the most recent year list the amounts reported for total assets, total liabilities, and total shareholders' equity. Does the accounting equation hold true? Are assets primarily financed with liabilities or shareholders' equity?
   c. Does Merck use accrual-based or cash-based accounting? How can you tell?

Please note: Internet Web sites are constantly being updated. Therefore, if the information is not found where indicated, please explore the Web site further to find the information.

Accruals and Deferrals: Timing Is Everything in Accounting

Here's Where You've Been . . .

In Chapter 2, you studied the qualities of the information in the financial statements. Accounting information should be useful. You also learned that GAAP requires accrual basis accounting—revenues are recognized when *earned* and expenses are *matched* to those revenues.

Here's Where You're Going . . .

In Chapter 3, you will learn more about how the financial statements show transactions in which the exchange of the cash and the exchange of goods and services happen at different times. These are accruals and deferrals.

Learning Objectives

When you are finished studying this chapter, you should be able to:

1. Define accrual accounting and explain how income is measured.

2. Explain *accruals* and how they affect the financial statements; describe and perform the adjustments related to accruals.

3. Explain *deferrals* and how they affect the financial statements; describe and perform the adjustments related to deferrals.

4. Construct the basic financial statements from a given set of transactions that include accruals and deferrals and recognize the effect of these transactions on actual financial statements.

5. Compute and explain *working capital* and the *quick ratio*.

6. Explain the business risks associated with financial records and accounting information.

Ethics Matters

When John Rigas, the former chairman and CEO of Adelphia Communications, was found guilty of bank and securities fraud and sentenced to 15 years in prison, it was not just the case of a CEO who looted a publicly traded communications company. John Rigas was the company's founder. He and his son, Timothy Rigas, were convicted of stealing over $2 billion from the company.

Some people believe that having someone like the founder of a company as part of the management team will help protect the company from management abuses. If a firm's managers have some ownership in the company, their interests should be aligned with those of the shareholders. Although there may be some truth in this, one thing is clear from the case of Adelphia: There is no substitute for ethical behavior. In this case, the founder of the company drove the company into bankruptcy to support a life of extreme luxury. For John Rigas, over 80 years old, the only luxury he may have left is the luxury of spending the last years of his life in jail.

L.O.1

Define accrual accounting and explain how income is measured.

Measuring Income

After its first month, Tom's Wear prepared a set of financial statements to measure and report the company's activity during that first month and to measure and report its financial position at the end of that month. Tom's Wear did both again for the second month.

At different points of time in the life of a company, owners, investors, creditors, and other interested parties want to know the company's financial position and accomplishments in order to make all kinds of evaluations and decisions, including whether or not the company is meeting its goals. The main goal is usually to make a profit; so measuring the profit the company has made during a specified period plays a big role in evaluating how successfully a company has been doing its business.

As you learned in Chapter 2, the income statement summarizes revenues and expenses for a period of time, usually a year. Net income can also be measured for a week, a month, or a quarter. For example, many companies provide quarterly financial information to their shareholders. That information would include net income for the quarter.

Accountants consider the continuous life of a business as being composed of discrete periods of time—months, quarters, or years. The way we divide the revenues and expenses among those time periods is a crucial part of accounting. That is why timing is everything in accounting. If revenue is *earned* (not necessarily *collected*) in a certain time period, you must be sure that it is included on the income statement for that period—not the one before and not the one after. If you have used some supplies during a period, then you need to include the cost of those supplies as part of the expenses on the income statement for that same period.

Sometimes you will see the income statement referred to as the *statement of operations* and other times as the *profit and loss statement*. However it is referred to, it will usually appear as the first financial statement in a company's annual report. Exhibit 3.1 shows the income statements for Chico's FAS Inc. When you see total sales of $1,404,575,000 for the year ended January 28, 2006, you know that all the sales made in that fiscal year—a year of business for the company—are included in that amount, even if some of the cash has not been collected from the customers by January 28, 2006. Similarly, the expenses listed are only the expenses incurred in that fiscal year, whether or not the company has paid for those expenses by January 28, 2006. Chico's has worked hard to get the amounts right.

EXHIBIT 3.1

**Income Statements
for Chico's**

Chico's had net sales of over
$1.4 billion during the fiscal year
ended January 28, 2006.
Investors depend on that
information, so Chico's works
hard to get it right.

Chico's FAS, Inc. and Subsidiaries
Consolidated Statements of Income
(In thousands, except per share amounts)

	Fiscal Year Ended		
	January 28, 2006	January 29, 2005	January 31, 2004
Net sales by Chico's/Soma stores	$1,095,938	$ 889,429	$ 698,100
Net sales by WH|BM stores	261,601	142,092	39,818
Net sales by catalog and Internet	36,151	26,831	22,780
Net sales to franchisees	10,885	8,530	7,801
Net sales	1,404,575	1,066,882	768,499
Cost of goods sold	547,532	411,908	297,477
Gross profit	857,043	654,974	471,022
General, administrative and store operating expenses	514,529	398,117	289,118
Depreciation and amortization	44,201	32,481	21,130
Income from operations	298,313	224,376	160,774
Interest income, net	8,236	2,327	888
Income before income taxes	306,549	226,703	161,662
Income tax provision	112,568	85,497	61,432
Net income	$ 193,981	$ 141,206	$ 100,230

Timing differences in accounting are differences between

- the time when a company earns revenue by providing a product or service to customers and the time when the cash is collected from the customers,

and

- the time when the company incurs an expense and the time when the company pays for the expense.

You will see in this chapter how to identify timing differences and present them on the financial statements.

As discussed in the previous chapter, you can think of the timing problems in accounting in two simple ways:

- action before dollars
- dollars before action

An example of action before dollars is when a sale is made *on account*. A customer buys on credit and agrees to pay later. The action of making the sale—the economic substance of the transaction—takes place before dollars are exchanged in payment. This type of transaction—action first, dollars later—is called an **accrual**.

In contrast, an example of dollars before action is when a firm buys insurance. By its nature, insurance must be purchased in advance of the time period to which it applies. Payment—when the dollars are exchanged—is made first, and the use of the insurance— the action provided by insurance protection—comes later. Dollars first, action later is called a **deferral**.

For timing differences, whether accruals or deferrals, we must look at the accounting information on each side of the difference and adjust that information before it can be presented on the financial statements.

Timing differences arise when revenues are earned and collected in different accounting periods. They also arise when expenses are incurred in one accounting period and paid for in another.

An **accrual** is a transaction in which the revenue has been earned or the expense has been incurred but no cash has been exchanged.

A **deferral** is a transaction in which the cash is exchanged before the revenue is earned or the expense is incurred.

L.O.2
Explain accruals and how
they affect the financial
statements; describe and
perform the adjustments
related to accruals.

Accruals

When the substance of a business transaction takes place before any cash changes hands, the accountant includes that transaction in the measurement of income. That is, if a firm has earned revenue, that revenue must be included on the income statement. If the firm incurred an expense to earn that revenue, that expense must be included on the income statement. Accruals can pertain to both revenues and expenses. There are two types of accruals that need a closer look:

- interest expense and interest revenue
- other expenses and revenues

Accruals for Interest Expense and Interest Revenue

The most common timing difference pertains to interest related to borrowing or lending money. When you borrow money, you pay interest for the use of that money. If you borrowed $500 from a bank on January 1, 2006, and agreed to repay it with 8% interest on January 1, 2007, you would pay back a total of $540. On January 1, 2006, when you borrow the money, you get the $500 cash, an asset, and you increase your liabilities. The accounting equation is increased on both sides by $500.

Assets	=	Liabilities	+	Shareholder's equity		
				Contributed capital	+	Retained earnings
+ 500 cash		+ 500 notes payable				

When you get ready to prepare the financial statements for the year ended December 31, 2006, you see that this liability—notes payable—is still on the books and will be listed on the balance sheet. That is because on December 31, 2006, you still owe the bank the full amount of the loan. What about the $500 cash you received? You may still have it, but it is more likely you spent it during the year to keep your business running. That is why you borrowed it.

What about the cost of borrowing the money—the interest expense? On December 31, 2006, one full year has passed since you borrowed the money. The passing of time has caused interest expense to be incurred.

- Interest expense is the cost of using someone else's money.
- Time passing is the action related to interest expense.

Although the action of using someone else's money during the year has taken place, the dollars have not been exchanged—the interest payment for using that money. To make the December 31, 2006, financial statements correct, you must show the interest expense of $40 ($500 × 8%, or $500 × 0.08) on the income statement. Also, you must show—on the balance sheet—the obligation called **interest payable**. It is a liability, indicating the bank's claim to the $40 as of December 31, 2006. The liability section of the balance sheet will show both the $500 loan and the $40 interest.

Remember that revenues and expenses are shown on the income statement. Then, before the balance sheet can be prepared, net income needs to be added to the beginning retained earnings balance to get the new retained earnings balance for the balance sheet. Even though revenues and expenses eventually increase retained earnings (part of shareholders' equity), these amounts are not considered part of retained earnings.

Interest payable is a liability. It is the amount a company owes for borrowing money (after the time period to which the interest applies has passed).

Assets	=	Liabilities	+	Shareholder's equity		
				Contributed capital	+	Retained earnings
		+ 40 interest payable				(40) interest expense

The adjustment increases liabilities and will eventually decrease retained earnings in the accounting equation. Making this adjustment is called accruing interest expense; the expense itself is called an accrual. Sometimes a company will label the amount of interest expense accrued as *accrued liabilities* or *accrued expenses*. Each expression means the same thing—an expense that will be paid in the future. Notice that the interest expense will be on the income statement for the period, even though the cash has not been paid yet.

Suppose you borrowed the $500 on July 1, 2006 (instead of January 1). In this case, you would have use of the money for only half of the year and therefore would have incurred only half a year of interest expense as of December 31, 2006. This is the formula for interest:

$$\text{Interest (I)} = \text{Principal (P)} \times \text{Rate (R)} \times \text{Time (T)}$$

Interest rates, like the 8% annual interest, always pertain to a year. As of December 31, 2006, the interest payable on the note would be $500 \times 0.08 \times 6/12 = 20. The last part of the formula gives the time as a percentage of a year, or the number of months out of 12. Whenever you accrue interest, you must be careful to count the months that apply. That will help you make sure you put the right amount of interest expense on the income statement for exactly the period of time you had use of the borrowed money.

If you borrowed the $500 on January 1, 2006, for one full year, what would happen when you pay the bank on January 1, 2007? On one side of the accounting equation, you will reduce cash by $540. The equation will be balanced by a reduction of $500 in notes payable plus the reduction of $40 in interest payable. There will be no expense recorded when you actually pay the cash. Remember, the action has already taken place, and the action resulted in interest expense in 2006. There is no interest expense in 2007 because you paid off the loan on January 1, 2007.

This is how timing differences work. The expense is recorded in one period, but the cash is paid in another period.

Assets	=	Liabilities	+	Shareholder's equity		
				Contributed capital	+	Retained earnings
		(40) interest payable				
(540) cash		(500) notes payable				

In most of our examples, a company will be borrowing money; however, sometimes a company lends money to another company or to an employee. A company that lends money accrues interest revenue during the time the loan is outstanding. The amount of interest revenue accrued at the time an income statement is prepared is calculated with the same formula used to calculate interest expense, $I = P \times R \times T$. The amount of interest revenue will increase assets—interest receivable—and will increase retained earnings—via interest revenue.

Suppose a company lends $200 to an employee on October 1 at 10% interest, to be repaid on January 1 of the following year. The transaction on October 1 decreases assets—cash—and also increases assets—other receivables. Because firms generally use *accounts receivable* to describe amounts customers owe the company, we call the amounts owed by others—meaning anyone who is not a customer—other receivables.

Assets	=	Liabilities	+	Shareholder's equity		
				Contributed capital	+	Retained earnings
(200) cash						
+ 200 other receivables						

On December 31, the company will accrue interest revenue. Why? Because some time has passed and interest revenue has been earned during that period. With interest, the action is the passage of time, so the action has taken place, but the cash will not change hands until the following January 1. You would record interest revenue of $5 ($200 \times 0.10 \times 3/12$).

You would also record interest receivable of $5. By doing all this, the financial statements would accurately reflect the following situation on December 31:

* The company has earned $5 of interest revenue as of December 31.
* The company has not received the interest revenue at December 31.

Because all revenues increase retained earnings, the interest revenue will be recorded under retained earnings in the accounting equation:

Assets	=	Liabilities	+	Shareholder's equity		
				Contributed capital	+	**Retained earnings**
+ 5 interest receivable						+ 5 interest revenue

When the company actually receives the cash for the interest on January 1, along with repayment of the $200 principal, it will not be recorded as interest revenue. Instead, the total $205 cash is recorded as an increase in cash and a decrease in the asset other receivables by $200 and the asset interest receivable by $5. The timing difference resulted in recording the interest revenue in one period and the cash collection in another.

Your Turn 3-1
Your Turn
Your Turn

1. **If you borrowed $1,000 at 7% (interest rates are always assumed to be per year), how much interest would you pay for having that money for only 6 months?**
2. **If you have an outstanding loan and you record interest expense before you actually make the cash payment for the interest, is this an accrual or a deferral? Why?**

Accruals for Other Revenues and Expenses

There are other types of revenues and expenses that must be accrued at the end of the period so that the financial statements will accurately reflect the business transactions for the period. For example, if you have provided services for a customer during 2007 but have not recorded those services (perhaps because you have not billed the customers yet), you want to be sure to record the revenue on the 2007 income statement. Why record this on the 2007 income statement? Because the action was completed in 2007. You cannot record any cash received for this action in 2007—because you have not received payment in 2007 as a result of your action in 2007. This is a timing difference, recorded as an accounts receivable.

Accrued revenue and receivables are often paired together in accruals. An increase in assets—accounts receivable—and an increase in retained earnings—revenue—both in the same amount, balance the accounting equation. Then, when the cash is actually collected—sometimes called **realized**—it is not recognized as revenue because it was already recognized in a previous period. That is, receipt of the cash in the following year is not recognized as revenue because the revenue was already recognized in the prior year.

> **Realized** means the cash is collected. Sometimes revenue is *recognized* before it is *realized*.

Exhibit 3.2 shows the current assets section of Talbots' balance sheet. At January 28, 2006, Talbots had accounts receivable amounting to $209,749,000. This is a significant amount of money! When you see receivables on a company's balance sheet, it means the related revenues have been earned and included on the income statement for that period even though the cash has not been collected yet.

Expenses may also need to be accrued. When you get to the end of an accounting period—when you prepare financial statements—you examine your records and business transactions to find any expenses that might have been incurred but not recorded. These are the expenses you have not paid for yet. (If you paid for them, you would have recorded them when you gave the cash to pay for them.) When you receive a bill for some expenses such as utilities, you likely will record the expense and the related accounts payable. If you have done that, you will not need to accrue it at the end of the period.

However, there are some typical expenses that companies do not record until the end of the period. These expenses must be accrued, which will result in an expense on the in-

EXHIBIT 3.2

Current Assets Section of Talbots' Balance Sheet

This is the current assets section of Talbots' balance sheet.

The Talbots', Inc. and Subsidiaries
From the Consolidated Balance Sheets
(Amounts in thousands)

Assets	January 28, 2006	January 29, 2005
Current Assets:		
Cash and cash equivalents	$ 103,020	$ 31,811
Customer accounts receivable—net	209,749	199,256
Merchandise inventories	246,707	238,544
Deferred catalog costs	6,021	5,118
Due from affiliates	7,892	9,073
Deferred income taxes	14,115	14,006
Prepaid and other current assets	33,157	29,589
Total current assets	$ 620,661	$ 527,397

come statement and some sort of payable in the liabilities section of the balance sheet. These expenses have been recognized—shown on the income statement—but the cash has not been paid yet.

One of the most common accruals is salary expense. Typically, a company will record salary expense when it pays its employees. (In the accounting equation, that transaction would reduce assets—cash—and reduce retained earnings via salary expense.) What do you do if the end of an accounting period does not coincide with payday? You need to record the salary expense for the work that your employees have done since the last time you paid them. You want to be sure to get the correct amount of salary expense on the income statement for the period. This accrual will increase liabilities—salaries payable—and decrease retained earnings via salaries expense. The action—the employees performing the work—has already taken place; but the cash will not be exchanged until the next payday, which will be in the next accounting period.

Suppose you are preparing the financial statements for the accounting period ended on December 31, 2008. That date is on a Wednesday. If you pay your employees every Friday, the last payday of the year is December 26, 2008. As of December 31, 2008, you will owe them for their work done on Monday, Tuesday, and Wednesday, December 29, 2008, through December 31, 2008. You will need to record the salary expense for those 3 days, even though you will not pay the employees until Friday, January 2, 2009. Recording this salary expense so it is recognized on the correct income statement is called accruing salary expense. This adjustment will increase liabilities—salaries payable—and decrease retained earnings by increasing salary expense.

What happens when January 2, 2009, arrives and you actually pay the employees? You will pay them for the week from December 29, 2008, through January 2, 2009. The expense for three of those days—December 29 through December 31—was recorded on December 31, 2008, so that it would be on the income statement for the fiscal year ended December 31, 2008. The expense for the other 2 days—January 1, 2009 and January 2, 2009—has not been recorded yet. The expense for those 2 days belongs on the income statement for the fiscal year ended December 31, 2009. When you pay the employees on January 2, 2009, you will reduce liabilities—the amount of the salaries payable you recorded on December 31, 2008, will be deducted from that account—and you will reduce retained earnings by recording salary expense for those 2 days in 2009.

Putting numbers in an example should help make this clear. Suppose the total amount you owe your employees for a 5-day workweek is $3,500. Look at the calendar in Exhibit 3.3—we are interested in the week beginning December 29.

Monday	Tuesday	Wednesday	Thursday	Friday
December 22	December 23	December 24	December 25	December 26
December 29	December 30	December 31	January 1	January 2
January 5	January 6	January 7	January 8	January 9

On December 31, you need to accrue 3 days' worth of salary expense. The $3,500 applies to 5 days, but you need to look at it as $700 per day. To accrue the salary expense for 3 days, you increase the liability salaries payable and decrease retained earnings via salary expense by $2,100. Why are you recording the salary expense and salaries payable even though you are not paying your employees until January 2? Because you want to have the expense for those 3 days on the income statement for the year ended December 31, 2008. How does this adjustment affect the accounting equation? Both the income statement and the balance sheet are affected by this accrual.

Assets	=	Liabilities	+	Shareholder's equity		
				Contributed capital	+	Retained earnings
		+ 2,100 salaries payable				(2,100) salary expense

On January 2, when you actually pay the employees for an entire week, you will give them cash of $3,500. How much of that amount is expense for work done in the year 2008 and how much is expense for work done in 2009? We already know that $2,100 is expense for 2008. The other 2 days' worth of work done and salary earned—$1,400—applies to 2009. Here is how the transaction on January 2—paying the employees for a full week of work—affects the accounting equation:

Cash is reduced; salaries payable is reduced; and retained earnings is reduced via salary expense.

Assets	=	Liabilities	+	Shareholder's equity		
				Contributed capital	+	Retained earnings
(3,500) cash		(2,100) salaries payable				(1,400) salary expense

Review the example and make sure you know why the adjustment on December 31 was necessary and how the amount was calculated. Notice that the salary expense recorded is only the amount of the January work.

Your Turn 3-2

Suppose ABC Company pays its employees a total of $56,000 on the 15th of each month for work done the previous month. ABC generally records salary expense when the employees are paid. If the ABC fiscal year-end is June 30, 2008, does any salary expense need to be accrued at year-end? If so, how much?

L.O.3
Explain deferrals and how they affect the financial statements; describe and perform the adjustments related to deferrals.

Deferrals

The word *defer* means "to put off or to postpone." In accounting, a deferral refers to a transaction in which the dollars have been exchanged before the economic substance of the transaction—the action—has taken place. It can refer to both revenues and expenses. As you read and study the examples that follow, remember that you are taking the point of view of the business.

Deferrals Related to Revenue

Unearned Revenue. Suppose a company decides to sell items on the Internet. The man who owns the company is a conservative fellow who is not too sure about this way of doing business, so he decides that he will not ship the products until he has received a customer's check and it has cleared the bank. When the company receives a check for $80 for an order, the owner must defer recognition of the revenue until the items have shipped. However, he immediately deposits the check. Technically, he does not have claim to the cash until he ships the items he sold. In fact, the claim to the cash belongs to the customer at the time the company receives and deposits the check. Here is how this cash receipt affects the accounting equation:

Assets	=	Liabilities	+	Shareholder's equity	
				Contributed + **capital**	**Retained earnings**
+ 80 cash		+ 80 unearned revenue			

Unearned revenue is a balance sheet account—a liability. It represents amounts a company owes to others—customers. This is called a *deferral* because the company is *putting off* the recognition of the revenue, that is, not showing it on the income statement until the revenue is actually earned. Please notice that the name of this liability is a bit unusual. It has the word revenue in it, but it is *not* an income statement account.

When the items sold are actually shipped, the company will recognize the revenue. This will be done by decreasing unearned revenue and increasing retained earnings via revenue. Here is how the accounting equation will be affected:

Assets	=	Liabilities	+	Shareholder's equity	
				Contributed + **capital**	**Retained earnings**
		(80) unearned revenue			80 sales revenue

Notice that the claim has changed hands—the claim no longer belongs to the customer. Now that the items have been shipped, the owner has claim to the $80 cash paid by the customer.

Another common example of deferred revenue is magazine subscriptions. Customers pay the company in advance, so the dollars are exchanged before the action—delivery of the magazine—takes place. When the customers pay, the cash must be deposited, but the revenue is not recognized. If the magazine company prepares a balance sheet after receiving the cash but before the magazines are actually delivered (the revenue has not been earned), the balance sheet will show the cash and the obligation to the customers—unearned revenue. That obligation will be removed from the balance sheet when the magazines are delivered.

The current liabilities section of the balance sheet for Time Warner Inc. at December 31, 2005 and 2004, are shown in Exhibit 3.4. Highlighted on the statement you will see $1,473 million of unearned revenue at the end of 2005 and $1,653 million at the end of 2006. The company calls it *deferred revenue*. It represents amounts Time Warner has collected from customers but has not yet earned by providing the related services. As the company earns those revenues, the earned amounts will be deducted from the liability and recognized as revenue.

Gift Certificates. Have you ever received a gift certificate or a gift card? Almost all retail firms are happy to sell gift cards. Suppose you decide to purchase a $50 gift card at Best Buy to give your cousin for his birthday. You want something easy to mail, and you are not sure what sort of gift he would like. When you pay $50 to Best Buy for a gift card, Best Buy records the cash—an asset—and a liability—unearned revenue. Some firms combine their

> A **deferral** is a transaction in which the cash is received or paid before the action takes place. The cash must be recorded, but recognition of the related revenue or expense is deferred. When we adjust that deferral to recognize any portion that may no longer need to be deferred, we are really *un*doing a deferral.

> **Unearned revenue** is a liability. It represents the amount of goods or services that a company owes its customers. The cash has been collected, but the action of *earning* the revenue has not taken place.

EXHIBIT 3.4

Deferred Revenue from Time Warner, Inc.

Time Warner has had over a billion dollars of deferred revenue at the end of each of the past two years, highlighted in the portion of its balance sheet shown here.

Time Warner Inc.
From the Consolidated Balance Sheet
December 31,
(millions)

	2005	2004
Liabilities and Shareholders' Equity		
Current liabilities		
Accounts payable	$ 1,380	$ 1,339
Participations payable	2,426	2,452
Royalties and programming costs payable	1,074	1,018
Deferred revenue	1,473	1,653
Debt due within one year	92	1,672
Other current liabilities	6,100	6,468
Current liabilities of discontinued operations	43	50
Total current liabilities	$ 12,588	$ 14,652

liability for gift cards with other liabilities on their balance sheet. Others have such a significant amount that the liability for gift cards is shown as a line item on the balance sheet. Look at Best Buy's balance sheet in Exhibit 3.5. You will see the liability *unredeemed* gift cards for $469 million at February 25, 2006. As the gift cards are redeemed or as they expire, Best Buy will recognize the related revenue.

EXHIBIT 3.5

Liabilities from Best Buy's Balance Sheet

The highlighted line shows that Best Buy had a significant amount of outstanding gift cards at the end of each of the fiscal years shown.

Best Buy Co., Inc.
Consolidated Balance Sheets
($ in millions)

	February 25, 2006	February 26, 2005
Liabilities and Shareholders' Equity		
Current Liabilities		
Accounts payable	$ 3,234	$ 2,824
Unredeemed gift card liabilities	469	410
Accrued compensation and related expenses	354	234
Accrued liabilities	878	844
Accrued income taxes	703	575
Current portion of long-term debt	418	72
Total current liabilities	6,056	4,959
Long-Term Liabilities	373	358
Long-Term Debt	178	528
Shareholders' Equity		
Preferred stock, $1.00 par value: Authorized—400,000 shares;		
Issued and outstanding—none	–	–
Common stock, $.10 par value: Authorized—1 billion shares;		
Issued and outstanding—485,098,000 and 492,512,000		
shares; respectively	49	49
Additional paid-in capital	643	936
Retained earnings	4,304	3,315
Accumulated other comprehensive income	261	149
Total shareholders' equity	5,257	4,449
Total Liabilities and Shareholders' Equity	$ 11,864	$ 10,294

Living Time Magazine collected $300,000 for 12-month subscriptions before it published its first issue in June 2008. How much revenue should the magazine company recognize for the fiscal year ended December 31, 2008? Explain what it means to *recognize* revenue in this situation.

Your Turn 3-3
Your Turn
Your Turn

Deferrals Related to Expenses

Four kinds of expenses are commonly paid in advance. We will first discuss expenses for insurance, rent, and supplies. The other is an advance payment for equipment used by a company for more than one fiscal period. All four expenses have in common that the timing of the cash disbursement precedes the actual use of the product or service purchased.

Insurance. Like any of us when we buy insurance, a company pays for insurance in advance of the service provided by the insurance company. In accounting, the advance payment for a service or good to be received in the future is considered the purchase of an asset. Recall from Chapter 2 that accountants call the asset *prepaid insurance*. Remember, assets are items of value that the company will use up to produce revenue. Until it is actually used, prepaid insurance is shown in the current asset section of the balance sheet. Suppose a firm paid $2,400 for 1 year of insurance coverage, beginning on October 1, the date of the payment to the insurance company. Here is how the payment would affect the accounting equation:

Assets	=	Liabilities	+	Shareholder's equity	
				Contributed + capital	Retained earnings
(2,400) cash + 2,400 prepaid insurance					

Purchasing the insurance policy is an asset exchange: Cash is exchanged for prepaid insurance. No expense is recorded when the payment is made because the benefit of the cost has not been used. The expense will be recognized when the company actually uses the insurance. The signal that the insurance is being used is the passing of time. As time passes, the insurance protection expires and the amount paid for insurance during that time becomes an expense. The firm makes the adjustment when it prepares the financial statements.

Suppose the firm wants to prepare the financial statements on December 31. How much of the insurance is still unused? That is the amount the firm must show as an asset on the December 31 balance sheet. How much has been used up? That is the amount the firm must show as an expense on the income statement.

News Flash

You have learned that deferring an expense means postponing recognition of that expense—keeping it off the income statement until sometime in the future. Fannie Mae, a giant provider of funding for home mortgages, is expected to recognize about $11 billion of losses that had been erroneously deferred! Oops! In May 2006, Fannie Mae agreed to pay a $400 million fine to the SEC as part of a settlement of accounting-fraud charges.

Here is the adjustment the firm makes before preparing the December 31 financial statements:

Assets	=	Liabilities	+	Shareholder's equity	
				Contributed capital +	**Retained earnings**
(600) prepaid insurance					(600) insurance expense

The firm has used up 3 months of the 12-month insurance policy already paid for. The firm paid $2,400 for the 12-month policy, so the monthly cost of insurance is $200. That means the total insurance expense for 3 months is $600, and the prepaid insurance remaining—insurance not yet used up—will be on the December 31 balance sheet in the amount of $1,800. Look at Exhibit 3.6 for another example with insurance.

Rent. Rent is also usually paid in advance. In the accounting records, prepaid rent is treated exactly the same way as prepaid insurance. When the company pays the cash for rent in advance, an asset called **prepaid rent** is recorded. The disbursement of cash for prepaid rent is an asset exchange. Suppose a company paid $9,000 to rent a warehouse for 3 months, beginning on November 1, the date of the payment. The way it would affect the accounting equation follows:

> **Prepaid rent** is an asset. It represents amounts paid for rent not yet used. The rent expense is deferred until the rented asset has actually been used—when the time related to the rent has passed.

Assets	=	Liabilities	+	Shareholder's equity	
				Contributed capital +	**Retained earnings**
(9,000) cash + 9,000 prepaid rent					

The asset *prepaid rent* is increased, and cash is decreased. Notice, no expense is recognized when the company makes the payment for the rent. Until it is actually used, prepaid rent is an asset. When would the rent expense be recognized, that is, when would it be put on the income statement? When the company prepares financial statements, it wants to be sure that the rent expense is shown correctly on the income statement. The amount paid was $9,000 for a period of 3 months, which is $3,000 per month. When the financial statements are prepared on December 31, 2 months of rent has been used—$6,000. To make sure the income statement reflects the expense for the period ended December 31, the company makes the following adjustment:

EXHIBIT 3.6

Deferred Expenses— Insurance

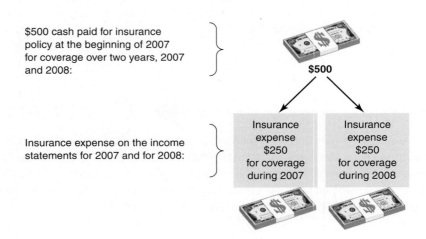

$500 cash paid for insurance policy at the beginning of 2007 for coverage over two years, 2007 and 2008:

$500

Insurance expense on the income statements for 2007 and for 2008:

Insurance expense $250 for coverage during 2007

Insurance expense $250 for coverage during 2008

a portion of that equipment cost each accounting period in which the equipment is used, hopefully to generate revenue.

The matching principle is the reason the cost of equipment is spread over several periods. Expenses and the revenues they help generate need to be on the same income statement—that is the heart of the matching principle. When it is hard to make a precise match with specific revenue (such as sales and cost of goods sold), the next best match is to put an expense on the income statement in the period in which the related asset is used. That is what you do with equipment—allocate the cost of the equipment to the periods the equipment is used.

Suppose a company purchases a computer for $5,000 cash. When the purchase is made, the company will record the acquisition of the new asset and the cash payment.

Assets	=	Liabilities	+	Shareholder's equity	
				Contributed capital	+ Retained earnings
(5,000) cash					
+ 5,000 computer					

If the firm were to classify the purchase as an expense at this point, it would be doing a very poor job of matching revenues and expenses. The firm wants to recognize the expense of the computer during the years in which it uses the computer.

The terminology that accountants use with equipment is different than the terminology used with other deferrals. Instead of calling the expense related to using the computer something logical like "computer expense," it is called **depreciation expense**. Do not confuse depreciation in this accounting context with depreciation commonly used to mean decline in market value.

> The **depreciation expense** is the expense for each period.

As the asset is used and the firm wants to reduce its amount in the accounting records, the accountant will not subtract the amount of the expense directly from the asset's purchase price. Instead, per GAAP, the firm will show the subtractions separately on the balance sheet. Exhibit 3.8 shows how Best Buy Co. Inc. presents this information.

Using real financial information to first learn an accounting concept can be difficult. An example with a fictitious company will help explain the accounting treatment of the cost of equipment and its depreciation expense over time. Sample Company purchased the computer for $5,000 on January 1, 2009, and recorded the asset exchange shown in the preceding accounting equation. Then, when Sample Company prepares its year-end financial statements, depreciation expense must be recognized. The shareholders' claims to the company assets are reduced via depreciation expense.

To calculate how much the asset cost should be reduced each year, Sample Company first must deduct the value it believes the asset will have—what it will be worth—when the company is finished using it. That amount is called the **residual value**. In this example, Sample Company plans to use the computer until it is worth nothing; that means the residual value is zero. The cost of the asset minus any residual value is divided by the number of accounting periods that the asset will be used. Usually, the time period for depreciation expense is a year. Because Sample plans to use the $5,000 computer for 5 years and has estimated its residual value to be zero, the annual depreciation amount will be $1,000.

> **Residual value,** also known as *salvage value,* is the estimated value of an asset at the end of its useful life. With most depreciation methods, residual value is deducted before the calculation of depreciation expense.

The total reduction in the dollar amount of equipment, at any particular point in time, is called **accumulated depreciation**. Each year, accumulated depreciation gets larger. Accumulated depreciation is not the same as depreciation expense. Accumulated depreciation is the total depreciation taken over the entire life of the asset, and depreciation expense is the amount of depreciation for a single year. Accumulated depreciation is called a **contra-asset** because it is the opposite of an asset. It is a deduction from assets. Accumulated depreciation is disclosed separately somewhere in the financial statements so that the original cost of the equipment is kept intact.

> The **accumulated depreciation** is the reduction to the cost of the asset. Accumulated depreciation is a contra-asset, deducted from the cost of the asset for the balance sheet.

On the balance sheet, the original cost of the equipment is shown along with the deduction for accumulated depreciation—the total amount of depreciation that has been

> A **contra-asset** is an amount that is deducted from an asset.

EXHIBIT 3.8

Assets from Best Buy's Balance Sheet

Best Buy has property and equipment that cost $4,836 million on February 25, 2006. The total amount of depreciation expense the firm has recorded over the life of these assets is $2,124 million.

Best Buy Co., Inc.
Consolidated Balance Sheets
($ in millions)

Assets	February 25, 2006	February 26, 2005
Current Assets		
Cash and cash equivalents	$ 681	$ 354
Short-term investments	3,051	2,994
Receivables	506	375
Merchandise inventories	3,338	2,851
Other current assets	409	329
Total current assets	7,985	6,903
Property and equipment		
Land and buildings	580	506
Leasehold improvements	1,325	1,139
Fixtures and equipment	2,898	2,458
Property under master and capital lease	33	89
	4,836	4,192
Less accumulated depreciation	2,124	1,728
Net property and equipment	2,712	2,464
Goodwill	557	513
Tradename	44	40
Long-term investments	218	148
Other assets	348	226
Total assets	$ 11,864	$ 10,294

The **book value** of an asset is the cost minus the accumulated depreciation related to the asset.

Carrying value is another expression for book value.

recorded during the time the asset has been owned. The resulting amount is called the **book value**, or **carrying value**, of the equipment. The book value is the net amount that is included when the total assets are added up on the balance sheet.

Here is the year-end adjustment to record depreciation of the asset after its first year of use:

Assets	=	Liabilities	+	Shareholder's equity	
				Contributed capital	+ Retained earnings
(1,000) accumulated depreciation					(1,000) depreciation expense

The accumulated depreciation is shown on the balance sheet as a *deduction* from the cost of the equipment. The depreciation expense is shown on the income statement. The book value of the asset is $4,000 (cost minus accumulated depreciation) at the end of the first year.

After the second year of use, Sample Company would again record the same thing—$1,000 more recorded as accumulated depreciation and $1,000 as depreciation expense. The amount of accumulated depreciation will then be $2,000. The amount of depreciation expense is only $1,000 because it represents only a single year—the second year—of depreciation expense. The accumulated depreciation refers to all the depreciation expense for the life of the asset through the year of the financial statement. The book value of the computer at the end of the second year is $3,000—$5,000 cost minus its $2,000 accumulated depreciation. See Exhibit 3.9 for another example.

Truck purchased on January 1, 2007. The truck will last for seven years. Cost is $49,000. No residual value.

EXHIBIT 3.9

Deferred Expenses— Depreciation

Cost of the truck will be spread over the income statements of the seven years the truck is used as depreciation expense. The expense is being **deferred**, that is *put off*, until the truck is actually used.

The cost of the asset is spread—as an expense—evenly (in this example) over the life of the asset.

Year ended December 31	2007	2008	2009	2010	2011	2012	2013
Depreciation expense	$7,000	$ 7,000	$ 7,000	$ 7,000	$ 7,000	$ 7,000	$ 7,000
Accumulated depreciation	$7,000	$14,000	$21,000	$28,000	$35,000	$42,000	$49,000

Tango Company purchased a computer on July 1, 2006, for $6,500. It is expected to last for 5 years and have a residual value of $500 at the end of the fifth year. How much depreciation expense would appear on the Tango December 31, 2006, income statement? What is the book value of the computer at the end of 2007?

Your Turn 3-6
Your Turn
Your Turn

Effects of Accruals and Deferrals on Financial Statements

L.O.4
Construct the basic financial statements from a given set of transactions that include accruals and deferrals and recognize the effect of these transactions on actual financial statements.

Now that you have learned the details of accrual and deferrals you are ready to put it all together in the construction of a set of financial statements. We will take Tom's Wear through its third month of business to see how timing differences affect the firm's financial statements. Then we will look at some real firms' financial statements to identify the effects of accruals and deferrals.

Tom's Wear Transactions for March

In Chapters 1 and 2, Tom's Wear completed its first two months of operations. Exhibit 3.10 shows the company's balance sheet at the end of the second month, which we prepared in Chapter 2.

EXHIBIT 3.10

Tom's Wear Balance Sheet at February 28, 2006

tom's wear

Tom's Wear, Inc.
Balance Sheet
At February 28, 2006

Assets		Liabilities and Shareholder's equity	
Cash	$ 6,695	Accounts payable	$ 800
Accounts receivable	150	Other payables	50
Inventory	100		
Prepaid insurance	125	Common stock	5,000
		Retained earnings	1,220
		Total liabilities and	
Total assets	$ 7,070	shareholder's equity	$ 7,070

EXHIBIT 3.11

Transactions for March 2006 for Tom's Wear

1 March 1	Purchased computer for $4,000 with $1,000 down and a 3-month, 12% note for $3,000. The computer is expected to last for 3 years and have a residual value of $400.	
2 March 10	Paid the rest of last month's advertising bill, $50.	
3 March 15	Collected accounts receivable of $150 from customers from February.	
4 March 20	Paid for February purchases—paying off the accounts payable balance of $800.	
5 March 24	Purchased 250 shirts @ $4 each for cash, $1,000.	
6 March 27	Sold 200 shirts for $10 each, all on account, for total sales of $2,000.	

These are the amounts that are carried over to the next month, so this is the March 1, 2006, balance sheet, too. We will now take Tom's Wear through the third month of business, with the transactions shown in Exhibit 3.11.

At the end of his third month, Tom prepares his financial statements to see how his business is progressing. We will see how each transaction affects the accounting equation. Then, look at the accounting equation worksheet in Exhibit 3.12 at the end of the example to see all of the transactions together.

Transaction 1: Purchase of a long-term asset Tom's Wear purchases a fixed asset that will last longer than 1 year; therefore, it will be classified as a long-term asset. Remember, current assets will be used up or converted to cash within 1 year. If the cost of an asset needs to be spread over more than 1 year, it is considered long term. The actual purchase of the asset is recorded as an asset exchange, not as an expense. Do not worry about depreciation expense and interest expense right now. That will be considered when it is time to prepare the financial statements. Here is how the purchase of the $4,000 computer with $1,000 down and a note payable of $3,000 with an annual interest rate of 12%, due in 3 months, affects the accounting equation:

Assets	=	Liabilities	+	Shareholder's equity		
				Contributed capital	+	**Retained earnings**
(1,000) cash		+ 3,000 notes				
+ 4,000 computer		payable				

The recognition of the expense related to the cost of the computer will be deferred—put off—until Tom's Wear has used the asset and is ready to prepare financial statements. The cash portion of the payment for the computer will be shown as an investing cash flow on the statement of cash flows.

Transaction 2: Cash disbursement to settle a liability Last month, Tom hired a company to do some advertising for his business. On February 28, 2006, Tom's Wear had not paid the full amount. Because the work was done in February, the expense was shown on the income statement for the month of February. In March, Tom's Wear pays cash of $50 to settle—eliminate—the liability. Here is how the cash disbursement affects the accounting equation:

Assets	=	Liabilities	+	Shareholder's equity		
				Contributed capital	+	**Retained earnings**
(50) cash		(50) other payables				

The action took place during February, so the expense was shown on that month's income statement. The cash is now paid in March, but no expense is recognized in

EXHIBIT 3.12

Transactions for Tom's Wear for March in the Accounting Equation Worksheet

The income statement is prepared first. Then, the net income can be used on the Statement of Changes in Shareholder's Equity. The total contributed capital and retained earnings from that statement are then used on the balance sheet. Finally, the cash transactions are reorganized for the statement of cash flows.

| | Assets | | | | | | = | Liabilities | | | | + | Shareholder's Equity | | | |
| | | | | | | Accumulated | | | | | | | Contributed Capital | Retained Earnings (RE) Beginning RE 1,220 | | |
	Cash	Accounts Receivable	Inventory	Prepaid Insurance	Computers	Depreciation, Computers		Accounts Payable	Other Payables	Interest Payable	Notes Payable		Common Stock	Revenues	Expenses	Dividends
Beginning Balances	$ 6,695	150	100	125				800	50				5,000			
March 1	(1,000)				4,000						3,000					
March 10	(50)								(50)							
March 15	150	(150)														
March 20	(800)							(800)								
March 24	(1,000)		1,000													
March 27		2,000	(800)											2,000	(800)	
Adjustment 1						(100)									(100)	
Adjustment 2				(50)											(50)	
Adjustment 3										30					(30)	
Ending Balances	$ 3,995	2,000	300	75	4,000	(100)	=	0	0	30	3,000		5,000	2,000	(980)	0 1,220
Check for equality			10,270					10,270								

— Income Statement — Statement of Changes in Shareholder's Equity — Balance Sheet — Statement of Cash Flows

115

March because that would be double counting the expense. An expense is recognized only once. The cash payment is an operating cash flow for the statement of cash flows.

Transaction 3: Collection of cash to settle a receivable At the end of last month, Tom's Wear had not received all the cash it was owed by customers. Because the sales were made during February, the revenue from those sales was shown on the income statement for the month of February. Because the cash for the sales was not collected at the time the sales were made, Tom's Wear recorded accounts receivable. Accounts receivable is an asset that will be converted to cash within the next year. When customers pay their bills, Tom's Wear records the receipt of cash and removes the receivable from its records. Here is how the collection of the cash affects the accounting equation:

Assets	=	Liabilities	+	Shareholder's equity	
				Contributed capital	+ Retained earnings
+ 150 cash (150) accounts receivable					

Revenue is not recorded when the cash is collected because the revenue was already recorded at the time of the sale. To count it now would be double counting. The cash collection is an operating cash flow for the statement of cash flows.

Transaction 4: Payment to vendor At the end of last month, the balance sheet for Tom's Wear showed accounts payable of $800. This is the amount still owed to vendors for February purchases. Tom's Wear pays this debt, bringing the accounts payable balance to zero. The cash payment is an operating cash flow for the statement of cash flows.

Assets	=	Liabilities	+	Shareholder's equity	
				Contributed capital	+ Retained earnings
(800) cash		(800) accounts payable			

Transaction 5: Purchase of inventory Tom's Wear purchases 250 shirts at $4 each, for a total of $1,000 and pays cash for the purchase. The cash payment is an operating cash flow for the statement of cash flows.

Assets	=	Liabilities	+	Shareholder's equity	
				Contributed capital	+ Retained earnings
(1,000) cash + 1,000 inventory					

Transaction 6: Sales Tom's Wear sells 200 shirts at $10 each, all on account. That means the company extended credit to its customers and Tom's Wear will collect later.

Assets	=	Liabilities	+	Shareholder's equity	
				Contributed capital	+ Retained earnings
+ 2,000 accounts receivable					+ 2,000 sales revenue

At the same time sales revenue is recorded, Tom's Wear records the reduction in inventory. The reduction in inventory is an expense called cost of goods sold.

Assets	=	Liabilities	+	Shareholder's equity	
				Contributed + capital	Retained earnings
(800) inventory					(800) cost of goods sold

Notice that the sale is recorded at the amount Tom's Wear will collect from the customer. At the same time, the reduction in the inventory is recorded at the cost of the inventory—200 shirts at a cost of $4 per shirt. This is a terrific example of the matching principle.

Notice that there is no explicit recording of profit in the company records. Instead, profit is a derived amount; it is calculated by subtracting cost of goods sold from the amount of sales. For this sale, the profit is $1,200. It is called the gross profit—also called gross margin—on sales. Other expenses must be subtracted from the gross margin to get to net profit, also called net income.

Up to this point, we have looked just at the routine transactions during the month ended March 31, 2006. At the end of the month, Tom's Wear will adjust the company records for any accruals and deferrals needed for accurate financial statements. Look back over the transactions and see if you can identify the adjustments needed.

Adjustments to the Accounting Records

A review of the transactions for March should reveal three adjustments needed at the end of March 2006:

1. Depreciation expense for the computer
2. Insurance expense for the month
3. Interest expense on the note payable

We will now look at each of the adjustments and how the amounts for those adjustments are calculated.

Adjustment 1: Depreciation The computer purchased on March 1 must be depreciated—that is, part of the cost must be recognized as depreciation expense during March. To figure out the depreciation expense, the residual value is subtracted from the cost of the asset, and then the difference is divided by the estimated useful life of the asset. In this case, the residual value is $400, so that amount is subtracted from the cost of $4,000. The remaining $3,600 is divided by 3 years, resulting in a depreciation expense of $1,200 per year. Because we are preparing monthly statements, the annual amount must be divided by 12 months, giving $100 depreciation per month. The adjustment is a reduction to assets and an expense.

Assets	=	Liabilities	+	Shareholder's equity	
				Contributed + capital	Retained earnings
(100) accumulated depreciation					(100) depreciation expense

The reduction to the cost of the computer accumulates each month, so that the carrying value of the asset in the accounting records goes down by $100 each month. In the accounting records, we do not simply subtract $100 each month from the computer's cost on the left side of the equation, because GAAP requires the cost of a specific asset and the total accumulated depreciation related to that asset to be shown separately.

The subtracted amount is called *accumulated depreciation*. After the first month, accumulated depreciation related to this particular asset is $100. After the second month, the accumulated depreciation will be $200. That amount—representing how

Notice, the residual value is deducted only in the calculation of the amount of depreciation expense. It is not deducted from the cost of the asset in the company's formal records.

much of the asset cost we count as used—is a contra-asset, because it reduces the recorded value of an asset.

The cost of an asset minus its accumulated depreciation is called the *book value* or *carrying value* of the asset. Each time depreciation expense is recorded, the accumulated depreciation increases, and the book value of the asset decreases.

Depreciation expense represents a single period's expense and is shown on the income statement.

Adjustment 2: Insurance expense In mid-February, Tom's Wear purchased 3 months' worth of insurance for $150, which is $50 per month. On the March 1 balance sheet, there is a current asset called prepaid insurance in the amount of $125. A full month of insurance expense needs to be recorded for the month of March. That amount will be deducted from prepaid insurance.

Assets	=	Liabilities	+	Shareholder's equity	
				Contributed capital	+ Retained earnings
(50) prepaid insurance					(50) insurance expense

Adjustment 3: Accruing interest expense On March 1, Tom's Wear signed a 3-month note for $3,000. The note carries an interest rate of 12%. (Interest rates are typically given as an annual rate.) Because the firm is preparing a monthly income statement, it needs to accrue 1 month of interest expense. The interest rate formula—Interest = Principal × Rate × Time—produces the following interest computation:

$$\text{Interest} = \$3{,}000 \times 0.12 \times 1/12 \text{ (1 month out of 12)} = \mathbf{\$30}$$

Assets	=	Liabilities	+	Shareholder's equity	
				Contributed capital	+ Retained earnings
		+ 30 interest payable			(30) interest expense

Notice that the calculation of the interest expense does not take into consideration the length of the note. The interest expense would be the same if this were a 6-month note or a 2-year note, or a note of any other length of time. Interest expense is calculated based on the time that has passed as a fraction of a year because the interest rate used is an annual rate.

These are the needed adjustments at March 31, 2006, for Tom's Wear to produce accurate financial statements according to GAAP.

Exhibit 3.12 shows all of the transactions and adjustments in the accounting equation worksheet. Notice how each financial statement is derived from the transactions.

Preparing the Financial Statements

First, Tom's Wear prepares the income statement. Revenues and expenses are found in the red-boxed columns of the accounting equation worksheet. Organized and summarized, they produce the income statement for Tom's Wear for March, shown in Exhibit 3.13. The income statement covers a period of time—in this case, it covers 1 month of business activity.

Second, Tom's Wear prepares the statement of changes in shareholder's equity—a summary of what has happened to equity during the period. It is shown in Exhibit 3.14. Like the income statement, the statement of changes in shareholder's equity covers a period of time—here, 1 month.

Third, Tom's Wear prepares the balance sheet—composed of three sections: assets, liabilities, and shareholder's equity, with the amount of each on the last day of the period. The assets are arranged in order of liquidity—how easily the asset can be converted to cash. Current assets will be used or converted to cash sometime during the next fiscal year. Long-term assets will last longer than 1 year.

Current liabilities are obligations that will be satisfied in the next fiscal year. Long-term liabilities are obligations that will not be repaid in the next fiscal year.

Shareholder's equity is shown in two parts—contributed capital and retained earnings. Because the balance sheet is a summary of all the transactions in the accounting equation, it should balance if there are no errors in your worksheet. The balance sheet is shown in Exhibit 3.15.

Tom's Wear, Inc.
Income Statement
For the Month Ended March 31, 2006

Sales revenue		$ 2,000
Expenses		
Cost of goods sold	$ 800	
Depreciation expense	100	
Insurance expense	50	
Interest expense	30	980
Net income		$ 1,020

EXHIBIT 3.13

Income Statement for Tom's Wear for March

Tom's Wear, Inc.
Statement of Changes in Shareholder's Equity
For the Month Ended March 31, 2006

Beginning common stock	$ 5,000	
Common stock issued during the month	0	
Ending common stock		$ 5,000
Beginning retained earnings	$ 1,220	
Net income for the month	1,020	
Dividends declared	0	
Ending retained earnings		2,240
Total shareholder's equity		$ 7,240

Tom's Wear, Inc.
Balance Sheet
At March 31, 2006

Assets		Liabilities and Shareholder's equity	
Current assets		Current liabilities	
Cash	$ 3,995	Interest payable	$ 30
Accounts receivable	2,000	Notes payable	3,000
Inventory	300	Total current liabilities	3,030
Prepaid insurance	75	Shareholder's equity	
Total current assets	6,370	Common stock	5,000
Computer (net of $100		Retained earnings	2,240
accumulated depreciation)	3,900	Total shareholder's equity	7,240
		Total liabilities and	
Total assets	$10,270	shareholder's equity	$10,270

EXHIBIT 3.15

Balance Sheet for Tom's Wear at March 31, 2006

Fourth, Tom's Wear prepares the statement of cash flows. Because the first three financial statements—income statement, statement of changes in shareholder's equity, and the balance sheet—are accrual based instead of cash based, these three financial statements do not provide detailed information about a company's cash—where it came from and how it

EXHIBIT 3.16

Statement of Cash Flows for Tom's Wear for March

tom's wear

Tom's Wear, Inc.
Statement of Cash Flows
For the Month Ended March 31, 2006

Cash from operating activities:

Cash collected from customers	$ 150	
Cash paid to vendors	(1,800)	
Cash paid for operating expense	(50)	
Net cash from operating activities		$ (1,700)
Cash from investing activities:		
Purchase of asset*	$(1,000)	(1,000)
Cash from financing activities:		0
Net increase (decrease) in cash		$ (2,700)
Beginning cash balance		6,695
Ending cash balance		$ 3,995

*Computer was purchased for $4,000. A note was signed for $3,000 and cash paid was $1,000.

was spent. The balance sheet gives only the total amount of cash on hand at the close of business on the last day of the fiscal period, and the income statement—the focus of financial reporting—gives no information about cash. This is why the statement of cash flows is needed. Even though accrual accounting does not base the measurement of income on cash, there is no debate about the importance of the sources and uses of cash to a business. The statement of cash flows gives the details of how the cash balance has changed from the first day of the period to the last day. The statement is shown in Exhibit 3.16.

Accruals and Deferrals on Real Firms' Financial Statements

The most apparent place on a set of financial statements to identify accruals and deferrals is the balance sheet. Most often, the transactions have been summarized in such a way that the income statement does not make accruals and deferrals obvious. For example, if a firm shows sales revenue on the income statement, the firm may or may not have collected the related cash. The place to find that information is the balance sheet.

Take a close look at Circuit City's balance sheets in Exhibit 3.17. Although there are many items on these statements that you are not familiar with, you should be able to see how much you have learned about financial statements in three short chapters. For example, you know that it is a classified balance sheet because there are subtotals for current assets and current liabilities. The assets are ordered by liquidity, with cash and cash equivalents at the beginning of the assets. Notice that Circuit City starts its current liabilities section with *merchandise payable*. This is what most companies would call *accounts payable*. As you look at more real firms' financial statements, you will find that each firm will use some unique terminology. Usually, you will be able to figure out what sort of account or amount it is. If you can not, take a look in the notes to the financial statements for more information.

Look down the balance sheet and see if you can identify specific accruals and deferrals that the company probably recorded when it was preparing its year-end balance sheet. Here are a few examples:

1. *Prepaid expenses.* This is listed as a current asset. It represents goods or services that have been paid for but not used. Putting this amount on the balance sheet is deferring the expense until the period in which the items are used. It is rare for the word *expense* to be on the balance sheet. Here it is the word *prepaid* that makes this an asset rather than an expense on the income statement.

2. *Accumulated depreciation.* Circuit City has several types of property and equipment. Notice that *accumulated depreciation* has been deducted from the recorded amounts for these assets, as indicated by the word *net*. In the firm's actual accounting records,

EXHIBIT 3.17

Circuit City Balance Sheets at February 28, 2006 and 2005

The three shaded items are just a few examples of accruals and deferral that can easily be picked out from Circuit City's balance sheet.

Circuit City Stores, Inc.
Consolidated Balance Sheets
(Amounts in thousands)

The word "expenses" is strange to see on the balance sheet. It's only an asset when "prepaid" describes it.

	At February 28	
	2006	2005
Assets		
Current assets:		
Cash and cash equivalents	$ 315,970	$ 879,660
Short-term investments	521,992	125,325
Accounts receivable, net of allowance for doubtful accounts	220,869	230,605
Merchandise inventory	1,698,026	1,455,170
Deferred income taxes	29,598	31,194
Income tax receivable	5,571	
Prepaid expenses and other current assets	41,315	23,203
Total current assets	2,833,341	2,745,157
Property and equipment, net of accumulated depreciation	839,356	726,940
Deferred income taxes	97,889	79,935
Goodwill	223,999	215,884
Other intangible assets, net of accumulated amortization	30,372	31,331
Other assets	44,087	40,763
Total assets	$4,069,044	$3,840,010
Liabilities and stockholders' equity		
Current liabilities:		
Merchandise payable	$ 850,359	$ 635,674
Expenses payable	202,300	170,629
Accrued expenses and other current liabilities	464,511	433,110
Accrued income taxes	75,909	75,183
Short-term debt	22,003	–
Current installments of long-term debt	7,248	888
Total current liabilities	1,622,330	1,315,484
Long-term debt, excluding current installments	51,985	19,944
Accrued straight-line rent and deferred rent credits	256,120	242,001
Accrued lease termination costs	79,091	90,734
Other liabilities	104,885	91,920
Total liabilities	2,114,411	1,760,083
Commitments and contingent liabilities [Notes 12, 13, 14, and 17]		
Stockholders' equity:		
Common stock, $0.50 par value; 525,000,000 shares authorized; 174,789,390 shares issued and outstanding (188,150,383 in 2005)	87,395	94,075
Capital in excess of par value	458,211	721,038
Retained earnings	1,364,740	1,239,714
Accumulated other comprehensive income	44,287	25,100
Total stockholders' equity	1,954,633	2,079,927
Total liabilities and stockholders' equity	$4,069,044	$3,840,010

Accumulated depreciation has already been deducted from the cost of the property and equipment (i.e., *net*), but the amount will be disclosed in the notes to the financial statements.

Here the word "expenses" is preceded by "accrued." The expenses have been incurred but not yet paid for.

UNDERSTANDING Business

Corporate Financial Performance and Corporate Social Performance

The goal of a corporation is to make money for its shareholders—that is, to increase shareholder value. It is the job of financial statements to report the corporation's financial performance. Where does a corporation's social responsibility fit in? Is there a relationship between financial performance and a corporation's social performance?

In the 2004 Moskowitz prize-winning report, "Corporate Social and Financial Performance: A Meta-Analysis," researchers found that there is a significant positive relationship between corporate financial performance and corporate social performance. The study provides evidence to dispel the notion that corporations cannot afford to be socially responsible.

In his book, *What Matters Most: How a Small Group of Pioneers Is Teaching Social Responsibility to Big Business and Why Big Business Is Listening*, Jeffrey Hollander argues that "introducing social responsibility into day-to-day business operations is an effective way of creating long-term sustainable growth and improved financial performance." Many organizations agree. In 2005, Apple Computer took back 6.2 million pounds of e-waste. Dell and HP have actually created business profit centers from computer recycling. In 2005, Dell took in 41 million pounds and HP took in 114 million pounds of material for recycling.

An organization called As You Sow began in 1992 and launched the Corporate Social Responsibility Program in 1997. Read about it on the group's Web site at www.asyousow.org. An important part of understanding business is understanding corporate responsibility.

---

accumulated depreciation is a contra-asset, representing the amount of the assets the company has recorded as depreciation expense over the life of the assets.

3. *Accrued expenses.* As part of the current liabilities (listed with accounts payable), accrued expenses are amounts that the company has recognized as expenses (i.e., put on the income statement). The company purchased these things on account. That is, the company still owes someone for these things. It could be things such as utilities payable or salaries payable—anything the company has used to generate revenue but has not yet paid for these goods or services. Again, there is the word *expense* on the balance sheet. Here it is preceded by the word *accrued*, which indicates that it is a liability rather than an expense on the income statement.

As you continue to learn about the underlying business transactions that are included in a company's financial statements, you will see more examples of accruals and deferrals that are an integral part of GAAP.

Applying Your Knowledge: Ratio Analysis

Working Capital

L.O.5
Compute and explain working capital and the quick ratio.

Working capital equals current assets minus current liabilities.

In Chapter 2, you learned about the current ratio and how it provides information about the company's liquidity and ability to meet its short-term obligations. **Working capital** is another measure used to evaluate liquidity. Working capital is defined as *current assets minus current liabilities*. The current ratio gives a relative measure of a company's ability to finance its operations, and the amount of working capital gives an absolute measure. Look at the information from the balance sheet of Circuit City in Exhibit 3.17. The working capital at February 28, 2006, was just over $1.2 billion.

$$\text{Working capital} = \text{Current assets} - \text{Current liabilities}$$

Calculate the working capital at February 28, 2005. If you subtract the current liabilities from the current assets, you should get $1,429,673,000, which is approximately $1.43 billion. Current assets have increased for Circuit City during the year, between the two balance sheet dates, from $2,745,157,000 to $2,833,341,000. During the same time, current liabilities have increased from $1,315,484,000 to $1,622,330,000. This looks like a significant decrease in working capital. Any company considering doing business with Circuit City might compute working capital for several years to identify any increases or decreases. This decrease could indicate a decrease in the company's ability to pay its current liabilities.

Quick Ratio

It is important that the information on the financial statements be accurate and reliable because it is used to help measure a company's ability to meet its short-term obligations. As you learned in Chapter 2, the *current ratio* is current assets divided by current liabilities. Another ratio similar to the current ratio is called the **quick ratio**, also known as the *acid-test ratio*. Instead of using all of a company's current assets in the numerator, the quick ratio uses only cash, short-term investments, and net accounts receivable. These three assets are the most liquid—easiest to convert to cash—so they are the most readily available for paying off current liabilities. You might see the quick ratio defined as *current assets minus inventories divided by current liabilities*. An investor or analyst will use the quick ratio as a stricter test of a company's ability to meet its short-term obligations. It measures a firm's ability to meet its short-term obligations even if the firm makes no additional sales.

$$\text{Quick Ratio} = \frac{\text{Cash} + \text{Accounts Receivable} + \text{Short-term Investments}}{\text{Current Liabilities}}$$

Use the information from Circuit City's balance sheet in Exhibit 3.17 to calculate both the current ratio that we studied in Chapter 2 and the quick ratio. At its fiscal year end February 28, 2005, Circuit City had current assets of $2.745 billion and current liabilities of $1.315 billion. The current ratio is

$$2.745 \div 1.315 = 2.09$$

At February 28, 2006, Circuit City had current assets of $2.833 billion and current liabilities of $1.622 billion. The current ratio is

$$2.833 \div 1.622 = 1.75$$

The current ratio has declined, but it is still quite respectable. Calculate the quick ratio to see if we can get some additional insight. The numerator is the total of cash, short-term investment, and accounts receivable. At February 28, 2005, the quick assets are (rounded):

$$\textbf{0.880} \text{ billion} + \textbf{0.125} \text{ billion} + \textbf{0.231} \text{ billion} = 1.236 \text{ billion}$$

The denominator is unchanged, so the quick ratio at February 28, 2005, is:

$$1.236 \text{ billion} \div 1.315 \text{ billion} = 0.94$$

Similarly, the quick assets at February 28, 2006, are the total of cash, short-term investments, and accounts receivable:

$$\textbf{0.316} \text{ billion} + \textbf{0.522} \text{ billion} + \textbf{0.221} \text{ billion} = 1.059 \text{ billion}$$

Again, the denominator is the same as that used in the current ratio:

$$1.059 \text{ billion} \div 1.622 \text{ billion} = 0.65$$

It is very difficult to draw any conclusion from one or two ratios or one or two years. Would you find Circuit City's ratios more useful if you knew the industry averages or the same ratios for Best Buy, one of Circuit City's major competitors? Calculate the current ratio and quick ratio for Best Buy when you take Your Turn 3-7.

Your Turn 3-7
Your Turn
Your Turn

Use the information from Best Buy's recent balance sheets to calculate the current ratio and the quick ratio at February 25, 2006. Are the ratios in line with the ones calculated for Circuit City?

Best Buy Co., Inc.
Consolidated Balance Sheet (partial)
$ in millions, except per share amounts

Assets	February 25, 2006
Current Assets	
Cash and cash equivalents	$ 681
Short-term investments	3,051
Receivables	506
Merchandise inventories	3,338
Other current assets	409
Total current assets	7,985
Total current liabilities	6,056

L.O.6
Explain the business risks associated with financial records and accounting information.

Business Risk, Control, and Ethics

In Chapters 1 and 2, we discussed the risks a business faces, particularly those risks associated with financial information. Now that you have learned how many transactions are reflected on the financial statements, we will look at the three most significant risks associated with this information:

1. Errors in recording and updating the financial accounting records
2. Unauthorized access to the financial accounting records
3. Loss of the data in the financial accounting records

No matter how transactions are recorded, the information system needs to address the risks of errors in recording the data, unauthorized access to the data, and potential loss of the data.

Errors in Recording and Updating the Accounting Records

Errors in recording transactions can lead to inaccurate records and reports. These errors can be costly, both for internal decision making and external reporting. The accuracy and completeness of the recording process are crucial for a firm's success. The controls that can minimize the risk of these errors include: (1) input and processing controls, (2) reconciliation and control reports, and (3) documentation to provide supporting evidence for the recorded transactions. These controls should be present in both manual and computerized accounting information systems.

• *Input and processing controls.* This control is designed to make sure that only authorized transactions are put into the system. For example, when a sales clerk enters a sale at a cash register, the clerk must put in an employee code before entering the data. Additional controls, such as department numbers and item numbers, help make sure that clerks enter the correct information. The computer program that controls this part of the accounting system may also have limits on the dollar amounts that can be entered. The design of the controls depends on the accounting information system and the business, but all firms should have controls to ensure the accuracy of the input and processing of the data that are recorded.

- *Reconciliation and control reports.* This control is designed to catch any errors in the input and processing of the accounting data. Computerized accounting systems are valuable because they make sure the accounting equation is in balance at every stage of the data entry. This type of equality with each entry is a control programmed into accounting software such as Peachtree and QuickBooks. Accounting software does not guarantee that all the transactions have been recorded correctly, but it does keep some errors from occurring.

- *Documentation to provide supporting evidence for the recorded transactions.* This control is designed to keep errors from occurring and also to catch errors that have occurred. The employee who puts the data into the accounting system will get that data from a document that describes the transaction. The information contained in the documentation can be compared to the data put into the accounting system. For example, when a book-publishing company such as Prentice Hall sends an invoice to Amazon.com for a shipment of books, Prentice Hall will keep a copy of this invoice to input the data into its accounting system. Prentice Hall may also use this invoice to verify the accuracy of the accounting entry by referring back to the original invoice.

Unauthorized Access to the Accounting Information

Unauthorized access is an obvious risk for any company's accounting system. Such access would expose a company to leaks of confidential data, errors, and the cover-up of theft. In manual systems, the records should be locked in a secure place so that they cannot be accessed by unauthorized employees. Computerized systems have user IDs and passwords to control access to the accounting system.

There are serious ethical issues related to a firm's data and computerized accounting systems. With the rapid expansion of the Internet and the development of wireless technologies, systems-related fraud has been on the rise. Firms must carefully screen all employees, but particularly those who are involved with developing and securing the firm's computer systems. No system is totally safe from fraud.

Loss or Destruction of Accounting Data

Imagine that you are working for several hours on a report for your marketing class, and you save your work on your hard drive. You decide to step out for a coffee with friends before wrapping up. While you are gone, the computer shuts down, and you cannot reboot. If you backed up your file, you are okay. If you did not, you must start the report from scratch.

The accounting information system contains data that are crucial parts of a company's operations, so there must be a backup and disaster-recovery plan. The 2001 terrorist attack on the World Trade Center is perhaps the most vivid example of why backup and disaster-recovery plans are important. Even before September 11, Fiduciary Trust International, a subsidiary of Franklin Templeton, used a method called remote shadowing, saving data simultaneously in two separate locations. Having an offsite facility with a copy of the data, created at the time of the transactions, enabled the company to conduct wire transfers for cash and securities on the date after the attacks. On Monday, September 17, Fiduciary was ready to resume its core business. Although the loss of accounting data is insignificant in comparison to the human loss suffered in this tragic event, it did bring the issue of lost and destroyed data to the attention of companies that were affected that day.

Chapter Summary Points

Accountants want the income statement to reflect the revenues and expenses for the period covered by the statement—none from the period before or the period after. Accountants also want the balance sheet to show the correct amount of assets and liabilities on the date of the statement. To do that, accountants must allocate revenues and expenses to the correct periods. This is done by making adjustments at the end of the accounting period.

- Sometimes a company purchases something and pays for it later. Sometimes a company earns revenue but collects the cash for that revenue later.

- Accountants do **not** base the recognition of revenues and expenses on the income statement on the collection of cash or on the disbursement of cash. Revenue and expenses are recognized—shown on the income statement—when the economic substance of the transaction has taken place. The economic substance of a transaction is the action of providing or receiving goods and services.
- When the action has been completed but the dollars have not yet changed hands, it is called an accrual. Action comes first, and payment for that action comes later. You accrue—build up or accumulate—revenue you have earned or expenses you have incurred, even though the cash has not been exchanged.
- In some situations, the payment comes first and the action for that payment comes later. Sometimes you pay in advance for goods or services; or sometimes your customers pay you in advance for those goods or services you will provide in a later period. These situations are called deferrals. Dollars are exchanged, but you defer recognition of the revenue or expense until the action of the transaction is complete.

Chapter Summary Problems

BB&B Decorating provides decorating services for a fee. Suppose BB&B Decorating began the month of January 2007 with the following account balances:

Cash	$ 200,000	
Supplies	20,000	Total
Equipment*	100,000	assets
Accumulated depreciation	(10,000)	$310,000
Miscellaneous payables	$ 40,000	
Salaries payable	4,000	
Long-term notes payable	50,000	Total
Common stock	126,000	liabilities & equity
Retained earnings	90,000	$310,000

*Equipment is depreciated by $10,000 each year, which is $833 per month.

The following transactions occurred during January 2007.

1. Purchased additional supplies for $12,000 on account (record the liability as miscellaneous payables)
2. Paid salaries owed to employees at December 31, 2006
3. Provided decorating services for $84,000 cash
4. Paid entire balance in miscellaneous payables (including purchase in item 1)
5. Purchased $15,000 worth of supplies on account (record as miscellaneous payables)
6. Paid 6 months' worth of rent on buildings for $6,000, starting on January 1, 2007
7. Made a payment on the long-term loan of $5,000, of which $4,950 was principal and $50 was interest for January

Additional information:

1. There was $5,000 worth of supplies left on hand at the end of the month.
2. The equipment is being depreciated at $833 per month.
3. At month-end, the following expenses for January (to be paid in February) had not been recorded:
utilities $ 350
salaries $4,600

Instructions

1. Set up an accounting equation worksheet and enter the beginning balances. Then, record each transaction including the needed adjustments. (Add any accounts you need.)
2. Prepare the four basic financial statements. For the statement of changes in shareholders' equity, prepare only the retained earnings portion of the statement.

Solution

	Cash	Supplies	Prepaid Rent	Equipment	Accumulated Depreciation, Equipment	Miscellaneous Payables	Salaries Payables	Interest Payables	L-T Notes Payable	Common Stock	Revenues	Expenses	Dividends
Assets						**= Liabilities**				**+ Contributed Capital**	**Retained Earnings (RE)** Beginning RE 90,000		
Beginning Balances	$200,000	20,000		100,000	(10,000)	40,000	4,000		50,000	126,000			
1.		12,000				12,000							
2.	(4,000)						(4,000)						
3.	84,000										84,000		
4.	(52,000)					(52,000)							
5.		15,000				15,000							
6.	(6,000)		6,000										
7.	(5,000)								(4,950)			(50)	
Adjustment 1		(42,000)										(42,000)	
Adjustment 2					(833)							(833)	
Adjustment 3							4,600					(4,600)	
Adjustment 4						350						(350)	
	0		(1,000)		(10,833)							(1,000)	
Balances	$217,000	5,000	5,000	100,000		316,167 = 15,350	4,600	0	45,050	126,000	84,000	(48,833)	0 90,000
Check for equality						316,167							

— Income Statement   — Statement of Changes in Shareholder's Equity   — Balance Sheet   — Statement of Cash Flows

---

BB&B Decorating
Income Statement
For the Month Ended January 31, 2007

Revenue	$ 84,000
Expenses	48,833
Net Income	$35,167

BB&B Decorating
Statement of Retained Earnings
For the Month Ended January 31, 2007

Retained Earnings:	
Beginning balance	$ 90,000
+ Net income	35,167
Ending Balance	$125,167

BB&B Decorating
Statement of Cash Flows
For the Month Ended January 31, 2007

Cash from operating activities	
Cash from customers	$ 84,000
Cash paid for operating expenses	(62,000)
Cash paid for interest	(50)
Net cash from operating activities	$ 21,950
Cash from investing activities	–
Cash from financing activities	
Cash paid on loan principal	(4,950)
Net increase in cash	17,000
Add beginning cash balance	200,000
Cash balance at January 31	$217,000

BB&B Decorating
Balance Sheet
At January 31, 2007

Assets	
Cash	$217,000
Supplies	5,000
Prepaid rent	5,000
Total current assets	227,000
Equipment (net of $10,833 accumulated depreciation)	89,167
Total assets	$316,167
Liabilities & Shareholder's Equity	
Liabilities	
Miscellaneous payables	15,350
Salaries payable	4,600
Total current liabilities	19,950
Long-term notes payable	45,050
Shareholder's Equity	
Common stock	126,000
Retained earnings	125,167
Total liabilities and shareholder's equity	$316,167

Key Terms for Chapter 3

Accrual (p. 99)
Accumulated depreciation
   (p. 111)
Book value (p. 112)
Carrying value (p. 112)
Contra-asset (p. 111)

Deferral (p. 99)
Depreciation expense
   (p. 111)
Interest payable (p. 100)
Prepaid rent (p. 108)
Realized (p. 102)

Residual value (p. 111)
Timing differences (p. 99)
Unearned revenue
   (p. 105)
Working capital (p. 122)

Answers to YOUR TURN Questions

CHAPTER 3

Your Turn 3-1

1. You would pay $1,000 \times 0.07 \times 1/2 = \$35$ in interest.
2. This is an accrual—the action of incurring the expense via the passage of time precedes the cash payment.

Your Turn 3-2

Yes, salary expense needs to be accrued. The expense for June would routinely be recorded on July 15 when the payment is made. To get the June salary expense on the income statement for the year ending June 30, ABC Company needs to accrue the expense. A month of salary expense for June is recorded as salary expense and salaries payable in the amount of $56,000.

Your Turn 3-3

Out of 12 months of magazines, 7 months have been delivered at December 31. That means 7/12 of the $300,000 collected in advance has actually been earned by December 31. When the cash was collected, the recognition of the revenue was deferred—put off or postponed—because it had not been earned. At December 31, the company recognizes $175,000 worth of revenue. That means it will put $175,000 worth of revenue on the income statement and reduce the liability *unearned revenue* on the balance sheet.

Your Turn 3-4

When Advantage Company made the rent payment on March 1, the company recorded a decrease in cash and an increase in the asset *prepaid rent*. Now, it is 10 months later, and 10 months' worth of rent has been used. That means it should be recorded as rent expense. The March 1 payment was $3,600 for 1 year, which means $300 per month. Now, 10 months at $300 per month = $3,000 must be deducted from prepaid rent and added to rent expense. Then, $3,000 of rent paid on March 1 will be shown on the income statement.

Your Turn 3-5

1. Konny started with $500 worth of supplies and then purchased an additional $650 worth, which made a total of $1,150 worth of supplies available for the company to use during the month. At the end of the month, there were $250 worth of supplies remaining. That means that the company must have used $900 worth ($1,150 – $250). Of the supplies remaining, $250 will be on the balance sheet as a current asset, *supplies*.
2. Supplies expense of $900 will be shown on the income statement for April.

Your Turn 3-6

The depreciable amount is the cost minus the residual (salvage) value, $6,500 - \$500 = \$6,000$. The estimated life is 5 years. Thus, the depreciation expense per year is $6,000/ 5 = \$1,200$ per year. Because the computer was purchased on July 1, 2006, only half a year of depreciation expense, $600, will be shown on the income statement for the year ending December 31, 2006. The book value = cost less accumulated depreciation (all the depreciation that has been recorded on the asset during its life) = $6,500 − $600 (for 2006) − $1,200 (for 2007) = $4,700 at December 31, 2007.

Your Turn 3-7

The current ratio is $7,985 ÷ $6,056 = 1.32.
The quick ratio is ($681 + $3,051 + $506) ÷ $6,056 = 0.70.
These ratios are a bit lower than the ones for Circuit City, but they appear to be reasonable.

Questions

1. How does accrual basis accounting differ from cash basis accounting?
2. What is deferred revenue?
3. What is accrued revenue?
4. What are deferred expenses?
5. What are accrued expenses?
6. What is interest and how is it computed?
7. Explain the difference between liabilities and expenses.
8. Name two common deferred expenses.
9. What does it mean to recognize revenue?
10. How does matching relate to accruals and deferrals?
11. What is depreciation?
12. Why is depreciation necessary?
13. What is working capital and what does it indicate?
14. What is the quick ratio and what does it measure?
15. What risks are associated with the financial accounting records?

Multiple-Choice Questions

1. Which of the following accounts is a liability?
   a. Depreciation expense
   b. Dividends
   c. Accumulated depreciation
   d. Unearned advertising fees
2. Which of the following is an example of an accrual?
   a. Revenue collected in advance
   b. Supplies purchased for cash but not yet used
   c. Interest expense incurred but not yet paid
   d. Payment for insurance policy to be used in the next 2 years
3. Which of the following is an example of a deferral?
   a. Cash has not changed hands and services have not been rendered.
   b. Services have been rendered but nothing has been recorded.
   c. A business never has enough cash.
   d. Resources have been purchased for cash but not yet used.
4. The carrying (book) value of an asset is
   a. An account with a credit balance that offsets an asset account on the balance sheet
   b. The original cost of an asset minus the accumulated depreciation
   c. The original cost of an asset
   d. Equivalent to accumulated depreciation
5. Receiving a payment for a credit sale made in a previous accounting period will
   a. Decrease assets and decrease shareholders' equity
   b. Increase assets and increases liabilities
   c. Have no net effect on total assets
   d. Increase revenues and increase assets

6. When a company pays cash in June to a vendor for goods purchased in May, the transaction will
   a. Increase cash and decrease inventory
   b. Decrease accounts payable and decrease cash
   c. Decrease accounts receivable and decrease cash
   d. Increase accounts payable and increase inventory

7. Z Company's accountant forgot to make an adjustment at the end of the year to record depreciation expense on the equipment. What effect did this omission have on the company's financial statements?
   a. Understated assets and liabilities
   b. Overstated assets and shareholders' equity
   c. Understated liabilities and overstated shareholders' equity
   d. Overstated assets and understated shareholders' equity

8. Phillip's Camera Store had a retained earnings balance of $1,000 on January 1, 2008. For year 2008, sales were $10,500 and expenses were $6,500. The company declared and distributed cash dividends of $2,500 on December 31, 2008. What was the amount of retained earnings on December 31, 2008?
   a. $4,000
   b. $1,500
   c. $2,500
   d. $1,500

9. When prepaid insurance has been used, the following adjustment will be necessary:
   a. Increase insurance expense, decrease cash.
   b. Increase prepaid insurance, decrease insurance expense.
   c. Increase insurance expense, increase prepaid insurance.
   d. Increase insurance expense, decrease prepaid insurance.

10. The quick ratio is
    a. Current liabilities divided by the sum of cash, accounts receivable, and short-term investments
    b. Current assets divided by current liabilities
    c. Accounts receivable divided by current assets
    d. The sum of cash, accounts receivable, and short-term investments divided by current liabilities

Short Exercises

SE3-1. *Analyze effect of transactions on net income.* (LO 1)
The following transactions occurred during a recent accounting period. For each, tell whether it (1) increases net income, (2) decreases net income, or (3) does not affect net income.
   a. Issued stock for cash
   b. Borrowed money from bank
   c. Provided services to customers on credit
   d. Paid rent in advance
   e. Used some of the supplies
   f. Paid salaries to employees for work done this year

SE3-2. *Calculate net income and retained earnings.* (LO 1)
Capboy Company earned $5,000 of revenues and incurred $2,950 worth of expenses during the period. Capboy also declared and paid dividends of $500 to its shareholders. What was net income for the period? Assuming this is the first year of operations for Capboy, what is the ending balance in retained earnings for the period?

SE3-3. *Account for interest expense.* (LO 1, 2)
UMC Company purchased equipment on November 1, 2008, and gave a 3-month, 9% note with a face value of $10,000. How much interest expense will be recognized on the income statement for the year ended December 31, 2008? What effect does this adjustment have on the statement of cash flows for 2008? Is this adjustment an accrual or deferral?

SE3-4. *Account for supplies expense.* (LO 1, 3)
MBI Corporation started the month with $600 worth of supplies on hand. During the month, the company purchased an additional $760 worth of supplies. At the end of the month, $390 worth of supplies was left on hand. What amount would MBI Corporation show as supplies expense on its income statement for the month? Is this adjustment an accrual or deferral?

SE3-5. *Account for insurance expense.* (LO 1, 3)
Bovina Company was started on January 1, 2005. During its first week of business, the company paid $3,600 for 18 months' worth of fire insurance with an effective date of January 1. When Bovina Company prepares its income statement for the year ended December 31, 2005, how much prepaid insurance will be shown on the balance sheet, and how much insurance expense will be shown on the income statement? Is this adjustment an accrual or deferral?

SE3-6. *Account for depreciation expense.* (LO 1, 3)
Suppose a company purchases a piece of equipment for $9,000 at the beginning of the year. The equipment is estimated to have a useful life of 3 years and no residual value. Using the depreciation method you learned about in this chapter, what is the depreciation expense for the first year of the asset's life? What is the book value of the equipment at the end of the first year? What is the book value of the equipment at the end of the second year?

SE3-7. *Account for insurance expense.* (LO 1, 3)
The correct amount of prepaid insurance shown on a company's December 31, 2007, balance sheet was $800. On July 1, 2008, the company paid an additional insurance premium of $400. On the December 31, 2008, balance sheet, the amount of prepaid insurance was correctly shown as $500. What amount of insurance expense would appear on the company's income statement for the year ended December 31, 2008? Is this adjustment an accrual or deferral?

SE3-8. *Account for unearned revenue.* (LO 1, 3)
Able Company received $4,800 from a customer on April 1 for services to be provided in the coming year in an equal amount for each of the 12 months beginning April. In the Able information system, these cash receipts are coded as unearned revenue. What adjustment will Able need to make when preparing the December 31 financial statements? What is the impact on the financial statements if the necessary adjustment is not made? Is this adjustment an accrual or deferral?

SE3-9. *Account for supplies expense.* (LO 1, 3)
Peter's Pizza started the month with $500 worth of supplies. During the month, Peter's Pizza purchased an additional $300 worth of supplies. At the end of the month, $175 worth of supplies remained unused. Give the amounts that would appear on the financial statements for the month for supplies expense and supplies on hand. Is this adjustment an accrual or deferral?

SE3-10. *Identify accounts.* (LO 1, 2, 3)
From the following list of accounts: (1) Identify the assets or liabilities that commonly require an adjustment at the end of the accounting period, and (2) indicate whether it relates to a deferral or accrual.

Cash

Accounts receivable

Prepaid insurance

Supplies

Building

Accumulated depreciation—building

Unearned revenue

Interest payable

Salaries payable

Common stock

Retained earnings

Sales revenue

Interest revenue

Depreciation expense

Insurance expense

Supplies expense

Utilities expense

Rent expense

SE3-11. *Account for unearned revenue.* (LO 1, 3)
On January 1, 2006, the law firm of Munns and Munns was formed. On February 1, 2006, the company received $18,000 from clients in advance for services to be performed monthly during the next 18 months. During the year, the firm incurred and paid expenses of $5,000. Is the adjustment for the service revenue an accrual or deferral? Assuming that these were the only transactions completed in 2006, prepare the firm's income statement, statement of cash flows, statement of retained earnings for the year ended December 31, 2006, and balance sheet at December 31, 2006.

SE3-12. *Calculate net income.* (LO 1, 4)
Suppose a company had the following accounts and balances at year-end:

Service revenue	$7,400
Interest revenue	$2,200
Unearned revenue	$3,250
Operating expenses	$1,500
Prepaid rent	$1,030

Prepare the income statement for the year.

SE3-13. *Calculate net income.* (LO 1, 4)
Suppose a company had the following accounts and balances at year-end:

Sales revenue	$5,400
Interest revenue	$1,200
Rent expense	$1,240
Other operating expenses	$3,050
Dividends	$1,000

Calculate net income by preparing the income statement for the year.

SE3-14. *Calculate working capital and quick ratio.* (LO 5)
Suppose a firm had a current ratio of 1.5 at year-end, with current assets of $300,000. How much working capital did the firm have? If current assets were made up of $50,000 accounts receivable, $100,000 cash, and $150,000 inventory, what was the quick ratio at year-end?

SE3-15. *Identify internal controls.* (LO 6)
You have been hired to assess the internal controls of Brown's Brick Company. The owner is concerned about the reliability of the data from the firm's accounting information system. What types of controls will you look for?

Exercises—Set A

E3-1A. *Account for salaries expense.* (LO 1, 2)
Royal Company pays all salaried employees biweekly. Overtime pay, however, is paid in the next biweekly period. Royal accrues salary expense only at its December 31 year-end. Information about salaries earned in December 2007 is as follows:

- Last payroll was paid on December 26, 2007, for the 2-week period ended December 26, 2007.
- Overtime pay earned in the 2-week period ended December 26, 2007 was $5,000.
- Remaining workdays in 2007 were December 29, 30, 31; no overtime was worked on these days.
- The regular biweekly salaries total $90,000.

Using a 5-day workweek, what will Royal Company's balance sheet show as salaries payable on December 31, 2007?

E3-2A. *Account for unearned revenue.* (LO 1, 3)
The TJ Company collects all service revenue in advance. The company showed a $12,500 liability on its December 31, 2006, balance sheet for unearned service revenue. During 2007, customers paid $50,000 for future services, and the income statement for the year ended December 31, 2007, reported service revenue of $52,700. What amount for the liability unearned service revenue will appear on the balance sheet at December 31, 2007?

E3-3A. *Account for interest expense.* (LO 1, 2)
Sojourn Company purchased equipment on November 1, 2006, and gave a 3-month, 9% note with a face value of $20,000. On maturity, January 31, the note plus interest will be paid to the bank. Fill in the blanks in the following chart:

	Interest expense (for the month ended)	Cash paid for interest
November 30, 2006	_____	_____
December 31, 2006	_____	_____
January 31, 2007	_____	_____

E3-4A. *Account for insurance expense.* (LO 1, 3)
Baker Company paid $3,600 on July 1, 2007, for a 2-year insurance policy. It was recorded as prepaid insurance. Use the accounting equation to show the adjustment Baker will make to properly report expenses when preparing the December 31, 2007 financial statements.

E3-5A. *Account for rent expense.* (LO 1, 3)
Susan rented office space for her new business on March 1, 2008. To receive a discount, she paid $3,600 for 12 months' rent in advance. How will this advance payment appear on the financial statements prepared at year-end, December 31? Assume no additional rent was paid in 2009. Use the following chart for your answers:

	Rent expense for the year	Prepaid rent at December 31
2008	_____	_____
2009	_____	_____

E3-6A. *Account for unearned revenue.* (LO 1, 3)
In November and December 2009, Uncle's Company, a newly organized magazine publisher, received $72,000 for 1,000 3-year (36-month) subscriptions to a new monthly magazine at $24 per year, starting with the first issue in March 2010. Fill in the following chart for each of the given years to show the amount of revenue to be recognized on the income statement and the related liability reported on the balance sheet. Uncle's Company's fiscal year-end is December 31.

	Revenue recognized during	Unearned revenue at December 31
2009	_____	_____
2010	_____	_____
2011	_____	_____
2012	_____	_____

E3-7A. *Account for insurance expense.* (LO 1, 3)
Yodel & Company paid $3,600 on June 1, 2008, for a 2-year insurance policy beginning on that date. The company recorded the entire amount as prepaid insurance. By using the

following chart, calculate how much expense and prepaid insurance will be reported on the year-end financial statements. The company's fiscal year-end is December 31.

	Insurance expense	Prepaid insurance at December 31
2008	_____	_____
2009	_____	_____
2010	_____	_____

E3-8A. *Account for depreciation expense.* (LO 1, 3)
Thomas Toy Company purchased a new delivery truck on January 1, 2006, for $25,000. The truck is estimated to last for 6 years and will then be sold, at which time it should be worth approximately $1,000. The company uses straight-line depreciation and has a fiscal year-end of December 31.

1. How much depreciation expense will be shown on the income statement for the year ended December 31, 2008?
2. What is the book value (also called carrying value) of the truck on the balance sheet for each of the 6 years beginning with December 31, 2006?

E3-9A. *Analyze timing of revenue recognition.* (LO 1, 2, 3)
Show each of the following transactions in the accounting equation. Then, tell whether or not the original transaction as given is one that results in the recognition of revenue or expenses.
   a. Dell Inc. paid its computer service technicians $80,000 in salaries for the month ended January 31.
   b. Shell Oil used $5,000 worth of electricity in its headquarters building during March. Shell received the bill, but will not pay it until sometime in April.
   c. In 2006, Chico's, FAS had $22 million in catalogue sales. Assume all sales were recorded as credit sales.
   d. Home Depot collected $59 million in interest and investment income during 2006.

E3-10A. *Account for rent expense.* (LO 1, 3)
BNP Company started the year with $3,000 of prepaid rent, $15,000 of cash, and $18,000 of common stock. During the year, BNP paid additional rent in advance amounting to $10,000. The rent expense for the year was $12,000. What was the balance in prepaid rent on the year-end balance sheet?

E3-11A. *Account for insurance expense.* (LO 1, 3)
Precore Company began the year with $6,500 prepaid insurance. During the year, Precore prepaid additional insurance premiums amounting to $8,000. The company's insurance expense for the year was $10,000. What is the balance in prepaid insurance at year-end?

E3-12A. *Account for rent expense and prepare financial statements.* (LO 4)
On March 1, 2007, Quality Consulting Inc. was formed when the owners contributed $35,000 cash in the business in exchange for common stock. On April 1, 2007, the company paid $24,000 cash to rent office space for the coming year. The consulting services generated $62,000 of cash revenue during 2007. Prepare an income statement, statement of changes in shareholders' equity, and statement of cash flows for the 10 months ended December 31, 2007, and a balance sheet at December 31, 2007.

E3-13A. *Account for depreciation expense and prepare financial statements.* (LO 3, 4)
Southeast Pest Control Inc. was started when its owners invested $20,000 in the business in exchange for common stock on January 1, 2006. The cash received by the company was immediately used to purchase a $15,000 heavy-duty chemical truck, which had no residual value and an expected useful life of 5 years. The company earned $13,000 of cash revenue during 2006. Prepare an income statement, statement of changes in shareholders' equity, and statement of cash flows for the year ended December 31, 2006, and a balance sheet at December 31, 2006.

E3-14A. *Classify accounts.* (LO 1, 4)

Tell whether each of the following items would appear on the income statement, statement of changes in shareholders' equity, balance sheet, or statement of cash flows. Some items may appear on more than one statement.

Interest receivable	Accounts payable
Salary expense	Common stock
Notes receivable	Dividends
Unearned revenue	Total assets
Net cash flow from investing activities	Net income
Insurance expense	Consulting revenue
Retained earnings	Depreciation expense
Prepaid insurance	Supplies expense
Cash	Salaries payable
Accumulated depreciation	Supplies
Prepaid rent	Net cash flow from financing activities
Accounts receivable	Land
Total shareholders' equity	Net cash flow from operating activities

E3-15A. *Analyze business transactions.* (LO 1, 2, 3)

Analyze the following accounting equation worksheet for Starwood Yacht Repair Corporation and explain the transaction or event that resulted in each entry.

	Assets					=	Liabilities			+	Shareholder's Equity		
											Contributed Capital	Retained Earnings	
	Cash	Supplies	Prepaid Insurance	Property & Equipment (P & E)	Accumulated Depreciation— P & E	Interest Payable	Salaries Payable	Long-term Notes Payable		Common Stock	Revenues	Expenses
a.	150,000									150,000		
b.	(125,000)			125,000								
c.	100,000							100,000				
d.	(500)	500										
e.	(650)		650									
f.	15,000										15,000	
g.		(375)										(375)
h.			(325)									(325)
i.							500					(500)
j.					(1,000)							(1,000)
k.						100						(100)

E3-16A. *Prepare financial statements.* (LO 1, 2, 3, 4)

Refer to E3-15A. Assume all beginning balances are zero. Prepare the four financial statements for the period ended December 31, 2009 (balance sheet at December 31, 2009).

E3-17A. *Compute working capital and quick ratio.* (LO 5)

Use the given information to calculate the amount of working capital and the quick ratio at December 31. Balances from December 31 balance sheet:

Cash	$5,460
Accounts receivable	2,500
Short-term investments	1,000
Inventory	2,350
Prepaid insurance	460
Current liabilities	9,200

E3-18A. *Identify internal controls.* (LO 6)

During Hurricane Katrina in 2005, James and Dory law firm in New Orleans lost most of their financial records. What advice could you give the firm as they prepare for another hurricane season?

Exercises—Set B

E3-1B. *Account for salaries expense.* (LO 1, 2)
Jack's Finance & Budget Consulting Inc. pays all salaried employees monthly on the first Monday following the end of the month. Overtime, however, is recorded as comp time for all employees. Jack's allows employees to exchange all comp time not used during the year for pay on June 30 and pays it on July 15. Jack's accrues salary expense only at its June 30 year-end. Information about salaries earned in June 2008 is as follows:

- Last payroll was paid on June 2, 2008, for the month ended May 31, 2008.
- Comp pay exchanged at year-end totals $150,000.
- The regular yearly salaries total $1,500,000.

Using a 12-month fiscal work year, what will Jack's Finance & Budget Consulting Inc.'s balance sheet show as salaries payable on June 30, 2008?

E3-2B. *Account for unearned revenue.* (LO 1, 3)
The Joe & Einstein Cable Company collects all service revenue in advance. Joe & Einstein showed a $16,825 liability on its June 30, 2008, balance sheet for unearned service revenue. During the following fiscal year, customers paid $85,000 for future services, and the income statement for the year ended June 30, 2009, reported service revenue of $75,850. What amount for the liability unearned service revenue will appear on the balance sheet at June 30, 2009?

E3-3B. *Account for interest expense.* (LO 1, 2)
The Muzby Pet Grooming Company purchased a computer on December 30, 2007, and gave a 4-month, 7% note with a face value of $6,000. On maturity, April 30, 2008, the note plus interest will be paid to the bank. Fill in the blanks in the following chart:

	Interest expense	Cash paid for interest
January 31, 2008	_____	_____
February 29, 2008	_____	_____
March 31, 2008	_____	_____
April 30, 2008	_____	_____

E3-4B. *Account for insurance expense.* (LO 1, 3)
More & Blue Painting Professionals Inc. paid $6,300 on February 1, 2008, for a 3-year insurance policy. In the More & Blue information system, this was recorded as prepaid insurance. Use the accounting equation to show the adjustment More & Blue will need to make to properly report expenses when preparing the June 30, 2008, financial statements.

E3-5B. *Account for rent expense.* (LO 1, 3)
Utopia Dance Clubs Inc. rented an old warehouse for its newest club on October 1, 2006. To receive a discount, Utopia paid $2,970 for 18 months of rent in advance. How will this advance payment appear on the financial statements prepared at year-end, December 31? Assume no additional rent is paid in 2007 and 2008. Use the following chart for your answers:

	Rent expense for the year	Prepaid rent at December 31
2006	_____	_____
2007	_____	_____
2008	_____	_____

E3-6B. *Account for unearned revenue.* (LO 1, 3)
In May and June 2010, Lynn Haven Gazette, a newly organized newspaper publisher, received $12,000 for 500 2-year (24-month) subscriptions to a new monthly community events newspaper at $12 per year, starting with the first issue in September 2010. Fill in the following chart for each of the given years to show the amount of revenue to be recognized

CHAPTER 3 • EXERCISES

on the income statement and the related liability reported on the balance sheet. Lynn Haven Gazette's fiscal year-end is June 30.

	Revenue recognized	Unearned revenue at June 30
2010	_____	_____
2011	_____	_____
2012	_____	_____

E3-7B. *Account for insurance expense.* (LO 1, 3)
All Natural Medicine Corporation paid $2,178 on August 1, 2009, for an 18-month insurance policy beginning on that date. The company recorded the entire amount as prepaid insurance. By using the following chart, calculate how much expense and prepaid insurance will be reported on the year-end financial statements. The company's year-end is December 31.

	Insurance expense	Prepaid insurance at December 31
2009	_____	_____
2010	_____	_____
2011	_____	_____

E3-8B. *Account for depreciation expense.* (LO 1, 3)
E. Hutson Pastries Inc. purchased a new delivery van on July 1, 2007, for $35,000. The truck is estimated to last for 5 years and will then be sold, at which time it should be worth nothing. The company uses straight-line depreciation and has a fiscal year-end of June 30.
   a. How much depreciation expense will be shown on the income statement for the year ended June 30, 2010?
   b. What is the book value (also called carrying value) of the truck on the balance sheet for each of the 5 years beginning with June 30, 2008?

E3-9B. *Analyze timing of revenue recognition.* (LO 1, 2, 3)
For each of the following transactions, tell whether or not the original transaction as shown is one that results in the recognition of revenue or expenses.
   a. On April 15, Mike's Pressure Cleaning Services Inc. paid its employees $3,000 in salaries for services provided.
   b. Mister Hsieh Fencing Company used $1,000 worth of radio advertising during April. Mister received the bill but will not pay it until sometime in May.
   c. During 2007, Tootie's Pet Training School Inc. earned $125,000 in service revenues. Assume all services were offered on account.
   d. Susan's Investment Company collected $130,000 in interest and investment income earned during 2008.

E3-10B. *Account for rent expense.* (LO 1, 3)
Florida's Number One Credit Solution Organization started the year with $1,850 of prepaid rent, $25,000 of cash, and $26,850 of retained earnings. During the year, Florida paid additional rent in advance amounting to $16,275. The rent expense for the year was $16,850. What was the balance in prepaid rent on the year-end balance sheet?

E3-11B. *Account for insurance expense.* (LO 1, 3)
J.B. Eriksen's Construction Company began the year with $18,500 prepaid insurance. During the year, J.B. Eriksen's prepaid additional insurance premiums amounting to $96,000. The company's insurance expense for the year was $104,500. What is the balance in prepaid insurance at year-end?

E3-12B. *Account for rent expense and insurance expense and prepare financial statements.* (LO 3, 4)
On February 1, 2010, Breeder's Choice Pet Trainers Inc. was formed when the owners invested $25,626 cash in the business in exchange for common stock. On March 1, 2010, the

company paid $22,212 cash to rent office space for the next 18 months and paid $3,414 cash for 6 months of prepaid insurance. The training services generated $115,725 of cash revenue during the remainder of the fiscal year. The company has chosen June 30 as the end of its fiscal year. Prepare an income statement, statement of changes in shareholders' equity, and statement of cash flows for the 5 months ended June 30, 2010, and a balance sheet at June 30, 2010.

E3-13B. *Account for depreciation expense and prepare financial statements.* (LO 3, 4)
Northeast Termite Specialists Inc. was started when its owners invested $32,685 in the business in exchange for common stock on July 1, 2010. Part of the cash received to start the company was immediately used to purchase a $19,875 high-pressure chemical sprayer, which had a $2,875 residual value and an expected useful life of 10 years. The company earned $68,315 of cash revenue during the year and had cash operating expenses of $27,205. Prepare an income statement, statement of changes in shareholders' equity, and statement of cash flows for the year ended June 30, 2011, and a balance sheet at June 30, 2011.

E3-14B. *Identify accounts.* (LO 1, 4)
From the following list of accounts: (1) identify the assets or liabilities that may require an adjustment at the end of the accounting period, and (2) indicate whether it relates to a deferral or accrual.

Cash	Common stock
Accounts receivable	Retained earnings
Prepaid insurance	Sales revenue
Prepaid rent	Interest revenue
Supplies	Equipment
Depreciation expense	Accumulated depreciation—equipment
Insurance expense	Unearned revenue
Supplies expense	Interest payable
Utilities expense	Salaries payable
Rent expense	Accounts payable
Interest receivable	Other operating expense

E3-15B. *Analyze business transactions from the accounting equation.* (LO 1, 2, 3)
Analyze the following transactions for Information Resource Services Inc. and explain the transaction or event that resulted in each entry.

	Cash	Accounts Receivable	Supplies	Prepaid Rent	Property & Equipment (P & E)	Accumulated Depreciation— P & E	Interest Payable	Salaries Payable	Long-term Notes Payable	Common Stock	Revenues	Expenses
a.	115,000									115,000		
b.	(112,500)				112,500							
c.	85,000								85,000			
d.	(1,000)		1,000									
e.	(825)			825								
f.	13,150										13,150	
g.			(615)									(615)
h.				(275)								(275)
i.								795				(795)
j.						(1,500)						(1,500)
k.							50					(50)

E3-16B. *Prepare financial statements.* (LO 1, 2, 3, 4)
Refer to E3-15B. Assume all beginning balances are zero. Prepare the four financial statements for the period ended June 30, 2007 (balance sheet at June 30, 2007).

E3-17B. *Compute working capital and quick ratio.* (LO 5)
Use the given information to calculate the amount of working capital and the quick ratio at December 31.

Balances from December 31 balance sheet:

Cash	$2,500
Accounts receivable	1,500
Short-term investments	4,000
Inventory	3,350
Prepaid rent	750
Current liabilities	9,000

Do you think the firm's quick ratio is high enough? Why or why not?

E3-18B. *Identify internal controls.* (LO 6)
What are some controls that a company might use to make sure its financial statements contain accurate information?

Problems—Set A

P3-1A. *Record adjustments and prepare income statement.* (LO 1, 2, 3, 4)
Selected amounts (at December 31, 2007) from Soul Tan, Polish & Refine Inc.'s information system appear as follows:

1.	Cash paid employees for salaries and wages	$ 300,000
2.	Cash collected from customers for service rendered	1,850,000
3.	Long-term notes payable	500,000
4.	Cash	150,000
5.	Common stock	60,000
6.	Equipment	840,000
7.	Prepaid insurance	30,000
8.	Inventory	250,000
9.	Prepaid rent	140,000
10.	Retained earnings	130,000
11.	Salaries and wages expense	328,000
12.	Service revenues	2,000,000

Required

a. There are five adjustments that need to be made before the financial statements can be prepared at year-end. For each, show the adjustment in the accounting equation.
   1. The equipment (purchased on January 1, 2007) has a useful life of 12 years with no salvage value. (An equal amount of depreciation is taken each year.)
   2. Interest accrued on the notes payable is $1,000 as of December 31, 2007.
   3. Unexpired insurance at December 31, 2007, is $7,000.
   4. The rent payment of $140,000 covered the 4 months from December 1, 2007, through March 31, 2008.
   5. Employees had earned salaries and wages of $28,000 that were unpaid at December 31, 2007.

b. Prepare an income statement for the year ended December 31, 2007, for Soul Tan, Polish & Refine Inc.

P3-2A. *Record adjustments and calculate net income.* (LO 1, 2, 3, 4)
The records of RCA Company revealed the following recorded amounts at December 31, 2006, before adjustments:

Prepaid insurance	$ 1,800
Cleaning supplies	2,800
Unearned service fees	3,000
Notes payable	5,000
Service fees	96,000
Wages expense	75,000

Truck rent expense	3,900
Truck fuel expense	1,100
Insurance expense	0
Supplies expense	0
Interest expense	0
Interest payable	0
Wages payable	0
Prepaid rent—truck	0

Before RCA prepares the financial statements for the business, adjustments must be made for the following items:

1. The prepaid insurance represents an 18-month policy purchased early in January.
2. A physical count on December 31 revealed $500 of cleaning supplies on hand.
3. On December 1, a customer paid for 3 months of service in advance.
4. The truck rent is $300 per month in advance. January 2007 rent was paid in late December 2006.
5. The bank loan was taken out October 1. The interest rate is 12% (1% per month) for 1 year.
6. On Wednesday, December 31, the company owed its employees for working 3 days. The normal workweek is 5 days with wages of $1,500 paid at the end of the week.

Required

    a. For each item, show the adjustment in the accounting equation.
    b. Prepare an income statement for the year ended December 31, 2006, for RCA Company.

Excel Template
www.prenhall.com/reimers

P3-3A. *Account for depreciable assets.* (LO 3)
Charlotte & Gary Motorcycle Repair Corporation purchased a machine on January 1, 2008, for $8,000 cash. Gary expects to use the machine for 4 years and thinks it will be worthless at the end of the 4-year period. The company will depreciate the machine in equal annual amounts.

Required

    a. Show the purchase of the machine and the first year's depreciation in the accounting equation.
    b. Show how the machine will be presented in the asset section of the balance sheet at December 31, 2008, and December 31, 2009, after appropriate adjustments.
    c. What amount of depreciation expense will be shown on the income statement for the year ended December 31, 2008? What amount will be shown for the year ended December 31, 2009?
    d. Calculate the total depreciation expense for all 4 years of the asset's life. What do you notice about the book value of the asset at the end of its useful life?

P3-4A. *Record adjustments.* (LO 1, 2, 3)
The following is a partial list of financial statement items from the records of Marshall's Company at December 31, 2008.

Prepaid insurance	$10,000
Prepaid rent	18,000
Interest receivable	0
Salaries payable	0
Unearned fee income	30,000
Interest income	10,000

Additional information includes the following:

1. The insurance policy indicates that on December 31, 2008, only 5 months remain on the 24-month policy that originally cost $18,000.
2. Marshall's has a note receivable with $2,500 of interest due from a customer on January 1, 2009.

3. The accounting records show that one-third of the fees paid in advance by a customer on July 1, 2008, has now been earned.
4. The company paid $18,000 for rent for 9 months starting on August 1, 2008.
5. At year-end, Marshall's owed $7,000 worth of salaries to employees for work done in December 2008. The next payday is January 5, 2009.

Required

    a. Use the accounting equation to show the adjustments that must be made prior to the preparation of the financial statements for the year ended December 31, 2008.

    b. Calculate the account balances that would be shown on Marshall's financial statements for the year ended December 31, 2008.

P3-5A. *Record adjustments.* (LO 1, 2, 3)
The following is a list of financial statement items from Sugar & Spice Cookie Company as of December 31, 2007:

Prepaid insurance	$ 6,000
Prepaid rent expense	10,000
Wages expense	25,000
Unearned subscription revenue	70,000
Interest expense	38,000

Additional information:

1. The company paid a $7,200 premium on a 3-year business insurance policy on July 1, 2006.
2. Sugar & Spice borrowed $200,000 on January 2, 2007, and must pay 11% interest on January 2, 2008, for the entire year of 2007.
3. The books show that $60,000 of the unearned subscription revenue has now been earned.
4. The company paid 10 months of rent in advance on November 1, 2007.
5. The company will pay wages of $2,000 for December 31 to employees on January 3, 2008.

Required

    a. Use the accounting equation to show the adjustments that must be made prior to the preparation of the financial statements for the year ended December 31, 2007.

    b. Calculate the account balances that would appear on the financial statements for the year ended December 31, 2007.

P3-6A. *Record adjustments.* (LO 1, 2, 3)
The Fruit Packing Company has the following account balances at the end of the year:

Prepaid insurance	$8,000
Unearned revenue	4,200
Wages expense	6,790
Taxes payable	4,168
Interest income	2,475

The company also has the following information available at the end of the year:

1. Of the prepaid insurance, $3,000 has now expired.
2. Of the unearned revenue, $2,000 has been earned.
3. The company must accrue an additional $1,500 of wages expense.
4. The company has earned an additional $500 of interest income, not yet received.

Required

    a. Use the accounting equation to show the adjustments indicated at year-end.

    b. Calculate the balances in each account after the adjustments.

    c. Indicate whether each adjustment is an accrual or deferral.

P3-7A. *Record adjustments and prepare financial statements.* (LO 1, 2, 3, 4)
The accounting records for Sony Snowboard Company, a snowboard repair company, contained the following balances as of December 31, 2006:

Assets		Liabilities and shareholders' equity	
Cash	$40,000	Accounts payable	$17,000
Accounts receivable	16,500	Common stock	45,000
Land	20,000	Retained earnings	14,500
Totals	$76,500		$76,500

The following accounting events apply to Sony's 2007 fiscal year:
- a. Jan. 1 The company acquired an additional $20,000 cash from the owners in exchange for common stock.
- b. Jan. 1 Sony purchased a computer that cost $15,000 for cash. The computer had a no salvage value and a 3-year useful life.
- c. Mar. 1 The company borrowed $10,000 by issuing a 1-year note at 12%.
- d. May 1 The company paid $2,400 cash in advance for a 1-year lease for office space.
- e. June 1 The company declared and paid dividends to the owners of $4,000 cash.
- f. July 1 The company purchased land that cost $17,000 cash.
- g. Aug. 1 Cash payments on accounts payable amounted to $6,000.
- h. Aug. 1 Sony received $9,600 cash in advance for 12 months of service to be performed monthly for the next year, beginning on receipt of payment.
- i. Sept. 1 Sony sold a parcel of land for $13,000 cash, the amount the company originally paid for it.
- j. Oct. 1 Sony purchased $795 of supplies on account.
- k. Nov. 1 Sony purchased short-term investments for $18,000. The investments pay a fixed rate of 6%.
- l. Dec. 31 The company earned service revenue on account during the year that amounted to $40,000.
- m. Dec. 31 Cash collections from accounts receivable amounted to $44,000.
- n. Dec. 31 The company incurred other operating expenses on account during the year of $5,450.

1. Salaries that had been earned by the sales staff but not yet paid amounted to $2,300.
2. Supplies worth $180 were on hand at the end of the period.

Based on the preceding transaction data, there are five additional adjustments (for a total of seven) that need to be made before the financial statements can be prepared.

Required
- a. Prepare an accounting equation worksheet and record the account balances as of December 31, 2006.
- b. Using the worksheet, record the transactions that occurred during 2007 and the necessary adjustments needed at year-end.
- c. Prepare all four financial statements for the year ended December 31, 2007 (balance sheet at December 31, 2007).

Excel Template
www.prenhail.com/reimers

P3-8A. *Record adjustments and prepare financial statements.* (LO 1, 2, 3, 4)
Transactions for Pops Company for 2007 were:

1. The owners started the business as a corporation by contributing $30,000 cash in exchange for common stock.
2. The company purchased office equipment for $8,000 cash and land for $15,000 cash.
3. The company earned a total of $22,000 of revenue of which $16,000 was collected in cash.
4. The company purchased $890 worth of supplies for cash.
5. The company paid $6,000 in cash for other operating expenses.

6. At the end of the year, the company owed employees $2,480 for work that the employees had done in 2007. The next payday, however, is not until January 4, 2008.

7. Only $175 worth of supplies was left at the end of the year.

The office equipment was purchased on January 1 and is expected to last for 8 years (straight-line depreciation, no salvage value).

Required

a. Use an accounting equation worksheet to record the transactions that occurred during 2007.

b. Record any needed adjustments at year-end.

c. Prepare all four financial statements for the year ended December 31, 2007 (balance sheet at December 31, 2007).

P3-9A. *Record adjustments and prepare financial statements.* (LO 1, 2, 3, 4)

On June 1, Joel Adams started a computer business as a corporation. Joel started the business by contributing $25,000 in exchange for common stock. He paid 2 months of rent in advance totaling $500. On June 3, Joel purchased supplies for $600 and two computers at a total cost of $6,500. Joel expects the computers to last for 3 years with no residual value. Joel hired an office assistant, agreeing to pay the assistant $800 per month to be paid $400 on June 15 and June 30. On June 27, Joel paid $300 for a radio advertisement to run immediately to announce the opening of the business. Joel earned $4,200 in June, of which he collected $2,800 in cash. At the end of the month, Joel had only $130 worth of supplies on hand.

Required

a. Use an accounting equation worksheet to record the transactions that occurred during the month of June and the adjustments that must be made prior to the preparation of the financial statements for the month ended June 30.

b. Prepare the four financial statements for Joel's company for the month ended June 30 (balance sheet at June 30).

P3-10A. *Record adjustments and prepare financial statements.* (LO 1, 2, 3, 4, 5)

The following is a list of accounts and their balances for Casa Bella Interiors at May 31 before adjustments and some additional data for the fiscal year ended May 31, 2006.

Casa Bella Interiors
Accounts and balances
31-May-06

Cash	$ 4,300
Accounts receivable	9,300
Notes receivable	1,000
Interest receivable	—
Prepaid rent	1,700
Supplies	400
Office equipment	23,400
Accumulated depreciation (office equipment)	(1,600)
Accounts payable	500
Salaries payable	—
Interest payable	—
Unearned service revenue	2,600
Long-term notes payable	8,400
Common stock	5,000
Additional paid-in capital	2,300

Retained earnings	5,000
Service revenue	19,800
Salary expense	4,650
Rent expense	
Depreciation expense	
Advertising expense	450

Additional data:

1. Depreciation on the office equipment for the year is $500.
2. Salaries owed to employees at year-end but not yet recorded or paid total $750.
3. Prepaid rent that has expired at year-end amounts to $800.
4. Interest due at year-end on the notes receivable is $120.
5. Interest owed at year-end on the notes payable is $840.
6. Unearned service revenue that has actually been earned by year-end totals $1,500.

Required

    a. Make the adjustments needed at year-end. (Use the accounting equation.)
    b. Prepare an income statement for the year ended May 31, 2006, and a balance sheet at May 31, 2006.

P3-11A. *Analyze business transactions and prepare financial statements.* (LO 1, 2, 3, 4)
The accounting department for Setting Sun Vacation Rentals recorded the following transactions for 2009, the first year of business. Setting Sun generates revenue by renting waterfront condominiums to vacationers to the area. When a reservation is made in advance, Setting Sun collects half the week's rent to hold the reservation. However, Setting Sun does not require reservations, and sometimes customers will come in to rent a unit the same day. These types of transactions require that Setting Sun's accounting department record some cash receipts as unearned revenues and others as earned revenues.

	Assets						=	Liabilities			+	Shareholder's Equity		
												Contributed Capital	Retained Earnings	
	Cash	Accounts Receivable	Supplies	Prepaid Rent	Property & Equipment (P & E)	Accumulated Depreciation— P & E		Interest Payable	Salaries Payable	Long-term Notes Payable		Common Stock	Revenues	Expenses
a.	115,000											115,000		
b.	(112,500)				112,500									
c.	85,000										85,000			
d.	(1,000)		1,000											
e.	(825)			825										
f.	13,150												13,150	
g.			(615)											(615)
h.				(275)										(275)
i.										795				(795)
j.						(1,500)								(1,500)
k.									50					(50)

Required

    a. Explain the transaction or event that resulted in each entry in the accounting equation worksheet.
    b. Did Setting Sun Vacation Rentals generate net income or net loss for the period ending December 31, 2009? How can you tell?
    c. Prepare the four financial statements at year-end.

Problems—Set B

P3-1B. *Record adjustments and prepare income statement.* (LO 1, 2, 3, 4)
Selected amounts (at December 31, 2008) from Budget Planning Company's accounting records are shown here. No adjustments have been made.

Cash paid to employees for salaries and wages	$ 400,000
Cash collected from customers for services rendered	2,220,000
Long-term notes payable	350,000
Cash	250,000
Common stock	30,000
Equipment	780,000
Prepaid insurance	140,000
Inventory	175,000
Prepaid rent	120,000
Retained earnings	330,000
Salaries and wages expense	428,000
Service revenue	3,000,000

Required

a. There are five adjustments that need to be made before the financial statements for the year ended December 31, 2008, can be prepared. Show each in an accounting equation worksheet.

   1. The equipment (purchased on January 1, 2008) has a useful life of 12 years with no salvage value (equal amount of depreciation each year).
   2. Interest on the notes payable needs to be accrued for the year in the amount of $40,000.
   3. Unexpired insurance at December 31, 2008, is $40,000.
   4. The rent payment of $120,000 was made on June 1. The rent payment is for 12 months beginning on the date of payment.
   5. Salaries of $58,000 were earned but unpaid at December 31, 2008.

b. Prepare an income statement for the year ended December 31, 2008, for Budget Planning Company.

P3-2B. *Record adjustments and calculate net income.* (LO 1, 2, 3, 4)
The records of Jimenez Electric Company showed the following amounts at December 31, 2007, before adjustments:

Prepaid insurance	$ 1,500
Supplies	3,500
Unearned service fees	4,000
Notes payable	30,000
Service fees	106,000
Salary expense	65,000
Prepaid rent	3,900
Insurance expense	0
Supplies expense	0
Rent expense	0
Interest expense	0
Interest payable	0
Wages payable	0

Before Mr. Jimenez prepares the financial statements for his business, adjustments must be made for the following items:

1. The prepaid insurance is for a 12-month policy purchased on March 1 for cash. The policy is effective from March 1, 2007, to February 28, 2008.
2. A count of the supplies on December 31 revealed $400 worth still on hand.
3. One customer paid for 4 months of service in advance on December 1. By December 31, 1 month of the service had been performed.
4. The prepaid rent was for 10 months of rent for the company office building, beginning June 1.
5. The company took out a bank loan on November 1, 2007. The interest rate is 12% (1% per month) for 1 year.
6. As of December 31, the company owed its employees $5,000 for work done in 2007. The next payday is in January 2008.

Required

    a. Show the adjustments in the accounting equation.

    b. Prepare an income statement for the year ended December 31, 2007, for Jimenez Electric Company.

Excel Template
www.prenhall.com/reimers

P3-3B. *Account for depreciable assets.* (LO 3)

Super Clean Dry Cleaning purchased a new piece of office equipment on January 1, 2009, for $18,000 cash. The company expects to use the equipment for 3 years and thinks it will be worthless at the end of the 3-year period. The company depreciates the equipment in equal annual amounts.

Required

    a. Show the adjustments in an accounting equation worksheet for the first 2 years of depreciation.

    b. Prepare the asset section of the balance sheet at December 31, 2009, and December 31, 2010, after appropriate adjustments.

    c. What amount of depreciation expense will be shown on the income statement for the year ended December 31, 2009? What amount will be shown for the year ended December 31, 2010?

    d. Calculate the total depreciation for the life of the asset. What do you notice about the book value of the asset at the end of its useful life?

P3-4B. *Record adjustments.* (LO 1, 2, 3)

The following is a partial list of financial statement items from the records of Starnes Company at December 31, 2006.

Prepaid rent	$20,000
Prepaid insurance	12,000
Service revenue	35,000
Wages expense	8,000
Unearned service revenue	18,000
Interest expense	5,000

Additional information includes the following:

1. The insurance policy indicates that on December 31, 2006, only 5 months remain on the 12-month policy that originally cost $12,000.
2. Starnes has a note payable with $2,500 of interest that must be paid on January 1, 2007.
3. The accounting records show that two-thirds of the service revenue paid in advance by a customer on March 1 has now been earned.
4. On August 1, the company paid $20,000 for rent for 10 months beginning on August 1.
5. At year-end, Starnes Company owed $500 worth of salaries to employees for work done in December. The next payday is January 3, 2007.

Required

    a. Use an accounting equation worksheet to record the adjustments that must be made prior to the preparation of the financial statements for the year ended December 31, 2006.

    b. Calculate the account balances that would be shown on Starnes' financial statements for the year ended December 31, 2006.

P3-5B. *Record adjustments.* (LO 1, 2, 3)

The following is a list of financial statement items from Chunky Candy Company as of June 30, 2008. Chunky's fiscal year is from July 1 to June 30.

Prepaid insurance	$ 3,600
Prepaid rent	5,000
Wages expense	12,000
Unearned revenue	30,000
Interest expense	0

Additional information:

1. The company paid a $3,600 premium on a 3-year insurance policy on January 1, 2008.
2. Chunky borrowed $100,000 on July 1, 2007, with an interest rate of 11%. No interest has been paid as of June 30, 2008.
3. The books show that $10,000 of the unearned revenue has now been earned.
4. The company paid 10 months of rent in advance on March 1, 2008.
5. Wages for June 30 of $1,000 will be paid to employees on July 3.

Required

a. Use the accounting equation to record the adjustments that must be made prior to the preparation of the financial statements for the fiscal year ended June 30, 2008.
b. Calculate the balances that would appear on the financial statements for the year ended June 30, 2008.

P3-6B. *Record adjustments.* (LO 1, 2, 3)
The Delphi Desk Company has the following amounts in its records at the end of the fiscal year:

Prepaid insurance	$5,000
Unearned revenue	3,700
Wages expense	6,790
Accounts payable	4,200
Interest revenue	1,235

The company also has the following information available at the end of the year:

1. Of the prepaid insurance, $1,000 has now expired.
2. Of the unearned revenue, $1,700 has been earned.
3. The company must accrue an additional $1,250 of wages expense.
4. A bill for $300 from the company that provides the desks that Delphi Desk Company sells arrived on the last day of the year. Nothing related to this invoice has been recorded or paid.
5. The company has earned an additional $500 of interest revenue, not yet received.

Required

a. Use an accounting equation worksheet to show the adjustments at the end of the year.
b. Calculate the balances in each account after the adjustments.
c. Indicate whether each adjustment is an accrual or deferral.

P3-7B. *Record adjustments and prepare financial statements.* (LO 1, 2, 3, 4)
The accounting records for Beta Company contained the following balances as of December 31, 2008:

Assets		Liabilities and Shareholders' Equity	
Cash	$50,000	Accounts payable	$17,500
Accounts receivable	26,500		
Prepaid rent	3,600	Common stock	48,600
Land	10,500	Retained earnings	24,500
Totals	$90,600		$90,600

The following accounting events apply to Beta's 2009 fiscal year:

a. Jan. 1   Beta purchased a computer that cost $18,000 for cash. The computer had a no salvage value and a 3-year useful life.
b. Mar. 1   The company borrowed $20,000 by issuing a 2-year note at 12%.
c. May 1   The company paid $6,000 cash in advance for a 6-month lease starting on July 1 for office space.
d. June 1   The company declared and paid dividends of $2,000 to the owners.

e. July 1   The company purchased land that cost $15,000 cash.

f. Aug. 1   Cash payments on accounts payable amounted to $5,500.

g. Aug. 1   Beta received $13,200 cash in advance for 12 months of service to be performed monthly for the next year, beginning on receipt of payment.

h. Sept. 1   Beta sold a parcel of land for $13,000, its original cost of the land.

i. Oct. 1   Beta purchased $1,300 of supplies on account.

j. Nov. 1   Beta purchased short-term investments for $10,000. The investments earn a fixed rate of 5% per year.

k. Dec. 31   The company earned service revenue on account during the year that amounted to $50,000.

l. Dec. 31   Cash collections from accounts receivable amounted to $46,000.

m. Dec. 31   The company incurred other operating expenses on account during the year that amounted to $5,850.

Additional information:

1. Salaries that had been earned by the sales staff but not yet paid amounted to $2,300.
2. Supplies on hand at the end of the period totaled $200.
3. The beginning balance of $3,600 in prepaid rent was completely used up by the end of the year.

Required

a. Set up an accounting equation worksheet and record the account balances as of December 31, 2008.

b. Record the transactions that occurred during 2009 and the necessary adjustments at year-end.

c. Prepare all four financial statements for the year ended December 31, 2009 (balance sheet at December 31, 2009).

Excel Template
www.prenhall.com/reimers

P3-8B. *Record adjustments and prepare financial statements.* (LO 1, 2, 3, 4)
Given the following transactions for Security Company for 2008:

1. The owners started the business as a corporation by contributing $50,000 cash in exchange for common stock.
2. Security Company purchased office equipment for $5,000 cash and land for $15,000 cash.
3. The company earned a total of $32,000 of revenue of which $20,000 was collected in cash.
4. The company purchased $550 worth of supplies for cash.
5. The company paid $6,000 in cash for other operating expenses.
6. At the end of the year, Security Company owed employees $3,600 for work that the employees had done in 2008. The next payday, however, is not until January 4, 2009.
7. Only $120 worth of supplies was left at the end of the year.
8. The office equipment was purchased on January 1 and is expected to last for 5 years. There is no expected salvage value, and the company wants equal amounts of depreciation expense each year related to this equipment.

Required

a. Use an accounting equation worksheet to record the transactions that occurred during 2008.

b. Record any adjustments needed at year-end.

c. Prepare all four financial statements for the year ended December 31, 2008 (balance sheet at December 31, 2008).

P3-9B. *Record adjustments and prepare financial statements.* (LO 1, 2, 3, 4)
On September 1, Irene Shannon started Shannon Check Verification Services as a corporation. Irene started the firm by contributing $37,000 in exchange for common stock. The new firm paid 4 months of rent in advance totaling $1,200 and paid 10 months of insurance in advance totaling $6,500. Both rent and insurance coverage began on September 1. On September 6, the firm purchased supplies for $800. The firm hired one employee to help Irene and

agreed to pay the assistant $1,000 per month, paid on the last day of each month. Shannon Check Verification Services paid $200 for a newspaper advertisement to announce the opening of the business. The firm earned service revenue of $6,200 in September, of which $6,000 was in cash. At the end of the month, the firm had only $100 worth of supplies on hand.

Required

    a. Using an accounting equation worksheet, record the transactions that occurred during the month of September and the adjustments that must be made prior to the preparation of the financial statements for the month ended September 30.

    b. Prepare the four financial statements for Shannon Check Verification Services for the month ended September 30 (balance sheet at September 30).

P3-10B. *Record adjustments and prepare financial statements.* (LO 1, 2, 3, 4)
Puppy Studs Inc. provides a stud service for serious dog breeders. The company's accountant prepared the following list of accounts with their unadjusted balances at the end of the fiscal year, March 31, 2007.

Cash	$ 52,200
Accounts receivable	47,500
Prepaid insurance	20,000
Prepaid rent	1,800
Supplies	10,350
Equipment	137,500
Accumulated depreciation	(1,700)
Accounts payable	3,500
Unearned service revenue	3,000
Long-term notes payable	35,000
Common stock	50,500
Additional paid-in capital	91,450
Retained earnings	87,120
Dividends	5,320
Service revenue	226,850
Miscellaneous operating expenses	149,450
Salary expense	75,000

Additional facts:

1. The company owes its employees $2,500 for work done in this fiscal year. The next payday is not until April.
2. $2,000 worth of the unearned service revenue has actually been earned at year-end.
3. The equipment is depreciated at the rate of $1,700 per year.
4. At year-end $600 worth of prepaid rent and $15,000 of prepaid insurance remains unexpired.
5. Interest on the long-term note for a year at the rate of 6.5% is due on April 1.
6. Supplies on hand at the end of the year amounted to $2,100.
7. On the last day of the fiscal year, the firm earned $20,000. The customer paid $15,000 with cash and owed the remainder on account. However, the accountant left early that day, so the day's revenue was not recorded in the accounting records.

Required

    a. Make the adjustments needed at year-end. (Use the accounting equation.)

    b. Prepare an income statement for the year ended March 31, 2007, and a balance sheet at March 31, 2007.

P3-11B. *Analyze business transactions and prepare financial statements.* (LO 1, 2, 3, 4)
The accounting department for SummerFest Promotions recorded the following transactions for the fiscal year ended June 30, 2008. SummerFest Promotions generates revenue

by selling tickets for local events such as concerts, fights, and sporting events. Sometimes tickets are sold in advance and sometimes customers will purchase their tickets the same day as the event. These types of transactions require that the SummerFest accounting department record some cash receipts as unearned revenues and others as earned revenues.

| | | Assets | | | | | = | Liabilities | | | | | + | Shareholder's Equity | | | |
| | | | | | | | | | | | | | | Contributed Capital | Retained Earnings | | |
	Cash	Accounts Receivable	Office Supplies	Prepaid Rent	Buildings	Accumulated Depreciation—P & E		Accounts Payable	Salaries Payable	Unearned Rent Revenue	Interest Payable	Long-term Notes Payable		Common Stock	Revenues	Expenses	Dividends
a.	150,000													150,000			
b.			475						475								
c.	(18,000)			18,000													
d.					375,000							375,000					
e.	16,000										16,000						
f.	(525)																(525)
g.	(475)								(475)								
h.	50,000														50,000		
i.											(10,000)				10,000		
j.			(300)													(300)	
k.				(7,000)												(7,000)	
l.												225				(225)	
m.						(2,000)										(2,000)	
n.	(7,500)																(7,500)
o.										5,500						(5,500)	

Required

a. Explain the transaction or event that resulted in each item recorded on the worksheet.

b. Did SummerFest Promotions generate net income or net loss for the fiscal year ended June 30, 2008? How can you tell?

c. Prepare the four financial statements at year-end.

Financial Statement Analysis

FSA3-1. (LO 2, 3, 4, 5)
Use the annual report from Staples to answer these questions:

a. Does Staples have any deferred expenses? What are they, and where are they shown?

b. Does Staples have accrued expenses? What are they, and where are they shown?

c. What is the difference between a deferred expense and an accrued expense?

d. Calculate the amount of working capital for the two most recent fiscal years. What information does this provide?

FSA3-2. (LO 2, 3, 4, 5)
Use Circuit City's balance sheet in Exhibit 3-17 on page 121 to answer these questions:

a. The current asset section shows prepaid expenses. What might these pertain to? Have the "expenses" referred to here been recognized (i.e., included on the period's income statement)?

b. The liabilities section shows accrued expenses. What does this represent? Have the associated expenses been recognized?

c. The liabilities section shows merchandise payable. Explain what this is and what Circuit City will do to satisfy this liability.

d. Calculate Circuit City's working capital at the balance sheet dates given. What information does this provide?

FSA3-3. (LO 2, 3, 4)
Use Carnival Corporation's balance sheet to answer these questions:

a. Which current asset reflects deferred expenses? Explain what it means to defer expenses, and give the adjustment to the accounting equation that was probably made to record this asset.

b. The liabilities section shows over $2 billion in customer deposits at November 30, 2005. Explain why this is a liability, and give the transaction (in the accounting equation) that resulted in this liability.

c. Calculate the current ratio for Carnival Corporation for both years shown. Comment on your results.

Carnival Corporation
Consolidated Balance Sheets
($ in millions, except par value)

	November 30, 2005	2004
Assets		
Current Assets		
Cash and cash equivalents	$ 1,178	$ 643
Short-term investments	9	17
Accounts receivable, net	408	409
Inventories	250	240
Prepaid expenses and other	370	419
Total current assets	2,215	1,728
Property and Equipment, Net	21,312	20,823
Goodwill	3,206	3,321
Trademarks	1,282	1,306
Other Assets	417	458
	$28,432	$27,636
Liabilities and Shareholder's Equity		
Current Liabilities		
Short-term borrowings	$300	$381
Current portion of long-term debt	1,042	681
Convertible debt subject to current put option	283	600
Accounts payable	690	631
Accrued liabilities and other	832	868
Customer deposits	2,045	1,873
Total current liabilities	5,192	5,034
Long-Term Debt	5,727	6,291
Other Long-Term Liabilities and Deferred Income	541	551
Commitments and Contingencies (Notes 7 and 8)		
Shareholder's Equity		
Common stock of Carnival Corporation; $.01 par value; 1,960 shares authorized; 639 shares at 2005 and 634 shares at 2004 issued	6	6
Ordinary shares of Carnival plc; $1.66 par value; 226 shares authorized; 212 shares at 2005 and 2004 issued	353	353
Additional paid-in capital	7,381	7,311
Retained earnings	10,233	8,623
Unearned stock compensation	(13)	(16)
Accumulated other comprehensive income	156	541
Treasury stock; 2 shares of Carnival Corporation at 2005 and 42 shares of Carnival plc at 2005 and 2004, at cost	(1,144)	(1,058)
Total shareholder's equity	16,972	15,760
Total liabilities and shareholders' equity	$28,432	$27,636

The accompanying notes are an integral part of these consolidated financial statements.

Critical Thinking Problems

Risk and Controls

Is there anything in the annual report of Staples, given in the book's appendix, that addresses how the firm protects its accounting data? Be sure to use the entire annual report to answer this question.

Ethics

DVD-Online Inc. is in its second year of business. The company is totally Web based, offering DVD rental to online customers for a fixed monthly fee. For $30 per month, a customer receives three DVDs each month, one at a time as the previous one is returned. No matter how many DVDs a customer uses (up to three), the fee is fixed at $30 per month. Customers sign a contract for a year, so DVD-Online recognizes $360 sales revenue each time a customer signs up for the service. The owner of DVD-Online, John Richards, has heard about GAAP, but he does not see any reason to follow these accounting principles. Although DVD-Online is not publicly traded, John does put the company's financial statements on the Web page for customers to see.

a. Explain how DVD-Online would account for its revenue if it did follow GAAP.
b. Explain to John Richards why he should use GAAP, and describe why his financial statements may now be misleading.
c. Do you see this as an ethical issue? Explain.

Group Problem

Use the balance sheet for Carnival Corporation shown in FSA 3-3. For each of the current assets and current liabilities, prepare a brief explanation of the nature of the item. For each current liability, explain how you think the company will satisfy the liability.

Internet Exercise: Darden

Please go to the www.prenhall.com/reimers Web site. Go to Chapter 3 and use the Internet Exercise company link. Or try www.dardenrestaurants.com.

IE3-1. If you were at a Darden property, what might you be doing? List two of the Darden chains.

IE3-2. Click on Investor Relations followed by Annual Report and Financials and then select the HTML version of the most recent annual report. Find the Balance Sheets under Financial Review by clicking next or using the "contents" scroll bar. Does Darden use a calendar year for its fiscal year? How can you tell?

IE3-3. Refer to the asset section.
a. List the title of one asset account that includes accrued revenue—amounts earned but not yet received in cash.
b. List the title of one asset account that includes amounts that have been paid for in cash but have not yet been expensed.
c. List the title of one asset account that includes amounts that will be depreciated.
d. For each account listed in a through c, identify the amount reported for the most recent year. Do these amounts still need adjusting? Explain why or why not.

IE3-4. List the amounts reported for total current assets and total current liabilities for the most recent year. Compute working capital. For Darden, what does the amount of working capital indicate?

IE3-5. For the two most recent years list the amounts reported for total assets, total liabilities, and total stockholders' equity. For each type of account, identify what the trend indicates. Does the accounting equation hold true both years?

Please note: Internet Web sites are constantly being updated. Therefore, if the information is not found where indicated, please explore the Web site further to find the information.

Acquisition and Use of Long-Term Operational Assets

Here's Where You've Been . . .

In Chapter 3, you learned:
- Accruals are transactions in which the exchange of cash comes after the exchange of the related goods and services.
- Deferrals are transactions in which the exchange of cash comes before the exchange of the related goods and services.

Both are part of accrual basis accounting.

Here's Where You're Going . . .

- You will learn to account for the purchase and use of buildings, manufacturing plants, equipment, natural resources, and intangible assets.
- You will learn how transactions related to long-term assets are presented on the financial statements.

Learning Objectives

When you are finished studying this chapter, you should be able to:

1. Explain how long-term assets are classified and how their cost is computed.

2. Explain and compute how tangible assets are written off over their useful lives and reported on the financial statements.

3. Explain and compute how intangible assets are written off over their useful lives and reported on the financial statements.

4. Explain how decreases in value, repairs, changes in productive capacity, and changes in estimates of useful life and salvage value of assets are reported on the financial statements.

5. Explain how the disposal of an asset is reflected in the financial statements.

6. Recognize and explain how long-term assets are reported on the financial statements, and prepare financial statements that include long-term assets.

7. Use return on assets (ROA) and the asset turnover ratio to help evaluate a firm's performance.

8. Identify and describe the business risks associated with long-term assets and the controls that can minimize those risks.

9. (Appendix) Explain how depreciation for financial statements differs from depreciation for taxes.

Ethics Matters

The bankruptcy of WorldCom in 2002 was the culmination of an $11 billion accounting fraud, the largest on record. Scott Sullivan, the former chief financial officer (CFO) received a 5-year prison sentence for his part in the fraud. Sentencing guidelines suggest 25 years for his crimes, but he was rewarded for his cooperation with government prosecutors in the case against former CEO Bernard Ebbers. Ebbers was sentenced to 25 years but is appealing both the conviction and the sentence.

Besides Sullivan and Ebbers, who will pay for the $11 billion fraud? Eleven former members of the WorldCom board of directors agreed to pay investors $20 million as partial compensation for the investors' losses. The directors will pay this money from their own pockets, in addition to any amounts paid by the insurance companies that provided liability insurance for the directors. The result of this type of settlement, similar to the agreement by the Enron directors to pay $13 million to investors, could be harmful to all investors in publicly traded companies. According to Daniel Akst, a writer for *The New York Times*, "it's hard to imagine a better system for driving away the kind of experienced, careful people you would want most to serve on any board."

So, who pays for frauds such as those at WorldCom and Enron? Employees, shareholders, and members of the board are just a few of the groups. ALL investors share the costs of the unethical behavior of corporate criminals in ways we are just beginning to recognize.

L.O.1
Explain how long-term assets are classified and how their cost is computed.

Acquiring Plant Assets

So far, you have studied the accounting cycle and know how transactions make their way to the financial statements. In this chapter, we will look at the purchase of long-term assets that are used in the operation of a business. Long-term assets purchased as investments or to resell are not considered *operational* assets, so the information in this chapter does not apply to them.

All businesses purchase long-term operational assets such as computers, copy machines, and furniture as well as short-term assets such as folders, paper, and pens. Acquiring long-term assets, often called fixed assets, is usually more complicated than acquiring short-term assets. Purchasing long-term assets is complex for several reasons. With long-term assets, a firm must put a great deal of care in selecting the vendor because the relationship could last for a significant amount of time. The monetary investment in long-term assets is typically much greater than the investment in short-term assets, and it is more difficult to dispose of long-term assets if the company makes a bad decision. For example, a new computer system for tracking inventory would cost a firm like Staples thousands of dollars more than the purchase of a new telephone for the employee lounge. If Staples' manager did not like the kind of phone that was purchased, it would be simple to give it away or donate it to the local Goodwill and buy another. What happens if the manager decides the wrong computerized inventory system was purchased? It is significantly harder to get rid of the long-term asset, and it could reflect poorly on the manager who made the decision to purchase the system in the first place.

Before a firm purchases a long-term asset, it must determine how much revenue that asset will generate and how much the asset will cost. The cost of a long-term asset must include all of the costs to get the asset ready for use. Long-term assets often require extensive setup and preparation before they become operational, and employees need to be trained to use them. If Staples purchases a new computerized inventory system, it may require new

> Capital expenditures are an important part of any firm's strategic plans. Wal-Mart spends billions of dollars every year to remodel and update its stores. In fact, in early 2006, Wal-Mart's budget for capital expenditures was estimated at $17 billion. Why would a firm spend that much money for renovations and remodeling? Sales growth at many of its stores has failed to keep pace with rivals such as Target, and Wal-Mart is determined to turn that trend around. Check out Wal-Mart's financial statements to see if the firm has actually carried out its ambitious plans.

hardware and software, and employees will need to be trained to use the new system. All of these costs will be recorded as part of the cost of the asset.

Considering all of these costs is part of the process of acquiring a long-term asset. Accountants then use these costs to account for the purchase and use of the asset. What assets to buy and how to pay for them are decisions that do not affect the income statement at the time of the purchase. Recording the purchase of a long-term asset affects the balance sheet and potentially the statement of cash flows. As you saw in Chapter 3, a business defers recognizing the expense of a long-term asset until the asset is actually used in the business. When the asset is used and the expense is recognized, the expense is called depreciation expense. This deferral is an example of a timing difference. We have purchased a long-term asset at one point in time in the past, and we will use that asset over a subsequent period of time.

Types of Long-Lived Assets: Tangible and Intangible

There are two categories of long-term assets: **tangible assets** and **intangible assets**. Exhibit 4.1 shows the long-term asset section of Staples' balance sheet, where you will see both types of long-term assets.

Common tangible assets are property, plant, and equipment (PPE). Common intangible assets are trademarks, patents, and copyrights. We will discuss these in detail later in the chapter.

> **Tangible assets** are assets with physical substance; they can be seen and touched.

> **Intangible assets** are rights, privileges, or benefits that result from owning long-lived assets that do not have physical substance.

Acquisition Costs

Consider the purchase of a long-term asset. The historical cost principle requires a company to record an asset at the amount paid for the asset—its cost. The cost for property, plant, and

From the Balance Sheet of Staples, Inc. (in thousands)	January 28, 2006	January 29, 2005
Property and equipment:		
Land and buildings	$ 705,978	$ 649,175
Leasehold improvements	884,853	762,946
Equipment	1,330,181	1,140,234
Furniture and fixtures	672,931	597,293
Total property and equipment	3,593,943	3,149,648
Less accumulated depreciation and amortization	1,835,549	1,548,774
Net property and equipment	1,758,394	1,600,874
Lease acquisition costs net of accumulated amortization	34,885	38,400
Intangible assets net of accumulated amortization	240,395	222,520
Goodwill	1,378,752	1,321,464
Other assets	119,619	106,578
Total long-term assets	$3,532,045	$3,289,836

These are *tangible* assets:

These are *intangible* assets:

EXHIBIT 4.1

From the Balance Sheet of Staples

You won't know the meaning of some terms Staples has used, but you will learn about them in this chapter.

equipment includes all expenditures that are reasonable and necessary to get an asset in place and ready for use. The reason for recording all of these costs on the balance sheet, as part of the cost of the asset, is to defer recognition of the expense until the asset is actually used to generate revenue. This is, as you know, the matching principle, which provides the foundation for accrual basis accounting. The assets are put on the balance sheet and then written off as expenses over the accounting periods in which they are used to generate revenue. The following are some common components of the cost of property, plant, and equipment.

1. When a firm purchases land to use as the location of a building or factory, the acquisition cost includes:
   a. Price paid for the land
   b. Real estate commissions
   c. Attorneys' fees
   d. Costs of preparing the land for use, such as clearing or draining
   e. Costs of tearing down existing structures
   In general, land is not depreciated. Because land typically retains its usefulness and is not consumed to produce revenue, its cost remains unchanged on the balance sheet as a long-term asset. Even if the land's value increases, financial statements will show the land at cost.
2. When a firm purchases a physical plant, the acquisition cost includes:
   a. Purchase cost of buildings or factories
   b. Costs to update or remodel the facilities
   c. Any other costs to get the plant operational
3. When a firm purchases equipment, the acquisition cost includes:
   a. Purchase cost
   b. Freight-in—cost to have the equipment delivered
   c. Insurance while in transit
   d. Installation costs, including test runs
   e. Cost of training employees to use the new equipment
4. When a firm constructs or renovates a building, the acquisition cost includes:
   a. Architects' or contractors' fees
   b. Construction costs
   c. Cost of renovating or repairing the building

In contrast to the accounting treatment of land, even if a firm expects a building to increase in value, the asset will be depreciated. In practice, most assets used in a business to generate revenues will decrease in value as they are used. Recall that depreciation is not meant to value an asset at its market value. Rather, it is the systematic allocation of the cost of an asset to the periods in which the asset is used by the firm to generate revenue.

Your Turn 4-1
Your Turn
Your Turn

For each of the following costs, tell whether it should be recorded as an asset or recorded as an expense at the time of the transaction.
1. Payment for employee salaries
2. Purchase of new delivery truck
3. Rent paid in advance
4. Rent paid in arrears (after use of the building)

Relative fair market value method is a way to allocate the total cost for several assets purchased together to each of the individual assets. This method is based on the assets' individual market values.

Basket Purchase Allocation

Calculating the acquisition cost of certain assets can be difficult. Buying a building with the land it occupies is an example of a "basket purchase" because two assets are acquired for a single price. For the accounting records, the firm must calculate a separate cost for each asset. Why? The firm will depreciate the building but it will not depreciate the land. The firm divides the purchase price between the building and land by using the **relative fair market**

UNDERSTANDING **Business**

Lease or Buy?

Generally accepted accounting principles (GAAP) try to make sure the financial statements reflect the substance of a company's transactions instead of the form of the transaction. Because a company's financial statements are so important to investors, creditors, and anyone who wants to evaluate a company's performance, how a transaction is reflected on those statements is very important to the company. Sometimes recording a transaction based on its substance may not be very appealing. A classic example is buying or leasing long-term assets. When a company buys an asset, it is shown on the balance sheet, and any amount that the company owes for the purchase of the asset must be shown on the balance sheet as a liability.

Suppose a company does not want to put any additional liabilities on its balance sheet. Then would a company lease an asset instead of buying it? Could the company simply record the expense of leasing the asset as the lease payments are made? If the form of the transaction is a lease but the substance is more like a purchase, the lease is called a capital lease, and GAAP says the transaction must be recorded like a purchase. In other words, a company cannot "hide" future financial commitments related to long-term leases by calling the transaction a lease and simply recognizing the expense when the payments are made. That means the company must record the asset on the balance sheet and also record the related long-term obligation of the future lease payments as a liability. Then the asset is de-

preciated, just like any other depreciable asset owned by the company.

The accounting standards have very specific rules about how to account for long-term leases. The criteria for deciding if a lease qualifies as a capital lease are very technical, numerous, and highly debated and discussed by standards-setting boards such as the Financial Accounting Standards Board (FASB) and the Securities and Exchange Commission (SEC). An accountant comes in handy when this issue comes up.

In the long-term assets section of a company's balance sheet, you will often see items called capitalized leases or leasehold improvements. Capitalized leases represent assets a company has, in substance, bought but the form of the purchase is a lease. Leasehold improvements are long-term assets in the form of additions and improvements to leased property. For example, if a company remodels the interior of a leased office building, the cost of the remodeling will be called leasehold improvements.

A company decides whether to lease an asset or to purchase an asset based on business factors such as (1) the type of asset and the risk of obsolescence, (2) the interest rate of the lease payments compared with the interest rate of a purchase, (3) the lease's renewal and purchase options, (4) the acceptable alterations to leased assets, and (5) the estimated useful life of the leased asset to the business. However, the accounting treatment should not influence the economic decision. It goes the other way—the economic decision influences the accounting treatment.

---

value method. Suppose a company purchased a building and its land together for one price of $100,000. The company would obtain a market price, usually in the form of an appraisal, for each item separately. Then, the company uses the relative amounts of the individual appraisals to divide the purchase price of $100,000 between the two assets. Suppose the building appraised at $90,000 and the land appraised at $30,000. The total appraised value is $120,000 ($90,000 + $30,000).

The building accounts for three-quarters of the total appraised value.

$$\$90,000 \div \$120,000 = 3/4$$

So, the accountant records the building at three-fourths of the total cost of the basket purchase.

$$3/4 \times \$100,000 = \$75,000$$

The cost assigned to the land will be the remaining $25,000.

$$\$100,000 - \$75,000 = \$25,000$$

Or if you want to calculate it,

$$1/4 \times \$100,000 = \$25,000$$

This same method—using an asset's proportion of the total appraised value of a group of assets—can be used for any number of assets purchased together for a single price.

Your Turn 4-2
Your Turn
Your Turn

Bargain Company paid $480,000 for a building and the land on which it is located. Independent appraisals valued the building at $400,000 and the land at $100,000. How much should Bargain Company record as the cost of the building and how much as the cost of the land? Why does the company need to record the costs separately?

L.O.2
Explain and compute how tangible assets are written off over their useful lives and reported on the financial statements.

To **capitalize** is to record a cost as an asset rather than to record it as an expense.

Amortization means to write off the cost of a long-term asset over more than one accounting period.

Depreciation is a systematic and rational allocation process to recognize the expense of long-term assets over the periods in which the assets are used.

Depletion is the amortization of a natural resource.

Using Long-Term Tangible Assets: Depreciation and Depletion

Now that you are familiar with the types of assets a firm may have and the costs associated with their acquisition, we are ready to talk about using the assets. Until property, plant, and equipment are put into use, their costs remain as assets on the balance sheet. As soon as the firm uses the asset to help generate revenue, the financial statements will show some amount of expense on the income statement. Recording a cost as an asset, rather than recording it as an expense, is called **capitalizing** the cost. That cost will be recognized as an expense during the periods in which the asset is used. Recall from Chapter 3 that depreciation is a systematic and rational allocation process to recognize the expense of long-term assets over the periods in which the assets are used. Depreciation is an example of the matching principle—matching the cost of an asset with the revenue it helps generate. For each year a company plans to use an asset, the company will recognize depreciation expense on the income statement.

If you hear or read, "The asset is worth $10,000 on our books," that does not mean the asset is actually worth that amount if it were sold. Instead, it means that $10,000 is the carrying value or book value of the asset in the accounting records—it is the amount not yet depreciated. It is called the carrying value because that is the amount at which we carry our assets on the balance sheet. The amount not yet depreciated is also known as the book value because it is the value of the asset on the accounting records. As you read about the specific methods of depreciating assets, refer to the vocabulary of depreciation in Exhibit 4.2.

Accountants primarily use three terms to describe how a cost is written off over several accounting periods. **Amortization** is the most general expression for writing off the cost of a long-term asset. **Depreciation** is the specific word that describes the amortization of certain kinds of property, plant, or equipment. **Depletion** is the specific term that describes the amortization of a natural resource. There is no specific term for writing off intangible assets, so accountants use the general term *amortization* to describe writing off the cost of intangible assets.

All of these terms—amortization, depreciation, and depletion—refer to allocating the cost of an asset to more than one accounting period.

Accountants use several methods of depreciation for the financial statements. We will discuss three of the most common:

1. Straight-line depreciation
2. Activity (units-of-production) depreciation
3. Declining balance depreciation

EXHIBIT 4.2

Depreciation Terminology

Term	Definition	Example
Cost or **acquisition cost**	The amount paid for the asset, including all amounts necessary to get the asset up and running	Staples purchases computer cash registers for its new store for $21,000.
Estimated useful life	How long the company plans to use the asset; may be measured in years or in units that the asset will produce	Staples plans to use these cash registers for 10 years.
Salvage value or **residual value**	Estimated value the asset will have when the company is done with it—the salvage value is the estimated market value on the anticipated disposal date	When Staples is done using the cash registers, the company plans to sell them for $1,000.
Depreciable base	*Cost* minus *salvage value*	The depreciable base is $21,000 − $1,000 = $20,000.
Book value or **carrying value**	*Cost* less *total depreciation* taken to date	If Staples uses the straight-line method, the company's depreciation expense will be $2,000 per year. After the first year, the book value will be $19,000 (= $21,000 − $2,000).

For each of the following, give the term for writing off the cost of the asset.
1. Equipment
2. Building
3. Oil well

Your Turn 4-3
Your Turn
Your Turn

Straight-Line Depreciation

Straight-line depreciation is the simplest way to allocate the cost of an asset to the periods in which the asset is used. This is the method we used in Chapter 3. Using this method, the depreciation expense is the same every period. To calculate the appropriate amount of depreciation expense for each accounting period, you follow several steps.

First, you must estimate the useful life of the asset. The firm should consider this estimate when purchasing an asset and use the estimate after the purchase to properly account for the cost of that asset.

Second, you estimate the **salvage value**, the amount you believe the asset will be worth when the company is finished using it. Salvage value is the amount you think someone will pay you for the used asset. Someone who knows a lot about the asset and the relationship between the use of the asset and its market value will estimate the salvage value. Salvage value is an estimate that you may need to revise more than once during the life of the asset.

Straight-line depreciation is a depreciation method in which the depreciation expense is the same each period.

Salvage value (also known as *residual value*) is the estimated value of an asset at the end of its useful life.

The useful life and the salvage value are related, and the firm should have made these estimates as part of the acquisition decision.

Third, you calculate the depreciable base—the amount you want to depreciate—by deducting the salvage value from the acquisition cost of the asset. This calculation gives the depreciable base.

Fourth, you divide the depreciable base—the difference between the asset's cost and its estimated salvage value—by the estimate of the number of years of the asset's useful life. This gives you the annual depreciation expense.

$$[\text{Acquisition cost} - \text{Salvage value}] \div \text{Estimated useful life in years}$$
$$= \text{Annual depreciation expense}$$

We will use an orange juice machine purchased by Holiday Hotels to demonstrate all of the depreciation methods. Exhibit 4.3 summarizes the information we need for all three depreciation methods.

Suppose Holiday Hotels purchases a new squeeze-your-own orange juice machine for its self-service breakfast bar. Such a machine is expensive and requires large supplies of fresh oranges. After considering the risks and rewards of purchasing the machine and evaluating the effect such a purchase would have on the financial statements, Holiday Hotels decides to purchase an $11,500 machine with an estimated useful life of 6 years. In addition to the invoice price of $11,500, delivery and installation costs amount to $1,000. Holiday will capitalize these costs as part of the acquisition cost of the asset. Holiday estimates that the machine will have a salvage value of $500 at the end of 6 years. After someone in the firm who is knowledgeable about the characteristics of the asset reviews and confirms the judgments about useful life and salvage value, Holiday will calculate the yearly depreciation expense.

First, Holiday calculates the depreciable base by subtracting the salvage value from the cost.

$$\text{Cost} = \$11,500 + \$1,000 = \$12,500$$
$$\text{Salvage value} = \$500$$
$$\text{Depreciable base} = \$12,500 - \$500 = \$12,000$$

EXHIBIT 4.3

Holiday Hotel's Orange Juice Machine

Cost	$11,500 invoice price + 1,000 delivery and installation costs $12,500
Useful life	6 years
Salvage value	$500
Estimated production during its useful life	240,000 glasses of juice

Then, Holiday divides the depreciable base by the number of years of useful life.

Annual depreciation expense = $12,000/6 years = $2,000 per year

Each year the income statement will include depreciation expense of $2,000, and each year the carrying value of the asset will be reduced by $2,000. This reduction in carrying value is accumulated over the life of the asset, so that the carrying value decreases each year. A company's accounting records always preserve the acquisition cost of the asset and disclose the cost on the balance sheet or in the notes, so Holiday will keep the total accumulated depreciation in a separate account and subtract it from the acquisition cost of the asset on the balance sheet. If Holiday bought the machine on January 1, 2006, and the company's fiscal year ends on December 31, then the income statement for the year ended December 31, 2006, would include depreciation expense of $2,000. The balance sheet would show the acquisition cost—$12,500—and the accumulated depreciation at December 31, 2006—$2,000. This is how the adjustment for depreciation expense would look in the accounting equation:

Assets	=	Liabilities	+	Shareholder's equity	
				Contributed capital	+ Retained earnings
Accumulated depreciation— Equipment (2,000)					Depreciation expense (2,000)

The equipment account will have a balance of $12,500 during the entire life of the asset. The accumulated depreciation account will have a balance of $2,000 after the 2006 depreciation is recorded. Here is how the asset is reported on the balance sheet at December 31, 2006:

	December 31, 2006
Equipment	$12,500
Less accumulated depreciation	(2,000)
Net book value	$10,500

In the following year, 2007, the income statement for the year would again include $2,000 depreciation expense. The straight-line method gets its name from the fact that the same amount is depreciated each year, so the depreciation expense could be graphed as a straight horizontal line across the life of the asset. The adjustment at the end of 2007 will be identical to the adjustment at the end of 2006. It will add $2,000 to the accumulated depreciation account, so the new balance is $4,000. Because the income statement is only for a single year, the depreciation expense will again be $2,000. The balance sheet at December 31, 2007, would show how the carrying value of our asset is declining, because on that date Holiday has used it for 2 years.

	December 31, 2007
Equipment	$12,500
Less accumulated depreciation	(4,000)
Net book value	$ 8,500

Exhibit 4.4 shows the depreciation expense and accumulated depreciation amounts for the year-end financial statements during the entire life of the asset. At the end of the useful life of the asset, the carrying value will equal the salvage value. Holiday has previously estimated that it could sell the asset at the end of its useful life for a price equal to its carrying value—$500.

EXHIBIT 4.4

Straight-Line Depreciation

The depreciation expense each year is always $2,000, as shown in the table and accompanying graph. The carrying value decreases over time, from $10,500 at December 31, 2006 to $500 at December 31, 2011.

Year	Depreciation Expense on the Income Statement	Accumulated Depreciation on Year-End Balance Sheet	Carrying or Book Value on the Year-End Balance Sheet
2006	$2,000	$ 2,000	$10,500
2007	$2,000	$ 4,000	$ 8,500
2008	$2,000	$ 6,000	$ 6,500
2009	$2,000	$ 8,000	$ 4,500
2010	$2,000	$10,000	$ 2,500
2011	$2,000	$12,000	$ 500

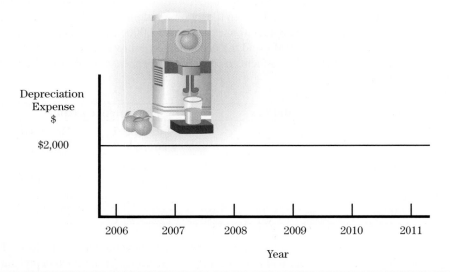

Your Turn 4-4
Your Turn
Your Turn

On January 1, 2006, Access Company purchased a new computer system for $15,000. The estimated useful life of the computer system was 5 years, with an estimated salvage value of $3,000. Using straight-line depreciation, how much depreciation expense will Access Company include on the income statement for the year ended December 31, 2007? Determine the book value of the asset on December 31, 2007.

Activity (Units-of-Production) Depreciation

Another way a firm determines depreciation expense is by estimating the productivity of the asset—how much the asset will produce during its useful life. How many units will the asset produce, or how much work will the asset do during its useful life? This way of determining depreciation expense is called the **activity method**, also known as the units-of-production method. Examples of activities are miles driven or units produced. If a company buys a car, it may decide to use it for 100,000 miles before trading it in. The activity method is similar to the straight-line method. The difference is that an estimate of the number of units of activity over the asset's life is used as the allocation base instead of an estimate of the number of years of useful life.

> **Activity method depreciation** is the method of depreciation in which useful life is expressed in terms of the total units of activity or production expected from the asset, and the asset is written off in proportion to its activity during the accounting period.

$$\frac{\text{Acquisition cost} - \text{Salvage value}}{\text{Estimate useful life in activity units}} = \text{Rate per activity unit}$$

$$\text{Rate} \times \text{Actual activity level for the year} = \text{Annual depreciation expense}$$

To use the activity method, Holiday needs to estimate how many units the machine will be able to produce during its useful life. Suppose Holiday estimates the machine will be able to produce 240,000 glasses of juice during its useful life. You calculate the depreciable base in exactly the same way when using activity depreciation as when using straight-line depreciation—subtract the expected salvage value from the cost. In this example, the depreciable base is $12,000 ($12,500 − $500). You then divide the depreciable base by the total number of units you expect to produce with the machine during its useful life.

Here is how the activity method of depreciation can be applied to Holiday's orange juice machine. Start by dividing the depreciable base—$12,000—by the estimated number of glasses of orange juice the machine will produce. That gives the depreciation rate.

$$\$12,000 \div 240,000 \text{ glasses} = \$0.05 \text{ per glass}$$

Holiday will use this rate of $0.05 per glass to depreciate the machine for each glass of juice it produces. Suppose the machine has a built-in counter that showed 36,000 glasses of juice were squeezed during the first year. The depreciation expense shown on the income statement for that year would be $1,800.

$$36,000 \text{ glasses} \times \$0.05 \text{ per glass} = \$1,800 \text{ depreciation expense}$$

That is the depreciation expense for the year, and the book value of the asset would decline by that amount during the year. It is important to keep a record of the book value of the asset so that Holiday Hotels does not depreciate the asset lower than its $500 estimated salvage value. The salvage value will equal the carrying value when the asset has reached the end of Holiday's estimate of the useful life.

Exhibit 4.5 shows the depreciation schedule for the orange juice machine, given the production levels for each year as shown.

EXHIBIT 4.5

Activity Depreciation

Year	Production Each Year— Number of Glasses of Orange Juice	Depreciation Rate × Number of Glasses of Juice *Rate: $0.05 per Glass	Depreciation Expense (Income Statement)	Accumulated Depreciation (Balance Sheet at the End of the Year)	Book Value of the Asset (Balance Sheet at the End of the Year)
2006	36,000	$0.05 × 36,000	$1,800	$ 1,800	$10,700
2007	41,000	$0.05 × 41,000	$2,050	$ 3,850	$ 8,650
2008	39,000	$0.05 × 39,000	$1,950	$ 5,800	$ 6,700
2009	46,000	$0.05 × 46,000	$2,300	$ 8,100	$ 4,400
2010	43,000	$0.05 × 43,000	$2,150	$10,250	$ 2,250
2011	35,000	$0.05 × 35,000	$1,750	$12,000	$ 500

Cost of machine of $12,500 minus salvage value of $500, gives a depreciable base of $12,000.
Total estimated production is 240,000 glasses.
*Rate = $12,000 ÷ 240,000 = $0.05 per glass.

With the activity depreciation method, the depreciation expense each year depends on how many units the asset produces each year. This method matches the expense to the amount of work performed by the asset. Although the book value is decreasing each year, the amount of depreciation expense will likely vary from year-to-year, as shown in both the table and graph. As always, accumulated depreciation is working its way up until it reaches the depreciable base—cost minus salvage value. That means the book value will be equal to the estimated salvage value at the end of its useful life.

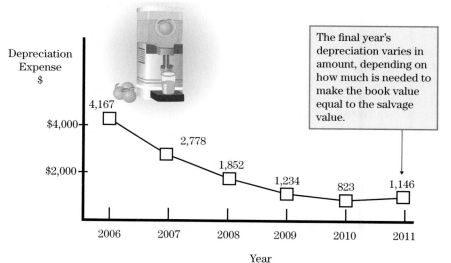

The final year's depreciation varies in amount, depending on how much is needed to make the book value equal to the salvage value.

Your Turn 4-5
Your Turn
Your Turn

Hopper Company purchased equipment on January 1, 2005, for $44,000. The expected useful life is 10 years or 100,000 units of activity, and its salvage value is estimated at $4,000. In 2005, 3,000 units were produced, and in 2006, 14,000 units were produced. Calculate the depreciation expense for 2005 and 2006 using activity depreciation.

Declining balance depreciation is an accelerated depreciation method in which depreciation expense is based on the declining book value of the asset.

Accelerated depreciation is a depreciation method in which more depreciation expense is taken in the early years of the asset's life and less in the later years.

Declining Balance Depreciation

You have learned about the straight-line depreciation method and the activity depreciation method. The third method is **declining balance depreciation**. This method is considered an **accelerated depreciation** method, one that allows more depreciation in the early years of an asset's life and less in the later years. The higher depreciation charges will occur in the early, more productive years when the equipment is generating more revenue. Depreciating more of the asset in the first few years also helps even out the total expenses related to an asset. In later years, the depreciation expense is lower but repair expenses are likely to be increasing.

The declining balance method speeds up an asset's depreciation by applying a constant rate to the declining book value of an asset. Frequently, firms use a version of the declining balance method called double-declining balance. The firm takes 200% of the straight-line rate to use as the annual depreciation rate. For example, if the useful life of an asset were 5 years, the straight-line rate would be one-fifth, or 20%. That is because 20% of the asset would be depreciated each year for 5 years using straight-line depreciation. The rate used for double-declining balance depreciation would be 40%, which is 200%, or twice, the straight-line rate. Here is how this method works and why it is called double-declining balance. Every year, the accountant depreciates the carrying value, or book value, of the asset by an amount equal to two divided by the useful life in years.

$$\text{Book value} \times (2/\text{Estimated useful life in years}) = \text{Yearly expense}$$

An example will help you see how this method works. Suppose the useful life of an asset is 4 years. The double-declining rate would be

$$2 \div 4 \text{ years} = 1/2$$

Alternatively, you could calculate the straight-line rate and then double it.

$$100\% \div 4 \text{ years} = 25\% \text{ per year} = \text{Straight-line rate}$$
$$\text{Double it: } 50\% = \text{Double-declining balance rate}$$

Using this depreciation method for Holiday Hotel's orange juice machine, the book value at the beginning of the first year is $12,500—its acquisition cost. Notice that the calculation of the annual depreciation expense ignores any salvage value because book value equals cost minus accumulated depreciation. Recall that the useful life of the juice machine is 6 years. So the depreciation rate is

$$2 \div 6 \text{ years} = 1/3$$

The depreciation expense for the first year is

$$1/3 \times \$12,500 = \$4,167$$

The book value on the balance sheet at December 31, 2006, will be

$$\$12,500 - \$4,167 = \$8,333$$

For the second year, the accountant again calculates the amount of depreciation as one-third of the *book value* (not the *cost*). For the second year, the depreciation expense is

$$1/3 \times \$8,333 = \$2,778 \text{ (rounded)}$$

The accumulated depreciation at the end of the second year is

$$\$4,167 + \$2,778 = \$6,945$$

The book value on the December 31, 2007, balance sheet is

$$\$12,500 - \$6,945 = \$5,555$$

Although salvage value is ignored in the calculation of each year's expense, you must always keep the salvage value in mind so that the book value of the asset is never lower than its salvage value. Exhibit 4.6 shows how Holiday Hotel's orange juice machine would be depreciated using double-declining balance depreciation.

Sometimes depreciation expense for the last year of the asset's useful life is more than the amount calculated by multiplying the book value by the double-declining rate, and sometimes it is less. When the asset has a large salvage value, the depreciation expense in the last year of the asset's must be less than the amount calculated using the double-declining depreciation rate and the carrying value. When the asset has no salvage value, the depreciation expense in the last year must be more than the calculated amount. The last year's depreciation expense will be the amount needed to get the book value of the asset equal to the salvage value.

EXHIBIT 4.6

Double-Declining-Balance Depreciation

Year	Depreciation Rate = 1/3 or 33.333%	Book Value Before Depreciating the Asset for the Year	Depreciation Expense for the Year	Accumulated Depreciation (At the End of the Year)	Book Value at the End of the Year: $12,500– Accumulated Depreciation
2006	.33333	$12,500	$4,167	$ 4,167	$8,333
2007	.33333	$ 8,333	$2,778	$ 6,945	$5,555
2008	.33333	$ 5,555	$1,852	$ 8,797	$3,703
2009	.33333	$ 3,703	$1,234	$10,031	$2,469
2010	.33333	$ 2,469	$ 823	$10,854	$1,646
2011	.33333	$ 1,646	$1,146*	$12,000	$ 500**

*The calculation of (0.33333 × $1,646) indicates depreciation expense of $549. Because this is the last year of its useful life and the book value after this year's depreciation should be $500, the depreciation expense must be $1,146 to bring the total accumulated depreciation to $12,000.

**The depreciation expense for Year 6 must be calculated to make this the book value at the end of the useful life—because the book value should be the estimated salvage value.

With double-declining depreciation, depreciation expense is larger in the early years of the asset's life and smaller in the later years. The book value is decreasing at a decreasing rate. Still, the balance in Accumulated Depreciation is working its way up until it reaches the cost minus salvage value. A firm always wants the book value of the asset to be equal to the estimated salvage value at the end of its useful life.

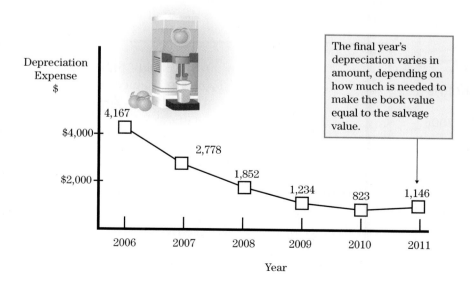

Depreciation Expense $

The final year's depreciation varies in amount, depending on how much is needed to make the book value equal to the salvage value.

4,167

$4,000

2,778

1,852

$2,000

1,234

823

1,146

2006   2007   2008   2009   2010   2011

Year

EXHIBIT 4.7

Depreciation Methods

Method	Formula for Depreciation Expense
Straight line	$\dfrac{\text{Acquisition cost} - \text{Salvage value}}{\text{Estimated useful life in years}} = \text{Yearly depreciation expense}$
Activity	$\dfrac{\text{Acquisition cost} - \text{Salvage value}}{\text{Estimated useful life in activity units}} = \text{Unit depreciation rate}$ $\text{Rate} \times \text{Actual activity level for the year} = \text{Yearly depreciation expense}$
Double-declining balance	$\text{Beginning-of-the-year book value} \times (2/\text{Estimated useful life in years}) = \text{Yearly depreciation expense}$

EXHIBIT 4.8

Comparison of Depreciation Expense by Year over the Life of the Orange Juice Machine for Holiday Hotels

Notice that the annual depreciation expense differs among the three methods, but the total depreciation expense taken over the life of asset is the same for all methods.

Year	Straight Line	Activity	Double-Declining Balance
2006	$ 2,000	$ 1,800	$ 4,167
2007	$ 2,000	$ 2,050	$ 2,778
2008	$ 2,000	$ 1,950	$ 1,852
2009	$ 2,000	$ 2,300	$ 1,234
2010	$ 2,000	$ 2,150	$ 823
2011	$ 2,000	$ 1,750	$ 1,146
Total depreciation expense during the life of the asset	$12,000	$12,000	$12,000

Exhibit 4.7 summarizes the calculations for the three depreciation methods.

Over the useful life of the asset, the same total depreciation expense will be recognized no matter which method is used. Exhibit 4.8 compares the depreciation expense of the orange juice machine with the three different depreciation methods.

Your Turn 4-6
Your Turn
Your Turn

An asset costs $50,000, has an estimated salvage value of $5,000, and has a useful life of 5 years. Calculate the amount of depreciation expense for the second year using the double-declining balance method.

Depletion. Now that you know how equipment and similar kinds of fixed assets are written off using various depreciation methods, we turn our attention to the way natural resources are written off. When a company uses a natural resource to obtain benefits for the operation of its business, the write-off of the asset is called depletion. For example, Cleveland-Cliffs, the largest producer of iron ore pellets in North America, uses depletion to expense iron ore. The company shows depreciation and depletion together on the balance sheet. Exhibit 4.9 shows the fixed asset portion of the firm's balance sheet.

EXHIBIT 4.9

Fixed Assets from Cleveland-Cliffs Balance Sheet at December 31, 2005

Cleveland-Cliffs
From the Balance Sheet
December 31, 2005
(in millions)

Properties
Plant and equipment $557.50
Minerals 421.80
979.30
Allowances* for depreciation and depletion .... (176.50)
Total properties $802.80

*This is another way of expressing "accumulated" depreciation and depletion amounts.

Often, all amounts of depreciation, depletion, and amortization are captured in a single total on the balance sheet.

Depletion is similar to the activity depreciation method, but it applies only to writing off the cost of natural resources. Examples of such natural resources are land being used for oil wells and mines. A depletion cost per unit is calculated by dividing the cost of the natural resource less any salvage value by the estimated units of activity or output available from that natural resource. The depletion cost per unit is then multiplied by the units pumped, mined, or cut per period to determine the total depletion related to the activity during the period.

Suppose that, on January 1, 2005, a company purchases the rights to an oil well in Texas for $100,000, estimating the well will produce 200,000 barrels of oil during its life. The depletion rate per barrel is:

$$\$100,000 \div 200,000 \text{ barrels} = \$0.50 \text{ per barrel}$$

If 50,000 barrels are produced in the year 2005, then the depletion related to the 50,000 barrels produced in 2005 will be:

$$\$0.50 \text{ per barrel} \times 50,000 \text{ barrels} = \$25,000$$

On the December 31, 2005, balance sheet, the book value of the oil rights will be:

$$\$100,000 - \$25,000 = \$75,000$$

Using Intangible Assets: Amortization

L.O.3
Explain and compute how intangible assets are written off over their useful lives and reported on the financial statements.

In addition to tangible assets, most firms have intangible assets, which are rights, privileges, or benefits that result from owning long-lived assets. Intangible assets have long-term value to the firm, but they are not visible or touchable. Their value resides in the rights and privileges given to the owners of the asset. These rights are often represented by contracts. Like tangible assets, they are recorded at cost, which includes all of the costs a firm incurs to obtain the asset.

If an intangible asset has an indefinite useful life, the asset is not amortized. However, the firm will periodically evaluate the asset for any permanent decline in value and then write it down if necessary. The idea here is that the balance sheet should include any asset that has future value to produce revenue for the firm, but the asset should never be valued at more than its fair value. Writing down an asset because of a permanent decline in value means reducing the amount of the asset and recording a loss that will go on the income statement.

Intangible assets that have a limited life are written off over their useful life or legal life, whichever is shorter, using straight-line amortization. That means an equal amount is expensed each year. Firms use an accumulated amortization account for each intangible asset because the accumulated amortization must be reported. Accumulated depreciation and accumulated amortization are often added together for the balance sheet presentation. Firms often have one or more intangible assets.

Copyrights

Copyright is a form of legal protection for authors of "original works of authorship," provided by U.S. law. When you hear the term copyright, you probably think of written works such as books and magazine articles. Copyright protection extends beyond written works to musical and artistic works and is available to both published and unpublished works. According to the 1976 Copyright Act, the owner of the copyright can

A **copyright** is a form of legal protection for authors of "original works of authorship," provided by U.S. law.

- copy the work
- use the work to prepare related material
- distribute copies of the work to the public by sale, rental, or lending
- perform the work publicly, in the case of literary, musical, dramatic, and choreographic works

• perform the work publicly by means of a digital audio transmission, in the case of sound recordings

All costs to obtain and defend copyrights are part of the cost of the asset. Copyrights are amortized using straight-line amortization over their legal life or their useful life, whichever is shorter.

Patents

A **patent** is a property right that the U.S. government grants to an inventor "to exclude others from making, using, offering for sale, or selling the invention throughout the United States or importing the invention into the United States for a specified period of time in exchange for public disclosure of the invention when the patent is granted." For example, Micron Technology filed for a patent for a computer memory device in February 2004. IBM obtained a patent for a vibration-driven wireless network in April 2000. Did you know that universities apply for hundreds of patents each year for their inventions? In 2004, the University of California applied for 424 patents—more patents than any other university.

As with copyrights, costs to defend patents are *capitalized* as part of the cost of the asset. Patents are amortized using straight-line amortization over their useful life or legal life, whichever is shorter. For example, most patents have a legal life of 20 years. However, a company may believe the useful life of a patent is less than that. If the company believes the patent will provide value for only 10 years, the company should use the shorter time period for amortizing the asset.

Trademarks

A **trademark** is a symbol, word, phrase, or logo that legally distinguishes one company's product from any others. One of the most recognized trademarks is Nike's swoosh symbol. In many cases, trademarks are not amortized because their useful lives are indefinite. Registering a trademark with the U.S. Patent and Trademark Office provides 10 years of protection, renewable as long as the trademark is in use.

Franchises

A **franchise** is an agreement that authorizes someone to sell or distribute a company's goods or services in a certain area. The initial cost of buying a franchise is the franchise fee, and this is the intangible asset that is capitalized. It is amortized over the life of the franchise if there is a limited life. If the life of the franchise is indefinite, it will not be amortized. In addition to the initial fee, franchise owners pay an ongoing fee to the company that is usually a percentage of sales. You might be surprised at some of the top franchises for 2005. They include Subway, Curves, and Quiznos.

Goodwill

Goodwill is the excess of cost over market value of the net assets when one company purchases another company. When the term *goodwill* is used in everyday conversation, it refers to favorable qualities. However, when you see goodwill on a company's balance sheet, you know that it is a result of purchasing another company for more than the fair market value of its net assets. Goodwill is an advanced topic for intermediate or advanced accounting courses. However, you should have a general understanding of goodwill because it appears on the balance sheet of many firms.

Suppose that The Home Depot purchased Pop's Hardware store for $950,000. The inventory and building—all of Pop's assets—were appraised at $750,000; and the small hardware store had no debt. Why would The Home Depot pay more than the market value for the net tangible assets of Pop's Hardware? Pop's Hardware store had been in business for many years, and the store had a terrific location and a loyal customer base. All of this is goodwill that Pop's had developed over years of business. GAAP does not allow a company to recognize its internally developed goodwill, so Pop's financial statements do not include goodwill. Now that The Home Depot has decided to purchase Pop's Hardware, however, the goodwill will be recorded. Here is how the transaction affects the accounting equation for Home Depot:

Assets	=	Liabilities	+	Shareholder's equity		
				Contributed capital	+	**Retained earnings**
(950,000) Cash						
750,000 Various assets						
200,000 Goodwill						

What happens to the intangible asset goodwill? Goodwill is not amortized because it is assumed to have an indefinite life. Even though goodwill is not amortized, companies must evaluate goodwill to make sure it is not overvalued on the balance sheet. Goodwill that has lost some of its value must be written down—that is, the asset is reduced and a loss is recorded. You can read about a firm's goodwill in the notes to the financial statements.

Research and Development Costs

Research and development (R&D) costs have benefits to the firm—at least that is the goal of R&D. However, R&D costs are expensed and are not capitalized as part of the cost of an asset because it is not clear that these costs represent something of value. Software development costs are considered research costs until they result in a product that is technologically feasible, so these costs must also be expensed as they are incurred. However, once the software is considered technologically feasible, the costs incurred from that point on are capitalized as part of the cost of the software. Deciding when a piece of software is technologically feasible is another example of how firms need to use judgment when making accounting decisions. The firm's developers and computer experts would make this judgment.

Changes after the Purchase of the Asset

We started the chapter with a discussion of the types and costs of long-term assets. Then, we discussed how the accounting records show the firm's use of those assets. Now we discuss how to adjust financial statements to record three things that may take place after an asset has been in use. First, the asset may lose value due to circumstances outside the firm's control. Second, the firm may make expenditures to maintain or improve the asset during its useful life. And third, the firm may need to revise its prior estimates of an asset's estimated life and salvage value.

L.O.4
Explain how decreases in value, repairs, changes in productive capacity, and changes in estimates of useful life and salvage value of assets are reported on the financial statements.

Asset Impairment

By now you know that accountants want to avoid overstating assets on the balance sheet or revenue on the income statement. A firm that is getting ready to prepare its financial statements must evaluate its long-term assets, including goodwill and other intangible assets, for **impairment**—a permanent reduction in the fair market value of an asset below its book value—if certain changes have occurred. Such changes include

Impairment is a permanent decline in the fair market value of an asset such that its book value exceeds its fair market value.

1. A downturn in the economy that causes a significant decrease in the market value of a long-lived asset
2. A change in how the company uses an asset
3. A change in the business climate that could affect the asset's value

An asset is considered impaired when the book value of the asset or group of assets is greater than its fair market value. Impairment is not easy to measure, but you will read about it in the notes to almost every set of financial statements. Because testing an asset for impairment can be quite difficult, it is a topic reserved for more advanced courses. However, you should be familiar with the terminology because you will see it in almost every annual report.

EXHIBIT 4.10

Disclosure About Asset Impairment in Darden Restaurants' Notes to the Financial Statements
The Notes to the Financial Statements provide important information about the amounts in the financial statements.

> From the Notes to the Financial Statements
> of Darden Restaurants, Inc.

In the fourth quarter of fiscal 2004, we recognized asset impairment charges of $37 million ($23 million after-tax) for the closing of six Bahama Breeze restaurants and the write-down of four other Bahama Breeze restaurants, one Olive Garden restaurant and one Red Lobster restaurant based on an evaluation of expected cash flows. During fiscal 2005, we recognized asset impairment charges of $6 million ($4 million after-tax) for the write-down of two Olive Garden restaurants, one Red Lobster restaurant and one Smokey Bones restaurant based on an evaluation of expected cash flows. The Smokey Bones restaurant was closed subsequent to fiscal 2005 while the two Olive Garden restaurants and one Red Lobster restaurant continued to operate.

A **capital expenditure** is a cost that is recorded as an asset, not an expense, at the time it is incurred. This is also called *capitalizing* a cost.

Exhibit 4.10 shows a portion of the disclosure made by Darden Restaurants Inc. regarding its reported asset impairment charges (losses) of $37 million in 2004 and $6 million in 2005. A company must disclose in the notes to the financial statements a description of the impaired asset and the facts and circumstances leading to the impairment.

Expenditures to Improve an Asset or Extend Its Useful Life

Another change in the value of an asset may be the result of the firm spending money to improve its assets. Any expenditure that will benefit more than one accounting period is called a **capital expenditure**. A capital expenditure is recorded as an asset when it is incurred, and it is expensed or amortized over the accounting periods in which it is used.

Just the opposite of a capital expenditure is an expenditure that does not extend the useful life or improve the asset. Any expenditure that will benefit only the current accounting period is expensed in the period in which it is incurred. It is sometimes called a *revenue expenditure*, although *expense* really captures its meaning in a more logical way.

Many companies establish policies that categorize purchased items as capital expenditures or revenue expenditures—expenses, often based on dollar amounts. The accounting constraint of materiality applies here so that small dollar amounts can simply be expensed.

Remodeling and improvement projects are capital expenditures because they will offer firms benefits over a number of years.

- remodeling, such as a new wiring system to increase the efficiency of the electrical system of a building
- improvements, such as a more energy-efficient air-conditioning system

Ordinary repairs are recognized as current expenses because they are routine and do not increase the useful life of the asset or its efficiency. Ordinary repairs, such as painting, tune-ups for vehicles, or cleaning and lubricating equipment are expenditures that are necessary to maintain an asset in good operating condition and are expensed as incurred.

Suppose the computer terminals at Staples' corporate offices need a monthly tune-up and cleaning. The cost of this maintenance would be an expense—recognized in the period the work was done. But suppose Staples upgraded its computer hardware to expand its capability or its useful life. This cost would be considered a capital expenditure and capitalized—recorded as part of the cost of the asset and depreciated along with the asset over its remaining useful life.

Revising Estimates of Useful Life and Salvage Value

Sometimes managers have used an asset for a period of time when it becomes clear that they need to revise their estimates of the useful life or the salvage value of the asset. Evaluating estimates related to fixed assets is an ongoing part of accounting for those assets. In accounting for long-term assets, revising an estimate is not treated like an error—you do not go back and correct any previous records or financial statements. Those amounts were correct at the time—because the best estimates at that time were used for the calculation. Suppose managers believe that a smoothly running machine will offer a useful life beyond the original estimate. The undepreciated balance—the book value of the asset—reduced by the estimated salvage value would be spread over the new estimated remaining useful life. Similarly, if managers come to believe that the salvage value of the machine will be greater than their earlier estimate, the depreciation will be recalculated with the new salvage value. This approach is similar to treating the undepreciated balance like the cost of the asset at the time of the revised estimates and using the new estimates of useful life and salvage value to calculate the depreciation expense for the remaining years of the asset's life.

Suppose Staples purchased a copy machine that cost $50,000, with an estimated useful life of 4 years and an estimated salvage value of $2,000. Using straight-line depreciation, a single year's depreciation is

$$\frac{\$50,000 - \$2,000}{4 \text{ years}} = \frac{\$48,000}{4 \text{ years}} = \$12,000 \text{ per year}$$

Suppose Staples has depreciated the machine for 2 years. That would make the book value $26,000.

$$\underset{\text{Cost}}{\$50,000} - \underset{\substack{\text{Depreciation} \\ \text{year 1}}}{\$12,000} - \underset{\substack{\text{Depreciation} \\ \text{year 2}}}{\$12,000} = \underset{\text{Book value}}{\$26,000}$$

As Staples begins the third year of the asset's life, the manager realizes that Staples will be able to use it for three *more* years—rather than two more years as we originally estimated—but now believes the salvage value at the end of that time will be $1,000—not $2,000 as originally estimated.

The depreciation expense for the first 2 years will not be changed. For the next 3 years, however, the depreciation expense will be different than it was for the first 2 years. The acquisition cost of $50,000 less $24,000 of accumulated depreciation gives us the undepreciated balance of $26,000. This amount is treated as if it were now the cost of the asset. The estimated salvage value is $1,000, and the estimated remaining useful life is 3 years. The calculation is

$$\frac{\$26,000 - 1,000}{3 \text{ years}} = \frac{\$25,000}{3 \text{ years}} = \$8,333 \text{ per year}$$

The asset will now be depreciated for 3 years at $8,333 per year. At the end of that time the book value of the asset will be $1,000 [$26,000 − ($8,333 per year × 3 years)].

Your Turn 4-7
Your Turn
Your Turn

At the beginning of 2005, White Company hired a mechanic to perform a major overhaul of its main piece of equipment at a cost of $2,400. The equipment originally cost $10,000 at the beginning of 2001, and the book value of the equipment on the December 31, 2004, balance sheet was $6,000. At the time of the purchase, White Company estimated that the equipment would have a useful life of 10 years and no salvage value. The overhaul at the beginning of 2005 extended the useful life of the equipment. White Company's new estimate is that the equipment will now last until the end of 2012—8 years from the date of the overhaul. Expected salvage value is still zero. White uses straight-line depreciation for all of its assets. Calculate the depreciation expense for White's income statement for the year ended December 31, 2006.

Selling Long-Term Assets

L.O.5
Explain how the disposal of an asset is reflected in the financial statements.

We have bought the long-term asset and used it—depreciating, depleting, or amortizing it over its useful life. Now, we deal with getting rid of an asset. Disposing of an asset means to sell it, trade it in, or simply toss it in the trash. When would a company sell an asset? Sometimes an asset is sold because it is no longer useful to the company. Other times an asset is replaced with a newer model, even though there is remaining productive capacity in the current asset. You calculate the gain or loss on the disposal of an asset by comparing the cash received for the sale of the asset—also known as cash proceeds—and the asset's book value at the time of disposal. One of three situations will exist:

1. Cash proceeds are greater than the book value. There will be a gain.
2. Cash proceeds are less than the book value. There will be a loss.
3. Cash proceeds are equal to the book value. There will be no gain or loss.

Suppose you decide to sell equipment that was purchased 7 years ago. At the time of the purchase, you estimated it would last 10 years. The asset cost $25,000, and you used straight-line depreciation with an estimated salvage value of zero. The depreciation expense each year was $2,500. Now, 7 years later, you sell the asset for $8,000. Is there a gain or loss on the sale? First, calculate the book value on the date you sold the asset:

$$\text{Book value} = \text{Cost} \quad - \text{Accumulated depreciation}$$
$$\text{Book value} = \$25,000 - (7 \text{ years} \times \$2,500 \text{ per year})$$
$$\text{Book value} = \$25,000 - \$17,500 = \$7,500$$

Then, subtract the book value from the cash proceeds to calculate the gain or loss on the sale.

$$\$8,000 - \$7,500 = \$500$$

Because the proceeds of $8,000 are larger than the book value of $7,500, there is a gain on the sale. A gain is a special kind of revenue that is shown on the income statement. A gain is special because it is not a normal part of business operations. You are not in business to buy and sell the equipment you use in your business, so the income from such a transaction is called a gain rather than simply called revenue.

Another way to calculate the gain or loss on the sale of an asset is to record the three amounts you know.

1. Record the receipt of cash.
2. Remove the asset and its accumulated depreciation.
3. Balance the transaction in the accounting equation with a gain or loss.

Assets	=	Liabilities	+	Shareholder's equity		
				Contributed capital	+	Retained earnings
8,000 Cash						
(25,000) Equipment						500
17,500						gain on sale
Accumulated depreciation						of equipment

Now suppose, instead, you sell the asset after 7 years for $5,000 rather than $8,000. Is there a gain or loss on the sale? You already know the book value is $7,500 at the date of the sale. Subtract the book value from the cash proceeds.

$$\$5,000 - \$7,500 = -\$2,500$$

Because the proceeds are less than the book value, there is a loss on the sale. A loss is a special kind of expense, and it is shown on the income statement.

Suppose you sold the asset for exactly the book value, $7,500. There would be no gain or loss on the sale. Look at the accounting equation below to see the effect of selling an asset for its book value.

Assets	=	Liabilities	+	Shareholder's equity		
				Contributed capital	+	Retained earnings
7,500 Cash						
(25,000) Equipment						
17,500						
Accumulated depreciation						

There is no gain or loss. Selling an asset for its book value, therefore, does not affect the income statement.

Perry Plants Company owned an asset that originally cost $24,000. The company sold the asset on January 1, 2005, for $8,000 cash. Accumulated depreciation on the day of sale was $18,000. Determine whether Perry should recognize a gain or a loss on the sale. If so, how much?

Your Turn 4-8
Your Turn
Your Turn

Presentation of Long-Term Assets on the Financial Statements

L.O.6
Recognize and explain how long-term assets are reported on the financial statements, and prepare financial statements that include long-term assets.

Reporting Long-Term Assets

In this chapter you have seen that both tangible and intangible long-term assets are recorded at the amount the firm paid for them. The assets are shown on the balance sheet in the last half of the asset section, after current assets. Because the carrying value of property, plant, and equipment (PPE) is the difference between the cost of the asset and its accumulated depreciation, accountants say that PPE is reported at its *amortized cost* or its *depreciated cost*. The notes to the financial statements are a good place to learn the types of assets, approximate age of the assets, and depreciation method(s) used.

The use of long-term assets is shown on the income statement with depreciation, depletion, and amortization expense. Often, the amount is included in the total of several accounts for presentation on the income statement.

The statement of cash flows will indicate any cash expenditures for PPE as cash used for investing activities. Any cash received from the sale of long-term assets will be shown as an inflow in the same section—cash from investing activities—of the statement. Remember that the gain or loss on the sale of a long-term asset, reported on the income statement, is *not* the cash related to the sale. The cash collected from the sale will appear on the statement of cash flows.

Exhibit 4.11 shows the asset section of Best Buy's balance sheet. The firm shows the various categories of fixed assets at their cost and then shows the deduction for accumulated depreciation. This is all the depreciation that the firm has taken on its property, plant, and equipment since their purchase. Some firms show only the net amount, leaving the details for the notes to the financial statements. In any case, you should be able to find or calculate the cost of a firm's long-term assets.

Preparing Statements for Tom's Wear

Since beginning in January 2006, Tom's Wear Company has now finished 3 months of business. Refresh your memory by reviewing Tom's March 31 balance sheet in Exhibit 4.12, before Tom's Wear begins the month of April. Tom's Wear has been struggling along, but Tom believes that he can make a big profit breakthrough if he can expand his business. His research indicates a large demand for his T-shirts, so he plans a major expansion in April. Read through each of the transactions and study how they have been entered in the accounting equation worksheet in Exhibit 4.13. Then, we will make the end-of-the-month adjustments and prepare the four financial statements.

Transaction 1 In April, Tom's Wear purchased a van for $25,000. The company paid an additional $5,000 to have it equipped with the racks for T-shirts. Tom's Wear financed the $30,000 at 10% per year for 5 years with a local bank. On March 31 of each year beginning in 2007, Tom's Wear will pay the bank the interest it owes for the year plus $6,000 of the $30,000 principal. Tom's Wear expects the van to be driven for approximately 200,000 miles and have a residual value of $1,000 at the end of its useful life. The company decided to depreciate the van using the activity method, based on miles.

Transaction 2 Tom's Wear hired an employee, Sam Cubby, for 20 hours per week to fold, sort, and deliver the shirts. Sam will earn $1,000 per month, payable on the fifth of the following month. Sam will not begin work until May.

Transaction 3 Tom's Wear received cash for the prior month of sales on account, settling the $2,000 accounts receivable on the March 31, 2006, balance sheet.

Best Buy Co., Inc.
Consolidated Balance Sheets (partial)

$ in millions	February 25, 2006	February 26, 2005
Assets		
Current assets:		
Cash and cash equivalents	$ 681	$ 354
Short-term investments	3,051	2,994
Receivables	506	375
Merchandise inventories	3,338	2,851
Other current assets	409	329
Total current assets	7,985	6,903
Property and equipment		
Land and buildings	580	506
Leasehold improvements	1,325	1,139
Fixtures and equipment	2,898	2,458
Property under master and capital lease	33	89
	4,836	4,192
Less accumulated depreciation	2,124	1,728
Net property and equipment	2,712	2,464
Goodwill	557	513
Tradename	44	40
Long-term investments	218	148
Other assets	348	226
Total assets	$11,864	$10,294

Transaction 4 Tom's Wear found several sporting goods stores to buy its shirts, so the firm must dramatically increase the inventory. Tom's Wear purchases 1,000 T-shirts at $4 each on account.

Transaction 5 Tom's Wear rented a warehouse in which to store its inventory. On April 15, the company paid $2,400 for 2 months of rent.

tom's wear

Tom's Wear, Inc.
Balance Sheet
At March 31, 2006

Assets		Liabilities and Shareholder's Equity	
Current assets		Current liabilities	
Cash	$ 3,995	Interest payable	$ 30
Accounts receivable	2,000	Notes payable	3,000
Inventory	300	Total current liabilities	3,030
Prepaid insurance	75	Shareholder's equity	
Total current assets	6,370	Common stock	5,000
Computer (net of $100		Retained earnings	2,240
accumulated		Total shareholder's equity	7,240
depreciation)	3,900		
		Total liabilities and	
Total assets	$10,270	shareholder's equity	$10,270

EXHIBIT 4.13

Accounting Equation Worksheet for Tom's Wear for April (before adjustments)

All of the transactions for April are shown in this accounting equation worksheet.

	Assets							=	Liabilities			+	Shareholder's Equity			
													Contributed Capital	Retained Earnings		
	Cash	Accounts Receivable	Inventory	Prepaid Insurance	Prepaid Rent	Property & Equipment (P&E)	Accumulated Depreciation— P&E	=	Accounts Payable	Interest Payable	Notes Payable		Common Stock		Revenues	Expenses
Beginning Balances	3,995	2,000	300	75		4,000	(100)	=		30	3,000	=	5,000	2,240		
1.						30,000					30,000					
2.	No entry required at this time.															
3.	2,000	(2,000)														
4.			4,000						4,000							
5.	(2,400)				2,400											
6.		8,000													8,000	
			(3,200)													(3,200)
7.	(300)															(300)
Ending Balances	3,295	8,000	1,100	75	2,400	34,000	(100)	=	4,000	30	33,000	=	5,000	6,740		

— Income Statement   — Statement of Changes in Shareholder's Equity   — Balance Sheet   — Statement of Cash Flows

Transaction 6 Tom's Wear arranged the sales of its shirts to a number of sporting good stores in the area. Each month Tom's Wear will deliver 800 shirts for $10 each to six different shops. The delivery will be made on the 15th of each month, and the customer will pay by the 10th of the subsequent month. The first deliveries are on April 15.

Transaction 7 Tom's Wear paid cash for $300 worth of operating expenses.

After you understand each of the transactions shown in Exhibit 4.13, you are ready to make the needed adjustments before the April financial statements can be prepared. As you read each of the explanations for the adjustments, follow along on the worksheet in Exhibit 4.14.

Adjustment 1 Tom's Wear needs to adjust prepaid insurance. On April 1, there was $75 worth of prepaid insurance on the balance sheet. Recall, Tom's Wear purchased 3 months of insurance on February 15 for a total cost of $150, which is $50 per month.

Adjustment 2 Another item that needs to be adjusted is prepaid rent. Tom's Wear paid $2,400 for 2 months of rent, beginning on April 15. On April 30, half a month's rent should be expensed.

Adjustment 3 Depreciation expense for the computer needs to be recorded. Recall, it is being depreciated at $100 per month.

Adjustment 4 Depreciation expense for the new van needs to be recorded. It cost $30,000 and has an estimated residual value of $1,000. It is being depreciated using the activity method based on an estimated 200,000 miles. During April, the van was driven 5,000 miles. The rate is $0.145 per mile ($29,000 depreciable base divided by 200,000 miles). The depreciation expense for April is $0.145 per mile × 5,000 miles = $725.

Adjustment 5 Interest expense on the note for the computer needs to be accrued. The 3-month, $3,000 note at 12% was signed on March 1. Interest for April will be $30 ($3,000 × 0.12 × 1/12).

Adjustment 6 Interest expense on the note for the van needs to be accrued. The $30,000 note at 10% was signed on April 1. Interest for April will be $250 ($30,000 × 0.10 × 1/12).

Using the accounting equation worksheet in Exhibit 4.14, you can see how the financial statements are derived. Study each of them by tracing the numbers from the worksheet to the appropriate financial statement, shown in Exhibit 4.15.

L.O.7
Use return on assets (ROA) and the asset turnover ratio to help evaluate a firm's performance.

Applying Your Knowledge—Ratio Analysis

You know how a firm records the purchase of long-term assets and how it accounts for the use of the assets. Now we will look at how you can use the information about long-term assets to help evaluate the performance of the firm.

Return on Assets

A company purchases assets to help generate future revenue. Recall the definition of an asset—something of value used by a business to generate revenue. A ratio that measures how well a company is using its assets to generate revenue is return on assets (ROA). ROA is an overall measure of a company's profitability. Like much of the terminology in accounting, the name of this ratio is descriptive. A company's return is what the company is getting back. We want to measure that return as a percentage of assets. So return on assets is literally *return*—net income—divided by *assets*.

$$\text{Return on assets} = \frac{\text{Net income} + \text{Interest expense}}{\text{Average total assets}}$$

This ratio measures a company's success in using its assets to earn income for the people financing the business—both owners and creditors. Because interest expense is

EXHIBIT 4.14

Accounting Equation Worksheet for Tom's Wear for April (with adjustments)

Notice that the adjustments have been added to the worksheet.

	Assets							=	Liabilities			+	Shareholder's Equity			
						Property &	Accumulated						Contributed Capital	Retained Earnings		
	Cash	Accounts Receivable	Inventory	Prepaid Insurance	Prepaid Rent	Equipment (P&E)	Depreciation—P&E	=	Accounts Payable	Interest Payable	Notes Payable	+	Common Stock		Revenues	Expenses
Beginning Balances	3,995	2,000	300	75		4,000	(100)	=		30	3,000		5,000	2,240		
1.						30,000					30,000					
2.	No entry required at this time.															
3.	2,000	(2,000)														
4.			4,000						4,000							
5.	(2,400)				2,400											
6.		8,000													8,000	
			(3,200)													(3,200)
7.	(300)															(300)
Adjustment																
1.				(50)												(50)
2.					(600)											(600)
3.							(100)									(100)
4.							(725)									(725)
5.										30						(30)
6.										250						(250)
Ending Balances	3,295	8,000	1,100	25	1,800	34,000	(925)	=	4,000	310	33,000		5,000	4,985		

— Income Statement   — Statement of Changes in Shareholder's Equity   — Balance Sheet   — Statement of Cash Flows

EXHIBIT 4.15

Financial Statements for Tom's Wear

The arrows should help you see the relationships between the financial statements.

Tom's Wear, Inc.
Income Statement
For the Month Ended April 30

Sales revenue		$8,000
Costs of goods sold		3,200
Gross profit		4,800
Other expenses		
Insurance	$ 50	
Rent	600	
Depreciation	825	
Interest	280	
Other operating expenses	300	2,055
Net income		$2,745

Tom's Wear, Inc.
Statement of Changes in Shareholder's Equity
For the Month Ended April 30

Common stock

Beginning balance	$5,000	
+ New stock issued	–	
Ending balance		$ 5,000
Retained earnings		
Beginning balance	$2,240	
+ Net income	2,745	
– Dividends	–	
Ending balance		4,985
Total shareholder's equity		$9,985

Tom's Wear, Inc.
Statement of Cash Flows
For the Month Ended April 30

Cash from operating activities

Cash collected from customers		$ 2,000
Cash paid for operating expenses		(2,700)
Net cash from operating activities		(700)
Cash from investing activities		0
Cash from financing activities		0
Net increase (decrease) in cash		(700)
Add beginning cash balance		3,995
Ending cash balance		$3,295

Tom's Wear, Inc.
Balance Sheet
At April 30

Assets

Cash	$3,295
Accounts receivable	8,000
Inventory	1,100
Prepaid insurance	25
Prepaid rent	1,800
Total current assets	14,220
Property & equipment (net of $925 accumulated depreciation)	33,075
Total assets	$47,295
Liabilities & Shareholder's Equity	
Liabilities	
Accounts payable	4,000
Interest payable	310
Short-term notes payable	3,000
Total current liabilities	7,310
Long-term notes payable	30,000
Shareholder's Equity	
Common stock	5,000
Retained earnings	4,985
Total liabilites and SH equity	$47,295

EXHIBIT 4.16

Return on Assets for Apple Computer and Dell

	Apple Computer, Inc. For the year ended September 24, 2005	Dell, Inc. For the year ended February 3, 2006
(dollars in millions)		
Net income plus interest expense	$ 1,335	$ 3,600
Average Assets	$ 9,800	$23,162
Return on Assets	13.62%	15.54%

part of what has been earned to pay creditors, it is added back to the numerator. Net income is the return to the owners, and interest expense is the return to the creditors. So you add interest expense back to net income for the numerator. The denominator is average total assets.

Using a ratio such as ROA gives financial statement users a way to standardize net income across companies. Exhibit 4.16 provides an example. For the fiscal year ended September 24, 2005, Apple Computers had a net income $1,335 and average assets of $9,800 (both in millions). The firm had no interest expense during the year. For the fiscal year ended February 3, 2006, Dell had net income of $3,572 and interest expense of $28, with average assets of $23,162 (all dollars in millions). Clearly, Dell is outperforming Apple Computers in total net income. But that comparison does not tell us how well each company is using its assets to make that net income. If we divide net income plus interest expense by average total assets, we will get the return on assets for the year.

It is clear in this comparison that Dell is earning a better return with its total assets than Apple Computer is earning with its assets. The industry average for firms in this industry for return on assets is 12.6%. Apple's ROA is 13.62% and Dell's ROA is 15.54% using the results from the fiscal years shown in Exhibit 4.16. You can find up-to-date information on the firms' ROA at www.moneycentral.msn.com.

Asset Turnover Ratio

Another ratio that helps us evaluate a firm's use of its assets is the asset turnover ratio. This ratio indicates how efficiently a company is using its assets. The ratio is defined as net sales divided by average total assets. The ratio answers the question: How many dollars of sales are generated by each dollar invested in assets?

$$\text{Asset turnover ratio} = \frac{\text{Net sales}}{\text{Average total assets}}$$

Look at Apple Computer and Dell again. Sales for Apple Computer for the fiscal year ended September 24, 2005, were $13,931 million, and sales for Dell for the fiscal year ended February 3, 2006, totaled $55,908 million. The asset turnover ratio for each is:

(dollars in millions)	Apple Computer	Dell
Sales	$13,931	$55,908
Average Assets	$9,800	$23,162
Asset Turnover Ratio	1.42	2.41

Asset turnover ratios vary significantly from industry to industry, so it is important to compare firms only in the same industry. Dell's use of its assets to generate revenue was quite a bit better than that of Apple Computer during this time period.

Remember that all ratios have this in common: To be meaningful, ratios must be compared to the ratios from other years with the same company or with other companies. Industry standards are also often available for common ratios to help investors and analysts evaluate a company's performance using ratio analysis.

Business Risk, Control, and Ethics

L.O.8
Identify and describe the business risks associated with long-term assets and the controls that can minimize those risks.

A firm risks losing long-term assets due to theft. This risk is not a problem with some large assets, such as a factory, but it is a very serious problem with smaller, mobile, fixed assets, such as cars, computers, and furniture and fixtures. Even large assets, such as buildings and factories, are at risk for damage due to vandalism, hurricanes, or terrorist activities. One of the major functions of any company's internal control system is to safeguard all assets from theft and damage—whether intentional or unintentional. The cost of safeguarding assets can be tremendous, as can the cost of replacing them if they are destroyed. The damage done to long-term assets by Hurricane Katrina in August 2005 to the Gulf Coast has amounted to billions of dollars.

Physical controls to safeguard assets may be as simple as a lock on a warehouse door, a video camera in a retail store, or a security guard who remains in an office complex overnight. Even when assets are protected in a secure facility with guards, fences, or alarms, the company must be sure that only the appropriate people have access to the assets.

Segregation of duties means that the person who has physical custody of an asset is not the same person who has record-keeping responsibilities for that asset.

Complete and reliable record keeping for the assets is also part of safeguarding assets. With assets such as cash and inventory, the people who are responsible for the record keeping for long-term assets should be different than the people who have physical custody of the assets. This is called **segregation of duties** and is a very common control.

Monitoring is another control to safeguard assets. This means that someone needs to make sure the other controls—physical controls, segregation of duties, and any other policies and procedures related to protecting assets—are operating properly. Often, firms have internal auditors—their own employees—who perform this function as part of their job responsibilities. You may recall that it was an internal auditor who first blew the whistle on the Enron fraud.

Intangible assets present special risks to a firm. Google's attempt to digitize all the books in the libraries of several major universities has brought new concerns over copyright laws. The value of these intangible assets on a firm's balance sheet and the potential costs of defending these rights can amount to significant sums of money. Technology and ethics have collided, resulting in many questions about the legal and ethical dimensions of current copyright laws.

News Flash

Google is scanning millions of books in an effort to advance its mission to organize all knowledge; but in 2005, some authors and publishing companies sued Google for copyright infringement. The argument is not over the books publishers currently keep in print; it is over the 25 million books considered "orphans." It is very difficult to track down the owner of the copyright. Jane Friedman, the CEO of HarperCollins Publishers, does not expect this lawsuit to be settled in her lifetime. But Kevin Kelly, in a *New York Times* article (May 14, 2006), feels sure that the technology will win out. He predicts that "all new works will be born digital, and they will flow into the universal library..."

Chapter Summary Points

- Assets that last longer than a year are classified as noncurrent (or long term) on the balance sheet. They are recorded at cost, including all of the costs necessary to get the asset ready for use.
- Long-term assets are written off over their useful lives. For plant and equipment, an asset may be written off using either straight-line, activity, or double-declining balance depreciation methods. Intangible assets with a definite life are written off, or amortized, using the straight-line method.
- Routine repair and maintenance costs are expensed as incurred, whereas improvements to the productive capacity or the useful life of an asset are capitalized as part of the cost of the asset.
- Any revisions in the useful life or the estimated salvage value of an asset are implemented at the time of the revision and in the future periods. Any past depreciation expense is *not* revised.
- When an asset is sold, the gain or loss is calculated as the difference between the proceeds (sales amount) and the book value (cost − accumulated depreciation) of the asset.

Chapter Summary Problems

Suppose Pencils Office Supply started the fiscal year with the following accounts and balances:

Balances at January 1, 2008

Account		
Cash	$390,000	
Accounts receivable	136,000	
Inventory	106,350	
Prepaid insurance	3,000	
Equipment	261,000	
Accumulated depreciation—Equipment	(75,800)	$820,550
Accounts payable	26,700	
Salaries payable	13,500	
Unearned revenue	35,000	
Long-term note payable	130,000	
Other long-term liabilities	85,000	
Common stock	250,000	
Retained earnings	280,350	$820,550

Suppose the company engaged in the following transactions during its fiscal year ended December 31, 2008:

1. The company purchased new equipment at the beginning of the fiscal year. The invoice price was $158,500, but the manufacturer of the equipment gave Pencils a 3% discount for paying cash for the equipment on delivery. Pencils paid shipping costs of $1,500 and paid $700 for a special insurance policy to cover the equipment while in transit. Installation cost was $3,000, and Pencils spent $6,000 training employees to use the new equipment. Additionally, Pencils hired a new supervisor at an annual salary of $40,000 to be responsible for the printing services area where the new equipment will be used. All payments were made in cash as the costs were incurred.
2. The company sold some old equipment with an original cost of $12,300 and related accumulated depreciation of $11,100. Proceeds from the sale amounted to $1,500.
3. The company collected cash of $134,200 on accounts receivable.

4. The company purchased $365,500 worth of inventory during the year, paying $200,000 cash, with the remainder purchased on account.
5. The company paid insurance premiums of $12,000.
6. The company paid $170,000 on accounts payable.
7. The company paid employees total cash for salaries of $72,250. (This includes the amount owed at the beginning of the year and the salary expense for the new supervisor.)
8. The company made sales to customers in the amount of $354,570. They collected $200,000 in cash, and the remainder was on account. (Inventory sold cost $110,000.) The company uses only one revenue account: Sales and service revenue.
9. The company paid $50,000 to reduce principal of the long-term note and paid interest of $10,400.
10. The company paid operating expenses in the amount of $30,000 in cash.

Other Information

A-1. The company owed salaries of $10,250 to employees at year-end (earned but not paid).

A-2. Insurance left unused at year-end amounted to $2,000.

A-3. The company estimates that the new equipment will last for 20 years and have a salvage value of $2,945 at the end of its useful life.

A-4. Previously purchased fixed assets are being depreciated at a rate of 10% per year.

A-5. Unearned service revenue of $21,000 has been earned at year-end.

Instructions

Set up an accounting equation worksheet. Enter the beginning balances, the transactions, and any needed adjustments at year-end. Then, prepare an income statement, statement of changes in shareholders' equity, the statement of cash flows—all for the fiscal year, and the balance sheet at December 31, 2008.

Solution

Pencils Office Supply
Income Statement
For the Year Ended December 31, 2008

Sales revenue		$375,570
Cost of goods sold		110,000
Gross profit		265,570
Gain on sale of asset		300
Other expenses		
Insurance expense	$ 13,000	
Salaries expense	69,000	
Depreciation expense	32,970	
Interest expense	10,400	
Other operating expense	30,000	(155,370)
Net income		$110,500

Pencils Office Supply
Statement of Changes in Shareholder's Equity
For the Year Ended December 31, 2008

Common stock		
Beginning balance	$250,000	
+ New contributions	–	
Ending balance		$250,000
Retained earnings		
Beginning balance	$280,350	
+ Net income	110,500	
– Dividends	–	
Ending balance		$390,850
Total shareholder's equity		$ 640,850

Pencils Office Supply
Statement of Cash Flows
For the Year Ended December 31, 2008

Cash from operating activities
Cash collected from customers	$ 334,200
Cash paid to vendors	(370,000)
Cash paid for insurance	(12,000)
Cash paid to employees	(72,250)
Cash paid for interest	(10,400)
Cash paid for other operating expenses	(30,000)
Net cash from (used for) operating activities	(160,450)
Cash from investing activities	
Proceeds from sale of equipment	1,500
Cash paid for purchase of equipment	(164,945)
Net cash from (used for) investing activities	(163,445)
Cash from financing activities	
Cash paid on long-term note payable	(50,000)
Increase (decrease) in cash during the year	(373,895)
Add beginning cash balance	390,000
Cash balance at April 30	$16,105

Pencils Office Supply
Balance Sheet
At December 31, 2008

Assets
Cash	$ 16,105
Accounts receivable	156,370
Inventory	361,850
Prepaid insurance	2,000
Total current assets	536,325
Equipment (net of $97,670 accumulated depreciation)	315,975
Total assets	$ 852,300
Liabilities & Shareholder's Equity	
Liabilities	
Accounts payable	22,200
Salaries payable	10,250
Unearned revenue	14,000
Total current liabilities	46,450
Long-term notes payable	80,000
Other long-term liabilities	85,000
Shareholder's Equity	
Common stock	250,000
Retained earnings	390,850
Total liabilities and SH equity	$ 852,300

Solution

Assets = Liabilities + Shareholder's Equity

	Cash	Accounts Receivable	Inventory	Prepaid Insurance	Property & Equipment (P&E)	Accumulated Depreciation—P&E	Accounts Payable	Salaries Payable	Unearned Revenue	Long-Term Notes Payable	Other Long-Term Liabilities	Common Stock (Contributed Capital)	Retained Earnings	Revenues	Expenses
BB*	390,000	136,000	106,350	3,000	261,000	(75,800)	26,700	13,500	35,000	130,000	85,000	250,000	280,350		
1.	(164,945)				164,945										
2.	1,500				(12,300)	11,100								300	
3.	134,200	(134,200)													
4.	(200,000)		365,500				165,500								
5.	(12,000)			12,000											
6.	(170,000)						(170,000)								
7.	(72,250)							(13,500)							(58,750)
8.	200,000	154,570	(110,000)											354,570	(110,000)
9.	(50,000)									(50,000)					
10.	(10,400)														(10,400)
	(30,000)														(30,000)
A†-1								10,250							(10,250)
A-2				(13,000)											(13,000)
A-3						(8,100)									(8,100)
A-4						(24,870)			(21,000)					21,000	(24,870)
A-5															
	16,105	156,370	361,850	2,000	413,645	(97,670)	22,200	10,250	14,000	80,000	85,000	250,000	390,850		
	852,300						852,300								

* BB = Beginning Balances

† A = Adjustment

Net income = 110,500

184

Key Terms for Chapter 4

Accelerated depreciation (p. 164)
Activity method depreciation (p. 162)
Amortization (p. 158)
Capital expenditure (p. 170)
Capitalize (p. 158)
Copyright (p. 167)

Declining balance depreciation (p. 164)
Depletion (p. 158)
Depreciation (p. 158)
Franchise (p. 168)
Goodwill (p. 168)
Impairment (p. 169)
Intangible assets (p. 155)
Patent (p. 168)

Relative fair market value method (p. 156)
Salvage value (p. 159)
Segregation of duties (p. 180)
Straight-line depreciation (p. 159)
Tangible assets (p. 155)
Trademark (p. 168)

Answers to YOUR TURN Questions

Chapter 4

Your Turn 4-1

1. Expense
2. Asset
3. Asset
4. Expense

Your Turn 4-2

Four-fifths of the costs (400,000/500,000 $\times$ \$480,000) = \$384,000 should be recorded as the cost of the building, and one-fifth of the cost (100,000/500,000 $\times$ \$480,000) = \$96,000 should be recorded as the cost of the land. These two costs need to be separated because the company will depreciate the building but not the land.

Your Turn 4-3

1. Depreciation
2. Depreciation
3. Depletion

Your Turn 4-4

Each year's depreciation is \$2,400 [(\$15,000 $-$ \$3,000)/5 years] per year, so that amount will be on the income statement for the year ended December 31, 2007. At December 31, 2007, the company will have taken 2 years' worth of depreciation, so the book value will be \$10,200 (\$15,000 $-$ \$4,800).

Your Turn 4-5

Rate = (\$44,000 $-$ \$4,000) $\div$ 100,000 = \$0.40 per unit
2005: 3,000 units $\times$ \$0.40 = \$1,200
2006: 14,000 units $\times$ \$0.40 = \$5,600

Your Turn 4-6

\$50,000 $\times$ 2/5 = \$20,000 for the first year
New book value = \$50,000 $-$ \$20,000 = \$30,000
\$30,000 $\times$ 2/5 = \$12,000 for the second year

Your Turn 4-7

\$6,000 $+$ \$2,400 = \$8,400 new depreciable amount
\$8,400/8 years remaining life = \$1,050 per year

Your Turn 4-8

There is a \$2,000 gain on the sale. The proceeds of \$8,000 are greater than the book value of \$6,000.

Questions

1. Describe the difference between tangible and intangible assets.
2. What is the difference between capitalizing and expensing a cost?
3. What is depreciation?
4. What does amortization mean?
5. Explain the difference between depreciation and depletion.
6. How do firms determine the cost of property, plant, and equipment?
7. What is a basket purchase? What accounting problem does this type of purchase create, and how do firms remedy the accounting problem?
8. What is the carrying value, or book value, of an asset? Is this value equal to the market value of the asset? Explain your answer.
9. What is the residual value, or salvage value, of an asset?
10. What is the difference between depreciation expense and accumulated depreciation? On which financial statement(s) do depreciation expense and accumulated depreciation appear?
11. How does depreciation apply the matching principle?
12. Explain the difference between the three depreciation methods allowed by GAAP.
13. What is a copyright and how is it accounted for?
14. What is a patent and how is it accounted for?
15. What does it mean for an asset to be impaired?
16. What types of costs related to long-term operational assets are capitalized and what types are expensed?
17. How is a gain or loss on the disposal of an asset calculated? On which financial statement(s) would the gain or loss appear?
18. How does goodwill arise?
19. How is the return on assets (ROA) ratio calculated and what does this ratio measure?
20. How is the asset turnover ratio calculated and what does this ratio measure?
21. List two types of controls that safeguard assets.

Multiple-Choice Questions

1. Which of the following is an intangible asset?
   a. Franchise
   b. Oil reserves
   c. Land
   d. Repairs
2. Depreciation is the systematic allocation of the cost of an asset
   a. Over the periods during which the asset is paid for
   b. Over the periods during which the market value of the asset decreases
   c. Over the periods during which the company uses the asset
   d. Over the life of the company
3. Writing off a cost means
   a. Putting the cost on the balance sheet as an asset
   b. Evaluating the useful life of the asset
   c. Recording the cost as an expense
   d. Deferring the expense
4. Suppose a firm purchases a new building for $500,000 and spends an additional $50,000 making alterations to it before it can be used. How much will the firm record as the cost of the asset?
   a. $500,000
   b. $550,000
   c. $450,000
   d. It depends on who performed the alterations.
5. Suppose a firm buys a piece of land with a building for $100,000. The firm's accountant wants to divide the cost between the land and building for the firm's financial records. Why?
   a. Land is always more expensive than buildings.

b. Land will not be depreciated but the building will be depreciated, so the accountant needs two different amounts.

c. Land will appreciate and its recorded cost will increase over time, whereas the building will be depreciated.

d. Depreciation expense will be separated from accumulated depreciation after the first year.

6. When an expenditure to repair an existing asset extends the useful life of the asset, the cost should be
   a. Classified as a revenue expenditure because it will result in increased revenue
   b. Capitalized and written off over the remaining life of the asset
   c. Expensed in the period of the repair
   d. Presented on the income statement or in the notes

7. When goodwill is determined to be impaired, a firm will
   a. Increase its book value to market value
   b. Sell it immediately
   c. Reduce the value of the goodwill with a charge against income (impairment loss)
   d. Reduce the value of the goodwill with a charge to paid-in capital (reduce paid-in capital)

8. When a company's balance sheet shows goodwill for $300,000, what does that mean?
   a. The company has developed a strong reputation valued at $300,000 if the company were to be sold.
   b. The company is worth $300,000 more than the balance sheet indicates.
   c. The company purchased another company and paid $300,000 more than the fair market value of the company's net assets.
   d. The company has invested $300,000 in new equipment during the period.

9. Suppose a firm purchased an asset for $100,000 and estimated, on the date of the purchase, its useful life as 10 years with no salvage value. The firm uses straight-line depreciation. After using the asset for 5 years, the firm changes its estimate of the remaining useful life to 4 years (a total of 9 years rather than the original 10 years). How much depreciation expense will the firm recognize in the sixth year of the asset's life?
   a. $12,500
   b. $10,000
   c. $11,111
   d. $31,111

10. Suppose a firm purchased an asset for $50,000 and depreciated it using straight-line depreciation for its 10-year useful life, with no salvage value. At the end of the seventh year of use, the firm decided to sell the asset. Proceeds from the sale were $17,500. What was the gain or loss from the sale of the asset? How did the sale affect the statement of cash flows?
   a. $2,500 loss; $2,500 cash outflow from investing activities
   b. $32,500 loss; $17,500 cash inflow from investing activities
   c. $17,500 gain; $17,500 cash inflow from investing activities
   d. $2,500 gain; $17,500 cash inflow from investing activities

Short Exercises

SE4-1. *Calculate the cost of an asset.* (LO 1)
Gruber Window Fashions bought a new wood-cutting machine as a part of its venture into manufacturing interior shutters. The invoice price of the machine was $90,000. Gruber also had the following expenses associated with purchasing this machine.

Delivery charge	$2,850
Installation	2,500
Power to run the machine for the first year	450

What amount should Gruber record on the books for this machine?

SE4-2. *Calculate the cost of an asset.* (LO 1)
Settler Company was quickly outgrowing its rented office space. The company decided that it could raise enough capital to buy land and build a new office building. The building was completed on September 15. Consider the following costs incurred for the new building.

Building materials	$110,000
Labor costs (including architect's fees)	205,000
Rental of equipment used in the construction	9,000
Maintenance on the building from Sept. 15 to Dec. 31	14,000

What amount should Settler Company record on the books for its new building?

SE4-3. *Account for basket purchase.* (LO 1)
Tylo Corporation obtained a building, its surrounding land, and a delivery truck in a lump-sum purchase for $230,000. An appraisal set the value of land at $180,000, the building at $145,000, and the truck at $25,000. At what amount should Tylo record each new asset on its books?

SE4-4. *Account for basket purchase.* (LO 1)
Villa Corporation purchased three buildings at a total cost of $960,000. The appraised values of the individual buildings were as follows:

Building 1	$600,000
Building 2	400,000
Building 3	200,000

What amounts should be recorded as the cost for each of the buildings in Villa Corporation's accounts?

SE4-5. *Calculate depreciation expense: straight-line.* (LO 2)
Calculate the annual straight-line depreciation expense for an asset that cost $12,000, has a useful life of 5 years, and has an estimated salvage value of $2,000.

SE4-6. *Calculate depreciation expense: activity method.* (LO 2)
Using the activity method, calculate the first 2 years of depreciation expense for a copy machine that cost $14,000, has an estimated useful life of 5 years or 50,000 copies, and has an estimated salvage value of $4,000. The number of copies produced each year is as follows:

Year 1	12,000
Year 2	10,500
Year 3	9,700
Year 4	9,100
Year 5	8,700

SE4-7. *Calculate depreciation expense: double-declining balance.* (LO 2)
Using the double-declining balance method, calculate the annual depreciation expense that will be recorded each year for an asset that cost $12,000, has a useful life of 5 years, and has an estimated salvage value of $2,000. Explain what accounting issue arises, if any, in the fourth and fifth years.

SE4-8. *Determine the cost of an asset.* (LO 1, 2)
If an asset with no salvage value is being depreciated at a rate of $1,000 per year using the straight-line method over a useful life of 6 years, how much did the asset cost?

SE4-9. *Calculate depreciation expense: straight-line.* (LO 2)
A machine is purchased on January 2, 2006, for $50,000, and it has an expected life of 4 years and no estimated salvage value. If the machine is still in use 5 years later, what amount of depreciation expense will be reported for the fifth year?

SE4-10. *Determine the useful life of an asset.* (LO 2)
Suppose an asset cost $20,000 and has an estimated salvage value of $2,000. At the end of 3 years, the carrying value of the asset is $11,000. What is the useful life of the asset? Assume straight-line depreciation.

SE4-11. *Calculate depletion.* (LO 2)
CNA Enterprises purchases an oil field and expects it to produce 1,000,000 barrels of oil. The oil field, acquired in January 2006, cost CNA $1.5 million. In 2006, 280,000 barrels were produced. In 2007, the oil field produced 350,000 barrels. What is the depletion for each of these years?

SE4-12. *Calculate depletion.* (LO 2)
Earthlink Mining purchased a copper mine for $12,000,000. The company expects the mine to produce 6,000,000 tons of copper over its 5-year useful life. During the first year of operations, the company extracts 750,000 tons of copper. How much depletion should Earthlink Mining record for the first year?

SE4-13. *Amortization of intangible assets.* (LO 3)
Edgewood Company obtained a patent for a new invention. The costs associated with the patent totaled $35,000. With the rapid development of new technology, Edgewood's engineers have estimated the invention will not have any value after 10 years. The patent has a legal life of 20 years. How will Edgewood amortize the cost of the patent?

SE4-14. *Amortization of intangible assets.* (LO 3)
Barclay Company purchased a patent for $50,000 on January 1, 2007. The estimated useful life is 10 years. The legal life is 20 years. What is the amortization expense for the fiscal year ended December 31, 2007?

SE4-15. *Analyze revenue and capital expenditures.* (LO 4)
For each of the following, tell whether it should be classified as (a) a revenue expenditure (expensed), (b) a capital expenditure (capitalized), or (c) neither.
    a. Paid $2,000 for routine repairs
    b. Paid cash dividends to shareholders
    c. Paid $6,000 for repairs that will extend the asset's useful life
    d. Purchased a patent for $5,000 cash
    e. Purchased a machine for $10,000 and gave a 2-year note
    f. Paid $50,000 for an addition to a building
    g. Paid $1,000 for routine maintenance on a machine

SE4-16. *Analyze revenue and capital expenditures.* (LO 4)
Categorize each of the following as a capital expenditure or a revenue expenditure (expense) for Dalton & Sons and explain why.
    a. In accordance with the long-term maintenance plan, paid for a newly reshingled roof (replacing similar old shingles)
    b. Built an annex to the building for the executive offices
    c. Improved the ventilation system to increase energy efficiency in the building
    d. Replaced parts in major equipment as needed

SE4-17. *Calculate depreciation expense with change in estimate of salvage value.* (LO 4)
On January 1, 2007, the Lance Corporation purchased a machine at a cost of $55,000. The machine was expected to have a useful life of 10 years and no salvage value. The straight-line depreciation method was used. In January 2009, the estimate of salvage value was revised from $0 to $6,000. How much depreciation should Lance Company record for 2009?

SE4-18. *Account for asset impairment.* (LO 4)
Delta Airlines has determined that several of its planes are impaired. The book value of the planes is $10 million, but the fair market value of the planes is $9 million. How should Delta treat this decline?

SE4-19. *Account for disposal of an asset.* (LO 5)
A machine is purchased on January 2, 2005, for $100,000. It has an expected useful life of 10 years and no salvage value. After 9 years, the machine is sold for $3,000 cash. Will there be a gain or loss on the sale? How much?

SE4-20. *Account for disposal of an asset.* (LO 5)
The Topspin Company sold some old equipment for $65,000. The equipment originally cost $100,000, had an estimated useful life of 10 years, and had no estimated salvage value. It was depreciated for 5 years using the straight-line method. In the year of the sale, what amount of gain or loss, if any, should Topspin Company report on its income statement?

SE4-21. *Prepare financial statements.* (LO 6)
At what value are fixed assets such as property, plant, and equipment shown on the balance sheet? How is that amount calculated?

SE4-22. *Calculate ratio analysis.* (LO 7)
Financial ratios are often used to evaluate a company's performance. What ratio(s) would provide information about how efficiently a company is using its assets?

SE4-23. *Identify risks and controls.* (LO 8)
Write a paragraph describing a specific risk associated with long-term assets and some possible controls that might minimize the risk.

SE4-24. *Identify risks and controls.* (LO 8)
Give an example of an industry with a particular interest in copyright laws. What risks do firms in that industry face?

SE4-25. *(Appendix) Explain depreciation for taxes.* (LO 9)
What kind of depreciation do firms use for taxes? Explain. Why would the IRS allow such depreciation?

Exercise—Set A

E4-1A. *Account for basket purchase.* (LO 1, 2)
Coca-Cola purchases a building and land for $180,000. An independent appraiser provides the following market values: building—$150,000; land—$50,000.
   a. How much of the purchase price should Coca-Cola allocate to each of the assets?
   b. If the building has a useful life of 10 years and an estimated salvage value of $35,000, how much depreciation expense should Coca-Cola record each year using the straight-line method?
   c. Using the double-declining balance method, what would the book value of the building be at the end of 3 years?

E4-2A. *Calculate the cost of an asset and depreciation expense.* (LO 1, 2)
Corona Company purchased land for $75,000 cash and a building for $300,000 cash. The company paid real estate closing costs of $8,000 and allocated that cost to the building and the land based on the purchase price. Renovation costs on the building were $35,000. Use the accounting equation to record the purchase of the property, including all related expenditures. Assume that all transactions were for cash and that all purchases occurred at the beginning of the year.
   a. Compute the annual straight-line depreciation, assuming a 20-year estimated useful life and a $10,000 estimated salvage value for the building.
   b. What would be the book value of the building at the end of the second year?
   c. What would be the book value of the land at the end of the second year?

E4-3A. *Calculate depreciation expense: straight-line and activity methods.* (LO 2)
Best-Goods Company purchased a delivery truck for $35,000 on January 1, 2006. The truck had an estimated useful life of 7 years or 210,000 miles. Best-Goods estimated the

truck's salvage value to be $5,000. The truck was driven 21,000 miles in 2006 and 31,500 miles in 2007.

    a. Compute the depreciation expense for 2006 and 2007, first using the straight-line method, then the activity method.

    b. Which method portrays more accurately the actual use of this asset? Explain your answer.

E4-4A. *Calculate depreciation expense: straight-line and double-declining balance methods.* (LO 2)

On January 1, 2006, Norris Company purchased equipment for $42,000. Norris also paid $1,200 for shipping and installation. The equipment is expected to have a useful life of 10 years and a salvage value of $3,200.

    a. Compute the depreciation expense for the years 2006 through 2008, using the straight-line method.

    b. Compute the depreciation expense for the years 2006 through 2008, using the double-declining balance method. (Round your answers to the nearest dollar.)

    c. What is the book value of the equipment at the end of 2008 under each method?

E4-5A. *Calculate depreciation under alternative methods.* (LO 2)

Avery Corporation bought a new piece of equipment at the beginning of the year at a cost of $15,400. The estimated useful life of the machine is 5 years, and its estimated productivity is 75,000 units. Its salvage value is estimated to be $400. Yearly production was: Year 1—15,000 units; Year 2—18,750 units; Year 3—11,250 units; Year 4—22,500 units; and Year 5—7,500 units. Complete a separate depreciation schedule for each of the three methods given for all 5 years. (Round your answers to the nearest dollar.)

    a. Straight-line method

    b. Activity method

    c. Double-declining balance method

E4-6A. *Calculate depreciation under alternative methods.* (LO 2)

Using the information from E4-5A, suppose the production in Year 5 was actually 9,000 rather than 7,500 units. How would this difference in production change the amount of depreciation for Year 5 under each method? Explain.

E4-7A. *Calculate depreciation under alternative methods.* (LO 2)

Propel Company bought a machine for $65,000 cash at the beginning of 2006. The estimated useful life is 5 years and the estimated salvage value is $5,000. The estimated productivity is 150,000 units. Units actually produced were 49,500 in 2006 and 36,000 in 2007. Calculate the depreciation expense for 2006 and 2007 under each of the three methods given. (Round your answers to the nearest dollar.)

    a. Straight-line method

    b. Activity method

    c. Double-declining balance method

E4-8A. *Calculate depletion.* (LO 2)

On January 1, 2008, American Oil Company purchased the rights to an offshore oil well for $45,000,000. The company expects the oil well to produce 9,000,000 barrels of oil during its life. During 2008, American Oil removed 315,000 barrels of oil.

    a. How much depletion should American Oil Company record for 2008?

    b. What is the book value of the oil rights at December 31, 2008, the end of the fiscal year?

E4-9A. *Amortize intangible assets.* (LO 3)

Becker and Associates registered a patent with the U.S. Patent and Trademark Office. The total cost of obtaining the patent was $165,000. Although the patent has a legal life of 20 years, the firm believes it will be useful for only 10 years. What will Becker and Associates record for its annual amortization expense? Show how it would be recorded in the accounting equation.

E4-10A. *Calculate goodwill.* (LO 3)
Carpenter Tools decides to acquire a small local tool company called Local Tools. Local Tools has net assets with a market value of $230,000 but Carpenter pays $250,000. Why? Use the accounting equation to record the purchase.

E4-11A. *Evaluate asset impairment.* (LO 4)
During its most recent fiscal year, Bargain Airlines grounded 10 of its 747s due to a potential problem with the wing flaps. Although the planes had been repaired by the end of the fiscal year, the company believed the problems indicated the need for an evaluation of potential impairment of these planes. The results of the analysis indicated that the planes had permanently declined in fair value by $120 million below their book value. What effect would this decline in value have on Bargain Airlines' net income for the year?

E4-12A. *Distinguish between capital and revenue expenditures (expenses).* (LO 1, 4)
Classify the following items as either a capital expenditure or a revenue expenditure (an expense).
   a. Changed oil in the delivery truck
   b. Replaced the engine in the delivery truck
   c. Paid sales tax on the new delivery truck
   d. Installed a new, similar roof on the office building
   e. Paid freight and installation charges for a new computer system
   f. Repainted the administrative offices
   g. Purchased and installed a new toner cartridge in the laser printer
   h. Replaced several missing shingles on the roof
   i. Trained an employee prior to using the new computer system
   j. Replaced the brake pads on the delivery truck

E4-13A. *Account for capital and revenue expenditures (expenses) and calculate depreciation expense.* (LO 2, 4)
Yester Mfg. Co. has had a piece of equipment for 6 years. At the beginning of the seventh year, the equipment was not performing as well as expected. First, Yester relubricated the equipment, which cost $150. Then, the company replaced some worn-out parts, which cost $520. Finally, at the beginning of the seventh year, the company completed a major overhaul of the equipment that not only fixed the machine but also added new functionality and extended its useful life by 3 years (to a total of 10 years) with no salvage value. The overhaul cost $10,000. (Originally, the machine cost $60,000, had a salvage value of $4,000, and had an estimated useful life of 7 years.)
   a. Which of these costs are capital expenditures? How would these amounts appear on the financial statements?
   b. Which are revenue expenditures? How would these amounts appear on the financial statements?
   c. Assuming Yester Mfg. uses the straight-line method of depreciation, how much depreciation expense will be reported on the income statements for years 7 through 10?

E4-14A. *Account for capital and revenue expenditures (expenses) and calculate depreciation expense.* (LO 2, 4)
Sharper Company operates a small repair facility for its products. At the beginning of 2006, the accounting records for the company showed the following balances for its only piece of equipment, purchased at the beginning of 2004:

Equipment	$115,000
Accumulated depreciation	20,000

During 2006, the following costs were incurred for repairs and maintenance on the equipment:

Routine maintenance and repairs	$ 650
Major overhaul of the equipment that improved efficiency	22,000

The company uses the straight-line method, and it now estimates the equipment will last for a total of 11 years with $5,000 estimated salvage value. The company's fiscal year ends on December 31.

    a. How much depreciation did Shaper Company record on the equipment at the end of 2005?

    b. After the overhaul at the beginning of 2006, what is the remaining estimated life of the equipment?

    c. What is the amount of depreciation expense the company will record for 2006?

E4-15A. *Account for disposal of an asset.* (LO 5)
Zellwiger Plumbing bought a van for $60,000. The van is expected to have a 10-year useful life and a salvage value of $4,000.

    a. If Zellwiger sells the van after 3 years for $20,000, would the company realize a gain or loss? How much? (Assume straight-line depreciation.)

    b. What would be the gain or loss if the company sold the van for $30,000 after 6 years?

E4-16A. *Account for disposal of an asset.* (LO 5)
Troy Wilson Athletic Gear purchased a packaging machine 4 years ago for $18,000. The machinery was expected to have a salvage value of $2,000 after an 8-year useful life. Assuming straight-line depreciation is used, calculate the gain or loss realized if after 4 years the machinery was sold for:

    a. $11,400

    b. $7,800

E4-17A. *Account for disposal of an asset.* (LO 5)
Dave's Delivery disposed of a delivery truck after using it 4 years. The records of the company provide the following information:

Delivery truck	$38,000
Accumulated depreciation	23,000

Calculate the gain or loss on the disposal of the truck for each of the following independent situations:

    a. Dave's Delivery sold the truck to Papa John's Pizza for $12,000.

    b. Dave's Delivery sold the truck to Cornerstone Grocery for $15,000.

    c. Dave's Delivery sold the truck to John's Plumbing for $16,000.

    d. The truck was stolen out of Dave's parking lot, and the company had no insurance.

E4-18A. *Account for disposal of an asset.* (LO 5)
Sweet Tooth Bakery disposed of an oven after using it for 4 years. The oven originally cost $40,000 and had associated accumulated depreciation of $29,000. Calculate the gain or loss on the disposal of the oven for each of the following situations:

    a. The company sold the oven to a homeless shelter for $8,000.

    b. The company sold the oven to a local restaurant for $10,000.

    c. The company gave the oven to a hauling company in return for hauling the oven to the local dump. The oven was totally worthless.

E4-19A. *Calculate gain or loss and cash flow.* (LO 5, 6)
Arco Incorporated sold assets with an original cost of $15,000 and accumulated depreciation of $9,000. If the cash proceeds from the sale were $7,000, what was the gain or loss on

the sale? On which financial statement would that amount be shown? How much would be shown on the statement of cash flows and in which section?

E4-20A. *Prepare financial statements.* (LO 6)
For each of the following, give the financial statement on which it would appear.
  a. Book value of fixed assets of $56,900
  b. Proceeds from sale of fixed assets of $20,000
  c. Loss on sale of fixed assets of $12,500
  d. Accumulated depreciation on equipment of $10,000
  e. Depreciation expense on equipment of $2,000
  f. Impairment write-down on assets of $45,000

E4-21A. *Calculate return on assets and asset turnover ratios.* (LO 7)
Using the Staples annual report in the appendix at the back of the book, calculate the following ratios for the most recent fiscal year and explain what each ratio measures:
  a. Return on assets (ROA)
  b. Asset turnover ratio

E4-22A. *Identify risks and controls.* (LO 8)
Look at Staples' annual report in the appendix at the back of the book. What types of fixed assets does the firm have? What risks do you think Staples faces with respect to these assets, and how is the firm controlling those risks?

Exercise—Set B

E4-1B. *Account for basket purchase.* (LO 1, 2)
Premium Bottling Company purchases a building and land for a total cash price of $200,000. An independent appraiser provides the following market values: building—$175,000; land—$75,000.
  a. How much of the purchase price should the company allocate to each of the assets?
  b. If the building has a useful life of 10 years and an estimated salvage value of $40,000, how much depreciation expense should Premium record each year using the straight-line method?
  c. Using the double-declining balance method, what would the book value of the building be at the end of 3 years?

E4-2B. *Calculate the cost of an asset and depreciation expense.* (LO 1, 2)
Wilson, Smith & Knight Beer Brewers purchased a building for $125,000 cash and the land for $275,000 cash. The company paid real estate closing costs of $6,000 and allocated that cost to the building and the land based on the purchase price. Renovation costs on the building were $45,000.
Use the accounting equation to record the purchase of the property, including all related expenditures. Assume that all transactions were for cash and that all purchases occurred at the beginning of the year.
  a. Compute the annual straight-line depreciation, assuming a 20-year estimated useful life and an $11,875 estimated salvage value for the building.
  b. What would be the book value of the building at the end of the fifth year?
  c. What would be the book value of the land at the end of the tenth year?

E4-3B. *Calculate depreciation expense: straight-line and activity methods.* (LO 2)
Walt's Water Pressure Company purchased a van for $45,000 on July 1, 2008. The van had an estimated useful life of 6 years or 250,000 miles. Walt's estimated the van's salvage value to be $3,000. The van was driven 25,000 miles in the year ended June 30, 2009, and 30,000 miles in the year ended June 30, 2010.
  a. Compute the depreciation expense for 2009 and 2010, first using the straight-line method, then the activity method.
  b. Which method portrays more accurately the actual use of this asset? Explain your answer.

E4-4B. *Calculate depreciation expense: straight-line and double-declining balance methods.* (LO 2)
On January 1, 2008, Hsieh & Wen's Gourmet Taste of Asia purchased kitchen equipment for $51,500. Hsieh & Wen's was also charged $1,650 for shipping and installation. The equipment is expected to have a useful life of 8 years and a salvage value of $3,150.
   a. Compute the depreciation expense for the years 2008 through 2010, using the straight-line method (December 31 is the fiscal year-end.).
   b. Compute the depreciation expense for the years 2008 through 2010, using the double-declining balance method. (Round your answers to the nearest dollar.)
   c. What is the book value of the equipment at the end of 2008 under each method?

E4-5B. *Calculate depreciation under alternative methods.* (LO 2)
Designer Jeans bought a new piece of equipment at the beginning of the year at a cost of $24,500. The estimated useful life of the machine is 4 years, and its estimated productivity is 85,000 units. Its salvage value is estimated to be $500. Yearly production for Year 1 was 34,000 units; Year 2 was 25,500 units; Year 3 was 19,125 units; and Year 4 was 6,375 units. Complete a separate depreciation schedule for each of the three methods given for all 4 years. (Round your answers to the nearest dollar.)
   a. Straight-line method
   b. Activity method
   c. Double-declining balance method

E4-6B. *Calculate depreciation under alternative methods.* (LO 2)
Using the information from E4-5B, suppose the production in Year 4 was actually 8,500 rather than 6,375 units. How would this change the amount of depreciation for Year 4 under each method? Explain.

E4-7B. *Calculate depreciation under alternative methods.* (LO 2)
Brother's Helper Manufacturing bought a machine for $172,000 cash at the beginning of 2007. The estimated useful life is 8 years and the estimated salvage value is $4,000. The estimated productivity is 265,000 units. Units actually produced were 92,750 in 2007 and 55,650 in 2008. Calculate the depreciation expense for 2007 and 2008 under each of the three methods given. (Round your answers to the nearest dollar.)
   a. Straight-line method
   b. Activity method
   c. Double-declining balance method

E4-8B. *Calculate depletion.* (LO 2)
On January 1, 2007, West Mountain Mining Company purchased the rights to a coal mine for $15,000,000. The company expects the coal mine to produce 10,000,000 pounds of coal. During 2007, West Mountain Mining removed 550,000 pounds of coal.
   a. How much depletion should West Mountain Mining Company record for 2007?
   b. What is the book value of the coal rights at December 31, 2007, the end of the fiscal year?

E4-9B. *Amortize intangible assets.* (LO 3)
Microtech registered a trademark with the U.S. Patent and Trademark Office. The total cost of obtaining the trademark was $55,000. Although the trademark has a legal life of 20 years, the firm believes it will be renewed indefinitely. What will Microtech record for its annual amortization expense?

E4-10B. *Calculate goodwill.* (LO 3)
Evans has decided to acquire a competitor firm. The competitor firm has assets with a market value of $430,000 and liabilities with a market value of $210,000, and Evans pays $250,000. Why? Use the accounting equation to record the purchase.

E4-11B. *Evaluate asset impairment.* (LO 4)
During its fiscal year ended June 30, Super Shippers Delivery Service had to decommission 1,500 delivery trucks due to a potential problem with the fuel tank. Although the trucks had

been repaired by the end of the fiscal year, the company determined the problems required an evaluation of potential impairment of these trucks. The results of the analysis indicated that the trucks had permanently declined in fair value by $7.5 million below their book value. What effect would this decline have on Super Shippers' net income for the year?

E4-12B. *Distinguish between capital and revenue expenditures (expenses). (LO 1, 4)*
Classify the following items as either a capital expenditure or a revenue expenditure (expense).
  a. Changed the filter in the moving van
  b. Painted the moving van
  c. Paid sales tax on the new moving van
  d. Installed a new energy-efficient air-conditioning system for the office building
  e. Cleaned and lubricated sewing equipment
  f. Performed routine yearly maintenance on copy machine
  g. Purchased and installed a new set of energy-efficient deep fryers
  h. Replaced several cracked tiles in company bathroom floor
  i. Trained an employee prior to using the new energy-efficient deep fryers
  j. Replaced the tires on the moving van

E4-13B. *Account for capital and revenue expenditures (expenses) and calculate depreciation expense. (LO 2, 4)*
Shiny & New Auto Mechanic Shop has had a piece of equipment for five years. At the beginning of the sixth year, it wasn't performing as well as it should have been. First, Shiny & New had the equipment serviced, which cost $175. Then, the company tried replacing some worn-out parts, which cost $480. Finally, at the beginning of the sixth year, it completed a major overhaul of the equipment that not only fixed the machine, but also added new functionality to it and extended the useful life by four years (to a total of ten years with five remaining) with no salvage value. The overhaul cost $20,000. (Originally, the machine cost $65,000, had a salvage value of $5,000, and an estimated useful life of six years.)
  a. Which of these costs are capital expenditures? How would these amounts appear on the financial statements?
  b. Which are revenue expenditures? How would these amounts appear on the financial statements?
  c. Assuming Shiny & New uses the straight-line method of depreciation, how much depreciation expense will be reported on the income statements for years six through ten?

E4-14B. *Account for capital and revenue expenditures (expenses) and calculate depreciation expense. (LO 2, 4)*
Global Electronics operates a manufacturing plant for production of its products. At the beginning of 2008, the accounting records for the company showed the following balances for its only piece of equipment, purchased at the beginning of 2005:

Equipment	$94,000
Accumulated depreciation	54,000

During 2008, the following cash costs were incurred for repairs and maintenance on the equipment:

Routine maintenance and repairs	$ 575
Major overhaul of the equipment that improved efficiency	30,000

The company uses straight-line depreciation and estimates the equipment will last for 5 years beginning in 2008 with a $4,000 estimated salvage value. The company's fiscal year ends on December 31.
  a. How much did the firm record for depreciation on the equipment at the end of 2008?

b. After the overhaul, at the beginning of 2008, what is the remaining estimated life?
c. What is the amount of depreciation expense the company will record for 2008?

E4-15B. *Account for disposal of an asset.* (LO 5)
Chesney Flower Shop purchased a delivery van for $51,000. The company expects the van to have an 8-year useful life and a salvage value of $3,000.
 a. If Chesney sells the van after 2 years for $40,500, would it realize a gain or loss? How much? (Assume straight-line depreciation.)
 b. What would be the gain or loss if the van were sold for $18,250 after 5 years?

E4-16B. *Account for disposal of an asset.* (LO 5)
Brenda Sue's Stitch & Sew purchased a sewing machine 4 years ago for $29,000. The company expects the machine to have a salvage value of $4,000 after a 10-year useful life. Assuming the company uses straight-line depreciation, calculate the gain or loss realized if the company sells the machine after 4 years for:
 a. $ 14,250
 b. $ 18,600

E4-17B. *Account for disposal of an asset.* (LO 5)
Kat & Jen's Solar Tan disposed of a high-pressure tanning bed that had been used in the business for 3 years. The records of the company provide the following information:

High-pressure tanning bed	$39,000
Accumulated depreciation	18,000

Calculate the gain or loss on the disposal of the tanning bed for each of the following independent situations:
 a. Kat & Jen's sold the tanning bed to Dark Bodies for $21,000.
 b. Kat & Jen's sold the tanning bed to a customer for $22,550.
 c. Kat & Jen's sold the tanning bed to Angela's Fitness Center for $18,000.
 d. The tanning salon was broken into and the tanning bed was stolen; Kat & Jen's had no insurance.

E4-18B. *Account for disposal of an asset.* (LO 5)
Crystal Clean Steamers disposed of an industrial wet/dry vacuum that had been used in the business for 5 years. The vacuum originally cost $51,000 and had associated accumulated depreciation of $32,500. Calculate the gain or loss on the disposal of the vacuum for each of the following situations:
 a. The company sold the vacuum to a local church for $16,250.
 b. The company sold the vacuum to a competitor for $21,475.
 c. The company called the city trash collectors to pick up the vacuum because it was totally worthless.

E4-19B. *Calculate gain or loss and cash flow.* (LO 5, 6)
Safin Incorporated sold assets with an original cost of $37,000 and accumulated depreciation of $30,000. If the cash proceeds from the sale were $4,000, what was the gain or loss on the sale? On which financial statement would that amount be shown? How much would be shown on the statement of cash flows and in which section?

E4-20B. *Prepare financial statements.* (LO 6)
For each of the following, give the financial statement on which it would appear.
 a. Book value of fixed assets of $56,900
 b. Proceeds from sale of fixed assets of $20,000
 c. Loss on sale of fixed assets of $12,500
 d. Accumulated depreciation on equipment of $10,000
 e. Depreciation expense on equipment of $2,000
 f. Impairment write-down on assets of $45,000

E4-21B. *Calculate return on assets and asset turnover ratios.* (LO 7)
Using the Office Depot annual report from the website that accompanies this text, calculate the following ratios for the most recent fiscal year and explain what each measures:
    a. Return on assets (ROA)
    b. Asset turnover ratio

E4-22B. *Identify risks and controls.* (LO 8)
Firms with large fixed assets such as land and factories often think that their assets are safe because they are too large to be stolen. What risks do you think exist for these firms with respect to such assets, and how might those risks be controlled?

Problem Set A

P4-1A. *Calculate capitalized cost and depreciation expense.* (LO 1, 2)
Acme Print Shop purchased a new printing press in 2007. The invoice price was $158,500, but the manufacturer of the press gave Acme a 2% discount for paying cash for the machine on delivery. Delivery costs amounted to $1,500, and Acme paid $500 for a special insurance policy to cover the press while in transit. Installation cost was $1,350, and Acme spent $3,000 training the employees to use the new press. Additionally, Acme hired a new supervisor at an annual salary of $65,000 to be responsible for keeping the press online during business hours.

Required

    a. What amount should be capitalized for this new asset?
    b. To calculate the depreciation expense for 2007, what other information do you need? Do you think the company should gather this information before purchasing the asset? Why or why not?

Excel Template
www.prenhall.com/reimers

P4-2A. *Calculate and analyze depreciation under alternative methods.* (LO 2)
On January 1, 2007, the Oviedo Manufacturing Company purchased equipment for $170,000. The estimated useful life of the equipment is 4 years, and the estimated salvage value is $10,000. The company expects the equipment to produce 480,000 units during its service life. Actual units produced were:

Year	Units
2007	100,800
2008	130,080
2009	139,200
2010	109,920

Required

    a. Calculate the depreciation expense for each year of the 4-year life of the equipment using
        1. Straight-line method
        2. Double-declining balance method
        3. Activity method (Round your answers to the nearest dollar.)
    b. How does the choice of depreciation methods affect net income in each of the years? How does the choice of depreciation methods affect the balance sheet in each of the years?

P4-3A. *Calculate and analyze depreciation under alternative methods.* (LO 2)
Federal Express purchased a new truck on January 1, 2007, at a cost of $100,000. The estimated useful life is 5 years with a salvage value of $10,000.

Required

    a. Prepare two different depreciation schedules for the truck—one using the straight-line method, and the other using the double-declining balance method. (Round to the nearest dollar.)

b. Determine which method would result in the greatest net income for the year 2007.
c. (Appendix) How would taxes affect management's choice between these two methods for the financial statements?

P4-4A. *Calculate and analyze depreciation under alternative methods.* (LO 2)
Peps Co. purchased a new machine at the beginning of 2006 for $6,400. The company expects the machine to last for 5 years and have a salvage value of $400. The estimated productive life of the machine is 100,000 units. Yearly production: in 2006—28,000 units; in 2007—22,000 units; in 2008—16,000 units; in 2009—14,000 units; in 2010—20,000 units.

Excel Template
www.prenhall.com/reimers

Required

a. Calculate the depreciation expense for each year of the 5-year life of the machine using
   1. Straight-line method
   2. Double-declining balance method (Round to the nearest dollar.)
   3. Activity method using units
b. For each method, give the amount of accumulated depreciation that would be shown on the balance sheet at the end of each year.
c. Calculate the book value of the machine at the end of each year for each method.

P4-5A. *Account for intangible assets.* (LO 3)
LB Company had the following balances in its intangible assets accounts at the beginning of the year. The patents have a remaining useful life of 10 years, and the copyright has a remaining useful life of 7 years.

Patents	$35,000
Copyright	21,000
Goodwill	40,000

Transactions during the year:

1. At the beginning of the year, LB filed for a new patent. The costs totaled $20,000. Its useful life is estimated at 10 years.
2. LB incurred R&D costs of $60,000 related to new product development. No new products have been identified.
3. LB evaluated the goodwill for impairment and reduced its book value by $2,000.
4. LB successfully defended one of its patents in court. Fees totaled $24,000.

Required

Show each of the transactions in the accounting equation, including any adjustments that would need to be made for the year-end financial statements. Then, prepare the intangible assets section of the balance sheet at year-end.

P4-6A. *Account for change in estimates for depreciation.* (LO 4)
In January 2004, Harvey's Hoola Hoop Company purchased a computer system that cost $37,000. Harvey's estimated that the system would last for 5 years and have a salvage value of $2,000 at the end of 2008. The company uses the straight-line method of depreciation. Analyze each of the following independent scenarios.
   a. Before the depreciation expense is recorded for the year 2006, computer experts tell Harvey's that the system can be used until the end of 2008 as planned but that it will be worth only $500.
   b. Before depreciation expense is recorded for the year 2006, Harvey's decides that the computer system will last only until the end of 2007. The company anticipates the value of the system at that time will still be $2,000.
   c. Before depreciation expense is recorded for the year 2006, Harvey's decides that the computer system will last until the end of 2008, but that it will be worth only $1,000 at that time.

  d. Before the depreciation expense is recorded for the year 2006, computer experts tell Harvey's that the system can be used until the end of 2012 if the company spends $4,000 on upgrades. However, the estimated salvage value at that time would be $0. Harvey's decides to follow the experts' advice and upgrade the computer system.

Required

Calculate the amount of depreciation expense related to the computer system Harvey's Hoola Hoop Company would report on its income statement for the year ended December 31, 2006, for each scenario.

P4-7A. *Account for disposal of an asset.* (LO 5)
Analyze each of the following independent scenarios.
  a. A truck that cost $25,000 had an estimated useful life of 5 years and no salvage value. After 4 years of using straight-line depreciation, the company sold the truck for $6,000.
  b. A machine that cost $50,000 had an estimated useful life of 12 years and a salvage value of $2,000. After 10 years of using straight-line depreciation, the company sold the completely worn-out machine for $400 as scrap.
  c. An asset that cost $40,000 had an estimated useful life of 4 years and a salvage value of $2,000. After 3 years of using double-declining balance depreciation, the company sold the asset for $11,000.
  d. A machine that cost $15,000 had an estimated useful life of 5 years and no salvage value. After 4 years of using straight-line depreciation, the company deemed the asset worthless and hauled it to the dump.

Required

For each scenario, calculate the gain or loss, if any, that would result upon disposal.

P4-8A. *Calculate depreciation under alternative methods and account for disposal of an asset.* (LO 2, 5)
Bella Interiors purchased a new sewing machine on January 2, 2007, for $48,000. The company expects the machine to have a useful life of 5 years and a salvage value of $3,000. The company's fiscal year ends on December 31.

Required

  a. Calculate the depreciation expense for the fiscal years 2007 and 2008 using each of the following methods:
   1. Straight-line method
   2. Double-declining balance method
  b. Assume that Bella Interiors decided to use the straight-line method and that the sewing machine was sold at the end of December 2009, for $27,000. What was the gain or loss on the sale? On which financial statement would the gain or loss appear? What information does this accounting calculation provide for future decisions?

P4-9A. *Calculate depreciation under alternative methods and account for disposal of an asset.* (LO 2, 5)
Perfect Heating and Air purchased a truck 3 years ago for $50,000. The company expects the truck to have a useful life of 5 years with no salvage value. The company has taken three full years of depreciation expense.

Required

  a. Assume that the company uses straight-line depreciation. If the truck is sold for $25,000, will there be a gain or loss on the sale? If so, how much? How will the sale affect the financial statements for the year?

b. Assume that the company uses double-declining balance depreciation. If the truck is sold for $15,000, will there be a gain or loss on the sale? If so, how much? How will the sale affect the financial statements for the year?

c. Assume the company uses straight-line depreciation and sells the truck for $20,000. Would there be a gain or loss on the sale? How would that change if the company had been using double-declining balance depreciation?

P4-10A. *(Appendix) Analyze and correct accounting errors related to long-term assets.* (LO 9)

Due to an umpire strike early in 2006, Umpire's Empire had some trouble with its information processing and some errors were made in accounting for certain transactions. Evaluate the following independent situations that occurred during the year:

a. At the beginning of 2006, a building and land were purchased together for $100,000. Even though the appraisers determined that 90% of the price should be allocated to the building, Umpire's decided to allocate the entire purchase price to the building. The building is being depreciated using the straight-line method over 40 years, with an estimated salvage value of $10,000.

b. During the year, Umpire did some R&D on a new gadget to keep track of balls and strikes. The R&D cost $20,000, and Umpire capitalized it. The company intends to write it off over 5 years, using straight-line depreciation with no salvage value.

c. Near the beginning of the year, Umpire spent $10,000 on routine maintenance for its equipment, and the accountant decided to capitalize these costs as part of the equipment. (Equipment is depreciated over 5 years with no salvage value.)

d. Umpire spent $5,000 to extend the useful life of some of its equipment. The accountant capitalized the cost.

Required

a. For each, describe the error made and list the effect, if any, that the uncorrected error would have on the following items for Umpire's 2006 financial statements: net income, long-term assets, and retained earnings. If there is no error, simply write N/A next to the item.

b. Describe the adjustments that would correct the company's accounting records and make the 2006 financial statements accurate. If there is no error, write N/A next to the item.

Problem Set B

P4-1B. *Calculate capitalized cost and depreciation expense.* (LO 1, 2)

The executives for Sea World bought a piece of property adjacent to the park with an old, run-down motel. The cost of the land with the old motel was $1,500,000. Real estate commissions and fees including the title search were $317,850. Sea World paid its attorney $15,000 to review the contract and complete the purchase of the land on July 1, 2008. The resort paid $25,750 for the old motel to be demolished and an additional $17,850 for sugar white sand to be hauled in to prepare the land for use. The company paid $80,000 for some palm trees for the new area. Sea World hired three new employees at a salary of $35,000 a year each to maintain the landscaping for the new area.

Required

a. What amount should be capitalized for this new asset?

b. Would there be any depreciation expense for land at the end of 2008? Explain your answer.

P4-2B. *Calculate and analyze depreciation under alternative methods.* (LO 2)

WTA Tennis Academy purchased a new ball machine at a cost of $18,000 at the beginning of January 2005. The machine was estimated to have a salvage value of $2,000 at the end

Excel Template
www.prenhall.com/reimers

of its useful life of 4 years. A machine like this is supposed to deliver 160,000 hours of service. The actual number of hours that the machine was used per year was:

Year	Hours
2005	40,000
2006	60,800
2007	39,200
2008	20,000

Required

    a. Calculate the depreciation expense for each year of the 4-year life of the ball machine using
        1. Straight-line method
        2. Activity method
        3. Double-declining method
    b. How does the choice of depreciation methods affect income in each of the years?
    c. How does the choice of depreciation methods affect the balance sheet in each of the years?

P4-3B. *Calculate and analyze depreciation under alternative methods.* (LO 2)
Sugar's Candy Company purchased an automated display rack on January 1, 2008, at a cost of $35,000. The company estimates the display rack has a useful life of 5 years with a salvage value of $5,000.

Required

    a. Prepare two different depreciation schedules for the display rack—one using the straight-line method and the other using the double-declining balance method. (Round to the nearest dollar.)
    b. Determine which method would result in the greater net income for the year 2010.
    c. How would taxes affect management's choice between these two methods for the financial statements?

Excel Template
www.prenhall.com/reimers

P4-4B. *Calculate and analyze depreciation under alternative methods.* (LO 2)
Clean Water Co. purchased a new water filter at the beginning of 2010 for $200,000. It is expected to last for 8 years and have a salvage value of $32,000. The estimated productive life of the machine is 200,000 units. Yearly production: in 2010—45,000 units; in 2011—29,000 units; in 2012—41,000 units; in 2013—22,000 units; in 2014—25,000 units; in 2015—15,000 units; in 2016—16,000 units; and in 2017—7,000 units.

Required

    a. Calculate the depreciation for each year using each of these depreciation methods:
        1. Straight-line method
        2. Activity method based on units
        3. Double-declining balance method (round to the nearest dollar)
    b. For each method, give the amount of accumulated depreciation that would be shown on the balance sheet at the end of each year.
    c. Calculate the book value of the water filter at the end of each year for each method.

P4-5B. *Account for intangible assets.* (LO 3)
Larkin Company had the following balances in its intangible asset accounts at the beginning of the year. The trademarks have a remaining useful life of 5 years, and the copyright has a remaining useful life of 10 years.

Trademarks	$85,000
Copyright	50,000
Goodwill	80,000

Transactions during the year:

1. At the beginning of the year, Larkin filed for a new trademark. The costs totaled $40,000. Its useful life is estimated at 5 years.
2. Larkin incurred R&D costs of $30,000, related to new product development. No new products have been identified.
3. Larkin evaluated the goodwill for impairment and reduces its book value by $20,000.
4. Larkin successfully defended its copyrights in court. Fees totaled $10,000.

Required

Show each of the transactions in the accounting equation, including any adjustments that would need to be made for the year-end financial statements. Then, prepare the intangible assets section of the balance sheet at year-end.

P4-6B. *Account for change in estimates for depreciation.* (LO 4)
In July 2006, Hallmark Company purchased a computer system that cost $7,000. The company estimates that the system will last for 5 years and will have a salvage value of $2,000. The company uses the straight-line method of depreciation and has a June 30 fiscal year-end. Analyze each of the following independent scenarios.

   a. Before depreciation expense is recorded for the fiscal year ended June 30, 2009, Hallmark decides that the computer system will last until June 30, 2011 but that it will be worth only $800 at that time.
   b. Before depreciation expense is recorded for the fiscal year ended June 30, 2009, Hallmark decides that the computer system will last only until June 30, 2010. The company anticipates the value of the system at that time will still be $2,000.
   c. Before depreciation expense is recorded for the fiscal year ended June 30, 2009, Hallmark decides that the computer system will last until June 30, 2011 but that it will be worth only $1,500 at that time.
   d. Before depreciation expense is recorded for the fiscal year ended June 30, 2009, Hallmark's computer experts decide that the system can be used until June 30, 2013 if the company spends $1,000 on upgrades. However, the estimated salvage value at that time would be 0. Hallmark decides to follow the experts' advice and upgrade the computer system.

Required

Calculate the amount of depreciation expense related to the computer system Hallmark will report on its income statement for the fiscal year ended June 30, 2009, for each scenario.

P4-7B. *Account for disposal of an asset.* (LO 5)
Analyze each of the following independent scenarios.

   a. A company van that cost $32,000 had an estimated useful life of 8 years and no salvage value. After 6 years of using straight-line depreciation, the company sold the van for $12,000.
   b. A copy machine that cost $35,000 had an estimated useful life of 5 years and a salvage value of $5,000. After 2 years of using double-declining balance depreciation, the company sold the copy machine for $10,000.
   c. A company truck that cost $48,000 had an estimated useful life of 7 years and a salvage value of $6,000. After 5 years of using straight-line depreciation and driving the truck many miles on tough terrain, the company sold the completely worn-out truck for $850 for spare parts.
   d. A state-of-the-art computer that cost $29,000 had an estimated useful life of 4 years and a salvage value of $2,000. After 3 years of using double-declining balance depreciation, the company sold the computer for $6,000.

Required

For each scenario, calculate the gain or loss, if any, that would result upon disposal.

P4-8B. *Calculate depreciation under alternative methods and account for disposal of an asset.* (LO 2, 5)

A&W Root Beer Company bought new brewery equipment on January 1, 2008, for $64,000. The company expects the equipment to have a useful life of 8 years and a salvage value of $8,000. The company's fiscal year ends on December 31.

Required

    a. Calculate the depreciation expense for the fiscal years 2008 and 2009 using each of the following methods:
        1. Straight-line method
        2. Double-declining balance method
    b. Assume that the company decided to use the double-declining balance method and that the brewery equipment was sold at the end of December 2009, for $42,000. What was the gain or loss on the sale? On which financial statement would the gain or loss appear? What information does this accounting calculation provide for future decisions?

P4-9B. *Calculate depreciation under alternative methods and account for disposal of an asset.* (LO 2, 5)

The Queen Grande View Hotel purchased a van 3 years ago for $62,000. The company expects the van to have a useful life of 4 years and a $10,000 salvage value. Queen Grande View has taken three full years of depreciation expense.

Required

    a. Assume that Queen Grande View uses straight-line depreciation. If the van is sold for $20,000, will there be a gain or loss on the sale? If so, how much? How will it affect Queen Grande View's financial statements for the year?
    b. Assume that Queen Grande View uses double-declining balance depreciation. If the van is sold for $9,750, will there be a gain or loss on the sale? If so, how much? How will it affect Queen Grande View's financial statements for the year?
    c. Assume Queen Grande View uses double-declining balance depreciation and sells the van for $23,000. Would there be a gain or loss on the sale? How would that change if Queen Grande View had been using straight-line depreciation?

P4-10B. *(Appendix) Analyze and correct accounting errors related to long-term assets.* (LO 9)

During 2007, Jule's Gym had some trouble with its information processing due to several hurricanes, and some errors were made in accounting for certain transactions. The firm uses straight-line depreciation for all of its long-term assets. Evaluate the following independent situations that occurred during the year:

    a. At the beginning of the year, a basket purchase of a building and land was made for $350,000. The appraisers indicated that the market value of the land was $135,000 and the market value of the building was $250,000. So, Jule's Gym allocated $135,000 of the purchase price to the land and the remainder of the purchase price to the building. The building has an estimated useful life of 20 years and an estimated salvage value of $25,000.
    b. The plumber spent a great deal of time repairing broken toilets in one of the gym's buildings this year. Total cost, which Jule's Gym capitalized, was $5,000. Jule's Gym decided it was best to leave it on the books as an asset and not write it off, because the toilets will be used for quite a few more years. (Use 20 years as the estimated remaining useful life of the toilets.)
    c. Jule's Gym purchased a new van. It cost $20,000 and is expected to last 3 years. It has a salvage value of $2,000. To properly equip it for transporting gym equipment between locations, the inside was customized at a cost of $6,000. The cost of the van was capitalized, and the cost of the customization was expensed.
    d. Jule's Gym spent $5,500 on routine maintenance of its exercise equipment. The cost was expensed.

Required

   a. For each, describe the error made and list the effect, if any, that the uncorrected error would have on the following items for Jule's Gym's 2007 financial statements: net income, long-term assets, and retained earnings. If there is no error, simply write N/A next to the item.

   b. Use the accounting equation to show the adjustments that would correct the company's accounting records and make the 2007 financial statements accurate. If there is no error, write N/A next to the problem.

Financial Statement Analysis

FSA4-1. *Analyze long-term assets on the balance sheet.* (LO 6)
Information from The Home Depot Annual Report is shown here.

Required

   a. Can you tell how much The Home Depot paid for the buildings it owns? If so, how do you know?

   b. Can you tell how much the buildings are worth (the market value)?

   c. Explain what you think is included in each category of Property and Equipment. (Hint: To explain Capital Leases, be sure to read the Understanding Business feature in the chapter.)

   d. The Home Depot says it is modernizing its stores and building many new stores. Is this supported by any of the information?

From the Balance Sheet of The Home Depot, at

(dollars in millions)	January 29 2006	January 30 2005
Property and Equipment at cost:		
Land	7,924	6,932
Buildings	14,056	12,325
Furniture, Fixtures and Equipment	7,073	6,195
Leasehold Improvements	1,207	1,191
Construction in Progress	843	1,404
Capital Leases	427	390
	31,530	28,437
Less Accumulated Depreciation and Amortization	6,629	5,711
Net Property and Equipment	24,901	22,726

FSA4-2. *Analyze long-term assets on the balance sheet.* (LO 6)
Information from the 2005 Sony Annual Report is given here.

From the Sony Corporation Balance Sheets at March 31

	Yen in millions		Dollars in millions (Note 3)
	2004	2005	2005
Property, plant and equipment (Notes 9 and 12):			
Land	189,785	182,900	1,709
Buildings	930,983	925,796	8,652
Machinery and equipment	2,053,085	2,192,038	20,486
Construction in progress	98,480	92,611	866
	3,272,333	3,393,345	31,713
Less—Accumulated depreciation	1,907,289	2,020,946	18,887
	1,365,044	1,372,399	12,826
Intangible assets			
Goodwill, net	299,024	283,923	
Intangibles, net	307,034	187,024	

From the Notes to the Financial Statements
Property, Plant and Equipment and Depreciation
Property, plant and equipment are stated at cost. Depreciation of property, plant and equipment is primarily computed on the declining-balance method for Sony Corporation and Japanese subsidiaries, except for certain semiconductor manufacturing facilities whose depreciation is computed on the straight-line method, and on the straight-line method for foreign subsidiary companies at rates based on estimated useful lives of the assets, principally, ranging from 15 years up to 50 years for buildings and from 2 years up to 10 years for machinery and equipment. Significant renewals and additions are capitalized at cost. Maintenance and repairs, and minor renewals and betterments are charged to income as incurred.

Goodwill and Other Intangible Assets
Goodwill and certain other intangible assets that are determined to have an indefinite life are not amortized and are tested for impairment on an annual basis and between annual tests if an event occurs or circumstances change that would more likely than not reduce the fair value below its carrying amount. Fair value for those assets is generally determined using a discounted cash flow analysis.

Intangible assets that are determined not to have an indefinite life mainly consist of artist contracts, music catalogs, acquired patent rights and software to be sold, leased or otherwise marketed. Artist contracts and music catalogs are amortized on a straight-line basis principally over a period of up to 40 years. Acquired patent rights and software to be sold, leased or otherwise marketed are amortized on a straight-line basis over 3 to 10 years.

Required
   a. What is Sony's primary method for depreciating its assets?
   b. How much did Sony pay for the machinery and equipment it owns?
   c. Are any of the assets listed as property, plant, and equipment not being depreciated?
   d. Can you tell how much depreciation expense Sony had for the fiscal year ended March 31, 2005?
   e. Explain what the $18,877 (in millions) of accumulated depreciation represents.
   f. Can you find a sentence in the notes that summarizes the accounting treatment for major overhaul or additions to assets discussed in the chapter?
   g. Describe how Sony evaluates goodwill for impairment.

FSA4-3. *Analyze long-term assets on the balance sheet.* (LO 2, 3, 5, 6)
Use the Staples annual report from the appendix at the back of the book to help you answer the following questions.
   a. What type of depreciable assets does Staples have? What methods does the company use to depreciate these assets?
   b. Does Staples have any intangible assets? What are they and how are they being written off?
   c. What can you tell about the age and/or condition of Staples long-term assets? Is the company continuing to invest in property, plant, and equipment?
   d. Is the company making good use of its assets? How can you evaluate this?

Critical Thinking Problems

Risk and Control

What kinds of risks does a firm like Office Depot face with respect to safeguarding its assets? What types of controls do you think it already has in place to minimize these risks? Are any specific controls mentioned in the 10-K report provided on the website for this book?

Ethics

Rachel works in a real estate office that is equipped with up-to-date copiers, scanners, and printers. She is frequently the only employee working in the office in the evenings and often has spare time to do personal work. She has begun to use the office equipment for her children's school reports and for her husband's business. Do you think Rachel's use of the office equipment is harmless, or is she behaving unethically? Why? If you believe her behavior is unethical, what controls could be in place to prevent it? Have you ever used office resources for personal tasks? Under what conditions could such use of office resources be justified?

Group Assignment

Select one of the three depreciation methods presented in the chapter. Discuss reasons why the method should be used and reasons why the method is not a good choice. Determine the method you think is most consistent with the objectives of financial reporting.

Internet Exercise: Best Buy

Best Buy is the number-one specialty retailer of consumer electronics, personal computers, entertainment software, and appliances. Best Buy has about 742 stores in 49 states, with heavy concentrations in the Midwest, Texas, California, and Florida.

IE4-1. Go to www.bestbuy.com, and select "For Our Investors" near the bottom of the page. Then, select Best Buy's most recent annual report in the PDF format. Use the consolidated balance sheets to answer the following questions. At the most recent year-end, examine Property and Equipment.
  a. What is the acquisition cost of these assets?
  b. What is the book value (carrying value)?
  c. What amount of the acquisition cost has already been expensed?
  d. Are any of the assets listed not being depreciated?

IE4-2. Use the notes to financial statements to answer the following questions (usually the information can be found in note 1):
  a. Find the heading Property and Equipment. What depreciation method does Best Buy use for property and equipment? What is the range of useful lives for buildings and for fixtures and equipment? Do these useful lives make sense?
  b. Find the heading Goodwill. What type of an asset is goodwill? Does Best Buy write off this asset? Explain what the company does.

IE4-3. On page 25 of Best Buy's annual report for its fiscal year ended February 25, 2006, there is a 5-year summary of financial highlights.
  a. Identify the amounts reported for total assets at the four most recent year-ends.
  b. Identify the amounts reported for Revenues and Net Earnings (net income) for the three most recent years.
  c. Compute the asset turnover ratio for the two most recent fiscal years. In which fiscal year did the company make best use of its assets? How can you tell?

Appendix 4

Depreciation and Taxes

L.O.9
Explain how depreciation for financial statements differs from depreciation for taxes.

Depreciation and Taxes

The accounting information a company presents on its financial statements is not the same information the company reports to the IRS on its federal income tax return. The company follows GAAP reporting standards when preparing financial statements because those statements are provided to shareholders, who are the owners of the company. The information for taxes is determined by the legal rules of the Internal Revenue Code. GAAP and the IRS require different information to be reported, so companies will use an information system that can produce two sets of data.

For depreciating fixed assets, corporations use a method called the **Modified Accelerated Cost Recovery System (MACRS)** to calculate the deduction for their tax returns. MACRS is allowed for tax purposes but not GAAP. The goal of MACRS is to give companies incentive to invest in new property, plant, and equipment. If an asset can be written off quickly—large depreciation deductions over a small number of years—the tax benefit from the depreciation deductions leaves the company more cash to invest in new assets.

How does more depreciation expense result in lower taxes? Suppose a company's income before depreciation and before taxes is $10,000. If depreciation expense for taxes is $2,000, then the company has taxable income of $8,000. Suppose the company's tax rate is 25%. Then, the company must pay $2,000 (= $8,000 × 0.25) in taxes. (Net income will be $6,000.)

Now, suppose the company can depreciate the assets using a more accelerated depreciation method that results in $4,000 worth of depreciation expense. Income before depreciation and taxes is $10,000, so income before taxes will be $6,000 (= $10,000 − $4,000). With a tax rate of 25%, the company will have to pay $1,500 in taxes. (Net income will be $4,500.)

When depreciation expense is larger, the amount of taxes a company must pay is smaller. A smaller tax bill means less cash has to be paid to the IRS, so the company's net cash flow for the year will be greater. However, as we have seen from comparing straight-line depreciation and double-declining balance depreciation, *over the life of an asset*, the total depreciation expense is the same no matter what method the company uses. The difference between the methods is reflected in the way the total depreciation is allocated to the years the asset is used. The reason a company wants to use an accelerated method like MACRS for tax purposes is so that the largest deductions are taken as soon as possible. Saving tax dollars *this* year is preferred to saving them *next* year because it is cash the company can use to buy assets that can increase production and therefore profits.

The Purchase and Sale of Inventory

Here's Where You've Been. . .

In Chapter 4, you learned about how a company accounts for long-term assets—property, plant, and equipment. You learned how assets are depreciated and how the information relevant to long-term assets is presented on the financial statements.

Here's Where You're Going. . .

In Chapter 5, you will learn how a company accounts for the purchase and sale of inventory. You will learn about LIFO and FIFO, two popular ways of keeping track of inventory purchases and sales.

Learning Objectives

When you are finished studying this chapter, you should be able to:

1. Calculate and record the purchase and sale of inventory.

2. Explain the two methods of inventory record keeping.

3. Define and calculate inventory using the four major inventory cost flow assumptions and explain how these methods affect the financial statements.

4. Analyze transactions and prepare financial statements with the purchase and sale of inventory.

5. Explain the lower-of-cost-or-market rule for valuing inventory.

6. Define and calculate the gross profit ratio and the inventory turnover ratio.

7. Describe the risks associated with inventory and the controls that minimize those risks.

8. (Appendix 5A) Describe and calculate the effect of inventory errors on the financial statements.

9. (Appendix 5B) Estimate inventory using the gross profit method.

Ethics Matters

Firms lose billions of dollars from inventory theft. Individual firms such as Bloomingdale's, Target, and Costco, will not talk about the numbers publicly, but the National Retail Federation gathers the data from hundreds of retailers. The bad news is that employee theft accounts for almost half of the over $30 billion annual losses from the disappearance of inventory.

What does that mean for a firm? Preston Turco, the owner of two specialty grocery stores in New York, uses elaborate security in his stores—special fraud detection software for cash registers, hidden cameras, store detectives, and an employee handprint identification device to clock his employees in and out. He has some other advice about reducing inventory theft: Hire and keep a happy and loyal staff.

We have all read about Ken Lay, Jeff Skilling, and Bernie Ebbers. They were at the very top level of management at the firms they looted. But very few of us have read about the deli clerk who switched higher price tags for lower ones and tried to bribe a cashier to look the other way. That clerk is now in prison, according to Mr. Turco. It turns out that ethics matter at all levels of a business.

L.O.1
Calculate and record the purchase and sale of inventory.

Acquiring and Selling Merchandise

An Operating Cycle

The operating cycle for a merchandising firm is a series of business activities that describes how a company takes cash and turns it into more cash. Exhibit 5.1 shows the operating cycle for a typical merchandising firm. For example, Target starts with cash, buys inventory, sells that inventory to customers, often creating accounts receivable, and then collects the cash from the customers. A firm's goal is to end up with more cash than it started with. For example, Target's net income for the fiscal year ended January 31, 2005, was over $3.1 billion, and the firm generated over $3.8 billion of net cash from operating activities. It was a very good year for Target.

Acquiring Merchandise for Sale

Now that you know about the operating cycle of a business, we will focus on the activity of purchasing the inventory. Acquiring goods to sell is an important activity for merchandising firms. Stroll down the aisle of Staples or Office Max and imagine keeping track of all that merchandise. All goods owned and held for sale in the regular course of business are considered *merchandise* inventory. In contrast, supplies and equipment are used by most firms rather than sold by those firms, in which case they would not be considered inventory. Only the items a firm sells are considered inventory. Most large corporations have large purchasing departments dedicated exclusively to acquiring inventory. Regardless of their size, firms must keep meticulous track of their inventory purchases through their information systems. An information system refers to the way the firm records and reports its transactions, including inventory and sales.

A merchandising firm records the inventory as a current asset until it is sold. According to the matching principle, inventory should be expensed in the period in which it is sold. So when it is sold, inventory becomes an expense—cost of goods sold. The sales of particular goods and the cost of those goods sold during the period are matched—put on the same income statement. You can see that the value of the inventory affects both the balance sheet and the income statement. Does the value of inventory matter? On its February 28, 2004, balance sheet, Best Buy had over $2.6 billion worth of inventory, making up over 30% of the company's total assets. That is a significant amount of the firm's assets.

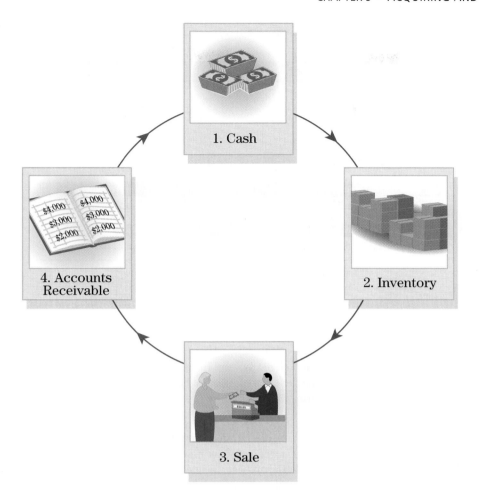

EXHIBIT 5.1

An Operating Cycle
This diagram shows a typical operating cycle of a merchandising firm. The firm begins with cash, then it purchases inventory, sells the inventory, and ends with the collection of cash.

We will look at the procedures for acquiring inventory and then focus on how to do the related record keeping.

Acquisition Process for Inventory

The process of acquiring inventory begins when someone in a firm decides to order merchandise for the inventory. The person requesting the purchase sends a document, called a purchase requisition, to the company's purchasing agent. For example, suppose that Office Depot needs to order paper. The manager of the appropriate department would submit a purchase requisition in either hard copy or electronic form to the purchasing agent. The purchasing agent selects a vendor to provide the paper, based on the vendor's prices, quality of goods or services needed, and the ability to deliver them in a timely manner. The purchasing agent specifies in a **purchase order**—a record of the company's request to a vendor for goods or services—what is needed, the prices, and the delivery time. A copy of the purchase order is sent to the vendor, and Office Depot keeps several copies for internal record keeping. An example of a purchase order is shown in Exhibit 5.2.

> A **purchase order** is a record of the company's request to a vendor for goods or services. It may be referred to as a P.O.

Office Depot's purchasing agent sends one copy of the purchase order to the receiving department and one to the accounts payable department. The receiving department will let the accounts payable department know when the goods have arrived. Accounts payable will pay for the goods when it receives an invoice from the vendor to match with the purchase order. The process can be much more complicated, but it always includes cooperation between departments so that the company pays for only the goods ordered and received.

Modern technology has provided shorter and more efficient ways to manage inventory. At Wal-Mart, for example, no one explicitly orders merchandise when it is needed. Using bar codes at the cash registers as each item is sold, the computerized inventory system is programmed to recognize when Wal-Mart should acquire more inventory, and the information

EXHIBIT 5.2

Purchase Order from Office Depot

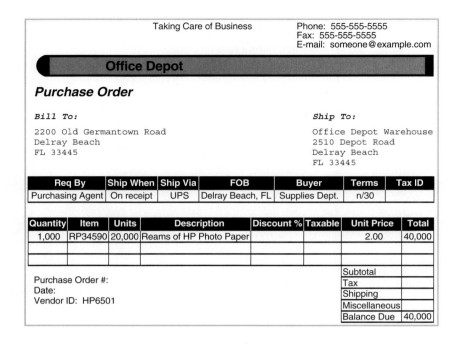

goes directly to the vendor's computerized system. Even when the process is automated, the underlying transaction is the same: Inventory is acquired from a vendor to be available to sell to a firm's customers, and the firm wants to be sure it pays for only the merchandise it has received.

Recording Purchases. Now that you are familiar with the procedures for purchasing inventory, you are ready to learn to account for its cost. The cost of acquiring inventory includes all costs the company incurs to purchase the items and get them ready for sale. Many people in the firm need details about the cost of inventory, including the person requesting the goods, the CFO, and the CEO. This inventory information is also needed for the financial statements.

There are two ways for firms to record their inventory transactions—perpetual and periodic. These two different methods describe the timing of the firm's inventory record keeping. When a company uses a **perpetual inventory system**, the firm records every purchase of inventory directly to the inventory account at the time of the purchase. Similarly, each time an item is sold, the firm will remove the cost of the item—the cost of goods sold—from the inventory account. That is the way Tom's Wear keeps track of its inventory. In the example that follows, Quality Lawn Mowers, a fictitious firm, will also use a perpetual inventory record-keeping system. We will discuss the **periodic inventory system** of record keeping—one in which the inventory account is updated only at the end of the period—later in the chapter.

We will use Quality Lawn Mowers for an example of how to account for the costs of inventory. Keep in mind that the company uses a perpetual inventory record-keeping system. Suppose that on June 1, Quality Lawn Mowers purchased 100 lawn mowers on account for $150 each from Black & Decker, a manufacturer of power tools and lawn mowers. This is how the transaction would be recorded in the accounting equation:

> The **perpetual inventory system** is a method of record keeping that involves updating the accounting records at the time of every purchase, sale, and return.

> The **periodic inventory system** is a method of record keeping that involves updating the accounting records only at the end of the accounting period.

Assets	=	Liabilities	+	Shareholders' equity		
					Contributed capital	+ Retained earnings
15,000 inventory		15,000 accounts payable				

Who Pays the Freight Costs to Obtain Inventory? The cost a company records in its inventory account is not always the amount quoted by the vendor. One reason is shipping costs. Remember that the cost of inventory includes all the costs to obtain the merchandise and get it ready to sell. When a merchandising firm pays for transportation costs for goods

EXHIBIT 5.3

Shipping Terms

Shipping terms determine who owns the goods, and at what point the owner pays the shipping costs. The firm that owns the goods while they are in transit must include the cost of those goods in its inventory.

Title passes here at *FOB shipping point*…or…Title passes here at *FOB destination*.

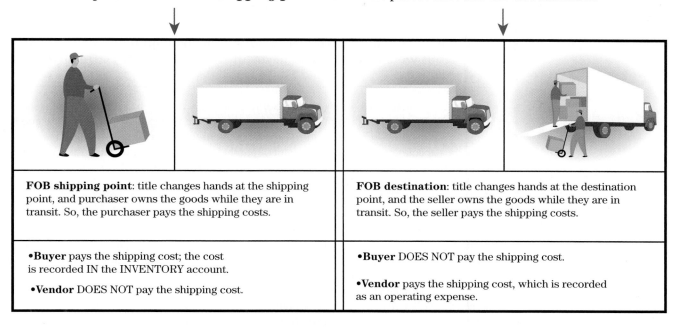

FOB shipping point: title changes hands at the shipping point, and purchaser owns the goods while they are in transit. So, the purchaser pays the shipping costs.	**FOB destination**: title changes hands at the destination point, and the seller owns the goods while they are in transit. So, the seller pays the shipping costs.
•**Buyer** pays the shipping cost; the cost is recorded IN the INVENTORY account. •**Vendor** DOES NOT pay the shipping cost.	•**Buyer** DOES NOT pay the shipping cost. •**Vendor** pays the shipping cost, which is recorded as an operating expense.

purchased, the freight cost is called freight-in and is considered part of the cost of the inventory. The shipping terms are negotiated between the buyer and the vendor.

If the terms of purchase are **FOB (free on board) shipping point**, title to the goods passes to the buyer at the shipping point (the vendor's warehouse), and the buyer is responsible for the cost of the transportation from that point on. If the terms are **FOB destination**, the vendor—Black & Decker—pays for the transportation costs until the goods reach their destination, when title passes to the buyer.

When you are the vendor and you pay the shipping costs for goods to be delivered to your customers, the expense goes on your income statement as freight-out or delivery expense. Freight-out is an operating expense, whereas freight-in is part of the cost of the inventory. Exhibit 5.3 shows the relationships among the FOB selling point, FOB destination, buyer, and vendor.

The details of inventory purchases, such as the shipping terms, can affect the cost of the inventory. A company must pay attention to these costs because such costs can make a difference in the profitability of the company.

Suppose the shipping cost for the 100 lawn mowers purchased by Quality Lawn Mowers was $343. If the shipping terms were FOB destination, then Black & Decker paid the shipping cost; and there is no record of the shipping cost in the books of Quality Lawn Mowers. However, suppose the terms were FOB shipping point. That means title changes hands at the point of shipping—the vendor's warehouse. Because Quality Lawn Mowers then owns the goods while they are in transit, Quality Lawn Mowers will pay the shipping costs. The $343 will be included as part of the cost of the inventory. Shipping costs are usually paid to the shipping company in cash. Here is how the transaction would be recorded in the accounting equation:

> **FOB (free on board) shipping point** means the buying firm pays the shipping costs. The amount is called freight-in and is included in the cost of the inventory.

> **FOB (free on board) destination** means that the vendor (selling firm) pays the shipping costs, so the buyer has no freight-in cost.

Assets	=	Liabilities	+	Shareholders' equity		
				Contributed capital	+	**Retained earnings**
343 inventory						
(343) cash						

Your Turn 5-1
Your Turn
Your Turn

In each separate situation, calculate the cost of the inventory purchased.

1. **Company A purchased merchandise FOB destination for $10,000. Terms were 2/10, n/30 and payment was made in 8 days. Freight cost was $90.**

2. **Company B purchased merchandise FOB shipping point for $10,000. Terms were 2/10, n/30 and payment was made in 29 days. Freight cost was $90.**

3. **Company C purchased merchandise FOB shipping point for $10,000. Terms were 2/10, n/30 and payment was made in 8 days. Freight cost was $90.**

Purchase Returns and Allowances. Some goods may need to be returned to the vendor because the firm ordered too much inventory, ordered the wrong items, or found the goods slightly damaged. When a firm returns goods, the transaction is called a *purchase return*. In the firm's accounting system, the amount of purchase returns will be deducted from the cost of the inventory. Because the company puts the cost of the items in the inventory account, the balance in that account will be decreased when goods are returned. The details of the returns will be noted in another part of the company's information system. The firm wants to know exactly how much merchandise it is returning in any given accounting period. A firm should be sure it understands the vendor's return policy. Often, near the end of the year, a vendor will institute a very liberal return policy to make a sale. Nevertheless, the firm should buy only the amount of inventory it actually needs, not a larger amount with the idea of returning it when the next accounting period starts.

Goods damaged or defective may be kept by the purchaser with a cost reduction called a *purchase allowance*. When a company has a purchase allowance, it is like getting a discounted purchase price so the inventory account will be reduced. A purchase allowance is different from a purchase return because the goods are kept by the purchaser in the case of a purchase allowance.

When an item is returned, accounts payable, which shows the amount a firm owes its vendors, will be reduced. The inventory account will be decreased because the goods have been returned. Suppose Quality Lawn Mowers returned two of the lawn mowers because they were defective. This is how the transaction would be recorded in the accounting equation:

Assets	=	Liabilities	+	Shareholders' equity		
				Contributed capital	+	Retained earnings
(300) inventory		(300) accounts payable				

Similarly, if a vendor gives the firm a purchase allowance, the amount owed to the vendor is reduced by subtracting the amount from accounts payable. There will also be a reduction in the balance in the inventory account to reflect the reduced cost. Purchase returns and purchase allowances are often grouped together in one expression—**purchase returns and allowances**.

Purchase Discounts. In addition to purchase returns and allowances, purchase discounts can also cause a difference between the vendor's quoted price and the cost to the purchasing firm. A **purchase discount** is a reduction in the purchase price in return for prompt payment. For example, a vendor offering a purchase discount for prompt payment from a customer would describe it in terms like this:

2/10, n/30

This term is read as "two-ten, net thirty" and means the vendor will give a 2% discount if the buyer pays for the entire purchase within 10 days of the invoice date. If not, the full amount is due within 30 days. A vendor may set any discount terms. What does 3/15, n/45 mean? The vendor will give a 3% discount if payment is made within 15 days. Otherwise,

Purchase returns and allowances are amounts that decrease the cost of inventory due to returned or damaged merchandise.

A **purchase discount** is a reduction in the price of an inventory purchase for prompt payment according to terms specified by the vendor.

full payment must be made within 45 days. The number of days a customer has to pay an invoice starts on the day after the date of the invoice. For example, an invoice dated June 15 with the terms 2/10, n/30 gives the customer until June 25 to pay with the discount applied. The full amount is due by July 15.

A firm should take advantage of purchase discount offers from vendors because it can amount to significant savings. If a vendor offers the terms 2/10, n/30, the vendor is actually charging the firm 36% annual interest to use the money if the firm does not pay within the discount period and waits until the last day, the 30th day. Here is how we calculated the high interest rate of 36%. If the discount period expires, and the firm has not paid until the 30th day after the invoice date, the firm is "borrowing" the money from the vendor for an additional 20 days. Because the firm did not pay within the discount period, the vendor has earned 2% in 20 days. And, 2% interest on a "loan" over 20 days is the same as a 36% annual rate, determined with the help of a simple ratio:

$$2\% \div 20 \text{ days} = x \div 360$$

Solve for x and you get x = 36% annual interest—if you consider a year as having 360 days. Some companies borrow the money from the bank (at 10% or 12% annual interest) to take advantage of purchase discounts.

Suppose Black & Decker offers Quality Lawn Mowers the terms 1/10, n/30. Quality takes advantage of this discount and pays for the inventory on June 9. Recall that it purchased the inventory on June 1, so the payment is made within the discount period. Quality Lawn Mowers owes the vendor $14,700 because $300 worth of merchandise from the original purchase of $15,000 was returned. The 1% discount amounts to $147. That means that the company will pay the vendor $14,553 ($14,700 − $147). Here is the way the transaction would be recorded in the accounting equation:

Assets	=	Liabilities	+	Shareholders' equity		
				Contributed capital	+	**Retained earnings**
(14,553) cash		(14,700) accounts				
(147) inventory		payable				

Before the payment, the balance in accounts payable was $14,700. So the entire $14,700 must be subtracted out of accounts payable. Because only $14,553 was actually paid, this is the amount deducted from the cash account. That leaves the discount amount to balance the accounting equation. This decreases the inventory account because inventory purchase was recorded at $14,700, which turned out not to be the cost of the inventory. The reduction of $147 adjusts the inventory account balance to the actual cost of the goods purchased.

If Quality Lawn Mowers did not pay within the discount period, the payment would be recorded with a reduction in accounts payable for $14,700 and a reduction in cash for $14,700.

Summary of Purchases for Quality Lawn Mowers. Let us review the activity in the inventory account for Quality Lawn Mowers. First, the original purchase of the 100 lawn mowers was recorded with an increase in inventory for $15,000. Then, Quality Lawn Mowers paid the shipping costs of $343. Next, Quality returned two lawn mowers—$300 worth of inventory. Finally, the company took advantage of the purchase discount. That reduced the value of the inventory by $147. The balance in the inventory account is now $14,896 for 98 lawn mowers. That is $152 per unit. This amount is called the **cost of goods available for sale**. If Quality had started the period with a beginning inventory, cost of goods available for sale would have included the amount of the beginning inventory. A simple way to think about the calculation of cost of goods available for sale is:

> **Cost of goods available for sale** is the total of beginning inventory plus the net purchases made during the period (plus any freight-in costs).

Beginning inventory	$ 0
+ Net purchases (this is total purchases less returns and allowances and discounts) 15,000 − 300 − 147	14,553
+ Shipping costs (freight-in)	343
= Cost of goods available for sale	$14,896

Your Turn 5-2
Your Turn
Your Turn

Jaden's Coffee Hut purchased 100 pounds of Columbian roast coffee beans to package and sell to its customers. The coffee cost $5 per pound, and Jaden's paid $100 for the bags in which to package the beans. When Jaden's received the invoice for $500 from the coffee importer, the accountant noticed that the payment terms were given as 2/10, n/30. The coffee beans were shipped FOB destination, and the shipping costs were $75. Jaden's accountant paid the coffee importer 5 days after the date on the invoice. The paper company that sold Jaden's the bags did not offer a discount, so Jaden's paid that firm a few weeks after receiving the invoice for $100. How much did Jaden's record in its inventory account related to these purchases?

Selling Merchandise

You now know how a company records the transactions related to the purchase of inventory. Now, we will look at what happens when the company sells the inventory.

Sales are reported net of returns, allowances, and any discounts given to customers. What you just learned about purchasing inventory also applies to selling the inventory, but everything is reversed. Instead of purchase returns and allowances, there will be *sales* returns and allowances. Instead of purchase discounts, there will be *sales* discounts.

The following are the typical business activities that take place when a firm makes a sale.

1. A customer places an order.
2. The company approves the order.
3. The warehouse selects the goods for shipment.
4. The company ships goods.
5. The company bills the customer for the goods.
6. The company receives payment for the goods.

Computers can perform some of these steps. Whether a firm performs the steps manually or with a computer, the objectives of those steps are the same.

- to ensure that the firm sells its goods or services to customers who will pay
- to ensure that the goods or services delivered are what the customers ordered
- to ensure that the customers are correctly billed and payment is received

Sales Process. For sales, revenue is typically recognized when the goods are shipped or when they are delivered, depending on the shipping terms. For example, when Intel ships computer chips to IBM with the terms FOB shipping point, the time the shipment leaves Intel will be the point at which Intel recognizes the revenue, not when the order is placed and not when IBM pays for the purchase. You know that the shipment of the goods is preceded by many crucial activities such as planning, marketing, and securing orders. Yet, no revenue is recognized until it is actually earned.

Exhibit 5.4 shows part of the note that IBM has included in the financial statements about its revenue recognition. Does payment need to be received before revenue is recognized at IBM? NO! Remember, GAAP is accrual accounting.

EXHIBIT 5.4

How Does IBM Recognize Revenue?

This is just a small part of IBM's note on revenue recognition.

The company recognizes revenue when it is realized or realizable and earned. The company considers revenue realized or realizable and earned when it has persuasive evidence of an arrangement, delivery has occurred, the sales price is fixed or determinable, and collectibility is reasonably assured. Delivery does not occur until products have been shipped or services have been provided to the client, the risk of loss has transferred to the client and client acceptance has been obtained, client acceptance provisions have lapsed, or the company has objective evidence that the criteria specified in the client acceptance provisions have been satisfied. The sale price is not considered to be fixed or determinable until all contingencies related to the sale have been resolved.

Recording Sales. When a sale is made, it is recorded as an increase in sales revenue, often simply called sales. Continuing our example with Quality Lawn Mowers, suppose the company sold 10 lawn mowers to Sam's Yard Service for $4,000 on account. This is the transaction in the accounting equation:

Assets	=	Liabilities	+	Shareholders' equity	
				Contributed capital	+ Retained earnings
4,000 accounts receivable					4,000 sales revenue

When a sale is made, the inventory will be reduced. Because Quality Lawn Mower has sold 10 lawn mowers, the cost of those mowers will be deducted from the balance in the inventory account. Recall that each lawn mower had a cost of $152. Removing the 10 mowers from inventory will reduce the inventory by $1,520 ($152 × 10). Cost of goods sold, an expense account, will increase by $1,520. This is the transaction in the accounting equation:

Assets	=	Liabilities	+	Shareholders' equity	
				Contributed capital	+ Retained earnings
(1,520) inventory					(1,520) cost of goods sold

Sales Returns and Allowances. A company's customers may return items, and the company may provide allowances on items it sells. These amounts will be recorded either as a reduction to sales revenue or in a separate account called **sales returns and allowances**. This account is an example of a **contra-revenue**, which will be deducted from sales revenue for the income statement. Often, you will simply see the term *net sales* on the income statement. This is gross sales minus the amount of returns and allowances. When a customer returns an item to the company, the customer's account receivable will be reduced (or cash will be reduced if the refund is made in cash). The sales returns and allowances account will be increased, and the balance in the account will eventually be deducted from sales revenue.

Suppose Sam's Yard Service, the company that purchased the 10 lawn mowers, discovers that one of them is dented and missing a couple of screws. Sam's Yard Service calls Quality Lawn Mowers to complain, and the salesman for Quality Lawn Mowers offers Sam's Yard Service an allowance of $100 on the damaged lawn mower. Sam's Yard Service agrees and will keep the lawn mower. Here is the transaction that Quality Lawn Mowers will record to adjust the amount of the sale and the amount Sam's Yard Service owes Quality Lawn Mowers:

> **Sales returns and allowances** is an account that holds amounts that reduce sales due to customer returns or allowances for damaged merchandise.

> A **contra-revenue** is an account that is an offset to a revenue account and therefore deducted from the revenue for the financial statements.

Assets	=	Liabilities	+	Shareholders' equity	
				Contributed capital	+ Retained earnings
(100) accounts receivable					(100) sales returns and allowances

Sales Discounts and Shipping Terms. The terms of sales discounts, reductions in the sales price for prompt payment, are expressed exactly like the terms you learned for purchases. A company will offer **sales discounts** to its customers to motivate them to pay promptly.

Suppose Quality Lawn Mowers offers Sam's Yard Service the terms 2/10, n/30 for the sale. If Sam's Yard Service pays its account within 10 days of the invoice date, Quality Lawn Mowers will reduce the amount due by 2%. This is an offer Sam's Yard Service should not refuse. Sam's Yard Service will pay $3,822, which is 98% of the amount of the invoice of $3,900. Recall the earlier $100 sales allowance that reduced the amount from $4,000 to $3,900.

> A **sales discount** is a reduction in the sales price of a product offered to customers for prompt payment.

Just as with sales returns and allowances, the amount of a sales discount could be subtracted directly from the sales revenue account, reducing the balance by $78. Whether or not you use a separate account to keep track of sales discounts, the income statement will show the net amount of sales. In this example, the calculation for net sales is

Sales revenue	$4,000
Sales allowance given	(100)
Sales discounts	(78)
Net sales	$3,822

Here is how the collection of cash from the customer is recorded in the accounting equation:

Assets	=	Liabilities	+	Shareholders' equity	
				Contributed capital	+ **Retained earnings**
3,822 cash (3,900) accounts receivable					(78) sales discounts

Notice two important things about the way the payment from Sam's Yard Service is recorded.

1. Sales discounts is a contra-revenue account like sales returns and allowances. The amount in the sales discounts account will be subtracted from sales revenue along with any sales returns and allowances to get *net sales* for the income statement.
2. Accounts receivable must be reduced by the full amount that Quality Lawn Mowers has recorded as Sam's Yard Service's accounts receivable balance. Even though the cash collected is less than this balance, Sam's Yard Service's account is paid in full with this payment, so the entire balance in Quality Lawn Mowers' accounting records for accounts receivable for Sam's Yard Service must be removed.

In addition to sales returns and allowances and sales discounts, a company will be concerned with shipping costs. You already learned about identifying the firm that pays for shipping by examining the shipping terms: FOB destination and FOB shipping point. When paying the shipping costs, the vendor will likely set prices high enough to cover the shipping. When the vendor pays the shipping costs, those costs are classified as operating expenses. Look back over Exhibit 5.3 on page 00. When you are working an accounting problem with shipping costs, be careful to properly identify your company as the purchaser or the vendor of the goods being shipped.

Summary of Purchases and Sales for Quality Lawn Mowers. A firm starts with beginning inventory, purchases additional inventory, and then sells some of the inventory. The calculation below shows what happened with Quality Lawn Mowers, providing a summary of the purchase and sales transactions.

Beginning inventory	$ 0
Purchases (net) ($15,000 − 300 − 147)	14,553
Freight-in	343
Cost of goods available for sale	14,896
Cost of goods sold	1,520
Ending inventory	$ 13,376

Sales Taxes. In addition to collecting sales revenue, most retail firms must also collect a sales tax for the state government. A sales tax is a percentage of the sales price. Suppose that Quality Lawn Mowers sold a mower to a customer for $400 and the sales tax rate is 4%. Quality collects the sales tax on behalf of the government, so it will owe the government whatever it collects. Here is how Quality Lawn Mowers would record receipt of $416 cash from the customer:

Assets	=	Liabilities	+	Shareholders' equity		
				Contributed capital	+	Retained earnings
416 cash		16 sales taxes payable				400 sales revenue

Fedco sold $3,000 worth of merchandise to a customer for cash. The sales tax was 5%. How much cash did Fedco receive? How much sales revenue did Fedco earn?

Your Turn 5-3
Your Turn
Your Turn

Recording Inventory: Perpetual Versus Periodic Record Keeping

L.O.2
Explain the two methods of inventory record keeping.

We have discussed buying and selling inventory. In our examples so far, the company used a perpetual inventory record-keeping system. With every transaction related to inventory, the inventory records were updated. As you learned earlier in the chapter, this is called a perpetual inventory system because it requires a continuous updating of the inventory records at the time of every purchase, every return, and every sale.

The other method, mentioned briefly earlier in the chapter, is called periodic. When a firm uses a periodic inventory system, the firm's accountant waits until the end of an accounting period to adjust the balance in the inventory account. The accounting system uses lots of different accounts to keep track of transactions rather than recording the transactions directly to the inventory account. Because of technology advances, an increasing number of companies are using perpetual inventory systems. For example, when you go shopping at Target and take your cart to the checkout counter, the cashier scans each of your items. The perpetual record-keeping system enables Target and stores such as Kroger, Safeway, and Macy's to do the equivalent of making the cost of goods sold adjustment at the time of sale. Of course, much more information is captured for the information system at the same time. Many companies have systems so sophisticated that the supplier of specific items will have access to the company's inventory via the Internet so that the supplying company is able to deliver goods to the purchasing company automatically. For example, Wal-Mart has many suppliers that automatically deliver goods when Wal-Mart's inventory records show that the inventory has fallen to some preset level.

Differences between Perpetual and Periodic Inventory Systems

One of the primary advantages of a perpetual system is that inventory records are always current, and a physical count can be compared to the records to see if there is any inventory shrinkage. Inventory shrinkage is a reduction in the inventory by damage, loss, or theft by either employees or customers. A perpetual system allows a company to identify shrinkage.

▶ *News Flash*

According to the National Retail Security Survey (http://retailindustry.about.com), this is how inventory shrinkage happens in the retail industry:

Employee theft	46%
Shoplifting	31%
Administrative errors	17%
Vendor fraud	6%

However, a perpetual system may be too cumbersome for firms that do not have up-to-date computerized support. A company may keep the physical count of its inventory current by recording each reduction in the amount of inventory sold without actually recording the cost of goods sold. That is a way to monitor the inventory for potential shrinkage without actually using a perpetual system for the accounting records.

When a company uses a periodic system, the accounting records are updated only at the end of the period. The firm must count the ending inventory and then calculate the amount for cost of goods sold. In other words, if the inventory is gone, it must have been sold. That means that any inventory shrinkage is not separately identified from the inventory sold. All missing inventory is considered inventory sold, and its cost will be included in the firm's cost of goods sold expense for the period.

Your Turn 5-4
Your Turn
Your Turn

Suppose a firm is very concerned about inventory theft. Which method of record keeping would be the best choice for this firm? Explain.

L.O.3
Define and calculate inventory using the four major inventory cost flow assumptions and explain how these methods affect the financial statements.

Inventory Cost Flow Assumptions

So far in this chapter, you have learned about the costs that must be included in the inventory. All costs to prepare the inventory for sale become part of the cost of the inventory and then, when the goods are sold, become part of the cost of goods sold expense. That is just the beginning of the story. Inventory costing gets more complicated when the cost of the merchandise changes with different purchases.

Suppose Oakley ships 120 pairs of its new sunglasses to Sunglass Hut. The cost to Sunglass Hut is $50 per pair. Then, suppose that just a month later, Sunglass Hut needs more of the popular sunglasses and buys another 120 pairs. This time, however, Oakley charges $55 per pair. If Sunglass Hut sold 140 pairs of Oakley sunglasses during the month to its customers, which ones did it sell? The problem is how to divide the cost of the inventory between the period's cost of goods sold and the ending (unsold) inventory.

We could determine the cost of goods sold if we knew how many pairs costing $50 were sold and how many pairs costing $55 were sold. Suppose Sunglass Hut has no method of keeping track of that information. The store simply knows 140 pairs were sold and 100 pairs are left in inventory. There were 240 pairs available for sale at a total cost of $12,600.

$$(120 \text{ pairs @ \$50 per pair}) + (120 \text{ pairs @ \$55 per pair})$$
$$= \$12,600 \text{ cost of goods available for sale}$$

How should the store allocate that amount—$12,600—between the 140 pairs sold (cost of goods sold) and the 100 pairs not sold (ending inventory) for the month?

Sunglass Hut will make an assumption about which pairs of sunglasses flowed out of inventory to customers and which pairs remain in inventory. Did the store sell all of the $50 pairs and some of the $55 pairs? Or did the store sell all of the $55 pairs and some of the $50 pairs? The assumption the store makes is called an inventory cost flow assumption, and it is made to calculate the cost of goods sold for the income statement and the cost of ending inventory for the balance sheet. The actual physical flow of the goods does not need to be consistent with the inventory cost flow assumption. The inventory manager could actually know that all of the $50 pairs could not have been sold because of the way shipments are stored below the display counter, yet the store is still allowed to use the assumption that the $50 pairs were sold first in calculating cost of goods sold. In accounting, we are concerned with inventory cost flow—that is, the flow of the costs associated with the goods that pass through a company—rather than with the actual physical movement of goods.

Generally accepted accounting principles (GAAP) allow a company to select one of several inventory cost flow assumptions. Studying several of these methods will help you understand how accounting choices can affect the amounts on the financial statements, even when the transactions are identical. There are four basic inventory cost flow assumptions used to calculate the cost of goods sold and the cost of ending inventory.

1. Specific identification
2. Weighted average cost
3. First-in, first-out (FIFO)
4. Last-in, first-out (LIFO)

Specific Identification

The **specific identification method** is one way of assigning the dollar amounts to cost of goods sold and ending inventory. Instead of assuming which inventory items are sold, a firm that uses specific identification actually keeps track of which goods were sold because the firm records the actual cost of the specific goods sold.

> The **specific identification method** is the inventory cost flow method in which the actual cost of the specific goods sold is recorded as cost of goods sold.

With the specific identification method, each item sold must be identified as coming from a specific purchase of inventory, at a specific unit cost. Specific identification can be used for determining the cost of each item of a small quantity of large, luxury items such as cars or yachts. However, this method would take too much time and money to use to determine the cost of each item of many identical items, like pairs of identical sunglasses. Companies that specialize in large, one-of-a-kind products, such as Boeing's 767-300ER airplane delivered to Ethiopian Airlines in June 2004, will definitely use specific identification. However, when you go into Foot Locker to buy a pair of Nike running shoes, the store accountant will not know exactly what the store paid Nike for that specific pair of shoes. The cost of goods sold will be determined by a method other than specific identification.

We will use a simple example to show how specific identification works. Exhibit 5.5 shows how a car dealership identifies the cost of each car sold, which is the amount the dealership paid the car manufacturer. Suppose you own a Volkswagen car dealership. You buy one Volkswagen for $22,000, a second for $23,000, and a third for $25,000. These three items for the inventory may look identical to a customer, but each car actually has its own unique VIN (vehicle identification number). You will know exactly what your dealership paid the manufacturer for each car. Suppose you sold two cars during the accounting period. What is the cost of goods sold? You will specifically identify the cars sold and their cost. If you sold the $22,000 car and the $25,000 car, then cost of goods sold would be $47,000 and ending inventory would be $23,000. However, if you sold the $23,000 car and the $25,000 car, then cost of goods sold would be $48,000 and ending inventory would be $22,000.

Weighted Average Cost

Few firms use specific identification because it is costly to keep track of each individual item in inventory. Instead, most firms use one of the other inventory cost flow assumptions: weighted average cost, FIFO, or LIFO. A firm that uses **weighted average cost** averages the cost of the items available for sale and then uses that weighted average cost to value both cost of goods sold and the ending inventory. An average unit cost is calculated

> **Weighted average cost** is the inventory cost flow method in which the weighted average cost of the goods available for sale is used to calculate the cost of goods sold and the ending inventory.

EXHIBIT 5.5

Inventory Cost Using Specific Identification

Each car's cost to the dealership is identified as the car is sold. The cost of goods sold will reflect the cost of each specific car sold.

$25,000

$23,000

$22,000

EXHIBIT 5.6

Weighted Average Inventory Costing

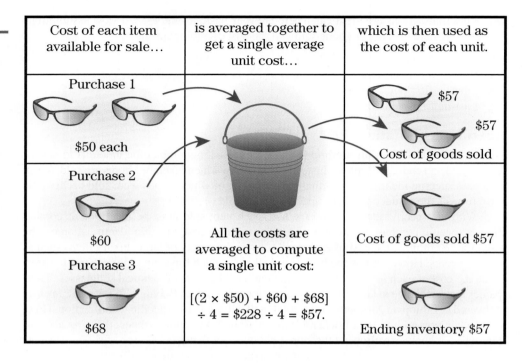

Cost of each item available for sale…	is averaged together to get a single average unit cost…	which is then used as the cost of each unit.
Purchase 1 $50 each		$57 / $57 Cost of goods sold
Purchase 2 $60	All the costs are averaged to compute a single unit cost: [(2 × $50) + $60 + $68] ÷ 4 = $228 ÷ 4 = $57.	Cost of goods sold $57
Purchase 3 $68		Ending inventory $57

by dividing the total cost of goods available for sale by the total number of units available for sale. This average unit cost is weighted because the number of units at each different price is used to weight the unit costs. The calculated average unit cost is applied to all units sold to get cost of goods sold and applied to all units remaining to get a value for ending inventory. Companies such as Best Buy, Intel, Starbucks, and Chico's use the weighted average cost method to calculate the cost of goods sold and the cost of ending inventory. Exhibit 5.6 shows how the weighted average cost method works for a shop that sells sunglasses.

Consider the sunglasses shown in Exhibit 5.6. The store purchased four pairs from the manufacturer. The first two pairs cost $50, the third pair cost $60, and the fourth pair cost $68. The total cost of goods available for sale is

$$(2 \times \$50) + \$60 + \$68 = \$228$$

Averaged over four pairs, the weighted average cost per pair is $57.

$$\$228 \div 4 = \$57$$

If the store now sold three pairs to customers, the cost of goods sold would be

$$3 \times \$57 = \$171$$

The ending inventory would be $57. Notice that the cost of goods sold of $171 plus the ending inventory of $57 adds up to $228, the cost of goods available for sale.

$171 cost of goods sold
+ 57 ending inventory
$228 cost of goods available for sale

Your Turn 5-5
Your Turn
Your Turn

A firm starts with 10 units in its beginning inventory at a cost of $1 each. During the first day of March, the firm purchases 20 units at a cost of $2 each. No other purchases were made. Between the 2nd and 31st of the month, the firm sold 15 units. How much was the cost of goods sold if the firm uses weighted average cost as its inventory cost flow assumption?

	The actual order of the items sold is not necessarily known, but the costs flow "as if" this were the flow of the goods:	
Cost of goods available for sale	Cost of goods sold	Ending inventory
Purchase 1 $50 each		
Purchase 2 $60		
Purchase 3 $68		
$228	**$160**	**$68**

EXHIBIT 5.7

FIFO Inventory Cost Flow Method

First-In, First-Out Method (FIFO)

The **first-in, first-out (FIFO)** method is the common assumption in inventory cost flow that the first items purchased are the first ones sold. The cost of the first goods purchased is assigned to the first goods sold. The cost of the goods on hand at the end of a period is determined from the most recent purchases. Apple Computers, Barnes & Noble, and Wendy's use FIFO.

We will use the four pairs of sunglasses we used earlier for the weighted average method to see how FIFO works. Suppose the glasses were purchased in the order shown in Exhibit 5.7. No matter which ones were actually sold first, the costs of the oldest purchases will become cost of goods sold. If the store sold three pairs, the cost of goods sold would be

$$\$50 + \$50 + \$60 = \$160$$

The ending inventory would be $68. Again notice that the cost of goods sold of $160 plus the ending inventory of $68 equals $228, the cost of goods available for sale.

$160 cost of goods sold
$\underline{+\ 68}$ ending inventory
$228 cost of goods available for sale

Last-In, First-Out Method (LIFO)

The **last-in, first-out (LIFO)** method is the inventory cost flow assumption that the most recently purchased goods are sold first. The cost of the last goods purchased is assigned to the cost of goods sold, so the cost of the ending inventory is assumed to be the cost of the goods purchased earliest. Firms from diverse industries use LIFO: Caterpillar, manufacturer of machinery and engines; Pepsico, the owner of PepsiCo Beverages North America and Frito-Lay; and McKesson Corporation, a pharmaceutical and health care company.

First-in, first-out (FIFO) is the inventory cost flow method that assumes the first items purchased are the first items sold.

Last-in, first-out (LIFO) is the inventory cost flow method that assumes the last items purchased are the first items sold.

EXHIBIT 5.8

LIFO Inventory Cost Flow Method

	The actual order of the items sold is not necessarily known, but the costs flow "as if" this were the flow of the goods:	
Cost of goods available for sale	Cost of goods sold	Ending inventory
Purchase 1  $50 each		
Purchase 2  $60		
Purchase 3  $68		
$228	**$178**	**$50**

We will use the four pairs of sunglasses again to see how LIFO works. Suppose the glasses were purchased in the order shown in Exhibit 5.8. No matter which ones were actually sold first, the costs of the most recent purchases will become cost of goods sold. If the store sold three pairs, the cost of goods sold would be:

$$\textbf{\$68 + \$60 + \$50 = \$178}$$

The ending inventory would be $50. Again notice that the cost of goods sold of $178 plus the ending inventory of $50 equals $228, the cost of goods available for sale.

$178 cost of goods sold
+ 50 ending inventory
$228 cost of goods available for sale

Firms that use LIFO must provide extra disclosures in their financial statements. Exhibit 5.9 shows an example of the disclosure about inventory provided by Tootsie Roll Industries. Although Tootsie Roll uses LIFO, it discloses information about the current cost

EXHIBIT 5.9

LIFO Disclosure in Notes to the Financial Statements

From Note 1 in Tootsie Roll Industries' 2005 Annual Report (dollars in millions)

Inventories:
Inventories are stated at cost, not to exceed market. The cost of substantially all of the Company's inventories ($51,969 and $54,794 at December 31, 2005 and 2004, respectively) has been determined by the last-in, first-out (LIFO) method. The excess of current cost over LIFO cost of inventories approximates $6,530 and $5,868 at December 31, 2005 and 2004, respectively.

Purchases	Cost of goods sold	Ending inventory
 $50 each $60 $68		
Weighted average cost	$57 + $57 + $57 = **$171**	**$57**
FIFO	$50 + $50 + $60 = **$160**	**$68**
LIFO	$68 + $60 + $50 = **$178**	**$50**

EXHIBIT 5.10

A Comparison of Weighted Average Cost, FIFO, and LIFO

This exhibit compares three methods for calculating the cost of goods sold and the cost of ending inventory—weighted average cost, FIFO, LIFO—using the example with four pairs of sunglasses. The three pairs of sunglasses sold and the pair left in ending inventory are not identifiable here to emphasize that the actual physical flow of goods does not matter to the inventory cost flow method.

of the ending inventory. Remember that LIFO inventory will be valued at the oldest costs because the more recent costs have gone to the income statement as cost of goods sold. The old inventory is often described as old "LIFO" layers. When a LIFO firm keeps a safety stock of inventory, never selling its entire inventory, those LIFO layers may be there for a long time. LIFO is controversial because a firm can make an extra purchase of inventory at the end of the period and change its cost of goods sold without making another sale. Whether or not it is ethical to buy extra inventory for the sole purpose of changing the period's cost of goods sold is something you should think about. Even if you believe it is not ethical, you should be aware that it can be done when using LIFO.

Take a look at Exhibit 5.10 for a comparison of three methods for calculating the cost of goods sold and the cost of ending inventory—weighted average cost, FIFO, and LIFO.

Jayne's Jewelry Store purchased three diamond and emerald bracelets during March. The price of diamonds has fluctuated wildly during the month, causing the supplying firm to change the price of the bracelets it sells to Jayne's Jewelry Store.

Your Turn 5-6
Your Turn
Your Turn

   a. On March 5, the first bracelet cost $4,600.
   b. On March 15, the second bracelet cost $5,100.
   c. On March 20, the third bracelet cost $3,500.

Suppose Jayne's Jewelry Store sold two of these bracelets for $7,000 each.

   1. Using FIFO, what is the cost of goods sold for these sales? What is the gross profit?
   2. Using LIFO, what is the cost of goods sold for these sales? What is the gross profit?
   3. Using weighted average cost, what is the cost of goods sold?

How Inventory Cost Flow Assumptions Affect the Financial Statements

Did you notice that the same set of facts and economic transactions in the examples you just studied resulted in different numbers on the financial statements for cost of goods sold and for ending inventory? In the following sections, you will learn how the firm's choice of inventory cost flow assumptions affects the financial statements.

Differences in Reported Inventory and Cost of Goods Sold Under Different Cost Flow Assumptions. Exhibit 5.11 shows inventory for Kaitlyn's Photo Shop. The shop sells a unique type of disposable camera that is relatively inexpensive. We will calculate the cost of goods sold and ending inventory for the month of January using weighted average cost, FIFO, and LIFO, first using periodic record keeping. Then, we will do each using perpetual record keeping.

No matter which method a company selects, the cost of goods available for sale—beginning inventory plus purchases—is the same. Here is a calculation for cost of goods available for sale.

$$\text{Cost of goods available for sale} = \text{Beginning inventory} + \text{purchases}$$

For Kaitlyn's Photo Shop for January, the cost of goods available for sale is $238.

$$\underset{\text{(8 cameras} \times \$10 \text{ each)}}{\$80} + \underset{\text{(5 cameras} \times \$12 \text{ each)}}{\$60} + \underset{\text{(7 cameras} \times \$14 \text{ each)}}{\$98} = \$238$$

The inventory cost flow assumption and record-keeping method determine how that dollar amount of cost of goods available for sale is divided between cost of goods sold and ending inventory.

Recall that a firm can update its accounting records with every sale—perpetual record keeping—or at the end of the accounting period—periodic record keeping. To keep the number of calculations to a minimum as you learn about inventory cost flow, we will start with periodic record keeping for the first examples. Then, we will repeat the examples using perpetual record keeping. No matter which record-keeping method a firm uses, the concept of cost flow differences between FIFO, LIFO, and weighted average cost is the same.

Weighted Average Cost—Periodic When the firm chooses a periodic record-keeping system, the computations for this method of keeping track of inventory are the simplest of all methods. Kaitlyn adds up beginning inventory and all purchases to get the cost of goods available for sale. Kaitlyn previously calculated that amount to be $238. Then, she divides $238 by the total number of cameras available for sale—that is the number of cameras that comprised the $238—to get a weighted average cost per camera. Kaitlyn had a total of 20 (8 + 5 + 7) cameras available for sale. Dividing $238 by 20 cameras gives $11.90 per camera. That weighted average unit cost is used to compute cost of goods sold and ending inventory:

$$\underset{\text{(Number of cameras sold)}}{11} \times \underset{\text{(per unit cost)}}{\$11.90} = \$130.90 \text{ cost of goods sold}$$

$$\underset{\substack{\text{(Number of cameras in} \\ \text{ending inventory)}}}{9} \times \underset{\text{(per unit cost)}}{\$11.90} = \$107.10 \text{ ending inventory}$$

Cost of goods sold ($130.90) and ending inventory ($107.10) add up to $238.

FIFO—Periodic At the end of the month, Kaitlyn's knows the total number of cameras sold in January was 11. Using FIFO, Kaitlyn's counts the oldest cameras in the inventory

EXHIBIT 5.11

Inventory Records for Kaitlyn's Photo Shop

January 1	Beginning Inventory	8 cameras	@ $10 each
January 8	Sales	3 cameras	@ $50 each
January 16	Purchase	5 cameras	@ $12 each
January 20	Sales	8 cameras	@ $55 each
January 30	Purchase	7 cameras	@ $14 each

as sold. The first items to go in the inventory are the first to go out to the income statement as cost of goods sold. So the firm counts the beginning inventory of 8 cameras at $10 each as the first part of cost of goods sold. On January 16, Kaitlyn's purchased 5 cameras, so the firm will include 3 of those as part of cost of goods sold, too. That makes 11 cameras sold during the month. The income statement will show $116 as expense, or cost of goods sold.

$$
\begin{aligned}
8 \text{ cameras} \times \$10 \text{ per unit} &= \$\ 80 \\
3 \text{ cameras} \times \$12 \text{ per unit} &= \$\ 36 \\
\text{Cost of goods sold} &= \mathbf{\$116}
\end{aligned}
$$

What is left in inventory on the balance sheet?

$$
\begin{aligned}
2 \text{ cameras} \times \$12 \text{ per unit} &= \$\ 24 \\
7 \text{ cameras} \times \$14 \text{ per unit} &= \$\ 98 \\
\text{Ending inventory} &= \mathbf{\$122}
\end{aligned}
$$

Notice that the cost of goods sold plus the ending inventory equals $238—the cost of goods available for sale during January. Exhibit 5.12 shows the FIFO inventory cost flow for Kaitlyn's Photo.

LIFO—Periodic When you use any inventory cost flow method with periodic record keeping, you start by calculating the total number of cameras sold during the month. We know that in January, Kaitlyn's Photo sold 11 cameras. Using LIFO, Kaitlyn counts cameras from the latest purchase as those sold first. The cost of the last items put in the inventory is the first

Beginning inventory 8 cameras @ $10 each		Cost of goods sold	
+ purchase 5 cameras @ $12 each		Cost of goods sold = $(8 \times \$10) + (3 \times \$12) = \$116$	
		Ending inventory	
+ purchase 7 cameras @ $14 each		Ending inventory = $(2 \times \$12) + (7 \times \$14) = \$122$	

EXHIBIT 5.12

FIFO Inventory Cost Flow Assumption for Kaitlyn's Photo Shop

Even though an inventory cost flow assumption does not need to mimic the physical flow of goods, it is a useful way to visualize what is happening. In this exhibit, think of each color of camera as representing the particular cost of a camera in that purchase. The green cameras cost $10 each; the red cameras cost $12 each; and the blue cameras cost $14 each. Kaitlyn's Photo starts with 8 cameras, purchases 5 more and then 7 more, and sells 11 cameras. That leaves 9 cameras in the ending inventory.

to go to the income statement as cost of goods sold. For LIFO, we start at the bottom of the list of purchases in the sequence in which the cameras were purchased.

The purchase on January 30 was 7 cameras, so Kaitlyn's counts the cost of those as part of cost of goods sold first.

The purchase on January 16 was 5 cameras, so the firm will count 4 of them in the cost of goods sold to get the total of 11 cameras sold.

$$
\begin{aligned}
7 \text{ cameras} \times \$14 \text{ per unit} &= \$\ 98 \\
4 \text{ cameras} \times \$12 \text{ per unit} &= \$\ 48 \\
\text{Cost of goods sold} &= \underline{\underline{\$146}}
\end{aligned}
$$

What is left in inventory on the balance sheet?

$$
\begin{aligned}
1 \text{ camera} \times \$12 \text{ per unit} &= \$12 \\
8 \text{ cameras} \times \$10 \text{ per unit} &= \$80 \\
\text{Ending inventory} &= \underline{\underline{\$92}}
\end{aligned}
$$

Notice that the cost of goods sold ($146) plus the ending inventory ($92) equals cost of goods available for sale ($238). Exhibit 5.13 shows the LIFO inventory cost flow for Kaitlyn's Photo.

Weighted Average Cost—Perpetual When a firm uses a perpetual inventory system, the inventory is reduced each time a sale is made. Technology makes it easy for a firm to use the perpetual system, but the calculations are a bit more complicated. Carefully trace the dates of the purchases and sales as you work through these examples.

EXHIBIT 5.13

LIFO Inventory Cost Flow Assumption for Kaitlyn's Photo Shop

Even though an inventory cost flow assumption does not need to mimic the physical flow of goods, it is a useful way to visualize what is happening. In this exhibit, think of each color of camera as representing the particular cost of a camera in that purchase. The green cameras cost $10 each, the red cameras cost $12 each, and the blue cameras cost $14 each. Kaitlyn's Photo starts with 8 cameras, purchases 5 more and then 7 more, and sells 11 cameras. That leaves 9 cameras in the ending inventory.

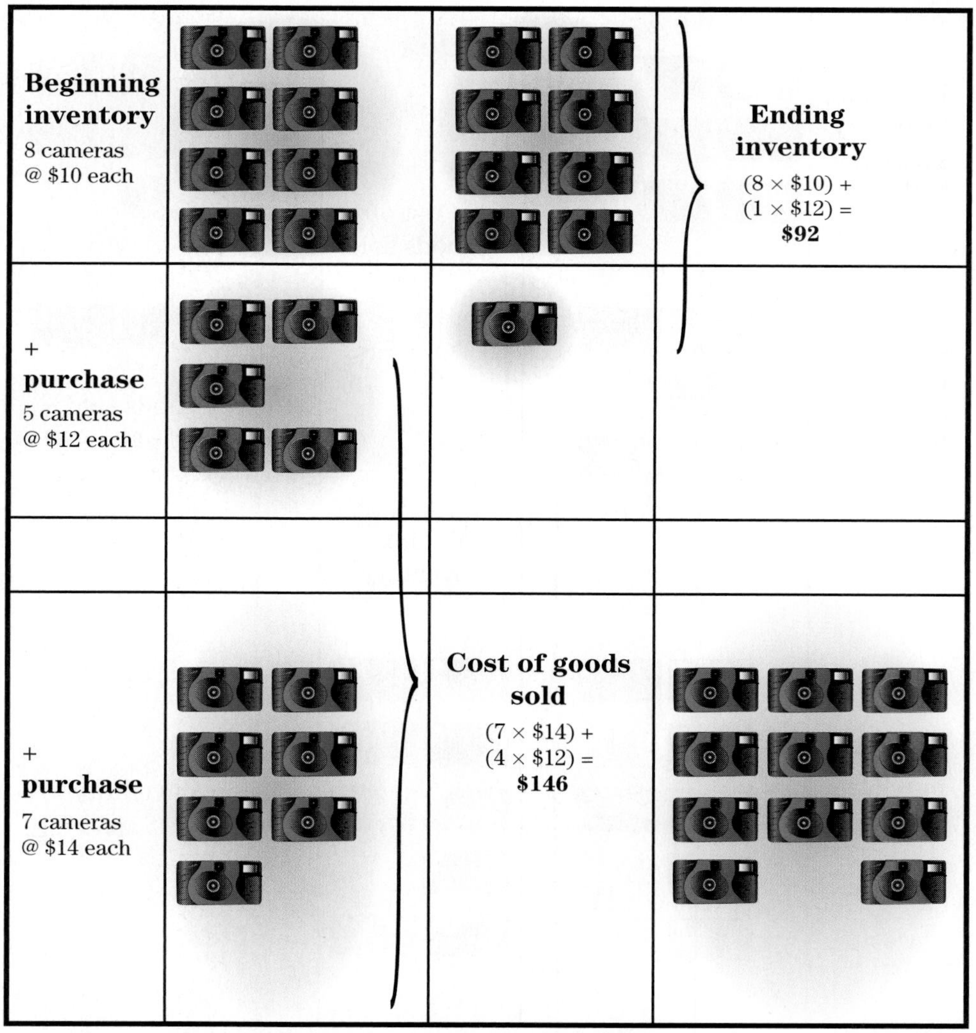

If a company were to select perpetual record keeping with the weighted average inventory cost flow assumption, the accountant would calculate a new weighted average cost every time a purchase is made and every time a sale is made. The method is often called *moving* weighted average because the average changes with every transaction. A modern firm's computer system can handle this record keeping with ease. However, it can be pretty messy to use the weighted average perpetual system with only a calculator.

When Kaitlyn's Photo sells three cameras on January 8, the weighted average cost of a camera is simply the cost carried in the beginning inventory. So the cost of goods sold for the January 8 sale is $30. That leaves five cameras at a cost of $10 each in the inventory. On January 16, Kaitlyn's purchases five cameras at $12 each. The weighted average cost for a camera is now

$$\frac{(5 \times \$10) + (5 \times \$12)}{10 \text{ total}} = \$11 \text{ each}$$

On January 20, Kaitlyn's Photo sells eight cameras. The cost of goods sold is $88, and there are two cameras left in the inventory at a weighted average cost of $11 each.

When the purchase of seven cameras at $14 each occurs on January 30, a new weighted average cost must be computed.

$$\frac{(2 \times \$11) + (7 \times \$14)}{9 \text{ total}} = \$13.33 \text{ each}$$

The cost of goods sold for the period is $88 + $30 = $118.
The ending inventory for the period is $120 (9 cameras × $13.33 each, rounded).

FIFO—Perpetual When a perpetual record-keeping system is used, the cost of goods sold for each sale must be calculated and recorded at the *time of the sale*. Only the cameras from the purchases as of the date of a sale—meaning prior and up to the date of a sale—are available to become part of the cost of goods sold. Perpetual record keeping requires you to pay attention to the dates on which goods are purchased and sold. Kaitlyn's first sale is on January 8. Only cameras from the beginning inventory are available for Kaitlyn's to use to calculate the cost of goods sold for the January 8 sale. The other purchases are in the future, and Kaitlyn's does not know anything about them on January 8.

The cost of goods sold for the January 8 sale is

3 cameras × $10 per camera = $30

Next, eight cameras were sold on January 20. Because the inventory cost flow assumption is FIFO, Kaitlyn's uses the cameras left in the beginning inventory as part of the cost of goods sold. So the cost of goods sold for the January 20 sale must start with the five cameras remaining in the beginning inventory—that will be 5 × $10 each = $50. To get the other three needed to make the total of eight sold, Kaitlyn's will count three from the January 16 purchase. That is 3 × $12 each = $36. So the total cost of goods sold for the January 20 sale is $86 ($50 + $36).

To summarize the cost of goods sold:

3 cameras × $10 each	= $ 30
5 cameras × $10 each	= $ 50
3 cameras × $12 each	= $ 36
Total cost of goods sold	= $116

What is left in ending inventory?

2 cameras × $12 each	= $ 24
7 cameras × $14 each	= $ 98
Total ending inventory	= $122

If you refer back to the FIFO periodic example, you will notice that doing all of the work to figure out the cost of goods sold using FIFO *perpetual* gives the same amount as FIFO *periodic*, which is much easier to calculate.

Is this coincidence, or is there a predictable pattern here? Look at the particular cameras that were assumed to be sold under the two methods. You will see that it is more than coincidence. No matter how the company does the actual record keeping, either FIFO method—perpetual or periodic—will give the same dollar amount of cost of goods sold and the same dollar amount of ending inventory for the period. Unfortunately, this is *not* true for LIFO.

LIFO—Perpetual Choosing LIFO perpetual makes life a bit more difficult for the accounting system than choosing FIFO. Each time a sale is made, the cost of goods sold is determined by using the *last* purchase as of the date of the sale. The amounts may differ slightly between LIFO periodic and LIFO perpetual because of timing differences between sales and purchases.

Kaitlyn's first sale is on January 8. Only cameras from the beginning inventory are available for Kaitlyn's to use to calculate the cost of goods sold for the January 8 sale. The other purchases are in the future, and Kaitlyn's does not know anything about them on January 8! The cost of goods sold for the January 8 sale is 3 cameras × $10 per camera = $30.

Next, eight cameras were sold on January 20. Because the inventory cost flow assumption is LIFO, Kaitlyn's uses the cameras from the most recent purchase as of January 20 to determine the cost of goods sold. So the cost of goods sold for the January 20 sale starts with the five cameras from the January 16 purchase. That is 5 × $12 each = $60. To get the remaining three cameras she needs for the total eight sold on January 20, Kaitlyn's will need to pick up three from the beginning inventory: 3 × $10 each = $30. So the total cost of goods sold for the January 20 sale is $90 ($60 + $30).

To summarize the cost of goods sold:

3 cameras × $10 each	= $ 30	Sale on January 8
5 cameras × $12 each	= $ 60	⎰ Sale on January 20
3 cameras × $10 each	= $ 30	⎱
Total cost of goods sold	= **$120**	

What is left in the ending inventory?

2 cameras × $10 each	= $ 20
7 cameras × $14 each	= $ 98
Total	= **$118**

If you look back at the example of LIFO periodic, you will see that it resulted in a slightly higher cost of goods sold, $146. That is because, under periodic record keeping, Kaitlyn's was allowed to "pretend" to have sold the inventory purchased on January 30. That is, the inventory cost flow assumption allowed an assumed flow of goods that could not possibly have taken place.

Conclusions About Inventory Cost Flow Assumptions. Firms use all of the combinations of the three inventory cost flow assumptions—weighted average, FIFO, and LIFO—and two record-keeping methods—perpetual and periodic. Accountants and firms have modified these methods to meet the needs of specific industries. Sometimes firms keep perpetual records of inventory in units but wait until the end of the period to calculate the cost of goods sold using the periodic method. You can see from the examples we have done that the method a company selects to account for inventory can make a difference in the reported cost of goods sold, inventory, and net income.

The cost of goods sold and ending inventory are shown in Exhibit 5.14 for weighted average, FIFO, and LIFO, all using periodic record keeping. In every case, notice that cost

EXHIBIT 5.14

Summary of Kaitlyn's Photo Inventory Data

Inventory Cost Flow Assumption	FIFO	LIFO	Weighted Average
Cost of goods sold	$116	$146	$131
Ending inventory	$122	$ 92	$107

Note: Amounts are rounded to the nearest dollar.

of goods sold and ending inventory together total $238, the cost of the goods available for sale. That is true for FIFO, LIFO, and weighted average using either a perpetual or a periodic system. You can read about how a firm makes this important calculation in the notes to the financial statements.

Jones Saddle Company had the following transactions during August 2008:

Purchased 30 units @ $20 per unit on August 10, 2008.
Purchased 20 units @ $21 per unit on August 15, 2008.
Purchased 20 units @ $23 per unit on August 21, 2008.
Sold 35 units @ $30 per unit on August 30, 2008.

Calculate the cost of goods sold using each of these inventory cost flow assumptions: (1) FIFO, (2) LIFO, and (3) weighted average cost. (In this case, perpetual and periodic produce the same answers because all purchases were made before any sales.)

Your Turn 5-7
Your Turn
Your Turn

Income Tax Effects of LIFO and FIFO. You see that the inventory cost flow assumption makes a difference in the amounts reported on the income statement for cost of goods sold and on the balance sheet for inventory. What effect do you think the inventory cost flow assumption has on the statement of cash flows? We will look at the income statement and the statement of cash flows for Kaitlyn's Photo for an explanation of what could make a company prefer one assumption over another. First, review Exhibit 5.14, which summarizes the calculation cost of goods sold under the three common methods.

Sales revenue and operating expenses are the same no matter what inventory cost flow assumption is used. Earlier we learned that sales revenue amounted to $590, and operating expenses, in addition to cost of goods sold, were $50 for the period. Now, look at Exhibit 5.15. Notice that we have added two new numbers: Operating expenses, paid in cash, of $50 and the income taxes of 30%. Exhibit 5.15 shows the income statement for each inventory cost flow assumption.

Before you decide that FIFO is best because it provides a higher net income, notice that this is true only in a period of increasing inventory costs. Additionally, we really need to look at the statement of cash flows to see what effect the inventory cost flow method has on cash flows. Exhibit 5.16 shows the statements of cash flow under each inventory cost flow assumption.

If you compare Exhibits 5.15 and 5.16, you will notice that although LIFO produces the lowest net income, it produces the largest net cash flow from operating activities. That is a direct result of the income tax savings from the lower net income. LIFO will yield the largest net cash flow in a period of rising costs of inventory. If Kaitlyn's uses LIFO instead of FIFO, she will save $9 on income taxes and have that money to spend on advertising or hiring new workers. Think of these savings in millions. Firms often save millions of dollars by using LIFO when inventory costs are rising. The disadvantage of using LIFO is that net income will be lower than it would have been with FIFO or weighted average cost.

EXHIBIT 5.15

Income Statements for Kaitlyn's Photo using Periodic Inventory with Various Cost Flow Assumptions

Recall that the cost of the inventory has been rising. That means LIFO will yield a higher cost of goods sold and a lower taxable income. Cost of Goods Sold and Income taxes are highlighted because those amounts are why LIFO income is lower than FIFO income.

Inventory Cost Flow Assumption	FIFO	LIFO	Weighted Average
Sales*	$590	$590	$590
Cost of goods sold	116	146	131
Operating expenses	50	50	50
Income before taxes	424	394	409
Income taxes (30%)	127	118	123
Net income	$297	$276	$286

*(3 × $50) + (8 × $55) = $590

EXHIBIT 5.16

Statements of Cash Flow for Kaitlyn's Photo Using Various Inventory Cost Flow Assumptions

All inventory methods produce the same cash flows for all items except income taxes.

Inventory Cost Flow Assumption	FIFO	LIFO	Weighted Average
Cash collected from customers	$590	$590	$590
Cash paid for inventory	238	238	238
Cash paid for operating expenses	50	50	50
Cash inflow before income taxes	302	302	302
Cash paid for income taxes	127	118	123
Net cash from operating activities	**$175**	**$184**	**$179**

How Do Firms Choose an Inventory Cost Flow Method? Now, think about some of the factors that might influence a firm's choice of inventory cost flow assumptions.

1. *Compatibility with similar companies.* A firm will often choose a method that other firms in the same industry use. Then, a manager can easily compare inventory levels to those of the competition. Also, investors like to compare similar companies without the complication of different inventory methods. Best Buy, for example, uses weighted average cost to value its inventory. Circuit City, a similar firm and competitor of Best Buy, also uses weighted average cost.

2. *Maximize tax savings and cash flows.* A firm may want to maximize tax savings and cash flows. As you saw in our analysis of Kaitlyn's Photo with various inventory methods, when inventory costs are rising, cost of goods sold is larger when a company uses LIFO rather than FIFO. There is a difference because the higher costs of the more recent purchases go to the income statement as cost of goods sold, and the older, lower costs are left on the balance sheet in inventory. Higher cost of goods sold expense results in a lower net income. Although financial accounting and tax accounting are usually quite different, the IRS requires any company that uses LIFO for income taxes to also use LIFO for its financial statements. This is called the LIFO conformity rule. So, if a firm wants to take advantage of lower income taxes when inventory costs are rising, the firm must also be willing to report a lower net income to its shareholders. Reducing income taxes is the major reason firms select LIFO. Read more about LIFO and taxes in *Understanding Business*.

3. *Maximize net income.* In a period of rising prices, a higher net income will come from using FIFO. That is because older, lower costs will go to the income statement as cost of goods sold. Suppose you are a CFO whose bonus depends on reaching a specific level of earnings. You may forego the tax benefits of LIFO to keep your net income higher with FIFO.

Whatever inventory cost flow method a firm uses, the method should be used consistently so that financial statements from one period can be compared to those from the previous period. A firm can change inventory cost flow methods only if the change improves the measurement of the firm's performance or financial position. Exhibit 5.17 gives an example of the type of disclosure a firm must make if it changes inventory cost flow methods.

EXHIBIT 5.17

Disclosure of a Change in Inventory Cost Flow Methods

This is just part of the inventory disclosure made by Books-A-Million in the notes to its January 29, 2005 financial statements. Notice the justification for the change in inventory methods, highlighted.

Inventories

Inventories are valued at the lower of cost or market, using the retail method. Market is determined based on the lower of replacement cost or estimated realizable value. Using the retail method, store and warehouse inventories are valued by applying a calculated cost to retail ratio to the retail value of inventories.

Effective February 2, 2003, the Company changed from the first-in, first-out (FIFO) method of accounting for inventories to the last-in, first-out (LIFO) method. Management believes this change was preferable in that it achieves a more appropriate matching of revenues and expenses. The impact of this accounting change was to increase "Costs of Products Sold" in the consolidated statements of operations by $0.4 million and $0.7 million for the fiscal years ended January 29, 2005 and January 31, 2004, respectively. This resulted in an after-tax decrease to net income of $0.3 million or $0.01 per diluted share for fiscal 2005 and an after-tax decrease to net income of $0.4 million or $0.02 per diluted share for fiscal 2004. The cumulative effect of a change in accounting principle from the FIFO method to LIFO method is not determinable. Accordingly, such change has been accounted for prospectively.

UNDERSTANDING Business

Inventory Cost Flow Assumptions and Taxes

Generally accepted accounting principles (GAAP) allow firms quite a bit of latitude in selecting a method of accounting for inventory costs. Last-in, first-out (LIFO) provides a tax benefit—lower taxes than first-in, first-out (FIFO)—in a period of rising prices. This is a real economic benefit that results from an accounting choice. In the past century, costs have been rising, so it would make sense for a company to take advantage of this tax savings by choosing LIFO for its inventory method. Yet, the most recent survey of accounting practices, reported in Accounting Trends & Techniques (2006), reports that only about 38% of firms use LIFO, many for only part of their inventories. What factors influence a firm's choice of inventory methods and why would a firm choose not to use LIFO?

Lower Earnings

If a firm uses LIFO for taxes, the firm must also use LIFO for financial reporting. This is called the LIFO conformity rule. This is an exception to the general rule that a firm may use one accounting method for financial statements and a different method for taxes. With respect to inventory, this required consistency means that choosing LIFO for taxes in a period of rising prices will result in lower reported profits for both taxes and financial statements. Why is that a problem?

Managers may worry that lower earnings will have a negative effect on the firm's stock price. Managers may have a compensation contract that is tied to earnings; so lower earnings may mean a smaller bonus.

Record-Keeping Costs

Inventory records associated with LIFO are more complicated to keep than inventory records associated with FIFO. If the tax benefit of using LIFO is small, it might not be worth the trouble. What would cause the tax benefit to be small or even nonexistent?

- A firm may not be paying much in taxes—due to losses in prior years that reduce taxes or special tax breaks, such as investment tax credits.
- The inventory levels may fluctuate a lot, so that old layers of LIFO inventory would have to be sold, causing a reversal of any tax benefit.
- The firm may turn over the inventory very rapidly, so that the inventory method would not have much effect on taxes.
- Costs in some industries are decreasing, so FIFO has the tax advantage in those cases.

Most of the time, the choice of an accounting method is difficult to trace to specific economic consequences. With inventory, however, the choice of accounting method can make a significant economic difference to a firm—real dollars. That makes selecting an inventory cost flow method an important business decision.

Explain the LIFO conformity rule. What is the usual relationship between accounting under GAAP and the IRS rules?

Your Turn 5-8
Your Turn
Your Turn

Applying Inventory Assumptions to Tom's Wear

Tom's Wear began in January 2006 and has now completed 4 months of operations. As the company completes its transactions for May, inventory prices are changing. For Tom's Wear, that means it must select an inventory cost flow assumption. If you look back at the first 4 months of transactions, you will see that inventory prices were constant at $4 per shirt. When inventory prices are constant, there is no need for a cost flow assumption. Every method produces the identical values for inventory and cost of goods sold. You will also recall that Tom's Wear recorded the reduction in inventory at the same time as the related sale. You have now learned that this method is called perpetual record keeping.

L.O.4
Analyze transactions and prepare financial statements with a record keeping and cost flow assumption.

EXHIBIT 5.18

Balance Sheet for Tom's Wear at May 1, 2006

tom's wear

Tom's Wear Balance Sheet at May 1, 2006	

Assets

Cash	$ 3,295
Accounts receivable	8,000
Inventory	1,100
Prepaid insurance	25
Prepaid rent	1,800
Total current assets	14,220
Equipment (net of $925 accumulated depreciation)	33,075
Total assets	$47,295

Liabilities & Shareholder's Equity
Liabilities

Accounts payable	4,000
Interest payable	310
Short-term notes payable	3,000
Total current liabilities	7,310
Long-term notes payable	30,000
Shareholder's Equity	
Common stock	5,000
Retained earnings	4,985
Total liabilities and shareholder's equity	$47,295

The balance sheet at May 1, 2006, is shown in Exhibit 5.18. As you know, it is the same as the balance sheet at April 30, 2006, from Exhibit 4.15. The transactions for May are shown in Exhibit 5.19. First, we will record each transaction in the accounting equation. Then, we will review the records to identify any needed adjustments.

Transaction 1: Payment for insurance Tom's Wear pays cash for insurance premium, $300 for 3 months; coverage starts May 15. The firm records all insurance payments to prepaid insurance. The expense will be recorded as an adjustment at the end of the month.

Assets	=	Liabilities	+	Shareholder's equity	
				Contributed capital	+ **Retained earnings**
(300) cash					
300 prepaid insurance					

Transaction 2: Collection on accounts receivable Tom's Wear collects $7,900 from customers who purchased shirts in prior months. No revenue is recognized because the revenue was already recognized when the sale was originally made. This collection simply exchanges one asset—accounts receivable—for another—cash.

Assets	=	Liabilities	+	Shareholder's equity	
				Contributed capital	+ **Retained earnings**
7,900 cash					
(7,900) accounts receivable					

EXHIBIT 5.19

Accounting Equation Worksheet for Tom's Wear for May

Assets = Liabilities + Shareholder's Equity

Retained Earnings (BB) = 4,985; ending Retained Earnings = 9,883 (Common Stock 5,000 | Revenues | Expenses)

Ref	Cash	Accounts Receivable	Inventory	Prepaid Insurance	Prepaid Rent	Prepaid Web Service	Equipment (Computer)	Acc. Depr. Equipment	Van	Acc. Depr. Van	Accounts Payable	Salaries Payable	Unearned Revenue	Interest Payable	Other Payables**	Short-Term Notes Payable	Long-Term Notes Payable	Common Stock	Revenues	Expenses
BB*	3,295	8,000	1,100	25	1,800		4,000	(200)	30,000	(725)	4,000			310		3,000	30,000	5,000		
1.	(300)			300																
2.	7,900	(7,900)																		
3.	(4,000)										(4,000)									
4.	(4,400)		4,400																	
5.	9,900												9,900							
6.		8,800	(3,200)																8,800	(3,200)
7.			4,200								4,200									
8.	(500)					300														(200)
9.	(3,000)															(3,000)				
A-1	(90)													(60) 250						(30) (250)
A-2			(1,800)										(4,950)						4,950	(1,800)
A-3				(75)																(75)
A-4					(1,200)															(1,200)
A-5						(50)														(50)
A-6								(100)		(870)										(100) (870)
A-7												723			277					(1,000)
A-8															77					(77)
	8,805	8,900	4,700	250	600	250	4,000	(300)	30,000	(1,595)	4,200	723	4,950	500	354	–	30,000	5,000	13,750	(8,852)

Check figures   55,610   55,610   9,883

* BB beginning balances
** The first entry of $277 is the amount Tom's Wear has withheld from Sam Cubbie's paycheck, and Tom's Wear will pay that to the government on Sam's behalf. The second entry of $77 is the amount Tom's Wear must pay the government as a matching payment for Sam's Social Security contributions, here given as $77.

Transaction 3: Payment on accounts payable Tom's Wear makes a payment of $4,000 on accounts payable. This pays off the current amount of the obligation.

Assets	=	Liabilities	+	Shareholder's equity		
				Contributed capital	+	**Retained earnings**
(4,000) cash		(4,000) accounts payable				

Transaction 4: Purchase of inventory Tom's Wear purchases 1,100 shirts at $4 each for cash.

Assets	=	Liabilities	+	Shareholder's equity		
				Contributed capital	+	**Retained earnings**
(4,400) cash						
4,400 inventory						

Transaction 5: Receipt of unearned revenue Tom's Wear agrees to sell the local school system 900 shirts for $11 each. Tom's Wear collects cash of $9,900 in advance of delivery. Half the shirts will be delivered on May 30, and the other half will be delivered in June.

Assets	=	Liabilities	+	Shareholder's equity		
				Contributed capital	+	**Retained earnings**
9,900 cash		9,900 unearned revenue				

Transaction 6: Sales Tom's Wear sells 800 shirts at $11 each, all on account. That means the company extended credit to its customers, and Tom's Wear will collect later.

Assets	=	Liabilities	+	Shareholder's equity		
				Contributed capital	+	**Retained earnings**
8,800 accounts receivable						8,800 sales revenue

At the same time sales revenue is recorded, Tom's Wear records the reduction in inventory. As you know, the reduction in inventory is an expense called cost of goods sold. At this point, all of the items in inventory cost the same amount—$4. Tom's Wear has decided to use FIFO, but there is no actual impact of that choice for this transaction. All of the shirts Tom's Wear sold cost $4, so cost of goods sold is $3,200. There were 275 shirts at $4 each in the beginning inventory, so those are assumed to be sold first. The remaining 525 shirts come from the recent purchase of 1,100 shirts at $4 each, leaving 575 shirts in the inventory.

Assets	=	Liabilities	+	Shareholder's equity		
				Contributed capital	+	**Retained earnings**
(3,200) inventory						(3,200) cost of goods sold

Transaction 7: Payment for Web design and for 6 months' worth of maintenance Tom's Wear hires Web designers to start a Web page for the firm. The firm pays $200 for Web design and $300 for 6 months' worth of maintenance fees. A full month of maintenance will be charged for May.

Assets	=	Liabilities	+	Shareholder's equity		
				Contributed capital	+	Retained earnings
300 prepaid Web service (500) cash						(200) miscellaneous operating expenses

Transaction 8: Purchase of inventory Tom's Wear purchases 1,000 shirts at a cost of $4.20 each, on account.

Assets	=	Liabilities	+	Shareholder's equity		
				Contributed capital	+	Retained earnings
4,200 inventory		4,200 accounts payable				

Transaction 9: Repayment of note with interest Tom's Wear started the month with a short-term note payable of $3,000. It was issued on March 1, so 3 months' worth of interest is also paid. The interest rate on the note is 12%. Previously, at the end of March and again at the end of April, the interest for the month was accrued. That is, each month $30 of interest expense and interest payable was recorded. So the payment of interest here for 3 months is $90, $60 of which was interest payable and $30 will be recorded as interest expense for May. The payment of the note and the payment of the interest are shown separately because it will be easier to construct the statement of cash flows if these are separate. The repayment of the note is a financing cash outflow, whereas the interest payment is an operating cash flow. Interest payments and receipts are always classified as cash from operating activities on the statement of cash flows.

Assets	=	Liabilities	+	Shareholder's equity		
				Contributed capital	+	Retained earnings
(3,000) cash (90) cash		(3,000) Short-term notes payable (60) interest payable				(30) interest expense

All of these routine transactions are recorded in the accounting equation worksheet in Exhibit 5.19. Now, Tom's Wear must make several adjustments before it can prepare the financial statements for May. To do this, the additional information that the van was driven 6,000 miles in May is needed. As you read about each adjustment, identify the entry in the accounting equation worksheet.

Adjustment 1: Insurance expense needs to be recorded. The total expense for May is $75. That is the total of $25 from the first half of the month (which uses up the beginning balance in prepaid insurance) and $50 for the second half of the month (from the new policy at $100 per month, beginning May 15).

Adjustment 2: Rent expense needs to be recorded. The amount is $1,200 for the month.

Adjustment 3: The Web service of $50 for May needs to be recorded.

Adjustment 4: Depreciation expense on the van (which was driven 6,000 miles during May) needs to be recorded (6,000 miles × $0.145 per mile = $870).

Adjustment 5: Depreciation expense needs to be recorded on the computer, $100 per month.

Adjustment 6: Half of the 900 shirts were delivered to the schools, so half of the unearned revenue needs to be recognized. That is, $4,950 in revenue should be recorded. The reduction in inventory must also be recorded. Recall that Tom's Wear is using FIFO. There are 575 shirts left that cost $4 each and a recent purchase of 1,000 shirts at $4.20 each. Using FIFO, the 450 shirts that were delivered (half of the 900 the school paid for in advance) are assumed to be from the oldest inventory, so the cost of goods sold is $450 \times \$4 = \$1,800$.

Adjustment 7: Sam Cubbie's salary for May needs to be accrued, and the employer's portion of the payroll taxes also needs to be accrued. You will learn more about this in the next chapter, so for now we will simply record $277 as the amount withheld from the employee's check. This amount will be passed on by Tom's Wear to the government (for Social Security and income taxes). We will also record a $77 payroll tax expense for Tom's Wear because the employer is also required to pay Social Security for its employees. No cash has been disbursed related to this work done by Cubbie. His salary for May is $1,000 per month and will be paid on the 5th of June.

Adjustment 8: Interest expense on the van note needs to be recorded. Recall that the note is $30,000 with an annual interest rate of 10%. One month's interest = $30,000 $\times\ 0.10 \times 1/12 = \$250$.

After the adjustments are made, the financial statements can be prepared. Make sure you can trace each amount on the financial statements in Exhibit 5.20 to the accounting equation worksheet in Exhibit 5.19.

Complications in Valuing Inventory: Lower-of-Cost-or-Market Rule

L.O.5
Explain the lower-of-cost-or-market rule for valuing inventory.

Inventory is an asset on the balance sheet, recorded at cost. As you have seen, that asset can be a significant amount. To make sure that inventory is not overstated, GAAP requires companies to compare the cost of their inventory at the end of the period with the market value of that inventory, based on either individual items or total inventory. For the financial statements, the company must use the lower of either the cost or the market value of its inventory. This is called the **lower-of-cost-or-market (LCM) rule**. When you study any company's annual report, the note about inventory methods will almost always mention that the lower-of-cost-or-market valuation rule has been applied.

The **lower-of-cost-or-market (LCM) rule** is the rule that requires firms to use the lower of either the cost or the market value (replacement cost) of its inventory on the date of the balance sheet.

Estimating the market value of inventory is the difficult part of the LCM rule. The market value used is **replacement cost**. That is the cost to buy similar inventory items from the supplier to replace the inventory. A company compares the cost of the inventory, as it is recorded in the accounting records, to the replacement cost at the date of the financial statements and uses the lower of the two values for the balance sheet. Although there are a few more complications in applying this rule, the concept is straightforward. Inventory must not be overstated. When the inventory value is reduced, the adjustment to reduce the inventory also reduces net income.

Replacement cost is the cost to buy similar items in inventory from the supplier to replace the inventory.

Comparing the cost of inventory to its current replacement cost is more than a simple accounting requirement. Information about the current replacement cost of inventory is important for formulating sales strategies related to various items in inventory and for inventory-purchasing decisions.

It is common for the inventory of companies such as T-Mobile and Sony to lose value or quickly become obsolete because of new technology. These companies cannot know the value of the inventory with certainty, so they will often estimate the reduction in inventory. Sometimes this is shown on the financial statements as an "allowance for obsolescence." Knowing how a company values its inventory is essential for analyzing a company's financial statements, and you will find this information in the notes to the financial statements.

Financial Statement Analysis

Gross Profit Ratio

L.O.6
Define and calculate the gross profit ratio and the inventory turnover ratio.

Each of the four financial statements is useful to investors and other users. For example, the balance sheet tells investors about a firm's financial position and its ability to meet its short-term obligations. The current ratio, quick ratio, and the amount of working capital you studied

EXHIBIT 5.20

Financial Statements for Tom's Wear for May 2006

tom's wear

Tom's Wear, Inc.
Income Statement
For the Month Ended May 31

Revenues:		
Sales		$13,750
Expenses:		
Cost of goods sold	3,200	
Insurance expense	75	
Rent expense	1,200	
Depreciation expense	970	
Salary expense	1,000	
Interest expense	280	
Other operating expenses	327	
		8,852
Net income		$ 4,898

Tom's Wear, Inc.
Statement of Changes in Shareholder's Equity
For the Month Ended May 31

Common stock:		
Beginning balance		$ 5,000
Stock issued during the month		–
Ending balance		$ 5,000
Retained earnings:		
Beginning balance		$ 4,985
+ Net income		4,898
– Dividends declared		–
Ending balance		$ 9,883
Total shareholder's equity		$14,883

Tom's Wear, Inc.
Statement of Cash Flows
For the Month Ended May 31

Cash from operating activities:		
Cash collected from customers	$17,800	
Cash paid to vendors	(8,400)	
Cash paid for operating expense	(800)	
Cash paid for interest	(90)	
		$ 8,510
Cash from investing activities:		
	–	
Cash from financing activities:		
Cash payment for loan	(3,000)	
		(3,000)
Increase in cash		$ 5,510
Add beginning cash balance		3,295
Ending cash balance		$ 8,805

Tom's Wear, Inc.
Balance Sheet
At May 31

Assets			
Current assets			
Cash			$ 8,805
Accounts receivable		8,900	
Inventory		4,700	
Prepaid insurance		250	
Prepaid rent		600	
Prepaid Web services		250	
Total current assets			23,505
Equipment (net of $300 accumulated depreciation)			3,700
Van (net of $1,595 accumulated depreciation)			28,405
Total assets			$ 55,610

Liabilities & Shareholder's Equity			
Current liabilities			
Accounts payable			$ 4,200
Interest payable			500
Unearned revenue			4,950
Salaries payable			723
Other payables			354
Total current liabilities			10,727
Notes payable			30,000
Total liabilities			40,727
Shareholder's Equity			
Common stock			5,000
Retained earnings			9,883
Total liabilities and SH equity			$ 55,610

EXHIBIT 5.21

Target Corporation: Consolidated Statement of Operations

Target's year-end for its fiscal year 2005 was January 28, 2006. Even though only a year is given at the top, you can find the exact date of the firm's year end on the balance sheet (not shown here).

Target Corporation
Consolidated Statements of Operations (partial)
(in millions)

	For fiscal years		
	2005	2004	2003
Sales	$ 51,271	$ 45,682	$ 40,928
Net credit card revenues	1,349	1,157	1,097
Total revenues	52,620	46,839	42,025
Cost of sales	34,927	31,445	28,389
Selling, general and administrative expenses	11,185	9,797	8,657
Credit card expenses	776	737	722
Depreciation and amortization	1,409	1,259	1,098
Earnings from continuing operations before interest expense and income taxes	4,323	3,601	3,159
Net interest expense	463	570	556
Earning from continuing operations before income taxes	3,860	3,031	2,603
Provision for income taxes	1,452	1,146	984
Earnings from continuing operations	2,408	1,885	1,619
Earnings from discontinued operations, net of taxes of $46 and $116	–	75	190
Gain on disposal of discontinued operations, net of taxes of $761	–	1,238	–
Net earnings	$ 2,408	$ 3,198	$ 1,809

Gross profit ratio is equal to the gross profit (sales minus cost of goods sold) divided by sales. It is a ratio for evaluating firm performance.

in earlier chapters are calculated from amounts on the balance sheet. In addition to an analysis of a firm's financial position and ability to meet its short-term obligations, investors are very interested in a firm's performance. That information comes from the income statement. An important ratio for measuring a firm's performance is the **gross profit ratio**, also called the gross margin ratio. You know that gross profit equals sales minus cost of goods sold. The gross profit ratio is defined as gross profit divided by sales. The ratio measures the portion of sales dollars a company has left after paying for the goods sold. The remaining amount must cover all other operating costs, such as salary expense and insurance expense, and be large enough to have something left over for profit.

We will calculate the gross profit ratio for Target from its income statement shown in Exhibit 5.21. For its fiscal year ended January 28, 2006 (fiscal 2005), Target's gross profit was $16,344 (51,271 − 34,927)—dollars in millions. The gross profit ratio—gross profit as a percent of sales—was 31.9%.

This ratio is very important to a retail company. As with all ratios, it is useful to compare this ratio across several years. Look at Target's income statement, and compute the gross profit ratio for its fiscal year ended January 29, 2005 (fiscal 2004). Divide the gross profit of $14,237 by sales of $45,682 (dollars in millions). You should see that Target's gross margin ratio has improved. For that fiscal year it was 31.2%, so it has increased by a small amount.

When an income statement is presented in a multiple-step format, calculating the gross profit ratio is straightforward. Look at the partial income statements of Barnes & Noble in Exhibit 5.22. From fiscal year 2003 to 2004, the gross profit increased, but sales also increased. Calculating the gross profit ratio for each year helps us evaluate a firm's performance. As shown in the last row of Exhibit 5.22, the gross profit ratio appears relatively constant—although a quarter percent could be a big improvement for the firm.

Barnes & Noble, Inc.
Consolidated Statements of Operations (partial)
For the fiscal year ended
(in thousands)

	Jan. 29, 2005	Jan. 31, 2004	Feb. 1, 2003
Fiscal Year	2004	2003	2002
Sales	$4,873,595	$4,372,177	$3,916,544
Cost of sales	3,386,619	3,060,462	2,731,588
Gross profit	1,486,976	1,311,715	1,184,956
Sales and administrative expenses	1,052,345	910,448	816,597
Depreciation and amortization	181,553	166,825	154,844
Pre-opening expenses	8,862	8,668	11,933
Impairment charge	–	–	25,328
Operating profit	$ 244,216	$ 225,774	$ 176,254
Gross profit ratio	30.51%	30.00%	30.26%

EXHIBIT 5.22

Partial Income Statements for Barnes & Noble

The income statements for Barnes & Noble are multiple-step statements, showing a subtotal for gross profit. That makes it easy to calculate the gross profit ratio.

A retail company is particularly interested in its gross profit ratio and how it compares to that of prior years or that of competitors. When managers talk about a product's margins, they are talking about the gross profit. There is no specific amount that signifies an acceptable or good gross profit. For example, the margin on a grocery store item is usually smaller than that of a new car because a grocery store turns over its inventory more frequently than does a car dealership. When a grocery store such as Kroger or Whole Foods Market buys a grocery item, such as a gallon of milk, the sales price of that item is often not much higher than its cost. Because a grocery store sells so many different items and a large quantity of each, the gross profit on each item does not need to be very big to accumulate into a sizable gross profit for the store. However, when a company sells larger items, such as cars, televisions, or clothing, and not so many of them, it needs to have a larger gross profit on each item. For its fiscal year ended September 25, 2005, Whole Food's gross profit ratio was 35%, whereas Chico's, with fiscal year-end, January 28, 2006 had a gross profit ratio of 61%.

Inventory Turnover Ratio

Merchandising companies make a profit by selling their inventory. The faster they sell their inventory, the more profit they make. Buying inventory and then selling it makes the inventory "turn over." After a company sells its inventory, it must purchase new inventory. The more often this happens, the more profit a company makes. Financial analysts and investors are very interested in how quickly a company turns over its inventory. Inventory turnover rates vary a great deal from industry to industry. Industries with small gross margins, such as the candy industry, usually turn over their inventories more quickly than industries with large gross margins, such as the auto industry.

News Flash

Have DVDs paid off for the movie studios? According to Ken Fisher of ARS Technica (http://arstechnica.com), profit margins on DVD sales are 50–60%, compared to 20–30% for VHS business. In 2004, U.S. theater revenues were approximately $9.4 billion, whereas DVD sales were $15 billion.

EXHIBIT 5.23

Inventory Turnover Ratios for Whole Foods and Chicos

(dollars in thousands) For fiscal year ended	Whole Foods Market, Inc. September 25, 2005	Chico's FAS January 28, 2006
(1) Sales	$ 4,701,289	$ 1,404,575
(2) Cost of goods sold	3,052,184	547,532
(3) Gross profit	1,649,105	857,043
Gross profit ratio (3) ÷ (1)	35.1%	61.0%
(4) Inventory, beginning of the year January 29, 2005	152,912	73,223
(5) Inventory, end of the year January 28, 2006	174,848	95,421
(6) Average inventory ((4) + (5)) ÷ 2	163,880	84,322
Inventory turnover ratio (2) ÷ (6)	18.62 times	6.49 times

> The **inventory turnover ratio** is defined as cost of goods sold divided by average inventory. It is a measure of how quickly a firm sells its inventory.

The **inventory turnover ratio** is defined as cost of goods sold divided by the average inventory on hand during the year. The ratio measures how many times a firm turns over its inventory during the year—how quickly a firm is selling its inventory. We will compare the inventory turnover ratio for Whole Foods, a large grocery chain, with that for Chico's FAS, a smaller specialty clothes store chain. The year's cost of goods sold for each firm is found on its income statement, and average inventory can be calculated from the beginning and ending inventory amounts shown on comparative balance sheets. To get the average, we will just add the year-end inventory balances and divide by two. The data and calculations are shown in Exhibit 5.23. Notice that although Whole Foods has a much lower gross profit ratio than Chico's, the firm turns over its inventory many more times each year than does Chico's.

Although managers want to turn over inventory rapidly, they also want enough inventory on hand to meet customer demand. Managers can monitor inventory by using the inventory turnover ratio to find out the number of days items stay in inventory. For Whole Foods, 365 (days in a year) divided by 18.62 (inventory turnover ratio) = 19.6 days. For Chico's, the average number of days in inventory is just over 56 days (365 ÷ 6.49). Managers closely watch both the inventory turnover ratio and average days in inventory.

Your Turn 5-9
Your Turn
Your Turn

Safeway reported inventory of $2,766.0 and $2,740.7 on its balance sheets at the end of the fiscal years 2005 and 2004, respectively. During the 2005 fiscal year (ended on the Saturday nearest December 31), the company's cost of goods sold was $27,301.1. (Numbers are in millions.) What was Safeway's inventory turnover ratio for the year? How many days, on average, did merchandise remain in the inventory?

L.O.7
Describe the risks associated with inventory and the controls that minimize those risks.

Business Risk, Control, and Ethics

Inventory is a very important asset and ties up a large percentage of a firm's cash. The firm must evaluate and control the risk of losing inventory. Have you ever read how much money retail companies lose from shoplifting? The 17th Annual Retail Theft Survey reported that over $4.7 billion was lost from shoplifting and employee theft in just 27 U.S. retail companies in 2004. It is no surprise that retail firms such as Macy's and Target are very concerned about inventory theft. All consumers pay for that loss in higher merchandise prices; therefore, good controls on inventory are important to both the company and the consumer.

Like any of a company's assets, the inventory must be protected from damage and theft. The policies and procedures we have discussed can help reduce the risks associated with the actual purchase of the inventory—selecting a reliable vendor and making sure the items received are the ones ordered. To safeguard inventory from theft, companies can use controls such as locking storage rooms and limiting access to the inventory. When you buy clothes from Abercrombie & Fitch or the GAP, you might notice a sensor attached to the clothing that the salesclerk must remove before you leave the store. You may have experienced the unpleasant beeping of a sensor if a store clerk forgets to remove the device. Other items such as CDs and DVDs will set off a beeper if you try to leave the store without having the cashier de-sensor them.

Inventory Obsolescence Reserve

Inventory represents a significant portion of our assets (38.1%). Our profitability and viability is highly dependent on the demand for our products. An imbalance between purchasing levels and sales could cause rapid and material obsolescence, and loss of competitive price advantage and market share. We believe that our product mix has provided sufficient diversification to mitigate this risk. At the end of each reporting period, we reduce the value by our estimate of what we believe to be obsolete, and we recognize an expense of the same amount, which is included in Cost of Sales in our consolidated statement of operations.

EXHIBIT 5.24

Tweeter Home Entertainment Group's Note About the Risk of Inventory Obsolescence
Tweeter Home Entertainment Group sells cutting-edge technologies that are at most risk for having obsolete inventory. The company, therefore, has an extensive note about inventory obsolescence.

Segregation of duties is a control that helps companies minimize the risk of losing inventory to error or theft. The person who keeps the inventory records should not be the same person who has physical control of the inventory. This separation of record keeping and physical control of assets makes it impossible for a single individual to steal the inventory and cover it up with false record keeping. When this control is in place and functioning properly, it would take collusion—two or more people getting together on the plan—to lose inventory in this way.

Large retail firms such as Target have extensive inventory controls. There are many places—from the receiving dock to the front door of the store—where Target must keep an eye on its inventory. When goods arrive at the receiving dock, a clerk will make a record of the type and amount of merchandise that has arrived on a copy of the original purchase order without any quantities listed. The firm wants the receiving clerk to independently check the type and amount of goods that have been received. This record will be sent to the accounts payable department, where a clerk in that department will compare the record of the goods received with the original purchase order, which was sent over earlier from the purchasing department. Do you see the controls in place to safeguard the incoming shipments of merchandise? Several different departments are keeping a record of the goods ordered and received. The receiving clerk sends the merchandise to the inventory department, where physical custody of the goods is separate from the record keeping, which we have seen is verified by several departments.

Inventory is such an important asset to a firm that financial analysts and investors are very concerned that it is properly reported on the financial statements. In addition to protecting inventory from damage and theft, firms risk losing inventory as a result of obsolescence. If you were the manager of Best Buy, you would hate to have a warehouse full of VHS tapes when DVDs are available. If you were the manager of CompUSA, you would hate to have an inventory full of Pentium 3 computers when Pentium 4, a much faster and more efficient model, became available.

Firms that deal with cutting-edge technologies are at most risk for having obsolete inventory. Sprint PCS or T-Mobile would not want to have a huge inventory of analog-only phones now that digital phones are the better choice. With the new Bluetooth technology, the cell phone business is at risk with its old inventories. Each year, a company's inventory is evaluated for obsolescence at the same time the lower-of-cost-or-market rule is applied. Inventory must be written off, which will increase the cost of goods sold, when it is deemed to be obsolete. For example, in the notes to its financial statements, Tweeter Home Entertainment Group, the owner of HiFi Buys, Electronic Interiors, Showcase Home Entertainment, and Sound Advice, has an extensive note about inventory obsolescence, shown in Exhibit 5.24.

Inventory losses have an ethical component. The obvious one is that unethical people may steal a firm's inventory. Less obvious is the opportunity that inventory provides for misstating the value of the firm's assets. Failure to write down inventory that has lost value means that earnings will be overstated by the amount of the decline in inventory. As you know by now, managers rarely want to recognize expenses that do not produce any revenue, and they often look for ways to boost earnings. Inventory valuation is an area where the flexibility of accounting standards can lead to manipulation of earnings. When you study a firm's financial statements, be sure to read the notes to the financial statements about the firm's policy on writing down its obsolete inventory.

Chapter Summary Points

- A firm records the purchase of inventory at cost. That includes all costs to get the inventory ready for sale. Shipping costs, purchase discounts, and purchase returns and allowances all must be considered in calculating the cost of inventory.
- When a firm sells the inventory, the firm must consider sales discounts and sales returns and allowances when calculating net sales revenue.
- Inventory record keeping can be done at the time of each sale—perpetual inventory system, or the record keeping can be done at the end of the period—periodic inventory system.
- If a firm does not specifically identify the inventory item sold at the time of the sale, the firm will select one of three common cost flow assumptions to value inventory sold. Making a cost flow assumption is necessary when inventory costs are not constant and the specific identification of inventory units sold is too costly. The three methods are weighted average cost; first-in, first-out (FIFO); and last-in, first-out (LIFO). When costs of inventory are changing, these methods most often will produce different amounts for cost of goods sold.
- To avoid overvaluing inventory, firms must compare the cost of their inventory to the market value of the inventory and value the inventory at the lower of the two. This is called the lower-of-cost-or-market rule for valuing inventory.
- The gross profit ratio and the inventory turnover ratio are both useful in evaluating a firm's performance with respect to inventory. Gross profit ratio is equal to the gross profit divided by sales. The inventory turnover ratio is equal to cost of goods sold divided by average inventory.
- Firms face the risk of inventory being lost, damaged, and stolen. Controls include physically guarding the inventory (security services, locks, and alarms) and regular record keeping to identify potential problems. Many firms, high-tech firms in particular, run the risk of having obsolete inventory. Again, regular monitoring of purchases and sales will help control this risk.

Chapter Summary Problems

To compare the inventory methods for TV Heaven, a retail firm that specializes in high-end televisions, we will look at a single item to keep the analysis simple. Our results will apply to the other items in the inventory as well. Suppose TV Heaven started March with an inventory of 50 plasma TVs that cost $2,010 each, for a total beginning inventory of $100,500. During March, the firm made the following purchases:

March 2	200 TVs for $2,000 each
March 10	150 TVs for $1,800 each
March 20	100 TVs for $1,500 each
March 29	50 TVs for $1,000 each

During March, the firm made the following sales:

March 5	110 TVs for $4,000 each
March 12	160 TVs for $4,000 each
March 25	150 TVs for $4,000 each

Instructions

1. Using *periodic inventory record keeping*, calculate the cost of goods sold for the month and the inventory at the end of the month. Do these calculations using three methods: weighted average cost, FIFO, and LIFO. All other operating expenses amounted to $250,000. Assume these are the only transactions for the period. Calculate net income using each of the three methods. Which method provides the highest net income? What is causing this method to produce the highest net income?

2. Using *perpetual inventory record keeping*, calculate the cost of goods sold for the month and the inventory at the end of the month. Do these calculations using three methods: weighted average cost, FIFO, and LIFO. All other operating expenses amounted to $250,000. Assume these are the only transactions for the period. Calculate net income using each of the three methods. Which method provides the highest net income? Explain why weighted average cost and LIFO produce different amounts under perpetual than they do under periodic.

Solution

1. **Periodic Inventory**

Cost of Goods Sold

	No. of Units	Unit Cost	Total Cost
Beginning inventory	50	$2,010	$100,500
Purchases Mar 2	200	$2,000	$400,000
Mar 10	150	$1,800	$270,000
Mar 20	100	$1,500	$150,000
Mar 29	50	$1,000	$ 50,000
Goods available for sale	550		$970,500
Units sold	420		

Cost of goods sold:

Weighted average cost	$970,500 ÷ 550	= $ 1,765	Ending Inventory:	
Cost of goods sold =	420 × $1,765	= $741,300	130 × $1,765 =	$229,450
FIFO	50 × $2,010 =	$100,500		
	200 × $2,000 =	$400,000		
	150 × $1,800 =	$270,000	80 × $1,800 =	$120,000
	20 × $1,500 =	$ 30,000	50 × $1,000 =	$50,000
Cost of goods sold	420	$800,500	Ending Inventory	$170,000
LIFO	50 × $1,000 =	$ 50,000		
	100 × $1,500 =	$150,000		
	150 × $1,800 =	$270,000	80 × $2,000 =	$160,000
	120 × $2,000 =	$240,000	50 × $2,010 =	$100,500
Cost of goods sold	420	$710,000	Ending Inventory	$260,500

Net Income

	Weighted Average Cost	FIFO	LIFO
Sales revenue	$1,680,000	$1,680,000	$1,680,000
Cost of goods sold	741,300	800,500	710,000
Gross profit	938,700	879,500	970,000
Other operating expenses	250,000	250,000	250,000
Net income	$ 688,700	$ 629,500	$ 720,000

Net income is highest using LIFO because the cost of the inventory is going down. More often, costs go up so companies use LIFO to minimize net income. In this case, the technology advances are likely driving down the cost of plasma TVs.

2. Perpetual Inventory

Cost of Goods Sold

	No. of Units	Unit Cost	Total Cost
Beginning inventory	50	$2,010	$100,500
Purchases Mar 2	200	$2,000	$400,000
Mar 10	150	$1,800	$270,000
Mar 20	100	$1,500	$150,000
Mar 29	50	$1,000	$ 50,000
Goods available for sale	550		$970,500
Units sold Mar 5	110		
Mar 12	160		
Mar 25	150		
Ending inventory	130		

Weighted average (WA) cost		Average unit cost	Cost of goods sold
WA cost on March 5	50 @ $2,010 200 @ $2,000	$500,500 ÷ 250 = $2,002 avg. cost	110 units × $2,002 = $220,220
WA cost on March 12	140 @ $2,002 150 @ $1,800	$550,280 ÷ 290 = $1,898 avg. cost (rounded)	160 units × $1,898 = $303,680
WA cost on March 25	130 @ $1,898 100 @ $1,500	$396,740 ÷ 230 = $1,725 avg. cost (rounded)	150 units × $1,725 = $258,750
Total cost of goods sold			$782,650
(Ending inventory)	80 @ $1,725 50 @ $1,000	$188,000 + 130= $1,446 per unit (rounded)	$188,000

Note: Under WA perpetual, the ending inventory plus cost of goods sold is $150 more than goods available for sale. This differential is due to rounding. If you carry out the calculations to several decimal places, you will eliminate this rounding error. This type of calculation is typically done in a computer program that will not round as we have done here.

FIFO

Sale on March 5 (110 units)	50 @ $2,010 60 @ $2,000	$220,500
Sale on March 12 (160 units)	140 @ $2,000 20 @ $1,800	$316,000
Sale on March 25 (150 units)	130 @ $1,800 20 @ $1,500	$264,000
Cost of goods sold		$800,500
FIFO ending inventory	80 @ $220,000 50 @ $1,000	$170,000

LIFO

Sale on March 5 (110 units)	110 @ $2,000	$220,000
Sale on March 12 (160 units)	150 @ $1,800 10 @ $2,000	$290,000
Sale on March 25 (150 units)	100 @ $1,500 50 @ $2,000	$250,000
Cost of goods sold		$760,000

LIFO ending inventory	50 @ $1,000	$210,500	
	30 @ $2,000		
	50 @ $2,010		

Net Income	Weighted Average Cost	FIFO	LIFO
Sales revenue	$1,680,000	$1,680,000	$1,680,000
Cost of goods sold	782,650	800,500	760,000
Gross profit	897,350	879,500	920,000
Other operating expenses	250,000	250,000	250,000
Net income	$ 647,350	$ 629,500	$ 670,000

When a firm uses perpetual record keeping, it cannot assume to have sold units that were not purchased by the date of the sale. On the other hand, when a firm uses periodic record keeping, every purchase made during the period—no matter how the purchase dates match up to the sales dates—is part of the calculation of cost of goods sold. For weighted average cost, the average is different because of the late purchase. For LIFO, that last and cheapest purchase can be counted in the cost of goods sold. (Under perpetual, it could not be used because it had not been purchased at the time of the last sale.)

Key Terms for Chapter 5

Contra-revenue (p. 217)
Cost of goods available
  for sale (p. 215)
First-in, first-out (FIFO)
  (p. 223)
FOB destination (p. 213)
FOB shipping point (p. 213)
Gross profit ratio (p. 240)
Inventory turnover ratio
  (p. 241)

Last-in, first-out (LIFO)
  (p. 223)
Lower-of-cost-or-market
  (LCM) rule (p. 238)
Periodic inventory system
  (p. 212)
Perpetual inventory system
  (p. 212)
Purchase discount (p. 214)
Purchase order (p. 211)

Purchase returns and
  allowances (p. 214)
Replacement cost (p. 238)
Sales discount (p. 217)
Sales returns and
  allowances (p. 217)
Specific identification
  method (p. 221)
Weighted average cost
  (p. 221)

Answers to YOUR TURN Questions

Chapter 5
Your Turn 5-1
1. $9,800 [$10,000 − 2% discount; vendor paid the freight]
2. $10,090 [Discount expired; buyer paid the freight]
3. $9,890 [$10,000 − 2% discount + $90 freight]

Your Turn 5-2

Coffee	98% of $500	$490
Bags		100
Total inventory cost		$590

Your Turn 5-3
Cash collected: $3,150
Revenue: $3,000

Your Turn 5-4
The firm should use perpetual. At the time of each sale, the inventory account will be reduced. When the period is over and the inventory is counted, any difference between the inventory amount shown in the records and the inventory amount identified by a physical count of the

inventory will be the amount of inventory shrinkage. If the firm used a periodic system, all inventory not present at the end of the period is assumed to be part of cost of goods sold.

Your Turn 5-5

The weighted average cost of a unit is: [($10 + $40)/30] = $1.66667 per unit
Cost of goods sold = 15 units × $1.66667 = **$25**

Your Turn 5-6

1. Cost of goods sold is $4,600 + $5,100 = $9,700; and the gross profit is $14,000 − $9,700 = $4,300.
2. Cost of goods sold is $3,500 + $5,100 = $8,600; and the gross profit is $14,000 − $8,600 = $5,400.
3. Weighted average cost of the bracelets is $13,200/3 = $4,400. The cost of goods sold for the sale of two bracelets would be 2 × $4,400 = $8,800.

Your Turn 5-7

1. FIFO: $705 [(30 × $20) + (5 × $21)]
2. LIFO: $775 [(20 × $23) + (15 × $21)]
3. $21.143 (rounded) × 35 = $740

Your Turn 5-8

The LIFO conformity rule says that if a firm uses LIFO for tax purposes, it must also use LIFO for accounting (GAAP) purposes. It is unusual for accounting and tax rules to overlap. Usually accounting rules (GAAP) do not follow tax law.

Your Turn 5-9

Inventory turnover ratio = 27,301.1 ÷ [(2,766.0 + 2,740.7) ÷ 2] = 9.92
Average days in inventory = 365 ÷ 9.92 = 36.79 days

Questions

1. Explain the terms *FOB shipping point* and *FOB destination*. What are the accounting and business implications of the shipping terms? Why is it important to know who owns goods during shipping?
2. What is the difference between freight-in and freight-out?
3. What is the difference between a purchase return and a purchase allowance? What is the effect of purchase returns and allowances on the overall cost of inventory to the buyer?
4. What is a purchase discount? What is the effect of a purchase discount on the overall cost of inventory to the buyer?
5. Explain the terms of a purchase described as *2/15, n/30*. Would you take advantage of this offer? Why or why not?
6. What is a contra-revenue account? Give two examples of contra-revenue accounts.
7. What is a sales discount? What is the effect of a sales discount on the total sales revenue of the seller?
8. What is the difference between a periodic and perpetual inventory system?
9. What is inventory shrinkage?
10. What is the difference between the physical flow of inventory and the inventory cost flow?
11. What are the common cost flow methods for accounting for inventory? Describe the differences.
12. If inventory costs are rising, which method (FIFO, LIFO, or weighted average cost) results in the highest net income? Explain your answer.
13. If inventory costs are rising, which method (FIFO, LIFO, or weighted average cost) results in the lowest net income? Explain your answer.
14. Does LIFO or FIFO give the best—most current—balance sheet value for the ending inventory? Why?
15. How do taxes affect the choice between LIFO and FIFO?

16. Does the periodic or perpetual choice affect the choice of a cost flow (LIFO versus FIFO) method? Explain.
17. What is the *lower-of-cost-or-market* rule and why is it necessary?
18. What does the gross profit percentage measure? How is it calculated?
19. What does the inventory turnover ratio measure? What does *average-days-in-inventory* mean?
20. What are some of the risks associated with inventory? How do managers minimize these risks?

Multiple-Choice Questions

1. When inventory is purchased, it is recorded as a(n) _____ and when sold it becomes a(n) _____.
   a. liability, withdrawal
   b. asset, expense
   c. liability, asset
   d. asset, contra-asset

Use the following information to answer the questions 2 through 5.
Inventory data for Newman & Frith Merchandisers Inc. is provided here. Sales for the period were 2,800 units. Each sold for $8. The company maintains a periodic inventory system.

Date		Number of Units	Unit Cost	Total Cost
January	Beginning inventory	1,000	$3.00	$ 3,000
February	Purchases	600	$3.50	$ 2,100
March	Purchases	800	$4.00	$ 3,200
April	Purchases	1,200	$4.25	$ 5,100
Totals		3,600		$13,400

2. Determine the ending inventory assuming the company uses the FIFO cost flow method.
   a. $3,400
   b. $2,400
   c. $9,200
   d. $10,000
3. Determine the cost of goods sold assuming the company uses the FIFO cost flow method.
   a. $3,400
   b. $10,000
   c. $10,200
   d. $2,400
4. Determine the ending inventory assuming the company uses the weighted average cost flow method.
   a. $2,300
   b. $3,300
   c. $9,800
   d. $2,976
5. Determine the gross profit assuming the company uses the LIFO cost flow method.
   a. $11,400
   b. $14,400
   c. $22,400
   d. $19,700
6. Using LIFO will produce a lower net income than using FIFO under which of the following conditions?
   a. Inventory costs are decreasing.
   b. Inventory costs are increasing.
   c. Inventory costs are not changing.
   d. Sales prices are decreasing.

Use the following information to answer questions 7 through 10.

Sales revenue	$480,000
Cost of goods sold	300,000
Sales discounts	20,000
Sales returns and allowances	15,000
Operating expenses	85,000
Interest revenue	5,000

7. What is the net sales revenue?
   a. $400,000
   b. $445,000
   c. $415,000
   d. $455,000
8. What is the gross profit?
   a. $145,000
   b. $105,000
   c. $140,000
   d. $90,000
9. What is the net income?
   a. $60,000
   b. $65,000
   c. $55,000
   d. $180,000
10. What is the gross profit percentage?
    a. 13.54%
    b. 14.61%
    c. 32.58%
    d. 21.67%

Short Exercises

SE5-1. *Calculate cost of inventory.* (LO 1)
Celebration Coordinators Corporation began operations on April 1. The following transactions took place in the month of April.
   a. Cash purchases of merchandise during April were $300,000.
   b. Purchases of merchandise on account during April were $400,000.
   c. The cost of freight to deliver the merchandise to Celebration was $25,000; the terms were FOB shipping point. The freight bill was paid in April.
   d. Celebration returned $22,000 of merchandise purchased in part a to the supplier for a full refund.
   e. The store manager's salary was $3,000 for the month.

Calculate the amount that Celebration Coordinators Corporation should record for the total cost of merchandise inventory purchased in April.

SE5-2. *Record purchase of merchandise inventory: perpetual inventory system.* (LO 1, 2)
Using the data from SE5-1, enter each of the transactions into the accounting equation for the month of April, assuming Celebration Coordinators Corporation uses a perpetual inventory system.

SE5-3. *Calculate cost of inventory.* (LO 1)
For each of the following independent situations, calculate the amount that the purchasing company would record as the cost of each inventory purchase.
   a. Invoice price of goods is $5,000. Purchase terms are 2/10, n/30 and the invoice is paid in the week of receipt. The shipping terms are F.O.B. shipping point, and the shipping costs amount to $200.
   b. Invoice price of goods is $3,000. Purchase terms are 4/10, n/30 and the invoice is paid in the week of receipt. The shipping terms are F.O.B. destination, and the shipping costs amount to $250.

c. Invoice price of goods is $2,500. Purchase terms are 2/10, n/30 and the invoice is paid 15 days after receipt. The shipping terms are F.O.B. shipping point, and the shipping costs amount to $250.

SE5-4. *Record sale of merchandise inventory: perpetual inventory system.* (LO 1, 2)
Brenda Bailey's Textiles Inc. uses a perpetual inventory system. Enter each of the following transactions into the accounting equation.

1. On February 12, Brenda Bailey's sold $500,000 of merchandise on account with terms 2/10, n/30. The cost of the merchandise sold was $230,000.
2. On February 16, the customer returned $100,000 of the merchandise purchased on February 12 because it was the wrong style. The cost of the merchandise returned was $46,000.
3. On February 20, the customer paid the balance due Brenda Bailey's.

SE5-5. *Calculate gross profit and gross profit ratio.* (LO 1, 6)
Brenda Bailey's started the month of February with $300,000 of inventory. Using the information in SE5-4, calculate the net sales revenue, cost of goods sold, and gross profit that would appear on Brenda Bailey's Textiles Inc. income statement for the month of February.

SE5-6. *Calculate cost of goods sold and ending inventory: weighted-average cost.* (LO 3)
Calculate the cost of goods sold and the cost of the ending inventory using the weighted average cost flow assumption. Assume periodic record keeping.

Sales	100 units at $15 per unit
Beginning inventory	90 units at $6 per unit
Purchases	60 units at $9 per unit

SE5-7. *Calculate cost of goods sold and ending inventory: FIFO.* (LO 3)
Using the data from SE5-6, calculate the cost of goods sold and the cost of the ending inventory using the FIFO periodic cost flow assumption.

SE5-8. *Calculate cost of goods sold and ending inventory: LIFO.* (LO 3)
Using the data from SE5-6, calculate the cost of goods sold and the cost of the ending inventory using the LIFO periodic cost flow assumption.

SE5-9. *Analyze effect of cost flow method on net income.* (LO 3)
Given the following information, calculate the amount by which net income would differ between FIFO and LIFO.

Beginning inventory	3,000 units at $100 per unit
Purchases	8,000 units at $130 per unit
Units sold	6,000 units at $225 per unit

SE5-10. *Analyze effect of cost flow method on gross profit.* (LO 3, 4)
Given the following information, calculate the amount by which gross profit would differ between FIFO and LIFO.

Beginning inventory	1,500 units at $55 per unit
Purchases	2,750 units at $58 per unit
Units sold	2,250 units at $99 per unit

SE5-11. *Apply the lower-of-cost-or-market rule.* (LO 5)
The following information pertains to item #007SS of inventory of Marine Aquatic Sales Inc.

	Per unit
Cost	$180
Replacement cost	181
Selling price	195

The physical inventory indicates 2,000 units of item #007SS on hand. What amount will be reported on The Marine Aquatic Sales Inc.'s balance sheet for this inventory item?

SE5-12. *Apply the lower-of-cost-or-market rule.* (LO 5)
In each case, select the correct amount for the inventory on the year-end balance sheet.

a.	Ending inventory at cost	$24,500
	Ending inventory at replacement cost	$23,000
b.	Ending inventory at cost	$27,000
	Ending inventory at replacement cost	$28,500

In addition to the amounts for the financial statements, what information does the comparison between cost and market provide to a company's management?

SE5-13. *Calculate the gross profit ratio, inventory turnover ratio, and average days in inventory.* (LO 6)
Using the following information, calculate inventory turnover ratio, the average days in inventory, and the gross profit ratio for Barkley Company for the year ended December 31, 2012. (Round to two decimal places.)

Sales	$ 125,000
Cost of goods sold	75,000
Ending inventory, December 31, 2011	15,275
Ending inventory, December 31, 2012	18,750
Net income	26,500

SE5-14. *Identify risk and control.* (LO 7)
What is obsolete inventory? Name two things a firm can do to protect itself from the associated risk.

SE5-15. *(Appendix A) Calculate inventory errors.* (LO 8)
How would each of the following inventory errors affect net income for the year? Assume each is the only error during the year.
   a. Ending inventory is overstated by $3,000.
   b. Ending inventory is understated by $1,500.
   c. Beginning inventory is understated by $3,000.
   d. Beginning inventory is overstated by $1,550.

SE5-16. *(Appendix B) Estimate inventory.* (LO 9)
Fantasy Games Inc. wants to estimate its ending inventory balance for its quarterly financial statements for the first quarter of the year. Given the following, what is your best estimate?

Beginning inventory	$75,800
Net sales	$92,500
Net purchases	$50,500
Gross profit ratio	20%

Exercises—Set A

E5-1A. *Record merchandising transactions: perpetual inventory system.* (LO 1, 2)
Assume the following transactions for Clark's Appliances Inc. took place during May. Clark's Appliances uses a perpetual inventory system. Enter each of the transactions into the accounting equation.

May 2	Purchased refrigerators on account at a total cost of $500,000; terms 1/10, n/30
May 9	Paid freight of $800 on refrigerators purchased from GE
May 16	Returned refrigerators to GE because they were damaged; received a credit of $5,000 from GE
May 22	Sold refrigerators costing $100,000 for $180,000 to Pizzeria Number 1 on account, terms n/30
May 24	Gave a credit of $3,000 to Pizzeria Number 1 for the return of a refrigerator not ordered; Clark's cost was $1,200

E5-2A. *Record merchandising transactions: perpetual inventory system.* (LO 1, 2)
The Fedora Company had a beginning inventory balance of $25,750 and engaged in the following transactions during the month of June.

June 2   Purchased $4,000 of merchandise inventory on account from Plumes Incorporated with terms 2/10, n/30 and FOB destination. Freight costs associated with this purchase were $225.

June 4   Returned $400 of damaged merchandise to Plumes Incorporated

June 6   Sold $7,000 of merchandise to Fancy Caps on account, terms 1/15, n/30 and FOB shipping point. Freight costs were $125. The cost of the inventory sold was $3,500.

June 9   Paid the amount owed to Plumes Incorporated

June 10   The Fedora Company granted Fancy Caps an allowance on the June 6 sale of $300 for minor damage found on several pieces of merchandise.

June 22   Received total payment owed from Fancy Caps

June 24   Paid sales salaries of $1,850

June 25   Paid the rent on the showroom of $1,200

Enter each of the transactions for the Fedora Company into the accounting equation, assuming they use a perpetual inventory system.

E5-3A. *Calculate cost of goods sold and ending inventory: periodic FIFO.* (LO 3, 4)
Name Brand TV Sales and Service began the month of May with two television sets in inventory, Model # TV5684; each unit cost $125. During May, five additional television sets of the same model were purchased.

May 10   Purchased two units at $127 each
May 13   Sold two units at $225 each
May 16   Purchased one unit at $130
May 18   Sold one unit at $225
May 23   Sold two units at $225 each
May 24   Purchased two units at $135 each

Assume Name Brand uses a periodic inventory system and the FIFO cost flow method.
a. Calculate the cost of goods sold that will appear on Name Brand's income statement for the month of May.
b. Determine the cost of inventory that will appear on Name Brand's balance sheet at the end of May.

E5-4A. *Calculate cost of goods sold and ending inventory: periodic LIFO.* (LO 3, 4)
Use the data in E5-3A to answer the following questions.

Assume Name Brand uses a periodic inventory system and the LIFO cost flow method.
a. Calculate the cost of goods sold that will appear on Name Brand's income statement for the month of May.
b. Determine the cost of inventory that will appear on Name Brand's balance sheet at the end of May.

E5-5A. *Calculate cost of goods sold and ending inventory: perpetual FIFO.* (LO 3, 4)
Use the data in E5-3A to answer the following questions.
Assume Name Brand uses a perpetual inventory system and the FIFO cost flow method.
a. Calculate the cost of goods sold that will appear on Name Brand's income statement for the month of May.
b. Determine the cost of inventory that will appear on Name Brand's balance sheet at the end of May.

E5-6A. *Calculate cost of goods sold and ending inventory: perpetual LIFO.* (LO 3, 4)
Use the data in E5-3A to answer the following questions.

Assume Name Brand uses a perpetual inventory system and the LIFO cost flow method.

    a. Calculate the cost of goods sold that will appear on Name Brand's income statement for the month of May.

    b. Determine the cost of inventory that will appear on Name Brand's balance sheet at the end of May.

E5-7A. *Calculate cost of goods sold and ending inventory: periodic weighted average cost.* (LO 3, 4)

The For Fish Company sells commercial fish tanks. The company began 2006 with 1,000 units of inventory on hand. These units cost $150 each. The following transactions related to the company's merchandise inventory occurred during the first quarter of 2006.

January 20	Purchased 500 units for $160 each
February 18	Purchased 600 units for $170 each
March 28	Purchased 400 units for $180 each
Total purchases	1,500 units

All unit costs include the purchase price and freight charges paid by For Fish. During the quarter ending March 31, 2006, sales totaled 1,700 units, leaving 800 units in ending inventory.

    Assume For Fish uses a periodic inventory system and the weighted average cost flow method.

    a. Calculate the cost of goods sold that will appear on For Fish Company's income statement for the quarter ending March 31.

    b. Determine the cost of inventory that will appear on For Fish Company's balance sheet at the end of March.

E5-8A. *Calculate cost of goods sold and ending inventory: perpetual weighted average cost.* (LO 3, 4)

Advanced Music Technology Inc. sells MP3 players. The company began the third quarter of the year on July 1, 2008, with 750 units of inventory on hand. These units cost $50 each. The following transactions related to the company's merchandise inventory occurred during the third quarter of 2008.

July 15	Sold 450 units for $150 each
August 29	Purchased 500 units for $90 each
September 15	Sold 450 units for $200 each
September 28	Purchased 500 units for $117.50 each
September 30	Sold 800 units for $250 each

All unit costs include the purchase price and freight charges paid by Advanced Music Technology.

    Assume Advanced Music Technology uses a perpetual inventory system and the weighted average cost flow method.

    a. Calculate the cost of goods sold that will appear on Advanced Music Technology's income statement for the quarter ending September 30.

    b. Determine the cost of inventory that will appear on Advanced Music Technology's balance sheet at the end of September.

E5-9A. *Apply the lower-of-cost-or-market rule.* (LO 5)

Use the following data to answer the following question.

Ending inventory at cost, December 31, 2011	17,095
Ending inventory at replacement cost, December 31, 2011	16,545
Cost of goods sold, balance at December 31, 2011	250,765
Sales revenue, balance at December 31, 2011	535,780
Cash, balance at December 31, 2011	165,340

What inventory amount will this firm report on its balance sheet at December 31, 2011?

E5-10A. *Apply the lower-of-cost-or-market rule.* (LO 5)
In each case, indicate the correct amount to be reported for the inventory on the year-end balance sheet.

  a. Ending inventory at cost $125,000
     Ending inventory at market $121,750
  b. Ending inventory at cost $117,500
     Ending inventory at market $120,250

E5-11A. *Calculate gross profit and gross profit percentage: FIFO and LIFO.* (LO 6)
Given the following information, calculate the gross profit and gross profit ratio under (a) FIFO periodic and under (b) LIFO periodic.

  Sales   200 units at $50 per unit
  Beginning inventory   60 units at $40 per unit
  Purchases   175 units at $45 per unit

E5-12A. *Calculate the inventory turnover ratio.* (LO 6)
A company calculated its inventory turnover for the past 2 years. This year the inventory turnover is 6.3, and last year the inventory turnover was 7.5. Use this data to answer the following questions.

  a. Will this change in the inventory turnover ratio be viewed as good news or bad news? Explain your answer.
  b. Does the change indicate that more or less capital has been tied up in inventory this year compared to last year?

E5-13A. *Identify risk and control.* (LO 7)
Suppose an unethical manager wanted to keep his firm's net income as high as possible for a particular quarter to make sure he would get his bonus. The inventory manager has informed him that some obsolete inventory should be written off. What effect does writing down the value of the inventory have on net income? How will the manager respond to the inventory manager?

E5-14A. *(Appendix A) Calculate inventory errors.* (LO 8)
Ian's Small Appliances reported cost of goods sold as follows.

	2005	2006
Beginning inventory	$130,000	$ 50,000
Purchases	275,000	240,000
Cost of goods available for sale	405,000	290,000
Ending inventory	50,000	40,000
Cost of goods sold	$355,000	$250,000

Ian's made two errors:

  1. 2005 ending inventory was understated by $5,000.
  2. 2006 ending inventory was overstated by $2,000.

Calculate the correct cost of goods sold for 2005 and 2006.

E5-15A. *(Appendix B) Estimate inventory.* (LO 9)
The following information is available for the Arizona Chemical Supply Company.

  Inventory, January 1, 2006 $240,000
  Net purchases for the month of January   750,000
  Net sales for the month of January   950,000
  Gross profit ratio (historical)   40%

Estimate the cost of goods sold for January and the ending inventory at January 31, 2006.

Exercises—Set B

E5-1B. *Record merchandising transactions: perpetual inventory system.* (LO 1, 2)
Assume the following transactions for Jennifer's Fix-It-Up Inc. took place during March.
Jennifer's uses a perpetual inventory system. Enter each of the transactions into the accounting equation.

March 3	Purchased televisions from Sanyo on account at a total cost of $650,000, terms 2/10, n/25
March 8	Paid freight of $1,000 on televisions purchased from Sanyo
March 16	Returned televisions to Sanyo because they were damaged. Received a credit of $15,000 from Sanyo.
March 22	Sold televisions costing $125,000 for $225,000 to Joe's Sport's Bar & Grille on account, terms n/15
March 28	Gave a credit of $2,800 to Joe's Sport's Bar & Grille for the return of a television not ordered. Jennifer's cost was $1,600.

E5-2B. *Record merchandising transactions: perpetual inventory system.* (LO 1, 2)
Discount Wines Inc. had a beginning inventory balance of $85,450 and engaged in the following transactions during the month of October.

October 2	Purchased $15,000 of merchandise inventory on account from Joe's Winery with terms 2/10, n/30 and FOB destination. Freight costs for this purchase were $750.
October 5	Returned $100 of damaged merchandise to Joe's
October 6	Sold $18,000 of merchandise to Tasty Catering Service on account, terms 2/15, n/30 and FOB shipping point. Freight costs were $155. The cost of the inventory sold was $10,500.
October 10	Paid the amount owed to Joe's
October 10	Discount granted Tasty an allowance on the October 6 sale of $200 for some soured wine.
October 23	Received payment from Tasty
October 29	Paid sales salaries of $1,500
October 31	Paid the rent on the warehouse of $1,450

Enter each of the transactions for Discount Wines Inc. into the accounting equation, assuming they use a perpetual inventory system.

E5-3B. *Calculate cost of goods sold and ending inventory: periodic weighted average cost.* (LO 3, 4)
Sandy's Clean Carpet Company sells commercial vacuums. The company's fiscal year begins July 1, 2006, and ends June 30, 2007. Sandy's began the year with 1,500 units of inventory on hand. These units cost $200 each. The following transactions related to the company's merchandise inventory occurred during the first quarter of the year.

July 15	Purchased 450 units for $195 each
August 28	Purchased 575 units for $190 each
September 10	Purchased <u>600</u> units for $185 each
Total purchases	1,625 units

All unit costs include the purchase price and freight charges paid by Sandy's Clean Carpet.
During the quarter ending September 30, 2006, sales in units totaled 1,950 units.
Assume Sandy's Clean Carpet uses a periodic inventory system and the weighted average cost flow method.
   a. Calculate the cost of goods sold that will appear on Sandy's Clean Carpet Company's income statement for the quarter ending September 30.
   b. Determine the cost of inventory that will appear on Sandy's Clean Carpet Company's balance sheet at the end of September.

E5-4B. *Calculate cost of goods sold and ending inventory: perpetual weighted average cost.* (LO 3, 4)
Cutting Edge Enterprises Inc. sells flat-screen televisions. The company began the last quarter of the year on October 1, 2009, with 750 units of inventory on hand. These units

cost $1,000 each. The following transactions related to the company's merchandise inventory occurred during the last quarter of 2009.

October 15	Sold 450 units for $3,000 each
October 29	Purchased 500 units for $1,800 each
November 15	Sold 450 units for $4,000 each
December 28	Purchased 500 units for $2,350 each
December 30	Sold 800 units for $5,000 each

All unit costs include the purchase price and freight charges paid by Cutting Edge Enterprises. Assume Cutting Edge uses a perpetual inventory system and the weighted average cost flow method.

a. Calculate the cost of goods sold that will appear on Cutting Edge Enterprises' income statement for the quarter ending December 31, 2009.

b. Determine the cost of inventory that will appear on Cutting Edge Enterprises' balance sheet at the end of December.

E5-5B. *Calculate cost of goods sold and ending inventory: periodic FIFO.* (LO 3, 4) Radio Tech. Sales & Service Inc. began the month of April with three top-of-the-line radios in inventory, Model # RD58V6Q; each unit cost $235. During April, nine additional radios of the same model were purchased.

April 9	Purchased three units at $230 each
April 11	Sold five units at $350 each
April 17	Purchased two units at $195 each
April 18	Sold one unit at $350
April 20	Sold two units at $350 each
April 28	Purchased four units at $180 each

Assume Radio Tech. uses a periodic inventory system and the FIFO cost flow method.

a. Calculate the cost of goods sold that will appear on Radio Tech.'s income statement for the month of April.

b. Determine the cost of inventory that will appear on Radio Tech.'s balance sheet at the end of April.

E5-6B. *Calculate cost of goods sold and ending inventory: periodic LIFO.* (LO 3, 4) Use the data in E5-5B to answer the following questions.

Assume Radio Tech. uses a periodic inventory system and the LIFO cost flow method.

a. Calculate the cost of goods sold that will appear on Radio Tech.'s income statement for the month of April.

b. Determine the cost of inventory that will appear on Radio Tech.'s balance sheet at the end of April.

E5-7B. *Calculate cost of goods sold and ending inventory: perpetual FIFO.* (LO 3, 4) Use the data in E5-5B to answer the following questions.

Assume Radio Tech. uses a perpetual inventory system and the FIFO cost flow method.

a. Calculate the cost of goods sold that will appear on Radio Tech.'s income statement for the month of April.

b. Determine the cost of inventory that will appear on Radio Tech.'s balance sheet at the end of April.

E5-8B. *Calculate cost of goods sold and ending inventory: perpetual LIFO.* (LO 3, 4) Use the data in E5-5B to answer the following questions.

Assume Radio Tech. uses a perpetual inventory system and the LIFO cost flow method.

a. Calculate the cost of goods sold that will appear on Radio Tech.'s income statement for the month of April.

b. Determine the cost of inventory that will appear on Radio Tech.'s balance sheet at the end of April.

E5-9B. *Apply the lower-of-cost-or-market rule.* (LO 5)
Use the following data to answer the following question.

Ending inventory at cost, June 30, 2010	$25,180
Ending inventory at replacement cost, June 30, 2010	25,130
Cost of goods sold, balance at June 30, 2010	150,550
Sales revenue, balance at June 30, 2010	275,625
Cash, balance at June 30, 2010	285,515

ASB Hardware Inc. uses a perpetual inventory system and the FIFO cost flow method to account for its inventory. What inventory amount will ASB Hardware report on its balance sheet at June 30, 2010?

E5-10B. *Apply the lower-of-cost-or-market rule.* (LO 5)
In each case, indicate the correct amount to be reported for the inventory on the year-end balance sheet.

a.	Ending inventory at cost	$275,000
	Ending inventory at market	$271,250
b.	Ending inventory at cost	$185,250
	Ending inventory at market	$187,550

E5-11B. *Calculate gross profit and gross profit ratio: FIFO and LIFO.* (LO 6)
Given the following information, calculate the gross profit and gross profit ratio under (a) FIFO periodic and under (b) LIFO periodic.

Sales	225 units at $30 per unit
Beginning inventory	105 units at $20 per unit
Purchases	180 units at $32 per unit

E5-12B. *Calculate the inventory turnover ratio.* (LO 6)
A company calculated its inventory turnover for the past 2 years. This year the inventory turnover is 7.2, and last year the inventory turnover was 8.3. Use this data to answer the following questions.
   a. Will this change in the inventory turnover ratio be viewed as good news or bad news? Explain your answer.
   b. Does the change indicate that more or less capital has been tied up in inventory this year compared to last year?

E5-13B. *Identify risk and control.* (LO 7)
Risks associated with inventory include (1) theft, (2) damage, and (3) obsolescence. For each item, give an example of a company you believe is seriously faced with this risk and explain why.

E5-14B. *(Appendix A) Calculate inventory errors.* (LO 8)
Tire Pro Company's records reported the following at the end of the fiscal year.

Beginning inventory	$ 80,000
Ending inventory	85,000
Cost of goods sold	295,000

A physical inventory count showed that the ending inventory was actually $78,000. If this error is not corrected, what effect would it have on the income statement for this fiscal year and the following fiscal year?

E5-15B. *(Appendix B) Estimate inventory.* (LO 9)
The records of Florida Tool Shop revealed the following information related to inventory destroyed in Hurricane Frances.

Inventory, beginning of period	$300,000
Purchases to date of hurricane	140,000
Net sales to date of hurricane	885,000
Gross profit ratio	55%

The company needs to file a claim for lost inventory with its insurance company. What is the estimated value of the lost inventory?

Problems—Set A

P5-1A. *Analyze purchases of merchandise inventory.* (LO 1)

Guppies & Mollies Inc. made the following purchases in July of the current year.

July 3   Purchased $7,500 of merchandise, terms 1/10, n/30, FOB shipping point
July 6   Purchased $4,100 of merchandise, terms 2/15, n/45, FOB shipping point
July 11 Purchased $8,600 of merchandise, terms 3/5, n/15, FOB destination

Required

a. For each of the purchases listed, how many days does the company have to take advantage of the purchase discount?
b. What is the amount of the cash discount allowed in each case?
c. Assume the freight charges are $250 on each purchase. What is the amount of freight that Guppies & Mollies must pay for each purchase?
d. What is the total cost of inventory for Guppies & Mollies for the month of July, assuming that all discounts were taken?

P5-2A. *Analyze purchases of merchandise inventory.* (LO 1)

Carrie & Runnels Bikes Plus Inc. made the following purchases in December of the current year.

December 5   Purchased $2,600 of merchandise, terms 3/10, n/30, FOB destination
December 14   Purchased $6,150 of merchandise, terms 1/10, n/60, FOB shipping point
December 24   Purchased $8,375 of merchandise, terms 2/05, n/20, FOB destination

Required

a. For each purchase, by what date is the payment due, assuming the company takes advantage of the discount?
b. For each purchase, when is the payment due if the company does not take advantage of the discount?
c. In each case, what is the amount of the cash discount allowed?
d. Assume the freight charges are $365 on each purchase. For which purchase(s) is Bikes Plus responsible for the freight charges?
e. What is the total cost of inventory for Bikes Plus for the month of December, assuming that all discounts were taken?

P5-3A. *Record merchandising transactions, prepare financial statements, and calculate gross profit ratio: perpetual inventory system.* (LO 1, 2, 4, 6)

At the beginning of February, Ace Distribution Company Inc. started with a contribution of $10,000 cash in exchange for common stock from its shareholders. The company engaged in the following transactions during the month of February.

February 2	Purchased merchandise on account from Enter Supply Co. for $7,100, terms 2/10, n/45
February 5	Sold merchandise on account to Exit Company for $6,000, terms 2/10, n/30 and FOB destination. The cost of the merchandise sold was $4,500.
February 6	Paid $100 freight on the sale to Exit Company
February 8	Received credit from Enter Supply Co. for merchandise returned for $500
February 10	Paid Enter Supply Co. in full
February 12	Received payment from Exit Company for sale made on February 5
February 14	Purchased merchandise for cash for $5,200
February 16	Received refund from supplier for returned merchandise on February 14 cash purchase of $350
February 17	Purchased merchandise on account from Inware Distributors for $3,800, terms 1/10, n/30

February 18	Paid $250 freight on February 17 purchase
February 21	Sold merchandise for cash for $10,350. The cost of the merchandise sold was $8,200.
February 24	Purchased merchandise for cash for $2,300
February 25	Paid Inware Distributors for purchase on February 17
February 27	Gave refund of $200 to customer from February 21. The cost of the returned merchandise was $135.
February 28	Sold merchandise of $3,000 on account with the terms 2/10, n/30. The merchandise cost $2,300.

Required

    a. Enter each transaction into the accounting equation, assuming Ace Distribution Company uses a perpetual inventory system. Start with the opening balances in cash and common stock described at the beginning of the problem.

    b. Calculate the balance in the inventory account at the end of February.

    c. Prepare the four financial statements (including multiple-step income statement) for the month of February.

    d. Calculate the gross profit ratio.

P5-4A. *Record merchandising transactions and prepare multi-step financial statement: perpetual inventory system.* (LO 1, 2, 4, 6)
The following transactions occurred during March 2007 at the Five Oaks Tennis Club.

March 3	Purchased racquets and balls on credit from Spaulding Company for $700, with terms 3/05, n/30
March 4	Paid freight of $50 on the March 3 purchase
March 6	Sold merchandise to members on credit for $400, terms n/30. The merchandise sold cost $300.
March 10	Received credit of $40 from Spaulding for a damaged racquet that was returned
March 11	Purchased tennis shoes from Reebok for cash for $3,000
March 13	Paid Spaulding Company in full
March 14	Purchased tennis shirts and shorts from Nike Sportswear on credit for $5,000, terms 2/10, n/45
March 15	Received credit of $50 from Nike Sportswear for damaged merchandise
March 18	Sold merchandise to members on account, $950, terms n/30. The cost of the merchandise sold was $500.
March 22	Received $650 in cash payment on account from members
March 24	Paid Nike Sportswear in full
March 26	Granted an allowance of $30 to members for tennis clothing that faded when washed. (Customers kept the clothes.)
March 30	Received $320 in cash payments on account from members
March 30	Paid cash operating expenses of $300 for the month

Required

    a. Suppose the Five Oaks Tennis Club started the month with cash of $8,000, merchandise inventory of $2,000, and common stock of $10,000. Enter each transaction into the accounting equation, assuming Five Oaks Tennis Club uses a perpetual inventory system.

    b. Calculate the cost of goods sold for March and the ending balance in inventory.

    c. Prepare the multiple-step income statement, and the statement of changes in shareholders' equity for the month of March, and the balance sheet at March 31.

    d. Calculate the gross profit ratio for Five Oaks. Explain what the ratio measures.

P5-5A. *Analyze accounting methods and prepare corrected income statement.* (LO 1, 2, 4)
You are the accountant for Baldwin Company, and your assistant has prepared the following income statement for the year ended September 30, 2007.

Baldwin Company
Income Statement
For the year ended September 30, 2007

Sales revenue		$850,000
Sales returns and allowances	$22,500	
Freight costs	14,300	(36,800)
Net sales		813,200
Expenses		
Cost of goods sold	540,000	
Selling expenses	150,000	
Insurance expense	20,000	
Administrative expenses	40,000	
Dividends	8,000	
Total expenses		758,000
Net income		$ 55,200

You have uncovered the following errors:

1. Sales revenue includes $5,000 of items that have been back-ordered. (The items have not been delivered to the customers, and the customers have not been billed for the items.)
2. Selling expenses includes $250 of allowances that were given to customers who received damaged products.
3. Insurance expense includes $100 worth of insurance that applies to 2008.
4. Administrative expenses include a loan made to worker who had some serious financial trouble and needed $500 to pay a hospital bill. The worker plans to repay the money by the end of December.

Required

a. Prepare a corrected multistep income statement for the year. Baldwin shows sales as the net amount only on its income statement.
b. Write a memo to your assistant explaining why each error you found is incorrect and what the correct accounting treatment should be.

P5-6A. *Analyze results of physical count of inventory and calculate cost of goods sold.* (LO 1, 2, 7, 8)
Beard Company uses a perpetual inventory system. The company's accounting records showed the following related to June 2006 transactions.

		Units	Cost
	Beginning inventory, June 1	200	$ 600
+	Purchases during June	1,700	5,100
=	Goods available for sale	1,900	$ 5,700
−	Cost of goods sold	1,500	4,500
=	Ending inventory, June 30	400	$ 1,200

On June 30, 2006, Beard conducted a physical count of its inventory and discovered there were only 375 units of inventory actually on hand.

Required

a. Using the information from the physical count, correct Beard's cost of goods sold for June.
b. *(Appendix A)* How would this correction change the financial statements for the year?
c. What are some possible causes of the difference between the inventory amounts in Beard's accounting records and the inventory amount from the physical count?

P5-7A. *Calculate cost of goods sold and ending inventory and analyze effect of each method on financial statements.* (LO 3, 4)

Excel Template
www.prenhall.com/reimers

Jefferson Company had the following sales and purchases during 2006, its first year of business.

January 5	Purchased 40 units at $100 each
February 15	Sold 15 units at $150 each
April 10	Sold 10 units at $150 each
June 30	Purchased 30 units at $105 each
August 15	Sold 25 units at $150 each
November 28	Purchased 30 units at $110 each

Required

Calculate the ending inventory, the cost of goods sold, and the gross profit for the December 31, 2006, financial statements under each of the following assumptions:

a. FIFO periodic
b. LIFO periodic
c. Weighted average cost periodic
d. How will the differences between the methods affect the income statement and balance sheet for the year?

P5-8A. *Calculate cost of goods sold and ending inventory; analyze effects of each method on financial statements; apply lower-of-cost-or-market rule; calculate inventory turnover ratio.* (LO 3, 4, 5, 6)

The following series of transactions occurred during 2007.

January 1	Beginning inventory was 70 units at $10 each
January 15	Purchased 100 units at $11 each
February 4	Sold 60 units at $20 each
March 10	Purchased 50 units at $12 each
April 15	Sold 70 units at $20 each
June 30	Purchased 100 units at $13 each
August 4	Sold 110 units at $20 each
October 1	Purchased 80 units at $14 each
December 5	Sold 50 units at $21 each

Required

a. Calculate the value of the ending inventory and cost of goods sold, assuming the company uses a periodic inventory system and the FIFO cost flow assumption.
b. Calculate the value of the ending inventory and cost of goods sold, assuming the company uses a periodic inventory system and the LIFO cost flow assumption.
c. Calculate the value of the ending inventory and cost of goods sold, assuming the company uses a periodic inventory system and the weighted average cost flow assumption.
d. Which of the three methods will result in the highest cost of goods sold for the year ended December 31, 2007?
e. Which of the three methods will provide the most current ending inventory value for the balance sheet at December 31, 2007?
f. How will the differences between the methods affect the income statement for the year and the balance sheet at year end?
g. At the end of the year, the current replacement cost of the inventory is $1,100. Indicate at what amount the company's inventory will be reported using the lower-of-cost-or-market rule for each method (FIFO, LIFO, and weighted average cost).
h. Calculate the company's inventory turnover ratio and days in inventory for the year for each method in items a, b, and c.

P5-9A. *Calculate cost of goods sold, ending inventory, and inventory turnover ratio.* (LO 3, 6)

The following merchandise inventory transactions occurred during the month of June for the Furlong Corporation.

June 1	Inventory on hand was 1,000 units at $8.00 each
June 7	Sold 750 units at $10.50 each

June 18	Purchased 2,000 units at $8.80 each
June 21	Sold 2,225 units at $10.50 each
June 27	Purchased 2,500 units at $10.00 each

Required

a. Assume Furlong uses a periodic inventory system and compute the cost of goods sold for the month ended June 30 and ending inventory at June 30 using each of the following cost flow methods:
   1. FIFO
   2. LIFO
   3. Weighted average cost
b. Using the information for item a, calculate the inventory turnover ratio and days in inventory for the month of June for each method.
c. Assume Furlong uses the perpetual inventory system and compute the cost of goods sold for the month ended June 30 and ending inventory at June 30 using each of the following cost flow methods:
   1. FIFO
   2. LIFO

P5-10A. *Analyze effect of cost flow method on financial statements and inventory turnover ratio.* (LO 2, 4, 6)
Green Bay Cheese Company is considering changing inventory cost flow methods. Green Bay's primary objective is to maximize profits. Currently, the firm uses weighted average cost. Data for 2006 are provided.

Beginning inventory (10,000 units)	$14,500
Purchases	
60,000 units at $1.50 each	$90,000
50,000 units at $1.60 each	80,000
70,000 units at $1.70 each	66,000
Sales	
130,000 units at $3.00 each	

Operating expenses were $120,000 and the company's tax rate is 30%.

Required

a. Prepare the multiple-step income statement for 2006 using each of the following methods:
   1. FIFO periodic
   2. LIFO periodic
b. Which method provides the more current balance sheet inventory balance at December 31, 2006? Explain your answer.
c. Which method provides the more current cost of goods sold for the year ended December 31, 2006? Explain your answer.
d. Which method provides the better inventory turnover ratio for the year? Explain your answer.
e. In order to meet Green Bay's goal, what is your recommendation to Green Bay Cheese Company? Explain your answer.

P5-11A. *Calculate cost of goods sold and ending inventory; analyze effects of each method on financial statements; apply lower-of-cost-or-market rule; calculate inventory turnover ratio.* (LO 3, 4, 5, 6)
The following information is for Manuel's Pharmacy Supply Inc. for the year ending December 31, 2010.
At January 1, 2010:

- Cash amounted to $19,375.
- Beginning inventory was $16,000 (160 units at $100 each).
- Contributed capital was $15,000.
- Retained earnings was $20,375.

Transactions during 2010:

- Purchased 150 units at $110 each
- Purchased 190 more units at $120 each
- Cash sales of 390 units at $200 each
- Paid $11,500 cash for operating expenses
- Paid cash for income tax at a rate of 30% of net income

Required

a. Compute the cost of goods sold for the year and ending inventory at December 31, 2010, using each of the following cost flow methods:
   1. FIFO periodic
   2. LIFO periodic
   3. Weighted average cost periodic
b. For each method, prepare the balance sheet at December 31, 2010, a multistep income statement, statement of cash flows, and statement of changes in shareholder's equity for Manuel for the year ended December 31, 2010.
c. What is income before taxes and net income after taxes under each of the three inventory cost flow assumptions? What observations can you make about net income from the analysis of the three methods?
d. At the end of the year, the current replacement cost of the inventory is $12,750. Indicate at what amount the company's inventory will be reported using the lower-of-cost-or-market rule for each method (FIFO, LIFO, and weighted average cost).
e. For each method, calculate the inventory turnover ratio and average days in inventory for the year ended December 31, 2010.

Excel Template
www.prenhall.com/reimers

P5-12A. *Calculate the gross profit ratio and inventory turnover ratio.* (LO 6)
The following information is from the financial statements of Afua's International Pasta Corporation.

For year ended (amounts in thousands)	June 30, 2009	June 30, 2008	June 30, 2007
Sales (domestic)	$416,049	$429,813	$445,849
Cost of sales	92,488	98,717	110,632
Inventory	17,030	16,341	12,659

Required

a. Calculate the gross profit ratio for the last 2 years shown.
b. Calculate the inventory turnover ratio for the last 2 years shown.
c. What information do these comparisons provide?

P5-13A. *(Appendix B) Estimate inventory.* (LO 9)
Hines Fruit Corp. sells fresh fruit to tourists on Interstate 75 in Florida. A tornado destroyed the entire inventory in late June. In order to file an insurance claim, Hazel and Euglenia, the owners of the company, must estimate the value of the lost inventory. Records from January 1 through the date of the tornado in June indicated that Hines Fruit Corp. started the year with $4,000 worth of inventory on hand. Purchases for the year amounted to $9,000, and sales up to the date of the tornado were $16,000. Gross profit percentage has traditionally been 30%.

Required

a. How much should Hazel and Euglenia request from the insurance company?
b. Suppose that one case of fruit was spared by the tornado. The cost of that case was $700. How much was the inventory loss under these conditions?

Problems—Set B

P5-1B. *Analyze purchases of merchandise inventory.* (LO 1)
Deborah Hartranft's Professional Costumers Inc. made the following purchases in November of the current year.

November 7   Purchased $2,500 of merchandise, terms 3/15, n/20, FOB shipping point

| November 12 | Purchased $4,300 of merchandise, terms 1/05, n/25, FOB destination |
| November 16 | Purchased $6,200 of merchandise, terms 2/10, n/40, FOB shipping point |

Required

a. For each of the listed purchases, how many days does the company have to take advantage of the purchase discount?
b. What is the amount of the cash discount allowed in each case?
c. Assume the freight charges are $115 on each purchase. What is the amount of freight that Professional Costumers must pay for each purchase?
d. What is the total cost of inventory for Professional Costumers for the month of November, assuming that all discounts were taken?

P5-2B. *Analyze purchases of merchandise inventory.* (LO 1)
International Sports Merchandising Inc. made the following purchases in August of the current year.

August 5	Purchased $12,200 of athletic shoes, terms 1/15, n/20, FOB destination
August 14	Purchased $11,600 of training gear, terms 2/10, n/15, FOB shipping point
August 19	Purchased $3,500 of tennis rackets and tennis balls, terms 3/05, n/10, FOB destination

Required

a. For each purchase, by what date is the payment due, assuming the company takes advantage of the discount?
b. For each purchase, when is the payment due if the company does not take advantage of the discount?
c. In each case, what is the amount of the cash discount allowed?
d. Assume the freight charges are $170 on each purchase. For which purchases is International Sports Merchandising responsible for the freight charges?
e. What is the total amount of inventory costs for the month of August, assuming that all discounts were taken?

P5-3B. *Record merchandising transactions, prepare financial statements, and calculate gross profit ratio: perpetual inventory system.* (LO 1, 2, 4, 6)
At the beginning of April, Morgan Parts Company Inc. started with a contribution of $20,000 cash in exchange for common stock from its shareholders. The company engaged in the following transactions during the month of April.

April 3	Purchased merchandise on account from Thompson Supply Co. for $5,000, terms 1/10, n/30
April 4	Sold merchandise on account to Brown Company for $3,500, terms 2/10, n/30. The cost of the merchandise sold was $1,500.
April 7	Paid $100 freight on the sale to Brown Company
April 8	Received credit from Thompson Supply Co. for merchandise returned for $500
April 10	Paid Thompson Supply Co. in full
April 15	Received payment from Brown Company for sale made on April 4
April 16	Purchased merchandise for cash for $3,200
April 17	Received refund from supplier for returned merchandise on April 16 cash purchase of $350
April 19	Purchased merchandise on account from Kelsey Distributors for $4,100, terms 2/10, n/30
April 20	Paid $350 freight on April 19 purchase

April 21	Sold merchandise for cash for $12,170. The cost of the merchandise sold was for $9,500.
April 24	Purchased merchandise for cash for $5,300
April 25	Paid Kelsey Distributors for purchase on April 19
April 27	Gave refund of $800 to customer from April 21. The cost of the returned merchandise was $535.
April 30	Sold merchandise of $2,000 on account with the terms 2/10, n/30. The merchandise cost $1,200.

Required

a. Enter each transaction into the accounting equation, assuming Morgan Parts Company Inc. uses a perpetual inventory system. Start with the opening balances in cash and common stock described at the beginning of the problem.
b. Calculate the balance in the inventory account at the end of April.
c. Prepare the four financial statements (including multiple-step income statement) for the month of April. (Balance sheet at April 30.)
d. Calculate the gross profit ratio.

P5-4B. *Record merchandising transactions and prepare single-step and multiple-step income statement: perpetual inventory system.* (LO 1, 2, 4, 6)
FOXX Supplier Inc. sells plant food to retail landscaping and gardening stores. At the beginning of May, FOXX Supplier had a $15,000 balance in cash and $15,000 in common stock. During the month of May, the following transactions took place.

May 3	Purchased 500 pounds of plant food on account from the manufacturer for $20 per pound. The terms were 1/10, n/30, FOB shipping point. Freight costs were $90.
May 6	Sold 50 pounds of plant food to Center Street Garden Supply for $35 per pound on account, with terms 2/10, n/30, FOB destination. Freight costs were $15.
May 10	Paid the manufacturer for the May 3 purchase
May 15	Received payment in full from Center Street Garden Supply
May 17	Sold 200 pounds of plant food to Perry's Plants on account for $34 per pound, with terms 1/10, n/30, FOB shipping point. Freight costs were $100.
May 19	Returned 10 pounds of spoiled plant food to the manufacturer and received cash payment of $20 per pound
May 20	Purchased 300 pounds of plant food on account from the manufacturer for $20 per pound. Terms were n/30, FOB destination. Freight costs were $50.
May 24	Sold 150 pounds of plant food to Sam's Pest Control for $24 each for cash. Sam's picked up the order, so there were no shipping costs.
May 31	Paid for the purchase on May 20
May 31	Declared and paid cash dividends of $150

Required

a. Enter each transaction into the accounting equation, assuming FOXX Supplier Inc. uses a perpetual inventory system. Start with the opening balances in cash and common stock described at the beginning of the problem.
b. Calculate the cost of goods sold for May and the ending balance in inventory.
c. Prepare the multiple-step income statement and the statement of changes in shareholders' equity for the month of May, and the balance sheet at May 31.
d. Calculate the gross profit ratio for FOXX Supplier. Explain what the ratio measures.

P5-5B. *Analyze accounting methods and prepare corrected income statement.* (LO 1, 2, 4)
You are the accountant for Celebration Company, and your assistant has prepared the following income statement for the year ended December 31, 2006.

Celebration Company
Income Statement
For the year ended December 31, 2010

Sales revenue		$650,000
Sales returns and allowances	$18,100	
Freight expenses	2,000	
Selling expenses	48,300	(68,400)
Net sales		581,600
Expenses		
Cost of goods sold	350,000	
Salary expenses	82,000	
Rent expense	10,000	
Administrative expenses	23,500	
Dividends	4,000	
Total expenses		469,500
Net income		$112,100

You have uncovered the following facts:

1. Sales revenue includes $6,000 of items that have been back-ordered. (The items have not been delivered to the customers, although the customers have paid for the items.)
2. Selling expenses includes $4,000 of allowances that were given to customers who received damaged products.
3. Rent expense includes $400 worth of rent that applies to 2011.
4. Salary expenses include $10,000 loaned to one of the executives for a boat.
   a. Prepare a corrected multistep income statement for the year. Celebration shows sales as the net amount only on its income statement.
   b. Write a memo to your assistant explaining why each error you found is incorrect and what the correct accounting treatment should be.

P5-6B. *Analyze results of physical count of inventory and calculate cost of goods sold.* (LO 1, 2, 7, 8)
Barney's Flowerpot Company uses a perpetual inventory system, so the cost of goods sold is recorded and the inventory records are updated at the time of every sale. The company's accounting records showed the following related to May 2008 transactions.

		Units	Cost
	Beginning inventory, May 1	300	$ 600
+	Purchases during June	4,000	8,000
=	Goods available for sale	4,300	$8,600
−	Cost of goods sold	3,300	6,600
=	Ending inventory, May 31	1,000	$2,000

On May 31, 2008, Barney conducted a physical count of its inventory and discovered there were actually 900 units of inventory on hand.

Required

   a. Using the information from the physical count, correct Barney's cost of goods sold for June.
   b. *(Appendix A)* How would this correction change the financial statements for the year?
   c. What are some possible causes of the difference between the inventory amounts in Barney's accounting records and the inventory amount from the physical count?

P5-7B. *Calculate cost of goods sold and ending inventory and analyze effect of each method on the financial statements.* (LO 3, 4)

Excel Template
www.prenhall.com/reimers

Washington Company had the following sales and purchases during 2009, its first year of business.

January 8	Purchased 125 units at $100 each
February 20	Sold 75 units at $150 each
April 13	Sold 35 units at $150 each
June 28	Purchased 235 units at $105 each
August 2	Sold 175 units at $150 each
November 24	Purchased 140 units at $110 each

Required

a. Calculate the ending inventory, the cost of goods sold, and the gross profit for the December 31, 2009, financial statements under each of the following assumptions:
   1. FIFO periodic
   2. LIFO periodic
   3. Weighted average cost periodic
b. How will the differences between the methods affect the income statement and balance sheet for the year?

P5-8B. *Calculate cost of goods sold and ending inventory; analyze effects of each method on financial statements; apply lower-of-cost-or-market rule; calculate inventory turnover ratio.* (LO 3, 4, 5, 6)

Hillary's Diamonique buys and then resells a single product. Here is some information concerning Hillary's inventory activity during the month of August 2008.

August 2	860 units on hand at a total value of $10,320
August 6	Sold 400 units at $14 per unit
August 8	Purchased 640 units at $11 per unit
August 12	Purchased 425 units at $10 per unit
August 15	Sold 600 units at $12 per unit
August 21	Purchased 300 units at $9 per unit
August 24	Sold 800 units at $16 per unit
August 31	Purchased 100 units at $8 per unit

Hillary's uses a periodic inventory system.

Required

a. Calculate the value of the ending inventory and cost of goods sold, assuming the company uses a periodic inventory system and the FIFO cost flow assumption.
b. Calculate the value of the ending inventory and cost of goods sold, assuming the company uses a periodic inventory system and the LIFO cost flow assumption.
c. Calculate the value of the ending inventory and cost of goods sold, assuming the company uses a periodic inventory system and the weighted average cost flow assumption.
d. Which of the three methods will result in the highest cost of goods sold for August?
e. Which of the three methods will provide the most current ending inventory value for Hillary's balance sheet at August 31, 2008?
f. How would the differences between the methods affect Hillary's income statement for August and balance sheet at August 31, 2008?
g. At the end of the year, the current replacement cost of the inventory is $6,730. Indicate at what amount the company's inventory will be reported using the lower-of-cost-or-market rule for each method (FIFO, LIFO, and weighted average cost).
h. Calculate the company's inventory turnover ratio and days in inventory for the month for each method in items a, b, and c.

P5-9B. *Calculate cost of goods sold, ending inventory, and inventory turnover ratio.* (LO 3, 6)

The following merchandise inventory transactions occurred during the month of November for Party Heaven Inc.

November 5	Inventory on hand was 2,000 units at a cost $4.00 each
November 12	Sold 1,500 units at $6.00 each

November 16   Purchased 4,000 units at $4.40 each
November 23   Sold 4,300 units at $6.00 each
November 29   Purchased 5,000 units at $5.00 each

Required

a. Assume Party Heaven uses a periodic inventory system and compute the cost of goods sold for the month ended November 30 and ending inventory at November 30 using each of the following cost flow methods:
   1. FIFO
   2. LIFO
   3. Weighted average cost

b. Using the information for item a, calculate the inventory turnover ratio and days in inventory for the month of November for each method.

c. Assume Party Heaven uses the perpetual inventory system and compute the cost of goods sold for the month ended November 30 and ending inventory at November 30 using each of the following cost flow methods:
   1. FIFO
   2. LIFO

P5-10B. *Analyze effect of cost flow method on financial statements and inventory turnover ratio.* (LO 2, 4, 6)

Castana Company is considering changing inventory cost flow methods. Castana's primary objective is to minimize their tax liability. Currently, the firm uses weighted average cost. Data for 2007 are provided.

Beginning inventory (2,000 units)	$10,000
Purchases	
5,000 units at $6 each	$30,000
4,000 units at $6.50 each	26,000
6,000 units at $7 each	42,000
Sales	
15,000 units at $10 each	$150,000

Operating expenses were $12,000 and the company's tax rate is 25%.

Required

a. Prepare the income statement for 2007 using each of the following methods:
   1. FIFO
   2. LIFO

b. Which method provides the more current balance sheet inventory balance at December 31, 2007? Explain your answer.

c. Which method provides the more current cost of goods sold for the year ended December 31, 2007? Explain your answer.

d. Which method provides the better inventory turnover ratio for the year? Explain your answer.

e. In order to meet Castana's goal, what is your recommendation to Castana Company? Explain your answer.

P5-11B. *Calculate cost of goods sold and ending inventory; analyze effects of each method on financial statements; apply lower-of-cost-or-market rule; calculate inventory turnover ratio.* (LO 3, 4, 5, 6)

The following information is for Decades of Music Corporation for the year ended June 30, 2007.

At July 01, 2006:

- Cash amounted to $27,000.
- Beginning inventory was $30,000 (750 units at $40 each).
- Contributed capital was $12,000.
- Retained earnings was $45,000.

Transactions during 2006 and 2007:

- Purchased 825 units at $41 each
- Purchased 375 more units at $43 each
- Sold 1,150 units at $56 each
- Paid $8,500 cash for operating expenses
- Paid cash for income taxes at a rate of 40% of net income

Required

    a. Compute the cost of goods sold and ending inventory at June 30, 2007, using each of the following cost flow methods:
        1. FIFO periodic
        2. LIFO periodic
        3. Weighted average cost periodic
    b. For each method, prepare the balance sheet at June 30, 2007, a multiple-step income statement, and statement of cash flows for Decades for the fiscal year ended June 30, 2007.
    c. What is income before taxes and net income after taxes under each of the three inventory cost flow assumptions? What observations can you make about net income from the analysis of the three methods?
    d. At the end of the year, the current replacement cost of the inventory is $33,000. Indicate at what amount the company's inventory will be reported using the lower-of-cost-or-market rule for each method (FIFO, LIFO, and weighted average cost).
    e. For each method, calculate the inventory turnover ratio and average days in inventory for the fiscal year ended June 30, 2007.

Excel Template
www.prenhall.com/reimers

P5-12B. *Calculate the gross profit ratio and inventory turnover ratio.* (LO 6)
The following information is from the financial statements of Toys for Toddlers Company.

For year ended (amounts in thousands)	December 31, 2007	December 31, 2006	December 31, 2005
Sales	$2,534,135	$2,187,438	$1,925,319
Cost of goods sold	1,634,562	1,383,665	1,229,277
Inventory	54,353	47,433	45,334

Required

    a. Calculate the gross profit ratio for the last 2 years shown.
    b. Calculate the inventory turnover ratio for the last 2 years shown.
    c. What information do these comparisons provide?

P5-13B. *(Appendix B) Estimate inventory.* (LO 9)
Cynthia's Cotton Candy Company sells cotton candy to visitors at a traveling county fair. During a drought a fire destroyed the entire inventory in late July. In order to file an insurance claim, Cynthia, the owner of the company, must estimate the value of the lost inventory. Records from January 1 through the date of the fire in July indicated that Cynthia's Cotton Candy Company started the year with $4,250 worth of inventory on hand. Purchases for the year amounted to $8,000, and sales up to the date of the fire were $17,500. Gross profit percentage has traditionally been 35%.

Required

    a. How much should Cynthia request from the insurance company?
    b. Suppose that one bag of cotton candy mix was spared by the fire. The cost of that bag was $50. How much was the inventory loss under these conditions?

Financial Statement Analysis

FSA5-1. *Analyze income statement.* (LO 6)
The income statements for *Williams-Sonoma Inc.* for the fiscal years ended January 29, 2006, and January 30, 2005, are shown here. Compare the company's performance for the

2 years. Is the company controlling its cost of inventory? Is the company controlling its other expenses well? Be able to support your answers.

Williams-Sonoma, Inc.
Consolidated Statements of Earnings

	Fiscal Year Ended	
(Dollars in thousands)	Jan. 29, 2006	Jan. 30, 2005
Net revenues	$ 3,538,947	$ 3,136,931
Cost of goods sold	2,103,465	1,865,786
Gross margin	1,435,482	1,271,145
Selling, general and administrative expenses	1,090,392	961,176
Interest income	(5,683)	(1,939)
Interest expense	1,975	1,703
Earnings before income taxes	348,798	310,205
Income taxes	133,932	118,971
Net earnings	$ 214,866	$ 191,234

FSA5-2. *Analyze inventory management.* (LO 6)
Use the information from Wet Seal Inc. to analyze the firm's inventory management. Calculate the gross profit ratio and the inventory turnover ratio for each year. How do you think Wet Seal is managing its inventory? What other information would be useful in answering this question? Do you think the firm's increasing losses are attributable to increasing costs of the goods the firm sells or increases in other operating costs?

The Wet Seal, Inc.
Consolidated Statements of Operations

	Fiscal Years Ended		
(In thousands)	January 28, 2006	January 29, 2005	January 31, 2004
Net sales	$ 500,807	$ 435,582	$ 517,870
Cost of sales	339,356	377,664	420,520
Gross margin	161,451	57,918	97,350
Selling, general and administrative expenses	172,154	161,856	159,181
Store closure costs	4,517	16,398	–
Asset impairment	989	41,378	–
Operating loss	(16,209)	(161,714)	(61,831)
Interest (expense) income, net	(13,000)	(2,111)	1,550
Loss before provision (benefit) for income taxes	(29,209)	(163,825)	(60,281)
Provision (benefit) for income taxes	330	27,509	(21,498)
Loss from continuing operations	(29,539)	(191,334)	(38,783)
Loss from discontinued operations, net of income taxes	–	(6,967)	(8,300)
Net loss	(29,539)	(198,301)	(47,083)
Accretion of non-cash dividends on convertible preferred stock (Note 7)	(23,317)	–	–
Net loss attributable to common stockholders	$ (52,856)	$ (198,301)	$ (47,083)

From the balance sheet at January 28, 2006
Inventory $25,475 (in thousands)

From the balance sheet at January 29, 2005
Inventory $18,372

From the balance sheet at January 31, 2004
Inventory $29,054

From the balance sheet at February 1, 2003
Inventory $30,886

FSA5-3. *Analyze inventory management.* (LO 7)
Use the information given to analyze Amazon.com's inventory management.

(in millions)	For the year ended Dec. 31, 2005	For the year ended Dec. 31, 2004	At Dec. 31, 2003
Sales	$ 8,490	$ 6,291	
Cost of sales	6,451	5,319	
Net income	$ 359	$ 588	
Inventory (at year end)	$ 566	$ 480	$ 294

Write a short report for Amazon.com's shareholders with your comments about its inventory management.

Critical Thinking Problems

Risks and Controls

In this chapter, you learned that retail firms are at risk that their inventory will become obsolete. What can a firm do to minimize this risk? What types of firms are most at risk? Least at risk? (LO 6)

Ethics

Jim's Music Company uses LIFO for inventory, and the company's profits are quite high this year. The cost of the inventory has been steadily rising all year, and Jim is worried about his taxes. His accountant has suggested that the company make a large purchase of inventory to be received during the last week in December. The accountant has explained to Jim that this would reduce his income significantly. (LO 3, 5)

a. Jim does not understand the logic of the accountant's suggestion. Explain how the purchase would affect taxable income.

b. Is this ethical? Jim is uncertain about the appropriateness of this action from a legal and an ethical standpoint.

Group Assignment

Select a retail firm that you think might be concerned about obsolete inventory and another that you believe would not be very concerned. Then, find the financial statements and calculate the inventory turnover ratio of these two firms for the past two fiscal years. Are your results what you expected? Explain what you expected to find and your results. (LO 6, 7)

Internet Exercise: GAP

Gap Inc. was founded in 1969 by Donald and Doris Fisher in San Francisco, California, with a single store and a handful of employees. Today, they are one of the world's largest specialty retailers with three of the most recognized brands in the apparel industry (Gap, Banana Republic, and Old Navy). Gap Inc. has more than 150,000 employees supporting about 3,000 stores in the United States, United Kingdom, Canada, France, and Japan. Go to www.gapinc.com.

IE5-1. Click on "Investors," followed by "Financials," and then "Annual Reports and Proxy." Download the latest annual report.

    a. Which inventory cost flow assumption is used to measure the cost of inventory? Does Gap Inc. value inventory at the lower-of-cost-or-market value? If so, how is market value determined? Does this policy comply with GAAP?

    b. For the three most recent years, list the amounts reported for Net Sales and Gross Profit. Is Net Sales increasing or decreasing? Is Gross Profit increasing or decreasing? Are these trends favorable or unfavorable? Explain your answer.

    c. Using the financial statements, calculate the inventory turnover ratio for the three most recent years. Did the inventory turnover ratio increase or decrease? What does this measure? What does Gap Inc. do to identify inventory that is slow moving and how is this inventory treated?

    d. For cost of goods sold, Gap Inc. uses Cost of Goods Sold and Occupancy Expenses. What is included in this amount?

IE5-2. Go back to "GAP Inc. homepage" and click on "Social Responsibility."

    a. Does Gap Inc. do anything to ensure its garment workers are treated fairly? If so, why is this important for Gap Inc. to do?
       Go back to "About GAP Inc."

    b. Click on "How Our Clothes Are Made." List and briefly describe Gap Inc.'s five steps of their product life cycle.

Please note: Internet Web sites are constantly being updated. Therefore, if the information is not found where indicated, please explore the annual report further to find the information.

Appendix 5A

L.O.8
Describe and calculate the effect of inventory errors on the financial statements.

Inventory Errors

You know that the cost of the beginning inventory plus the cost of purchases equals the cost of goods available for sale. The cost of goods available for sale is then divided between the cost of goods sold and the ending inventory. That is,

Beginning inventory
+ Purchases
= Cost of goods available for sale
− Ending inventory
= Cost of goods sold

Because inventory directly affects cost of goods sold, a major expense, errors in the calculation of beginning inventory or ending inventory will affect net income. Tracing the effects of errors requires slow, focused deliberation. To show how inventory errors can affect income, here is a simple numerical example that shows an ending inventory error and a beginning inventory error. Read each description below and study the related examples.

Ending Inventory Errors

Suppose a firm has the correct amount for beginning inventory and the correct amount for purchases. Then, cost of goods available for sale is correct. If the ending inventory is overstated, cost of goods sold must be understated. Why? Because ending inventory and cost of goods sold are the two parts of cost of goods available for sale. Cost of goods sold is an expense. If the expense deducted from sales is too small, the result is that net income will be too large. Suppose you have correctly calculated the cost of goods available for sale (beginning inventory + purchases) to be $10. Those goods will either be sold—and become part of cost of goods sold—or they will not be sold—and will still be part of the inventory.

So, the cost of goods available for sale consists of two parts—cost of goods sold and ending inventory. Suppose the correct ending inventory is $2, but you erroneously give it a value of $3. If ending inventory is incorrectly valued at $3, then cost of goods sold will be valued at $7. Remember, the ending inventory and cost of goods sold must add up to $10 in this example. What is wrong with cost of goods sold? If ending inventory is actually $2, then cost of goods sold should be $8. See what happens? You understate cost of goods sold when you overstate the ending inventory. Anytime you understate an expense, you will overstate net income.

If ending inventory is too small—understated, cost of goods sold must be too large—overstated. The result is that net income will be understated. Let us use the same example, in which the cost of goods available for sale was correctly computed at $10. If ending inventory is actually $2 but you erroneously understate it as $1, then cost of goods sold will be valued as $9. It should be $8. So, an understatement in ending inventory has caused an overstatement of cost of goods sold. If you overstate an expense, then you will understate net income.

Beginning Inventory Errors

If ending inventory is overstated in 2006, then beginning inventory in 2007 will be overstated. After all, it is the same number. Errors in the ending inventory will, therefore, affect two consecutive years—ending inventory one year and beginning inventory the following year. If beginning inventory is overstated, then the cost of goods available for sale is overstated. If

	Calculated Amounts	Correct Amounts
Beginning Inventory	$ 1 (understated from prior year error)	$ 2
+ Purchases	+ $15	+ $15
Cost of Goods Available for Sale	$16	$17
− Ending Inventory	$ 6	$ 6
Cost of Goods Sold	$10	$11

EXHIBIT 5A.1

Error in the Beginning Inventory

ending inventory is counted correctly, then cost of goods sold will be overstated. So, net income will be understated. Let us continue the previous example. If you value beginning inventory at $3 (and the correct value is $2) and you correctly add the purchases for the second year—say, $15 worth—then, the cost of goods available for sale will be $18. Keep in mind, the correct amount is $17. At year-end, you count the ending inventory correctly at $6. The calculated cost of goods sold would be $12. Ending inventory and cost of goods sold must total $18. However, we know that the true cost of goods available for sale is $17. If the correct ending inventory is $6, then the correct cost of goods sold is $11. The calculated cost of goods sold was overstated by $1. When an expense is overstated, then net income will be understated.

If beginning inventory is understated, then the cost of goods available for sale is understated. If ending inventory is counted correctly, then cost of goods sold will be understated. So, net income will be overstated. Try thinking about the example in the format given in Exhibit 5A.1.

As you can see, when you understate the beginning inventory, you will naturally understate cost of goods sold. This understated expense will result in an overstatement of net income.

Note that over a period of 2 years the errors will counterbalance—they will cancel each other out. However, it is important that the financial statements be correct each year, not every other year, so a company will correct inventory errors if they are discovered, rather than wait for the errors to cancel each other out.

Berry Corporation miscounted the ending inventory at December 31, 2007. The balance sheet reported inventory of $360,000, but $25,000 worth of items were omitted from that amount. Berry reported net income of $742,640 for the year. What effect did this inventory error have on Berry's cost of goods sold for the year? What is the correct net income for the year ended December 31, 2007?

Answer: Ending inventory was understated, so cost of goods sold was overstated. Too much expense was deducted, so net income should have been higher by $25,000 for a correct net income of $767,640.

Your Turn 5A-1
Your Turn 5A-1
Your Turn 5A-1

Appendix 5B

L.O. 9
Estimate inventory using the gross profit method.

Gross Profit Method of Estimating Ending Inventory

There are times when a company might want to *estimate* the cost of the ending inventory rather than counting the units to calculate the cost. For example, if a company prepares monthly or quarterly financial statements, GAAP allows ending inventory to be estimated for reporting on those financial statements. This saves a company the trouble of counting the inventory every quarter. Also, if the inventory is destroyed or stolen, the company will have a reliable estimate of the cost of the destroyed inventory for the insurance claim.

First, you must know the usual gross profit percentage—the gross profit ratio you learned about in Chapter 5—for the company. Gross profit percentage is gross profit divided by sales. You can calculate the gross profit ratio using prior years' sales and cost data. Then, you multiply that percentage by the sales for the period, which gives the estimated gross profit. You then subtract the estimated gross profit from sales to get the estimated cost of goods sold. Because you know (a) beginning inventory (from the last period's financial statements), (b) purchases (from your records), and (c) an estimate for cost of goods sold, you can estimate ending inventory.

For example, suppose Super Soap Company lost its entire inventory in a flood on April 16. Super Soap had prepared a set of financial statements on March 31, when the inventory on hand was valued at $2,500. During the first part of April, purchases amounted to $3,500. The usual gross profit percentage in this business is 40%. If Super Soap had sales of $8,200 during the first 16 days of April, how much inventory was lost?

1. If sales were $8,200 and the usual gross profit percentage is 40%, then the gross profit would be $3,280.
2. If sales were $8,200 and gross profit is $3,280, then cost of goods sold would be $4,920. In other words, if the gross profit percentage is 40%, then the other 60% must be the cost of goods sold. So 60% of $8,200 = cost of goods sold = $4,920.
3. Beginning inventory + purchases − cost of goods sold = ending inventory. $2,500 + $3,500 − $4,920 = $1,080. This is our best estimate of the lost inventory.

Your Turn 5B-1
Your Turn 5B-1
Your Turn 5B-1

Suppose Base Company began May with inventory of $2,000 and purchased $8,000 worth of inventory during the first half of May. Sales for the first half of May amounted to $12,000.

Then, a fire destroyed the remaining inventory. Base Company has had a gross profit ratio of approximately 30% for the first 4 months of the year. Approximately how much inventory did Base Company lose in the fire?

Answer: $12,000 × 0.7 = Cost of goods sold
$8,400 worth of inventory has been sold.
$10,000 − $8,400 = $1,600 worth of inventory must have been lost in the fire.

Payment for Goods and Services: Cash and Accounts Receivable

Here's Where You've Been . . .

In Chapter 5, you learned about how a company acquires and accounts for inventory. You learned to value inventory with cost flow assumptions such as LIFO and FIFO and how that information is shown on a company's financial statements.

Here's Where You're Going . . .

When you are finished with Chapter 6, you should understand how a company accounts for cash and accounts receivable. You will learn how that information is presented on the financial statements.

Learning Objectives

When you are finished studying this chapter, you should be able to:

1. Explain how a firm controls cash and prepares a bank reconciliation.

2. Describe how cash is reported on the financial statements.

3. Calculate bad debts expense and explain how a firm evaluates and reports accounts receivable.

4. Explain the difference between sales on credit and credit card sales.

5. Account for and report notes receivable.

6. Explain how a firm accounts for product warranties.

7. Prepare financial statements that include bad debts and warranties.

8. Analyze a firm's accounts receivable with ratio analysis.

9. Identify the risks and controls associated with cash and receivables.

Ethics Matters

Fraud can happen anywhere. On May 27, 2006, a New York City priest, Monsignor John G. Woolsey, pleaded guilty to second-degree grand larceny. He was accused of stealing over $830,000 from his former church. The district attorney said that Woolsey "hid money in a secret bank account, falsified church records to conceal his thefts, and lied to the archdiocese about how he was spending church money." (*The New York Times*, May 27, 2006, p. B2. "Priest Asks Mercy after Pleading Guilty to Theft from Parish," by A. Hartocollis.)

Controls are not just for business firms trying to make a profit. Even not-for-profit organizations are susceptible to fraud. Cash is a particularly vulnerable asset, and controls need to be in place and operating to protect an organization's cash.

L.O.1

Explain how a firm controls cash and prepares a bank reconciliation.

Controlling Cash

You have learned how a firm buys and accounts for long-term assets, the infrastructure of a business. Then, as you learned in Chapter 5, a firm provides goods or services to its customers. Buying and selling inventory are the primary business activities of merchandising firms. Now, we turn to the collection of the payment for the goods and services a firm provides.

Customers usually have two choices when paying for goods and services: cash or credit. A company will analyze the risks associated with a method of payment and then put controls in place to minimize those risks. For example, if a company collects a lot of cash, it may keep large amounts in a locked safe. That is a control that helps protect the firm from robbery. If a company makes sales on credit, it is important that the company keep accurate records so that the customers can be properly billed for the sales. Millions of dollars of revenue are lost by businesses each year because either they miss capturing revenue they have earned or they miss collecting payment for goods and services they have delivered. By studying cash and the related controls, you will see how a company protects one of its most important assets.

Firms often keep a very significant amount of cash. For example, at the end of 2005, Hershey Foods had over $67 million in cash and cash equivalents. That is a lot of money, and Hershey's management wants to make sure it is safe. Because cash is often the target of misappropriation, firms must keep tight control of this asset.

Assignment of Responsibilities for Cash

A key control you learned about in Chapter 5 is the segregation of duties. For cash, segregation of duties means the person who has the physical custody of cash—anyone who has actual physical access to cash at any time and who can write checks and make deposits—cannot be the same person who does the record keeping for cash. If the same person had responsibility for both, it would be easy for that person to keep some of the cash and alter the records to hide the theft.

News Flash

Do firms keep cash as a safety net, or could it be a good investment? In 2006, the Federal Reserve, the governmental agency that sets interest rates, boosted the short-term interest rate up to its highest level since 2001. Sometimes, it is a good idea to keep cash in the short term. Read about it in *The Wall Street Journal*, "Thanks to the Fed, Cash Is Almost Exciting," by Kelly K. Spors, July 2, 2006.

Simply having two people involved in the same task can help protect a firm from fraud. For example, if the firm typically receives cash and checks in the mail from its customers, having two people open the envelopes together is a common practice. Stealing money would require collusion—two or more people working together to commit fraud. At banks, you will often see two people counting cash together. Having people share this responsibility decreases both errors and fraud.

Bank Reconciliations

Almost all companies use banks to help them keep track of and safeguard their cash. The bank assists its customers by providing a periodic bank statement. A **bank statement** is a summary of the activity in a bank account—deposits, checks, debit card transactions—usually sent monthly to the account owner. An example is shown in Exhibit 6.1.

> A **bank statement** is a summary of the activity in a bank account sent each month to the account holder.

EXHIBIT 6.1

Bank Statement

AB Andover Bank
Andover, MA 01844

Statement Date
June 30, 2006

Account Statement

Jessica's Chocolate Shop
15 Main Street
Andover, MA 01844

356814
ACCOUNT NUMBER

Balance Last Statement	Deposits and Credits		Checks and Debits		Balance This Statement
May 31, 2006	No.	Total Amount	No.	Total Amount	June 30, 2006
19,817.02	12	20,579.05	12	12,509.93	27,886.14

DEPOSITS AND CREDITS		CHECKS AND DEBITS			DAILY BALANCE	
Date	Amount	Date	No.	Amount	Date	Amount
6-2	733.30	6-2	235	560.50	6-2	19,989.82
6-3	689.50	6-3	236	1,450.00	6-3	19,229.32
6-6	3,000.00	6-4	237	1,090.50	6-4	18,138.82
6-7	4,000.00	6-5	238	1,500.48	6-5	16,638.34
6-8	999.28	6-6	239	890.60	6-6	18,747.74
6-9 CM	1,070.00	6-7	240	1,500.87	6-7	21,246.87
6-11	1,500.72	6-8	241	468.90	6-8	21,777.25
6-12	750.25	6-11	242	2,220.85	6-9	22,847.25
6-13	1,205.50	6-12	243	1,300.08	6-11	22,127.12
6-27	1,200.00	6-29	NSF	225.65	6-12	21,577.29
6-29	3,450.80	6-29	452	875.85	6-13	22,782.79
6-30	1,979.70	6-30	DM	50.00	6-27	23,982.79
		6-30	461	375.65	6-29	26,332.09
					6-30	27,886.14

Symbols: **ATM** Automatic Teller Machine   **CM** Credit Memo   **EC** Error Correction
NSF Not Sufficient Funds   **DM** Debit Memo   **INT** Interest Earned   **SC** Service Charge

Reconcile Your Account Promptly

A **bank reconciliation** is a comparison between the cash balance in the firm's accounting records and the cash balance on the bank statement to identify the reasons for any differences.

Someone in the firm will perform a **bank reconciliation**, which involves comparing the cash balance in the accounting records and the bank statement cash balance for that month. A bank reconciliation is more than simply part of the record keeping for cash. The bank reconciliation is a crucial part of controlling cash. As we all know, the bottom line in our checkbook or ATM spending records seldom agrees with the bottom line on our monthly bank statement. That is true for a business, too: The cash balance in a firm's records seldom agrees with the cash balance on its monthly bank statement. The two cash balances do not agree because there are transactions that are recorded in one place but not recorded in the other place due to timing differences. Sometimes the bank knows about a transaction that the firm has not recorded on its books, and sometimes the firm knows about a transaction that the bank has not recorded on its books. For example, a firm may make a deposit on the last day of June, but the deposit may not appear on the June bank statement due to the bank's delay in recording the deposit. Even more often, the checks a firm has written may not have reached the bank for payment—that is, the checks have not cleared the bank at the date of the bank statement. In other words, the bank does not know about those transactions on the date of the bank statement. The monthly bank statement, which contains all of the deposits, checks, ATM transactions, and other miscellaneous items, must be reconciled to the cash balance in the accounting records.

Your Turn 6-1
Your Turn
Your Turn

What is the purpose of a bank reconciliation? How often would a firm prepare one?

Steps in the Reconciliation. Reconciling the monthly bank statement to the general ledger cash account is an important element of internal control and requires two major steps.

1. Start with the balance on the monthly bank statement, called the balance per bank, and make adjustments for all the transactions that have been recorded in the firm's books but not recorded in the bank's books because the bank did not get the transaction recorded as of the date of the bank statement.
2. Start with the firm's cash balance, called the balance per books, and make adjustments for all the transactions that the bank has recorded but have not been recorded on the firm's books.

After the above steps are complete, each section of the bank reconciliation should show the same reconciled cash balance. That balance will be the actual amount of cash the firm had on the date of the bank statement. The actual amount is called the true cash balance. A firm reconciling a bank statement divides a worksheet into two parts, as shown in Exhibit 6.2.

Reconciling Items. The right side of Exhibit 6.2 shows items that will need adjustments in the firm's books. Adjustments will never be required for transactions already recorded in the general ledger. The left part of Exhibit 6.2 shows **deposits in transit** and **outstanding checks**. No adjustments will be needed for these items because they have already been recorded in the firm's accounting records, and the bank will eventually receive and record those transactions in its records.

A **deposit in transit** is a bank deposit the firm has made but is not included on the month's bank statement because the deposit did not reach the bank's record-keeping department in time to be included on the current bank statement.

Performing a bank reconciliation enables a firm to

1. Locate any errors, whether made by the bank or by the firm
2. Make adjustments to the cash account in the firm's books for transactions the bank has recorded but the firm has not yet recorded in its cash account

An **outstanding check** is a check the firm has written but has not yet cleared the bank. That is, the check has not been presented to the bank for payment.

The bank reconciliation begins with the balance per bank and the balance per books as of the bank statement date. Each of these balances is then adjusted to arrive at the true cash balance. A bank reconciliation has eight common adjustments. Three common adjustments may be needed to make the bank statement balance with the firm's records.

1. Deposits in transit are added to the balance per bank.
2. Outstanding checks are deducted from the balance per bank.
3. Errors made by the bank may require additions or deductions.

EXHIBIT 6.2

Format for Bank Reconciliation

To prepare a bank reconciliation, an accountant would create a worksheet divided into two parts: the Bank Statement (on the left) and the General Ledger Cash Account (on the right). Focus on the types of adjustments. We'll use the example dollar amounts later in Exhibits 6.3 and 6.4.

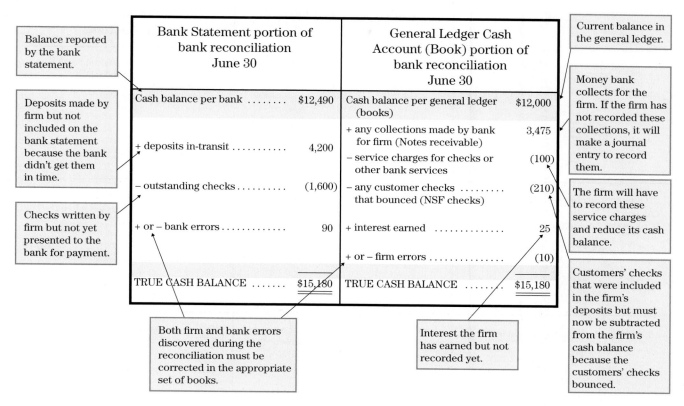

Five common adjustments may be needed to make the firm's cash record balance with the bank statement.

1. Collections made by the bank on behalf of the firm are added to the balance per books.
2. Service charges by the bank appear on the bank statement and are deducted from the balance per books.
3. A customer's non-sufficient-funds (NSF) check is deducted from the balance per books.
4. Interest earned on a checking account is added to the balance per books.
5. Errors made by the firm may require additions or deductions.

Exhibit 6.3 shows how each item on the bank side is treated in the bank reconciliation, and Exhibit 6.4 shows how each item on the books side is treated in the reconciliation. The dollar amounts come from the example in Exhibit 6.2. Remember that a bank reconciliation is not part of the formal records of the firm. It is just a worksheet, and any changes that the firm needs to make to its records must be done by formally recording the changes in the firm's accounting system.

Exhibit 6.4 shows the information already included in the calculation of the bank's balance at the date of the bank statement but unknown to the firm until the bank statement is received.

An Example of a Bank Reconciliation and the Adjustments. We will use the relevant information from ABC Light Company to prepare a bank reconciliation. Make sure you can identify where each amount is included in the reconciliation.

EXHIBIT 6.3

Items Used on the Bank Side of a Bank Reconciliation

There are actually an unlimited number of adjustments that may need to be made, but these are the five most common.

Item	What happens to the item during the bank reconciliation?	What happens to the item in the firm's books?
1. Deposits in transit—deposits the firm made too late for the bank to include them on the bank statement	Adjustment is needed to add the total amount of the deposits, $4,200, to the balance per bank.	No adjustment is needed because the cash was already added when the deposits were made.
2. Outstanding checks—checks the firm has written, but they haven't cleared the bank at the time of the bank statement	Adjustment is needed to deduct the total amount of the outstanding checks, ($1,600), from the balance per bank, $12,490.	No adjustment is needed because the cash was already deducted when the checks were written.
3. Any errors the bank has made	Suppose the bank should have recorded a deposit as $980 but instead recorded it as $890. In this case, add $90 to the bank's balance.	No adjustment is needed because the bank's records are wrong. The firm had the deposit recorded correctly. The firm would call the bank to have the error corrected.

ABC Light Company

Information from the bank statement:	
Balance per bank statement, June 30, 2006	$4,890
Note receivable ($1,000) and interest ($30) collected by bank for ABC Light Co.	1,030
Bank service charges	10
Customer check returned and marked "NSF"	100
Information from ABC's accounting records:	
Company books cash balance, June 30, 2006	1,774
Checks outstanding on 6/30/06: No. 298	1,300
304	456
306	2,358
Deposit made after bank hours by ABC Light Co. on 6/30/06	1,750

Keep these two additional facts in mind as you prepare the bank reconciliation.

1. The bank statement showed the bank had mistakenly charged ABC Light Company for a $150 check that was written by the ABC Chemical Company.
2. During June, ABC Light Company's bookkeeper recorded payment of an account payable incorrectly as $346. The check was paid by the bank in the correct amount of $364.

EXHIBIT 6.4

Items Used on the Book Side of a Bank Reconciliation

Item	What happens to the item during the bank reconciliation?	What happens to the item in the firm's books?
1. Amounts collected by the bank on behalf of the firm; in this example, a notes receivable 	Add $3,475 to the balance per books.	Increase cash and decrease notes receivable by $3,475.
2. Service charges—amounts the bank charges for its services 	Deduct $100 from the balance per books.	Decrease cash and increase bank expenses by $100.
3. Non-sufficient-funds (NSF) checks—checks the firm received from customers and deposited that bounced! 	Deduct $210 from the balance per books.	Increase (to restore) accounts receivable (specific account) and decrease cash by $210.
4. Interest earned on the bank account balance 	Add $25 to the balance per books.	Increase cash and increase interest revenue by $25.
5. Any errors the firm has made in its records 	Suppose the firm recorded a check it wrote to a vendor in payment of accounts payable for $480 when the check was actually $490. In this case, deduct $10 from the balance per books.	Decrease accounts payable and decrease cash by $10.

ABC Light Company
Bank Reconciliation
June 30, 2006

Balance per bank statement, June 30, 2006	$ 4,890
Add: Deposits in transit*	1,750
Bank error	150
Deduct: Outstanding checks (#298, #304, #306)	(4,114)
True cash balance, June 30, 2006	$ 2,676
Balance per books, June 30, 2006	$ 1,774
Add: Note and interest collected by bank	1,030
Deduct: Bank charges	(10)
NSF check	(100)
Company error (+ $346 − $364 = $18)	(18)
True cash balance, June 30, 2006	$ 2,676

> The true cash balance is found on both sides of the completed bank reconciliation.

(*Company has made the deposit, but it was not recorded by the bank as of the date of the bank statement.)

As you learned earlier in the chapter, a bank reconciliation is simply a worksheet— it is not a formal part of the firm's accounting system. Nothing included on the worksheet actually corrects the accounting records. The accounting records will need to be adjusted to account for every item on the "balance per books" part of the reconciliation. Here are the adjustments that ABC Light Company would make to bring its accounting records up to date following the bank reconciliation:

Assets	=	Liabilities	+	Shareholders' equity	
				Contributed + capital	Retained earnings
1,030 cash					
(1,000) notes receivable					30 interest revenue
(10) cash					
(100) cash					(10) bank expense
100 accounts receivable					
(18) cash		(18) accounts payable			

Often a firm's bank statement will have *debit memos* and *credit memos*. The debit memos are charges to the firm's account, reducing the balance in the account. The credit memos are additions to the account, increasing its balance. The bank statement might include a debit memo for new checks that were ordered. In contrast, the bank would include a credit memo for any interest the account has earned. Accountants use debits and credits to increase and decrease account balances. Even though you may not ever need to know how the accounting debit-credit system works, you may actually see the terms used in business. For example, the name for your "debit" card comes from the accounting entry that a bank makes when you use money from your account. When you hear the terms debit and credit used in business, you can be sure that the meaning is derived from the accounting meanings of those terms and used from the viewpoint of that business. If you want to know more about how the accounting debit-credit system works, you can read about it in Appendix A.

Your Turn 6-2
Your Turn
Your Turn

ABC Light Company's unadjusted book balance amounted to $2,400. The company's bank statement included a debit memo for bank service charges of $100. There were two credit memos in the bank statement. One was for $300, which represented a collection that the bank made for ABC. The second credit memo was for $100, which represented the amount of interest that ABC had

earned during the accounting period. Outstanding checks amounted to $250, and there were no deposits in transit. Based on this information, what is ABC's true cash balance?

Reporting Cash

Cash is an asset you will find on two financial statements: the balance sheet and the statement of cash flows. On the balance sheet, the amount of cash a firm has on the date of the balance sheet is reported. A firm often has a number of cash accounts—checking accounts and savings accounts in various banks. For example, a firm will often have a special bank account for its payroll. All of the firm's cash accounts will be combined for presentation on the balance sheet. Exhibit 6.5A shows how Hershey Foods reports cash on its balance sheet.

Cash Equivalents. On the balance sheet of Hershey Foods, the first asset is *Cash and cash equivalents*. It is the first asset listed on almost all balance sheets. **Cash equivalents** are highly liquid investments with a maturity of 3 months or less that a firm can easily convert into a known amount of cash. U.S. Treasury Bills are a common cash equivalent. The notes to the financial statements disclose how a firm defines its cash equivalents. Exhibit 6.5B shows the note defining cash equivalents from the financial statements of Hershey Foods. Although it is infrequent, a negative balance in cash should be listed as a current liability. This balance would indicate that a firm has had checks cleared in excess of its available cash. As you might guess, a firm does not want to have a negative cash balance.

The Statement of Cash Flows. In addition to its prominent place on the balance sheet, cash has its very own statement. As you learned in previous chapters, the statement of cash flows describes all of the cash flows for the period, which explains the change in cash from one balance sheet to the next. The amount of cash shown on the latest balance sheet will be the bottom line in the statement of cash flows. The statement of cash flows is an important financial statement because a business cannot survive if it does not have enough cash to pay its employees, vendors, rent, and other expenses.

L.O.2
Describe how cash is reported on the financial statements.

Cash equivalents are highly liquid investments with a maturity of 3 months or less that a firm can easily convert into a known amount of cash.

Hershey Foods Corporation
Comparative Balance Sheets (partial)
(in millions)

	At December 31, 2005	At December 31, 2004
Assets		
Current assets:		
Cash and cash equivalents	$ 67,183	$ 54,837
Accounts receivable—trade (net)	559,289	408,930
Inventories	610,284	557,180
Prepaid expenses and other	172,184	176,747
Total current assets	$1,408,940	$1,197,694

EXHIBIT 6.5A

Current Asset Section of Hershey Foods Corporation Comparative Balance Sheets

The current asset section of the balance sheet starts with cash and cash equivalents, followed by accounts receivable.

From the notes to the financial statements of Hershey Foods Corporation:

CASH EQUIVALENTS. Cash equivalents consist of highly liquid debt instruments, time deposits, and money market funds with original maturities of three months or less. The fair value of cash and cash equivalents approximates the carrying amount.

EXHIBIT 6.5B

Disclosure About Cash and Cash Equivalents

This note to the financial statements of Hershey Foods Corporation defines "cash equivalents" as it is used by the firm.

L.O.3
Calculate bad debts expense and explain how a firm evaluates and reports accounts receivable.

Accounts Receivable and Bad Debts Expense

As you know, often firms sell goods and services on account, which means they extend credit to customers and collect the cash later. We will look at why firms extend credit and how firms record transactions in accounts receivable.

Extending Credit

Accounts receivable is a current asset that arises from sales on credit; it is also the total amount customers owe the firm.

When a firm makes a sale on account, the amount is recorded in **accounts receivable**, sometimes simply called *receivables*. Why would a firm make sales on account? Extending credit to customers attracts business. Whereas many retail firms use bank credit cards to satisfy customer demand to delay payment, those firms that buy and sell from other firms simply extend credit to their customers. Most firms will deal only with vendors who allow payment to be made sometime after delivery of the goods.

Exhibit 6.5A shows Hershey Foods' current asset section of its December 31, 2005, and December 31, 2004, balance sheets. Notice that the second asset listed is *Accounts receivable trade (net)*. The balance in accounts receivable is the total amount owed to the firm by its customers. Sometimes a firm will call the amounts owed by customers *trade* accounts receivable to distinguish them from amounts owed by others who are not customers. When a person or firm that is not a customer owes the firm, the firm will call them *other* receivables.

For example, Hershey may lend money to another company to cover a cash shortfall. This would be recorded in *other receivables*. Unfortunately, a firm cannot expect to collect 100% of its accounts receivable balance. That is, not all customers will pay what they owe. For example, some customers are unable to pay as a result of a downturn in the economy or as a result of bankruptcy. If the amount a firm collects from credit sales as a percentage of total accounts receivable is low, the uncollected amounts will be costly to the firm. Every firm makes its own judgment about the percentage of uncollectible accounts it is comfortable with—there is no rule or specific amount. Having customers who do not pay is part of doing business, and a firm designs its credit policy to strike an acceptable balance between maximizing sales and minimizing the accounts receivable that are never paid.

Most companies offer credit to their customers, and they often have significant amounts of accounts receivable. Under GAAP, when a firm reports accounts receivable on its balance sheet, the amount must be what the firm expects to collect. The amount is called the net realizable value (NRV) of accounts receivable. Notice in Exhibit 6.5A that the term "net" follows the accounts receivable account title. Net means Hershey has deducted the amount the firm believes is uncollectible from total accounts receivable. A firm generally uses a method called the **allowance method** to calculate the uncollectible amount.

The **allowance method** is a method of accounting for bad debts in which the amount of the uncollectible accounts is estimated at the end of each accounting period.

A firm using GAAP applies the matching principle by putting the expense of having nonpaying customers on the same income statement as the revenue from sales made to those customers. To make this match, Hershey will estimate and record as an expense the amount it believes it will not collect each period. Accounts receivable that a firm cannot collect are called *bad debts*, and the expense to record bad debts is called *bad debts expense*.

Recording Uncollectible Accounts

Bad debts expense is the expense to record uncollectible accounts receivable.

To understand how firms account for bad debts, we will start by looking at the way a firm would record bad debts in the accounting equation. Then, we will discuss how a firm arrives at the dollar amounts. To record **bad debts expense**, a firm will make an adjustment at the end of the accounting period. The adjustment starts with an increase to an expense called bad debts expense. This adjustment puts the expense on the income statement for the period. Now we need to balance the accounting equation. Because the accounts that will not be collected have not been identified at year-end when the expense is estimated, the amount cannot be directly deducted from accounts receivable. The balance in accounts receivable is simply the total of all the individual customers' outstanding account balances, so the firm would have to know the name of the person who is not paying to deduct the amount directly from accounts receivable.

The **allowance for uncollectible accounts** is a contra-asset account, the balance of which represents the total amount the firm believes it will not collect from its total accounts receivable.

The amount that a firm estimates it will not collect—its uncollectible accounts—is put in a separate account called the **allowance for uncollectible accounts**. This account is a contra-asset and is used to hold the deductions from accounts receivable until the firm can identify specific accounts that are bad and take them off the firm's books. The balance in the allowance for uncollectible accounts is the amount that will appear on the balance sheet as a deduction from accounts receivable. Here is the adjustment a firm makes when it wants to record $5,000 as bad debts expense.

Assets	=	Liabilities	+	Shareholders' equity	
				Contributed + capital	Retained earnings
(5,000) allowance for uncollectible accounts					(5,000) bad debts expense

The amount remaining when you subtract the balance in the allowance for uncollectible accounts from the total amount of accounts receivable is called the carrying value of accounts receivable. Accountants use this terminology consistently for many different amounts on the balance sheet. Do you recall the name of the remainder when accumulated depreciation is subtracted from the cost of equipment? It is called the book value or carrying value of equipment on the balance sheet. For accounts receivable, the remainder is also called the net realizable value.

To summarize, the allowance for uncollectible accounts is a contra-asset account. The contra-asset holds the subtractions from accounts receivable, representing uncollectible accounts. Those credits cannot be deducted directly from accounts receivable because at the time the accountant records the bad debts expense, the firm does not know exactly whose accounts will go unpaid.

UNDERSTANDING Business

Managing Accounts Receivable

Accounts receivable is commonly one of a company's largest current assets. Because current assets support operations, managing the size of those assets and the timing of their use or conversion to cash is a crucial business activity.

How does a company control the size of its accounts receivable? The obvious way is to set credit policies that help achieve the desired level of credit sales and related collections. If the amount of a company's accounts receivable is larger than the company desires, it can tighten credit policies to reduce the amount of credit sales or it can increase collection efforts to speed up the collection of the related cash. If a company has a small amount of accounts receivable and is willing to increase that amount, the company may want to loosen its credit policies.

Companies often do that when they want to increase sales. There are other, less obvious ways for a company to manage its accounts receivable. If a company has a large amount of accounts receivable and it needs cash for operations, the company may sell its accounts receivable to a bank or finance company. This is called *factoring* accounts receivable, and the buyer is called a factor. When a company sells accounts receivable to a factor, the factor will keep a percentage of the value of the accounts receivable, similar to a credit card provider.

For example, if a company sold $100,000 worth of accounts receivable, the factor would pay the company a percentage of the face value of the receivables—often between 97% and 98%. The company removes the total accounts receivable from its records and records the remaining 2% or 3% as factoring expense. The factor takes ownership of the accounts receivable and collects the accounts receivable as they come due.

Managing accounts receivable is an important part of the sales and collection business process. Accounting information—the size and collection time for accounts receivable—provides crucial input for the decisions in this process.

Methods of Estimating Bad Debts Expense

Now that you know the terminology involved in accounting for bad debts, we will look at the procedures accountants use to estimate those bad debts. Using the allowance method, there are two ways of estimating uncollectible accounts expense: the percentage of sales method and the accounts receivable method.

Allowance Method—Percentage of Sales Method. The percentage of sales method focuses on the income statement and the amount of the current period's sales for which collection will likely not be made. For the purpose of putting the most meaningful amount on the income statement, the question is: How much of the sales revenue will go uncollected? The bad debts expense is recorded as a percentage of credit sales, and the balancing amount is an addition to the allowance for uncollectible accounts. This reduces assets because it will be subtracted from accounts receivable.

Suppose you own a firm that has credit sales of $100,000 a year. To prepare your financial statements, you need to estimate the portion of those sales for which you will not collect payment. You must estimate the amount of bad debts expense based on past experience because you cannot predict exactly which customers will not pay their bills. Suppose you believed 2% of your credit sales would be uncollectible. You would record bad debts expense of $2,000 and report the net accounts receivable of $98,000—$100,000 minus the allowance for uncollectible accounts of $2,000—on the balance sheet.

Allowance Method—Accounts Receivable Method. The second method of calculating the allowance for uncollectible accounts and corresponding bad debts expense is the accounts receivable method. This method focuses on the balance sheet. A firm starts by estimating how much of the year-end balance of accounts receivable it believes it will not collect. This estimate reduces the amount of accounts receivable on the balance sheet so that a firm reports the amount it estimates it will collect, the net realizable value. To put the most meaningful amount on the balance sheet, the question is: How much of the total amount of accounts receivable will go uncollected? (The question for the sales method is: What percentage of credit sales will not be collected?)

> An **aging schedule** is an analysis of the amounts owed to a firm by the length of time they have been outstanding.

Most often firms use an **aging schedule** to estimate this amount. An aging schedule is a list of the individual accounts that make up the total balance in accounts receivable categorized by how long the payment has been outstanding. Another way to estimate the amount is to take a percentage of the total balance in accounts receivable.

Using the accounts receivable method of estimating the balance needed in the allowance for uncollectible accounts is sometimes called the *aging method* and sometimes called the *percent of accounts receivable method*. Both names are simply more specific names for the accounts receivable method. Using this method, the bad debts expense equals the amount needed to get the balance in the allowance for uncollectible accounts to the amount to be subtracted from accounts receivable to make it equal to the net realizable value.

Hershey Foods uses the accounts receivable method (aging method) to estimate uncollectible accounts. Read how the firm describes the method in Exhibit 6.6. Notice that the firm mentions using the allowance method, assessing the collectibility of accounts, and using aging analysis to make its estimates.

EXHIBIT 6.6

Hershey Foods' Description of its Allowance for Uncollectible Accounts from Its 10-K for the Year Ended December 31, 2005

Hershey makes it clear that estimating uncollectible accounts involves a number of factors, all of which are subject to change.

In the normal course of business, the Company extends credit to customers that satisfy pre-defined credit criteria. The Company believes that it has little concentration of credit risk due to the diversity of its customer base. Accounts Receivable–Trade, as shown on the Consolidated Balance Sheets, were net of allowances and anticipated discounts. An allowance for doubtful accounts is determined through analysis of the aging of accounts receivable at the date of the financial statements, assessments of collectibility based on historical trends and an evaluation of the impact of current and projected economic conditions. The Company monitors the collectibility of its accounts receivable on an ongoing basis by analyzing the aging of its accounts receivable, assessing the credit worthiness of its customers and evaluating the impact of reasonably likely changes in economic conditions that may impact credit risks. Estimates with regard to the collectibility of accounts receivable are reasonably likely to change in the future.

How would a firm estimate bad debts expense using the balance in accounts receivable as the starting point? Suppose the balance in accounts receivable for Good Guys Co. at December 31, 2006, before any adjustments have been made, is $42,550. In this example, we have not even been told the amount of sales. To use the accounts receivable method, Good Guys Co. decides to prepare an aging schedule of accounts receivable, as shown in Exhibit 6.7. As you just learned, an aging schedule is an analysis of the amounts owed to a firm by the length of time they have been outstanding. As accounts become more overdue, they are increasingly unlikely to be collected.

Based on the aging of accounts receivable, management estimates the uncollectible amount at the end of the year to be $2,078. You can see how that total is calculated in Exhibit 6.7. So the net realizable value—the amount of accounts receivable the firm thinks it will collect—is $40,472. That is the total $42,550 minus $2,078. That amount is what Good Guys wants the balance sheet to show—the book value—at December 31, 2006. GAAP requires the firm to disclose the total accounts receivable balance and its net realizable value. Some companies show the details on the balance sheet, and others include the details in the notes to the financial statements. Exhibit 6.8 shows how Good Guys might present its accounts receivable.

In the first year of using the allowance method, with a zero balance in the allowance account, Good Guys estimated uncollectible accounts of $2,078. This is the adjustment that Good Guys will make at the end of the period.

Assets	=	Liabilities	+	Shareholders' equity	
				Contributed + capital	Retained earnings
(2,078) allowance for uncollectible accounts					(2,078) bad debts expense

Customer	Total	Current	1–30	31–60	61–90	Over 90
J. Adams	$500	$300	$200			
K. Brown	$200	$200				
L. Cannon	$650		$300	$350		
M. Dibbs	$600				$200	$400
Other customers	$41,500	$25,000	$10,000	$3,000	$2,500	$1,000
	$43,450	$25,500	$10,500	$3,350	$2,700	$1,400
Estimated percentage uncollectible		1%	3%	8%	20%	50%
Total estimated bad debts	$2,078	$255	$315	$268	$540	$700

Number of days past due

The amounts in this row are totals of many individual customers' accounts.

The sum of these amounts is $2,078.

EXHIBIT 6.7

Aging Schedule of Accounts Receivable
Notice that the amounts owed to the firm decrease with age. That's because most of the customers who purchased items on account pay their bills on time. Also notice that the percentages used to estimate the uncollectible portion increases as the age of the accounts increases. In this example, if an account is overdue by more than 90 days, there is a 50% chance it will never be collected.

EXHIBIT 6.8

Balance Sheet Presentation of Accounts Receivable

Balance Sheet, December 31, 2006

Current Assets:	
Accounts receivable	$42,550
Allowance for uncollectible accounts	(2,078)
Net accounts receivable	$40,472

Remember that rather than deducting the $2,078 directly from accounts receivable, the accountant will keep that amount in a separate allowance account, a contra-asset account, and show it on the balance sheet as a deduction from accounts receivable. Bad debts expense appears on the income statement as an operating expense.

Writing Off a Specific Account

During the following year, 2007, the firm will identify specific bad accounts and remove them from the books. That is when the firm finds out that a specific customer is not going to be able to pay his or her outstanding accounts receivable. When the firm eventually identifies the specific bad account and wants to remove it from the books, it will be done by deducting the amount from accounts receivable and also removing the amount from the allowance for uncollectible accounts. Removing the amount from accounts receivable reduces assets. Removing the amount from the allowance for uncollectible accounts *increases* assets by reducing the amount that will be deducted from accounts receivable on the balance sheet. That means there is no net effect on assets when the account is actually written off. There is no bad debts expense recorded when the firm actually writes off a specific customer's account using the allowance method. That is because the firm already recognized the bad debts expense when the accountant made the bad debts estimate for the adjustments at the time of the preparation of the financial statements.

When the firm writes off a specific account, the accountant is simply reclassifying an unnamed bad debt to a *named* bad debt. This is the transaction the firm would record to write off a specific account in the amount of $100.

Assets	=	Liabilities	+	Shareholders' equity	
				Contributed + capital	Retained earnings
(100) accounts receivable					
100 allowance for uncollectible accounts					

Only when you use the allowance method with accounts receivable as the basis for estimating bad debts expense do you adjust your new estimate for any over- or underestimation you made in the previous accounting period. If you write off more bad debts than you had estimated (i.e., you underestimated bad debts expense), you will end up with a shortage (negative balance) in the allowance for uncollectible accounts. However, you will adjust that balance in the allowance for uncollectible accounts when you do the end-of-period adjustments so that it will have the desired balance for the end-of-period balance sheet. If you write off fewer bad debts than you had estimated (i.e., you overestimated bad debts expense), you will end up with a bit extra (positive balance) in the allowance for uncollectible accounts. The next example will show you what to do if this happens.

Recall that Good Guys recorded $2,078 in its allowance for uncollectible accounts at December 31, 2006. This amount will be used for 2007 write-offs. Suppose the firm identifies M. Dibbs, who owes the firm $600, as an uncollectible account customer in February 2007. That means the firm's accountant or credit manager feels sure that the firm will not be able to collect his specific account. The effect on the accounting equation is a reduction in both the allowance for uncollectible accounts and accounts receivable. There is no effect on the net amount of accounts receivable. Writing off a specific account is a matter of cleaning up the firm's books. Instead of remaining an unidentified bad account, the firm can now put a name with $600 worth of bad debts. The firm already recognized the expense with the estimate it made at the end of the prior year, so no expense is recognized when a specific name is put with the uncollectible account. Here is the way the firm would write off Dibbs' account.

Assets	=	Liabilities	+	Shareholders' equity	
				Contributed + capital	Retained earnings
(600) accounts receivable, Dibbs 600 allowance for uncollectible accounts					

Can you see what happens when you write off a specific account? With the allowance method, there is no effect on a firm's *net* accounts receivable when the firm writes off a specific account. Instead, the firm removes the account from its accounts receivable and removes an equal amount from the allowance.

	Balances on year-end balance sheet after adjustments	Effect of writing off Dibbs' account	Balances after writing off Dibbs' account
Accounts receivable	$42,550	(600)	$41,950
Allowance for uncollectible accounts	(2,078)	600	(1,478)
Net accounts receivable	$40,472		$40,472

Suppose that, by the end of the year, Good Guys has identified and written off $1,400 of accounts in addition to Dibbs' account, for a total of $2,000 worth of specific bad accounts. This process of identifying and writing off continues throughout the year as the accounts are identified. That means last year's estimate of bad debts of $2,078 was $78 more than the total of the accounts actually identified and written off. The firm will ignore that difference and estimate the next year's bad debts expense in the same way as it did for the prior year. Good Guys will prepare another aging schedule and again make an estimate of uncollectible accounts. Follow along by looking at the additions and subtractions from the relevant accounts in Exhibit 6.9. Suppose credit sales for the year amounted to $100,000 and collections totaled $90,550, leaving a balance in accounts receivable of $50,000. Here is a summary of the activity in accounts receivable for the year.

- Beginning balance was $42,550 (ending 2006 balance).
- Add credit sales of $100,000.
- Deduct collections of $90,550.
- Deduct the total write-offs of $2,000.

This activity leaves an ending balance of $50,000 in accounts receivable. Suppose an aging schedule produced an estimate of uncollectible accounts of $2,500. Good Guys wants the balance sheet to use this estimate as the reduction in accounts receivable, showing the book value or carrying value of accounts receivable as $47,500. Now, Good Guys must take into consideration that it has a balance in the allowance account from last year's recording of bad debts expense. Good Guys will record bad debts expense this year of only $2,422 ($2,500 − $78). The amount carried over from last year, $78, is still in the allowance for uncollectible accounts, so the firm needs to add only $2,422 to the allowance for uncollectible accounts to get the total $2,500 needed for the balance sheet. So the firm's bad debts expense in the second year would be $2,422, and the allowance for uncollectible accounts balance at year-end will be the desired $2,500. The accounts receivable balance of $50,000 will be reduced by the allowance of $2,500 to give net accounts receivable of $47,500.

Study the summary of this example in Exhibit 6.9 to make sure you understand the procedures for estimating and recording bad debts expense and the procedures for actually writing off a specific account.

EXHIBIT 6.9

Allowance for Uncollectible Accounts Using Accounts Receivable to Estimate Bad Debts Expense

This example begins with an accounts receivable balance of $42,550. The allowance for uncollectible accounts is recorded along with bad debts expense for the year ended Dec. 31, 2006, for $2,078. During 2007, the firm has credit sales of $100,000 and collections of $90,550. Both are shown in AR, along with accounts written off. During the year, $2,000 worth of bad debts are identified and written off: Dibbs for $600 and another batch totaling $1,400. Writing off these accounts reduce both AR and the allowance for uncollectible accounts. At December 31, 2007, the balance in the allowance is $78, reflecting an amount left over from the prior year. When the estimate of bad debts at Dec. 31, 2007, of $2,500 is calculated, it is reduced by the $78 left over from the prior year. The adjustment to record bad debts expense for 2007 increases the allowance (which reduces assets) and increases bad debts expense (which reduces retained earnings).

	Accounts Receivable	Allowance for Uncollectible Accounts	Bad Debts Expense
Beginning balances from Dec. 31, 2006, financial statements	$42,550	$2,078	$2,078 to income statment
Credit sales in 2007	100,000		
Cash collections in 2007	(90,550)		
Write-offs in 2007	(600) (1,400)	(600) (1,400)	
Balance before adjustment	$50,000	$ 78	
Desired ending balance		$2,500	
Bad debts expense ($2,500 – 78) (amount needed to get desired balance in allowance)		$2,422	$2,422 to income statment

▨ Amounts on the Dec. 31, 2007, balance sheet

When the accounts receivable method for estimating the allowance is used, the balance in the *allowance for uncollectible accounts* account and the bad debts expense are guaranteed to be equal only in the first year. After that, they would be equal only if the estimate of bad debts at the end of the previous year is exactly equal to the accounts identified as uncollectible and written off in the subsequent year—and that rarely happens. Each year, the expense usually contains a small adjustment for the over- or underestimate from the previous year's entry.

Making the adjustment for the allowance for uncollectible accounts is part of the adjusting entries the firm records at the end of the accounting period. The amount of the bad debts estimate affects net income. To help ensure their bonuses or good salary increases, unethical managers could manipulate bad debts estimates to inflate net income. Watch for this when you read about firms' accounting problems in the news.

Exhibit 6.10 provides a summary of the allowance method for bad debts. Refer to the exhibit when you are trying to learn the differences between the methods of calculating the amounts for the allowance for uncollectible accounts and bad debts expense.

Your Turn 6-3
Your Turn
Your Turn

Suppose at the end of the year, Pendleton Corp. records showed the following:

Allowance for doubtful accounts (excess from prior year)	**$100 balance**
Bad debts expense*	**-0-**
Accounts receivable	**$10,000**

*Bad debts expense has a zero balance because no adjustments have been made.

EXHIBIT 6.10

Allowance Methods of Accounting for Bad Debts

Method of Estimating Bad Debts Expense	Procedure	Effect on Income Statement	Effect on Balance Sheet
Sales method	Take a % of credit sales to record as bad debts expense.	Reduces income with bad debts expense.	Reduces assets with an increase in the allowance for uncollectible accounts (a contra-asset).
Accounts receivable method	Prepare an aging schedule or use a single percentage of the total balance in accounts receivable to estimate the balance needed in the allowance for uncollectible accounts	Reduces income with bad debts expense	Reduces assets with an increase in the allowance for uncollectible accounts (a contra-asset).
For both methods:	Writing off a specific account under both methods:	No effect on income statement	No net effect on the balance sheet

Pendleton estimated the end-of-year uncollectible accounts receivable to be $500, based on an aging schedule of accounts receivable.
1. **Calculate the amount of bad debts expense that should be shown on the income statement for the year.**
2. **What will be the net accounts receivable on the year-end balance sheet?**

The Direct Write-off Method

As you have learned, when a firm reports accounts receivable on its balance sheet, the amount must be what the firm expects to collect—that amount is the real asset. Most publicly traded firms use the allowance method because GAAP requires it when a firm has a significant amount of bad debts. There is another option called the **direct write-off method**. Using this method, a firm does not make any estimates of bad debts. The bad debts expense is recorded only when a specific account is identified as uncollectible. A firm uses the direct write-off method only when it has so few bad debts that almost all accounts receivable will be collected. Otherwise, the firm would be violating GAAP because it would not be matching the bad debts expense with the appropriate sales revenue.

The **direct write-off method** is a method of accounting for bad debts in which they are recorded as an expense in the period in which they are identified as uncollectible.

The accountant removes the "bad" account from the accounting records by deducting it from accounts receivable. The bad debts expense account is increased. Using the direct write-off method, a firm reports total accounts receivable on the balance sheet. Here is the transaction the firm records when it discovers that Jane Doe, who owes the firm $200, will not pay.

Assets	=	Liabilities	+	Shareholders' equity	
				Contributed + capital	Retained earnings
(200) accounts receivable, J. Doe					(200) bad debts expense

Remember that the direct write-off method is not considered GAAP. Very few firms that extend credit to customers use this method if they follow GAAP because specific bad debts

EXHIBIT 6.11

Accounting for Uncollectible Accounts

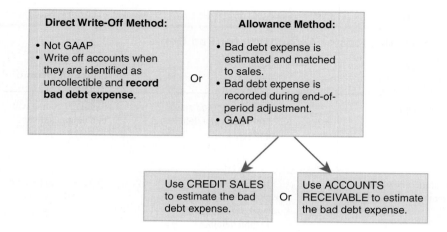

are written off in the period they are discovered rather than in the earlier period of the sale, which violates the matching principle.

Exhibit 6.11 shows the relationships between the methods of accounting for bad debts that you have learned.

L.O.4

Explain the difference between sales on credit and credit card sales.

Credit Card Sales

One way to avoid the risk of extending credit to your customers is to accept payment with their credit cards. Banks or other financial institutions—also known as credit card companies—issue credit cards; and the users often must pay the issuer a fee to use the card. The credit card companies take the responsibility for evaluating a person's credit-worthiness, and they also handle billing the customers and collecting payments. If a company allows customers to use a credit card to pay for their purchases, the company must pay the credit card company for these services. This is an important business decision, especially for small companies. The cost of allowing customers to make purchases using credit cards must be compared with the benefits. The most significant cost is the credit card expense. Benefits may include increasing the number of customers and eliminating the risks associated with extending credit to customers. In addition, the company does not need to keep track of customers' credit, payments, and outstanding balances; and will not face any problems with late or uncollectible accounts.

This is how credit card sales are handled. The company will submit all the credit card sales receipts to the credit card company, and the credit card company will pay the company immediately. The amount the company receives will not be the gross amount of the sales. It will be a smaller amount because the credit card company will deduct a percentage of total sales as its fee for the services it provides. The company classifies the fees withheld by the credit card company as operating expenses.

Suppose that Wally's Tire Company accepts **MasterCard**, and total credit card sales for the day were $1,000. Suppose the **MasterCard** fee is 5% of sales. Wally's would record the sales for the day in its accounting records as follows.

Assets	=	Liabilities	+	Shareholders' equity	
				Contributed capital	+ Retained earnings
950 accounts receivable **MasterCard**					1,000 sales revenue (50) credit card expense

When the company receives payment from **MasterCard**—typically daily or weekly, depending on the procedures for submitting credit card receipts to **MasterCard**—the company will record the increase in cash and the decrease in accounts receivable.

Lots of people buy goods and services using credit. In May 2006, consumer debt reached an all-time high of $2.174 trillion. Revolving debt—primarily credit cards—grew to a high of $812.5 billion.

Magic Cow Company made a sale for $5,000 to a customer during December. The customer paid with MasterCard. MasterCard charges Magic Cow Company a fee of 3% of sales for its services. How much sales revenue will Magic Cow record related to this sale? How much cash will Magic Cow collect related to this sale?

Your Turn 6-4
Your Turn
Your Turn

Notes Receivable

You have learned about the most significant receivables a firm has—accounts receivable. Another common receivable is a **promissory note**, which is a written promise to pay a specified amount of money at a specified time. The person or firm making the promise to pay is called the **maker**, and the person or firm receiving the money is called the **payee**. A promissory note is also called a *notes* receivable. The main differences between accounts receivable and notes receivable related to accounting are time and interest.

First, notes receivable usually have a collection period longer than accounts receivable. For example, with accounts receivable, a firm usually expects a customer to pay an account within 30 days of the invoice date. Recall that many companies offer their customers terms such as 2/10, n/30, where 30 designates the maximum length of time a customer may take to pay. If a customer is late with a payment, the firm often imposes a late charge. A note receivable usually has a time period longer than a month associated with it, and the customer or firm who owes the money will pay interest along with the principal repayment. Frequently, a firm will renegotiate an overdue account receivable by allowing the customer to sign a promissory note giving the customer more time to pay and charging interest on the note.

Second, accounts receivable generally have no interest charges, whereas a note receivable always has interest charges. The firm calculates the interest on a note receivable in the same way it calculates interest on any debt:

$$\text{Interest} = \text{Principal} \times \text{Rate} \times \text{Time}$$

If the note is a short-term note, which the firm will classify as a current asset, the length of the note is less than a year. When calculating interest on a short-term note, be sure to keep the interest rate and the time period in the same units. Interest rates are always recorded on a note as annual rates, so the time period must be expressed as a portion of a year. A simple example will demonstrate the procedure for calculating the interest on a note.

Suppose Procter and Gamble allowed Pop's Grocery Store to renegotiate an overdue account receivable with a promissory note, dated May 1. The amount of the note is $5,000, due in 3 months, at an interest rate of 8%. This is how Procter and Gamble would record the note.

Assets	=	Liabilities	+	Shareholders' equity	
				Contributed + capital	**Retained earnings**
(5,000) accounts receivable, Pop's Grocery					
5,000 notes receivable, Pop's Grocery					

When Pop's repays the note, it will also pay 3 months' worth of interest. This is the transaction as it would be recorded in the accounting equation.

L.O.5
Account for and report notes receivable.

A **promissory note** is a written promise to pay a specified amount of money at a specified time.

The **maker** of a note is the person or firm making the promise to pay.

The **payee** of a note is the person or firm receiving the money.

Assets	=	Liabilities	+	Shareholders' equity	
				Contributed + capital	Retained earnings
(5,000) notes receivable, Pop's Grocery 5,100 cash					100 interest revenue*

*Interest = 5,000 × 0.08 × 3/12 = $100

If a note is outstanding when a firm is ready to prepare financial statements, any interest that the firm has earned but not recorded must be accrued. The firm will calculate interest for the time that has passed and record interest revenue and interest receivable.

Your Turn 6-5
Your Turn
Your Turn

Dell Products allowed a customer to give a note receivable in payment of a delinquent accounts receivable. The note was a 6-month note for $3,000, and the interest rate was 8%. If the note was issued on September 1, how would the note and any related interest be reported on Dell's December 31 balance sheet?

L.O.6
Explain how a firm accounts for product warranties.

Warranties

A significant amount of a company's time and attention related to the sales and collection cycle is devoted to collections. As we have seen, there are crucial issues related to cash and the collection of accounts receivable for a business to handle. However, there is one more issue related to sales that is very important and has become increasingly important in our customer-service-oriented business world: warranties.

Why would a company provide a warranty on a product or service? Just like the decision to offer credit sales, it is a sales and marketing tool; and whether or not to provide a warranty is one of the strategic decisions a company must make. For financial statement purposes, a company wants to recognize warranty expense at the time of the sale of the product. Why? The matching principle applies to this situation. Revenues and expenses that go together should be on the same income statement. The company does not know exactly how much it will cost to honor the warranty, so the cost must be estimated. Because the company is not actually disbursing the cash to fix or replace the item yet—at the time of the sale—a liability is recorded along with the warranty expense. It is an adjustment made either at the time of the sale or when it is time to prepare financial statements. Liabilities are increased by the same amount as warranty expense.

The accounting treatment that requires estimates of future warranty costs reflects the underlying business process. It is crucial for a company to consider and estimate such costs to make sound business decisions. These future costs may be significant, and the accounting rules force companies to record these costs when the sale is made instead of when the warranty is honored. What happens when the cash is actually paid to fix a product with a warranty? No expense is recorded. Instead, the liability previously set up is reduced. So actual expenditures result in a reduction in cash or some other asset (used to fix the item) and an equal reduction in the amount of the liability.

Suppose Brooke's Bike Company sold 100 bicycles during June and provided a 1-year warranty. The accountant estimated that future repairs and replacement related to the June sales would be approximately $30 per bicycle. (No expenditures were made related to the warranties during the month of June.) What amount of warranty expense would appear on the income statement for the month ended June 30? Brooke's Bike Company would want to show the entire amount, $3,000, as an expense for the month. What is the amount of the June 30 liability (warranty payable or estimated warranty liability)? The total $3,000 would be shown as a liability on the balance sheet.

Assets	=	Liabilities	+	Shareholders' equity	
				Contributed + capital	Retained earnings
		3,000 estimated warranty liability			(3,000) warranty expense

Suppose July was a slow month, and Brooke's Bike Company did not sell any bicycles. However, there were several bicycles, from sales in June, that were repaired in July. The repairs cost Brooke's Bike Company $250. What amount of warranty expense would appear on the income statement for the month ended July 31? None. Brooke's Bike Company recognized the expense when the sale was made, so no expense is recognized when the repairs are made. The cost of the repairs is deducted from the amount "owed" to the customers. So the amount of the July 31 liability (warranty payable or estimated warranty liability) is $2,750 ($3,000 − $250).

Assets	=	Liabilities	+	Shareholders' equity	
				Contributed capital	+ Retained earnings
(250) cash		(250) estimated warranty liability			

Suppose that August was another slow month for bicycle sales (none were made), but again Brooke's Bike Company did some repairs related to the warranties on previous sales. The total spent was $500. What amount of warranty expense would appear on Brooke's Bike Company's income statement for the month ended August 31? What is the amount of the August 31 liability (warranty payable or estimated warranty liability)?

Your Turn 6-6
Your Turn
Your Turn

Tom's Wear for June

L.O.7
Prepare financial statements that include bad debts and warranties.

When Tom began his T-shirt business, the firm's first customers were a few of Tom's friends, so collection of accounts receivable was not a problem. Then, the firm branched out to sporting goods stores and local schools. Again, bad debts did not represent a significant problem, so Tom's Wear did not use the allowance method of accounting for bad debts. However, since hiring Sam to manage the inventory flow, Tom has been able to devote his time to increasing sales. The firm's customer base has now grown to a size that makes it necessary for the firm to give serious attention to the collectibility of its accounts receivable. The June 1 balance sheet is shown in Exhibit 6.12, followed by the transactions for June (Exhibit 6.13). Make sure you understand how each transaction was posted to the accounting equation in Exhibit 6.14 before you go on to the adjustments.

Adjustment 1: As part of the month-end adjustments, Tom's Wear has decided to set up an allowance for uncollectible accounts. The firm will use the sales method and, after consulting with some local businesses and some accountants, Tom will set up an allowance equal to 3% of credit sales. Credit sales of $44,000 × 3% = $1,320.

Adjustment 2: Tom has also decided that his firm should offer a warranty against defects in its T-shirts. Tom estimates that 2% of total sales will provide an adequate amount for future warranty obligations. Total sales of $48,950 × 2% = $979.

Both of these decisions are based on the matching principle. The firm wants to match the bad debts and warranty expenses with the sales to which they pertain, even though the firm does not know how many customers will not pay or how many customers will return a T-shirt.

Adjustment 3: Depreciation needs to be recorded on the van and on the computer. The van was driven 8,000 miles in June. The depreciation rate is $0.145 per mile (see page 000, so the depreciation expense for the van is $1,160. The computer is being depreciated at $100 per month.

Adjustment 4: Interest on the long-term note for the van needs to be accrued. $30,000 principal × 10% × 1/12 = $250.

Adjustment 5: Insurance for the month is $100. (Insurance policy for 3 months was purchased for $300 and coverage began on May 15.)

Adjustment 6: Rent expense for the month is $1,200. (Two months' worth of rent was purchased for $2,400 in June.)

Adjustment 7: Web costs for the month were $50.

EXHIBIT 6.12

Balance Sheet for Tom's Wear at June 1

tom's wear

Tom's Wear, Inc.
Balance Sheet
At June 1, 2006

Assets		Liabilities and Shareholder's Equity	
Current assets		**Current liabilities**	
Cash	$ 8,805	Accounts payable	$ 4,200
Accounts receivable	8,900	Interest payable	500
Inventory	4,700	Unearned revenue	4,950
Prepaid insurance	250	Salaries payable	723
Prepaid rent	600	Other payables	354
		Current portion of	
Prepaid Web services	250	long-term debt*	6,000
		Total current liabilities	16,727
Total current assets	23,505	Notes payable	24,000
		Total liabilities	40,727
Equipment (net of $300 accumulated depreciation)	3,700	**Shareholder's Equity**	
Van (net of $1,595 accumulated depreciation)	28,405	Common stock	5,000
		Retained earnings	9,883
		Total liabilities and	
Total assets	$55,610	shareholder's equity	$55,610

*Tom's Wear noticed that it previously failed to classify the $6,000 payment on the note payable due in the coming year as a current liability. The beginning June balances reflect the correction.

Adjustment 8: Sam Cubbie's salary for June must be accrued. Salary is $1,000 and payroll taxes withheld total $277. So salaries payable is $723. Tom's Wear must also accrue its part of the matching FICA, which is $77.

After the worksheet in Exhibit 6.14 is complete, you are ready to prepare the financial statements. You will find them in Exhibit 6.15. Make sure you can trace amounts from the financial statements back to the worksheet.

EXHIBIT 6.13

Transactions for Tom's Wear for June 2006

1	June 1	Pays cash of $2,400 for two months of rent on the warehouse, beginning June 15
2	June 5	Pays Sam Cubbie's May salary and related payroll taxes
3	June 10	Delivers the second half of the shirts to the school system—450 shirts—and recognizes revenue of $4,950
4	June 12	Pays accounts payable of $4,200
5	June 14	Signs a contract with the school system to deliver 500 shirts per month for September through December, at a price of $10 per shirt; the shirts will be delivered on the last day of the month with the invoice attached to the delivery; Tom has serious competition for this deal, so he decides to offer the purchase terms, 2/10, n/30, to the school system to secure the contract
6	June 20	Purchases 5,000 T-shirts from a new vendor; the cost of the shirts is only $3.79 each, but the shipping terms are free on board (FOB) shipping point; the shipping costs for the month are $50; Tom's Wear pays cash for the shipping, but makes the purchase on account
7	June 20	Tom's sales efforts pay off with the addition of several sporting goods stores as customers; during June, the company sells 4,000 shirts to various stores for $11 each; all sales are on account
8	June 21	Collects $8,800 on accounts receivable
9	June 30	Miscellaneous operating expenses paid in cash amount to $600 for the month
10	June 30	Pays a dividend of $1,000

EXHIBIT 6.14

Accounting Equation Worksheet for Tom's Wear for June

Assets = Liabilities + Shareholder's Equity

Assets

Ref	Cash	Accounts Receivable	Allowance for Uncollectible Accounts	Inventory**	Prepaid Insurance	Prepaid Rent	Prepaid Web Service	Equipment (Computer)	Acc.Depr. Equipment	Van	Acc. Depr. Van
BB*	$8,805	8,900		4,700	250	600	250	4,000	(300)	30,000	(1,595)
1.	(2,400)					2,400					
2.	(1,077)										
3.				(1,865)							
4.	(4,200)										
5. No entry required											
6.	(50)			19,000							
7.		44,000		(15,470)							
8.	8,800	(8,800)									
9.	(600)										
10.	(1,000)										
A-1			(1,320)								
A-2											
A-3									(100)		(1,160)
A-4											
A-5					(100)						
A-6						(1,200)					
A-7							(50)				
A-8											
	$8,278	44,100	(1,320)	6,365	150	1,800	200	4,000	(400)	30,000	(2,755)

Liabilities + Shareholder's Equity

Ref	Accounts Payable	Salaries Payable	Unearned Revenue	Interest Payable	Other Payables	Warranties Payable	Current Portion of Long-Term Notes Payable	Long-Term Notes Payable	Common Stock	Revenues	Expenses	Dividends
BB*	4,200	723	4,950	500	354	–	6,000♦	24,000♦	5,000			
1.												
2.		(723)			(354)							
3.			(4,950)							4,950	(1,865)	
4.	(4,200)											
5. No entry required												
6.	18,950											
7.										44,000	(15,470)	
8.												
9.											(600)	
10.												(1,000)
A-1											(1,320)	
A-2						979					(979)	
A-3											(1,260)	
A-4				250							(250)	
A-5											(100)	
A-6											(1,200)	
A-7					277						(327)	
A-8		723			77						(800)	
	18,950	723	–	750	354	979	6,000	24,000	5,000	48,950	(24,171)	(1,000)

Retained Earnings: BB 9,883 · 34,662

Check figures: 90,418 = 90,418

♦ Tom's Wear's accountant noticed that the firm had not separated out the current portion of the long-term note payable, so it was corrected at the beginning of June.

* BB beginning balances

** Beginning inventory:
125 shirts @ $4 each
1,000 shirts @ $4.20 each
Total cost $4,700

June 10 sale
125 @ $4 = $ 500
325 @ $4.20 = 1,365
CGS = $1,865

June 20 purchase
5,000 @ $3.80 each
(with freight) = $19,000

June 20 sale
675 @ $4.20 = ($2,835)
3,325 @ $3.80 = ($12,635)
CGS = ($15,470)

Ending inventory:
1,675 shirts @ $3.80 = $6,365

EXHIBIT 6.15

Financial Statements for Tom's Wear for June 2006

Tom's Wear, Inc.
Income Statement
For the Month Ended June 30

Revenues:		
Sales		$ 48,950
Expenses:		
Cost of goods sold	17,335	
Insurance expense	100	
Rent expense	1,200	
Depreciation expense	1,260	
Salary expense	1,000	
Interest expense	250	
Warranty expense	979	
Bad debts expense	1,320	
Other operating expenses	727	24,171
Net income		$ 24,779

Tom's Wear, Inc.
Statement of Changes in Shareholder's Equity
For the Month Ended June 30

Common stock:		
Beginning balance	$ 5,000	
Stock issued during the month	—	
Ending balance	$ 5,000	
Retained earnings:		
Beginning balance	$ 9,883	
+ Net income	24,779	
– Dividends	(1,000)	
Ending balance	$ 33,662	
Total shareholder's equity		

Tom's Wear, Inc.
Statement of Cash Flows
For the Month Ended June 30

Cash from operating activities:		
Cash collected from customers	8,800	
Cash paid to vendors	(4,200)	
Cash paid for operating expense	(4,127)	473
Cash from investing activities:		
		—
Cash from financing activities:		
Dividends paid	(1,000)	(1,000)
Decrease in cash		$ (527)
Add beginning cash		8,805
Ending cash balance		$ 8,278

Tom's Wear, Inc.
Balance Sheet
At June 30

Assets			
Current assets			
Cash			$ 8,278
Accounts receivable			
(net of allowance of $1,320)	42,780		
Inventory	6,365		
Prepaid insurance	150		
Prepaid rent	1,800		
Prepaid Web services	200		
Total current assets			59,573
Equipment (net of $400			
accumulated depreciation)	3,600		
Van (net of $2,755			
accumulated depreciation)	27,245		
Total assets			$ 90,418

Liabilities & Shareholder's Equity			
Current liabilities			
Accounts payable			$ 18,950
Interest payable			750
Warranty liability			979
Salaries payable			723
Current portion of long-			
term note payable			6,000
Other payables			354
Total current liabilities			27,756
Notes payable			24,000
Total liabilities			51,756
Shareholder's Equity			
Common stock			5,000
Retained earnings			33,662
Total liabilities and			
shareholder's equity			$ 90,418

Applying Your Knowledge: Ratio Analysis

L.O.8
Analyze a firm's accounts receivable with ratio analysis.

Keeping control of cash through the bank reconciliation process helps ensure the correct numbers are getting to the financial statements. It is important that the numbers about sales and accounts receivable are accurate because managers and others use those numbers to measure the firm's ability to meet its short-term obligations. When the current ratio is computed—current assets divided by current liabilities—the numerator includes accounts receivable, because it is a current asset. Another ratio similar to the current ratio that you learned about in Chapter 3 is called the quick ratio, also known as the acid-test ratio. Instead of using all of a firm's current assets in the numerator, the quick ratio uses only cash, short-term investments, and net accounts receivable. These three assets are the most liquid—easiest to convert to cash—so they are the most available for paying off current liabilities. An investor or analyst will use the quick ratio as a stricter test of a firm's ability to meet its short-term obligations.

Another important ratio that involves accounts receivable is the **accounts receivable (AR) turnover ratio**. This ratio—net credit sales divided by average net accounts receivable—measures how quickly a firm collects its accounts receivable. The ratio tells how many times, on average, the process of selling on account and collecting the receivables is repeated during the period. Exhibit 6.16 shows the three ratios managers can use to evaluate liquidity and receivables.

The **accounts receivable (AR) turnover ratio** is a ratio that measures how quickly a firm collects its accounts receivable. It is defined as credit sales divided by average accounts receivable.

Exhibit 6.17 shows information from the financial statements for Hershey Foods and the calculation of the AR turnover ratio. The denominator of this ratio is the average of the beginning balance and ending balance of net accounts receivable. This particular ratio is useful for a firm to track over time to make sure receivables are being collected promptly.

Here is how the AR turnover ratio was calculated to be 9.99 times.

$$\frac{\$4,835,974}{(\$559,289 + \$408,930) \div 2} = \frac{\$4,835,974}{\$484,109.5} = 9.99$$

If the average turnover of accounts receivable is 9.99 times, we can calculate how long it takes for Hershey Foods, on average, to collect its accounts receivable. If we divide 365—the number of days in a year—by the AR turnover ratio, we will get the number of days it takes, on average, to collect its accounts receivable. For the fiscal year ending (FYE) December 31, 2005, we will divide 365 days by 9.99 times = 36.87 days. That means that it takes a little over a month for Hershey Foods to collect its accounts receivable. For FYE 2004, we divided 365 by 10.85 = 33.64 days. From FYE 2004 to 2005, Hershey Foods has slightly increased its average number of days to collect its accounts receivable, which is not considered an improvement. Notice that the higher the AR turnover ratio (10.85 times vs. 9.99 times), the faster the firm is collecting its accounts receivable.

Ratio	Description	Equation	When to Use
Current Ratio	Measure of liquidity	$\dfrac{\text{Total current assets}}{\text{Total current liabilities}}$	To evaluate a firm's ability to meet its short-term obligations
Quick Ratio or Acid-Test Ratio	Strict measure of liquidity	$\dfrac{\text{Cash} + \text{Short-term investments} + \text{Net receivable accounts}}{\text{Total current liabilities}}$	To evaluate quite conservatively a firm's ability to meet its short-term obligations
Accounts Receivable Turnover Ratio	Measure of rate of accounts receivable collections, another measure of liquidity	$\dfrac{\text{Net credit sales}}{\text{Average net accounts receivable}}$	To measure how quickly a firm is collecting its receivables. Another indication of a firm's ability to meet its short-term obligations

EXHIBIT 6.16

Three Liquidity Ratios Involving Accounts Receivable

EXHIBIT 6.17

Hershey Foods Corporation: Accounts Receivable Turnover Ratio

The accounts receivable (AR) turnover ratio equals credit sales divided by average net accounts receivable. Often, however, financial statements do not provide separate amounts for cash and credit sales, so we use total sales for the numerator. It's very important to be consistent in the calculation of ratios that are compared over time and from company to company. For example, if you use total sales to compute the AR turnover ratio at the end of this year, then you must also use total sales next year to have a basis for comparison.

(in thousands)	December 31, 2005	December 31, 2004	December 31, 2003
Receivables (net)*	$559,289	$408,930	$407,612
Sales*	$4,835,974	$4,429,248	
AR Turnover Ratio	9.99 times	10.85 times	

* Balance sheet amounts are as of the date shown, and sales are for the fiscal year ended on the date shown.

If we calculate the AR turnover ratio for a retail firm, the turnover ratio will be higher and the average number of days to collect its accounts receivable will be lower than our calculations for a wholesale firm like Hershey Foods. That is because a wholesale firm extends credit to almost all customers and, therefore, does not have as many cash sales as a retail firm. When we use total sales as our numerator in the ratio, which include cash sales, we are slightly underestimating the time it takes to collect an account. For example, look at the information in Exhibit 6.18 for Books-A-Million, a retail firm.

The AR turnover ratio is

$$\frac{\$503,751}{(\$9,668 + \$6,543) \div 2} = \frac{\$503,751}{\$8,105.5} = 62.15$$

To get the average number of days to collect its accounts receivable, we divide 365 days by 62.15, which is 5.87 days. That is significantly shorter than the average 37 days Hershey Foods takes to collect its credit sales! Most of the sales for Books-A-Million are cash, and the amount of credit sales is not disclosed separately. Using a sales amount that includes cash sales makes the AR turnover ratio much higher because it artificially inflates the numerator.

Internally, managers will use only credit sales in the calculation of the AR turnover ratio. For external users, that information may not be available. Different industries and even different firms in the same industry may have very different AR turnover ratios. As you have learned, you must use ratio analysis carefully.

EXHIBIT 6.18

Books-A-Million: Accounts Receivable and Sales

A retail firm will turn over its receivables very quickly. Remember that the total sales dollars includes cash sales.

(Dollars in thousands)	AR at 1/28/06	AR at 1/29/05	Sales for FYE 1/28/06
	$9,668	$6,543	$503,751

Suppose a firm has beginning AR of $10,500 and ending AR of $12,500. Credit sales for the period amounted to $120,000. What is the accounts receivable turnover ratio, and how long does it take, on average, to collect an outstanding account?

Your Turn 6-7
Your Turn
Your Turn

Business Risk, Control, and Ethics

You have learned about two of the most important assets a firm has—cash and receivables. Now we are ready to resume our discussion about the way a firm makes sure the risks related to these assets are minimized. Remember that an important purpose of internal controls is to be sure a firm's assets are safeguarded and that the related financial records are accurate and reliable.

Earlier in the book, you learned about one of the most important controls a firm can have: segregation of duties. This control means that the person who is responsible for the record keeping related to an asset does not have physical custody or access to the asset. This is an extremely important control in safeguarding cash.

In addition to segregation of duties, there are three more key controls that help a firm safeguard its assets and enhance the accuracy and reliability of its financial records: (1) clear assignment of responsibility for physical control of the assets, (2) specific procedures for documentation related to the assets, and (3) independent internal verification of the data. We will look at each of these more closely as they relate to cash and accounts receivable.

L.O.9
Identify the risks and controls associated with cash and receivables.

Clear Assignment of Responsibility

The responsibility for safeguarding cash can be assigned to a variety of people in the firm. For example, in some retail stores, each cashier is responsible for safeguarding the cash in their own register. At the end of each shift, the money is counted and the amount compared to the register's recorded sales. If a cashier is short by $10, it will be that cashier's responsibility to make up the $10 shortage. As shown in Exhibit 6.19, when new cashiers come on duty, they will have their own cash drawers for which they are responsible.

Specific Procedures for Documentation

Documentation procedures are another critical control for cash and accounts receivable. Have you ever returned an item to a department store? You may have been asked to fill out a form with your name, address, and the reason for the return. One reason for this procedure, shown in Exhibit 6.20, is to provide documentation for the refund. Either a cash refund or a credit to your account, if your purchase was on account, must be accompanied by supporting documentation to help ensure that refunds are granted only for legitimate returns.

EXHIBIT 6.19

Clear Assignment of Responsibility

EXHIBIT 6.20

Documentation Procedures

EXHIBIT 6.21

Independent Internal Verification of Data

Independent Internal Verification of Data

Have you ever purchased something from a store that has a sign by the cash register that reads: IF YOU DO NOT GET A RECEIPT, YOUR PURCHASE IS FREE? That sign is a control to be sure that every cashier is properly recording all sales. Cashiers will not be able to take your cash and put it in their pockets without ringing it up on the cash register to produce a receipt. Why? Because if they were to do that, you would ASK for a receipt and get your purchase free as well! You are helping the owners make sure they get their cash and that the sale is properly documented. Exhibit 6.21 gives an example of this type of control.

Your Turn 6-8
Your Turn
Your Turn

Explain why cashiers would not be able to pocket money from purchases if they were forced to give receipts.

Chapter Summary Points

- Cash is one of the most important assets a firm has. It is easy to steal because its ownership cannot be easily identified. Control of cash is crucial, and one of the most important controls is a bank reconciliation. That is a worksheet that reconciles the firm's cash balance with the bank statement balance at the end of each month.
- Cash is reported on the balance sheet along with very liquid investments called cash equivalents. Cash is also the focus of its own financial statement, the statement of cash flows, which gives all the sources and uses of cash during an accounting period.
- When a firm offers credit to its customers, the resulting asset is called accounts receivable. On the balance sheet, accounts receivable is a current asset and should reflect the

net amount the firm expects to collect. If the firm has a significant amount of bad debts (i.e., customers who will not pay), then the firm must estimate the amount of bad debts and deduct it from gross accounts receivable to get the net realizable value of accounts receivable to report on the balance sheet. This is called the allowance method of accounting for bad debts. This means that bad debts expense will be recognized as an estimate so that the firm can match the bad debts expense with the related sales. When a specific customer is identified as one who will not pay, the account is written off but no expense is recognized at that time. (The expense was already recognized in the period of the sale.)

• Credit card sales are almost like cash to a business. The credit card company reimburses the firm and is paid a fee for the service. The risk is much less than that of extending the firm's own credit to its customers. For example, if you use a Macy's charge account, the risk is greater to Macy's than if you had used your **MasterCard** to make a purchase at the department store.

• Notes receivable are amounts owed to the firm, often by customers who have been slow in paying their accounts and have negotiated new payment terms that include interest.

• Firms use accounts receivable to help evaluate a firm's financial position and performance. Both the current and quick ratios use accounts receivable in the numerator to measure short-term liquidity, and the accounts receivable turnover ratio (credit sales divided by average accounts receivable) measures how quickly the firm is collecting its accounts receivable.

• Controls are especially important with respect to cash. Three of them are: (1) clear assignment of responsibility, (2) specific procedures for documentation, and (3) independent internal verification of the data.

Chapter Summary Problems

The following transactions took place during Choco Drops fiscal year ended December 31, 2007.

1. Sold $900,000 of merchandise on account with the terms 2/10, n/30. Cost of goods sold was $270,000.
2. Collected payment for 80% of the sales within the discount period.
3. Accepted a 3-month note from Nature's Grocery Store Chain for $8,000 on October 1, 2007 (due on January 1, 2008), with an interest rate of 6%, in payment of its $8,000 outstanding balance in accounts receivable.
4. Had $98,000 of cash sales. Cost of goods sold was $29,400.
5. Wrote off a bad account for $4,000 after the bankruptcy court approved a reorganization plan for one of its struggling customers.
6. Incurred operating expenses $75,600, paid in cash.

Instructions

1. Post each of the transactions on an accounting equation worksheet. The firm started the year with a balance of $150,000 in accounts receivable and a balance of $4,500 in the allowance for uncollectible accounts. The balance in the inventory account was $500,000. The other beginning balances are not given and not required for the problem. (These came from the December 31, 2006, balance sheet.)
2. Make the adjustment to book bad debts expense. Choco Drops uses the allowance method of accounting for uncollectible accounts, based on a percentage of the ending balance in accounts receivable. (Use the same percentage—3%—the firm used to calculate the bad debts expense for 2006. Also, be sure to accrue interest receivable on the note in Transaction 3 above.)
3. Prepare an income statement for the year ended December 31, 2007.

Solution

Accounting Equation Worksheet for Choco Drops

	Assets						= Liabilities +		Shareholder's Equity			
										Contributed Capital	Retained Earnings	
	Cash	Accounts Receivable	Allowance for Uncollectible Accounts	Short-term Notes Receivable	Interest Receivable	Inventory	Accounts Payable	Common Stock	Revenues	Expenses	Dividends
BB*		150,000	(4,500)					500,000				
1.		900,000								900,000		
						(270,000)					(270,000)	
2.	705,600	(720,000)								(14,400)		
3.		(8,000)		8,000								
4.	98,000									98,000		
						(29,400)					(29,400)	
5.		(4,000)	4,000									
6.	(75,600)										(75,600)	
A-1			(9,040)								(9,040)	
A-2					120						120	
	728,000	318,000	(9,540)	8,000	120	200,600		–		983,720	(384,040)	

Choco Drops
Income Statement
For the year ended December 31, 2007

Sales	$ 998,000	
Sales discounts	(14,400)	
Net sales		$ 983,600
Interest revenue		120
Expenses		
Cost of goods sold	$ 299,400	
Bad debts expense*	9,040	
Operating expenses	75,600	(384,040)
Net income		$ 599,680

*Desired balance in allowance	= 3% of $318,000 = $9,540
Remaining balance at year end	= $500
Needed addition to get desired balance	= $9,040

Key Terms for Chapter 6

Accounts receivable (p. 286)
Accounts receivable (AR) turnover ratio (p. 301)
Aging schedule (p. 288)
Allowance for uncollectible accounts (p. 286)

Allowance method (p. 286)
Bad debts expense (p. 286)
Bank reconciliation (p. 280)
Bank statement (p. 279)
Cash equivalents (p. 285)
Deposit in transit (p. 280)

Direct write-off method (p. 293)
Maker (p. 245)
Outstanding check (p. 280)
Payee (p. 295)
Promissory note (p. 295)

Answers to YOUR TURN Questions

Chapter 6

Your Turn 6-1

The purpose of a bank reconciliation is to provide a control to protect cash. The amount of cash reported on the bank statement (an independently calculated balance) must be reconciled to the cash reported in the accounting records. A firm would prepare a bank reconciliation as often as the bank provided a statement, usually once each month.

Your Turn 6-2

To find the solution, you need to know the following information.

Balance per books	$2,400
Deduct service charges	−100
Add collection	+300
Add interest revenue	+100
True cash balance	**$2,700**

Outstanding checks are ignored because we are working with only the "balance per books" side of the reconciliation.

Your Turn 6-3

1. $400 ($500 desired balance − $100 remaining balance before adjustments)
2. $9,500 ($10,000 − $500)

Your Turn 6-4

Magic Cow will record revenue of $5,000. Cash collected will be 97% of $5,000 = $4,850. The remaining 3%, or $150, will be recorded as credit card expense.

Your Turn 6-5

Current assets: Notes receivable $3,000
Interest receivable $80 [$3,000 × 0.08 × 4/12]

Your Turn 6-6

1. No warranty expense would be on the August income statement.
2. The liability would be $2,250 ($2,750 − $500).

Your Turn 6-7

1. Sales of $120,000 divided by average AR [$11,500 = ($10,500 + $12,500) ÷ 2] = 10.43 times.
2. Days to collect: 365 days ÷ 10.43 = 35 days

Your Turn 6-8

To get the receipt to print, the transaction must be entered into the cash register or computer. If cash collected is reconciled to the records (from the register or computer), any missing amounts would be apparent.

Questions

1. What is a bank reconciliation and what does it determine?
2. What are two common adjustments made to the balance per bank on the bank reconciliation?
3. Describe two common adjustments made to the balance per books on the bank reconciliation.
4. Once the bank reconciliation is complete, which adjustments are recorded in the accounting records?
5. What does true cash balance refer to?
6. Identify and explain the financial statements on which cash is reported.
7. Describe how accounts receivable arise. What does the balance in accounts receivable represent?
8. How do trade receivables differ from other receivables?
9. Define net realizable value, book value, and carrying value as they relate to accounts receivable.
10. Explain the difference between the direct write-off method and the allowance method of accounting for bad debts. Which method is preferred and why?
11. If a company uses the allowance method of accounting for bad debts, what effect does writing off a specific account have on income?
12. Describe the two allowance methods used to estimate the amount of bad debts expense that appears on the income statement.

13. Which method of calculating the allowance for uncollectible accounts focuses on the income statement? Explain.
14. Which method of calculating the allowance for uncollectible accounts focuses on the balance sheet? Explain.
15. What are the advantages and disadvantages of allowing customers to make purchases with credit cards?
16. What is the difference between accounts receivable and notes receivable?
17. For financial statement purposes, when is the expense related to warranties recognized? Why? How is the cost of repairing a product under warranty accounted for?
18. What is the formula to calculate the accounts receivable turnover ratio, and what does the formula measure?
19. How does a firm use its accounts receivable turnover ratio to determine the average number of days it takes to collect its accounts receivable?
20. Explain how the segregation of duties serves as a major control for safeguarding cash.
21. Explain why it is important to have physical control of cash.

Multiple-Choice Questions

Use the following information for questions 1–4. Fred's Supply Store just received its monthly bank statement from Local Street Bank. The bank gives a balance of $45,000. Fred's accounting clerk has calculated that outstanding checks amount to $20,000. Fred's Supply Store made a deposit of $5,000 on the last day of the month, and it was not included on the bank statement. Bank service fees, not yet recorded on the store's books, were shown on the statement as $35. The bank statement also included an NSF check returned from a new customer in the amount of $250.

1. What is the store's true cash balance at the end of the month?
   a. $25,000
   b. $30,000
   c. $29,715
   d. $29,750
2. How should outstanding checks be treated on the bank reconciliation?
   a. They should be deducted from the balance per books.
   b. They should be added to the balance per books.
   c. They should be deducted from the balance per bank.
   d. They should be added to the balance per bank.
3. Which items would need to be recorded in a journal entry for Fred's Supply Store's accounting records?
   a. Outstanding checks and the deposit in transit
   b. NSF check
   c. Bank service fee
   d. Both NSF check and bank service fee
4. What was the cash balance in the general ledger before Fred's Supply Store began the bank reconciliation?
   a. $30,285
   b. $30,250
   c. $45,250
   d. $25,285

Use the following information to answer multiple-choice questions 5 and 6. At the end of the year, before any adjustments are made, the accounting records for Sutton Company show a balance of $100,000 in accounts receivable. The allowance for uncollectible accounts has a credit balance of $2,000. (This means last year's estimate was too large by $2,000.) The company uses accounts receivable to estimate bad debts expense. An analysis of accounts receivable results in an estimate of $27,000 of uncollectible accounts.

5. The bad debts expense on the income statement for the year would be
   a. $27,000
   b. $25,000
   c. $23,000
   d. $29,000

6. Net realizable value of the receivables on the year-end balance sheet would be
   a. $100,000
   b. $75,000
   c. $73,000
   d. $77,000

7. Suppose a firm uses the percentage of sales method for estimating bad debts expense. The firm has credit sales for the year of $200,000 and a balance of $80,000 in accounts receivable. The firm estimates that 2% of its credit sales will never be collected. What is the bad debts expense for the year?
   a. $1,600
   b. $2,000
   c. $4,000
   d. $3,600

8. Scott Company uses the allowance method of accounting for bad debts. During May, the company found out that one of its largest customers filed for bankruptcy. If Scott Company decides to write off the customer's account, what effect will doing that have on Scott Company's net income for the period?
   a. Bad debts expense will decrease income.
   b. Writing off the receivable will decrease income.
   c. Both a and b will happen.
   d. There is no effect on net income.

9. Merry Maids Inc. sells vacuum cleaners to McKenzie-Grace Corporation for $1,000. McKenzie-Grace pays Merry Maids with the company VISA card. VISA charges Merry Maids a 3% fee for all VISA sales. How would this transaction affect the accounting equation?
   a. Increase assets $1,000, increase net retained earnings $1,000
   b. Decrease assets $1,000, decrease net retained earning $1,000
   c. Increase assets $970, increase net retained earnings $970
   d. Not enough information

10. Advanced Music Technology Inc. estimated that its warranty costs would be $900 for items sold during the current year. During the year Advanced paid $750 to repair merchandise that was returned by customers. What is the amount of warranty expense for the current year?
    a. $750
    b. $900
    c. $150
    d. Cannot be determined

Short Exercises

SE6-1. *Analyze bank reconciliation items.* (LO 1)
For each item below, indicate whether or not the **balance per books** should be adjusted. For each item that affects the balance per books, indicate whether the item should be added to (+) or subtracted from (−) the balance per books.

Item	Balance per books adjusted?	+/−
Outstanding checks	No	n/a
Service charge by bank		
NSF check from customer		
Deposits in transit		
Error made by the bank		
Note receivable collected by the bank		

SE6-2. *Analyze bank reconciliation items.* (LO 1)

For each item below, indicate whether or not the **balance per bank** should be adjusted. For each item that affects the balance per bank, indicate whether the item should be added to (+) or subtracted from (−) the balance per bank.

Item	Balance per bank adjusted?	+/−
Outstanding checks	Yes	—
Service charge by bank		
NSF check from customer		
Deposits in transit		
Error made by the bank		
Note receivable collected by the bank		

SE6-3. *Calculate the true cash balance.* (LO 1)

At March 31, OAS Company has the following information available about its cash account.

Cash balance per bank	$6,000
Outstanding checks	$1,500
Deposits in transit	$1,200
Bank service charge	$ 100

Determine the true cash balance per bank at March 31.

SE6-4. *Calculate the true cash balance.* (LO 1)

Use the following information to calculate the true reconciled cash balance:

Bank statement shows interest earned for month	$50
Bank statement shows service charges for month	$10
Book shows deposits in transit	$75
Book shows outstanding checks	$25

	Books	Bank
Balance	$100	$90
Interest earned for month	_____	_____
Service charges for month	_____	_____
Outstanding deposits	_____	_____
Outstanding checks	_____	_____
Balance	_____	_____
True cash balance	_____	_____

SE6-5. *Calculate the true cash balance.* (LO 1)

On the April bank statement, the ending balance as of April 30 was $10,650.35. The cash balance in the general ledger was $11,150.81. Consider the following information:

Outstanding checks	$1,562.71
Interest earned on the account	$ 45.65
NSF check from Bailey's Textiles Inc.	$1,094.38
Deposits in transit	$1,015.16

What is the company's true cash balance at April 30?

SE6-6. *Analyze errors in a bank reconciliation.* (LO 1)

Name Brand Electronics' accountant wrote a check to a supplier for inventory in the amount of $1,060 but erroneously recorded it on the company's books as $1,600. She discovered this when she saw the monthly bank statement and noticed that the check had cleared the bank for $1,060. How would this be handled on the bank reconciliation? Enter the transaction into the accounting equation Name Brand's accountant needs to make to correct its accounting records.

SE6-7. *Determine bad debts expense using the percentage of sales method.* (LO 3)

Paris & Nicole Bakery has a liberal credit policy and has been experiencing a high rate of uncollectible accounts. The company estimates that 4% of credit sales become bad debts. Due to the significance of this amount, the company uses the allowance method for accounting for bad debts. During 2007, credit sales amounted to $450,000. The year-end accounts receivable balance was $217,000. What was the bad debts expense for the year?

SE6-8. *Determine bad debts expense using the percentage of sales method.* (LO 3)
The 2006 year-end unadjusted trial balance shows

Accounts receivable (AR)	$ 50,000
Allowance for uncollectible accounts	$ (1,000)
Net sales	$200,000

Using the percentage of sales method, the company estimates 2% of sales will become uncollectible. What is the bad debts expense for 2006? What will be the net realizable value of accounts receivable on the year-end balance sheet?

SE6-9. *Determine bad debts expense using the accounts receivable method.* (LO 3)
On July 1, 2007, a company's accounts receivable balance was $17,800, the allowance for uncollectible accounts balance was $(1,200), and the common stock balance was $16,600. This information came from the June 30, 2007, balance sheet. During the 2007–2008 fiscal year, the company reported $154,000 of credit sales and wrote off $800 of specific receivables as uncollectible. Cash collections of receivables were $138,000 for the year. The company estimates that 3% of the year-end accounts receivable will be uncollectible. Use the accounting equation to help determine bad debts expense for the year ended June 30, 2008.

SE6-10. *Determine bad debts expense using the accounts receivable method.* (LO 3)
At the end of the year, before any adjustments are made, the accounting records for Briggs Company show a balance of $200,000 in accounts receivable. The allowance for uncollectible accounts has a balance of $(2,000). The company uses accounts receivable to estimate bad debts expense. An analysis of accounts receivable accounts results in an estimate of $30,000 of uncollectible accounts. What is the bad debts expense for the year? What is the net realizable value of accounts receivable on the year-end balance sheet?

SE6-11. *Determine bad debts expense using the accounts receivable method.* (LO 3)
Bett Company had the following balances at year-end prior to recording any adjustments:

Credit sales	$160,000
Accounts receivable	$ 30,000
Allowance for uncollectible accounts	$ 100 shortfall[a]

[a] Bett wrote off $100 more accounts during the year than estimated (i.e., allowance was too small this year).

Following completion of an aging analysis, the accountant for Bett Company estimated that $1,100 of the receivables would be uncollectible. What amount of bad debts expense would Bett show on the year's income statement? What information would be disclosed on the balance sheet?

SE6-12. *Determine bad debts expense using the accounts receivable method.* (LO 3)
The 2007 year-end unadjusted trial balance shows

Accounts receivable (AR) $ 65,000
Allowance for uncollectible accounts   ($750) (excess from last year's estimate)
Net sales $525,000

Using the accounts receivable method, the company estimates $6,250 of ending accounts receivable will be uncollectible. What is the bad debts expense for 2007? What will be the net realizable value of accounts receivable on the year-end balance sheet?

SE6-13. *Determine bad debts expense using the direct write-off method.* (LO 3)
Fashions Marketing Inc. sells merchandise to department stores and boutiques. Fashions has always used the direct write-off method of accounting for bad debts because of very tight credit policies and predominately cash sales. During 2007, credit sales were $115,823 and the year-end balance in accounts receivable was $62,187. Fashions estimates that about 2.5% of the accounts receivable will not be collected. Unfortunately, just prior to the end of 2007, one of Fashions' best customers filed for bankruptcy and has informed Fashions that it will not be able to pay its outstanding balance of $31,775. That amount, however, is included in Fashions' $62,187 accounts receivable balance. Use the accounting equation to show how Fashions should record the $31,775 bad debt in its accounting records. What amount of bad debts expense will Fashions recognize on the income statement for the year ended December 31, 2007?

SE6-14. *Write off uncollectible accounts.* (LO 3)
Chastain's Upholstery has determined that Global Builders' accounts receivable balance of $5,500 is uncollectible. Use the accounting equation to show how Chastain's would write off the account using (a) the direct write-off method and (b) the allowance method for bad debts.

SE6-15. *Account for credit card sales.* (LO 4)
Jordan Beauty Supply accepts **Discover** from its customers. **Discover** charges Beauty Supply 3.5% of sales for its services. During the 2006–2007 fiscal year, Jordan's customers used **Discover** to purchase $65,000 worth of merchandise. How much did Jordan show as sales on the income statement for the year ended June 30, 2007? How much cash did Jordan actually receive from these sales?

SE6-16. *Account for credit card sales.* (LO 4)
Fried Foods Corporation accepts **MasterCard** from its customers. **MasterCard** charges Fried Foods a fixed fee of $125 per month plus 4.25% of **MasterCard** sales. If Fried Foods had **MasterCard** sales of $600,000 during 2006, how much did Fried Foods pay **MasterCard** for its service?

SE6-17. *Analyze notes receivable.* (LO 5)
On May 1, 2006, Bob's Music renegotiated its overdue account balance of $2,500 with Spectrum Electronics by signing a 2-month promissory note at an interest rate of 9%. What is the principal amount of the note? What is the due date of the note? How much will Bob's Music repay on the due date of the note?

SE6-18. *Account for warranties.* (LO 6)
Nunez Ethnic Specialties Inc. began the year with $30,000 in its warranty liability. During the year, the firm spent $20,000 to honor past warranties. Will the $20,000 be the warranty expense for the year? Why or why not?

SE6-19. *Account for warranties.* (LO 6, 7)
Key Company offers a 3-year warranty on its premium door locks. During the year, the company had sales of $100,000. Related to the sales, warranty costs should be approximately $3,000 per year. How much warranty expense related to these sales will Key Company's income statement show in the year of the sales? How much warranty expense related to these sales will Key Company have in the 2 years after the sales?

SE6-20. *Calculate accounts receivable turnover ratio.* (LO 8, 9)
Candid Company had the following balances.

	December 31, 2007	December 31, 2006
Receivables, net	$ 325,000	$ 285,000
Sales (all credit)	$1,757,000	$1,248,700

Calculate the accounts receivable turnover ratio for 2007. On average, how many days does it take Candid Company to collect its accounts receivable?

Exercises—Set A

E6-1A. *Prepare a bank reconciliation.* (LO 1)
The bank statement for Asaf's Plumbing had an ending balance as of March 31 of $42,765.88. Also listed on the statement was a service charge for $27.50. Check 1305 that Asaf wrote to pay for equipment purchased March 25 had not cleared the bank yet—the amount was $6,725.15. Deposits in transit were $3,185.64. Asaf's bank collected a $1,100 note for him in March. After reviewing the bank statement and canceled checks, Asaf discovered that the bank mistakenly deducted $1,185.19 from his account on a check that was written by Asaf's Landscaping. Calculate the true cash balance as of March 31.

E6-2A. *Prepare a bank reconciliation.* (LO 1)
The advertising firm Carolyn & Co. had the following information available concerning their cash account for the month of July.

Balance per Carolyn & Co. books, July 31	$18,280.54
Outstanding checks	6,440.29
NSF check from customer	2,800.00
Note collected by bank	3,000.00
Deposits in transit	5,860.50
Miscellaneous fees:	
Charge for collection of note	25.00
Order for checks	62.50
Interest earned on bank account	421.38

Calculate the true cash balance as of July 31.

E6-3A. *Prepare a bank reconciliation.* (LO 1)
Prepare a bank reconciliation for Samantha Vartan's Coffee Shop at April 30 using the following information.

Balance per USA Bank statement at April 30	$9,297.21
Outstanding checks	4,815.68
NSF checks from customer	2,851.77
Deposits in transit	6,772.89
Interest revenue	305.77
Service charge	75.00
Cash balance per Samantha Vartan's records at April 30	13,875.42

Enter adjustments into the accounting equation needed to update the company's cash balance. What is the net effect on net income? Will net income be increased or decreased? By what amount?

E6-4A. *Prepare a bank reconciliation.* (LO 1)
Prepare a bank reconciliation at December 31 for Sandra Warren's Smoothies using the following information.

Company's cash account balance, December 31	$6,275.34
Bank statement ending balance, December 31	4,607.51
Deposits in transit	2,504.57
Outstanding checks:	
4431	581.62
4432	246.12

Sandra found an error in the books: Check 4429 for $123.75 was correctly deducted from the bank account, but was mistakenly recorded in the books as $132.75.

E6-5A. *Identify and correct errors in a bank reconciliation.* (LO 1)
Janie Johnson is having trouble with the bank reconciliation at January 31. Her reconciliation is shown.

Cash balance per books	$4,015
Less deposits in transit	590
Add outstanding checks	730
Adjusted balance per books	$4,155
Cash balance per bank	$3,700
Add NSF check	430
Less bank service charge	25
Adjusted balance per bank	$4,105

a. Identify the errors Janie made in the preparation of the bank reconciliation.
b. What is the correct cash balance?
c. Enter adjustments into the accounting equation needed to update the company's cash balance.

E6-6A. *Determine the effects of transactions using the allowance method.* (LO 3)
Health & Nutrition Inc. uses the allowance method to account for bad debts. Indicate the effect that each of the following independent transactions will have on gross accounts receivable, the allowance for uncollectible accounts, net accounts receivable, and bad debt expense. Use (+) for increase, (−) for decrease, and (0) for no effect.
a. A customer pays her bill.
b. Of $450,000 in sales, 3.15% is estimated to be uncollectible.
c. Of $215,000 in accounts receivable, 4% is estimated to be uncollectible. Last year, an excess of $500 beyond what was expected was written off.

E6-7A. *Determine bad debts expense using the percentage of sales method.* (LO 3)
Brazwells at Bradford Inc. uses the allowance method to account for bad debts. During 2007, the company recorded $925,000 in credit sales. At the end of 2007, account balances were accounts receivable, $140,000 and allowance for uncollectible accounts, $(4,000). If bad debt expense is estimated to be 2.5% of credit sales, how much bad debt expense will be on the year-end income statement?

E6-8A. *Analyze effects of accounts receivable transactions using the percentage of sales method.* (LO 3)
At the beginning of 2008, Darcy's Floor Coverings had the following account balances: accounts receivable, $325,000 and allowance for uncollectible accounts, $(7,500). During the year, credit sales were $825,000, sales returns and allowances were $31,750, and $10,000 of specific customer accounts were written off. At year-end, Darcy's estimated that 5% of net credit sales were uncollectible.
a. Record the transactions (including beginning balances) into the accounting equation for 2008.
b. What is the net realizable value of accounts receivable at year-end?
c. What amount of bad debts expense will appear on the income statement for the year ended December 31, 2008?

E6-9A. *Determine bad debts expense using the percentage of accounts receivable method.* (LO 3)
A company started the year with accounts receivable of $20,000 and an allowance for uncollectible accounts of $(2,500). During the year, sales (all on account) were $80,000 and cash collections for sales amounted to $77,000. Also, $2,400 worth of uncollectible ac-

counts were specifically identified and written off. Then, at year-end, the company estimated that 5% of ending AR would be uncollectible.
  a. Record the transactions (including beginning balances) into the accounting equation.
  b. What amount will be shown on the year-end income statement for bad debts expense?
  c. What is the balance in the allowance for uncollectible accounts after all adjustments have been made?

E6-10A. *Determine bad debts expense using the percentage of accounts receivable method.* (LO 3)
Cairo Toyota Inc. uses the allowance method for bad debts and adjusts the allowance for uncollectible accounts to a desired amount based on an aging of accounts receivable. At the beginning of 2007, the allowance account had a balance of $(18,000). During 2007, credit sales totaled $480,000 and receivables of $14,000 were written off. The year-end aging indicated that a $21,000 allowance for uncollectible accounts was required. Record the transactions (including the beginning balances) into the accounting equation. What is the bad debts expense for 2007? What information will be disclosed on the balance sheet at year-end? What information does this provide someone who is evaluating Cairo Toyota's annual performance?

E6-11A. *Record credit card sales.* (LO 4)
Executive Air Travel Inc. accepts cash or credit card payment from customers. During April, Executive provided $215,000 worth of flight tickets to customers who used VISA to pay for their trips. VISA charges Executive 3% of ticket sales for card services. Give the journal entry that Executive will record for these ticket sales. Why would Executive accept VISA?

E6-12A. *Analyze and record notes receivable.* (LO 5)
On October 1, 2009, ACME Athletic Equipment Company purchased athletic equipment on account for $10,500 from Sporting Goods Unlimited with terms 2/10, n/30. On November 1, ACME renegotiated its accounts receivable by signing a 3-month promissory note at an interest rate of 10%. Record the transactions in the accounting equation that would be recorded on October 1 and November 1 for both companies. Determine the due date of the note and prepare the transaction (using the accounting equation) to record the collection of the note on the books of both companies.

E6-13A. *Account for warranties.* (LO 6)
When Park Avenue Pet Shop sells a puppy, it provides a health warranty for the little critter. If a puppy becomes ill in the first 2 years after the sale, Park Avenue Pet Shop will pay the vet bill up to $300. Because this is normally a significant expense for the shop, the accountant insists that Park Avenue Pet Shop record an estimated warranty liability at the end of every year before the financial statements are prepared. On December 31, 2006, the accountant made the appropriate entry to record that liability based on sales for the year of 1,500 puppies. On March 30, 2007, the store received a $50 vet bill from one of its customers, who had bought a puppy in 2006. Park Avenue Pet Shop wrote a check for $50 to reimburse the puppy's owner.
  a. Enter the transaction into the accounting equation to record the estimated warranty liability at December 31, 2006.
  b. Enter the transaction into the accounting equation to record the payment of the vet bill on March 30, 2007. What effect did this payment have on the 2007 financial statements of Park Avenue Pet Shop?

E6-14A. *Calculate accounts receivable turnover ratio.* (LO 8)
Using the data from E6-8A, calculate the accounts receivable turnover ratio for 2008. On average, how many days does it take Darcy's Floor Coverings to collect its accounts receivable?

E6-15A. *Identify risks and controls.* (LO 9)
Why would a firm offer customers a free purchase if the customer is not offered a receipt?

E6-16A. *Identify risks and controls.* (LO 9)
Give two examples of physical controls of cash in a retail store like Target.

Exercises—Set B

E6-1B. *Prepare a bank reconciliation.* (LO 1)
The bank statement for Rodney's Lawn Maintenance had an ending balance as of October 31 of $25,450.85. Also listed on the statement was a service charge for $21. Check 1825, which Rodney wrote to pay for equipment purchased October 30, had not cleared the bank yet—the amount was $5,415. Deposits in transit were $7,850.25. Rodney's bank collected a $1,275 note for him in October. After reviewing the bank statement and canceled checks, Rodney discovered that the bank mistakenly deducted $1,875.93 from his account on a check that was written by Rogers's Lawn Maintenance.
Calculate the true cash balance as of October 31.

E6-2B. *Prepare a bank reconciliation.* (LO 1)
The marketing firm Razzle & Dazzle Inc. had the following information available concerning their cash account for the month of May. (LO 1)

Balance per Razzle & Dazzle Inc. books, May 31	$15,375.21
Outstanding checks	8,720.85
NSF check from customer	1,650.00
Note collected by bank	4,650.00
Deposits in transit	8,215.50
Miscellaneous fees:	
Charge for collection of note	75.00
Order for checks	32.50
Interest earned on bank account	84.62

Calculate the true cash balance as of May 31.

E6-3B. *Prepare a bank reconciliation.* (LO 1)
Prepare a bank reconciliation for Josey's Fresh Deli at June 30 using the following information.

Balance per USA National Bank statement at June 30	$15,023.05
Outstanding checks	4,215.83
NSF checks from customer	250.68
Deposits in transit	2,452.87
Interest revenue	251.32
Service charge	15.00
Cash balance per Josey's records at June 30	13,274.45

Enter adjustments into the accounting equation needed to update the company's cash balance. What is the net effect on net income? Will net income be increased or decreased? By what amount?

E6-4B. *Prepare a bank reconciliation.* (LO 1)
Prepare a bank reconciliation at August 31 for Randy's Toy Box using the following information.

Company's cash account balance, August 31	$6,500.00
Bank statement ending balance, August 31	5,100.44
Deposits in transit	2,504.57
Outstanding checks:	
4051	1,052.15
4056	25.59

There was an error in Randy's books. Check 4052 for $825.69 was correctly deducted from the bank account, but was mistakenly recorded in the books as $852.96.

E6-5B. *Identify and correct errors in a bank reconciliation.* (LO 1)
Newman Killingsfield is having trouble with the bank reconciliation at March 31. His reconciliation is shown.

Cash balance per bank	$7,578.65
Add NSF check	305.00
Less bank service charge	31.00
Adjusted balance per bank	$8,824.25
Cash balance per books	$9,362.65
Less deposits in transit	1,875.00
Add outstanding checks	427.00
Adjusted balance per books	$7,959.65

a. Identify the errors Newman made in the preparation of the bank reconciliation.
b. What is the correct cash balance?
c. Enter adjustments into the accounting equation needed to update the company's cash balance.

E6-6B. *Determine bad debts expense using the percentage of sales method.* (LO 3)
Extreme Sport Inc. uses the allowance method to account for bad debts. During 2007, the company recorded $650,000 in credit sales. At the end of 2007, account balances were accounts receivable, $185,000 and allowance for uncollectible accounts, $(5,000). If bad debts expense is estimated to be 4% of credit sales, how much bad debts expense will be on the year-end income statement?

E6-7B. *Analyze effects of accounts receivable transactions using the percentage of sales method.* (LO 3)
At the beginning of 2009, Runnels' Art Supply had the following account balances: accounts receivable, $285,000 and allowance for uncollectible accounts, $(8,250). During the year, credit sales were $965,000, sales returns and allowances were $18,250, and $5,750 of specific customer accounts were written off. At year-end, Runnels' estimated that 6% of net credit sales were uncollectible.
   a. Record the transactions (including beginning balances) into the accounting equation for 2009.
   b. What is the net realizable value of accounts receivable at year-end?
   c. What amount of bad debts expense will appear on the income statement for the year ended December 31, 2009?

E6-8B. *Determine bad debts expense using the percentage of accounts receivable method.* (LO 3)
A company started the year with AR of $15,000 and an allowance of $(3,500). During the year, sales (all on account) were $110,000 and cash collections for sales amounted to $105,000. Also, $2,000 worth of uncollectible accounts were specifically identified and written off. Then, at year-end, the company estimated that 15% of ending AR would be uncollectible. Record the transactions (including beginning balances) into the accounting equation.
   a. What amount will be shown on the year-end income statement for bad debts expense?
   b. What is the balance in the allowance account after all adjustments have been made?

E6-9B. *Analyze effects of accounts receivable transactions using the percentage of accounts receivable method.* (LO 3)
Designer Jean Industries began 2008 with accounts receivable of $1,650,000 and a balance in the allowance for uncollectible accounts of $(26,000). During 2008, credit sales totaled $7,290,000 and cash collected from customers totaled $8,280,000. Actual write-offs of

specific accounts receivable in 2008 were $23,000. At the end of the year, an accounts receivable aging schedule indicated a required allowance of $27,500. No accounts receivable previously written off were collected.

    a. Record the transactions (including the beginning balances) into the accounting equation for 2008.

    b. What is the net realizable value of accounts receivable at year-end?

    c. What is the bad debts expense for the year 2008?

E6-10B. *Analyze accounts receivable disclosures and ratio analysis.* (LO 3, 8)
Use the following information from the financial statements of Prestige Furniture Inc.

Current assets (amounts in thousands)	February 29, 2012	February 28, 2011
Cash and cash equivalents	$ 28,706	$ 67,100
Receivables, less allowance of $50,948 in 2012 and $39,100 in 2011	788,906	530,314

    a. Does Prestige Furniture have significant credit sales? If so, what evidence supports your opinion?

    b. Can you tell what bad debts expense was for the fiscal year ending February 29, 2012?

    c. Sales for the year ending on February 29, 2012, were $3,434,840,000. Compute the accounts receivable turnover ratio and comment on what it tells you about the Prestige Furniture credit and collection policies. What would make the ratio more useful for this assessment?

E6-11B. *Analyze credit options.* (LO 4)
Jamie, the owner of Suitcases Unlimited, is trying to decide whether to extend credit to his customers or to accept **MasterCard**, or both. Suppose Jamie expects to sell approximately $170,000 worth of merchandise each quarter if he offers his customers one of these choices. What costs and benefits should Jamie consider in making his decision? Explain the difference in the two alternatives.

E6-12B. *Analyze and record notes receivable.* (LO 5)
On April 1, 2010, Tropical Aquatics purchased aquariums and equipment on account, for $25,000 from Tanks In All Shapes & Sizes Inc. with terms 3/15, n/30. On May 1, Tropical Aquatics renegotiated its accounts receivable by signing a promissory note for 2 months at an interest rate of 8%. Use the accounting equation to record the transactions on April 1 and May 1 for both companies. Determine the due date of the note and use the accounting equation to record the collection of the note on the books of both companies.

E6-13B. *Account for warranties.* (LO 6)
When M, K, & Boyd Pools Plus installs a pool, it provides a 3-year warranty (from the date of the sale) for any repairs needed that are not considered general maintenance. If a pool should need to be repaired in the first 3 years after the sale, M, K, & Boyd will repair the pool for a cost of up to $1,000. Because this is normally a significant expense, the accountant insists that M, K, & Boyd record an estimated warranty liability at the end of every year before the financial statements are prepared. For the year ended June 30, 2008, the accountant made the appropriate entry to record that liability based on sales and installations for the year of 360 pools. On January 1, 2009, M, K, & Boyd paid $750 to an independent contractor to repair a pool for one of its customers, who had purchased the pool on March 15, 2008.

    a. Enter the transaction into the accounting equation to record the estimated warranty liability at June 30, 2008.

    b. Enter the transaction into the accounting equation to record the payment of the repair bill on January 1, 2009. For the year ended June 30, 2009, what effect did this payment have on the financial statements of M, K, & Boyd Pools Plus?

E6-14B. *Calculate accounts receivable turnover ratio.* (LO 8)
Using the data from E6-7B, calculate the accounts receivable turnover ratio for 2009. On average, how many days does it take Runnels' Art Supply to collect its accounts receivable?

E6-15B. *Identify cash controls.* (LO 9)
Name three ways a firm can lose cash. How can these frauds be detected?

E6-16B. *Identify cash controls.* (LO 9)
Explain why it is so crucial for a firm to have good controls over its cash.

Problems—Set A

P6-1A. *Calculate the beginning book balance.* (LO 1)
Consider the following information about Lee Ann Vintage Shop for the month of January.

- Deposits in transit as of January 31 totaled $5,625.10.
- Interest revenue earned during the month was $875.
- Bank service charges amounted to $65.
- The bank deducted from Lee Ann Vintage Shop's account a check for $181.05 that was written by Lee Ann Retro Furniture Company.
- The following checks were still outstanding as of the bank statement date:

13012	$ 450.75
13008	620.82
13014	215.31

- The Lee Ann Vintage Shop accountant recorded a deposit of $215 as $251.
- The bank returned a check from a customer as NSF in the amount of $762.35.
- The balance per the bank at January 31 totaled $36,115.72.

Required

Determine the January 31 cash balance that appears on Lee Ann Vintage Shop's books prior to the bank reconciliation. (Hint: compute the true cash balance first.)

P6-2A. *Prepare a bank reconciliation.* (LO 1)
Country's Copies ending cash balance for April was $8,877.12. The owner deposited $757.24 on April 30 that did not appear on the bank statement. The bank collected a note of $2,500 for Country's Copies, of which $125 was interest, and charged them $20 for the service. The ending balance on the bank statement for April was $10,917.60. After comparing the company's records with the bank statement, checks totaling $550.98 were found to be outstanding. Besides the collection fee, there was $25 in other service charges. Also, the statement showed that Country's Copies earned $225 in interest revenue on the account and that checks amounting to $415.26 turned out to be NSF. Finally, an error in recording was discovered: Check 5624 for $813.40 was paid to one of Country's Copies' vendors. The bank incorrectly deducted $831.40 from Country's Copies' account, referencing Check 5624.

Excel Template
www.prenhall.com/reimers

Required

a. Prepare a bank reconciliation at April 30.
b. Prepare the necessary adjustments to the accounting equation to update the records of Country's Copies.

P6-3A. *Prepare a bank reconciliation.* (LO 1)
On May 31, 2007, Sharp Company had a cash balance in its general ledger of $6,675. The company's bank statement from National Bank showed a May 31 balance of $8,240. The following facts have come to your attention.

1. Sharp's May 31 deposit of $1,000 was not included on the bank statement because it was dropped in the night depository after bank hours on May 31.
2. The bank's general service charge for the month was $100.

3. The bank collected a note receivable of $1,500 for Sharp Company along with an additional $58 for interest. The bank deducted a $30 fee for this service. Sharp Company had not accrued any interest on the note.
4. Sharp's bookkeeper erroneously recorded a payment to Williams Company for $192 as $129. The check cleared the bank for the correct amount of $192.
5. Sharp's outstanding checks at May 31 totaled $1,200.

Required

    a. Prepare a bank reconciliation as of May 31.
    b. Prepare the necessary adjustments to the accounting equation to update the records of Sharp Company.

P6-4A. *Identify and correct errors in a bank reconciliation.* (LO 1)
Analyze the following errors that appeared on White Electric's bank statement and in the accounting records.

1. The bank recorded a deposit of $300 as $30.
2. The company's bookkeeper mistakenly recorded a deposit of $240 as $420.
3. The company's bookkeeper mistakenly recorded a payment of $450 received from a customer as $45 on the bank deposit slip. The bank caught the error and made the deposit for the correct amount.
4. The bank statement shows a check that was written by the company for $392 was erroneously paid (cleared the account) as $329.
5. The bookkeeper wrote a check for $275 but erroneously wrote down $257 as the cash disbursement in the company's records.

Required

For each error, describe how the correction would be shown on the company's bank reconciliation.

Excel Template
www.prenhall.com/reimers

P6-5A. *Analyze the effects of accounts receivable transactions using the percentage of sales method.* (LO 3, 8)
Evaluate the following scenarios, assuming both companies use the net credit sales as the basis for estimating bad debts expense:

1. At year-end, Bonnie Company has accounts receivable of $112,000. The allowance for uncollectible accounts has a balance prior to adjustment of $(400). Net credit sales for the year were $315,000 and 3% is estimated to be uncollectible.
2. At year-end, Clyde Company has accounts receivable of $220,000. The allowance for uncollectible accounts has a balance prior to adjustment of $200. Net credit sales for the year were $175,000 and 3% is estimated to be uncollectible.

Required

For each situation, compute the following:
    a. The bad debts expense for the year
    b. The balance in the allowance for uncollectible accounts account at year-end
    c. The net realizable value of accounts receivable at year-end
    d. Assuming Bonnie Company had an accounts receivable balance of $105,000 at the beginning of the year, what is Bonnie's accounts receivable turnover ratio for the year?
    e. Assuming Clyde Company had an accounts receivable balance of $226,000 at the beginning of the year, what is Clyde's accounts receivable turnover ratio for the year?

P6-6A. *Determine bad debts expense using the percentage of accounts receivable method.* (LO 3)
Evaluate the following scenarios, assuming both companies use the accounts receivable method of estimating bad debts expense.

1. At year-end, Tate Company has accounts receivable of $89,000. The allowance for uncollectible accounts has a balance prior to adjustment of $(750). An aging schedule prepared on December 31 indicates that $2,100 of Tate's accounts receivable is uncollectible. Net credit sales were $325,000 for the year.
2. At year-end, Bradley Company has accounts receivable of $75,250. The allowance for uncollectible accounts has a balance prior to adjustment of $625. An aging schedule prepared on December 31 indicates that $3,200 of Bradley's accounts receivable is uncollectible. Net credit sales were $452,000 for the year.

Required

For each situation, compute the following:
  a. The bad debts expense for the year
  b. The balance in the allowance for uncollectible accounts at year-end
  c. The net realizable value of accounts receivable at year-end
  d. Based solely on the data provided, how many days it takes each company to collect its receivables, and which company is doing a better job of collecting its receivables. Explain your answer.

P6-7A. *Account for accounts receivable, notes receivable, and credit card sales transactions.* (LO 3, 4, 5)
Storkville Baby Boutique had the following transactions during the first half of 2006.

Jan 2	Sold merchandise on account to Tiny Tots Toys, $24,000 with terms 1/10, n/30. The cost of the merchandise sold was $18,000.
Feb 3	Accepted a 90-day, 10% note for $24,000 from Tiny Tots Toys on account from the Jan 2 sale.
Feb 4	Sold merchandise on account to Stuffed Animals Unlimited, $22,500 with terms 2/10, n/45. The cost of the merchandise sold was $17,250.
Feb 9	Received $10,000 of the amount due from Stuffed Animals Unlimited from the Feb 4 sale. (No sales discount is applied unless amount owed is paid in full.)
Mar 22	Accepted a 60-day, 10% note for the remaining balance on Stuffed Animals Unlimited account from the Feb 4 sale.
Mar 25	Sold merchandise on account to Little Angels Boutique, $22,000 with terms 2/10, n/30. The cost of the merchandise sold was $16,500.
Mar 31	Storkville began accepting VISA on March 1 with deposits submitted monthly. The deposits for the month totaled $44,000. (Cost of merchandise sold was $25,000.) VISA charges a 2% fee.
Apr 30	Wrote off the Little Angels Boutique account as uncollectible after receiving news that the company declared bankruptcy. Storkville Baby Boutique uses the allowance method for accounting for uncollectible accounts.
Apr 30	April's VISA sales totaled $52,000. Cost of goods sold was $27,000.
May 4	Received payments in full from Tiny Tots Toys.
May 21	Received payment in full from Stuffed Animals Unlimited.
May 31	May's VISA sales totaled $65,000. Cost of goods sold was $34,000.
June 5	Sold merchandise on account to Tiny Tots Toys, $22,000 with terms 1/10, n/30. The cost of the merchandise was $16,850.
June 10	Sold merchandise on account to Stuffed Animals Unlimited, $35,000 with terms 2/10, n/45. The cost of the merchandise sold was $29,000.
June 15	Collected the amount due from Tiny Tots Toys for the June 5 sale.
June 22	Collected the amount due from Stuffed Animals Unlimited for the June 10 sale.
June 30	June's VISA sales totaled $28,000. Cost of goods sold was $18,000.
June 30	Storkville Baby Boutique has $156,000 in accounts receivable and an allowance account with a negative balance of $700. The net credit sales

for the first 6 months of the year were $650,000, and cash sales were $115,000. Assume that Storkville Baby Boutique uses the credit sales method of accounting for uncollectible accounts. The firm's historical data indicates that approximately 2.5% of net credit sales are uncollectible.

Required

Prepare the accounting equation entries to record the above transactions. Round to the nearest dollar.

P6-8A. *Account for warranties.* (LO 6, 7)

In 2005, Best Buy Inc. had sales of $70,000 of its new video recorders. The company gives a 2-year warranty with the purchase of a video recorder. When Best Buy recorded the sales, the company also estimated that it would spend $6,000 to honor those warranties. When the company prepared its annual financial statements for 2005, no video recorders had been brought in for repair. In January 2006, however, 20 people brought in their broken video recorders, and Best Buy spent a total of $450 repairing them (at no charge to the customers, because the video recorders were under warranty). Assume no additional sales were made in January 2006 (i.e., no new warranties were given in January).

Required

    a. How much warranty expense related to the sales of video recorders would Best Buy show on an income statement for the year 2005?

    b. Would Best Buy have a warranty liability on the balance sheet at the end of 2005? If so, how much?

    c. How much warranty expense would Best Buy show on an income statement for the month of January 2006 related to these video recorders?

    d. Would Best Buy have a warranty liability on the balance sheet at January 31, 2006? If so, how much?

P6-9A. *Calculate accounts receivable turnover ratio.* (LO 8)

Information from Mystic Corporation's balance sheet at December 31, 2008, and income statement for the year ended December 31, 2008 is as follows.

Cash	$ 35,000
Cost of goods sold	350,000
Unearned revenue	15,000
Rent expense	12,000
Accounts receivable, net	73,000
Accounts payable	10,000
Equipment, net	225,000
Interest payable	1,350
Net income	65,000
Inventory	350,000
Salaries payable	15,000
Marketable securities	15,000
Office supplies	5,000
Prepaid insurance	12,000
Land	75,000
Long-term notes payable	110,000
Sales revenue	775,000
Interest expense	1,500
Insurance expense	5,000

Required

    a. Calculate the corporation's accounts receivable turnover ratio. The accounts receivable balance at December 31, 2007, was $87,000. (Round to two decimal places.) Explain what the accounts receivable turnover ratio measures.

    b. On average, how many days does it take Mystic to collect its receivables?

Problems—Set B

P6-1B. *Calculate the beginning bank balance.* (LO 1)

Excel Template
www.prenhall.com/reimers

- Consider the following about Computer Tech's cash account for the month of April. Cash per Computer Tech's records was $85,834.99.
- $16,008.13 in customer payments were received April 30 but not deposited until May 1.
- Checks totaling $22,461.87 were issued in April but had not cleared the bank as of the statement date (April 30).
- According to the bank statement, service charges for April were $54.50, and the bank collected a $4,900 note on April 19.

Required

Determine the April 30 cash balance that appears on Computer Tech's bank statement. (Hint: compute the true cash balance first.)

P6-2B. *Prepare a bank reconciliation.* (LO 1)

Nance's Cosmetic Center's ending cash balance for February was $8,624.37. The owner deposited $905.66 on February 28 that did not appear on the bank statement. The bank collected a note of $500, of which $25 was interest, for Nance's Cosmetic Center and charged them $15 for the service. The ending balance on the bank statement for February was $8,570.83. After comparing the company's records with the bank statement, checks totaling $481.12 were found to be outstanding. Besides the collection fee, there was $45 in other service charges. Also, the statement showed that Nance's Cosmetic Center earned $112.75 in interest revenue on the account and that checks amounting to $109.75 turned out to be NSF. Finally, an error in recording was discovered: Check 6715 for $419.63 was paid to one of Nance's Cosmetic Center's vendors. The bank incorrectly deducted $491.63 from Nance's Cosmetic Center's account, referencing Check 6715.

Required

    a. Prepare a bank reconciliation at February 28.
    b. Prepare the necessary adjustments to the accounting equation to update the records of Nance's Cosmetic Center.

P6-3B. *Prepare a bank reconciliation.* (LO 1)

On June 30, 2007, Roddick Company had a cash balance in its general ledger of $11,595. The company's bank statement from Bank One showed a June 30 balance of $12,540. The following facts have come to your attention.

1. Roddick's June 30 deposit of $2,500 was not included on the bank statement because it was dropped in the night depository after bank hours on June 30.
2. The bank's general service charge for the month was $40.
3. The bank collected a note receivable of $2,000 for Roddick Company along with an additional $58 for interest. The bank deducted a $10 fee for this service. Roddick Company had not accrued any interest on the note.
4. Roddick's bookkeeper erroneously recorded a payment to Federer Company for $892 as $829. The check cleared the bank for the correct amount of $892.
5. Roddick's outstanding checks at June 30 totaled $1,500.

Required

    a. Prepare a bank reconciliation as of June 30.
    b. Prepare the necessary adjustment to the accounting equation to update the records of Roddick.

P6-4B. *Identify and correct errors in a bank reconciliation.* (LO 1)

Analyze the following errors that appeared on Pet Superstore's bank statement and in the accounting records.

1. The bank recorded a deposit of $450 as $4,500.
2. The company's bookkeeper mistakenly recorded a deposit of $750 as $570.

3. The company's bookkeeper mistakenly recorded a payment of $175 received from a customer as $17.50 on the bank deposit slip. The bank caught the error and made the deposit for the correct amount.
4. The bank statement shows a check that was written by the company for $970 was erroneously paid (cleared the account) as $935.
5. The bookkeeper wrote a check for $805 but erroneously wrote down $850 as the cash disbursement in the company's records.

Required

For each error, describe how the correction would be shown on the company's bank reconciliation.

Excel Template
www.prenhall.com/reimers

P6-5B. *Analyze the effects of accounts receivable transactions using the percentage of sales method.* (LO 3, 8)
Evaluate the following scenarios, assuming both companies use the net credit sales as the basis for estimating bad debts expense:

1. At year-end, Nash Company has accounts receivable of $84,000. The allowance for uncollectible accounts has a balance prior to adjustment of $(300). Net credit sales for the year were $250,000 and 3% is estimated to be uncollectible.
2. At year-end, Bridges Company has accounts receivable of $83,000. The allowance for uncollectible accounts has a balance prior to adjustment of $400. Net credit sales for the year were $250,000 and 3% is estimated to be uncollectible.

Required

For each situation described above, compute the following:
   a. The bad debts expense for the year
   b. The balance in the allowance for uncollectible accounts account at year-end
   c. The net realizable value of accounts receivable at year-end
   d. Assuming Nash Company had an accounts receivable balance of $76,000 at the beginning of the year, what is Nash's accounts receivable turnover ratio for the year?
   e. Assuming Bridges Company had an accounts receivable balance of $85,000 at the beginning of the year, what is Bridges' accounts receivable turnover ratio for the year?

P6-6B. *Determine bad debts expense using the percentage of accounts receivable method.* (LO 3)
Evaluate the following scenarios, assuming both companies use the accounts receivable method of estimating bad debts expense.

1. At year-end, Vio Company has accounts receivable of $14,000. The allowance for uncollectible accounts has a balance prior to adjustment of $(300). An aging schedule prepared on December 31 indicates that $1,100 of Vio's accounts receivable is uncollectible. Net credit sales were $125,000 for the year.
2. At year-end, Demato Company has accounts receivable of $25,700. The allowance for uncollectible accounts has a balance prior to adjustment of $400. An aging schedule prepared on December 31 indicates that $2,300 of Demato's accounts receivable is uncollectible. Net credit sales were $240,000 for the year.

Required

For each situation, compute the following:
   a. The bad debts expense for the year
   b. The balance in the allowance for uncollectible accounts at year-end
   c. The net realizable value of accounts receivable at year-end
   d. Based solely on the data provided, how many days it takes each company to collect its receivables, and which company is doing a better job of collecting its receivables. Explain your answer.

P6-7B. *Account for accounts receivable, notes receivable, and credit card sales transactions.* (LO 3, 4, 5)

Baby Trails Toys had the following transactions during the first half of 2009.

Jan 2	Sold merchandise on account to Thumbelina & Company, $14,000 with terms 1/10, n/30. The cost of the merchandise sold was $8,000.
Feb 4	Sold merchandise on account to Teddy Bears Incorporated, $12,500, with terms 2/10, n/45. The cost of the merchandise sold was $7,500.
Feb 9	Received $1,000 of the amount due from Teddy Bears Incorporated from the Feb 4 sale. (No sales discount is applied unless amount owed is paid in full.)
Feb 3	Accepted a 90-day, 10% note for $14,000 from Thumbelina & Company on account from the Jan 2 sale.
Mar 22	Accepted a 60-day, 8% note for the remaining balance on Teddy Bears Incorporated account from the Feb 4 sale.
Mar 25	Sold merchandise on account to Tots R Us, $12,000 with terms 2/10, n/30. The cost of the merchandise sold was $6,250.
Mar 31	Baby Trails began accepting **MasterCard** on March 1 with deposits submitted monthly. The deposits for the month totaled $24,000. **MasterCard** charges a 3% fee. The cost of merchandise sold was $13,000.
Apr 30	Wrote off the Tots R Us account as uncollectible after receiving news that the company declared bankruptcy. Baby Trails Toys uses the allowance method for accounting for uncollectible accounts.
Apr 30	April's **MasterCard** sales totaled $30,000.
May 4	Received payment in full from Thumbelina & Company.
May 21	Received payment in full from Teddy Bears Incorporated.
May 31	May's **MasterCard** sales totaled $45,000. Cost of goods sold was $18,000.
June 5	Sold merchandise on account to Thumbelina & Company, $12,000 with terms 1/10, n/30. The cost of the merchandise was $6,850.
June 10	Sold merchandise on account to Teddy Bears Incorporated, $15,000, with terms 2/10, n/45. The cost of the merchandise sold was $9,000.
June 15	Collected the amount due from Thumbelina & Company for the June 5 sale.
June 22	Collected the amount due from Teddy Bears Incorporated for the June 10 sale.
June 30	June's **MasterCard** sales totaled $40,000. Cost of good sold $25,000.
June 30	Baby Trails Toys has $250,000 in accounts receivable and an allowance account with a negative balance of $1,500. The net credit sales for the first 6 months of the year were $890,000, and cash sales were $95,000. Assume that Baby Trails Toys uses the sales method of accounting for uncollectible accounts. The firm's historical data indicates that approximately 3% of net credit sales are uncollectible.

Required

Prepare the accounting equation entries to record the transactions. Round to the nearest dollar.

P6-8B. *Account for warranties.* (LO 6, 7)

Laurienzo's Frames prepares monthly financial statements. The following took place during the month of July at Laurienzo's Frames.

1. $5,000 worth of frames was sold. Each is guaranteed for 12 months. Any defective frame will be repaired or replaced free of charge during that period.
2. Laurienzo estimated that it would cost $600 during the next year to honor the warranties on the July sales.
3. During August, Laurienzo spent $250 dollars to honor warranties related to July sales.

Required

 a. What amount of warranty expense would be shown on the income statement for July?
 b. What amount of warranty liability would be shown on the July 31 balance sheet?
 c. What amount of warranty expense would be shown on the income statement for August?
 d. What effect did recording the warranty expense have on owner's equity?
 e. What effect did spending the $250 in August have on owner's equity?

P6-9B. *Calculate accounts receivable turnover ratio.* (LO 8)
Information from River Corporation's balance sheet at December 31, 2008 and income statement for the year ended December 31, 2008 is as follows.

Cash	$ 15,000
Cost of goods sold	515,000
Unearned revenue	25,000
Rent expense	24,000
Accounts receivable, net	115,000
Accounts payable	13,000
Equipment, net	165,000
Interest payable	1,780
Net income	48,000
Inventory	212,000
Salaries payable	12,000
Marketable securities	8,000
Office supplies	1,250
Prepaid insurance	6,000
Land	35,000
Long-term notes payable	60,000
Sales revenue	1,825,000
Interest expense	1,350
Insurance expense	800

Required

 a. Calculate the corporation's accounts receivable turnover ratio. The accounts receivable balance at December 31, 2007, was $122,000. (Round to two decimal places.) Explain what the accounts receivable turnover ratio measures.
 b. On average, how many days does it take River to collect its receivables?

Financial Statement Analysis

FSA6-1. *Analyze accounts receivable and calculate accounts receivable turnover ratio.* (LO 3, 8)
Use the following information from the financial statements of Winnebago to answer the questions.

From current assets (amounts in thousands)	August 26, 2006	August 27, 2005
Cash and cash equivalents	$24,934	$19,484
Receivables, less allowance for doubtful accounts ($164 and $270, respectively)	20,859	40,910

 a. Does Winnebago have significant credit sales? If so, what evidence supports your opinion?
 b. Sales for the fiscal year ending on August 26, 2006, were $864,403 (in thousands). Compute the accounts receivable turnover ratio and comment on

what it tells you about Winnebago's credit and collection policies. What would make the ratio more useful for this assessment?
   c. Can you tell what bad debts expense was for the fiscal year ending August 26, 2006? Explain.

FSA6-2. *Analyze accounts receivable and credit sales.* (LO 3, 4)
An examination of the balance sheet of Family Dollar Stores Inc. shows no allowance for bad debts.
   a. Under what conditions would a company be allowed to omit this account from the balance sheet? Does this make sense for Family Dollar Stores Inc.?
   b. Many of Family Dollar Stores Inc. customers pay with credit cards. How do you think those sales are reflected on the financial statements?

FSA6-3. *Analyze accounts receivable and calculate accounts receivable turnover ratio.* (LO 3, 8)
The following information has been adapted from the annual financial statements of General Mills Inc.

From the Balance Sheet:

May 28, 2006, and May 29, 2005
in millions

	May 28, 2006	May 29, 2005
ASSETS		
Current Assets		
Cash and cash equivalents	$ 647	$ 573
Trade accounts receivable, less allowance of $18 and $19, in 2006 and 2005 respectively	1,076	1,034
Inventories	1,055	1,037
Prepaid expenses, deferred income taxes and other current assets	398	411
Total Current Assets	3,176	3,055
Property, plant, and equipment, net	2,997	3,111
Goodwill and intangible assets, net	10,259	10,216
Other assets	1,775	1,684
Total Assets	$18,207	$18,066

From the Income Statement:

Fiscal years ended May 28, 2006, and May 29, 2005 dollars in millions	2006	2005
Net revenues	$11,640	$11,244
Cost of sales	6,966	6,834
Gross profit	$ 4,674	$ 4,410

   a. What are the total amounts of accounts receivable for the 2 years given *before* considering the possible uncollectible accounts? That is, what are gross accounts receivable?
   b. Do you think the company has a significant amount of bad debts? Why or why not?
   c. Shortly after the financial statements were released, the company was notified that a major customer, who owes the company over $10,000, had filed for bankruptcy. If the company had received that information before the financial statements were released, what amounts might have been changed to reflect the accounting for the account receivable of the bankrupt customer? Explain.
   d. Calculate the accounts receivable turnover ratio for 2006 and 2005. (Net accounts receivable at the end of 2004 was $1,010 million.) Also, calculate the number of days it takes, on average, to collect an accounts receivable. Explain this information to the company's management.

Critical Thinking Problems

Risks and Controls

a. Suppose one person opens the cash receipts (checks received in the mail), makes the bank deposits, and keeps the accounts receivable records. What potential problems could arise from the lack of separation of duties?

b. Why would a store offer a free purchase to a customer who does not receive a receipt?

Ethics

You work in the billing and collections department of a small corporation. The firm's sales terms are 2/10, n/30; and most of the customers pay within the discount period. Over the years, you have become quite friendly with the finance manager of one of the customers. One day, he calls and asks you to change the date on your last invoice to his company to give him an extra week to pay and still be within the discount period. He offers to take you to dinner at the city's finest restaurant in exchange for this little favor.

It would be a simple change in the records, and no one would ever know. It would, you think, also create some goodwill with the customer. Would you make the change? Why or why not?

Group Assignment

The information given here was taken from Sears' balance sheet at the end of two fiscal years. In groups, discuss the potential reasons for the changes in the current assets from 2002 to 2003. Then, search the Internet for information to help you explain the changes. (The fiscal year ends on the Saturday nearest December 31.)

Sears, Roebuck and Co. Consolidated Balance Sheets *In millions*	2003	2002
ASSETS		
Current assets		
Cash and cash equivalents	$ 9,057	$ 1,962
Credit card receivables	1,998	32,563
Less allowance for uncollectible accounts	42	1,832
Net credit card receivables	1,956	30,731
Other receivables	733	891
Merchandise inventories, net	5,335	5,115
Prepaid expenses and deferred charges	407	535
Deferred income taxes	708	749
Total current assets	$18,196	$39,983

Internet Exercise: Intel Corporation

Intel, by far the world's number one maker of semiconductor chips, commands more than 80% of the PC microprocessor market. Compaq and Dell are Intel's largest customers. Go to http://www.intel.com and complete the following exercises.

IE6-1. Under "Quotes and Research" enter the company symbol INTC, the stock symbol of the Intel Corp., and then choose Financials. Find the annual income statement to answer the following questions.

a. Identify the amounts reported for total (net sales) revenue for the three most recent years.

b. In general, who are Intel's customers? Who are Intel's two largest customers? Do you think Intel primarily has credit sales or cash sales? Why? Does Intel extend credit to its customers, or do Intel's customers use credit cards to pay the amounts owed?

IE6-2. Find the annual balance sheet to answer the following questions.
   a. Identify the amounts reported for trade accounts receivable, net for the three most recent year-ends. Does this represent amounts owed by customers or amounts that the company estimates it will actually collect from customers?
   b. Does Intel use the allowance method or the direct write-off method to record uncollectible accounts? How can you tell?

IE6-3. Refer to the balance sheet to answer the following questions.
   a. Compute the accounts receivable turnover ratio for the two most recent years. In which year did the company collect receivables the quickest? How can you tell?
   b. For the most recent year, how long does it take on average for Intel to collect its accounts receivable? Do you think the credit terms might be n/45 or n/60? Explain why.

Accounting for Liabilities

Here's Where You've Been . . .

In Chapter 6, you learned how a company accounts for cash and accounts receivable and how that information is presented on the financial statements. You have learned about the major assets on the balance sheet, and now we will turn to the liability section of the balance sheet.

Here's Where You're Going . . .

When you are finished with Chapter 7, you should understand how firms account for both current and long-term liabilities and how they are presented on the financial statements.

Learning Objectives

When you are finished studying this chapter, you should be able to:

1. Define a definitely determinable liability and explain how payroll is recorded.

2. Explain how long-term notes and mortgages work.

3. Record the issue of bonds and payment of interest to bondholders.

4. Prepare financial statements that include payroll and long-term debt.

5. Explain capital structure and compute the debt-to-equity and the times-interest-earned ratios.

6. Identify the major risk associated with long-term debt and the related controls.

7. (Appendix) Calculate the present value of future cash flows.

Ethics Matters

Dennis Kozlowski, former CEO of Tyco International, and Mark Swartz, the firm's former CFO, could not convince a jury that the $150 million they received from Tyco was authorized compensation. They were also found guilty of secretly selling company shares of stock while artificially inflating the price of the stock. Kozlowski received hundreds of millions of dollars in salary and bonuses, including $70 million in 2002, his final year with the firm. That was the legal part!

The only defense Kozlowski had was that he was either ignorant or foolish, and jurors could not quite buy it. Kozlowski evidently took huge amounts of money that were never reported in Tyco's corporate filings or in Kozlowski's personal tax returns.

One of the lessons of Tyco and the other dozens of scandals of the early 2000s, according to Kurt Eichenwald of *The New York Times* (June 19, 2005), is that "corporate executives who want the big pay had better turn in spectacular, precision performance, legal analysts say. Otherwise, if a scandal blows up inside the company, their own compensation may prove their undoing."

L.O.1
Define a definitely determinable liability and explain how payroll is recorded.

Types of Liabilities

You have learned how a firm acquires and accounts for many of its assets—inventory, property, and equipment—and operating items, such as insurance and supplies. Now we will see that a firm pays for those assets with current liabilities and long-term liabilities. Liabilities, as you know, represent amounts a company owes its creditors. Creditors are the people and other firms that sold something to the company or have loaned money to the company and expect to be repaid. A liability is recognized—recorded in the accounting records so that it will appear on the balance sheet—when an obligation is incurred. For example, when The Home Depot receives merchandise from Black & Decker, The Home Depot records the asset in its inventory account and the liability in accounts payable. Liabilities are based on past transactions and are generally recognized when incurred.

There are three types of liabilities: definitely determinable liabilities, estimated liabilities, and contingent liabilities. We learned about an estimated liability in Chapter 6 where we discussed warranties. Because a firm wants to match warranty expense with the sale of the warranted item, the firm estimates and records an estimate of that future expense. **Estimated liabilities** involve judgment in arriving at the amount to record for the obligation.

A **contingent liability** is not actually a liability at all. It is a potential liability that depends on a future event related to some past action. Contingent liabilities are disclosed in the notes to the financial statements. As long as the potential loss is simply reasonably possible (not probable), there is no actual recording in the firm's books. The firm must disclose the details of the possible liability in the notes. A typical example is a lawsuit in progress.

In this chapter, the liabilities we discuss are definitely determinable liabilities. Exhibit 7.1 shows the liability section of The Home Depot's balance sheet. As we discuss various liabilities, you may want to refer back to this exhibit.

Estimated liabilities are obligations that have some uncertainty in the amount, such as the cost to honor a warranty.

Contingent liabilities are potential liabilities that depend on a future event related to some past action.

Definitely determinable liabilities are obligations that can be measured exactly.

Definitely Determinable Liabilities

Definitely determinable liabilities are liabilities that can be measured exactly. When Walgreens purchases drugs from pharmaceutical supplier McKesson Corporation, Walgreens knows the cost of the drugs and will record the liability at its exact amount. The company will record the amount of the obligation and an increase in inventory. Examples of liability accounts are accounts payable, bank loans or lines of credit, and notes payable.

EXHIBIT 7.1

Balance Sheet from The Home Depot
Focus on the liability section of The Home Depot's balance sheet. You may want to refer to it as you study the chapter.

The Home Depot, Inc. and Subsidiaries
Consolidated Balance Sheets

amounts in millions, except per share data	January 29, 2006	January 30, 2005
Assets		
Current assets:		
Cash and cash equivalents	$ 793	$ 506
Short-term investments	14	1,659
Receivables, net	2,396	1,499
Merchandise inventories	11,401	10,076
Other current assets	742	533
Total current assets	15,346	14,273
Property and equipment, at cost:		
Land	7,924	6,932
Buildings	14,056	12,325
Furniture, fixtures and equipment	7,073	6,195
Leasehold improvements	1,207	1,191
Construction in progress	843	1,404
Capital leases	427	390
	31,530	28,437
Less accumulated depreciation and amortization	6,629	5,711
Net property and equipment	24,901	22,726
Notes receivable	348	369
Cost in excess of the fair value of net assets acquired	3,286	1,394
Other assets	601	258
Total assets	$ 44,482	$ 39,020
Liabilities and Stockholder's Equity		
Current liabilities:		
Short-term debt	$ 900	$ —
Accounts payable	6,032	5,766
Accrued salaries and related expenses	1,176	1,055
Sales taxes payable	488	412
Deferred revenue	1,757	1,546
Income taxes payable	388	161
Current installments of long-term debt	513	11
Other accrued expenses	1,647	1,504
Total current liabilities	12,901	10,455
Long-term debt, excluding current installments	2,672	2,148
Other long-term liabilities	977	871
Deferred income taxes	1,023	1,388
Stockholder's equity:		
Common stock, par value $0.05; authorized: 10,000 shares; issued 2,401 shares at January 29, 2006 and 2,385 shares at January 30, 2005; outstanding 2,124 shares at January 29, 2006 and 2,185 shares at January 30, 2005	120	119
Paid-in capital	7,287	6,650
Retained earnings	28,943	23,962
Accumulated other comprehensive income	409	227
Unearned compensation	(138)	(108)
Treasury stock, at cost, 277 shares at January 29, 2006 and 200 shares at January 30, 2005	(9,712)	(6,692)
Total stockholder's equity	26,909	24,158
Total liabilities and stockholder's equity	$ 44,482	$ 39,020

In Exhibit 7.1, The Home Depot's balance sheet for the year ended January 29, 2006, shows accounts payable of $6,032 million. That is the amount The Home Depot owes its suppliers, and it is a definitely determinable liability. When Office Depot buys paper from International Paper Company on account, Office Depot's accountant will increase the balance in its inventory account, increasing an asset, and will increase the balance in accounts payable. Some accrued liabilities, such as salaries payable and interest payable, are usually definitely determinable.

Payroll

Payroll is an example of a common business expense that results in a definitely determinable, current liability. The government requires firms to supply them with the amounts of federal, state, and social security taxes each worker pays, so firms have to record more information about payroll than other accounts on the balance sheet. Accounting for payroll can take significant company resources, so frequently a company will hire another company such as Automatic Data Processing (ADP) to manage its payroll. Learning a little about payroll will help you understand your next check from your employer and will help you see how liabilities are recorded.

Suppose The Home Depot hires a former police officer to guard the company's headquarters building for a salary of $500 per week. That amount is the employee's gross pay. As you may know from your work experience, gross pay is not the amount the employee takes home. Exhibit 7.2 shows where each piece of a paycheck goes. From the gross pay amount, the company makes several deductions. First, the company withholds income taxes. To withhold taxes means that the employer, The Home Depot, deducts money from the employee's pay and sends it to the U.S. government. In doing so, The Home Depot is acting as an *agent* for the government. Second, the U.S. government requires the company to deduct social security taxes at the current legal rate (6.2% as this book was going to press) and Medicare taxes at the current legal rate (1.45% as this book was going to press). These two amounts must be "matched" by the employer. That means in addition to being an agent for the government, the company must also make its own payment. The company's payment is classified as payroll tax expense.

We will calculate the various amounts that The Home Depot must withhold from the $500 gross pay of the security guard. Assuming 20% is withheld for federal income taxes (FIT), The Home Depot would deduct $100. We will use social security taxes (FICA) at 6.2%, which amounts to $31.00, and Medicare taxes at 1.45%, which amounts to $7.25. So the amount The Home Depot will pay the employee is

$$\$500.00 - \$100.00 - \$31.00 - \$7.25 = \$361.75$$
$$\text{Gross pay} - \text{FIT} - \text{FICA} - \text{Medicare} = \text{Net pay}$$

The $361.75 cash that The Home Depot pays the employee is called net pay or net wages. The withheld amounts are payable to the various governmental agencies designated. Here is how the company's accountant would record the disbursement to the employee.

EXHIBIT 7.2

Where Does Your Paycheck Go?

Everybody wants a piece of the payroll pie. The amounts that are withheld in this example don't include health insurance premiums, state income taxes, or retirement contributions. Most people take home even less than 72% of their gross pay.

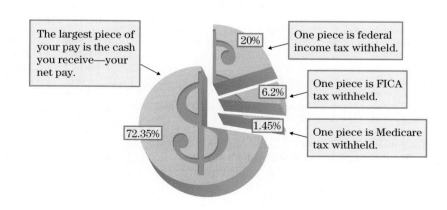

The largest piece of your pay is the cash you receive—your net pay.

One piece is federal income tax withheld. 20%

One piece is FICA tax withheld. 6.2%

One piece is Medicare tax withheld. 1.45%

72.35%

Assets	=	Liabilities	+	Shareholders' equity	
				Contributed capital	+ Retained earnings
(361.75) cash		100.00 FIT payable 31.00 FICA payable 7.25 Medicare taxes payable			(500) salary expense

When The Home Depot makes a payment to the government for social security and Medicare, the company will "match" those amounts. Often, these payments are made through the firm's bank. A company "deposits" its payroll taxes, which actually means the bank forwards the payment to the government for the company. Here is how The Home Depot would record the payment to the government, including the company's portion.

Assets	=	Liabilities	+	Shareholders' equity	
				Contributed capital	+ Retained earnings
(176.50) cash		(100.00) FIT payable (31.00) FICA payable (7.25) Medicare taxes payable			(38.25) payroll tax expense

There are other taxes the employer must pay to state and federal agencies, such as state and federal unemployment taxes. These are part of the employer's payroll expense.

Sandy earned $1,500 at her job at Paula's Bookstore during February. Sandy has 20% of her gross pay withheld for federal income taxes, 6.2% withheld for social security (FICA) taxes, and 1.45% withheld for Medicare taxes. What will be the net amount of Sandy's February paycheck? How will Paula's Bookstore record the payment to Sandy?

Your Turn 7-1
Your Turn
Your Turn

Long-Term Notes Payable and Mortgages

L.O.2
Explain how long-term notes and mortgages work.

You have learned how companies record current liabilities. In this section, you will learn how companies record long-term liabilities. When a company borrows money for longer than 1 year, that obligation is usually called a long-term note payable. Long-term notes differ from short-term notes in several ways. Recall from Chapter 2 that short-term notes are debt obligations that a company will repay in 1 year or sooner. A company may repay long-term notes in a lump sum at the note's maturity or with a series of equal payments over the life of the note. A car loan is an example of a loan with payments made over the life of the loan. The monthly payments are a combination of interest and principal. With each monthly payment, the borrower is paying that month's interest on the loan as well as paying back a small part of the principal balance due. Each month when the bank calculates the interest on the outstanding principal balance, the interest amount becomes a smaller portion of the payment. Why? Because the total amount of each payment stays the same, but the principal decreases. A larger part of each monthly payment is, therefore, available to reduce the outstanding principal.

Exhibit 7.3 shows why the interest amount on a loan becomes smaller for a loan of $100,000 with a 15-year term and an interest rate of 10% per year. The annual payment is the same every year, but the portion of the payment that is interest expense decreases, while the portion of the payment that reduces the outstanding principal balance increases.

A mortgage loan is a note payable that gives the lender a claim against that property if the borrower does not make payments. Like most long-term notes, mortgage loans are debt

EXHIBIT 7.3

Payments Comprised of Interest and Principal

This graph shows the payment schedule for a $100,000 loan for 15 years at 10% annual interest. There will be 15 annual payments of approximately $13,147 each. With each payment, the principal balance is reduced, so there is less interest expense each year. Because the payment stays the same, more of the payment goes toward reducing the principal each year. The graph shows how the proportion of interest in each payment decreases over time, while the proportion of principal in each payment increases over time.

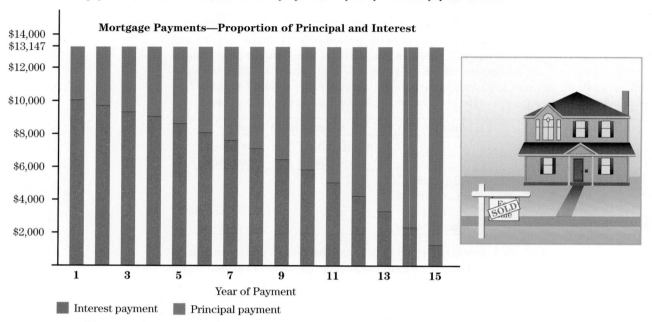

obligations commonly repaid in periodic installments—each payment is part principal and part interest.

Suppose you sign, on January 1, a $100,000, 3-year mortgage with SunTrust with an 8% annual interest rate to buy a piece of land. Payments are to be made annually on December 31 of each year in the amount of $38,803.35. How did SunTrust figure out that annual payment for the $100,000 loan for 3 years at 8% annual interest? The amount of the annual payment is based on a concept called the time value of money. "Time value of money" means there is value in having money for a period of time. That value is the interest the money can earn if invested.

The bank gives you $100,000 today, so you must repay that amount plus interest for the time you have that amount or any part of it. The bank calculates what it would receive if it invested the $100,000 for 3 years at an interest rate of 8%. That is the amount the bank expects to receive from you. The value today of the sum of those three payments in the future—a $38,803.35 payment at the end of each of the next 3 years—is called the **present value** (PV) of those three payments. Each payment is discounted to an amount equivalent to having the money today. When an amount of money earns interest, then that interest will itself earn interest during the time it is invested. Interest computed on both the principal and any interest earned but not paid or received is called compound interest.

Discounting the cash flows strips the amounts of the interest built in for the passage of time, bringing the cash flows back to equivalent dollars today. In this example, the dollars today amount to $100,000. The interest rate used in the calculation of present value amounts is also called the **discount rate**. In this example, the discount rate is 8%. In our mortgage example, $100,000 is the present value. SunTrust has calculated the three annual payments to be $38,803.35. The present value of those three payments, discounted at the interest rate of 8% per year, equals $100,000.

In this example, payments are annual, and the first payment will be made at the end of the first year of the loan. After the three payments, both the principal and the interest will be repaid. You can read about how to calculate present value in Appendix 7A at the end of this

The **present value** is the value today of a given amount to be invested or received in the future, assuming compound interest.

Discounting means to compute the present value of future cash flows.

The **discount rate** is the interest rate used to compute the present value of future cash flows.

Mortgage Balance		Annual Payment	Interest Portion of Payment (8% × mortgage balance)	Amount of Mortgage Reduction (annual payment − interest portion)
Beginning balance $100,000.00	1st	$38,803.35	$8,000.00	$30,803.35
After 1st payment $ 69,196.65	2nd	$38,803.35	$5,535.73	$33,267.62
After 2nd payment $ 35,929.03	3rd	$38,803.35	$2,874.32	$35,929.03
After 3rd payment -0-				

EXHIBIT 7.4

Amortization Schedule for a Mortgage

chapter. As you read how to make the computations, refer to Exhibit 7.4, which shows how each payment reduces the outstanding principal. This is called an amortization schedule for this loan.

How much of the first payment is interest expense and how much goes toward paying back the principal? Remember, interest is the cost of using someone else's money. The interest is based on the amount of the principal, the interest rate, and the amount of time for which the money is borrowed.

$$\text{Interest} = \text{Principal} \times \text{Rate} \times \text{Time}$$

The bank lends you $100,000 on Day 1 of the note. On Day 365, you make a $38,803.35 payment to the bank. The interest on the $100,000 for the year that has just passed is

$100,000 principal × 0.08 annual interest × 1 year = $8,000

You borrowed the entire $100,000 for a full year, so you multiply the principal by the annual rate and by the 1-year duration to get the interest expense for the year. Of the $38,803.35 payment, $8,000 is interest, so the remaining portion of the payment—$30,803.35—is repayment of principal. Here is how the first payment would be recorded.

Assets	=	Liabilities	+	Shareholders' equity		
				Contributed capital	+	Retained earnings
(38,803.35) cash		(30,803.35) mortgage payable				(8,000) interest expense

The principal of the mortgage has been reduced. In other words, the outstanding balance is lower—meaning you have less of the bank's money at the end of the first year.

Therefore, the interest owed the bank for the second year will be smaller than the interest paid for the first year. That is because the interest rate will be applied to a smaller principal—that is, a smaller outstanding balance. Again, we use the interest formula to calculate the portion of the payment that is interest for the second year, and then subtract the interest from the total payment to calculate the amount of the payment that reduces the principal.

- Outstanding balance due at the start of the second year: $69,196.65 ($100,000 original principal − $30,803.35 reduction in principal from the first payment)
- Interest expense for year 2: $69,196.65 principal for year 2 × 0.08 interest rate × 1 year = $5,535.73

The amount of interest you owe the bank is smaller each year because the outstanding balance of the note is smaller each year. At the end of year 2, the bank receives the second payment of $38,803.35. As the preceding calculation shows, $5,535.73 of that payment is interest expense. The rest of the payment—$33,267.62 ($38,803.35 − $5,535.73)—reduces the outstanding balance. After the second payment, the outstanding balance is $35,929.03. For the third payment of $38,803.35.

New principal = $35,929.03

Interest expense for year 3 = $35,929.03 × 0.08 × 1 = $2,874.32

When you subtract the interest of $2,874.32 from the third payment of $38,803.35, the remaining $35,929.03 reduces the principal—in this case, to zero. Is it just coincidence that the remaining outstanding balance is exactly that amount? No, the bank did the present value calculations with the principal, interest rate, and length of the loan so that it would come out to exactly that amount at the end of the third year.

Your Turn 7-2
Your Turn
Your Turn

Tompkins Corporation purchased a building on January 1 by signing a long-term $600,000 mortgage with monthly payments of $5,500. The mortgage carries an interest rate of 9% per year. How much of the first payment is interest and how much is principal?

UNDERSTANDING Business

Financing Your Business: Using A Line of Credit

Almost every company will need to borrow money during its life—sometimes to maintain a positive cash flow for regular operations and sometimes to expand or make other major changes to the business. Selecting the type of financing to obtain is a major business decision. In this chapter, the focus is on long-term financing. One common way to help a company manage its cash flow without long-term borrowing is called a line of credit. This is an excellent choice for financing the regular operations of a business.

What is a line of credit? It is an arrangement between a company and its bank in which the bank allows the company to borrow money for routine operating expenses up to the maximum amount of the credit line. The interest rate charged by the bank for this type of loan is usually much lower than the interest rate for credit card purchases, but it may be a bit higher than a typical bank loan for a specific amount and term. There is typically a short repayment "window" for a line of credit—60 to 90 days.

What kind of business should use a line of credit? First, the business must be a profitable, established business. Second, the business should have predictable cash flows. A line of credit works best when there is a predictable, temporary, short-term shortage of cash. The amount used—the amount borrowed—needs to be repaid in a short time to make a line of credit a cost-

effective financing choice. Having a line of credit is also a good choice for a company that does not have a current cash flow problem but would like a backup in case of a cash flow problem.

When is a line of credit a poor financing choice? If your company needs to make large purchases of major long-term assets, then a loan with a longer term and a lower interest rate would be a better type of financing. If the cash shortage is more than temporary, the company should make a long-term plan for a solution. It is also not a good idea to use a line of credit to pay employees. Payroll is an expense that should be a priority for a company's regular cash inflow. In most cases, a company that must borrow money to meet its payroll needs to rethink its financial situation.

What does a business need to provide to get a line of credit? One of the most important items a company should have is a set of financial statements, particularly a balance sheet and an income statement. In addition to the basic financial statements, a company should have a detailed schedule of projected cash inflows and outflows. Other important items are several years of tax returns, a list of current bank accounts, a current business plan, and appraisals of any assets that might be used as collateral.

Check out the financial statements of some well-known companies. You will find information about their lines of credit in the notes to the financial statements.

Long-Term Liabilities: Raising Money by Issuing Bonds

Long-term notes and mortgages are one way to borrow money with repayment over an extended period of time. Often, companies want to raise large amounts of money to build new stores or warehouses. One way to borrow this money is to issue bonds to the general public.

What Is a Bond?

A **bond** is an interest-bearing, long-term note payable issued by corporations, universities, and governmental agencies. Issuing bonds means a company is borrowing money from individual investors as well as other companies that want to invest. A bond certificate is a written agreement that specifies the company's responsibility to pay interest and repay the principal to the bondholders at the end of the term of the bond. The bond certificate will show the interest rate, the face amount of the bond, and the term of the bond. Exhibit 7.5 shows an actual bond certificate.

There are three main reasons why a company would borrow money by issuing bonds rather than going to a bank for a loan.

1. Firms can borrow more money from issuing bonds than a bank may be willing to lend.
2. Bondholders are typically willing to lend money for a longer time. Many bonds are 15-, 20-, or 30-year bonds. Some banks will not lend businesses money for such long periods

L.O.3
Record the issue of bonds and payment of interest to bondholders.

A **bond** is an interest-bearing, long-term note payable issued by corporations, universities, and governmental agencies.

EXHIBIT 7.5

Bond Certificate

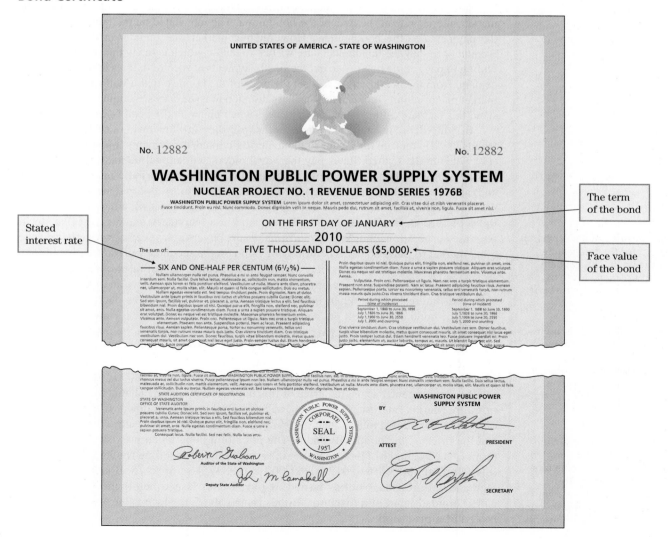

of time. Bondholders are willing to lend money for a long time because they can convert bonds into cash at any time by selling the bond to another investor in the bond market.

3. The rate of interest on a bond—the rate the borrower pays the bondholder—is commonly lower than the rate on loans charged by banks. Banks pay one rate of interest to people who deposit their money in saving accounts—the savings rate of interest—but charge a higher interest rate to lend money—the borrowing rate of interest.

A disadvantage to a firm of borrowing money by issuing bonds is that the firm may be restricted from borrowing additional money from other sources, or the firm may be required to maintain a certain debt-to-equity ratio—the ratio of liabilities to shareholders' equity. These restrictions, called bond covenants, are specified in the bond agreement to protect the interests of the bondholders. Recall that creditors, including bondholders, have priority over the claims of owners.

More about Bonds

Corporations issue bonds to raise money. Most bonds issued in the United States pay the bondholders annual or semiannual interest payments during the life of the bonds. The interest rate is given on the face of the bond. At a specific future date, called the maturity date, bondholders also receive a lump sum payment equal to the face amount of the bond. The face amount is also referred to as the stated value or the par value of the bond. Most bonds are issued with a face value in multiples of $1,000. The company borrowing the money is selling—or issuing—a legally binding promise to repay the buyer. The initial buyer is not really "buying" but rather lending the price paid for the bond.

The calculation of the payments to the bondholders is completely independent of the market interest rate at the date of the bond issue. The rate stated on the bonds determines the payments to the bondholders. However, the market rate of interest determines the amount of money the bondholders are willing to lend—which is really the amount they are willing to pay for the bonds—to get the fixed payments at specified times in the future. The demand from the bond market will set the price of the bond so that it will earn exactly the market rate of return. To make the business decision to issue bonds, a company must understand this fact and estimate the cash proceeds when planning the bond issue.

Bondholders are creditors of the company; they are not owners of the company. Bonds usually require the issuer to make periodic interest payments. Most bonds issued (i.e., sold) in the United States pay the bondholders semiannual interest payments during the life of the bonds. Bondholders are entitled to receive periodic interest payments and, at a specific future date called the maturity date, a lump sum payment equal to the amount given on the face of the bond. Most bonds are issued with a face value in multiples of $1,000. Bonds can be bought and sold in a secondary market. Just like stock, after the corporation completes the original issue, buyers and sellers get together via the bond market to trade bonds. The price of a bond on the secondary market will be different from the original bond price, depending on whether interest rates have increased or decreased since the date of the original bond issue. Bond prices have an inverse relationship with interest rates: When interest rates increase, bond prices decrease, and vice versa. The bond market will price the bond to yield the market rate for investments with similar risk. Because interest payments on a bond are fixed, when the market rate of interest goes down, those fixed rates look better. For example, suppose a $1,000 bond pays 9% interest per year. If the market rate of interest is 9%, the bond would sell for $1,000. If the market rate of interest goes up to 10%, this 9% bond of $1,000 is not as attractive as other investments. Thus, the price of this bond will go down. That is the inverse relationship: Market interest rate goes up, and the bond price goes down. If the market rate of interest goes down to 8%, then the 9% bond of $1,000 is a very attractive investment; and the price of the bond will go up. The price of a bond when it is issued is stated in terms of a percentage of its face value. If a bond is stated as selling for 98 3/8, that means it is selling for 98 3/8% of $1,000 ($1,000 × 0.98375), or $983.75. Bonds issued at the face amount are called **bonds issued at par**. Bonds issued below the face value are called **bonds issued at a discount**. Bonds issued above the face value are called **bonds issued at a premium**.

Bonds issued at par are bonds issued for the face value of the bond. This happens when the market rate of interest is equal to the bond's stated rate of interest.

Bonds issued at a discount are bonds issued for an amount less than the face value of the bond. This happens when the market rate of interest is greater than the bond's stated rate of interest.

Bonds issued at a premium are bonds issued for an amount more than the face value of the bond. This happens when the market rate of interest is less than the bond's stated rate of interest.

EXHIBIT 7.6

Types of Bonds

Type of Bond	Feature of the Bond or Description of the Bond
Secured	Give the bondholders a claim to a specific asset of the company in case of default
Unsecured (also known as debenture)	Are not linked to specific assets and are issued on the general credit of the company
Term	All mature on the same date
Serial	Mature periodically over a period of several years
Convertible	Give the bondholder the option of exchanging the bond for common stock
Callable	May be retired—called—prior to maturity at the option of the issuer for a specified amount of money
Zero interest (also known as zero coupon)	Pay no interest over the life of the bonds. (Interest is paid at the end of the life of the bond at the same time the principal is repaid.)
Junk	Have been downgraded by a bond-rating agency to below investment grade. (Ratings range from AAA—low risk bonds—to C or D. When a bond is rated BB or below, it is called a junk bond.)

- A bond that is selling at 100 is selling at par—100% of its face value.
- A bond selling below 100 is selling at a discount.
- A bond selling above 100 is selling at a premium.

There are many types of bonds. The common types are shown in Exhibit 7.6.

If a $1,000 bond is selling for 95 1/2, how much cash does the bondholder pay for the bond? If a $1,000 bond is selling for 102, how much cash does the bondholder pay for the bond?

Your Turn 7-3
Your Turn
Your Turn

Issuing Bonds Payable: Getting the Money

First, we will discuss how the market sets the price for a bond. Then, we will look at the details of a bond issued at various prices. Suppose Muzby Minerals issued a $1,000, zero interest bond due in 6 years. That means the bondholder will lend the company some amount of money—which we have not calculated yet—for a payment of $1,000 6 years from now. Zero interest means that no interest will be paid during the life of the bond. This type of bond is sometimes called a zero coupon bond. How much would you pay for this bond? Clearly, you would pay something less than $1,000. That is because $1,000 cash today is worth more than $1,000 cash in 6 years. You could invest the $1,000 today and have more than $1,000 in 6 years because you could earn interest on the money.

The amount you would pay for this $1,000, 6-year, zero interest bond is the amount you would need to invest today to have it grow to $1,000 in 6 years. Recall from our discussion of mortgages that this amount is its present value, and finding the present value of a future cash flow is called discounting the future amount. You would pay the present value for the bond to receive $1,000 in 6 years. To calculate the bond's price, you need to know the market rate of interest. That is the interest rate investors demand for lending money to the firm. The **market rate of interest** for a particular bond is considered the interest rate that an investor could earn in an equally risky investment. Suppose the market rate of interest is 4%. How much would you pay for the $1,000, 6-year, zero interest bond? You would pay the present value of $1,000 discounted back 6 years using 4%. That value is $790.31. You would lend Muzby Minerals $790.31, and the firm would pay you $1,000 at the end of 6 years. If you could find a bank to pay you 4% annually on your deposit of $790.31, it would grow to be $1,000 in 6 years.

> *Note to students: You can read about the time value of money in the appendix to the chapter. If you have not studied the time value of money previously, you will need to read the appendix before you go on.*

The **market rate of interest** is the interest rate that an investor could earn in an equally risky investment.

Bonds Issued at Par. Most bonds are not zero interest but instead have interest payments made to the bondholders over the life of the bond. Suppose Muzby Minerals issued a $1,000 bond for 6 years with a stated interest rate of 5%. Exhibit 7.7 shows the cash flows associated with this bond.

If the market rate of interest and the stated rate of interest on the bond are the same, investors will pay exactly the face value for the bonds. As you learned in the last section, bonds issued with a stated rate equal to the market rate are said to be issued at par. This is how Muzby Minerals would record the issue of a $1,000 bond at par.

Assets	=	Liabilities	+	Shareholders' equity		
					Contributed capital	+ Retained earnings
1,000 cash		1,000 bonds payable				

Bonds Issued at a Discount. However, if the market rate were more than 5%, investors would pay less for the bond than the face value because it would not take an amount as high as $1,000 today to cover the future 5% interest payments and the principal payment at the end of the life of the bonds. The present value of the cash flows would be less than $1,000, so the bonds would sell at less than par. When bonds are issued with a stated rate less than the market rate, the bonds are said to be issued at a discount.

Suppose the market rate of interest was 5.5% when the bond was issued. Because investors would require this return, the bonds must sell for less than $1,000. To calculate the issue price, you take the present value of the future cash flows associated with the bond. In other words, how much will the bondholders pay to receive $50 at the end of each of the next 6 years along with $1,000 at the end of year 6?

There are several ways to calculate the present value of these cash flows, and you should be sure to review Appendix 7A, Time Value of Money, if you have any difficulty understanding how these calculations are done. In this example, we will use values from present value tables such as those found in Appendix 7A.

PV of $50 payments for 6 years using a discount rate of 5.5% =

50	×	4.9955	=	$249.78	
payments		PV of an annuity 5.5%, 6 years		PV of the interest payments	

plus the PV of $1,000 in 6 years =

$1,000	×	0.72524	=	$725.24	
payment		PV of $1 5.5%, 6 years		PV of the payment	

$975.02

EXHIBIT 7.7

Cash Flows Defined by a Six-Year, $1,000, 5% Bond

It may be helpful to think of a bond as a series of cash payments. When a firm issues a bond, it is selling the bondholder a series of future payments. How much the bondholder will pay for those cash payments depends on the market rate of interest at the time the bonds are issued.

Year	0	1	2	3	4	5	6
Cash flow to bondholder		$50	$50	$50	$50	$50	$50 $1,000

Each cash flow is discounted back to today's value.

The issue price of this bond would be $975.02. This is how Muzby Minerals would record the issue of this bond.

Assets	=	Liabilities	+	Shareholders' equity	
				Contributed capital	+ **Retained earnings**
975.02 cash		1,000.00 bonds payable (24.98) discount on bonds payable			

The account called **discount on bonds payable** is a contra-liability account. You learned about contra-accounts in Chapter 3. Every contra-account has a partner account. For example, the contra-account *accumulated depreciation* is partnered with a fixed asset account such as *equipment*. Discount on bonds payable is shown on the balance sheet with its partner account bonds payable, and it is a deduction from the balance in bonds payable. Contra-accounts are considered valuation accounts. They are used to value the associated asset or liability. In the long-term liabilities portion of the balance sheet, the bond would be reported net of the balance in its discount account. The net value of bonds payable is also called the **carrying value** of the bonds. This is how the bond would be reported on the balance sheet on the date of issue.

Bonds payable	$1,000.00
Less discount on bonds payable	(24.98)
Net bonds payable	$ 975.02

> **Discount on bonds payable** is a contra-liability that is deducted from bonds payable on the balance sheet; it is the difference between the face value of the bond and its selling price, when the selling price is less than the face (par) value.

> The **carrying value** of a bond is the amount that the balance sheet shows as the net value of the bond, similar in meaning to the carrying value of a fixed asset. It is equal to the face value of the bond minus any discount or plus any premium.

Suppose Action Company issues a $1,000, 10-year, 11.5% bond at a time when the market interest rate is 12%. What are the proceeds—cash received by Action Company—from this bond issue?

Your Turn 7-4
Your Turn
Your Turn

Bonds Issued at a Premium. If, on the other hand, the market rate of interest were less than 5%, investors would have to pay more for the bond than the face value because it would take more than $1,000 today to cover the future 5% interest payments and the principal payment at the end of the life of the bonds. The present value of the cash flows would be greater than $1,000, so the bonds would sell for more than par value. When bonds are issued with a stated rate higher than the market rate, the bonds are said to be issued at a premium. The amount of the proceeds in excess of par is called the **premium on bonds payable**.

Suppose the market rate of interest was 4.5% when the bond was issued. Because investors would require this return and the market would price the bonds to yield this return, the bonds would sell for more than $1,000. Think of the extra amount as that needed to help the company meet interest payments of 5%, the face rate. Just as with a discount situation, the issue price is equal to the present value of the future cash flows associated with the bond. In other words, how much will the bondholders pay to receive $50 at the end of each of the next 6 years along with $1,000 at the end of year 6?

> **Premium on bonds payable** is an adjunct-liability that is added to bonds payable on the balance sheet; it is the difference between the face value of the bond and its selling price, when the selling price is more than the face (par) value.

The present value of the future cash flows is calculated as follows.

PV of $50 payments for 6 years using a discount rate of 4.5% =

50 × 5.15787 = $257.89 ⎤

plus the PV of $1,000 in 6 years =   ⎬ $1,025.79

1,000 × 0.76790 = $767.90 ⎦

The issue price of this bond would be $1,025.79. This is how Muzby Minerals would record the issue of this bond.

Assets	=	Liabilities	+	Shareholders' equity	
				Contributed + capital	Retained earnings
1,025.79 cash		1,000.00 bonds payable 25.79 premium on bonds payable			

The amount of the face value of the bond (bonds payable at $1,000) and the premium on bonds payable (at $25.79) are both liabilities. They appear next to each other on the balance sheet. **Premium on bonds payable** is called an adjunct liability. Adjunct means an add-on and describes the relationship between bonds payable and premium on bonds payable. The premium on bonds payable is a partner of the bonds payable liability it is paired with, and they are added together on the balance sheet. This is how this bond would be shown on the balance sheet—its carrying value—on its issue date.

Bonds payable	$1,000.00
Plus premium on bonds payable	25.79
Net bonds payable	$1,025.79

Your Turn 7-5
Your Turn
Your Turn

Suppose HPS Company issues a $1,000 face value, 10-year, 11.5% bond, with interest payable annually. At the time of issue, the market interest rate is 10%. How much money will HPS get for the bond?

Paying the Bondholders

Remember, no matter how much the bondholder pays for the bond—whether the issue price is above or below the price stated on the bond—the series of payments is established by what is printed on the face of the bond. That series of cash flows is what the bondholder is buying. In this example with a single bond issued by Muzby Minerals, the cash flows are set at $50 interest annually and a lump sum of $1,000 at maturity.

However, there are some complications related to the accounting records of the firm that issued the bonds. Now we will turn to the accounting for bonds issued for more or less than the face value.

Amortizing Bond Discounts and Premiums: Effective Interest Method. Bond discounts and bond premiums are written off over the life of the bonds. The carrying value of the bond on the date of maturity needs to be its face value because that is exactly the amount of the liability on the date of maturity. That means the amount of the discount or premium must be reduced over the life of the bond until it reaches zero. The amortization of bond premiums or discounts is a natural result of calculating the correct amount of interest expense for the period when the company makes an interest payment to the bondholder. Remember, the amount of the cash payments to the bondholders is established before the bond is issued. **But when bonds are issued at a discount or at a premium, the cash payment and the interest expense are not equal.**

Amortizing a Discount To show how a discount is written off, we will continue the example of a bond issued at a discount—a $1,000 bond issued for $975.02. The stated rate of interest on the bond is 5% and the market rate of interest is 5.5%. When the bonds are issued, the carrying value of the liability, which equals bonds payable minus the discount, is $975.02 ($1,000 − $24.98). Each time interest is paid to the bondholders, a portion of the discount is written off. The amount of the write-off is the difference between the interest expense and the cash interest payment to the bondholders.

Suppose the bond is issued on January 1. The first interest payment to the bondholders, on December 31, will be $50 ($1,000 × 0.05 × 1 year). The interest expense—shown on the income statement—is not equal to the cash interest payment to the bondholders. The interest expense is calculated using the usual interest rate formula.

$$\text{Interest} = \text{Principal} \times \text{Rate} \times \text{Time}$$

In this case, the principal amount borrowed is $975.02. That is the amount the bondholders actually lent the company on the date of the bond issue. The interest rate the bondholders are actually earning is 5.5%— the market rate at the date of issue, and the time period is 1 year.

$$\$975.02 \times 5.5\% \times 1 \text{ year} = \$53.63$$

The difference between the cash interest payment of $50 and the interest expense of $53.63 is the amount that reduces the discount. After the payment is made, the discount is reduced by $3.63. The discount that began with $24.98 at issue is now reduced to $21.35. The same thing happens each time a payment is made. The amount of the discount is reduced. The accounting terminology for that process is called writing off or *amortizing* the discount, and this method is called the effective interest method of amortization. The value of the bonds payable minus the unamortized discount is called the carrying value or book value of the bonds. Remember, that is the net amount added to the total liabilities on the balance sheet. Over the life of the bonds, the discount is amortized, so that the carrying value of the bonds at the date of maturity is exactly the face value. In other words, the amount of the discount is reduced—a portion at each interest payment date—to zero over the life of the bond.

When the firm makes the $50 payment of the bondholders on the first interest payment date, the firm actually owes the bondholder an additional $3.63. Because the payment to the bondholder is fixed, the extra $3.63 will be added to the outstanding principal balance of $975.02. After the first interest payment, the new principal balance is $978.65 ($975.02 + $3.63). The $3.63—the difference between the interest expense and the interest payment—is amortization of the discount. The payment to the bondholder of $50 and the discount amortization affects the accounting equation as follows:

Assets	=	Liabilities	+	Shareholders' equity	
				Contributed capital	+	Retained earnings
(50) cash		3.63 discount on bonds payable			(53.63) interest expense

Remember that the discount is a contra-liability. That is, the discount is subtracted from the bonds payable. As it is amortized, a smaller amount is subtracted from the face value of the bonds, until zero is subtracted from bonds payable. Thus, a reduction in the discount is actually an increase in total liabilities.

Without getting too technical, we will try to reason out why issuing a bond at a discount results in interest expense that is greater than the actual cash payment to the bondholder. Because the interest rate in the market is higher than the interest rate the bond is paying, the difference between the $1,000 face amount to be repaid and the $975.02 issue price may be thought of as some extra interest—in addition to the periodic interest payments—that the bond issuer must pay to borrow the $975.02. Each time an interest payment is made to the bondholder, a small portion of the discount is written off as interest expense. At the maturity date of the bond, the discount will be zero.

The amortization table for this bond is shown in Exhibit 7.8. Notice what happens over the life of the bond. The payment is exactly the same each year. However, because a discount is used to reduce the face value of the bonds to the amount actually owed, the discount must get smaller. What is the goal? You want the discount to be zero at maturity. A discount of zero means the book value of the bonds equals the face value of the bonds.

EXHIBIT 7.8

Amortization Schedule for a Bond Issued at a Discount

In this case, a $1,000 bond with a stated interest rate of 5% has been issued at a discount because the market rate of interest is 5.5%. To sell the bond, the firm must offer it at a discount. The actual return to the bondholder will be 5.5%.

	(1) Beginning carrying value	(2) Cash payment $1,000 \times 0.05$	(3) Interest expense $(1) \times .055$	(4) Amortization of discount $(3) - (2)$	(5) Ending carrying value $(1) + (4)$
Year 1	$975.02	$50.00	$53.63	$3.63	$ 978.65
Year 2	978.65	50.00	53.83	3.83	982.47
Year 3	982.47	50.00	54.04	4.04	986.51
Year 4	986.51	50.00	54.26	4.26	990.77
Year 5	990.77	50.00	54.49	4.49	995.26
Year 6	995.26	50.00	54.74	4.74	1,000.00

Your Turn 7-6
Your Turn
Your Turn

Try this example with semiannual interest payments. Just divide the annual interest rate by 2 and count the periods as the number of 6-month periods.

Knollwood Corp. issued $200,000 of 6% per year, 20-year bonds at 98 on January 1, 2003. The market rate of interest was approximately 6.5%. Interest is paid on June 30 and on December 31. The company uses the effective interest method of amortization. How much interest expense will Knollwood show on the income statement for the year ending December 31, 2003? What is the carrying value of the bonds on the balance sheet at December 31, 2003?

Amortizing a Premium   We will now use the same bond but assume it was issued at a premium. Recall, the market rate of interest of 4.5% is lower than the stated rate on the bond of 5%, so the bondholder will pay a premium for the bond's series of payments. In this example, the amount the bondholder pays—which we should not forget is actually a loan to the firm—is $1,025.79 for the bond. Just as it is calculated for a bond issued at a discount, the interest expense for bonds issued at a premium is calculated using the market rate interest. For the first year, the interest expense is

$$\textbf{Interest = Principal} \times \textbf{Rate} \times \textbf{Time}$$
$$\text{Interest} = \$1,025.79 \times 4.5\% \times 1 \text{ year} = \$46.16$$

When the bond issuer makes the cash payment of $50, that amount pays the bondholder the interest for the first year plus a small amount of the principal. The amount of principal paid off is the difference between the cash interest payment and the interest expense.

$$\$50 \text{ payment} - \$46.16 \text{ interest expense} = \$3.84$$

This $3.84 is amortization of the premium on bonds payable. The premium of $25.79 will be reduced a little bit each time the bond issuer makes an interest payment to the bondholder, until the premium is zero at maturity. At maturity, the bond issuer pays the bondholder the $1,000 face amount. The following shows how the interest payment to the bondholder affects the accounting equation.

Assets	=	Liabilities	+	Shareholders' equity	
				Contributed capital	+ Retained earnings
(50) cash		(3.84) premium on bonds payable			(46.16) interest expense

Issuing a bond at a premium results in interest expense (to the bond issuer) that is less than the actual cash payment of interest to the bondholder because the 4.5% interest rate in the market is lower than the 5% interest rate specified on the bond. With that in mind, we can think of the premium the bondholder paid as a payment in advance to the bond issuer to help meet the 5% payment due the bondholder. Each time a cash payment for interest is made to the bondholder, a little of the premium is written off. How much? The difference between the cash interest payment and the interest expense will be the amount of the premium amortization. At maturity, the premium will be zero.

	(1) Beginning carrying value	(2) Cash payment $1,000 × 0.05	(3) Interest expense (1) × .045	(4) Amortization of premium (2) – (3)	(5) Ending carrying value (1) – (4)
Year 1	$1,025.79	$50.00	$46.16	$3.84	$1,021.95
Year 2	1,021.95	50.00	45.99	4.01	1,017.94
Year 3	1,017.94	50.00	45.81	4.19	1,013.74
Year 4	1,013.74	50.00	45.62	4.38	1,009.36
Year 5	1,009.36	50.00	45.42	4.58	1,004.78
Year 6	1,004.78	50.00	45.22	4.78	1,000.00

EXHIBIT 7.9

Amortization Schedule for a Bond Issued at a Premium

In this case, a $1,000 bond with a stated interest rate of 5% has been issued at a premium because the market rate of interest is 4.5%. The bondholder must pay more than the face to buy the bond. The actual return to the bondholder will be 4.5%.

The amortization table for this bond is shown in Exhibit 7.9. Notice what happens over the life of the bond. The payment is exactly the same each year. However, because a premium is used to increase the face value of the bonds beyond the amount that will actually be owed at maturity, the premium must get smaller. What is the goal? You want the premium to be zero at maturity. A premium of zero means the book value of the bonds equals the face value of the bonds.

On January 1, 2007, Wood Corp. issued $200,000 of 20-year, 10% interest bonds when the market rate of interest was 9%. Interest is paid annually on December 31. The company uses the effective interest method of amortization. How much interest expense will Wood show on the income statement for the year ending December 31, 2007? What is the carrying value of the bonds on the balance sheet at December 31, 2007?

Your Turn 7-7
Your Turn
Your Turn

Straight-Line Amortization of Bond Discounts and Premiums. In addition to the effective interest method of amortizing a bond discount or premium, there is another method sometimes used called the straight-line method. Straight-line amortization simply divides the premium or discount equally over the number of interest payment periods. The effective interest method makes logical sense with respect to interest expense being calculated on the outstanding principal, but there is no particular logic to the straight-line method. It is a simple calculation, much easier than the effective interest method, and this simplicity is its only attractive feature. Straight-line amortization often does a poor job of matching and is not part of generally accepted accounting principles (GAAP). However, if the straight-line method and the effective interest method produce similar amounts for interest expense and for net bonds payable, the accounting standards allow the use of the straight-line method of amortization.

We will look at the last example—6-year bonds, 5% stated rate, $1,000 face value, market rate at issue of 4.5%—and see how straight-line amortization works. Recall, the bond will be issued at a premium, and we calculated the issue price to be $1,025.79. The difference between the face value of $1,000 and the issue price of $1,025.79 is a premium. We

---

▶ *News Flash*

If you invest in corporate bonds, would you be worried about your money? According to some experts, corporate debt is beginning to worry bondholders. As more corporate executives turn to debt for cash they need to "feed investors with share repurchases, dividends, and empire-building exercises," some bondholders are beginning to worry. During the first half of 2006, the amount of investment-grade bonds issued by nonfinancial companies increased by 72% over a year earlier.

(*Source:* "Corporate Debt Begins to Worry Bond Investors," by Serena Ng, *The Wall Street Journal*, July 11, 2006, p. C1.)

EXHIBIT 7.10

Straight-Line Amortization of a Bond Issued at a Premium

The premium of $25.79 is simply divided evenly over the life of the bond when straight-line amortization is used.

	(1) Beginning carrying value	(2) Cash payment $1,000 × 0.05	(3) Amortization of premium $25.79 ÷ 6	(4) Interest expense (2) – (3)	(5) Ending carrying value
Year 1	$1,025.79	$50.00	$4.30	$45.70	$1,021.49
Year 2	1,021.49	50.00	4.30	45.70	1,017.19
Year 3	1,017.19	50.00	4.30	45.70	1,012.89
Year 4	1,012.89	50.00	4.30	45.70	1,008.60
Year 5	1,008.60	50.00	4.30	45.70	1,004.30
Year 6	1,004.30	50.00	4.30	45.70	1,000.00

have already seen how the premium of $25.79 would be amortized using the effective interest method, shown in Exhibit 7.9. Now we will amortize the premium using the straight-line method. First, divide the premium by the number of interest payments to the bondholders. That means the same amount will be amortized each time an interest payment is made. In this example, in which the premium is $25.79, the amount of premium amortized will be $4.30 (rounded) per year. The amortization schedule using straight-line amortization is shown in Exhibit 7.10.

To use the straight-line method of amortization, you do not need to know the market interest rate to calculate the interest expense. Each period the interest expense is the same; the amortization of the discount or premium is the same; and, of course, the payment is the same. You can see how that makes the calculations easy. However, remember that it is only permissible to use the straight-line method when the interest expense calculated with this method is not significantly different than the interest expense calculated using the effective interest method. The numbers in this example are small, and the difference does not seem to be significant. When a company has hundreds of thousands or even millions of dollars of bonds outstanding, the two methods can produce vastly different amounts of interest expense.

Tom's Wear for July

L.O.4
Prepare financial statements that include payroll and long-term debt.

When Tom started his T-shirt business in January, he borrowed a small amount of money from his mom. Now that he has the business up and running, Tom decides he needs more space for inventory and for the actual business operations. This is crucial if he wants to take advantage of the demand for his shirts. Tom finds an excellent deal on a small office complex with a large warehouse; so he goes to his local bank and secures a mortgage loan for $75,000, the cost of the office complex. The transactions for July are shown in Exhibit 7.11, and the balance sheet at July 1 is shown in Exhibit 7.12. Remember that this is the same as the June 30 balance sheet from Chapter 6, Exhibit 6.15.

Here is some additional information needed to make the month-end adjustments.

1. The van was driven 10,000 miles this month.
2. Bad debts expense and warranty expense are calculated based on the same percentages as Tom's Wear used in June: 3% of credit sales for bad debts and 2% of sales for warranties.

First, we will use an accounting equation worksheet to record the transactions and the necessary adjustments. Then prepare the four basic financial statements for Tom's Wear for the month of July. As usual, we will simply ignore income taxes.

Trace each transaction in Exhibit 7.11 to the accounting equation worksheet in Exhibit 7.13. At the bottom of the worksheet, you can find some details of the more complex transactions. The inventory transactions are summarized, and the computations for the payroll are provided. After you study the transactions, look at the adjustments, A-1 through A-9. Identifying the needed adjustments is often the job of a firm's accounting staff.

From the accounting equation worksheet, you can prepare the financial statements. Exhibit 7.14 shows the four basic financial statements. You should be able to see where the amounts on the financial statements have come from on the accounting equation worksheet.

EXHIBIT 7.11

Transactions for Tom's Wear for July

1 July 1	For a new office complex, Tom's Wear borrows $75,000 at an annual interest rate of 8% for a term of 15 years. The terms of the loan call for quarterly payments of principal and interest. The first payment will be made on September 30. (Even though you won't record the actual payment until September 30, can you figure out what the payment will be?) As part of the decision to buy the office complex, the firm had an appraisal done on the land and building. Recall, we discussed "market basket" purchases in Chapter 4. Tom's Wear must separate the cost of the land and building, so the firm can depreciate only the building. The land was appraised at 10% of the purchase price and the building at 90%. The building has an estimated useful life of 40 years and an estimated residual value of $5,100. The firm will use straight-line depreciation.
2 July 5	Pays Sam's June salary and deposits the related payroll taxes (Check out the July 1 balance sheet for the accrued amounts.)
3 July 10–30	Collects cash on accounts receivable of $37,000.
4 July 12	Pays accounts payable of $18,950.
5 July 14	Tom's Wear has been concentrating on increasing sales, so the firm must increase inventory purchases as well. The firm has found a supplier who will give a significant discount with a large-quantity purchase, so the company purchases 10,000 T-shirts. The cost is $3.60 each. The shipping terms are FOB destination. Tom's Wear makes the purchase on account.
6 July 20	Tom's Wear finds out that Big Bend Sports has closed and filed for bankruptcy. The firm writes off their account, which has a balance of $1,000.
7 July 15–30	Tom's Wear's sales efforts continue to pay off with the addition of several more sporting goods stores as customers. During July, the firm sells 9,000 shirts for $11 each to 18 different stores. All sales are on account.
8 July 15–30	During July, 200 shirts are returned with defects. Tom's Wear replaces all of them with new shirts.
9 July 15–30	Pays other operating expenses of $2,600 for the month.
10 July 30	Tom's Wear has hired more people so the payroll has increased. Gross pay (including Sam Cubbie's salary) for July is $3,251.28. FICA is 6.2%; FIT is 20%; Medicare tax is 1.45%. Remember that Tom's Wear must match the FICA and Medicare taxes. Actual cash payments to the employees and payment for the withholding taxes are paid the following month.
11 July 30	Pays dividends of $2,000.

EXHIBIT 7.12

Tom's Wear Balance Sheet at July 1

tom's wear

Tom's Wear, Inc.
Balance Sheet
At July 1

Assets		Liabilities & Shareholder's Equity	
Current assets		**Current liabilities**	
Cash	$ 8,278	Accounts payable	$ 18,950
Accounts receivable		Interest payable	750
(net of allowance of $1,320)	42,780	Warranty liability	979
Inventory	6,365	Salaries payable	723
Prepaid insurance	150	Current portion of long-	
Prepaid rent	1,800	term note payable	6,000
Prepaid Web services	200	Other payables	354
Total current assets	59,573	Total current liabilities	27,756
		Notes payable	24,000
		Total liabilities	51,756
Equipment (net of $400			
accumulated depreciation)	3,600	**Shareholder's Equity**	
Van (net of $2,755 accumulated		Common stock	5,000
depreciation)	27,245	Retained earnings	33,662
		Total liabilities and	
		shareholder's equity	$ 90,418
Total assets	$ 90,418		

EXHIBIT 7.13

Accounting Equation Worksheet for Tom's Wear for July

Assets = Liabilities + Shareholder's Equity

	Cash	Accounts Receivable	Allowance for Uncollectible Accounts	Inventory**	Prepaid Insurance	Prepaid Rent	Prepaid Web Service	Equipment (Computer)	Acc. Depr. Equipment	Van	Acc. Depr. Van	Land	Buildings	Acc. Depr. Bldg.	Accounts Payable	Salaries Payable	Interest Payable	Other Payables▲	Warranties Payable	Current Portion of Mortgage Payable▼	Mortgage Payable	Current Portion of Long-Term Notes Payable	Long-Term Notes Payable	Common Stock	Revenues	Expenses	Dividends
BB*	8,278	44,100	(1,320)	6,365	150	1,800	200	4,000	(400)	30,000	(2,755)	7,500	67,500		18,950	723	750	354	979	2,710	72,290	6,000	24,000	5,000			
1.	(1,077)																										
2.	37,000	(37,000)																									
3.	(18,950)			36,000											(18,950)												
4.															36,000												
5.																											
6.		(1,000)	1,000																								
7.		99,000																							99,000		
8.				(32,735)																						(32,735)	
9.	(2,600)			(720)															(720)							(2,600)	
10.																										(3,500)	
11.	(2,000)															2,352		1,148									(2,000)
A-1					(100)																					(100)	
A-2						(1,200)																				(1,200)	
A-3							(50)																			(50)	
A-4									(100)																	(100)	
A-5											(1,450)															(1,450)	
A-6														(130)												(130)	
A-7																	250									(250)	
A-8																	500									(500)	
A-9			(2,970)																							(2,970)	
A-10																			1,980							(1,980)	
	20,651	105,100	(3,290)	8,910	50	600	150	4,000	(500)	30,000	(4,205)	7,500	67,500	(130)	36,000	2,352	1,500	1,148	2,239	2,710	72,290	6,000	24,000	5,000	99,000	(47,565)	(2,000)
															236,336										83,007		

Check figures = 236,336

* BB beginning balances
** Beginning inventory:
1,675 shirts @ 3.80 = $ 6,365
Purchases
10,000 @ 3.60 = $ 36,000

Sale of 9,000 shirts:
1,675 @ 3.80 = $6,365
+ 7,325 @ 3.60 = $26,370
Total CGS $ (32,735)
Returns $ (720)
EI $ 8,910

Payroll computations:

	Gross pay	FICA	Medicare	FIT	Match
	$3,251.28	6.20%	1.45%	20%	7.65%
		201.58	47.14	650.26	248.72

Net pay = $3,251.28 − 201.58 − 47.14 − 650.26 = $2,352 (rounded)
Salary expense = $3,251.28 + 248.72 = $3,500

▲Other payables = FICA + Medicare + FIT + Match = 1147.7 = $1,148 (rounded)

▼Current portion of long-term mortgage:

Payment at 8%, 15 years, quarterly payment =
2% quarterly, 60 payments, PV = $75,000 =
PV of an annuity, 2%, 60 periods *PMT = 75,000
PMT = 75,000 ÷ 34.7608 = $2,157.60

Beginning mortgage balance	2%	Payment	Reduction in mortgage balance
75,000.00	1,500.00	2,157.60	657.60
74,342.40	1,486.85	2,157.60	670.75
73,671.65	1,473.43	2,157.60	684.17
72,987.48	1,459.75	2,157.60	697.85
72,289.63	1,445.79	2,157.60	711.81
71,577.82	1,431.56	2,157.60	726.04
70,851.78	1,417.04	2,157.60	740.56

Payments due in the coming year: $2,710.37

EXHIBIT 7.14

Financial Statements
for Tom's Wear
for July 2006

Tom's Wear, Inc.
Income Statement
For the Month Ended July 31

Revenues:		
Sales		$ 99,000
Expenses:		
Cost of goods sold	$ 32,735	
Insurance expense	100	
Rent expense	1,200	
Depreciation expense	1,680	
Salary expense	3,500	
Interest expense	750	
Warranty expense	1,980	
Bad debts expense	2,970	
Other operating expenses	2,650	
		47,565
Net income		$ 51,435

Tom's Wear, Inc.
Statement of Changes in Shareholder's Equity
For the Month Ended July 31

Common stock		
Beginning balance		$ 5,000
New stock issued during the month		–
Ending balance		$ 5,000
Retained earnings:		
Beginning balance		$ 33,662
+ Net income		51,435
– Dividends		(2,000)
Ending balance		$83,097
Total shareholder's equity		$ 88,097

Tom's Wear, Inc.
Statement of Cash Flows
For the Month Ended July 31

Cash from operating activities:		
Cash collected from customers	$ 37,000	
Cash paid to vendors	(18,950)	
Cash paid for operating expense	(3,677)	
		$ 14,373
Cash from investing activities:		–
Cash from financing activities:		
Dividends paid	(2,000)	
		(2,000)
Increase in cash		$ 12,373
Add beginning cash		8,278
Ending cash balance		$20,651

Tom's Wear, Inc.
Balance Sheet
At July 31

Assets			Liabilities & Shareholder's Equity		
Current assets			Current liabilities		
Cash		$20,651	Accounts payable		$ 36,000
Accounts receivable (net of			Interest payable		1,500
$3,290 allowance for uncollectible			Warranty liability		2,239
accounts)		101,810	Salaries payable		2,352
Inventory		8,910	Other payables		1,148
Prepaid insurance		50	Current portion of		
Prepaid rent		600	mortgage payable		2,710
Prepaid Web services		150	Current portion of long-		
Total current assets		132,171	term notes payable		6,000
			Total current liabilities		51,949
Land		7,500	Mortgage payable		72,290
Equipment (net of $500			Notes payable		24,000
accumulated depreciation)		3,500	Total liabilities		148,239
Van (net of $4,205					
accumulated depreciation)		25,795	Shareholder's Equity		
Building (net of $130			Common stock		5,000
accumulated depreciation)		67,370	Retained earnings		83,097
			Total liabilities and		
			Shareholder's equity		$236,336
Total assets		$236,336			

L.O.5
Explain capital structure and compute the debt-to-equity and the times-interest-earned ratios.

Capital structure is the combination of debt and equity that a firm uses to finance its business.

Financial leverage is the use of borrowed funds to increase earnings.

Applying Your Knowledge:
Financial Statement Analysis

You know that the two ways to finance a business are debt and equity. The combination of debt and equity that a company chooses is called its **capital structure**. That is because debt and equity are the two sources of capital, and every company can choose the proportion of each that makes up its total capital.

When should a company borrow money? A very simplistic cost-benefit analysis would suggest that when the benefit of borrowing the money—what it can earn for the business—exceeds the cost of borrowing the money—interest expense—then borrowing money is a good idea. Look back at The Home Depot's balance sheet in Exhibit 7.1 on page 333. The Home Depot's total debt is $17,573 million at January 29, 2006. That is almost 40% of its financing (debt + shareholders' equity = $44,482 million at January 29, 2006). How does the company's percentage of total debt compare with other firms in related industries? At February 3, 2006, Lowe's had total liabilities of $10,343 million and total debt plus shareholders' equity of $24,682 million. Debt is almost 42% of Lowe's capital structure. There is no rule about how much debt a firm should have. If you take a finance course, you will study the topic of optimal capital structure and find there is no simple answer.

Closely related is the concept of **financial leverage**, which means using borrowed funds to increase earnings. If a company earns more with the money it borrows than it must pay to borrow that money, it is called positive financial leverage. Suppose Anna Chase has invested $50,000 in her new business and has no debt. If the business earns $5,000 net income during the year, then she has earned a return on her investment of 10%. Suppose Anna wants to expand her business. She might earn an additional $5,000 the next year if she borrows an additional $50,000. If the after-tax cost of borrowing the money is 8%, then Anna would be taking advantage of financial leverage if she borrows the money. That is because earnings could increase by more than the cost of borrowing the money. The new total income for the second year—$5,000 + $5,000 − $4,000 interest—would be $6,000. Anna's return on equity for the second year is $6,000 ÷ $50,000 = 12%.

Two financial ratios measure a company's debt position and its ability to meet its interest payments. The first is the **debt-to-equity ratio**.

$$\text{Debt-to-equity ratio} = \frac{\text{Total liabilities}}{\text{Total shareholders' equity}}$$

This ratio compares the amount of creditors' claims to the assets of the firm with owners' claims to the assets of the firm. A firm with a high debt-to-equity ratio is often referred to as a highly leveraged firm. A debt-to-equity ratio around 100% (half debt and half equity) is quite common. Exhibit 7.15 shows the debt-to-equity ratios for McDonald's and Wendy's.

The second ratio related to long-term debt is called the **times-interest-earned ratio**. This ratio measures a company's ability to meet its interest obligations.

$$\text{Times-interest-earned ratio} = \frac{\text{Income from operations}}{\text{Interest expense}}$$

It is important to make sure you have excluded the company's interest expense from the numerator. The ratio measures the number of times operating income can cover interest ex-

EXHIBIT 7.15
Debt-to-Equity Ratios for McDonald's and Wendy's

	McDonald's At Dec. 31, 2005	Wendy's At January 1, 2006
Total debt	$ 10,140	$ 1,382
Total shareholder's equity	$ 15,146	$ 2,059
Debt-to-equity ratio	66.9%	67.1%

	McDonald's FYE Dec. 31, 2005	Wendy's FYE January 1, 2006
	(dollars in thousands)	
Income from operations	$ 4,021,600	$ 377,183
Interest expense	$ 356,100	$ 46,405
Times-interest-earned ratio	11.29 times	8.13 times

EXHIBIT 7.16

Times-Interest-Earned Ratios for McDonald's and Wendy's

pense. The more interest expense a company has, the smaller the ratio will be. If a company has any trouble covering its interest expense, that company clearly has too much debt.

Look at the times-interest-earned ratios for McDonald's and Wendy's, each with a capital structure of about two-thirds debt and one-third equity. Exhibit 7.16 shows the income from operations, the interest expense, and the times-interest-earned ratio for both firms. Both firms appear to have no trouble meeting their interest payments.

The details of a company's long-term debt are often found in the notes to the financial statements, rather than on the face of the balance sheet, so it is important to study these notes. For example, the liabilities section of Sherwin Williams' balance sheet, shown in Exhibit 7.17, shows only the basic amounts of long-term obligations, whereas the notes give the details.

EXHIBIT 7.17

Details of Long-Term Debt from the Financial Statements of Sherwin Williams

This shows both the liabilities from the balance sheet and the notes that provide the related details.

From the Financial Statements of Sherwin Williams
(thousands of dollars)

From Liabilities and Shareholder's Equity Section

	At December 31,		
	2005	2004	2003
Total current liabilities	$1,554,371	$1,520,137	$1,154,170
Long-term debt	486,996	488,239	502,992
Postretirement benefits other than pensions	226,526	221,975	216,853
Other long-term liabilities	370,690	392,849	349,736
Minority interest		3,705	
Total shareholder's equity	1,730,612	1,647,246	1,458,857
Total Liabilities and Shareholder's Equity	$4,369,195	$4,274,151	$3,682,608

From the Notes to the Financial Statements:

Note 7 (Debt)

	Due Date	Amounts Outstanding		
		2005	2004	2003
6.85% Notes	2007	$ 197,595	$ 198,143	$ 203,173
7.375% Debentures	2027	139,932	139,929	149,921
7.45% Debentures	2097	146,948	146,942	147,932
5% to 8.5% Promissory Notes	Through 2007	1,021	1,725	1,285
9.875% Debentures	2016	1,500	1,500	1,500
Long-term debt before FAS No. 133 adjustments		486,996	488,239	503,811
Fair value adjustments to 6.85% Notes in accordance with FAS No. 133				(819)
		$486,996	$488,239	$502,992

L.O.6
Identify the major risk
associated with long-term
debt and the related
controls.

Business Risk, Control, and Ethics

The primary risk for a company associated with long-term debt is the risk of not being able to make the debt payments. The more debt a business has, the more risk there is that the company will not be able to pay the debt as it becomes due. That would result in serious financial trouble, possibly even bankruptcy. For The Home Depot, this does not seem to be a problem. As you just read, the firm's debt is approximately 40% of its capital structure, a much lower percentage than many firms. The inability of a firm to pay its debt is a significant risk for the creditors and investors, too. If a company has trouble making its debt payments, you would not like to be one of its creditors or an investor.

There are two major things a company can do to minimize the risk associated with long-term debt.

1. Be sure a thorough business analysis accompanies any decision to borrow money. This is where the concept of positive financial leverage comes in. The company must make sure there is a high probability of earning a higher return with the borrowed funds than the interest costs associated with borrowing the funds. How high the probability should be is an individual business decision. The more money involved, the higher the probability should be.

2. Study the characteristics of various types of debt—terms, interest rates, ease of obtaining the money—and evaluate their attractiveness in your specific circumstances, given the purpose of the loan and the financial situation of the company. For example, bonds are more flexible than a bank loan because the terms and cash flows can be varied, but a bank loan can be arranged more quickly than a company can issue bonds. As you know, debt shows up on a firm's balance sheet. When a firm structures a transaction to keep debt off of its balance sheet, it is called off-balance-sheet financing. An example would be for a firm to structure the acquisition of an asset as an operating lease rather than a purchase. The topic is a bit complicated for an introductory course, but you should be familiar with the expression and its general meaning. Off-balance-sheet financing is not always illegal or a violation of GAAP, but there are well-known cases where GAAP was violated to keep debt off a firm's balance sheet. This was the major fraud at Enron. The firm used creative bookkeeping to keep debt off the balance sheet that actually should have been shown there. The Enron bankruptcy shows that ethics touches every aspect of accounting, even how debt is recorded.

Your Turn 7-8
Your Turn
Your Turn

Calculate the debt-to-equity ratio for Sherwin Williams for each of the years shown in Exhibit 7.17. What trend do you see, and how might an investor interpret it?

News Flash

By keeping debt off of its balance sheet, a firm can make its balance sheet look stronger than it may actually be. Doing this is called off-balance-sheet financing. Now the Financial Accounting Standards Board (FASB) is trying to close some of the loopholes in the rules that allow this. In July 2006, the FASB and the International Accounting Standards Board (IASB) agreed to begin a joint project to develop a new, consistent accounting standard for leases. Critics of the current rules on lease accounting have suggested that it enables firms to leave hundreds of billions of dollars of debt off their balance sheets.

Chapter Summary Points

- A definitely determinable liability is one whose amount is known, and it is recorded when incurred. A typical example is payroll. The firm knows how much to record for salary expense. The firm serves as an agent for the government to collect social security, Medicare, and income taxes from the employee.
- Long-term mortgages usually have payments that include both principal and interest. To calculate the portion of the payment that is interest expense, multiply the interest rate (adjusted for the appropriate time period; e.g., a monthly rate for a monthly payment) by the outstanding principal balance just before the payment. Then, subtract that amount of interest from the payment to find the amount of principal reduction.
- Bonds are debt instruments issued by a firm to borrow money from the capital markets (general public). They may be issued at par, at a discount, or at a premium. The bonds are shown on the balance sheet—the carrying value—at a "net" amount. Any applicable discount (or premium) is deducted from (or added to) the face value of the bonds.
- Capital structure refers to the proportion of debt and equity a firm has. Debt-to-equity ratio is, as it sounds, the firm's total debt divided by the firm's equity. Times-interest-earned ratio is defined as operating income (or net income + interest expense) divided by interest expense. It tells investors and creditors how easy or difficult it was for the firm to meet the current period's interest obligation.
- The major risk for the firm is that it will not be able to make its debt payments. The best controls for this risk are sound financial planning and the profitable operation of the firm.

Chapter Summary Problems

The following transaction took place during HPC Company's most recent fiscal year.

1. On February 1, the first day of the fiscal year, HPC Company issued $5,000,000 worth of 10-year, 8% bonds at 98. At the time, the market rate was approximately 8.3%. Interest is payable annually on February 1. The discount will be amortized using the effective interest method.
2. HPC Company borrowed $10,000,000. The loan is for 20 years at 6.5% with quarterly payments of $224,260. HPC borrowed the money on the last day of the third quarter of the fiscal year and made the first payment on the last day of the fiscal year.
3. HPC spent $55,780 to honor warranties on products sold previously.
4. HPC purchased $675,000 worth of inventory on account. The firm uses a perpetual record-keeping inventory system.
5. HPC paid vendors $563,000 for part of the merchandise purchased in 4.
6. Of the beginning amount of unearned revenue, HPC earned $57,000 during the year.
7. HPC received $25,990 in advance from customers for products to be delivered next year.
8. HPC estimated it will spend $50,000 in the next 2 years honoring warranties related to this year's sales. (Two-year warranties are given for all products.)

Suppose HPC started the year with the following liability accounts and balances.

Accounts payable	$75,500
Unearned revenue	$57,960
Warranty payable	$68,950

Instructions

1. Show each of the transactions in the accounting equation.
2. Give the adjustments that HPC needs to make as the result of these transactions at year end.
3. Prepare the liability section of HPC's balance sheet at the end of the fiscal year.

Solution

	Assets			=	Liabilities							+	Shareholder's Equity		
										Discount on	Long-Term		Contributed Capital	Retained Earnings	
	Cash	Accounts Receivable	Inventory		Accounts Payable	Unearned Revenue	Warranties Payable	Interest Payable	Bonds Payable	Bonds Payable	Notes Payable		Common Stock	Revenues	Expenses
BB				=	75,500	57,960	68,950								
1.	4,900,000								5,000,000	(100,000)					
2.	10,000,000										10,000,000				
3.	(55,780)						(55,780)								
4.			675,000		675,000										
5.	(563,000)				(563,000)										
6.						(57,000)								57,000	
7.	25,990					25,990									(50,000)
8.							50,000								(162,500)
9.	(202,998)										(40,498)				(406,700)
A-1								400,000		6,700					
	14,104,212	–	675,000		187,500	26,950	63,170	400,000	5,000,000	(93,300)	9,959,502			57,000	(619,200)

Supporting Computations

Bonds:
    Interest expense for bonds:
        $\$4,900,000 \times 0.083 = \$406,700$

    Interest payment:
        $\$5,000,000 \times 0.08 = \$400,000$

    Discount amortization:
        $\$406,700 - \$400,000 = \$ 6,700$

Liabilities Section of the Year-End Balance Sheet:

Current Liabilities:	
Accounts payable	$ 187,500
Interest payable	400,000
Unearned revenue	26,950
Warranty liability	63,170
**Current portion of long-term debt	168,681
Total current liabilities	846,301
Long-Term Liabilities:	
**Notes payable	9,790,821
Bonds payable (net of a discount of 93,300)	4,906,700
Total liabilities	$ 15,543,822

** A partial amortization schedule for the long-term loan with quarterly payments is shown. In the next fiscal year, four of those payments will be due. Only the principal portion is recorded as a current liability because the interest has not yet been incurred at the end of the year. The total current portion is the sum of the highlighted values in the "Principal reduction" column. The remaining amount of the note payable, highlighted in the "Beginning principal" column, is shown as a long-term liability.

	Beginning Principal	Quarterly Interest (6.5 ÷ 4) 0.01625	Payment	Principal Reduction	
					Payment made
Q1, Y1	10,000,000	162,500	202,998	40,498	
Q2, Y1	9,959,502	161,842	202,998	41,156	Next year's
					payment of
Q3, Y1	9,918,346	161,173	202,998	41,825	principal
Q4, Y1	9,876,521	160,493	202,998	42,505	$168,681
Q1, Y2	9,834,016	159,803	202,998	43,195	
Q2, Y2	9,790,821				
	Long-term portion				

Key Terms for Chapter 7

Bond (p. 339)
Bonds issued at a discount (p. 340)
Bonds issued at a premium (p. 340)
Bonds issued at par (p. 340)
Capital structure (p. 352)

Carrying value (p. 343)
Contingent liabilities (p. 332)
Debt-to-equity ratio (p. 352)
Definitely determinable liabilities (p. 332)

Discount on bonds payable (p. 343)
Discount rate (p. 336)
Discounting (p. 336)
Estimated liabilities (p. 332)
Financial leverage (p. 352)

Market rate of interest (p. 341)
Premium on bonds payable (p. 343)
Present value (p. 336)
Times-interest-earned ratio (p. 352)

Answers to YOUR TURN Questions

Chapter 7

Your Turn 7-1

Sandy's paycheck will be in the amount of $1,085.25.
 This is how the transaction would be recorded.

Assets	=	Liabilities	+	Shareholders' equity	
				Contributed capital	+ Retained earnings
(1,085.25) cash		300.00 FIT payable 93.00 FICA payable 21.75 Medicare taxes payable			(1,500) salary expense

Your Turn 7-2

The interest is $600,000 × 9% × 1/12 = $4,500. The total payment is $5,500, so the principal reduction is the remaining $1,000.

Your Turn 7-3

A $1,000 bond issued at 95 1/2 will sell for $955.
A $1,000 bond issued at 102 will sell for $1,020.

Your Turn 7-4

The PV of the interest payments = $115 × 5.65022 = $649.78
The PV of the principal payment = $1,000 × 0.32197 = $321.97
The proceeds—cash received for the bond = $971.75

Your Turn 7-5

The PV of the interest payments = $115 × 6.14457 = $ 706.63
The PV of the principal payment = $1,000 × 0.38554 = $ 385.54
The proceeds—cash received for the bond = $1,092.17

Your Turn 7-6

Interest expense (as opposed to interest payment) is calculated by multiplying the bond's carrying value (the loan) by the market rate of interest. The amount of proceeds (selling price of the bonds) equals the carrying value of the bonds on the date of the first interest payment. Proceeds amounted to $196,000 (98% of $200,000).Thus, $196,000 × 0.065 × 1/2 = $6,370 is the interest expense for the first 6 months. Because the payment (fixed by the par value of the bond and the stated interest rate) for the 6 months is $6,000 ($200,000 × 6% × 1/2), the difference of $370 will be subtracted from the discount on bonds payable. That will increase the carrying value of the bonds to $196,370 after the first interest payment. Then, at December 31, 2003, Knollwood will accrue interest expense for the last half of the year; the expense is $196,370 × 0.065 × 1/2 year = $6,382. The payment is $6,000, so the difference of $382 will be subtracted from the discount. The carrying value of the bonds on December 31, 2003, will be $196,752. The total interest expense for the year is $6,370 + $6,382 = $12,752.

Your Turn 7-7

First, you must calculate the proceeds of the bond issue by taking the present value of the cash flows—the PV of the $20,000 interest payments (20 of them) and the PV of the $200,000 payment at maturity.

PV of $20,000 (20 years, 9%) = $182,570.91
PV of $200,000 paid at maturity = $ 35,686.18
Issue price (proceeds) = $218,257.09

On the first interest payment, the interest expense, which will be shown on the income statement, is **$19,643.14** (9% × $218,257.09).
The cash payment to the bondholders is **$20,000.00**.
The difference of **$356.86** is the amortization of the premium.
The carrying value, shown on the December 31 balance sheet, is **$217,900.23** ($218,257.09 − $356.86).

Your Turn 7-8

2005: $2,638,583 (total liabilities) ÷ $1,730,612 (total equity) = 1.52%
2004: $2,626,905 (total liabilities) ÷ $1,647,246 (total equity) = 1.59%
2003: $2,223,751 (total liabilities) ÷ $1,458,857 (total equity) = 1.52%
The ratio appears to be fairly stable, but we would need some industry comparisons for a meaningful analysis.

Questions

1. What are the two main sources of financing for a business?
2. What is the difference between a definitely determinable liability and an estimated liability? Give examples of both.
3. What is a mortgage?
4. When installment loan payments on a mortgage are made, the amount paid reduces cash. What other two items on the financial statements are affected?
5. What is the difference between how bonds are repaid compared to other forms of financing that require installment payments?
6. What advantage is there to obtaining financing using bonds compared to getting a loan from a bank?
7. What does the expression *time value of money* mean?
8. How are the interest payments associated with a bond calculated?
9. Explain the difference between the stated rate and the effective rate of interest on a bond.
10. What is another name for the face value of a bond?
11. When is a bond issued at a discount? When is a bond issued at a premium?
12. How is the carrying value of a bond computed? At maturity, what is the carrying value of a bond that was issued at a premium?
13. What are zero coupon bonds and how do they differ from bonds with a stated rate?
14. How is the debt-to-equity ratio calculated, and what does this ratio measure?
15. How is the time-interest-earned ratio calculated, and what does this ratio measure?

16. To what does the term *capital structure* refer?

17. Explain financial leverage.

Multiple-Choice Questions

1. On January 1, 2007, Sonata Company issued 10-year bonds with a face value of $400,000 and a stated rate of 10%. The cash proceeds from the bond issue amounted to $354,120. Sonata Company will pay interest to the bondholders annually. How much cash will Sonata pay the bondholders on the first payment date?
   a. $40,000
   b. $48,000
   c. $35,412
   d. $42,494

2. Refer to the information in multiple-choice question 1. How did the market interest rate compare to the stated rate on the date the bonds were issued?
   a. The market rate is higher than the stated rate.
   b. The market rate is lower than the stated rate.
   c. Both rates are the same.
   d. It cannot be determined.

3. Partco hired a secretary for $900 a week. The secretary's first paycheck had 20% withheld for income taxes, 6.2% for social security, and 1.45% for Medicare taxes. What is Partco's total salary expense related to this payment?
   a. $68.85
   b. $968.85
   c. $651.15
   d. $720.00

4. All of the following are current liabilities except
   a. Salaries payable
   b. Mortgage payable
   c. Unearned revenue
   d. Accounts payable

5. The amount a company owes its employees for current work done is
   a. Shown on the balance sheet as pension liability
   b. Shown as a current liability
   c. Called postretirement benefits on the balance sheet
   d. Not shown on the balance sheet

6. Liabilities are often estimated because
   a. The related expense needs to be recorded to match the appropriate revenues.
   b. It gives managers a way to manage assets.
   c. They are usually not disclosed until they are settled.
   d. The related assets are already recorded.

7. Bonds issued with a stated interest rate that is higher than the prevailing market rate are issued at
   a. A premium
   b. A discount
   c. Par
   d. Cannot be determined

8. A $1,000 bond with a stated rate of 8% is issued when the market rate is 10%. How much interest will the bondholders receive each year?
   a. $100
   b. $80
   c. $20
   d. $800

9. The carrying value of a bond is the
   a. Face value
   b. Face value minus any discount or plus any premium
   c. Face value minus any interest paid
   d. Amount of principal and interest owed to the bondholders

10. Positive financial leverage means that a company
   a. Has more debt than equity
   b. Earns more with borrowed money than the cost of borrowing it
   c. Has the correct amount of debt
   d. Has more equity than debt

Short Exercises

SE7-1. *Classify liabilities.* (LO 1)
Tell whether each of the following liabilities is definitely determinable or an estimate: accounts payable, unearned revenue, and warranty liability.

SE7-2. *Classify liabilities.* (LO 1)
Taylor Company has the following obligations at December 31: (a) a note payable for $10,000 due in 6 months, (b) unearned revenue of $12,500, (c) interest payable of $15,000, (d) accounts payable of $60,000, and (e) note payable due in 2 years. For each obligation, indicate whether it should be classified as a current liability.

SE7-3. *Account for payroll.* (LO 1)
Jimmy Paycheck earned $1,500 per month as the manager of a recording studio. Jimmy has 25% of his earnings withheld for federal income taxes. There are no other amounts withheld except for those required by the federal government. What are the other amounts that must be deducted from Jimmy's earnings? Calculate the net amount Jimmy will receive on his next paycheck.

SE7-4. *Account for mortgages.* (LO 2)
Fastrac Corporation is considering borrowing some money and is evaluating the different options for financing. As the chief financial officer, write a memo to the corporation's board of directors explaining the difference between how a mortgage is repaid and how a bond is repaid.

SE7-5. *Account for mortgages.* (LO 2)
Nunez Company has arranged to borrow $25,000 for 5 years at an interest rate of 8%. The annual payments will be $6,261.41. When Nunez makes its first payment at the end of the first year of the loan, how much of the payment will be interest?

SE7-6. *Account for mortgages.* (LO 2)
Feathers and Furs borrowed $75,000 to buy a new faux fur storage facility. The company borrowed the money for 10 years at 12%, and the monthly payment is $1,076.03. When the company makes the first monthly payment, by how much will the payment reduce the principal of the loan?

SE7-7. *Account for mortgages.* (LO 2)
Curtain Company borrowed $10,000 at 9% for 7 years. The loan requires annual payments of $1,986.91. When Curtain Company makes the first annual payment, how much of the payment will be interest and how much will reduce the principal of the loan?

SE7-8. *Account for mortgages.* (LO 2)
On July 1, 2006, Maxine's Equipment Company signed a long-term note with the local bank for $50,000. The term of the note was 10 years, at an annual interest rate of 8%. If Maxine's makes annual payments of $7,451.47, beginning on June 30, 2007, how much of the first payment will be interest?

SE7-9. *Account for bonds.* (LO 3)
If a $1,000 bond is selling at 95, how much cash will the issuing company receive? If a $1,000 is selling at par, how much cash will the issuing company receive? If a $1,000 is selling at 101, how much cash will the issuing company receive?

SE7-10. *Account for bonds.* (LO 3)
If $100,000 of 8% bonds is issued (sold) for $95,000, was the market rate of interest at the time of issue higher or lower than 8%? What is the amount of the annual interest payments to be received by the bondholders?

SE7-11. *Account for bonds.* (LO 3)
For each of the following situations, tell whether the bond described will be issued at a premium, at a discount, or at par.

    a. Colson Company issued $200,000 worth of bonds with a stated interest rate of 10%. At the time of issue, the market rate of interest for similar investments was 9%.

    b. Dean Company issued $100,000 worth of callable bonds with a stated rate of 12%. At the time of issue, the market rate of interest for similar investments was 9%.

    c. Liddy Company issued $200,000 worth of bonds with a stated rate of 8%. At the time of issue, the market rate of interest for similar investments was 9%.

SE7-12. *Account for bonds.* (LO 3)
For each of the following, compute the proceeds from the bond issue.

    a. Haldeman Hair Systems issued $20,000 worth of bonds at 106.

    b. Erlichman Egg Company issued $100,000 worth of bonds at 99.

    c. Carl's Cutlery Company issued $500,000 worth of bonds at 96 1/2.

SE7-13. *Account for bonds.* (LO 3)
Altoona Company was able to issue (sell) $200,000 of 9% bonds for $220,000 because its credit rating is excellent and market interest rates have fallen. How much interest will be paid in cash during the first year? Will the interest expense be higher or lower than the interest payment?

SE7-14. *Calculate the debt-to-equity ratio.* (LO 5)
Suppose that for 2006 GM's current assets totaled $57,855 (in millions), total assets totaled $449,999 (in millions), current liabilities totaled $71,264 (in millions) and total liabilities totaled $424,424 (in millions). Calculate the debt-to-equity ratio for GM for 2006.

SE7-15. *Calculate the times-interest-earned ratio.* (LO 5)
Suppose that for 2006, GM's total revenues were $185,524 (in millions), interest expense was $9,464 (in millions), income tax expense was $731 (in millions), and income from operations was $2,981 (in millions). Calculate the times-interest-earned ratio for GM for 2006.

SE7-16. *Identify risk and controls.* (LO 6)
GuGa's Shirt Company wants to borrow $35,000. What should the company consider before proceeding?

Exercises—Set A

E7-1A. *Classify liabilities.* (LO 1)
For each item in the list, tell whether it is a definitely determinable liability, an estimated liability, or neither.

    a. Amount owed to vendor for purchase of inventory
    b. Potential loss from pending lawsuit
    c. Amount of warranty obligations
    d. Amount of loan payment due next year
    e. Amount of vacation pay to accrue for employees for next year

E7-2A. *Account for payroll.* (LO 1)
A company has gross payroll of $30,000, federal income tax withheld of $6,000, FICA (social security) taxes withheld of $1,860, and Medicare taxes withheld of $435.

    a. How much will the balance sheet show for salaries payable (to employees)?
    b. How much will the income statement show for salary expense?
    c. What type of liability is salaries payable?

E7-3A. *Account for payroll.* (LO 1)
During February, Winter Company's employees earned wages of $50,000. Social security (FICA) withheld was $2,500; federal income taxes withheld were $3,500; and employees' contributions to United Way withheld totaled $500. Use the accounting equation to record wages expense and wages payable at the end of February. Winter Company will pay employees their February wages and the payroll taxes during the first week in March.

E7-4A. *Account for long-term liabilities.* (LO 2, 4)
Stephen's Storage Company needed some long-term financing and arranged for a $100,000, 20-year mortgage loan on December 31, 2006. The interest rate is 9% per year, with $11,000 (rounded) payments made at the end of each year.
    a. What is the amount of interest expense related to this loan for 2007?
    b. What amount of liability should appear on the 12/31/07 balance sheet?
    c. What is the amount of interest expense related to this loan for 2008?
    d. What amount of liability should appear on the 12/31/08 balance sheet?

E7-5A. *Account for long-term liabilities.* (LO 2, 4)
Grace's Gems purchased some property on December 31, 2008, for $100,000, paying $20,000 in cash and obtaining a mortgage loan for the other $80,000. The interest rate is 8% per year, with $2,925 payments made at the end of March, June, September, and December.
    a. What amounts should appear as interest expense on the quarterly income statements and as liabilities on the quarterly balance sheets during 2009?
    b. What amount of interest expense should appear on the income statement for the year ended December 31, 2009?

E7-6A. *Account for long-term liabilities.* (LO 2, 4)
Suppose Dell Corporation signed a $500,000, 10-year, 8% note payable to finance the expansion of its business on January 1, 2008. The terms provide for semiannual payments of $36,791 on June 30 and December 31, 2008. On the December 31 balance sheet, how much will Dell show as the principal of this note payable?

E7-7A. *Account for long-term liabilities.* (LO 2)
On April 1, Mark Hamm borrowed $15,000 on an 8-month, 6% note from State Bank of New York to open a business, Gymnastics World. The debt was in the company's name. The note and interest will be repaid on November 30.
    a. Use the accounting equation to show how Gymnastics World would record the receipt of the funds.
    b. Suppose Gymnastics World wants to prepare an income statement for the month of April. Use the accounting equation to show how the firm will accrue interest for the month.
    c. Assume that Gymnastics World accrues the interest expense related to this note at the end of each month. What is the balance in the interest payable account September 30?
    d. Use the accounting equation to show how the firm would record the transaction on November 30, when the loan is repaid with the interest.

Excel Template
www.prenhall.com/reimers

E7-8A. *Account for bonds.* (LO 3)
On December 31, 2006, Bert's Batteries Inc. issued $10,000 worth of 10% bonds at 94. These are 10-year bonds with interest paid annually on December 31.
    a. What are the interest payments for the first 2 years?
    b. Was the market interest rate higher or lower than 10% at the date of issue?
    c. Will the interest expense be higher or lower than the interest payment?

Excel Template
www.prenhall.com/reimers

E7-9A. *Account for bonds.* (LO 3)
On December 31, 2008, Carl's Cartons Inc. issued $100,000 worth of 9% bonds at 104. The interest on these bonds is paid annually on December 31.
    a. What are the interest payments for the first 2 years?
    b. Was the market interest rate higher or lower than 9% at the date of issue?
    c. Will the interest expense be higher or lower than the interest payment?

E7-10A. *Account for bonds.* (LO 3)
On January 1, 2008 Amico Company issued $200,000, 10%, 5-year bonds at face value. Interest is payable on January 1. Use the accounting equation to record the following.
    a. The bond issue

b. The accrual of interest on December 31, 2008
c. The payment of interest on January 1, 2009

E7-11A. *Account for bonds.* (LO 3)
On December 31, 2006, Dave's Delivery Service issued $10,000 worth of 10% bonds at approximately 89. These are 10-year bonds with interest paid semiannually on June 30 and December 31.
   a. What are the interest payments for the first 2 years?
   b. Was the market interest rate higher or lower than 10% at the date of issue?
   c. Will the interest expense be higher or lower than the interest payment?

E7-12A. *Account for bonds.* (LO 3)
On June 30, 2008, Ellie's Electronics issued $20,000 face value of 10% bonds at 105. They were 10-year bonds with interest paid semiannually, on December 31 and June 30.
   a. What are the interest payments for the first 2 years?
   b. Was the market interest rate higher or lower than 10% at the date of issue?
   c. Will the interest expense be higher or lower than the interest payment?

E7-13A. *Account for bonds.* (LO 3)
On June 30, 2006, Fred's Fudge Co. issued $50,000 worth of 10% bonds for $50,000. The interest is paid annually on June 30.
   a. What are the interest payments for the first 2 years?
   b. Was the market interest rate higher or lower than 10% at the date of issue?
   c. Will the interest expense be higher or lower than the interest payment?

E7-14A. *Calculate proceeds from bond issue and interest expense using the effective interest method.* (LO 3, 4)
On June 30, 2007, Mako Company issued $50,000 worth of 5-year, 10% bonds when the market rate was 9%. The interest is paid annually on June 30.
   a. What are the proceeds from the bond issue?
   b. What is the annual interest payment?
   c. What is the amount of interest expense on the date of the first interest payment?
   d. How would the bonds payable and the interest expense be shown on the year-end financial statements (June 30, 2008)?

E7-15A. *Calculate proceeds from bond issue and interest expense using the effective interest method.* (LO 3, 4)
On September 30, 2008, Maury Company issued $100,000 worth of 10-year, 6% bonds when the market rate was 7%. The interest is paid annually on September 30.
   a. What are the proceeds from the bond issue?
   b. What is the annual interest payment?
   c. What is the amount of interest expense on the date of the first interest payment?
   d. How would the bonds payable and the interest expense be shown on the year-end financial statements (Sept. 30, 2009)?

E7-16A. *Prepare an amortization schedule for bond issued at a discount.* (LO 3)
Jamison Corporation issued $100,000, 8%, 10-year bonds on January 1, 2007, when the market rate of interest was 10%. Proceeds were $87,711. Interest is payable annually on January 1. Jamison uses the effective interest method to amortize bond premiums and discounts. Prepare an amortization schedule for the life of the bonds.

E7-17A. *Prepare an amortization schedule for bond issued at a premium.* (LO 3)
Heimer Company issued $180,000, 11%, 10-year bonds on January 1, 2006, when the market rate of interest was 10%. The proceeds were $191,060. Interest is payable annually on January 1. Heimer uses the effective interest method to amortize bond premiums and discounts. Prepare an amortization schedule for the life of the bonds.

Use the following financial data for eBay Inc. to answer E7-18A and E7-19A.

From the Consolidated Balance Sheet of e-Bay

	December 31,	
	2004	2005
	(dollars in thousands)	
Assets		
Total current assets	$ 2,911,149	$ 3,183,237
Total assets	$ 7,991,051	$ 11,788,986
Liabilities & shareholder's equity		
Total current liabilities	$ 1,084,870	$ 1,484,935
Total liabilities	1,262,710	1,741,005
Total shareholder's equity	6,728,341	10,047,981
Total liabilities and shareholder's equity	$ 7,991,051	$ 11,788,986

eBay Inc.
Consolidated Statement of Income (partial)

	Year Ended December 31,		
	2003	2004	2005
	(in thousands, except per share amounts)		
Net revenues	$2,165,096	$3,271,309	$4,552,401
Cost of net revenues	416,058	614,415	818,104
Gross profit	1,749,038	2,656,894	3,734,297
Operating expenses:			
Sales and marketing	567,565	857,874	1,230,728
Product development	159,315	240,647	328,191
General and administrative	332,668	415,725	591,716
Payroll tax on employee stock options	9,590	17,479	13,014
Amortization of acquired intangible assets	50,659	65,927	128,941
Total operating expenses	1,119,797	1,597,652	2,292,590
Income from operations	629,241	1,059,242	1,441,707
Interest and other income, net	36,573	77,867	111,148
Interest expense	(4,314)	(8,879)	(3,478)
Income before cumulative effect of accounting change, income taxes and minority interests	661,500	1,128,230	1,549,377
Provision for income taxes	(206,738)	(343,885)	(467,285)
Minority interests	(7,578)	(6,122)	(49)
Income before cumulative effect of accounting change	447,184	778,223	1,082,043
Cumulative effect of accounting change, net of tax	(5,413)	–	–
Net income	$ 441,771	$ 778,223	$1,082,043

E7-18A. *Calculate the debt-to-equity ratio.* (LO 5)
Using the information provided for eBay Inc., calculate the debt-to-equity ratio at December 31, 2004 and December 31, 2005. Provide an explanation of what this ratio measures and whether the ratio has improved from 2004 to 2005.

E7-19A. *Calculate the times-interest-earned ratio.* (LO 5)
Using the information provided for eBay Inc., calculate the times-interest-earned ratio for 2004 and 2005. Provide an explanation of what this ratio measures and whether the ratio has improved from 2004 to 2005.

E7-20A. *Calculate payments using time value of money concepts.* (LO 7)
For each of the following, calculate the payment each loan would require. Assume the payments are made at the end of the period in each case. Interest rates are annual rates.

Excel Template
www.prenhall.com/reimers

    a. Principal = $30,000; interest rate = 5%; term = 5 years; payments = annual
    b. Principal = $30,000; interest rate = 8%; term = 5 years; payments = annual
    c. Principal = $30,000; interest rate = 8%; term = 10 years; payments = annual
    d. Principal = $30,000; interest rate = 8%; term = 10 years; payments = semi-annual
    e. Principal = $30,000; interest rate = 12%; term = 5 years; payments = monthly

Exercises—Set B

E7-1B. *Classify liabilities.* (LO 1)
For each item in the list below, tell whether it is a definitely determinable liability, an estimated liability, or neither.

    a. Amount of cash revenue received from customer that is unearned
    b. Corporate income tax for the year
    c. Coupons unredeemed at the end of the year (some percentage expected to be redeemed)
    d. Amount of salaries payable to accrue at the end of the year
    e. Account payable owed to vendor for purchase on credit

E7-2B. *Account for payroll.* (LO 1)
If a company has gross payroll of $30,000, federal income tax withheld of $6,000, and FICA (social security) taxes withheld of $2,295.

    a. How much will the balance sheet show for salaries payable (to employees)?
    b. How much will the income statement show for salary expense?
    c. What type of liability is salaries payable?

E7-3B. *Account for payroll.* (LO 1)
During March, The Wessue Coffee Emporium's employees earned wages of $18,000. Social security (FICA) withheld was $1,377; federal income taxes withheld were $3,600; and employees' contributions to the American Red Cross withheld totaled $175. Use the accounting equation to record wages expense and wages payable at the end of March. Wessue will pay employees their March wages and will pay the withholding taxes during the first week in April.

E7-4B. *Account for long-term liabilities.* (LO 2)
Don & Brenda's Gourmet Bread Shop needed some long-term financing and arranged for a $250,000, 15-year mortgage loan on December 31, 2007. The interest rate is 5.5% per year, with $24,906 payments made at the end of each year.

    a. What is the amount of interest expense related to this loan for 2008?
    b. What amount of liability should appear on the 12/31/08 balance sheet?
    c. What is the amount of interest expense related to this loan for 2009?
    d. What amount of liability should appear on the 12/31/09 balance sheet?

E7-5B. *Account for long-term liabilities.* (LO 2, 4)
Molly Merry's Accounting Firm purchased some property on December 31, 2006, for $150,000, paying $30,000 in cash and obtaining a mortgage loan for the other $120,000. The interest rate is 12% per year, with $8,065 payments made at the end of March, June, September, and December.

    a. What amounts should appear as interest expense on the quarterly income statements and as liabilities on the quarterly balance sheets during 2007?
    b. What amount of interest expense should appear on the year 2007 year-end income statement?

E7-6B. *Account for long-term liabilities.* (LO 2)
Suppose Cindy & Owen Cold Desserts Inc. signed a $185,000, 9-year, 6% note payable to finance the expansion of its business on January 1. The terms provide for semiannual payments of $13,451 on June 30 and December 31. Use the accounting equation to record Cindy & Owen's receipt of the proceeds of the loan and the first two payments.

E7-7B. *Account for long-term liabilities.* (LO 2, 4)
On March 1, Delvis Cromartie borrowed $7,500 on a 5-month, 8% note from Florida First Bank & Trust to open a business, Orchids & Such Nursery. The debt was in the company's name. The note and interest will be repaid on July 31.
   a. Use the accounting equation to record the receipt of the funds.
   b. Suppose Orchids & Such Nursery wants to prepare an income statement for the month of March. Use the accounting equation to accrue interest for the month.
   c. Assume that Orchids & Such Nursery accrues the interest expense related to this note at the end of each month. What is the balance in the interest payable account May 31?
   d. Use the accounting equation to record the transaction on July 31, when the loan is repaid with the interest.

E7-8B. *Account for bonds.* (LO 3)
On June 30, 2007, Jamie's Suitcases & Travel Inc. issued $25,000 worth of 8% bonds at 106. These are 5-year bonds with interest paid annually on June 30.
   a. What are the interest payments for the first 2 years?
   b. Was the market interest rate higher or lower than 8% at the date of issue?
   c. Use the accounting equation to record the interest expense and payment for June 30, 2008.

E7-9B. *Account for bonds.* (LO 3)
On February 28, 2009, Newman & Spears Enterprises Inc. issued $150,000 worth of 7% bonds at 92. The interest on these bonds is paid annually on February 28.
   a. What are the interest payments for the first 2 years?
   b. Was the market interest rate higher or lower than 7% at the date of issue?
   c. Will the interest expense be higher or lower than the interest payment?

E7-10B. *Account for bonds.* (LO 3)
On January 1, 2009 A&A Construction Inc. issued $300,000, 8%, 10-year bonds at face value. Interest is payable on January 1. Use the accounting equation to record the following.
   a. The bond issue
   b. The accrual of interest on December 31, 2009
   c. The payment of interest on January 1, 2010

E7-11B. *Account for bonds.* (LO 3)
On June 30, 2008, McCorvey's Lawn Service issued $7,500 worth of 6% bonds at approximately 102. These are 5-year bonds with interest paid semiannually on December 31 and June 30.
   a. What are the interest payments for the first 2 years?
   b. Was the market interest rate higher or lower than 6% at the date of issue?
   c. Will the interest expense be higher or lower than the interest payment?

E7-12B. *Account for bonds.* (LO 3)
On December 31, 2007, State of the Art Electronics issued $40,000 face value of 12% bonds at 96. They were 8-year bonds with interest paid semiannually, on June 30 and December 31.
   a. What are the interest payments for the first 2 years?
   b. Was the market interest rate higher or lower than 12% at the date of issue?
   c. Use the accounting equation to record the interest expense and payment for June 30 and December 31, 2008.

E7-13B. *Account for bonds.* (LO 3)
On June 30, 2008, Nikki C. Records Inc. issued $35,000 worth of 8% bonds for $35,000. The interest is paid annually on June 30.

a. What are the interest payments for the first 2 years?
b. Was the market interest rate higher or lower than 8% at the date of issue?
c. Will the interest expense be higher or lower than the interest payment?

E7-14B. *Calculate proceeds from bond issue and interest expense using the effective interest method.* (LO 3, 4)
On March 30, 2008, Canine Company issued $80,000 worth of 10-year, 6% bonds when the market rate was 5%. The interest is paid annually on March 30.
 a. What are the proceeds from the bond issue?
 b. What is the annual interest payment?
 c. What is the amount of interest expense on the date of the first interest payment?
 d. How would the bonds payable and the interest expense be shown on the year-end (March 30, 2009) financial statements?

E7-15B. *Calculate proceeds from bond issue and interest expense using the effective interest method.* (LO 3, 4)
On June 30, 2007, Feline Company issued $750,000 worth of 5-year, 7% bonds when the market rate was 6%. The interest is paid annually on June 30.
 a. What are the proceeds from the bond issue?
 b. What is the annual interest payment?
 c. What is the amount of interest expense on the date of the first interest payment?
 d. How would the bonds payable and the interest expense be shown on the year-end (June 30, 2008) financial statements?

E7-16B. *Prepare an amortization schedule for bond issued at a premium.* (LO 3)
Designer Clothes Inc. issued $200,000, 10%, 10-year bonds on July 1, 2007, when the market rate of interest was 8%. Proceeds were $226,840. Interest is payable annually on July 1. Designer uses the effective interest method to amortize bond premiums and discounts. Prepare an amortization schedule for the life of the bonds.

E7-17B. *Prepare an amortization schedule for bond issued at a discount.* (LO 3)
Panama City Tan Solutions Inc. issued $75,000, 7%, 15-year bonds on July 1, 2008, when the market rate of interest was 9%. The proceeds were $62,909. Interest is payable annually on July 1. Panama City Tan uses the effective interest method to amortize bond premiums and discounts. Prepare an amortization schedule for the life of the bonds.

Use the following financial data for Netflix Inc. to answer E7-18B and E7-19B.

Netflix, Inc.
Consolidated Balance Sheet (adapted)
(in thousands, except per share amounts)

	December 31,	
	2004	2005
	(dollars in thousands)	
Assets		
Total current assets	$ 187,346	$ 243,691
Total assets	$ 251,793	$ 364,681
Liabilities & Shareholder's Equity		
Total current liabilities	$ 94,910	$ 137,587
Total liabilities	95,510	138,429
Total shareholder's equity	156,283	226,252
Total liabilities and shareholder's equity	$ 251,793	$ 364,681

Netflix, Inc.
Consolidated Statements of Income
(in thousands, except per share data)

| | Year ended December 31, | | |
	2003	2004	2005
Revenues	$ 270,410	$ 500,611	$ 682,213
Cost of revenues:			
Subscription	147,736	273,401	393,788
Fulfillment expenses	31,274	56,609	70,762
Total cost of revenues	179,010	330,010	464,550
Gross profit	91,400	170,601	217,663
Operating expenses:			
Technology and development	17,884	22,906	30,942
Marketing	49,949	98,027	141,997
General and administrative	9,585	16,287	29,395
Stock-based compensation	10,719	16,587	14,327
Gain on disposal of DVDs	(1,209)	(2,560)	(1,987)
Total operating expenses	86,928	151,247	214,674
Operating income	4,472	19,354	2,989
Other income (expense)			
Interest and other income	2,457	2,592	5,753
Interest and other expense	(417)	(170)	(407)
Income before income taxes	6,512	21,776	8,335
Provision for (benefit from) income taxes	–	181	(33,692)
Net income	$ 6,512	$ 21,595	$ 42,027

E7-18B. *Calculate the debt-to-equity ratio.* (LO 5)
Using the information provided for Netflix Inc., calculate the debt-to-equity ratio at December 31, 2004 and December 31, 2005. Provide an explanation of what this ratio measures and whether the ratio has improved from 2004 to 2005.

E7-19B. *Calculate the times-interest-earned ratio.* (LO 5)
Using the information provided for Netflix Inc., calculate the times-interest-earned ratio for 2004 and 2005. Provide an explanation of what this ratio measures and whether the ratio has improved from 2004 to 2005.

E7-20B. *Calculate payments using time value of money concepts.* (LO 7)
For each of the following, calculate the payment each loan would require. Assume the payments are made at the end of the period in each case. Interest rates are annual rates.
  a. Principal = $25,000; interest rate = 6%; term = 5 years; payments = annual
  b. Principal = $25,000; interest rate = 9%; term = 5 years; payments = annual
  c. Principal = $35,000; interest rate = 7%; term = 8 years; payments = annual
  d. Principal = $35,000; interest rate = 7%; term = 8 years; payments = semiannual
  e. Principal = $40,000; interest rate = 12%; term = 3 years; payments = monthly

Problems—Set A

P7-1A. *Account for current liabilities.* (LO 1, 4)
On March 1, 2007, the accounting records of Stein Company showed the following liability accounts and balances.

Accounts payable	$21,600
Short-term notes payable	10,000
Interest payable	800
Unearned service revenue	12,500

1. On March 1, Stein Company signed a 3-month note for $12,000 at 7.5%.
2. During March, Stein Company paid off the $10,000 short-term note and the interest payable shown on the March 1 balance sheet.
3. Stein paid off the beginning accounts payable.
4. During the month, Stein purchased $25,000 of merchandise on account.
5. Also during March, Stein's employees earned salaries of $36,000. Withholdings related to these wages were $2,232 for social security (FICA), $3,800 for federal income tax, and $1,140 for state income tax. The company will pay March salaries and taxes withheld on April 1. No entry had been recorded for salaries or payroll tax expense as of March 31.

Required

    a. Use the accounting equation to show each of the transactions.
    b. Use the accounting equation to show the adjustments needed for interest on the notes payable and for salary expense and payroll tax expense.
    c. Prepare the current liabilities section of the balance sheet at March 31, 2007.

P7-2A. *Account for notes payable with periodic payments of principal and interest.* (LO 2) The SD Company engaged in the following transactions related to long-term liabilities during 2006.

Excel Template
www.prenhall.com/reimers

1. On March 1, the company borrowed $25,000 for a machine. The loan is to be repaid in equal annual payments of $6,344 at the end of each of the next 5 years (beginning February 28, 2007); the interest rate is 8.5%.
2. On October 1, the company borrowed $120,000 from Suwannee Local Bank at an interest rate of 7.25%. The loan is for 10 years, and SD Company will make annual payments of $17,283 on September 30 of each year.

Required

    a. For each loan, prepare an amortization schedule for the first four payments. Show the reduction in principal and the interest expense for each payment.
    b. What total interest expense related to these two loans would SD Company show on its income statement for the year ended December 31, 2006?
    c. How much interest payable would SD Company show on its balance sheet at December 31, 2006?

P7-3A. *Account for notes payable with periodic payments of principal and interest.* (LO 2) Joe Brinks is making plans to finance the following projects.

1. Purchase a truck for $30,000 to be repaid in equal monthly payments of $601 over the next 5 years. The bank has quoted an interest rate of 7.5%.
2. Purchase a piece of land, whose owner is offering to sell it to Joe for $25,000. The seller would accept five annual payments of $6,595 at 10%.
3. Sell some old equipment for $4,000. Joe is willing to accept quarterly payments of $546 for the next 2 years at an interest rate of 8%.
4. Purchase land and building for $50,000, with a down payment of $5,000, and semiannual payments of $3,095 for the next 10 years at an interest rate of 6.5%.

Required

For each independent scenario, show the transactions in the accounting equation for the first two payments.

(Note: If you are familiar with calculating the present value of an annuity, you should be able to calculate the payments in each case with the given information. Check it out to see if you can calculate the payment given.)

P7-4A. *Account for bonds payable.* (LO 3) Jule's Jewels issued $20,000 worth of 10-year bonds at 103 1/2. The bonds have a stated rate of 7%.

Required

    a. Was the interest rate at the time of issue higher or lower than 7%? How do you know?

    b. What were the proceeds from the bond issue?

    c. Will the interest expense each period be higher or lower than the interest payment?

    d. Will the book value of the bonds be higher or lower than $20,000 after 5 years?

P7-5A. *Account for bonds payable.* (LO 3)
Matrix Construction issued $2 million of its 5% bonds on July 1, 2006, at 99. The bonds mature on June 30, 2011. Interest is payable semiannually on June 30 and December 31.

Required

    a. What were the proceeds from the bond issue?

    b. Was the interest rate at the time of issue higher or lower than 5%?

    c. Will interest expense be higher or lower than the interest payment?

    d. What will the book value of the bonds be at maturity?

P7-6A. *Account for bonds using time value of money concepts.* (LO 3, 4)
Newman Corporation issued $100,000 of bonds on January 1, 2006. The bonds mature on January 1, 2016. Interest is payable annually on December 31. The stated rate of interest is 8%, and the market rate of interest was 10% at the time of issue.

Required

    a. Calculate the proceeds for the bond issue. How would issuing the bonds affect the financial statements for Newman (on the date of issue)?

    b. Prepare an amortization schedule for the first 3 years of the life of the bonds, showing the interest expense and the carrying value at the end of each interest period. Newman uses the effective interest method for amortizing discounts and premiums.

    c. How much interest expense related to these bonds would Newman show on its income statement for the year ended December 31, 2007? (Assume effective interest method.)

    d. Calculate the interest expense for the year ended December 31, 2007, using the straight-line method of amortization. Then, compare that amount to the amount calculated using the effective interest method. Which method do you think Newman should use and why?

Problems—Set B

P7-1B. *Account for current liabilities.* (LO 1, 4)
On May 1, 2006, the accounting records of Sea Salt Company showed the following liability accounts and balances.

Accounts payable	$35,600
Short-term notes payable	15,000
Interest payable	950
Unearned service revenue	6,000

  1. On May 1, Sea Salt Company signed a 6-month note for $20,000 at 6%.

  2. During March, Sea Salt Company paid off the $15,000 short-term note and the interest payable shown on the May 1 balance sheet.

  3. The company also paid off the beginning balance in accounts payable.

  4. During the month, Sea Salt purchased $40,000 of merchandise on account.

  5. Also during May, Sea Salt's employees earned salaries of $25,000. Withholdings related to these wages were $1,550 for social security (FICA), $5,000 for federal income tax, and $2,500 for state income tax. The company will pay May salaries and taxes withheld on June 1. No entry had been recorded for salaries or payroll tax expense as of May 31.

Required

a. Use the accounting equation to record the transactions described.

b. Show how Sea Salt Company would record the interest on the notes payable and the salary expense and payroll tax expense.

c. Prepare the current liabilities section of the balance sheet at May 31, 2006.

P7-2B. *Account for notes payable with periodic payments of principal and interest.* (LO 2, 4) The McIntyre Company engaged in the following transactions related to long-term liabilities during 2006.

Excel Template
www.prenhall.com/reimers

1. On July 1, the company borrowed $50,000 for a new piece of office equipment. The loan is to be repaid in equal annual payments of $8,701 at the end of each of the next 8 years (beginning June 30, 2007); and the interest rate McIntyre is paying for this loan is 8%.

2. On October 1, the company borrowed $200,000 from Shell Point Local Bank at an interest rate of 9.5%. The loan is for 10 years, and McIntyre will make annual payments of $31,853 on September 30 of each year.

Required

a. For each loan, prepare an amortization schedule for the first four payments. Show the reduction in principal and the interest expense for each payment.

b. What total interest expense related to these two loans would McIntyre Company show on its income statement for the year ended December 31, 2006?

c. How much interest payable would McIntyre show on its balance sheet at December 31, 2006?

P7-3B. *Account for notes payable with periodic payments of principal and interest.* (LO 2) Black Company is making plans to finance the following projects.

1. Purchase a boat for $50,000 to be repaid in equal monthly payments of $977.51 over the next 6 years. The bank has quoted an interest rate of 12%.

2. Purchase a property for $125,000. The seller would accept 10 semiannual payments of $15,411.37 at 8% (annual rate).

3. Sell some old equipment for $8,000. Joe is willing to accept quarterly payments of $1,092 for the next 2 years at an interest rate of 8% (annual rate).

4. Purchase land and building for $250,000, with a down payment of $50,000, and semiannual payments of $16,048.52 for the next 10 years at an interest rate of 10% (annual rate).

Required

For each situation, use the accounting equation to show how the firm would record the first two payments.

P7-4B. *Account for bonds payable.* (LO 3) Glassworks Inc. issued $150,000 worth of 6-year bonds with a stated interest rate of 7.5% and interest payable annually on December 31. The bonds were issued at 98. The bonds were issued on January 1, 2007. The fiscal year-end for Glassworks Inc. is December 31.

Required

a. Was the interest rate at the time of issue higher or lower than 7.5%? Explain.

b. Will the interest payment be more or less than the interest expense each year?

c. Will the carrying value be more or less than $150,000 after 3 years? After 4 years? At maturity?

P7-5B. *Account for bonds payable.* (LO 3) Venus Rug Company issued $80,000 worth of 10-year bonds at 103. The bonds have a stated rate of 9%.

Required

a. What were the proceeds from the bond issue?
b. Describe the change in carrying value of the bonds over the 10-year life.
c. Will interest expense be larger or smaller than the interest payment each year?

P7-6B. *Account for bonds using time value of money concepts.* (LO 3, 4)
Morgan Corporation issued $1,000,000 of bonds on January 1, 2007. The bonds mature on January 1, 2015. Interest is payable annually each December 31. The stated rate of interest is 11%, and the market rate of interest was 10% at the time of issue.

Required

a. Calculate the proceeds for the bond issue. How would issuing the bonds affect the financial statements for Morgan (on the date of issue)?
b. Prepare an amortization schedule for the first 4 years of the life of the bonds, showing the interest expense and the carrying value at the end of each interest period. Morgan uses the effective interest method for amortizing discounts and premiums.
c. How much interest expense related to these bonds would Morgan show on its income statement for the year ended December 31, 2011? (Assume effective interest method.)
d. Calculate the interest expense for the year ended December 31, 2011, using the straight-line method of amortization. Then, compare that amount to the amount calculated using the effective interest method. Which method do you think Morgan should use and why?

Financial Statement Analysis

FSA7-1. *Calculate debt-to-equity ratio and analyze financial data.* (LO 5, 6)
The following information comes from balance sheet of Nordstrom Inc.

Nordstrom, Inc.
Consolidated Balance Sheets (partial)
(amounts in thousands)

	January 28, 2006	January 29, 2005
Liabilities and Shareholder's Equity		
Current liabilities:		
Accounts payable	$ 540,019	$ 482,394
Accrued salaries, wages and related benefits	285,982	287,904
Other current liabilities	409,076	354,201
Income taxes payable	81,617	115,556
Current portion of long-term debt	306,618	101,097
Total current liabilities	1,623,312	1,341,152
Long-term debt, net	627,776	929,010
Deferred property incentives, net	364,382	367,087
Other liabilities	213,198	179,147
Shareholder's equity		
Common stock, no par value: 1,000,000 shares authorized 269,549 and 271,331 shared issued and outstanding	685,934	552,655
Unearned stock compensation	(327)	(299)
Retained earnings	1,404,366	1,227,303
Accumulated other comprehensive earnings	2,708	9,335
Total shareholder's equity	2,092,681	1,788,994
Total liabilities and shareholder's equity	$ 4,921,349	$ 4,605,390

a. Calculate the debt-to-equity ratio for the years shown.
b. Who would be interested in this information and why?
c. Suppose you were considering investing in some stock. What do you think of the change in this ratio from one year to the next?
d. If Nordstrom Inc. has bonds payable, where do you think they might be included on the balance sheet?
e. What risks are associated with the long-term debt on Nordstrom's balance sheet?

FSA7-2. *Calculate debt-to-equity ratio and analyze financial data.* (LO 5, 6)
The following information comes from the balance sheet of The Talbots Inc.

The Talbots, Inc. and Subsidiaries
Consolidated Balance Sheets (partial)
(amounts in thousands except share data)

	January 28, 2006	January 29, 2005
Liabilities and Shareholder's Equity		
Current Liabilities:		
Accounts payable	$ 85,343	$ 65,070
Accrued income taxes	37,909	27,196
Accrued liabilities	121,205	110,372
Total current liabilities	244,457	202,638
Long-term debt	100,000	100,000
Deferred rent under lease commitments	110,864	109,946
Deferred income taxes	–	5,670
Other liabilities	63,855	55,288
Commitments		
Stockholder's Equity:		
Common stock, $0.01 par value; 200,000,000 authorized; 77,861,128 shares and 76,940,134 shares issued, respectively, and 53,359,556 shares and 54,123,667 shares outstanding, respectively	779	769
Additional paid-in capital	455,221	432,912
Retained earnings	783,397	715,580
Accumulated other comprehensive loss	(16,682)	(17,142)
Deferred compensation	(13,403)	(11,821)
Treasury stock, at cost; 24,501,572 and 22,816,467 shares, respectively	(582,344)	(531,710)
Total stockholder's equity	626,968	588,588
Total Liabilities and Stockholder's Equity	$1,146,144	$1,062,130

---

a. Calculate the debt-to-equity ratio for the years shown.
b. Who would be interested in this information and why?
c. Suppose you were considering investing in some Talbots' stock. What do you think of the change in this ratio from one year to the next?
d. If Talbots has bonds payable, where do you think they might be included on the balance sheet?
e. What risks are associated with the long-term debt on the balance sheet of The Talbots Inc.?

FSA7-3. *Calculate the debt-to-equity and times-interest-earned ratios and analyze financial data.* (LO 5, 6)

Use Office Depot's financial statements, which can be found on the book's website, to answer the following questions.

    a. What types of debt does Office Depot have? Where did you find this information?

    b. Compute the times-interest-earned ratio and the debt-to-equity ratio for at least two consecutive years. What information do these ratios provide?

    c. Does Office Depot mention any risks associated with its long-term debt? If so, where?

Critical Thinking Problems

Risks and Controls

One of the risks of borrowing money is changing interest rates. For example, if a company issues bonds when the market rate is 7%, what happens if the market rate goes down while the bonds are outstanding? Name some actions a company could take to control for this risk. For several companies that have outstanding long-term debt, read the notes to the financial statements that address this interest rate risk.

Ethics

Lucy Shafer wants to borrow $100,000 to expand her dog-breeding business. She is preparing a set of financial statements to take to the local bank with her loan application. She currently has an outstanding loan from her uncle for $50,000. Lucy's uncle is letting her borrow the money at a very low interest rate, and she does not need to make any principal payments for 5 years. Due to the favorable terms of the loan from her uncle, Lucy has decided that it is not significant enough to disclose on her financial statements. Instead, Lucy has classified the $50,000 as contributed capital, and the interest payments are included in miscellaneous expenses on Lucy's income statement.

    a. What are the effects of Lucy's classifications of her uncle's loan and the related interest payments on the financial statements?

    b. Are there any ratios that might be of interest to the local bank that will be misstated by Lucy's actions?

    c. Do you think Lucy's actions are unethical? Suppose Lucy's uncle agrees to be a partner in the company until Lucy can afford to buy his share by repaying the $50,000 with interest. Does that change your opinion?

Group Assignment

With the class divided into groups, assign one of the following companies to each group.

    Southwest Airlines
    Delta Airlines
    United Airlines
    Northwest Airlines
    Alaska Airlines

For your company, analyze the liability section of the balance sheet. For each liability, write a short description. Use information from the notes to help you. Then, calculate the debt-to-equity ratio for the years with available information. What tentative conclusions can you draw about the debt position of your airline?

Internet Exercise: Starbucks

Starbucks Corp. is the number one specialty coffee retailer, operating more than 8,300 coffee shops. The company also sells coffee beans to restaurants, businesses, airlines, and hotels and offers mail-order and online shopping.

IE7-1. Under "Quotes & Research" enter the company symbol SBUX, the stock symbol of the Starbucks Corp., and then choose Financials. Find the Annual Balance Sheet. Identify amounts reported for total liabilities and total shareholders' equity at the three most recent year-ends.

IE7-2. Calculate the debt-to-equity ratio (total liabilities to total shareholders' equity) for each year-end.

IE7-3. Do owners or creditors have more claims on the Starbucks' assets? How can you tell?

IE7-4. What types of financial risks apply to Starbucks?

Appendix 7A

Time Value of Money and Present Values

The Time Value of Money

If you ever used a credit card or borrowed money for longer than one year, you have experience with the *time value of money*. The term means that money has value over time. That's because money that you invest can earn interest. A person would prefer to receive a dollar today rather than receive a dollar a year from now because the dollar received today can earn interest during the year. Then, it will be worth *more* than a dollar a year from now.

Simple Versus Compound Interest

We calculated the interest on the principal of a loan in several chapters, including Chapter 9. When interest is computed on the principal only, it is called *simple interest*. Simple interest usually applies to short-term loans, which are loans with terms of one year or less.

When interest is computed on the principal of a loan *plus* any interest that has been earned but not collected or paid, it is called *compound interest*. The interest earned during a year is added to the original principal, and that new larger amount is used to calculate the interest earned during the next year. Each year, the interest is calculated on a larger amount. The larger amount comes from adding each successive year's earned interest to the prior year's interest plus the initial principal.

Exhibit 7A.1 shows what happens to $1,000 if you invest it today and watch it grow over 10 years. You can easily see that compound interest makes your money grow much faster than simple interest.

You can use the concept of compound interest to do the following:

Calculate the amount of money you need to deposit today—the *present value* of a future amount—to grow to a specific amount by some future date.

Let's work through an example.

How much money will you have in 10 years if you deposit $1,000 today and it earns 10% interest per year?

- If the money earns simple interest, you'll have $2,000 at the end of 10 years. Each year, the principal of $1,000 will earn $100.
- If the money earns compound interest, you'll have $2,594 at the end of 10 years. Each year, the principal *plus the previously earned interest* will earn interest.

Present Value

Sometimes we want to know how much a future amount is worth today. For example, when we calculate the issue price of a bond, we are taking those future cash flows and calculating what they are worth today. That is, we want to know the present value of the future cash flows.

Present Value of a Single Amount. The present value of a sum of money to be received in the future is the value in *today's dollars*. If you are promised a payment of $100 one year

EXHIBIT 7A.1

Simple Versus Compound Interest

Deposit today at 10% annual interest	You'll have this much at the end of **Year 1**	...at the end of **Year 2**	...at the end of **Year 3**	...at the end of **Year 4**	...at the end of **Year 5**	...at the end of **Year 6**	...at the end of **Year 7**	...at the end of **Year 8**	...at the end of **Year 9**	You'll have this much at the end of **Year 10**
Simple interest										
$1,000	$1,100	$1,200	$1,300	$1,400	$1,500	$1,600	$1,700	$1,800	$1,900	$2,000
Compound interest										
$1,000	$1,100	$1,210	$1,331	$1,464	$1,611	$1,772	$1,949	$2,144	$2,358	$2,594

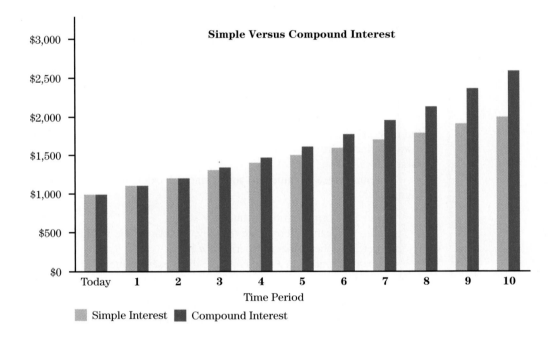

from today, how much is this worth today? In other words, how much would you have to deposit today to have it grow to be $100 in a year? That's what happens when you make a deposit at a bank today and the amount grows to a larger future value. Here's the formula for calculating future value:

$$FV_n = PV(1 + i)^n$$

where n = the number of periods
i = the interest rate (adjusted for the time period)
PV = the present value of the future sum of money
FV_n = the future value of the investment at the end of n periods

If we solve the equation for PV, we get

$$PV = FV_n \left(\frac{1}{(1 + i)^n} \right)$$

Let's figure out the present value of $100 one year from now at an annual interest rate of 10%.

$$PV = \$100\ (1/(1 + 0.10)^1)$$
$$PV = \$100\ (0.90909)$$
$$PV = \$90.91$$

This calculation shows that having $90.91 today is equivalent to having $100 in one year, when the annual interest rate is 10%. We can check it out logically: If we deposit $90.91 today and it earns 10% interest per year, at the end of the year we will have $100 (90.01 × 1.10 = 100.001).

Let's figure out the present value of $100 two years from now at an annual interest rate of 10%:

$$PV = \$100\ (1/(1 + 0.10)^2)$$
$$PV = \$100\ (0.82644628)$$
$$PV = \$82.6446$$

This calculation shows that having $82.6446 today is equivalent to having $100 in two years, when the interest rate is 10%. We can check it out logically: If we deposit $82.6446 today and earn 10% interest, we will have $90.909 [= 82.6446 (1 + 0.10)] after one year. Then, our $90.909 has a year to earn 10% interest, so at the end of the second year we will have $99.9999—which rounds to $100.

Fortunately, we do not have to use the formula to calculate the present value of a future amount. We can use a present value table, a financial calculator, or Excel. Let's look at a present value table first.

The present value table is based on $1. Find the factor from the table in Exhibit 7A.2 and multiply the factor by the dollars in our problem. Find the 10% column and the 2-year row. The factor from the table is 0.82645. Multiply that factor by $100, and the present value is $82.645.

Compute present value on your financial calculator (some calculators may differ slightly):

- Enter $100 for the future value (**FV** key).
- Enter 10 for the interest rate (**i%** key, sometimes the I/Y key).
- Enter 2 for the number of periods (**n** key).
- Press **CPT** and then **PV** to compute the present value.

You should see $82.645 in the display.

As you learned in the chapter, finding the present value of a future amount is called discounting the cash flow, and when discounting a cash flow, the interest rate is called the discount rate.

Present Value of an Annuity. In addition to discounting a single amount—often referred to as a *lump sum*—we may need to calculate the present value of a *series* of payments. A stream of deposits or payments that are the same and made periodically over equally spaced intervals is called an **annuity**. Its name comes from the idea of *annual* payments, because most annuities are annual. The present value of an annuity has many practical applications. Most present value problems involving annuities have payments at the end of the period, and they are called **ordinary annuities**. First, let's look at a simple example to see how the formulas work. Then, we'll look at some examples that should be familiar to you—buying a motorcycle or a car by borrowing money and making payments to repay the loan.

Annuity A series of equal cash receipts on cash payments over equally space intervals of time.

Ordinary annuities An annuity whose payments are made at the end of each interval or period.

EXHIBIT 7A.2

From the Present Value of $1 Table

(n) periods	8%	9%	10%	11%
1	0.92593	0.91743	0.90909	0.90090
2	0.85734	0.84168	**0.82645**	0.81162
3	0.79383	0.77218	0.75131	0.73119
4	0.73503	0.70843	0.68301	0.65873

John wants to have $5,000 in five years. How much should he deposit to-day to have $5,000 in five years if the annual interest rate is 10%? In other words, what is the present value of $5,000 in five years? Try using the formula, the present value table, and your financial calculator (if you have one).

Your Turn 7-9
Your Turn
Your Turn

Suppose you are selling your old motorcycle and a friend offers you a series of four payments of $500 each at the end of each of the next four years. How much is your friend actually offering for your motorcycle? It's *not* simply 4 × $500, or $2,000, because of the time value of money. Getting $500 a year from now is *not* the same as getting $500 today. To find out how much a series of four payments of $500 over the next four years is worth today, you need to use an appropriate interest rate and discount the payments to get the present value of each payment. Suppose the interest rate is 5% per year.

The first payment, made at the end of one year, will be discounted back one year. The second payment, made at the end of two years, will be discounted back two years. And so on, for the third and fourth payments. The present value of the series of payments will be the sum of the individual present value amounts. Here's how it looks in the formula:

$$PV = FV_n\left(\frac{1}{(1 + i)^n}\right)$$

$$PV = \$500(1/(1 + .05)^1) = 500(0.95238) = \$\ 476.19$$
$$PV = \$500(1/(1 + .05)^2) = 500(0.90703) = \$\ 453.51$$
$$PV = \$500(1/(1 + .05)^3) = 500(0.86384) = \$\ 431.92$$
$$PV = \$500(1/(1 + .05)^4) = 500(0.82270) = \$\ 411.35$$
$$\text{Total } PV = \$1,772.97$$

This calculation shows that, if you could deposit $1,772.97 today to earn 5%, you would be indifferent between receiving $1,772.97 today and receiving four payments of $500 each at the end of each of the next four years. Another way to express the same idea is that your friend is paying you $1,772.97 for your motorcycle by offering you the four $500 annual payments. The difference between the total payments of $2,000 and the $1,772.97 price of the motorcycle is interest.

The present value of an annuity table, shown in Exhibit 7A.3, compiles the individual factors from the present value of $1 table in Exhibit 7A.2. Use the present value of an annuity table to solve the same problem. Find the column for 5% and the row for 4 (periods), and you'll see the factor of 3.54595. If you multiply the payment of $500 by the factor 3.54595 you'll get **$1,772.98**. (It's off a cent due to rounding the factors above.)

Compute present value on your financial calculator.

• Enter $500 as the payment (**PMT** key);
• Enter 4 as the number of periods (**n** key);
• Enter 5 as the interest rate (**i%** or the I/Y key); then
• Press the **CPT** key, followed by the **PV** key.

You'll see $1,772.98 in the display. That's the present value of the series of payments.

(n) periods	4%	5%	6%	7%
3	2.77509	2.72325	2.67301	2.62432
4	3.62990	**3.54595**	3.46511	3.38721
5	4.45182	4.32948	4.21236	4.10020
6	5.24214	5.07569	4.91732	4.76654

EXHIBIT 7A.3

Present Value of an Annuity Table

EXHIBIT 7A.4

Present Value of an Annuity Table

(n) periods	0.50%	1%	2%	3%
35	32.03537	29.40858	24.99862	21.48722
36	**32.87102**	30.10751	25.48884	21.83225
37	33.70250	30.79951	25.96945	22.16724
38	34.52985	31.48466	26.44064	22.49246

Let's look at buying a car as an example. Suppose you find a car that you want to buy for $23,000. You have $1,000 for a down payment, and you'll have to borrow $22,000. If you borrow the money for three years at an annual interest rate of 6%, how much will be your monthly payments? Pay special attention to the timing of the payments in this situation. Rather than making annual payments, you'll be making monthly payments. To accommodate this payment plan, you'll need to make sure your time periods, n, and your interest rate, $i\%$, are both expressed with the same time frame. If the period is a month, the annual interest rate must be changed to a monthly interest rate. You are borrowing money for 36 periods (= 3 years × 12 months per year) at a rate of 1/2% (= 0.50% or .005) per month (that's an annual rate of 6%).

In this case, you have the present value—that's the amount you are borrowing for the car. Calculate the *series of payments* using the present value of an annuity table, shown in Exhibit 7A.4, and then try it with a financial calculator.

Present Value of a $1 Table

The Present Value of a Single Amount ($1)

$$PV = \frac{1}{(1+r)^n}$$

Periods	0.50%	1%	2%	3%	4%	5%	6%	7%	8%	9%	10%	11%	12%	13%	14%	15%
1	0.99502	0.99010	0.98039	0.97087	0.96154	0.95238	0.94340	0.93458	0.92593	0.91743	0.90909	0.90090	0.89286	0.88496	0.87719	0.86957
2	0.99007	0.98030	0.96117	0.94260	0.92456	0.90703	0.89000	0.87344	0.85734	0.84168	0.82645	0.81162	0.79719	0.78315	0.76947	0.75614
3	0.98515	0.97059	0.94232	0.91514	0.88900	0.86384	0.83962	0.81630	0.79383	0.77218	0.75131	0.73119	0.71178	0.69305	0.67497	0.65752
4	0.98025	0.96098	0.92385	0.88849	0.85480	0.82270	0.79209	0.76290	0.73503	0.70842	0.68301	0.65873	0.63552	0.61332	0.59208	0.57175
5	0.97537	0.95147	0.90573	0.86261	0.82193	0.78353	0.74726	0.71299	0.68058	0.64993	0.62092	0.59345	0.56743	0.54276	0.51937	0.49718
6	0.97052	0.94205	0.88797	0.83748	0.79031	0.74622	0.70496	0.66634	0.63017	0.59627	0.56447	0.53464	0.50663	0.48032	0.45559	0.43233
7	0.96569	0.93272	0.87056	0.81309	0.75992	0.71068	0.66506	0.62275	0.58349	0.54703	0.51316	0.48166	0.45235	0.42506	0.39964	0.37594
8	0.96089	0.92348	0.85349	0.78941	0.73069	0.67684	0.62741	0.58201	0.54027	0.50187	0.46651	0.43393	0.40388	0.37616	0.35056	0.32690
9	0.95610	0.91434	0.83676	0.76642	0.70259	0.64461	0.59190	0.54393	0.50025	0.46043	0.42410	0.39092	0.36061	0.33288	0.30751	0.28426
10	0.95135	0.90529	0.82035	0.74409	0.67556	0.61391	0.55839	0.50835	0.46319	0.42241	0.38554	0.35218	0.32197	0.29459	0.26974	0.24718
11	0.94661	0.89632	0.80426	0.72242	0.64958	0.58468	0.52679	0.47509	0.42888	0.38753	0.35049	0.31728	0.28748	0.26070	0.23662	0.21494
12	0.94191	0.88745	0.78849	0.70138	0.62460	0.55684	0.49697	0.44401	0.39711	0.35553	0.31863	0.28584	0.25668	0.23071	0.20756	0.18691
13	0.93722	0.87866	0.77303	0.68095	0.60057	0.53032	0.46884	0.41496	0.36770	0.32618	0.28966	0.25751	0.22917	0.20416	0.18207	0.16253
14	0.93256	0.86995	0.75788	0.66112	0.57748	0.50507	0.44230	0.38782	0.34046	0.29925	0.26333	0.23199	0.20462	0.18068	0.15971	0.14133
15	0.92792	0.86135	0.74301	0.64186	0.55526	0.48102	0.41727	0.36245	0.31524	0.27454	0.23939	0.20900	0.18270	0.15989	0.14010	0.12289
16	0.92330	0.85282	0.72845	0.62317	0.53391	0.45811	0.39365	0.33873	0.29189	0.25187	0.21762	0.18829	0.16312	0.14150	0.12289	0.10686
17	0.91874	0.84438	0.71416	0.60502	0.51337	0.43630	0.37136	0.31657	0.27027	0.23107	0.19784	0.16963	0.14564	0.12522	0.10780	0.09293
18	0.91414	0.83602	0.70016	0.58739	0.49363	0.41552	0.35034	0.29586	0.25025	0.21199	0.17986	0.15282	0.13004	0.11081	0.09456	0.08081
19	0.90959	0.82774	0.68643	0.57029	0.47464	0.39573	0.33051	0.27651	0.23171	0.19499	0.16351	0.13768	0.11611	0.09806	0.08295	0.07027
20	0.90506	0.81954	0.67297	0.55368	0.45639	0.37689	0.31180	0.25842	0.21455	0.17843	0.14864	0.12403	0.10367	0.08678	0.07276	0.06110
21	0.90056	0.81143	0.65978	0.53755	0.43883	0.35894	0.29416	0.24151	0.19866	0.16370	0.13513	0.11174	0.09256	0.07680	0.06383	0.05313
22	0.89608	0.80340	0.64684	0.52189	0.42196	0.34185	0.27751	0.22571	0.18394	0.15018	0.12285	0.10067	0.08264	0.06796	0.05599	0.04620
23	0.89162	0.79544	0.63416	0.50669	0.40573	0.32557	0.26180	0.21095	0.17032	0.13778	0.11168	0.09069	0.07379	0.06014	0.04911	0.04017
24	0.88719	0.78757	0.62172	0.49193	0.39012	0.31007	0.24698	0.19715	0.15770	0.12640	0.10153	0.08170	0.06588	0.05323	0.04308	0.03493
25	0.88277	0.77977	0.60953	0.47761	0.37512	0.29530	0.23300	0.18425	0.14602	0.11597	0.09230	0.07361	0.05882	0.04710	0.03779	0.03038
30	0.86103	0.74192	0.55207	0.41199	0.30832	0.23138	0.17411	0.13137	0.09938	0.07537	0.05731	0.04368	0.03338	0.02557	0.01963	0.01510
35	0.83982	0.70591	0.50003	0.35538	0.25342	0.18129	0.13011	0.09366	0.06763	0.04899	0.03558	0.02592	0.01894	0.01388	0.01019	0.00751
40	0.81914	0.67165	0.45289	0.30656	0.20829	0.14205	0.09722	0.06678	0.04603	0.03184	0.02210	0.01538	0.01075	0.00753	0.00529	0.00373

(PV = present value, r = interest rate per period in decimal form, n = number of periods)

EXHIBIT 7A.6

Present Value of an Annuity Table

The Present Value of Annuity $1.00 in Arrears*

$$PV_a = \frac{1}{r}\left[1 - \frac{1}{(1+r)^n}\right]$$

Periods	0.50%	1%	2%	3%	4%	5%	6%	7%	8%	9%	10%	11%	12%	13%	14%	15%
1	0.99502	0.99010	0.98039	0.97087	0.96154	0.95238	0.94340	0.93458	0.92593	0.91743	0.90909	0.90090	0.89286	0.88496	0.87719	0.86957
2	1.98510	1.97040	1.94156	1.91347	1.86609	1.85941	1.83339	1.80802	1.78326	1.75911	1.73554	1.71252	1.69005	1.66810	1.64666	1.62571
3	2.97025	2.94099	2.88388	2.82861	2.77509	2.72325	2.67301	2.62432	2.57710	2.53129	2.48685	2.44371	2.40183	2.36115	2.32163	2.28323
4	3.95050	3.90197	3.80773	3.71710	3.62990	3.54595	3.46511	3.38721	3.31213	3.23972	3.16987	3.10245	3.03735	2.97447	2.91371	2.85498
5	4.92587	4.85343	4.71346	4.57971	4.45182	4.32948	4.21236	4.10020	3.99271	3.88965	3.79079	3.69590	3.60478	3.51723	3.43308	3.35216
6	5.89638	5.79548	5.60143	5.41719	5.24214	5.07569	4.91732	4.76654	4.62288	4.48592	4.35526	4.23054	4.11141	3.99755	3.88867	3.78448
7	6.86207	6.72819	6.47199	6.23028	6.00205	5.78637	5.58238	5.38929	5.26037	5.03295	4.86842	4.71220	4.56376	4.42261	4.28830	4.16042
8	7.82296	7.65168	7.32548	7.01969	6.73274	6.46321	6.20979	5.97130	5.74664	5.53482	5.33493	5.14612	4.96764	4.79877	4.63886	4.48732
9	8.77906	8.56602	8.16224	7.78611	7.43533	7.10782	6.80169	6.51523	6.24689	5.99525	5.75902	5.53705	5.32825	5.13166	4.94637	4.77158
10	9.73041	9.47130	8.98259	8.53020	8.11090	7.72173	7.36009	7.02358	6.71008	6.41766	6.14457	5.88923	5.65022	5.42624	5.21612	5.01877
11	10.67703	10.36763	9.78685	9.25262	8.76048	8.30641	7.88687	7.49867	7.13896	6.80519	6.49506	6.20652	5.93770	5.68694	5.45273	5.23371
12	11.61893	11.25508	10.57534	9.95400	9.38507	8.86325	8.38384	7.94269	7.53608	7.16073	6.81369	6.49236	6.19437	5.91765	5.66029	5.42062
13	12.55615	12.13374	11.34837	10.63496	9.98565	9.39357	8.85268	8.35765	7.90378	7.48690	7.10336	6.74987	6.42355	6.12181	5.84236	5.58315
14	13.48871	13.00370	12.10625	11.29607	10.56312	9.89864	9.29498	8.74547	8.24424	7.78615	7.36669	6.98187	6.62817	6.30249	6.00207	5.72448
15	14.41662	13.86505	12.84926	11.93794	11.11839	10.37966	9.71225	9.10791	8.55948	8.06069	7.60608	7.19087	6.81086	6.46238	6.14217	5.84737
16	15.33993	14.71787	13.57771	12.56110	11.65230	10.83777	10.10590	9.44665	8.85137	8.31256	7.82371	7.37916	6.97399	6.60388	6.26506	5.95423
17	16.25863	15.56225	14.29187	13.16612	12.16567	11.27407	10.47726	9.73622	9.12164	8.54363	8.02155	7.54879	7.11963	6.72909	6.37286	6.04716
18	17.17277	16.39827	14.99203	13.75351	12.65930	11.68959	10.82760	10.05909	9.37189	8.75563	8.20141	7.70162	7.24967	6.83991	6.46742	6.12797
19	18.08236	17.22601	15.67846	14.32380	13.13394	12.08532	11.15812	10.33560	9.60360	8.95011	8.36492	7.83929	7.36578	6.91797	6.55037	6.19823
20	18.98742	18.04555	16.35143	14.87747	13.59033	12.46221	11.46992	10.59401	9.81815	9.12855	8.51356	7.96333	7.46944	7.02475	6.62313	6.25933
21	19.88798	18.85698	17.01121	15.41502	14.02916	12.82115	11.76408	10.83553	10.01680	9.29224	8.64869	8.07507	7.56200	7.10155	6.68696	6.31246
22	20.78406	19.66038	17.65805	15.93692	14.45112	13.16300	12.04158	11.06124	10.20074	9.44243	8.77154	8.17574	7.64465	7.16951	6.74294	6.35866
23	21.67568	20.45582	18.29220	16.44361	14.85684	13.48857	12.30338	11.27219	10.37106	9.58021	8.88322	8.26643	7.71843	7.22966	6.79206	6.39844
24	22.56287	21.24339	18.91393	16.93554	15.24696	13.79864	12.55036	11.46933	10.52876	9.70661	8.98474	8.34814	7.78432	7.28288	6.83514	6.43377
25	23.44564	22.02316	19.52346	17.41315	15.62208	14.09394	12.78336	11.65358	10.67478	9.82258	9.07704	8.42174	7.84314	7.32998	6.87293	6.46415
30	27.79405	25.80771	22.39646	19.60044	17.29203	15.37245	13.76483	12.40904	11.25778	10.27365	9.42691	8.69379	8.05518	7.49565	7.00266	6.56598
35	32.03537	29.40858	24.99862	21.48722	18.66461	16.37419	14.49825	12.94767	11.65457	10.56682	9.64416	8.85524	8.17550	7.58557	7.07005	6.61661
40	36.17223	32.83469	27.35548	23.11477	19.79277	17.15909	15.04620	13.33171	11.92461	10.75736	9.77908	8.95105	8.24378	7.63438	7.10504	6.64178

*Payments (or receipts) at the end of each period, r = interest rate per period in decimal form, n = number of periods in which a payment is made or received)
(PV_a = present value of an annuity.)

Accounting for Shareholders' Equity

Here's Where You've Been . . .

You learned how a firm accounts for and reports current and long-term liabilities.

Here's Where You're Going . . .

You will learn how a company accounts for and reports contributions from owners, payment of dividends, and retained earnings.

Learning Objectives

When you are finished studying Chapter 8, you should be able to:

1. Explain how a company finances its business with equity.

2. Account for the payment of cash dividends and calculate the allocation of dividends between common and preferred shareholders.

3. Define treasury stock, explain why a company would purchase treasury stock, and account for its purchase.

4. Explain stock dividends and stock splits.

5. Define retained earnings and account for its increases and decreases.

6. Prepare financial statements that contain equity transactions.

7. Compute return on equity and earnings per share, and explain what these ratios mean.

8. Recognize the business risks associated with shareholders' equity and the related controls.

Ethics Matters

Stock options are a common form of compensation for executives of large corporations. A stock option given as executive compensation is a privilege that gives the receiver the right, but not the obligation, to buy shares of the firm's stock at a specified price within a certain period or on a specific date. When the firm's stock price increases above the amount specified in the option, the executive can make quite a lot of money by buying the stock at the lower amount specified in the option and then either keeping the stock or selling it for the higher market price.

In July 2006, Gregory L. Reyes, the chief executive of Brocade Communications Systems, was charged by the Justice Department in connection with a company scheme to issue backdated options. Dozens of firms are being investigated for "rigging the timing of option grants to jack up their value, to the benefit of executives and the detriment of shareholders" ("Making Your Own Luck," *The New York Times* editorial, June 25, 2006). Stock options made Mr. Reyes a very rich man, and he will need some of that wealth to pay his attorneys to try to keep him out of jail.

L.O.1

Explain how a company finances its business with equity.

Components of Shareholders' Equity in a Corporation—Contributed Capital

Every business has owners. As you learned in Chapter 1, there are three general forms of business organization.

1. Sole proprietorships
2. Partnerships
3. Corporations

No matter which form a business takes, it needs money—contributions—from the owners to operate. With sole proprietorships and partnerships, individual owners use their own money or borrow money from family, friends, or banks. Corporations have access to more money because they sell stocks to investors. In this chapter, we will focus on how the firm acquires and accounts for money from owners.

The claims of the owners to the assets of the firm are called shareholders' equity or stockholders' equity. Recall there are two major parts to stockholders' equity—contributed capital and retained earnings. Each part is recorded and reported on the balance sheet as a separate amount. Contributed capital is the amount owners have invested in the corporation. Contributed capital is subdivided into two parts: capital stock and additional paid-in capital.

Stock—Authorized, Issued, and Outstanding

In return for their contributions, the owners receive shares of stock, representing ownership equal to the fair value of those contributions. The form of capital contributions is usually cash, but contributions of other assets are possible.

When a corporation is formed, the state in which the firm incorporates requires an agreement that specifies the characteristics of the firm. For example, the charter sets a maximum number of shares of stock it can issue, called **authorized shares**. **Issued shares** are shares offered and sold to shareholders—in batches, during times when a company needs capital.

Exhibit 8.1 shows the shareholders' equity section of Linens 'n Things Inc. at January 1, 2005, and January 3, 2004. Notice the number of shares of common stock authorized is

Authorized shares are shares of stock that are available for a firm to issue per its corporate charter.

Issued shares are shares of stock that have been offered and sold to shareholders.

EXHIBIT 8.1

From the Balance Sheet of
Linens 'n Things
Consolidated Balance Sheets

(in thousands, except share amounts)

Shareholders' Equity Section of the Balance Sheet of Linens 'n Things

As you read about the different parts of shareholders' equity, refer to this information from the balance sheet of Linens 'n Things.

LINENS·N·THINGS
Your Home Super Store

	January 1, 2005	January 3, 2004 restated
Shareholders' equity		
Preferred stock ($0.01 par value; 1,000,000 shares authorized; none issued and outstanding)	–	–
Common stock ($0.01 par value; 135,000,000 shares authorized; 45,460,467 shares issued and 45,200,896 shares outstanding at January 1, 2005; 45,052,255 shares issued and 44,793,619 shares outstanding at January 3, 2004)	455	450
Additional paid-in capital	372,627	362,483
Retained earnings	440,914	380,393
Accumulated other comprehensive gain	2,619	1,391
Treasury stock, at cost; 259,571 shares at January 1, 2005 and 258,636 shares at January 3, 2004	(7,262)	(7,340)
Total shareholders' equity	809,353	737,377
Total liabilities and shareholders' equity	$1,591,884	$1,467,456

135 million and the number of shares issued is 45,460,467 at January 1, 2005. An issued share of stock does not need to remain outstanding. Firms can purchase their own stock in the stock market. **Outstanding shares** are owned by stockholders rather than by the corporation.

When a company buys back its stock, those shares of stock are called **treasury stock**. Any stock that has been issued by a company may be either outstanding, which is owned by investors, or treasury stock, which is held in the company's treasury. Notice in Exhibit 8.1 that Linens 'n Things has a significant amount of treasury stock (259,571 shares at January 1, 2005), shown at the end of the shareholders' equity section where it is subtracted from total shareholders' equity.

Exhibit 8.2 shows the relationships among authorized shares, issued shares, outstanding shares, and treasury shares.

Common Stock

Common stock, as the name suggests, is the most common type of capital stock representing ownership of a corporation. All corporations must have common stock. The owners of common stock have the right to

1. Vote for members of the board of directors
2. Share in the corporation's profits
3. Share in any assets left if the corporation must dissolve (for example, if the company goes out of business due to bankruptcy)
4. Acquire more shares when the corporation issues new stock, often referred to as a preemptive right

The corporate charter determines a fixed per-share amount called the **par value** of the stock. Par value is an arbitrary amount and has no real meaning in today's business environment, and most states do not require a par value. The corporation must maintain a specific amount of capital, as determined by the state or contained in the corporate charter. That amount could be the total par value of the outstanding stock. Frequently, however,

Outstanding shares are shares of stock that are owned by stockholders.

Treasury stock are shares of stock that have been repurchased by the issuing firm.

Common stock is the most widespread form of ownership in a corporation; common shareholders have a vote in the election of the firm's board of directors.

Par value is the monetary amount assigned to a share of stock in the corporate charter. It has little meaning in today's business environment.

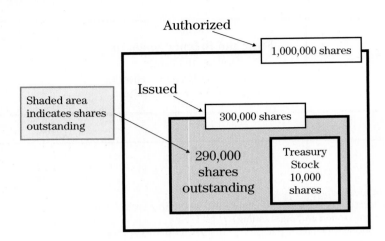

other means are used to determine the legal capital to protect creditors. Exhibit 8.1 shows that Linens 'n Things common stock has a par value of $0.01 per share. If you know the par value per share of the common stock and you know the dollar amount in the common stock account, you can calculate the number of shares that have been issued. Use the balance sheet in Exhibit 8.1 to see how that can be done. At January 1, 2005, the common stock account has a balance of $455,000, and the par value of the stock is $0.01 per share. To calculate the number of shares issued, divide the common stock balance by the par value per share to see how many shares are represented by the balance in the common stock account.

$$\frac{\$455,000}{\$0.01} = 45,500,000 \text{ shares}$$

Because the common stock account balance was rounded to $455,000, the number of shares from the calculation will also be rounded. The actual number of shares issued is 45,460,467. Our rounded calculation shows 45,500,000 shares.

Stock is usually sold for more than its par value. In some states, it is a legal requirement that stock sell for at least par value. Suppose the par value of a company's stock is $2 per share, the market price of the stock on the date the stock is issued is $10 per share, and the company issues 100 shares. Here is how to calculate the dollar amount that will be recorded as common stock.

$$\$2 \text{ par per share} \times 100 \text{ shares} = \$200$$

The amount of $200 will be shown on the balance sheet in an account separate from any contributions in excess of the par value. The remaining $8 per share will be credited to another paid-in capital account.

$$\$8 \text{ excess over par (per share)} \times 100 \text{ shares} = \$800$$

The total par value amount—$200—is called common or capital stock, and the excess contributions amount—$800—is called additional paid-in capital. Both amounts are reported on the balance sheet. Exhibit 8.3 shows how the amount of cash from the issue of stock is divided between the two paid-in capital accounts. Remember that paid-in capital designates both capital stock and additional paid-in capital. All amounts of contributed capital are called paid-in capital.

Suppose the corporate charter of Chicane Barkery authorizes 50 million shares of common stock at par value $0.01 per share. Suppose the company issues 300,000 shares at $15 per share. Here is how the firm would record the transaction.

Cash ($10 per share)	Common Stock at par ($2 per share)	Additional Paid-In Capital ($8 per share)
Company receives cash from issuing stock	**The amount, $10, is divided between two accounts: common stock and additional paid-in capital**	
Stock Value: 100 × $10 per share = $1,000	**Common Stock:** 100 × $2 per share = $200 + **Additional Paid-In Capital:** 100 × ($10 – $2) per share = $800	

EXHIBIT 8.3

Recording the Issue of Stock

One hundred shares of stock are issued for $10 each. Par value is $2 per share. The proceeds from the stock issue, $1,000, is divided between two accounts: Common Stock and Additional Paid-in Capital.

Assets	=	Liabilities	+	Shareholders' equity	
				Contributed capital	+ Retained earnings
4,500,000 cash				3,000 common stock 4,497,000 additional paid-in capital	

How would this transaction be shown on Chicane Barkery's financial statements? Suppose the company is issuing the stock for the first time. The shareholders' equity section of the balance sheet would show this information in the part of the statement that shows contributed capital.

Contributed capital	
Common stock (par value $0.01 per share; 50 million shares authorized; 300,000 shares issued and outstanding)	$ 3,000
Additional paid-in capital	4,497,000

Preferred Stock

In addition to common stock, corporations may have a second type of capital stock—**preferred stock**. Owners of preferred stock must receive their dividends before the common shareholders and also have a preferred claim on assets. If a firm goes out of business, the preferred shareholders receive assets that remain after the creditors have been paid. The common shareholders then get any remaining assets. However, the owners of preferred stock usually do not have voting rights.

Preferred stock are shares of stock that represent a special kind of ownership in a corporation. Preferred shareholders do not get a vote but they do receive dividends before the common shareholders.

UNDERSTANDING Business

Why Do Companies Have Preferred Stock?

One way a firm can obtain needed funds is to issue preferred stock. Just like issuing common stock, issuing preferred stock is a source of financing. Preferred stock is a special class of stock that has certain features that common stock does not have. These features can include shareholders' rights: to receive dividends before the common shareholders receive any dividends, to receive a share of the assets in the event of bankruptcy before common shareholders get any, and to exchange their preferred stock for common stock under certain conditions.

Preferred stock may be bought back by the issuing corporation directly from the shareholders (this means it is "callable" preferred stock), and preferred shareholders do not get a vote in running the company. Because of the features of the stock, preferred shareholders may seem more like creditors than owners.

Because the holders of preferred stock are more like creditors, preferred stock may be used as a weapon in a hostile takeover attempt—when someone tries to buy enough of the target company's stock to get the majority of shares so that the person (or a company), the new buyer, will be able to take over and run the target com-

pany. Often, the corporate charter gives the board of directors (BOD) complete discretion about when and how to offer preferred stock. If necessary, the BOD can issue a very large number of shares of preferred stock to make a takeover more difficult. The newly issued preferred stock will be issued to the current shareholders at a reduced rate, and the shareholders will convert it to common stock.

This way to defend against a hostile takeover is an example of a poison pill. In general, a poison pill is a strategy that firms use to discourage a hostile takeover by another company. The firm attempts to make its stock less attractive to the potential acquiring firm.

Of the total amount of all stock a firm issues, the BOD can set a maximum amount that a single outside party may acquire. If an outsider acquires a number of shares of the firm's stock exceeding that amount, the BOD will activate the poison pill. Poison pills became a great defense in the 1980s when they were devised to prevent hostile takeovers that were prevalent at that time. The poison pill is a trigger point that, once activated, means the BOD can, in this example, issue preferred stock at a reduced rate to current stockholders. This, in turn, increases the price of taking over a company to an outside party and in most cases kills the takeover efforts by the outside party.

Your Turn 8-1
Your Turn
Your Turn

Suppose General Mills issued 10,000 shares of $1 par per share common stock for $20 per share. How would the company record this transaction?

Cash Dividends

People buy stock in a corporation because they hope the value of the corporation will increase. Selling stock for more than its cost is one way the shareholder can make money on the investment. The other way is by receiving distributions from the firm. The distributions shareholders receive from the earnings of the corporation are called **dividends**. The board of directors decides the amount of dividends to be paid and when they will be paid to the shareholders. The directors are also free not to pay dividends at any time they believe it is in the best interest of the corporation. The board of directors may want to reinvest the available cash in the business by buying more equipment or inventory.

EXHIBIT 8.4

Notes to General Electric and Papa John's Financial Statements

General Electric	Papa John's
WE DECLARED $9.6 BILLION IN DIVIDENDS IN 2005. *Per-share dividends of $0.91 were up 11% from 2004, following a 6% increase from the preceding year. In December 2005, our Board of Directors raised our quarterly dividend 14% to $0.25 per share. We have rewarded our shareowners with over 100 consecutive years of dividends, with 30 consecutive years of dividend growth, and our dividend growth for the past five years has significantly outpaced that of companies in the Standard & Poor's (S&P) 500 stock index.*	*Since our initial public offering of common stock in 1993, we have not paid dividends on our common stock, and have no current plans to do so.*

Some firms, like General Electric, consistently pay a dividend. Other firms, like Papa John's, do not pay dividends. Compare the note to the financial statement for General Electric (left) and Papa John's (right).

Microsoft Corporation, for example, was started in 1975 and did not pay a dividend until 2003. Some firms traditionally pay a dividend, and others have never paid a dividend. Exhibit 8.4 shows excerpts from the notes to the financial statements of General Electric and Papa John's that explain the dividend policy. Notice that General Electric pays a dividend and Papa John's does not. Often new companies do not pay any dividends because they want to reinvest all of their earnings in the business. Established companies often do not have the growth potential of new firms and can attract investors with regular dividend payments.

Important Dates Related to Dividends

When the board of directors decides that a cash dividend will be paid, there are three important dates: the declaration date, the date of record, and the payment date.

Declaration Date. The dividend declaration date is the date on which the board of directors decides a dividend will be paid and announces it to shareholders. On this date, a legal liability called dividends payable is created. The amount of this liability is balanced in the accounting equation with a reduction to a temporary account called *dividends* or directly deducted from retained earnings. If a firm uses a dividends account, its balance will be deducted from retained earnings at the end of the accounting period. Dividends are not deducted from the contributed capital account because they are a distribution of earnings, not a distribution of the shareholders' original paid-in capital. Here is how a firm would record the declaration of $50,000 dividends to be divided among the shareholders.

Assets	=	Liabilities	+	Shareholders' equity	
				Contributed capital	+ Retained earnings
		50,000 dividends payable			(50,000) dividends or retained earnings

Remember, dividends are not included as an expense on the income statement because they are not related to generating revenue. Rather than a deduction from a company's earnings, dividends are considered a distribution of a company's earnings to owners in proportion to their share of ownership.

Date of Record. The date of record is used to determine exactly who will receive the dividends. Anyone owning the stock on this date is entitled to the dividend. After a corporation originally sells stock to investors, they are free to trade—sell and buy—shares of stock with other people. Whoever owns the stock on the date of record will receive the dividend. A stockholder may own the stock for only 1 day and receive the full dividend amount. After this date, stock is said to be ex-dividend. That is, if it is traded after the date of record, the new owner will not get the dividend. The firm does not record anything in its accounting records on the date of record.

Payment Date. The payment date is when the cash is actually paid to the shareholders. This payment has the same effect on the accounting equation as the payment of any liability: Assets (cash) are reduced and liabilities (dividends payable) are reduced.

Assets	=	Liabilities	+	Shareholders' equity		
				Contributed capital	+	Retained earnings
(50,000) cash		(50,000) dividends payable				

Distribution of Dividends between Common and Preferred Shareholders

The corporation must give holders of preferred stock a certain amount of dividends before common stockholders can receive any dividends. Dividends on preferred stock are usually fixed at a percentage of the par value of the stock. For example, preferred stock characterized as 10% preferred ($100 par) will receive a dividend of $10 in any year the corporation's board of directors declares a dividend. The preferred shareholders must get their $10 per preferred share before the common shareholders receive any dividends. The board of directors has discretion about whether or not to pay dividends to the preferred shareholders, but the board does not decide on the amount of the dividend for the preferred shareholders. The dividend for preferred shareholders is typically shown on the face of the preferred stock certificate. There are two types of preferred stock—cumulative and noncumulative.

- Cumulative preferred stock means the fixed dividend amount accumulates from year to year, and the entire amount of all past unpaid dividends must be paid to the preferred shareholders before any dividends can be paid to the common shareholders. Most preferred stock is cumulative preferred stock.
- With noncumulative preferred stock, the board determines whether or not to make up any missed dividends to the preferred shareholders. Any dividends owed to holders of cumulative preferred stock from past years but undeclared are called dividends in arrears. The corporation does not consider such dividends liabilities but does disclose them in the notes to the financial statements. Only after a dividend is actually declared is it considered a liability.

An Example of Dividend Payment

Suppose JG Company has the following stock outstanding.

- 1,000 shares of 9%, $100 par, cumulative preferred stock
- 50,000 shares of $0.50 per share par common stock

The company last paid dividends in December 2005. With the 2005 payment, JG paid all dividends through December 31, 2005. There were no dividends in arrears prior to 2006. No dividends were paid in 2006. On October 1, 2007, the board of directors declares a total of $30,000 in dividends for its shareholders to be paid on December 15, 2007 to all shareholders of record on November 1, 2007. How much of the dividend will go to the preferred shareholders, and how much will go to the common shareholders?

First, calculate the annual dividend for the preferred shareholders.

$$1,000 \text{ shares} \times \$100 \text{ par value} \times 0.09 = \$9,000$$

Because the preferred stock is cumulative and no dividends were paid to the preferred shareholders in 2006, JG must first pay the 2006 dividend of $9,000 to the preferred shareholders. Then, JG must pay the current year's (2007) $9,000 dividend to the preferred shareholders. The company pays a total of $18,000 to the preferred shareholders, and the remaining $12,000 goes to the common shareholders. On the date of declaration, October 1, the company incurs the legal liability for the dividend payment. Here is how the company records the transaction.

Assets	=	Liabilities	+	Shareholders' equity		
				Contributed capital	+	Retained earnings
		18,000 dividends payable, preferred shareholders 12,000 dividends payable, common shareholders				(30,000) dividends or retained earnings

On the declaration date, the company records the liability. If JG were to prepare its balance sheet, it would show a current liability called dividends payable. This liability is a debt owed to the shareholders for dividends. A corporation may list the liability to common shareholders separately from the liability to preferred shareholders, as shown in the preceding example, or the corporation may combine the preferred and common dividends into one amount for total dividends payable.

On December 15, when JG actually pays the cash to the shareholders to fulfill the obligation, cash is reduced and the liability—dividends payable—is removed from the records. Here is how the company records the transaction.

Assets	=	Liabilities	+	Shareholders' equity		
				Contributed capital	+	Retained earnings
(30,000) cash		(18,000) dividends payable, preferred shareholders (12,000) dividends payable, common shareholders				

Suppose the preferred stock was noncumulative. Then, JG would pay only the current year's dividend of $9,000 to the preferred shareholders, and the remaining $21,000 would go to the common shareholders.

A corporation has 10,000 shares of 8% cumulative preferred stock and 20,000 shares of common stock outstanding. Par value for each is $100. No dividends were paid last year, but this year $200,000 in dividends is paid to stockholders. How much of this $200,000 goes to the holders of preferred stock?

Your Turn 8-2

Treasury Stock

Companies can trade—buy and sell—their own stock on the open market. (The timing of these transactions is controlled by SEC rules.) Treasury stock refers to common stock that has been issued and subsequently purchased by the company that issued it. Once it is purchased by the company, the stock is considered treasury stock until it is resold or retired—taken completely out of circulation.

L.O.3
Define treasury stock, explain why a company would purchase treasury stock, and account for its purchase.

Why Do Firms Buy Their Own Stocks?

There are five common reasons why companies purchase shares of their own stock.

1. *To have stock to distribute to employees for compensation plans.* When a firm wants to give employees or corporate executives shares of stock, the firm will often use treasury shares. Issuing new shares is a costly and time-consuming project, with many requirements set by the SEC, so firms typically issue new shares only to raise a significant amount of money.

2. *To return cash to the shareholders using a way that is more flexible for both the firm and the shareholder than paying cash dividends.* Firms that have a great deal of cash

EXHIBIT 8.5

PetsMart Purchases Its Own Common Stock

Share Purchase Programs

In April 2000, the Board of Directors approved a plan to purchase the Company's common stock. In March 2003, the Board of Directors extended the term of the purchase of the Company's common stock for an additional three years through March 2006 and increased the authorized amount of annual purchases to $35,000,000. In September 2004, the Board of Directors approved a program, which replaced the March 2003 program, authorizing the purchase of up to $150,000,000 of the Company's common stock through fiscal year 2005. During the first quarter of fiscal 2005, the Company purchased approximately 3,618,000 shares of its common stock for $105,001,000, which completed the authorized purchase of $150,000,000 of the Company's common stock under the September 2004 program.

In June 2005, the Board of Directors approved a program authorizing the purchase of up to $270,000,000 of the Company's common stock through fiscal 2006. During fiscal 2005, the Company purchased approximately 6,322,000 shares of its common stock for $160,001,000, under the June 2005 program.

will often buy their own stock as a way to get the cash to the shareholders. The firm has complete flexibility over when to buy the stock and how much to buy, and the individual shareholders have complete flexibility over whether or not they sell their shares back to the company. This flexibility benefits the firm and the shareholder. The firm can control the mix of debt and equity in its capital structure. For example, it can reduce equity by buying back stock. The shareholders can decide when to take cash out of their investment in the firm by deciding whether or not to sell back their stock.

3. *To increase the company's earnings per share.* When a firm decreases the number of shares outstanding, earnings per share will increase with no change in net income due to the mathematics of the EPS calculation. However, a firm must consider that the cash used to buy back the stock would have earned some return—at least interest revenue—that would increase the numerator by some amount.

4. *To reduce the cash needed to pay future dividends.* When a firm reduces the number of shares outstanding, the total cash needed for dividends decreases. Treasury shares do not receive dividends.

5. *To reduce chances of a hostile takeover.* Top management or the board of directors may help their firm resist a takeover by making sure the treasury stock is distributed or sold to the right people—those who would resist the takeover. Buying stock also reduces cash reserves, which are a popular attraction for takeover attempts. Boards of directors decide if and when a firm will pursue a strategy to buy back their shares. It has become quite common, and you can read about it in the firm's notes to the financial statements.

Exhibit 8.5 shows an excerpt from the notes to the financial statements of PetsMart for the fiscal year ended January 29, 2006. Notice that PetsMart has a very active stock repurchase program. Over half of the firms that trade on the New York Stock Exchange regularly purchase their own stock.

Accounting for the Purchase

The purchase of treasury stock reduces a company's assets (cash) and reduces shareholders' equity. Suppose Papa John's decided to buy back some of the stock it had previously issued. Treasury stock is most often recorded at cost. Here is what the company will record if it buys back 100 shares at $16 per share.

Assets	=	Liabilities	+	Shareholders' equity		
				Contributed capital	+	Retained earnings
(1,600) cash				(1,600) treasury stock		

The par value and how much the stock was previously issued for do not matter. Using the cost method, treasury stock is simply recorded at the amount the firm pays to repurchase it. Under the cost method, the following procedures are used.

• Treasury stock holdings for the company are shown as a reduction in the total of shareholders' equity on the balance sheet. Therefore, treasury stock is a type of shareholders' equity. Unlike other equity accounts, however, the cost of treasury stock reduces shareholders' equity. Due to its presence in the shareholders' equity section of the balance sheet and its negative effect on total equity, the treasury stock account is called a contra-equity account and is subtracted from total shareholders' equity.

• No gains or losses are recorded in the company's financial records when a company purchases treasury stock or later resells it. Even if a company acquired one of its own shares for $4 and later sold it for $6, the company would not show a gain of $2. Instead, the company would have more money come in from the sale of stock—which is contributed capital.

Suppose a company originally issued 100,000 shares of $1 par common stock for $15 per share. Several years later, the company decides to buy back 1,000 shares of common stock. The stock is selling for $50 per share at the time of the stock repurchase. (a) How would the transaction be recorded in the accounting equation? (b) After the transaction, how many shares are issued and how many shares are outstanding?

Your Turn 8-3
Your Turn
Your Turn

Selling Treasury Stock

If treasury stock is sold, the shares sold will be removed from the treasury stock account at the amount the firm paid for the stock when it was repurchased. If the treasury stock is sold at a price higher than its cost, the excess will be classified as paid-in capital from treasury stock transactions.

Suppose a firm purchased 1,000 treasury shares at $50 per share. A year later, the firm sells half of the shares for $60 each. Removing 500 shares of treasury stock at $50 cost will increase total shareholders' equity by reducing the balance in the treasury stock account, a contra-equity account. Here is how the firm would record selling 500 shares of stock that cost $50 per share for $60 per share.

Assets	=	Liabilities	+	Shareholders' equity		
				Contributed capital	+	**Retained earnings**
30,000 cash				25,000 treasury stock		
				5,000 paid-in capital from treasury stock transactions		

 *News Flash*

How much of their own stock do firms buy back? You might be surprised to learn that Texas Instruments, for example, bought back $4.15 billion worth of its own stock during its 2005 fiscal year. Dell bought back 205 million shares at a cost of $7.2 billion during its fiscal year ended February 3, 2005. In July 2006, Microsoft announced plans of "a stock-buyback program that includes a $20 billion tender offer for shares to be completed August 17 [2006] and authorization for as much as $20 billion in additional buybacks through 2011." (*The Wall Street Journal*, July 21, 2006, p. A3)

There would be 500 shares remaining in the treasury stock account, each at a cost of $50. Suppose the firm sold those shares for $48 per share. As in the previous example, the treasury stock must be removed from the total amount of treasury stock at its cost. In this example, instead of having additional paid-in capital, the firm would reduce a paid-in capital account to balance the accounting equation. The difference between the cost and the reissue price—$2 per share × 500 shares = $1,000—would be deducted from paid-in capital from treasury stock transactions. Here is how a firm would record selling 500 treasury shares—that originally cost the company $50 per share—for a reissue price of $48.

Assets	=	Liabilities	+	Shareholders' equity	
				Contributed + **capital**	**Retained** **earnings**
24,000 cash				25,000 treasury stock (1,000) paid-in capital from treasury stock transactions	

If the amount in the account paid-in capital from treasury stock transactions were insufficient to cover the $2 decrease in stock price, then retained earnings would be reduced by the amount needed to balance the accounting equation.

Reporting Treasury Stock

Treasury stock is most often reported as a deduction from shareholders' equity on the balance sheet. Exhibit 8.6 shows how the shares Abercrombie & Fitch has repurchased are reported on its balance sheet. You will see that treasury stock, a contra-equity account, is deducted from total shareholders' equity. Always remember, there are never any gains or losses from treasury stock transactions. Exchanges between a company and its owners—issue of stock, payment of dividends, and purchase or sale of treasury stock—do not affect the income statement.

Your Turn 8-4
Your Turn
Your Turn

> Surety Corporation started the year 2005 with 125,000 shares of common stock with par value of $1 issued and outstanding. The issue price of these shares averaged $6 per share. During 2005, Surety purchased 1,000 shares of its own stock at an average price of $7 per share. How would Surety report its treasury stock on the balance sheet at December 31, 2005?

L.O.4
Explain stock dividends and stock splits.

Stock Dividends and Stock Splits

You have learned about issuing stock and buying back stock. There are two other transactions that a company may have with stock: a stock dividend and a stock split.

Stock Dividends

Stock dividends are new shares of stock that are distributed to the company's current shareholders.

A corporation may want to pay a dividend to shareholders but not have sufficient cash on hand. Instead of giving the shareholders cash, the corporation may give the shareholders additional shares of stock in the company. This is called a **stock dividend**. Recording the stock dividend simply reclassifies amounts in the shareholders' equity accounts. The corporation that issues a stock dividend converts retained earnings to contributed capital, thereby giving the stockholders a more direct claim to that portion of equity. A stock dividend is not income to the shareholder.

GAAP distinguishes between a small stock dividend—usually considered less than 25% of a company's outstanding stock—and a large stock dividend—greater than 25% of a company's outstanding stock. For a small stock dividend, the company uses the market value of the stock to record the transaction because a small stock dividend has a negligible

EXHIBIT 8.6

From the Balance Sheet of Abercrombie & Fitch

Abercrombie & Fitch
Consolidated Balance Sheets (partial)

(Thousands)	January 28, 2006	January 29, 2005
Shareholder's equity		
Class A common stock—$.01 par value: 150,000,000 shares authorized and 103,300,000 shares issued at January 28, 2006 and January 29, 2005, respectively	1,033	1,033
Paid-in capital	161,678	140,251
Retained earnings	1,357,791	1,076,023
Accumulated other comprehensive income	(796)	–
Deferred compensation	26,206	15,048
Treasury stock, at average cost 15,573,789 and 17,262,943 shares at January 28, 2006 and January 29, 2005, respectively	(550,795)	(563,029)
Total shareholder's equity	995,117	669,326
Total liabilities and shareholder's equity	$1,789,718	$1,386,791

From the notes to the financial statements:
The Company repurchased 1,765,000 shares, 11,150,500 shares, and 4,401,000 shares of its Class A Common Stock pursuant to previously authorized stock repurchase programs in Fiscal 2005, Fiscal 2004, and Fiscal 2003, respectively. As of January 28, 2006, the Company had 5,683,500 shares remaining available to repurchase under the 6,000,000 shares authorized by the Board of Directors in August 2005.

effect on a stock's market price. For a large stock dividend, the company uses the par value of the stock to record the transaction because a large stock dividend puts so much new stock in the market that the market price per share adjusts to the increased number of shares.

Suppose a company declares and issues a 10% stock dividend to its current shareholders. The stock has a par value of $1 per share, and the current market price is $18 per share. The company will record the stock dividend at its market value. Before the stock dividend, the company has 150,000 shares outstanding. Therefore, the company will issue 15,000 new shares (150,000 × 10%) to shareholders. Here is how this company will record the stock dividend.

Assets	=	Liabilities	+	Shareholders' equity		
				Contributed capital	+	**Retained earnings**
				15,000 common stock 255,000 additional paid-in capital		(270,000) retained earnings

This is sometimes called capitalizing retained earnings. Exhibit 8.7 shows how the equity section of the balance sheet is affected by a stock dividend. When considering stock dividends, remember that stock dividends do not increase any shareholder's percentage of ownership in the company. If you owned 5% of the company before the stock dividend, you own 5% of the company after the stock dividend. After the dividend, your 5% includes more shares—but every shareholder's portion of ownership remains the same.

Stock Splits

Stock splits occur when a corporation increases the number of shares outstanding and proportionately decreases the par value per share. It is different than a stock dividend. The outstanding shares are "split" into two or more shares with a corresponding division of the par

A **stock split** is the division of the current shares of stock by a specific number to increase the number of shares outstanding.

EXHIBIT 8.7

Shareholders' Equity Before and After a Stock Dividend

A stock dividend does not change total shareholders' equity. It simply takes a small portion of retained earnings and reclassifies it as additional paid-in capital.

Shareholder's Equity

	Before Stock Dividend	After Stock Dividend
Shareholder's Equity		
Common stock, $1 par	$ 150,000	$165,000
Additional paid-in capital	600,000	855,000
Total paid-in capital	750,000	1,020,000
Retained earnings	950,000	680,000
Total shareholder's equity	$1,700,000	$1,700,000

value. Sometimes a firm will call in all the old shares and reissue new shares. Other times, the firm will issue additional split shares with a notice to the shareholders of a change in par value of all shares.

Suppose you own 100 shares of Target stock. It has a par value of $1 a share and a market value of $24 a share. Suppose Target's board of directors votes to split the stock 2 for 1. After the split, instead of having 100 shares with a par value of $1 per share, you have 200 shares with a par value of $0.50 per share. Theoretically, a stock split should not affect the stock price beyond splitting the price in the same proportions as the stock split. For example, if a share was trading for $24 before a 2-for-1 split, a new share should trade for $12. However, a stock split almost always results in a small increase in the price of the stock beyond its proportionate share of the original price. The price of the share in this example would trade for something greater than $12. Some finance experts believe that the stock is now easier to trade at the lower price, which equates to increased demand, which, in turn, results in an increased stock price. Companies record the details of the stock split parenthetically in the shareholders' equity part of the financial statements. There is nothing formally recorded in the accounting records.

Your Turn 8-5
Your Turn
Your Turn

1. **Compare a stock split and a stock dividend.**
2. **Suppose you own 1,500 shares, which is 3%, of ABC Company's outstanding stock. If ABC declares a 2-for-1 stock split, how many shares will you own? What percentage ownership will your shares now represent?**

L.O.5
Define retained earnings and account for its increases and decreases.

Retained earnings is the total earnings of a firm since its inception, reduced by any net losses, that have not been distributed to shareholders.

Retained Earnings

Retained earnings is the amount of all the earnings of the firm—since its beginning—that have not been distributed to the stockholders. Retained earnings may also be called earned capital.

Retained earnings includes

1. Net incomes since the day the company began, minus
2. Any net losses since the day the company began, minus
3. Any dividends declared since the company began.

Because retained earnings is a part of shareholders' equity, the change in retained earnings during the period is contained in the statement of changes in shareholders' equity. Sometimes the part of the shareholders' equity statement that provides the details of the changes in retained earnings is shown separately and called a statement of retained earnings.

Your Turn 8-6
Your Turn
Your Turn

Suppose B&B Company started the year with retained earnings of $84,500. During the year, B&B had net income of $25,600 and declared cash dividends of $12,200. What was the ending balance in retained earnings?

Tom's Wear Issues New Stock

When a privately owned company decides it wants to offer ownership to the public—to raise a significant amount of capital, the form of the business organization must be a corporation. (A sole proprietorship or a partnership wanting to offer ownership to the public must first change its form to a corporation.) The first public offering of stock on one of the stock exchanges is called an initial public offering (IPO). Much like the work done before a company issues bonds, a company must do a great deal of work to prepare for an IPO. The Securities and Exchange Commission (SEC) requires the company to provide many reports, including a set of financial statements contained in a report called a prospectus. Remember, the job of the SEC is to protect the public.

In August, Tom decides his company could raise a great deal of capital by "going public." The company has a substantial amount of debt, and Tom decides it would be a good long-term strategy to increase the company's equity. As you know, a company's creditors and owners have claim to the company's assets, and the relationship between the amount of debt and the amount of equity in a company is called the company's capital structure. Tom decides that his company's capital structure is weighted too heavily toward debt, and he wants to increase the cash available to pay off some of that debt. To increase his company's equity, Tom will offer the opportunity to the general public to become part owners in Tom's Wear.

Exhibit 8.8 shows the balance sheet for Tom's Wear at the beginning of August. This is the July 31 balance sheet you saw in Chapter 7 (Exhibit 7.14). The first transaction for August is the Tom's Wear IPO. Although the form of the company has been a corporation, Tom's Wear has a lot of work to do to prepare to go public. The SEC requirements for this IPO are extensive, and we will let the investment bankers do the work behind the scenes. These are finance, accounting, and legal experts in the area of IPOs. The accounting changes in the balance sheet depend on the characteristics of the debt and equity of the company and the agreements the creditors and owners make. We will make it very simple for Tom's Wear, but in a real-world IPO, transactions could be much more complicated.

L.O.6
Prepare financial statements that contain equity transactions.

EXHIBIT 8.8

Balance Sheet for Tom's Wear at August 1

tom's wear

Tom's Wear, Inc.
Balance Sheet At August 1

Assets		Liabilities & Shareholder's Equity	
Current assets		Current liabilities	
Cash	$ 20,651	Accounts payable	$ 36,000
Accounts receivable		Interest payable	1,500
(net of $3,290 allowance		Warranty liability	2,239
for uncollectible accounts)	101,810	Salaries payable	2,352
Inventory	8,910	Other payables	1,148
Prepaid insurance	50	Current portion of	
Prepaid rent	600	mortgage payable	2,710
Prepaid Web services	150	Current portion of	
		long-term notes payable	6,000
Total current assets	132,171		
		Total current liabilities	51,949
Land	7,500		
Equipment (net of $500		Mortgage payable	72,290
accumulated depreciation)	3,500	Notes payable	24,000
Van (net of $4,205		Total liabilities	148,239
accumulated depreciation)	25,795		
Building (net of $130		Shareholder's Equity	
accumulated depreciation)	67,370		
		Common stock	5,000
		Retained earnings	83,097
		Total liabilities and	
Total assets	$ 236,336	shareholder's equity	$ 236,336

Tom works with an investment banking firm and an accounting firm to prepare the stock offering—the IPO. The investment bankers do the legal work and essentially buy the stock and then offer it to the public. The accountants prepare extensive financial information, required by the SEC, in a document called a prospectus. (For simplicity, we will assume that all of their fees have been deducted from the issue price of the stock.) Tom's Wear's corporate charter has 50,000,000 shares of common stock authorized with a par value of $0.01. Tom's personal ownership, which we have simply referred to as common stock without any details of the number of shares, is actually 500,000 shares. (Recall, his contribution was $5,000.) Tom wants to retain a majority of the stock so that he can retain control of the company, so Tom's Wear decides to issue 250,000 additional common shares in this initial offering. The shares are issued at $5 per share.

Assets	=	Liabilities	+	Shareholders' equity		
				Contributed capital	+	**Retained earnings**
1,250,000 cash				2,500 common stock 1,247,500 additional paid-in capital		

The remaining August transactions for Tom's Wear are given in Exhibit 8.9. Trace each one to the accounting equation worksheet in Exhibit 8.10. Then, study the list of adjustments. To make the necessary adjustments, you will need the following information.

1. Tom's Wear employees drove the van 20,000 miles in August. So the depreciation on the van is $2,900 (20,000 miles × 0.145 per mile).

EXHIBIT 8.9

August Transactions for Tom's Wear, Inc.

1	August 1	Tom's Wear issues stock for $1,250,000.
2	August 2	Tom's Wear pays the salaries payable of $2,352 and the payroll taxes of $1,148 recorded as "Other Payables."
3	August 10	Collects cash on accounts receivable of $96,000
4	August 12	Pays accounts payable of $30,000
5	August 14	Tom has been concentrating on increasing sales, so he must increase inventory purchases as well. With the new inflow of cash from the stock offering, Tom's Wear decides to buy 25,000 shirts. He gets a quantity discount from the vendor, paying $3.50 for each shirt. He pays cash for the purchase.
6	August 20	Tom's Wear finds out that Play Ball Sports Shop has closed and filed bankruptcy. He writes off the account, which has a balance of $3,000.
7	August 15–30	Tom's sales efforts continue to pay off with the addition of several more customers. Tom's Wear lowers the price slightly, and he is able to dramatically increase sales. During August, Tom's Wear sells 20,151 shirts at $10 each. All sales are on account.
8	August 15–30	During August, 300 shirts are returned with defects, and Tom's Wear replaces them with new shirts.
9	August 15–30	Miscellaneous operating expenses amount to $42,500 for the month, paid in cash.
10	August 30	The payroll has grown considerably because Tom has hired several new employees, including an on-site manager to run the warehouse. He has also put himself on the management payroll. Tom's Wear has hired a firm to handle his payroll because he has hired several new employees. The firm sends the payroll company a check for $22,000 by the 30th of each month to cover the monthly payroll and payroll tax expenses. The payroll company pays the employees and the payroll taxes and charges a fee based on the number of employees. Tom's Wear records the total expense as salary expense for financial statement purposes.
11	August 30	Tom's Wear pays for insurance to cover the business from August 15 to December 31 for a total of $675.
12	August 31	By the end of the month, Tom sees that he needs to increase the number of delivery vans and purchase some new office equipment. Tom's Wear pays cash for two vans for a total cost of $100,000 and new office equipment for $100,000.

EXHIBIT 8.10

Accounting Equation Worksheet for Tom's Wear for August

	Cash	Accounts Receivable	Allowance for Uncollectible Accounts	Inventory**	Prepaid Insurance	Prepaid Rent	Prepaid Web Service	Equipment (Computer)	Acc. Depr. Equipment	Van	Acc. Depr. Van	Land	Buildings	Acc. Depr. Bldg.	=	Accounts Payable	Salaries Payable	Interest Payable	Other Payables*	Warranties Payable	Current Portion of Mortgage Payable	Current Portion of Long-Term Notes Payable	Mortgage Payable	Long-Term Notes Payable	+	Common Stock	Additional Paid-In Capital	Revenues	Expenses	Dividends
BB	$20,651	105,100	(3,290)	8,910	50	600	150	4,000	(500)	30,000	(4,205)	7,500	67,500	(130)	=	36,000	2,352	1,500	1,148	2,239	2,710	6,000	72,290	24,000	+	5,000	–			83,097
1.	1,250,000																									2,500	1,247,500			
2.	(3,500)																		(1,148)											
3.	96,000	(96,000)																												
4.	(30,000)															(30,000)														
5.	(87,500)			87,500																										
6.		(3,000)	3,000																											
7.		201,510																										201,510		
8.			(70,776)																										(70,776)	
9.	(42,500)		(1,060)																	(1,050)									(42,500)	
10.	(22,000)																												(22,000)	
11.																														
12.	(200,000)			675				100,000		100,000																				
A-1																														
A-2																													(2,900)	
A-3			(6,045)																										(2,015)	
A-4					(125)															2,015									(6,045)	
A-5							(600)																						(600)	
A-6							(50)																						(125)	
A-7																													(50)	
A-8									(100)									250											(100)	
A-9																		500											(130)	
A-10											(130)																		(250)	
																													(500)	
	880,476	207,610	(6,385)	24,584	600	100	100	104,000	(600)	130,000	(7,105)	7,500	67,500	(260)	=	6,000	–	2,250	–	3,204	2,710	6,000	72,290	24,000	+	7,500	1,247,500	201,510	(147,991)	
																														136,616

Assets total 1,508,070   Liabilities total   Equity total

* BB beginning balances

** Beginning inventory:

2,475 shirts @ 3.60 =	$ 8,910		
Purchases			
25,000 @ 3.50 =	$ 87,500		
Sales			
201,161 shirts:			
2,475 @ 3.60 =	$8,910		
17,676 @ 3.50 =	$61,866	$(70,776)	
Shirts replaced			
300 @ 3.50		$ (1,050)	
Ending Inventory		$ 24,584	

Check figures   1,508,070   1,508,070

399

2. Due to fewer than expected warranty issues, Tom's Wear has decided to record only 1% of sales for potential warranty problems. Warranty expense will be $2,015 ($201,510 × 1%).

3. Allowance for uncollectible accounts will remain at 3% of credit sales. So bad debts expense will be $6,045 ($201,510 × 3%).

In addition to these adjustments, Tom's Wear must make the following routine month-end adjustments.

4. Rent—$600 for August
5. Insurance—$125 ($50 + $75) for August
6. Web service—$50 for August
7. Depreciation on computer ($100 per month)

EXHIBIT 8.11

tom's wear   **Financial Statements for Tom's Wear for August 2006**

Tom's Wear, Inc.
Income Statement
For the Month Ended August 31

Revenues:		
Sales		$ 201,510
Expenses:		
Cost of goods sold	70,776	
Insurance expense	125	
Rent expense	600	
Depreciation expense	3,130	
Salary expense	22,000	
Interest expense	750	
Warranty expense	2,015	
Bad debts expense	6,045	
Other operating expenses	42,550	147,991
Net income		$ 53,519

Tom's Wear, Inc.
Statement of Changes in Shareholder's Equity
For the Month Ended August 31

Common stock		
Beginning balance	$	5,000
New issue of stock—par value		2,500
		7,500
Additional paid-in capital for new issue		1,247,500
Ending balance		$ 1,255,000
Retained earnings:		
Beginning balance	$	83,097
+ Net income		53,519
– Dividends		–
Ending balance		$ 136,616
Total shareholder's equity		$ 1,391,616

Tom's Wear, Inc.
Statement of Cash Flows
For the Month Ended August 31

Cash from operating activities:		
Cash collected from customers	96,000	
Cash paid to vendors	(117,500)	
Cash paid for operating expense	(68,675)	(90,175)
Cash from investing activities:		
Purchase of vans and office equipment		(200,000)
Cash from financing activities:		
New stock issue		1,250,000
Increase in cash		$ 959,825
Add beginning cash		20,651
Ending cash balance		$ 980,476

Tom's Wear, Inc.
Balance Sheet
At August 31

Assets		Liabilities & Shareholders' Equity	
Current assets		Current liabilities	
Cash	$ 980,476	Accounts payable	$ 6,000
Accounts receivable		Interest payable	2,250
(net of $6,335 allowance		Warranty liability	3,204
for uncollectible accounts)	201,275	Current portion of	
Inventory	24,584	mortgage payable	2,710
Prepaid insurance	600	Current portion of	
Prepaid Web services	100	long-term notes payable	6,000
Total current assets	1,207,035	Total current liabilities	20,164
		Mortgage payable	72,290
Land	7,500	Notes payable	24,000
Equipment (net of $600			
accumulated depreciation)	103,400	Total liabilities	116,454
Vans (net of $7,105			
accumulated depreciation)	122,895	Shareholders' Equity	
Building (net of $260			
accumulated depreciation)	67,240	Common stock	7,500
		Additional paid-in capital	1,247,500
		Retained earnings	136,616
Total assets	$ 1,508,070	Total liabilities and shareholders' equity	$ 1,508,070

8. Depreciation on building ($62,400/40 = $1,560 per year; $130 per month)
9. Interest on van loan ($30,000 × 0.10 = $3000 per year; $250 per month)
10. Interest on mortgage ($75,000 × 0.08 = $6,000; $500 per month)

All of these adjustments are shown on the accounting equation worksheet in Exhibit 8.10. After you understand all of the entries on the worksheet, trace the numbers to the financial statements shown in Exhibit 8.11.

Applying Your Knowledge: Ratio Analysis

The shareholders' equity of a firm can provide information useful for financial statement analysis. There are two ratios that help us evaluate the return to shareholders.

1. Return on equity
2. Earnings per share

L.O.7
Compute return on equity and earnings per share, and explain what these ratios mean.

Return on Equity

Return on equity (ROE) measures the amount of income earned with each dollar of common shareholders' investment in the firm. To calculate ROE, we need the amount of common shareholders' equity at the beginning and at the end of the accounting period. Common shareholders' equity is all the equity except the preferred shareholders' equity. The ratio uses common shareholders' equity because common shareholders are considered to be the true owners of the firm. Then, we use the net income, reduced by the amount of preferred dividends declared, for the numerator. The reason for deducting preferred dividends from net income is that we are calculating the return to the common shareholder. The ratio takes preferred shareholders out of both the numerator and denominator. Recall that common shareholders are entitled to the earnings of the firm only after preferred dividends are paid. Return on equity tells us how well the company is using the common shareholders' contributions and earnings retained in the business.

Exhibit 8.12 shows the information needed to calculate Papa John's return on equity for two consecutive years. The size of the return needs to be compared to other similar companies or to industry standards for a meaningful analysis of a firm's performance. Notice that Papa John's ROE has increased quite significantly—from about 15.6% to about 30.7%. Any analyst would want to get more information about such a significant increase. Remember that when we calculate the ratios, we use a simple average of beginning and ending common shareholders' equity for the denominator.

Earnings Per Share

Earnings per share (EPS) is perhaps the most well-known and used ratio because analysts and investors use current earnings to predict future dividends and stock prices. This ratio is the per-share portion of net income of each common shareholder.

$$\text{Earnings per share} = \frac{\text{Net income–Preferred dividends}}{\text{Weighted average number of common shares outstanding}}$$

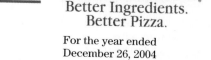

EXHIBIT 8.12

Return on Equity for Papa John's International

(dollars in thousands)	For the year ended December 25, 2005	For the year ended December 26, 2004
Net income	$46,056	$23,221
Average common equity	$(161,279 + 139,223) / 2 = $150,251	$(139,223 + 159,272) / 2 = $149,248
Return on equity	30.7%	15.6%

EXHIBIT 8.13

Presentation of Earnings Per Share on an Income Statement (Statement of Operations)

By now you should be getting used to the variety of terms accountants have for the same thing. Dollar Tree Stores doesn't have anything labeled *earnings per share*. Instead, the firm calls it *net income* per share.

Dollar Tree Stores, Inc.
Consolidated Statements of Operations

(In thousands, except per share data)	Year Ended January 28, 2006	Year Ended January 29, 2005	Year Ended January 31, 2004
Net sales	$3,393,924	$3,126,009	$2,799,872
Cost of sales (Note 4)	2,221,561	2,013,470	1,781,459
Gross profit	1,172,363	1,112,539	1,018,413
Selling, general and administrative expenses (Notes 8 and 9)	889,124	818,988	724,816
Operatiing income	283,239	293,551	293,597
Interest income	6,020	3,860	2,648
Interest expense (Note 6)	(14,041)	(9,241)	(7,493)
Income before income taxes	275,218	288,170	288,752
Provision for income taxes (Note 3)	101,300	107,920	111,169
Net income	$ 173,918	$ 180,250	$ 177,583
Basic net income per share (Note 7):			
Net income	$ 1.61	$ 1.59	$ 1.55
Diluted net income per share (Note 7):			
Net income	$ 1.60	$ 1.58	$ 1.54

See accompanying Notes to Consolidated Financial Statements.

The "earnings" in the numerator of this ratio begins with net income. Because EPS is designated as the earnings for the common shareholders, preferred dividends must be deducted from net income. An investor, who saw the corporation's net income increase year after year, might be fooled into thinking that he was doing better each year. The investor might be worse off, however, if the amount of common stock outstanding has been increasing, because those increases could dilute the investor's portion of the earnings. Even though net income went up, it must be shared among many more owners. EPS helps an investor predict stock prices, which is why it is a popular ratio. All financial statements provide EPS because it is required by GAAP. EPS is the most common indicator of a company's overall performance. EPS are forecast by financial analysts, anticipated by investors, managed by business executives, and announced with great anticipation by major corporations.

Dollar Tree Stores Inc.'s income statement in Exhibit 8.13 shows two amounts for earnings per share. The first is called basic net income per share. This is a straightforward calculation of net income divided by the weighted average number of common shares outstanding. The second is called diluted net income per share. This is a "what-if" calculation: What if all of the potential securities that could have been converted into common stock actually had been converted to common stock at year-end? Those securities could be securities such as convertible bonds or exercised stock options, both of which could be exchanged for shares of common stock. If you were a shareholder, you might want to know the worst-case scenario for your EPS. That is referred to as the diluted EPS. Calculations for diluted EPS can be complicated and are done by a company's accountant when the annual financial statements are prepared.

Business Risk, Control, and Ethics

L.O.8
Recognize the business risks associated with shareholders' equity and the related controls.

Generally, we have been looking at the risks faced by the firm. We will now look at the risks associated with shareholders' equity from an owner's point of view.

Risks Faced by Owners

Anyone who purchases a share of stock in a company risks losing that money. At the same time, however, there is the potential of earning a corresponding significant return. In the first few months of 2000, technology stocks were booming. It was called the dot-com boom because so many of the new firms were Internet-based. In March 2000, the NASDAQ (National Association of Securities Dealers Automated Quotation System) closed at a peak of 5,048.62, more than double its value just 14 months before. Many investors reaped the reward of the stock price increases. Then, prices began to fall. One day after reaching its peak, the NASDAQ lost almost 3% of its value. By October 2002, it had dropped to 1,114.11, a loss of 78% of its peak value. The dot-com boom had become the dot-com bust.

Many investors made money in the dot-com boom, and some technology firms did not lose their value. For example, if you bought a share of stock in eBay in July 2002, you paid approximately $14 for that share of stock. You could have sold it in January of 2005 for over $57. This is the reward side of the risk associated with equity ownership for an individual investor.

How can the risk of stock ownership be controlled? The best way to minimize the risks of stock ownership is to diversify your investments. If you own stock in many different types of firms, the stock prices of some should go up when others are going down. For example, if you own stock in a firm in the retail grocery business, such as Kroger, it might be wise to balance that investment with stock in a restaurant, such as Darden, the parent company of Olive Garden and Red Lobster. Then, if the popular trend is to eat at home, the grocery store stock might increase in value. If eating out becomes more popular, then the restaurant stock might become more valuable. This example is quite simplistic, and finance experts have a much more complicated concept of diversification. The bottom line, however, is quite straightforward. Do not put all your eggs in one basket.

Other risks of stock ownership result from the problems associated with the separation of ownership and management that is common in today's corporation. Considering the potential damage that can result from the actions of unethical management, investors considering ownership in a large corporation must take this risk seriously. Controls that monitor the behavior and decisions of management—such as boards of directors and independent audits—will help minimize these risks. Many of these risks are addressed by the Sarbanes-Oxley Act of 2002, which you can read more about in Chapter 11.

Public or Private?

Since the passage of the Sarbanes-Oxley (SOX) Act of 2002, firms are rethinking the costs and benefits of being a publicly traded company. There are advantages of the corporate form of business organization, particularly when the corporation's stock is available for widespread ownership via the capital markets. It is easier for a firm to raise funds, and stock provides an excellent source of bonuses for managers.

Many people believe that fewer firms are going public because the legal requirements have increased. According to Inc. Magazine ("What Does Sarbanes-Oxley Mean for Companies That Want to Go Public?" by Amy Feldman, September 2005), the "added costs of Sarbanes-Oxley are one reason, among many, that IPO-ready companies are now larger and more established than they used to be." We will talk more about the requirements of the new law in Chapter 11.

 *News Flash*

Has Sarbanes-Oxley Caused the Decline in IPOs?

The Sarbanes-Oxley Act of 2002 (SOX) introduced many new and costly requirements for firms that trade on the U.S. stock exchanges. The number of initial public offerings (IPOs) dropped from 236 in 2004 to 205 in 2005 (*IPO Watch Europe, Review of the Year 2005*, PricewaterhouseCoopers). Many people believe the cost of the SOX requirements has caused the recent reduction in IPOs. But not everyone agrees. "Don't blame America's declining IPO business on Sarbanes-Oxley," according to Daniel Gross (Moneybox.com, August 2, 2006, *www.slate.com/id/2147063/*). Instead, compare the costs of an IPO in the United States to those in London, Hong Kong, or Shanghai. It seems that the cost of an IPO in the United States is much higher than the cost in most overseas markets.

Chapter Summary Points

- Corporations raise money by issuing preferred stock and common stock. The number of shares of stock can be classified as authorized, issued, and outstanding.
- Preferred shareholders get their dividends before the common shareholders. The amount of the dividend is fixed by the par value and the percentage given on the stock certificate. The remaining dividends, out of the total declared by the board of directors, go to the common shareholders. Remember, a firm is not required to pay dividends. Some, like Papa John's, have never paid a cash dividend.
- Treasury stock is stock a firm has issued and later repurchased on the open market. A firm might buy its own stock to have shares available for employees and managers as part of compensation packages.
- A stock dividend is a dividend consisting of shares of stock rather than cash. Each shareholder receives an amount of stock that will maintain the predivided proportion of ownership. A stock split is when the company reduces the par value per share and increases the number of shares proportionately. For example, if you own 5 shares of $3 par stock and the company enacts a 3-for-1 split, the new par value of the stock is $1 per share and you will now own 15 shares. This reduces the market price of the stock. (No entry is made in the formal accounting records for stock splits.)
- The balance in retained earnings is the sum of all the net incomes minus any net losses and minus any dividends declared over the entire life of the company. It is the company's earnings that have been kept in the company.
- Return on equity is defined as net income for the common shareholders divided by average common shareholders' equity. It measures a company's profitability. Earnings per share is defined as net income divided by the weighted average number of shares outstanding (again, common shareholders only). This measures each common shareholder's proportionate share of net income.
- The biggest risk related to stock ownership is the potential for a decrease in the value of your stock. Because owners and managers are often different, the owners may have a problem monitoring the decisions of the managers. For firms, the risk of being publicly traded relates to the complicated requirements set forth by the SEC and the Sarbanes-Oxley Act.

Chapter Summary Problems

Suppose that Pia's Pizza engaged in the following transactions in the fiscal year ended December 28, 2007.

1. The company issued 100,000 shares of common stock, par value of $0.01 per share, for $24 per share.
2. Cash revenues for the year amounted to $100,690,000, and cash expenses amounted to $50,010,000.
3. The company declared cash dividends of $300,000.
4. The company repurchased 25,000 shares of its own stock (treasury stock) for an average cost of $22 per share.

Instructions

Use the accounting equation to show how Pia's Pizza would record each of the transactions. Then, update the shareholders' equity section of Pia's Pizza's balance sheet by filling in the shaded areas.

Pia's Pizza
Shareholder's Equity Section of the Balance Sheet
(in thousands)

	At 12/28/07	12/28/06
Shareholder's Equity:		
Preferred stock ($0.01 par value per share; authorized		
5,000,000 shares; no shares issued)		
Common stock ($0.01 par value per share;		
authorized 50,000,000 shares;		
xxxxxx shares issued in 2007 and		
31,716,105 shares issued in 2006)		$ 317
Additional paid-in capital-common stock		219,584
Accumulated other comprehensive income(loss)	(3,116)	(3,116)
Retained earnings		293,921
Treasury stock (xxxxxx shares in 2007,		
and 13,603,587 shares in 2006 at cost)		(351,434)
Total Shareholder's equity		$ 159,272

Pia's Pizza
Shareholder's Equity Section of the Balance Sheet
(in thousands)

	At 12/28/07	12/28/06
Shareholder's Equity:		
Preferred stock ($0.01 par value per share; authorized		
5,000,000 shares; no shares issued)		
Common stock ($0.01 par value per share;		
authorized 50,000,000 shares;		
31,816,105 shares issued in 2007 and		
31,716,105 shares issued in 2006)	$ 318	$ 317
Additional paid-in capital-common stock	221,983	219,584
Accumulated other comprehensive income(loss)	(3,116)	(3,116)
Retained earnings	344,301	293,921
Treasury stock (13,628,587 shares in 2007,		
and 13,603,587 shares in 2006 at cost)	(351,984)	(351,434)
Total Shareholder's equity	$ 211,502	$ 159,272

Solution

Assets	=	Liabilities	+	Shareholders' equity	
				Contributed capital	+ Retained earnings
1. 2,400,000 cash				1,000 common stock 2,399,000 additional paid-in capital	
2. 100,690,000 cash (50,010,000) cash					100,690,000 revenues 50,010,000 expenses
3.		300,000 dividends payable			(300,000) dividends
4. (550,000) cash				(550,000) treasury stock	

Key Terms for Chapter 8

Authorized shares (p. 384)	Outstanding shares (p. 385)	Stock dividend (p. 394)
Common stock (p. 385)	Par value (p. 385)	Stock split (p. 395)
Dividends (p. 388)	Preferred stock (p. 387)	Treasury stock (p. 385)
Issued shares (p. 384)	Retained earnings (p. 396)	

Answers to YOUR TURN Questions

Chapter 8

Your Turn 8-1

Assets	=	Liabilities	+	Shareholders' equity		
				Contributed capital	+	Retained earnings
200,000 cash				10,000 common stock 190,000 additional paid-in capital		

Your Turn 8-2

($100 × 10,000 × 0.08) = $80,000 for last year and $80,000 for this year for a total of $160,000 to the preferred shareholders. The remaining $40,000 goes to the common shareholders.

Your Turn 8-3

Assets	=	Liabilities	+	Shareholders' equity		
				Contributed capital	+	Retained earnings
(50,000) cash				(50,000) treasury stock		

One hundred thousand shares are issued and 99,000 shares are outstanding.

Your Turn 8-4

Treasury stock would be deducted from shareholders' equity. The amount would be $7,000, the cost of repurchasing the shares of stock.

Your Turn 8-5

(1) A stock split is a division of the par value of the stock and an increase in the number of shares owned by each shareholder, proportionate to the presplit ownership distribution. A stock dividend is a distribution of stock to the current shareholders as a dividend, similarly maintaining the predividend distribution of ownership. (2) You will own 3,000 shares, which will still be 3% of the outstanding stock.

Your Turn 8-6

$84,500 + $25,600 − $12,200 = $97,900

Questions

1. What are the two primary ways for a company to finance its business?
2. What is the difference between common stock and preferred stock?
3. Explain how par value affects the issuance of common stock and preferred stock.
4. What is the difference between paid-in capital and additional paid-in capital on the balance sheet?

5. What are the two ways that shareholders can make money on an investment in a corporation's stock?
6. Are dividends expenses of a corporation? Explain why or why not.
7. What are the three dates corporations consider when issuing a dividend?
8. What is the difference between cumulative and noncumulative preferred stock?
9. What are dividends in arrears?
10. What is treasury stock and why might a company acquire it?
11. What effect does the purchase of treasury stock have on a company's financial statements?
12. Would treasury stock be considered authorized, issued, or outstanding? Explain your answer.
13. Explain the difference between stock dividends and cash dividends.
14. What is the effect of a stock dividend on a company's financial statements?
15. What is a stock split and what effect does it have on a company's shareholders' equity?
16. What are the two sections of the shareholders' equity section of the balance sheet? Explain what each section reports.
17. How is return on equity calculated? What does this ratio measure?
18. Explain how earnings per share (EPS) is calculated. What does this ratio measure?
19. Of all the financial ratios you have studied, which is the only one that is reported in the financial statements? On which financial statement will it appear?

Multiple-Choice Questions

1. Which of the following *does not* affect retained earnings?
   a. Net income for the period
   b. Dividends declared for common shareholders
   c. Repayment of the principal of a loan
   d. All of the above affect retained earnings.
2. Preferred stock is stock that is
   a. Trading above the price of common stock
   b. Issued and later repurchased
   c. Bought and sold to smooth a company's earnings
   d. Given priority over common stock for dividends
3. Treasury stock is
   a. A company's own stock that it has repurchased and added to its short-term trading securities (current assets) as an investment
   b. A company's own stock that is considered issued but not outstanding
   c. A company's own stock that may be used to "manage" earnings—it could be sold for a gain when the price of the stock increases to help a company meet its earnings forecast
   d. Booked as an increase to assets and a decrease to shareholders' equity when it is purchased
4. The two major components of shareholders' equity are
   a. Preferred stock and common stock
   b. Contributed capital and paid-in capital
   c. Contributed capital and retained earnings
   d. Common stock and treasury stock
5. The purchase of treasury stock will
   a. Increase assets and shareholders' equity
   b. Decrease assets and shareholders' equity
   c. Have no effect on assets or shareholders' equity
   d. Decrease assets but have no effect on shareholders' equity
6. If a company purchased 50 shares of its own stock for $10 per share and later sold it for $12 per share, the company would
   a. Record a gain of $2 per share
   b. Record an increase to retained earnings of $100
   c. Show a gain on the sale
   d. Show an increase of $100 of paid-in capital

7. The number of shares of stock designated as *issued* on the year-end balance sheet are those shares that
   a. Were issued during the year
   b. Have been issued during the firm's life
   c. Are authorized to be issued
   d. Have been repurchased during the year

8. When treasury stock is reissued for more than the company paid to buy it, the difference is
   a. A gain that will increase the firm's income
   b. Included in sales revenue for the period
   c. Added to an additional paid-in capital account
   d. Given to the current shareholders as a dividend

9. The payment of dividends is
   a. Required by corporate law
   b. Determined by the firm's board of directors
   c. Related in amount to the firm's earnings per share
   d. Determined by the Securities and Exchange Commission

10. Return on equity measures how well a firm is using
    a. Owners' original contributions to the firm
    b. Creditors' investment in the firm
    c. Shareholders' total investment in the firm, both contributed and earned
    d. Its assets

Short Exercises

SE8-1. *Classify stock. (LO 1)*
Delta Corporation's corporate charter authorizes the company to sell 450,000,000 shares of $1.50 par common stock. As of December 31, 2006, the company had issued 180,915,000 shares for an average price of $4 each. Delta has 57,000,000 shares of treasury stock. How many shares of common stock will be disclosed as authorized, issued, and outstanding on the December 31, 2006, balance sheet?

SE8-2. *Classify stock. (LO 1)*
Sunshine Corporation began operations on July 1, 2005. When Sunshine's first fiscal year ended on June 30, 2006, the balance sheet showed 200,000 shares of common stock issued and 195,000 shares of common stock outstanding. During the second year, Sunshine repurchased 10,000 shares for the treasury. No new shares were issued in the second year. On the balance sheet at June 30, 2007, how many shares would be classified as issued? How many shares are outstanding?

SE8-3. *Record issuance of common stock. (LO 1)*
Vest Corporation sells and issues 100 shares of its $10 par value common stock at $11 per share. Show how this transaction would be recorded in the accounting equation.

SE8-4. *Analyze effect of issuance of common stock on financial statements. (LO 1)*
Ice Video Corporation issued 5,000 shares of $0.01 par value common stock for $32.50 per share. How much cash did Ice Corporation receive from the stock issue? How will the transaction be shown in the shareholders' equity section of the balance sheet?

SE8-5. *Analyze effect of issuance of common stock on financial statements. (LO 1)*
If a company issues 10,000 shares of $1 par common stock for $8.50 per share, what is the effect on total paid-in capital? What is the effect on additional paid-in capital (also known as paid-in capital in excess of par)?

SE8-6. *Analyze effect of issuance of common stock on financial statements. (LO 1)*
Stockton Company reported total shareholders' equity of $58,000 on its December 31, 2006, balance sheet. During 2006, it reported net income of $4,000, declared and paid a cash dividend of $2,000, and issued additional common stock of $20,000. What was total shareholders' equity at the beginning of the year, on January 1, 2006?

SE8-7. *Analyze effect of dividends on financial statements. (LO 2)*
On December 15, 2008, the board of directors of Seat Corporation declared a cash dividend, payable January 8, 2009, of $1.50 per share on the 100,000 common shares outstanding. The accounting period ends December 31. How will this be reflected on the balance sheet at December 31, 2008?

SE8-8. *Distribute dividend between preferred and common shareholders. (LO 2)*
In 2006, the board of directors of Tasty Bakery Corporation declared total dividends of $40,000. The company has 2,000 shares of 6%, $100 par, preferred stock. There are no dividends in arrears. How much of the $40,000 will be paid to the preferred shareholders? How much will be paid to the common shareholders?

SE8-9. *Calculate number of outstanding shares of preferred stock. (LO 2)*
Taxi Company paid $30,000 to its preferred shareholders in 2007. The company has issued 6%, $100 par, preferred stock and there were no dividends in arrears. How many shares of preferred stock were outstanding on the date of record?

SE8-10. *Distribute dividend between preferred and common shareholders. (LO 2)*
Bates Corporation has 7,000 shares of 5%, $100 par, cumulative preferred stock outstanding and 50,000 shares of $1 par common stock outstanding. If the board of directors declares $80,000 of total dividends and the company did not pay dividends the previous year, how much will the preferred and common shareholders receive?

SE8-11. *Analyze effect of treasury stock on financial statements. (LO 3)*
Fitness and Fashion Corporation decided to buy back some of its own stock to have on hand for end-of-year bonuses. If there were 30,000 shares issued and outstanding before the stock repurchase and the company bought 590 shares, how many shares were classified as issued and how many as outstanding after the treasury stock purchase?

SE8-12. *Record purchase of treasury stock. (LO 3)*
If Fitness and Fashion Corporation paid $10 per share for 590 shares of its own stock, how would the transaction be shown in the accounting equation? How would the transaction be reflected in the shareholders' equity section of the balance sheet?

SE8-13. *Record sale of treasury stock. (LO 3)*
Suppose Fitness and Fashion Corporation paid $10 per share for 590 shares of its own common stock on August 30, 2007, and then resold these treasury shares for $11.50 per share on September 25, 2007. Show the transaction on September 25, 2007, in the accounting equation. What effect does this transaction have on the shareholders' equity section of the balance sheet?

SE8-14. *Analyze effect of stock dividend on financial statements. (LO 4)*
Zorro Company declared and issued a 10% stock dividend on June 1, 2006. Before this dividend was declared and issued, there were 220,000 shares of $0.10 par common stock outstanding. After the stock dividend, how many shares are outstanding? What is the par value of each share?

SE8-15. *Analyze effect of stock split on financial statements. (LO 4)*
Romax Company announced a 2-for-1 stock split on its common stock. Before the announcement, there were 120,000 shares of $1 par common stock outstanding. Determine how many shares of common stock will be outstanding after the stock split. What will be the par value of each share? What effect does the stock split have on total shareholders' equity?

SE8-16. *Calculate retained earnings balance. (LO 5)*
On January 1, 2007, Harrison Corporation started the year with a $422,000 balance in retained earnings. During 2007, the company earned net income of $130,000 and

declared and paid dividends of $20,000. Also, the company received cash of $450,000 from a new issue of common stock. What is the balance in retained earnings on December 31, 2007?

SE8-17. *Calculate return on equity. (LO 6)*
Use the following data to calculate the return on equity for Mighty Motors (MM) Inc. At the beginning of 2008, MM's current assets totaled $57,855 (in millions), total assets totaled $449,999 (in millions), and total liabilities totaled $424,424 (in millions). For the year ended December 31, 2008, net income was $3,822 (in millions). At the end of 2008, the current assets were $62,397 (in millions), total assets were $369,053 (in millions), and total liabilities were $361,960 (in millions). Mighty Motors has no preferred stock. Calculate the return on equity (ROE) for MM for 2008. Make sure you use *average* shareholders' equity in your calculation.

SE8-18. *Calculate net income amount using return on equity ratio. (LO 6)*
Octevo Corporation had a return on shareholders' equity (ROE) of 12% in 2006. If total average shareholders' equity for Octevo Corporation was $500,000 and the company has no preferred stock, what was net income for 2006?

SE8-19. *Calculate earnings per share. (LO 6)*
Spikes Inc. started and ended the year with 400,000 shares of common stock issued and outstanding. Net income was $35,000. Calculate earnings per share (EPS) for the year.

SE8-20. *Identify risks and controls. (LO 7)*
What is the major risk of stock ownership and what can be done to minimize the risk?

Exercises—Set A

E8-1A. *Analyze equity section of balance sheet. (LO 1, 5)*
PetsMart reported the following information on the financial statements included with its 2004 annual report. Were any new shares of common stock issued between February 1, 2004, and January 30, 2005? Did the company report a net income for the year ended January 30, 2005? Explain how you know.

(dollars in thousands)	Jan. 30, 2005	Feb. 1, 2004
Common stock, par value $0.0001		
Authorized: 250,000,000 shares;		
Issued and outstanding 149,517,000 shares at Jan. 30, 2005	15	
144,813,000 shares at February 1, 2004		14
Paid-in capital	792,400	705,265
Retained earnings	286,380	132,544

E8-2A. *Classify stock and prepare shareholders' equity section of balance sheet. (LO 1, 5)*
Redmon Company's corporate charter allows it to sell 200,000 shares of $1 par value common stock. To date, the company has issued 50,000 shares for a total of $125,000. Last month, Redmon repurchased 1,000 shares for $3 per share.
   a. If Redmon were to prepare a balance sheet, how many shares would it show as authorized, issued, and outstanding?
   b. In addition to the shareholders' equity given above, Redmon Company also has $350,000 in retained earnings. Using this information, prepare the shareholders' equity section of Redmon Company's balance sheet.

E8-3A. *Record stock transactions. (LO 1, 3)*
Show how each of the following transactions affects the accounting equation.

April 1	Issued 50,000 shares of $0.01 par value common stock for cash of $300,000
June 1	Issued 1,000 shares of $100 par value preferred stock for cash at $120 per share
June 30	Purchased 2,000 shares of treasury stock for $6 per share (i.e., the company bought its own common stock in the stock market)

E8-4A. *Analyze effects of stock transactions on financial statements. (LO 1, 3)*
Refer to the information in E8-3A. How many shares of common stock will be classified as issued at June 30? How many shares will be classified as outstanding?

E8-5A. *Analyze effects of dividends on financial statements. (LO 2)*
Glenco Company had a net income of $250,000 for the year ended December 31, 2006. On January 15, 2007, the board of directors met and declared a dividend of $0.50 per share for each of the 300,000 outstanding shares of common stock. The board voted to make the actual distribution on March 1 to all shareholders of record as of February 1. What is (a) the date of declaration, (b) the date of record, and (c) the date of payment? If Glenco Company were to prepare a balance sheet on January 30, 2007, how would it report the dividends (if at all)?

E8-6A. *Distribute dividend between preferred and common shareholders. (LO 2)*
Framer Company has 4,000 shares of 9%, $100 par, cumulative preferred stock outstanding and 10,000 shares of $1 par value common stock outstanding. The company began operations on January 1, 2008. The cash dividends declared and paid during each of the first 3 years of Framer's operations are shown. Calculate the amounts that went to the preferred and the common shareholders (SHs) each year.

Year	Total Dividends Paid	Dividends to Preferred SHs	Dividends to Common SHs
2008	$120,000		
2009	60,000		
2010	80,000		

E8-7A. *Analyze equity section of balance sheet. (LO 1, 2)*
Jazz Company had the following stockholders' equity section on the December 31, 2007, balance sheet.

Preferred stock, 8%, $100 par, cumulative	$1,250,000
Common stock, $2 par value	800,000
Paid-in capital in excess of par, common stock	3,500,000
Retained earnings	3,467,000
Total	$9,017,000

a. How many shares of common stock are classified as issued?
b. How many shares of common stock are outstanding?
c. How many shares of preferred stock are outstanding?
d. What was the average selling price of a share of common stock?
e. If $150,000 of dividends was declared and there were no dividends in arrears, how much of the dividend would go to the common shareholders?

E8-8A. *Record stock transactions. (LO 1, 2, 3)*
Quicksilver Corporation is authorized to issue both preferred and common stock. Quicksilver's preferred stock is $200 par, 5% preferred stock. During the first month of operations, the company engaged in the following transactions related to its stock. Show each of the following transactions in the accounting equation.

Jan. 1	Issued 30,000 shares of $1 par value common stock for cash at $51 per share
Jan. 10	Issued 1,000 shares of preferred stock at par

Jan. 15	Purchased 2,000 shares of common stock to be held in the treasury for $53 per share
Jan. 20	Issued 40,000 shares $1 par value common stock for cash at $56 per share
Jan. 21	Sold 1,500 shares of the treasury stock purchased on the 15th for $56 per share
Jan. 31	Declared a $25,000 dividend

E8-9A. *Prepare equity section of the balance sheet. (LO 1, 2, 3)*
Use the data from E8-8A to prepare the shareholders' equity section of the balance sheet at January 31. Retained earnings at month-end are $125,000.

E8-10A. *Analyze equity accounts. (LO 1, 2, 3, 5)*
The following balances were shown on the year-end balance sheets for 2006 and 2007 for Columbia Company. For each item, give the most likely reason for the change from one year to the next.

	12/31/06	12/31/07	Explanation
Common stock	$ 45,000	$ 50,000	
Paid-in-capital	$200,000	$230,000	
Retained earnings	$182,500	*$200,000	
Treasury stock	$ (3,450)	$ (5,450)	

Net income for the year was $20,000.

E8-11A. *Analyze equity section of balance sheet. (LO 1, 2, 3)*
Answer the following questions using the shareholders' equity section of Camp Corporation's balance sheet at December 31.

Shareholders' equity	
Preferred stock, cumulative, 10,000 shares authorized, 3,000 shares issued and outstanding	$ 300,000
Additional paid-in capital, preferred stock	30,000
Common stock, $0.10 par, 750,000 shares authorized, 600,000 shares issued	60,000
Additional paid-in capital, common stock	234,000
Retained earnings	975,000
	1,599,000
Less: Treasury stock (8,000 common shares)	(85,200)
Total shareholders' equity	$1,513,800

a. How many shares of common stock are outstanding?
b. On average, what was the issue price of the common shares issued?
c. What is the par value of the preferred stock?
d. If the total annual dividend on preferred stock is $24,000, what is the dividend rate on preferred stock?
e. On average, how much per share did the company pay for the treasury stock?

E8-12A. *Record stock transactions. (LO 1, 2, 3, 4)*
On the first day of the fiscal year, Zenith Corporation had 190,000 shares of $1 par common stock issued and outstanding, and the retained earnings balance was $350,000. Show how each of the following transactions would affect the accounting equation.
  a. Issued 10,000 additional shares of common stock for $15 per share
  b. Distributed a 10% stock dividend
  c. Issued 5,000 additional shares of common stock for $14 per share
  d. Declared a cash dividend on outstanding shares of $1.20 per share
  e. Paid the dividend declared in item d
  f. Purchased 500 shares of treasury stock for $15 per share
  g. Sold 200 shares of treasury stock for $17 per share

h. Sold 250 shares of treasury stock for $14 per share
i. Declared 2-for-1 stock split

E8-13A. *Prepare equity section of the balance sheet. (LO 1, 2, 3, 4)*
Use the data from E8-12A to prepare the shareholders' equity section of the balance sheet at year-end.

E8-14A. *Prepare equity section of the balance sheet. (LO 1, 3, 5)*
The following account balances can be found in the general ledger of Abco Corporation at year-end. Prepare the shareholders' equity section of the balance sheet.

Retained earnings	$ 870,000
Treasury stock (8,000 common shares at cost)	64,000
Common stock ($1 par, 600,000 shares authorized, 200,000 shares issued)	200,000
Additional paid-in capital, common stock	1,500,000
Preferred stock ($10 par value, 9%, 80,000 shares authorized, 15,000 shares issued)	150,000
Additional paid-in capital, preferred stock	45,000

E8-15A. *Calculate return on equity and earnings per share. (LO 6)*
The following financial information is available for Cable Corporation at the end of its two most recent fiscal years. The company has no preferred stock. Calculate (1) return on equity and (2) earnings per share. What do the ratios indicate about the company's performance during the year?

(amounts in thousands)	2006	2005
Weighted average common shareholders' equity	$1,328	$1,150
Dividends declared for common shareholders	500	485
Net income	2,015	1,422
Average number of common shares outstanding during the year	2,186	1,950

E8-16A. *Analyze effects of equity transactions on financial statements. (LO 1, 2, 3, 4, 5)*
Analyze the following transactions and indicate the dollar increase (+) or decrease (−) each has on the balance sheet. If there is an overall change in shareholders' equity, also indicate whether contributed capital, retained earnings, or treasury stock is affected. If the transaction has no effect on the balance sheet, enter NA for that item. The first row is filled in for you as an example.

	Assets	Liabilities	Shareholders' Equity	Equity Section Affected
Issued 1,000 shares of $1 par common stock at par	+1,000		+1,000	Contributed capital
Issued 1,500 shares of $1 par common stock for $14				
Declared a cash dividend of $.25 per share				
Paid the $.25 cash dividend				
Purchased 200 shares of treasury stock for $17 per share				
Sold 100 shares of treasury stock for $17 per share				
Distributed a 10% common stock dividend				
Announced a 2-for-1 stock split				
Issued 2,000 shares of $100 par, 4% noncumulative preferred stock				

E8-17A. *Identify risks and controls. (LO 8)*
Explain what it means to diversify stock ownership. Why would an investor diversify?

Exercises—Set B

E8-1B. *Analyze equity section of balance sheet. (LO 1, 5)*
Outback Steakhouse reported the following information on the financial statements included with its 2005 annual report. Were any new shares of common stock issued during the year ended December 31, 2005? Did the company report a net income for the year ended December 31, 2005? Explain how you know.

(in thousands except per share amounts)	December 31, 2005	December 31, 2004
Common stock, par value $0.01		
Authorized: 200,000 shares;		
Issued: 78,750 shares at Dec. 31, 2005; 78,750 shares at Dec. 31, 2004	788	788
Outstanding: 74,854 shares at Dec. 31, 2005 73,767 shares at Dec. 31, 2004		
Additional paid-in capital	291,035	271,109
Retained earnings	1,104,423	1,025,447

E8-2B. *Classify stock and prepare shareholders' equity section of balance sheet. (LO 1, 5)*
Womack Grove Entertainment Inc.'s corporate charter allows it to sell 300,000 shares of $2 par value common stock. To date, the company has issued 100,000 shares for a total of $275,000. Last month, Womack Grove repurchased 500 shares for $3.75 per share.
   a. If Womack Grove were to prepare a balance sheet, how many shares would it show as authorized, issued, and outstanding?
   b. In addition to the shareholders' equity given above, Womack Grove also has $415,000 in retained earnings. Using this information, prepare the shareholders' equity section of Womack Grove Entertainment Inc.'s balance sheet.

E8-3B. *Record stock transactions. (LO 1, 3)*
Show how each of the following transactions would be recorded in the accounting equation.

October 1	Issued 75,000 shares of $0.10 par value common stock for cash of $187,500
December 1	Issued 1,500 shares of $125 par value preferred stock for cash at $150 per share
December 31	Purchased 10,000 shares of treasury stock (i.e., the company bought its own common stock in the stock market) for $2.50 per share

E8-4B. *Analyze effects of stock transactions on financial statements. (LO 1, 3)*
Refer to the information in E8-3B. How many shares of common stock will be classified as issued at December 31? How many shares will be classified as outstanding?

E8-5B. *Analyze effects of dividends on financial statements. (LO 2)*
Rich Land Inc. had a net income of $315,000 for the year ended June 30, 2008. On July 15, 2008, the board of directors met and declared a dividend of $0.25 per share for each of the 500,000 outstanding shares of common stock. The board voted to make the actual distribution on September 1 to all shareholders of record as of August 1. What is (a) the date of declaration, (b) the date of record, and (c) the date of payment? If Rich Land Inc. were to prepare a balance sheet on July 30, how would the dividends be reported (if at all)?

E8-6B. *Distribute dividend between preferred and common shareholders. (LO 2)*
Lawver Electronics Inc. has 8,000 shares of $150 par, 12% cumulative preferred stock outstanding and 15,000 shares of $2 par value common stock outstanding. The company began operations on January 1, 2007. The cash dividends declared and paid during each of the

first 3 years of Lawver's operations are shown below. Calculate the amounts that went to the preferred shareholders and the common shareholders (SHs) each year.

Year	Total Dividends Paid	Dividends to Preferred SHs	Dividends to Common SHs
2007	$150,000		
2008	125,000		
2009	176,000		

E8-7B. *Analyze equity section of balance sheet. (LO 1, 2)*
Market Street Music Corporation had the following stockholders' equity section on the December 31, 2007, balance sheet.

Preferred stock, $150 par, 6% cumulative	$2,250,000
Common stock, $1 par value	400,000
Paid-in capital in excess of par, common stock	1,020,000
Retained earnings	5,325,000
Total	$8,995,000

a. How many shares of common stock are classified as issued?
b. How many shares of common stock are outstanding?
c. How many shares of preferred stock are outstanding?
d. What was the average selling price of a share of common stock?
e. If $175,000 of dividends was declared and there were $35,000 dividends in arrears, how much of the dividend would go to the common shareholders?

E8-8B. *Record stock transactions. (LO 1, 2, 3)*
Dark Knight Comics Inc. is authorized to issue both preferred and common stock. Dark Knight's preferred stock is $175 par, 8% preferred stock. During the first month of operations, the company engaged in the following transactions related to its stock. For each of the following transactions, show how it would be recorded in the accounting equation.

July 1	Issued 40,000 shares of $.50 par value common stock for cash at $42 per share
July 8	Issued 1,500 shares of preferred stock at par
July 14	Purchased 2,750 shares of common stock to be held in the treasury for $43 per share
July 22	Issued 35,000 shares $.50 par value common stock for cash at $47 per share
July 26	Sold 1,750 shares of the treasury stock purchased on the 14th for $47 per share
July 31	Declared a $22,500 dividend

E8-9B. *Prepare equity section of the balance sheet. (LO 1, 2, 3)*
Use the data from E8-8B to prepare the shareholders' equity section of the balance sheet at July 31. Retained earnings at month-end are $125,000.

E8-10B. *Analyze equity accounts. (LO 1, 2, 3, 5)*
The following balances were shown on the year-end balance sheets for 2007 and 2008 for High Note Publishing Company. For each item, give the most likely reason for the change from one year to the next.

	12/31/07	12/31/08	Explanation
Common stock	$ 35,000	$ 43,000	
Paid-in capital	$115,000	155,000	
Retained earnings	$142,000	*$160,500	
Treasury stock	$ (2,125)	$ (2,625)	

*Net income for the year was $22,750.

E8-11B. *Analyze equity section of balance sheet. (LO 1, 2, 3)*
Answer the following questions using the shareholders' equity section of Fantasy Films Corporation's balance sheet at June 30.

Shareholders' equity	
Preferred stock, cumulative, 15,000 shares authorized,	
4,000 shares issued and outstanding	$ 420,000
Additional paid-in capital, preferred stock	40,000
Common stock, $0.05 par, 500,000 shares authorized,	
250,000 shares issued	12,500
Additional paid-in capital, common stock	675,000
Retained earnings	1,005,000
	2,152,500
Less: Treasury stock (4,000 common shares)	(13,000)
Total shareholders' equity	$2,139,500

a. How many shares of common stock are outstanding?
b. On average, what was the issue price of the common shares issued?
c. What is the par value of the preferred stock?
d. If the total annual dividend on preferred stock is $25,200, what is the dividend rate on preferred stock?
e. On average, how much per share did the company pay for the treasury stock?

E8-12B. *Record stock transactions. (LO 1, 2, 3, 4)*
On the first day of the fiscal year, JKB Construction Inc. had 185,000 shares of $.50 par common stock issued and outstanding, and the retained earnings balance was $165,000. Show each of the following transactions in the accounting equation.
a. Issued 15,000 additional shares of common stock for $16 per share
b. Distributed a 20% stock dividend
c. Issued 10,000 additional shares of common stock for $15 per share
d. Declared a cash dividend on outstanding shares of $1.10 per share
e. Paid the dividend declared in item d
f. Purchased 1,000 shares of treasury stock for $16 per share
g. Sold 250 shares of treasury stock for $18 per share
h. Sold 200 shares of treasury stock for $15 per share
i. Declared 2-for-1 stock split

E8-13B. *Prepare equity section of the balance sheet. (LO 1, 2, 3, 4)*
Use the data from E8-12B to prepare the shareholders' equity section of the balance sheet at year-end.

E8-14B. *Prepare equity section of the balance sheet. (LO 1, 3, 5)*
The following account balances can be found in the general ledger of Athletics Supply Corporation at year-end. Prepare the shareholders' equity section of the balance sheet.

Retained earnings	$ 450,000
Treasury stock (4,000 common shares at cost)	36,000
Common stock ($2 par, 500,000 shares authorized,	
175,000 shares issued)	350,000
Additional paid-in capital, common stock	2,712,500
Preferred stock ($8 par value, 8%, 90,000 shares authorized,	
20,000 shares issued)	160,000
Additional paid-in capital, preferred stock	50,000

E8-15B. *Calculate return on equity and earnings per share. (LO 6)*
The following financial information is available for Sugar Treats Corporation at the end of its two most recent fiscal years. The company has no preferred stock. Calculate (1) return

on equity and (2) earnings per share. What do the ratios indicate about the company's performance during the year?

(amounts in thousands)	2006	2005
Weighted average common stockholders' equity	$1,560	$1,235
Dividends declared for common stockholders	300	265
Net income	3,010	1,565
Average number of common shares outstanding during the year	2,050	1,635

E8-16B. *Analyze effects of equity transactions on financial statements. (LO 1, 2, 3, 4, 5)*
Analyze the following transactions and indicate the dollar increase (+) or decrease (−) each has on the balance sheet. If there is an overall change in shareholders' equity, also indicate whether contributed capital, retained earnings, or treasury stock is affected. If the transaction has no effect on the balance sheet, enter NA for that item. The first row is filled in for you as an example.

	Assets	Liabilities	Shareholders' Equity	Equity Section Affected
Issued 1,000 shares of $.50 par common stock at par	**+500**		**+500**	**Contributed capital**
Issued 2,500 shares of $.50 par common stock for $6.50				
Declared a cash dividend of $.50 per share				
Paid the $.50 cash dividend				
Purchased 175 shares of treasury stock for $9 per share				
Sold 65 shares of treasury stock for $9 per share				
Distributed a 5% common stock dividend				
Announced a 2-for-1 stock split				
Issued 5,000 shares of $75 par, 6% noncumulative preferred stock				

E8-17B. *Identify risks and controls. (LO 8)*
Explain the risks associated with the separation of ownership and management. Can you think of a way to minimize those risks?

Problems—Set A

P8-1A. *Account for stock transactions. (LO 1)*
Restoration Corporation was started on January 1, 2007. The company is authorized to issue 30,000 shares of 6%, $100 par value preferred stock and 800,000 shares of common stock with a par value of $1 per share. The following stock transactions took place during 2007.

Jan. 3	Issued 10,000 shares of common stock for cash at $4 per share
April 1	Issued 5,000 shares of preferred stock for cash at $105 per share
June 1	Issued 40,000 shares of common stock for cash at $4.50 per share
Sept. 1	Issued 1,000 shares of preferred stock for cash at $102 per share
Dec. 1	Issued 15,000 shares of common stock for cash at $5 per share

Required

a. Show each transaction in the accounting equation.
b. Prepare the contributed capital portion of the stockholders' equity section of the balance sheet at December 31, 2007.

P8-2A. *Analyze and record stock dividend transactions. (LO 4)*
As of December 31, 2007, Chips Company had 100,000 shares of $10 par value common stock issued and outstanding. The retained earnings balance was $125,000. On January 15, 2008, Chips Company issued a 5% stock dividend to its common shareholders. At the time of the dividend, the market value of the stock was $15 per share.

Required

    a. Show how the stock dividend would affect the accounting equation.
    b. How many shares of stock are outstanding after the stock dividend?
    c. If you owned 3% of the outstanding common stock of Chips Company before the stock dividend, what is your percentage ownership after the stock dividend?

Excel Template
www.prenhall.com/reimers

P8-3A. *Analyze and record stock transactions and prepare equity section of balance sheet. (LO 1, 2, 3, 4, 5)*
The following information pertains to the equity accounts of Fragrant Soap Company Inc.

1. Contributed capital on January 1, 2007, consisted of 70,000 issued and outstanding shares of common stock with par value of $0.50; additional paid-in capital in excess of par of $350,000; and retained earnings of $500,000.
2. During the first quarter of 2007, Fragrant Soap Company issued an additional 10,000 shares of common stock for $6 per share.
3. On June 15, the company declared a 2-for-1 stock split.
4. On September 30, the company distributed a 10% stock dividend. The market price of the stock on that date was $5 per share.
5. On October 1, the company declared a dividend of $0.25 per share to be paid on October 31.
6. Near the end of the year, the company's CEO decided the company should buy 1,000 shares of its own stock. At that time, the stock was trading for $6 per share in the stock market.
7. Net income for 2007 was $49,500.

Required

    a. Show how each of the transactions would affect the accounting equation.
    b. Prepare the shareholders' equity section of the balance sheet at December 31, 2007.

P8-4A. *Record stock transactions, prepare equity section of balance sheet, and calculate ratios. (LO 1, 2, 3, 5, 6)*
On January 1, 2007, the Expedite Corporation's shareholders' equity account balances were as follows.

Preferred stock (6%, $100 par noncumulative, 25,000 shares authorized)	$ 500,000
Common stock ($5 par value, 8,000,000 shares authorized)	4,500,000
Additional paid-in capital, preferred stock	20,000
Additional paid-in capital, common stock	6,300,000
Retained earnings	20,380,000
Treasury stock–common (5,000 shares, at cost)	70,000

During 2007, Expedite Corporation engaged in the following transactions.

Jan. 5	Issued 10,000 shares of common stock for $15 per share
Feb. 9	Purchased 2,000 additional shares of common treasury stock at $13 per share
June 1	Declared the annual cash dividend on preferred stock, payable June 30
Dec. 1	Declared a $0.25 per share cash dividend to common stockholders payable December 31, 2007

Net income for the year was $2,330,000.

Required

    a. Show each of the transactions in the accounting equation.

    b. Prepare the shareholders' equity section of the balance sheet at December 31, 2007.

    c. Calculate earnings per share and return on common stockholders' equity.

P8-5A. *Prepare equity section of balance sheet. (LO 1, 2, 5)*

On October 1, 2006, Marble Company had 400,000 shares of $2 par common stock issued and outstanding. The shareholders' equity accounts at October 1, 2006, had the following balances.

Common stock	$ 800,000
Additional paid-in capital	2,400,000
Retained earnings	9,800,000

The following transactions occurred during the fiscal year ended September 30, 2007.

  1. On October 30, issued 30,000 shares of 9%, $100 par, cumulative preferred stock at $102.

  2. On November 30, reacquired 8,000 shares of common stock for $8.50 per share.

  3. On December 1, declared a cash dividend of $0.45 per share on the common stock outstanding, payable on December 31, 2006, to shareholders of record on November 15.

  4. Paid dividends to preferred shareholders on December 31, 2006.

  5. Net income for the year ended September 30, 2007, was $3,875,000.

Required

Prepare the shareholders' equity section of Marble's balance sheet at September 30, 2007.

P8-6A. *Analyze equity section of balance sheet. (LO 1, 2, 3, 5)*

The following information is from the equity sections of the comparative balance sheets for Wildwood Company.

	December 31, 2007	December 31, 2006
Common stock ($10 par)	$420,000	$400,000
Additional paid-in-capital	326,000	306,000
Retained earnings	55,000	51,000
Total shareholders' equity	$801,000	$757,000

Net income for the year ended December 31, 2007, was $70,000.

Required

    a. How many shares of common stock were issued to new shareholders during 2007?

    b. What was the average issue price of the stock issued during 2007?

    c. What was the amount of dividends declared during 2007?

    d. Did the company have any treasury shares at the end of 2007?

P8-7A. *Analyze equity section of balance sheet. (LO 1, 2, 5)*

At December 31, 2006, Plasma Company reported the following on its comparative balance sheet (amounts in thousands).

	December 31, 2006	December 31, 2005
Common stock		
Authorized: 1,200 shares		
Issued: 950 shares at 2006	$ 475	
900 shares at 2005		$ 450
Paid-in capital in excess of par	19,000	17,550
Retained earnings	45,500	31,300

Required

a. What is the par value of the company's common stock?
b. Did the company issue any new shares during the fiscal year ended December 31, 2006?
c. What was the approximate (average) issue price of the stock issued during the year?
d. Did Plasma Company earn net income (loss) during the year? Assuming no dividends were paid, how much was net income (loss)?

P8-8A. *Analyze equity section of balance sheet. (LO 1, 2, 3, 4)*
The following information is from the equity section of the comparative balance sheets of Aloha Cruises Inc.

Aloha Cruises, Inc.
Consolidated Balance Sheets

(amounts in thousands, except share data)

Shareholders' equity:	June 30, 2006	June 30, 2005
Common stock, $0.10 par value; 250,000 shares issued and _____ shares outstanding at June 30, 2006; and 220,000 shares issued and _____ shares outstanding at June 30, 2005.	$ 25.0	$ 22.0
Additional paid-in-capital	3,580	3,014
Retained earnings	8,237	7,450
Treasury stock, at cost, 14,200 shares at June 30, 2006, and 12,000 shares at June 30, 2005.	213	171.6

Required

a. What was the average issue price per share of the 250,000 shares classified as "issued" at June 30, 2006? (Round the answer to the nearest cent.)
b. What was the average issue price of the 30,000 shares of common stock issued during the fiscal year ending June 30, 2006?
c. How many shares were outstanding at June 30, 2006? How many shares were outstanding at June 30, 2005?
d. How many shares did the company buy back during the year? What was the average cost of a share of the treasury shares purchased during the year? (Assume no treasury stock was sold during the year.)
e. If no dividends were paid, what was net income for the year ending June 30, 2006?

Problems—Set B

P8-1B. *Account for stock transactions. (LO 1)*
Simba Corporation was started on July 1, 2006. The company is authorized to issue 100,000 shares of 5%, $100 par value preferred stock and 1,800,000 shares of common stock with a par value of $2 per share. The following stock transactions took place during the fiscal year ended June 30, 2007.

Issued 40,000 shares of common stock for cash at $23.50 per share
Issued 10,000 shares of preferred stock for cash at $101 per share
Issued 40,000 shares of common stock for cash at $24.80 per share
Issued 7,000 shares of preferred stock for cash at $102 per share
Issued 25,000 shares of common stock for cash at $25 per share

Required

a. Show each transaction in the accounting equation.
b. Prepare the contributed capital portion of the shareholders' equity section at June 30, 2007.

P8-2B. *Analyze and record stock dividend transactions. (LO 4)*

At December 31, 2007, Robby's Shoe Company had 200,000 shares of $5 par common stock issued and outstanding. The retained earnings balance was $165,000. On January 15, 2008, Robby's issued a 3% stock dividend to its common shareholders. At the time of the dividend, the market value of the stock was $20 per share.

Required

 a. How would the stock dividend be shown in the accounting equation?

 b. How many shares of stock are outstanding after the stock dividend?

 c. If you owned 5% of the outstanding common stock of Robby's Shoe Company before the stock dividend, what is your percentage ownership after the stock dividend?

P8-3B. *Analyze and record stock transactions and prepare equity section of balance sheet. (LO 1, 2, 3, 4, 5)*

The following information pertains to All Batteries Company Inc.

Excel Template
www.prenhall.com/reimers

 1. Contributed capital on October 1, 2006, consisted of 50,000 issued and outstanding shares of common stock with par value of $1; additional paid-in capital in excess of par of $250,000; and retained earnings of $400,000.

 2. During the first quarter of the fiscal year, All Batteries Company issued an additional 20,000 shares of common stock for $8 per share.

 3. On March 15, the company declared a 2-for-1 stock split.

 4. On June 30, the company distributed a 5% stock dividend. The market price of the stock on that date was $6 per share.

 5. On July 1, the company declared a dividend of $0.50 per share to be paid on July 31.

 6. During September 2007, All Batteries Company's CEO decided the company should buy 600 shares of its own stock. At that time, the stock was trading for $7 per share.

 7. Net income for the year ended September 30, 2007, was $87,500.

Required

 a. Show each of the transactions in the accounting equation.

 b. Prepare the shareholders' equity section of the balance sheet at September 30, 2007.

P8-4B. *Record stock transactions, prepare equity section of balance sheet, and calculate ratios. (LO 1, 2, 3, 5, 6)*

On January 1, 2008, the Premier Corporation shareholders' equity account balances were as follows.

Preferred stock (8%, $100 par noncumulative, 15,000 shares authorized)	$ 400,000
Common stock ($1 par value, 5,000,000 shares authorized)	1,000,000
Additional paid-in capital, preferred stock	20,000
Additional paid-in capital, common stock	21,500,000
Retained earnings	50,450,000
Treasury stock–common (10,000 shares, at cost)	230,000

During 2008, Premier Corporation engaged in the following transactions.

Jan. 7	Issued 5,000 shares of common stock for $25 per share
Feb. 8	Purchased 1,000 additional shares of common treasury stock at $24 per share
June 1	Declared the annual cash dividend on preferred stock, payable June 30
Dec. 1	Declared a $0.30 per share cash dividend to common stockholders payable December 31, 2008

Net income for the year was $1,980,000.

Required

    a. Show the transactions in the accounting equation.
    b. Prepare the shareholders' equity section of the balance sheet at December 31, 2008.
    c. Compute earnings per share and return on common shareholders' equity.

P8-5B. *Prepare equity section of balance sheet. (LO 1, 2, 5)*
On July 1, 2006, Philbrick Company had 500,000 shares of $1 par common stock issued and outstanding. The shareholders' equity accounts at July 1, 2006, had the following balances.

Common stock	$ 500,000
Additional paid-in capital	36,500,000
Retained earnings	22,700,000

The following transactions occurred during the fiscal year ended June 30, 2007.

1. On July 30, issued 50,000 shares of $100 par value, 6% cumulative preferred stock at $103.
2. On October 1, reacquired 20,000 shares of common stock for $76 per share.
3. On December 1, declared a cash dividend of $2.50 per share on the common stock outstanding, payable on December 31, 2006, to shareholders of record on November 15.
4. Paid dividends to preferred shareholders on December 31, 2006.
5. Net income for the year ended June 30, 2007, was $5,150,000.

Required

Prepare the shareholders' equity section of Philbrick's balance sheet at June 30, 2007.

P8-6B. *Analyze equity section of balance sheet. (LO 1, 2, 3, 5)*
The following information was shown on the recent comparative balance sheets for Paul's Dot-Com Company.

	December 31, 2006	December 31, 2005
Common stock ($1 par)	$520,000	$400,000
Additional paid-in-capital	326,000	296,000
Retained earnings	65,000	50,000
Total shareholders' equity	$911,000	$746,000

Net income for the year ended December 31, 2006, was $75,000.

Required

    a. How many shares of common stock were issued to new shareholders during 2006?
    b. What was the average issue price of the stock issued during 2006?
    c. What was the amount of dividends declared during 2006?
    d. Did the company have any treasury shares at the end of 2006?

P8-7B. *Analyze equity section of balance sheet. (LO 1, 2, 5)*
At June 30, 2007, High Quality Mining Company reported the following on its comparative balance sheet, which included 2006 amounts for comparison (amounts in millions).

	June 30 2007	2006
Common stock		
Authorized: 2,500 shares		
Issued: 1,450 shares in 2007	$ 14,500	
1,400 shares in 2006		$ 14,000
Paid-in capital in excess of par	4,350	2,890
Retained earnings	15,500	14,300

Required

    a. What is the par value of the company's common stock?
    b. Did the company issue any new shares during the fiscal year ended June 30, 2007?

c. What was the approximate (average) issue price of the stock issued during the year?
d. Did High Quality Mining Company earn net income (loss) during the year? Assuming no dividends were paid this year, what was net income (loss)?

P8-8B. *Analyze equity section of balance sheet. (LO 1, 2, 3, 4)*
This information is from the equity section of the comparative balance sheets of Tick Tock Inc.

Tick Tock Inc.
Consolidated Balance Sheets

(amounts in thousands, except share data)

Shareholders' equity:	September 30, 2008	September 30, 2007
Common stock, $0.10 par value; 450,000 shares issued and _____ shares outstanding at September 30, 2008; and 425,000 shares issued and _____ shares outstanding at September 30, 2007.	45.0	42.5
Additional paid-in-capital	9,475	8,925
Retained earnings	25,237	21,450
Treasury stock at cost, 21,340 shares at Sept. 30, 2008, and 17,148 shares at Sept. 30, 2007	(448.1)	(343)

Required
a. What was the average issue price per share of the 450,000 shares classified as "issued" at September 30, 2008? (Round the answer to the nearest cent.)
b. What was the average issue price of the 25,000 shares of common stock issued during the fiscal year ending September 30, 2008?
c. How many shares were outstanding at September 30, 2008? How many shares were outstanding at September 30, 2007?
d. How many shares did the company buy back during the year? What was the average cost of a share of the treasury shares purchased during the year? (Assume no treasury stock was sold during the year.)
e. If no dividends were paid, what was net income for the year ending September 30, 2008?

Financial Statement Analysis

FSA8-1. *Analyze equity section of balance sheet. (LO 1, 2, 5)*
The Coca-Cola Company reported the following information on its comparative balance sheet at December 31 (amounts in millions).

	December 31 2005	December 31 2004
Common stock, par value _____		
Authorized: 5,600 shares		
Issued: 3,507 shares in 2005	$ 877	
3,500 shares in 2004		$ 875
Capital surplus	5,492	4,928
Reinvested earnings	31,299	29,105
Treasury stock, at cost 1,138 and 1,091 shares, respectively	(19,644)	(17,625)

a. Explain what capital surplus and reinvested earnings each represent.
b. What is the approximate par value of Coca-Cola's common stock?

   c. How many new shares of common stock did the company issue during the fiscal year ended December 31, 2005?

   d. What was the approximate (average) issue price of the stock issued during the year?

   e. Did Coca-Cola earn a net income during the year?

   f. If Coca-Cola paid dividends of $1.12 per share, what would you estimate net income for the year to be?

FSA8-2. *Analyze equity section of balance sheet. (LO 1, 3)*

The following information is from the comparative balance sheets of Linens 'n Things.

**Adapted from *Linens 'n Things Inc. & Subsidiaries*
Consolidated Balance Sheets**

(in thousands, except share amounts)

Shareholders' equity:	January 1, 2005	January 3, 2004
Preferred stock, *$0.01 par value, 1,000,000 shares authorized; none issued and outstanding*	-	-
Common stock, *$0.01 par value; 135,000,000 shares authorized; 45,460,467 shares issued and _____ shares outstanding at January 1, 2005; and 45,052,255 shares issued and _____ shares outstanding at January 3, 2004.*	$ 455	$ 450
Additional paid-in-capital	372,627	362,483
Retained earnings	440,914	380,393
Other comprehensive gain (loss)	2,619	1,391
Treasury stock, *at cost, 259,571 shares at January 1, 2005, and 258,636 shares at January 3, 2004*	(7,262)	(7,340)
Total shareholders' equity	$809,353	$737,377

   a. How many shares of common stock were outstanding at January 1, 2005?

   b. How many shares of common stock were outstanding at January 3, 2004?

   c. What was the average issue price per share of the 45,460,467 shares classified as "issued" at January 1, 2005? (Round the answer to the nearest cent.)

   d. How many shares of treasury stock did the company purchase during the fiscal year ended January 1, 2005? (Assume no treasury stock was sold during the year.)

   e. What was the average price per share paid for the treasury shares purchased during the fiscal year ended January 1, 2005? (Assume no treasury stock was sold during the year.)

   f. What was the average issue price of the shares of common stock issued during the fiscal year ended January 1, 2005?

FSA8-3. *Analyze equity section of balance sheet. (LO 6)*

Use the annual report of Office Depot, found on the book's website, to answer the following.

   a. Does Office Depot buy back its own stock? Where, in the financial statements, is this disclosed? Explain the treasury stock transaction(s) that took place during the most recent fiscal year.

   b. Compute the return on equity for the two most recent consecutive years. What information do these ratios provide?

CHAPTER 8 • INTERNET EXERCISE: HERSHEY FOODS CORPORATION   425

Critical Thinking Problems

Business Risk

What kinds of risks do the owners of Office Depot face? Would you prefer to be a creditor or an owner of Office Depot? Explain why.

Ethics

AVX Electronics is very close to bringing a revolutionary new computer chip to the market. The company fears that it could soon be the target of a takeover by a giant telecommunications company if this news were to leak before the product is introduced. The current AVX management intends to redistribute the company's stock holdings so its managers will have a larger share of ownership. So, management has decided to buy back 20% of the company's common stock while the price is still quite low and distribute it to the managers—including themselves—as part of the company's bonus plan. Are the actions of AVX management ethical? Explain why this strategy would reduce the risk of a hostile takeover. Was any group hurt by this strategy?

Group Assignment

In groups, select two companies that you would invest in if you had the money. Find their financial statements on the Internet and examine the shareholders' equity section of their balance sheets. What does your analysis tell you about each firm? Is this a good investment? Explain your findings and conclusion.

Internet Exercise: Hershey Foods Corporation

Hershey is the market leader, ahead of Mars Inc., in the U.S. candy market. The company makes such well-known chocolate and candy brands as Hershey's Kisses, Reese's peanut butter cups, Twizzlers licorice, Jolly Rancher, Mounds, Super Bubble gum, and Kit Kat (licensed from Nestlé). Its products are sold throughout North America and exported to over 90 countries.

Go to www.hersheys.com

IE 8-1. Explore "Investor's Relations." In what city is the Hershey factory located? The current stock quote (market price) of Hershey's stock is how much per share? Is this market price reflected on the Hershey balance sheet? If it is, where is it found?
Access the most recent annual report and find the consolidated balance sheets to answer the following questions. (Note: These financial statements are read with an Acrobat Reader, which may be downloaded free by clicking on Get Acrobat Reader.)

IE 8-2. How many types of stock have been authorized and issued? For the most recent year, how many shares are issued and are outstanding?

IE 8-3. For the most recent year-end, identify total stockholders' equity. Of this total, how much was contributed by shareholders for issued shares? On average, how much did shareholders pay per issued share? Is the average issue price more or less than the current market price? Give an explanation for this difference.

IE 8-4. For the most recent year-end, what amount of stockholders' equity is earned capital? What is the name of the earned capital account? Did earned capital increase or decrease compared with the previous year? What might cause this change?

IE 8-5. Has the company reacquired any of its common stock? How you can tell? What is reacquired stock called? When a company reacquires stock does total stockholders' equity increase or decrease? Why might a company want to reacquire issued shares?

IE 8-6. (Optional) For a study break, visit Hershey's Kidztown at www.kidztown.com and go to "Fun and Games" to play. (Hope you have fun.)

Preparing and Analyzing the Statement of Cash Flows

Here's Where You've Been . . .

You learned how a company accounts for and reports contributions from owners, payment of dividends, and retained earnings.

Here's Where You're Going . . .

You will learn two ways to prepare and present the statement of cash flows. This will increase your understanding of the difference between cash basis and accrual basis accounting.

Learning Objectives

When you are finished studying this chapter, you should be able to:

1. Explain the importance of the statement of cash flows and the three classifications of cash on the statement of cash flows.

2. Explain the difference between the direct method and the indirect method of preparing the statement of cash flows.

3. Convert accrual amounts to cash amounts.

4. Prepare the *cash flows from operating activities* section of the statement of cash flows using the direct method.

5. Prepare the *cash flows from operating activities* section of the statement of cash flows using the indirect method.

6. Prepare the *cash flows from investing activities* section and the *cash flows from financing activities* section of the statement of cash flows.

7. Perform general analysis of the statement of cash flows and calculate free cash flow.

8. Use the statement of cash flows and the related controls to evaluate the risk of investing in a firm.

Ethics Matters

Fraud is not restricted to publicly-held companies and privately-owned companies. Even the public sector is subject to fraud. Ethical behavior is needed everywhere! Here are just a few of the problems uncovered in an examination of the records of Hempstead Sanitary District No. 1 in Nassau County in New York.

Nonexistent time sheets for sanitation workers. Poor controls over nearly $1 million in cash receipts. A phantom garbage truck that had officially been "disposed of" but was nonetheless seen rumbling down the street. "Unreasonable" bills for out-of-state conferences—including a $676 steak dinner for four. (Source: "Tale of the Five-Hatted Accountant," by Vivian S. Toy, *The New York Times*, September 18, 2005, p. 3, Sec 14LI.)

L.O.1

Explain the importance of the statement of cash flows and the three classifications of cash on the statement of cash flows.

The Importance of the Statement of Cash Flows

The statement of cash flows—one of the four financial statements a company must prepare as part of generally accepted accounting principles (GAAP)—shows all the cash the company has received and all the cash the company has disbursed during the accounting period. Each cash flow relates to one of three business activities—operating, investing, or financing activities. Exhibit 9.1 shows a summary of the information presented on the statement of cash flows.

Thousands of companies go bankrupt each year because they fail to plan their cash flows effectively. When the time comes to pay their bills, they do not have enough cash on hand. Preparing a cash budget is a crucial activity for all companies. It is more complicated than just estimating cash inflows and outflows for the accounting period. The sources of cash and the uses of cash must be estimated in detail—both the amounts of cash and when cash is needed. Each month, projected cash inflows and outflows must be budgeted by source and use. With this level of detail, a company can plan ahead for any cash shortage by (1) securing a line of credit from a local bank, (2) borrowing the money, or (3) altering the timing of its receipts (tightening up credit policies) or disbursements (postponing purchases).

A cash budget is a detailed plan of a company's estimated cash receipts and estimated cash disbursements, with very specific forecasts of the sources, uses, and the timing of the cash flows. The budgeted cash flows in the cash budget can then be compared with actual cash flows, and the comparison is the basis for planning and evaluating performance. To compare the actual cash flows for an accounting period with the period's cash budget, a company must produce details about the actual sources of cash and actual uses of cash from the company's records. Comparing actual cash flows with budgeted cash flows gets a company ready to prepare the next period's budgeted cash flows. Even though the focus of financial reporting is fi-

News Flash

Large U.S. companies have lots of cash!

Cash is piling up at many large U.S. firms. According to *The Wall Street Journal* ("Capital Pains: Big Cash Hoards," by Ian McDonald, July 21, 2006, p. C1), the 174 S&P Industrials (a sector that excludes financial firms) had over $295 billion in cash in the first quarter of 2006. "That amount equals more than 7% of the companies' stock-market value, the highest level in nearly two decades."

EXHIBIT 9.1

The Statement of Cash Flows

A firm's statement of cash flows will include every cash inflow and outflow. The cash flows are divided into three categories: operating, investing, and financing.

	Operating	**Investing**	**Financing**
Types of transactions	Cash related to the day-to-day activities of running the business—revenue and expense transactions	Cash related to buying and selling assets that the firm plans to use for longer than one year	Cash receipts and disbursements related to loans (principal only); cash contributions from and distributions to owners
Examples			
Inflows	Cash collections from customers	Cash proceeds from the sale of land or building	Cash proceeds from a new stock issue
Outflows	Cash paid to vendors for inventory	Cash paid for new land or building	Cash dividends paid to shareholders
Cash flows are generally related to these balance sheet accounts	Current assets and current liabilities	Long-term assets	Long-term liabilities and shareholder's equity

nancial statements for shareholders and investors, the information about cash flows is equally useful to managers of a company.

Since Tom started his T-shirt business in January 2006, we have prepared the four basic financial statements for his business every month, including the statement of cash flows. The way we have prepared the statement of cash flows has been to

1. Identify every cash transaction on our accounting equation worksheet, and then
2. Classify each cash amount as one of three types: operating, investing, or financing.

When we use a separate column in the accounting equation worksheet for cash transactions, we simply take each addition of cash and each subtraction of cash; then we classify each cash flow as cash from operating activities, cash from investing activities, or cash from financing activities. Because a real company has a much more complex accounting system, needed to handle thousands or millions of transactions, examining each transaction is not a feasible way for a company to prepare the statement of cash flows. In this chapter, we will discuss how the statement is actually prepared.

Two Methods of Preparing and Presenting the Statement of Cash Flows

GAAP describes two ways of preparing the statement of cash flows: the **direct method** and the **indirect method**. These two methods are named for the way in which the operating section of the statement of cash flows—cash from operating activities—is prepared, either directly—by converting every number on the income statement to its cash amount—or indirectly—by starting with net income and adjusting it until you have the net cash from operating activities. For the other two sections, investing and financing, there is only one way to compute the cash flows: The transactions are directly identified. Thus, in any discussion

> The **direct method** shows every cash inflow and outflow to prepare the statement of cash flows.

> The **indirect method** starts with net income and makes adjustments for items that are not cash to prepare the statement of cash flows.

L.O.2
Explain the difference between the direct method and the indirect method of preparing the statement of cash flows.

EXHIBIT 9.2

Comparison of the Direct and Indirect Methods for the Statement of Cash Flows

Statement of Cash Flows
(cash from operating activities only)

Direct Method		Indirect Method	
Cash from operating activities:		Cash from operating activities:	
Cash collected from customers	$500	Net income	$330
Cash paid for supplies	(30)	– increase in accounts receivable	(100)
Cash paid to vendors for inventory	(200)	– increase in supplies	(10)
Net cash from operating activities	$270	+ increase in accounts payable	50
		Net cash from operating activities	$270

Both methods result in the same total cash from operating activities.

about different methods of preparing a statement of cash flows, the difference between the direct method and the indirect method applies only to cash from operating activities.

Before we discuss the two different methods in detail, we will look at a simple example of the difference between these methods of preparing the statement of cash flows. We will start with the first month of business for a simple company with the following transactions.

1. Purchase of inventory for $250—paid cash of $200 to vendor with the remaining $50 on account (accounts payable)
2. Sales of all inventory for $600—$500 for cash and $100 on account (accounts receivable)
3. Purchase of supplies for cash of $30—used $20 worth of them, with $10 worth remaining for next month

Net income is calculated as follows.

$600	–	$250	–	$20	=	$330
Sales		Cost of goods sold		Supplies expense		Net income

Cash collected and disbursed is calculated next.

$500	–	$200	–	$30	=	$270
Cash sales		Inventory purchases		Supplies purchase		Net cash flow

This change from accrual basis numbers to cash basis numbers can be done in the two ways shown in Exhibit 9.2—direct or indirect. The direct method examines each item on the income statement, one by one. In contrast, the indirect method is more mechanical: Net income is adjusted for all the changes in the current assets and current liabilities, excluding cash and noncash items from the income statement. You may want to study the transactions and the exhibit again after you learn more about how to prepare the statements. Notice the only cash flows in this example are cash flows from operating activities; and both methods produce the same amount of net cash from operating activities.

Both methods of preparing the operating section of the statement of cash flows require information about the underlying transactions so the cash can be separated from the accrual accounting numbers. For example, the amount of sales must be examined to get the actual cash collected from making those sales. Supplies expense must be examined to get the actual cash paid for supplies. Doing this converts accrual-based amounts to cash-based amounts.

Your Turn 9-1
Your Turn
Your Turn

What is the major difference between the direct and indirect methods of presenting the statement of cash flows? What are the similarities?

Accrual Accounting Versus Cash Basis Accounting

L.O.3
Convert accrual amounts to cash amounts.

As you know, companies that follow GAAP maintain their accounting records using the accrual basis. Preparing the statement of cash flows is actually converting the records of the business to cash basis. That is what you see in Exhibit 9.2. There are many reasons why accrual basis accounting and cash basis accounting are not generally the same.

For example, a company will record a sale and recognize the revenue on the income statement when the merchandise is shipped or delivered. Does the company always receive the cash at that time? No. Thus, the amount of revenue earned from sales for an accounting period may not be the same as the amount of cash collected during the period. At the end of the accounting period, when the company is preparing its financial statements, customers may still owe the company some money—there may be outstanding accounts receivable. That is one reason the cash collected from sales might not equal the amount of the sales for a specific accounting period.

Also, the company may have collected cash during the current period from sales made during the prior accounting period—accounts receivable from the prior year may have been collected in the current year. Thus, to calculate the cash collected from customers for the statement of cash flows, we must consider and make an adjustment for the change in accounts receivable.

Suppose a company began 2007 with accounts receivable of $500. These accounts receivable were recorded during 2006, when the revenue from the sales was recognized. All sales are made on credit; and during 2007, the company had sales of $3,000. At the end of 2007, the balance in accounts receivable was $600. How much cash was collected from customers during 2007? Because accounts receivable started with a balance of $500 and ended with a balance of $600, the increase represents sales that have not been collected from the customers. Therefore, although sales amounted to $3,000, only $2,900 worth of those sales must have been collected in cash.

Another way to think about it is first to suppose that customers paid off their old accounts of $500. If total sales were $3,000 and if an ending accounts receivable balance was $600, then $2,400 of the current sales must have been collected. The beginning balance of $500 was collected plus current sales of $2,400 have been collected—making the total cash collected from customers during the period equal to $2,900. This is the sort of reasoning that must be applied to each item on the income statement to prepare the statement of cash flows using the *direct* method.

The amount for every item on the income statement is potentially different from the cash paid or received for it. As we just discussed, the dollar amount of sales is potentially different from cash collected from customers. Cost of goods sold is potentially different from cash paid for inventory. Insurance expense is potentially different from the cash paid to the insurance company—and so on, for all items on the income statement.

The change in a current asset or a current liability will reflect the difference between the accrual-based income statement amount and the cash amount. Consider an expense on the income statement. Suppose salary expense is shown on the year's income statement as $75,000. For the statement of cash flows, we want to show cash paid to employees as an operating cash outflow. What could make salary expense different from cash paid to employees?

First, we could have paid some employees cash that we owed them from last year. The cash payment would reduce the liability salaries payable. If we did pay some salaries we owed at the beginning of the year, that cash paid would be in addition to any current year's salary paid to employees. What else could make *cash paid to employees* different from salary expense? We could have incurred salary expense that will not be paid until next year. In other words, we recognized some salary expense that did not get paid to the employees. We must have recorded it as salaries payable. In both cases, the difference between salary expense and *cash paid to employees* is reflected in the change in salaries payable from the beginning of the year to the end of the year. This is the sort of reasoning that must be applied to each current asset and each current liability (excluding cash) on the balance sheet to prepare the statement of cash flows.

Suppose we started the year with salaries payable of $690. Our salary expense for the year, as shown on the income statement, is $75,000. If the balance in salaries payable is $500 at year-end, how much cash was actually paid to employees? First, we must have paid off the amount we owed at the beginning of the year, $690. Then, because the ending balance in salaries payable is $500, we must have paid only $74,500 ($75,000 − $500) of the current year's salary expense. Thus, the total cash paid to employees is $75,190 ($690 + $74,500).

Another way to interpret what happened is to say that we paid the full $75,000 of this year's expense in cash and we paid down our salaries payable by $190 ($690 down to $500). That total is $75,190.

Your Turn 9-2
Your Turn
Your Turn

Robo Company began the year with $25,000 in accounts receivable. During the year, Robo's sales totaled $50,000. At year-end, Robo had an accounts receivable balance of $15,000. How much cash did Robo collect from customers during the year? How is that amount of cash classified on the statement of cash flows?

L.O.4

Prepare the *cash flows from operating activities* section of the statement of cash flows using the direct method.

Preparing the Statement of Cash Flows: Direct Method

Now you are ready to learn the procedures for preparing a statement of cash flows. First, the cash from operating activities section of the statement of cash flows is prepared using one of the following two methods we have already discussed.

1. Direct method: Each item on the accrual-based income statement is converted to cash.
2. Indirect method: Net income is the starting point, and adjustments are made by adding and subtracting amounts necessary to convert net income into net cash from operating activities.

After you have determined the cash flows from operating activities, you determine the cash flows from investing activities and cash flows from financing activities. You will learn about them later in the chapter.

The direct method of computing cash flows from operating activities begins with an analysis of the income statement. Item by item, every amount on the statement is analyzed to determine how much cash was actually collected or disbursed related to that item.

The first item on the income statement is usually revenue. What makes revenue on the income statement different from cash collected from customers? Any cash collected for sales in previous periods—that is, accounts receivable—must be counted as cash collected even though it is not included as revenue. Conversely, any sales for the period for which cash has not been collected must be excluded from cash collections. Both cash collected but not counted as revenue and cash not collected but included in revenue can be identified by looking at the change in accounts receivable during the period.

We will use Tom's Wear's third month of business—March—to see how this works. We start at the beginning of the income statement, shown in Exhibit 9.3 (first seen as Exhibit 3.13), for the month and analyze each amount to change it from accrual to cash.

Sales on the income statement for March amounted to $2,000. What we need to know for the statement of cash flows is how much cash was collected from customers during March. We need to see how accounts receivable changed during the month. On March 1, Tom's Wear had $150 worth of accounts receivable, and on March 31 the firm had $2,000 worth of accounts receivable. By comparing the balance sheet at the beginning of the month with the balance sheet at the end of the month, both shown in Exhibit 9.4, we can see accounts receivable increased by $1,850. The amount of the change in accounts receivable came from the current period's sales not collected.

Analyze what happened to accounts receivable. It started with $150. Then during the month, credit sales of $2,000 were made (sales on the income statement). The ending balance in accounts receivable is $2,000. Thus, the cash collected from customers must have

tom's wear

Tom's Wear, Inc.
Income Statement
For the Month Ended March 31, 2006

Sales revenue		$2,000
Expenses		
Cost of goods sold	800	
Depreciation expense	100	
Insurance expense	50	
Interest expense	30	(980)
Net income		$1,020

EXHIBIT 9.4

Comparative Balance Sheet for Tom's Wear, Inc.

tom's wear

Tom's Wear, Inc.
Balance Sheet
At March 1 and March 31, 2006

	March 31	March 1		March 31	March 1
Cash	$ 3,995	$6,695	Accounts payable	$ 0	$ 800
Accounts receivable	2,000	150	Other payables	0	50
Inventory	300	100	Interest payable	30	0
Prepaid insurance	75	125	Notes payable	3,000	0
Prepaid rent	0	0	Total liabilities	$ 3,030	$ 850
Equipment (net of $100 accumulated depreciation)	3,900	0	Common stock	5,000	5,000
			Retained earnings	2,240	1,220
			Total liabilities and shareholder's equity		
Total assets	$10,270	$7,070	shareholder's equity	$10,270	$7,070

been $150 ($2,000 − $1,850). If you go back and look at the transactions for Tom's Wear during March (in Chapter 3), you will find $150 was exactly the amount of cash the company collected from customers.

Continuing down the March income statement, the next item is cost of goods sold of $800. This is the cost of the merchandise sold during the month. How does that compare with the amount of cash paid to vendors during the month? Did Tom's Wear sell anything it bought the previous month from the beginning inventory; or did the company buy more goods in March than it actually sold in March? We need to look at what happened to the amount of inventory during the month. The beginning inventory balance was $100. The ending inventory balance was $300. That means Tom's Wear bought enough inventory to sell $800 worth and to build up the inventory by an additional $200. Thus, purchases of inventory must have been $1,000. Did Tom's Wear pay cash for these purchases of inventory?

To see how the purchase of $1,000 worth of inventory compares with the cash paid to vendors, we look at the change in accounts payable (to vendors). The beginning balance in accounts payable was $800, and the ending balance was zero. That means Tom's Wear must have paid $1,000 to vendors for the month's purchases and the $800 owed from February. Thus, the total paid to vendors was $1,800.

The next expense on the March 31 income statement is depreciation expense. Depreciation expense is a noncash expense. That means we do not have any cash outflow when

Tom's Wear, Inc.
Partial Statement of Cash Flows
For the Month Ended March 31, 2006

Cash from operating activities		
Cash collected from customers		$ 150
Cash paid to vendors		(1,800)
Cash paid for advertising		(50)
Net increase (decrease) in cash from operating activities		$(1,700)

we record depreciation expense. The cash we spend to buy equipment is considered an investing cash flow, and the periodic depreciation does not involve cash. Depreciation is one expense we can skip when we are calculating cash from operating activities using the direct method.

Insurance expense of $50 is shown on the March 31 income statement. How much cash was actually paid for insurance? When a company pays for insurance, the payment is generally recorded as prepaid insurance. Examining the change in prepaid insurance will help us figure out how much cash was paid for insurance during the month. Prepaid insurance started with a balance of $125 and ended with a balance of $75. Because the decrease in prepaid insurance is exactly the same as the insurance expense, Tom's Wear must not have paid for any insurance this month. All the expense came from insurance that was paid for in a previous period.

The last expense we need to consider is interest expense. On the income statement for March, we see interest expense of $30. Did Tom's Wear pay that in cash? On the balance sheet, the company began the month with no interest payable and ended the month with $30 interest payable. If it started the month without owing any interest and ended the month owing $30, how much of the $30 interest expense did the company pay for with cash? None. Tom's Wear must not have paid any cash for interest because it owes the entire amount of the expense at year-end.

Tom's Wear paid out one more amount of cash related to operating activities during the month. Can you find it? On the March 1 balance sheet, there is $50 that Tom's Wear owed; it is called other payables. By the end of March, that payable has been reduced to zero. Only one thing could have caused that reduction: a cash payment to settle the obligation related to advertising. Thus, we will also put the cash outflow of $50 on the statement of cash flows.

To summarize, we have "translated" the accrual amounts found on the income statement to cash amounts for the statement of cash flows. The cash collected from customers was $150. Tom's Wear paid its vendors cash of $1,800. It also paid $50 of other payables. Net cash flow from operating activities was $(1,700). The operating section of the statement of cash flows using the direct method is shown in Exhibit 9.5.

Remember, Exhibit 9.5 shows only the cash flow from operating activities. To explain the entire change in cash from March 1 to March 31, the investing and financing cash flows must be included.

Your Turn 9-3
Your Turn
Your Turn

Flex Company began the year 2006 with $350 of prepaid insurance. For 2006, the company's income statement showed insurance expense of $400. If Flex Company ended the year with $250 of prepaid insurance, how much cash was paid for insurance during 2006? On the statement of cash flows, how would that cash be classified?

Preparing the Statement of Cash Flows: Indirect Method

L.O.5
Prepare the *cash flows from operating activities* section of the statement of cash flows using the indirect method.

Even though the Financial Accounting Standards Board (FASB) suggested that companies use the direct method of preparing the statement of cash flows, more than 90% of companies use the indirect method. That is because most accountants think it is easier to prepare the statement of cash flows using the indirect method. Also, the requirement that a company using the direct method provide a reconciliation of net income to net cash from operating activities means more work for the company using the direct method.

Preparing the statement of cash flows using the indirect method—applied just to the operating section of the statement of cash flows—starts with net income. Following net income, any amounts on the income statement that are noncash must be added or subtracted to leave only cash amounts. Typical noncash items are depreciation and amortization expenses and any gains or losses on the sale of assets. Remember that a gain or loss on the sale of a long-term asset is not cash; it is the difference between the book value of the asset and the proceeds from the sale. (We will include the proceeds from the sale in the cash from investing activities section of the statement of cash flows.)

We will start with net income for Tom's Wear for March. Exhibits 9.3 and 9.4 show the numbers we need to prepare the statement of cash flows using the indirect method.

The net income for March was $1,020. The first adjustment we make is to add back any noncash expenses such as depreciation. For Tom's Wear, we must add back to net income the $100 depreciation expense. When we calculated the net income of $1,020, we subtracted $100 that was not a cash outflow. Thus, we must add it back to net income to change net income to a cash number.

Then, just as you did when you prepared the statement of cash flows using the direct method, you will evaluate every amount on the income statement for its relationship to cash flows. Recall that in the direct method, we use changes in accounts receivable to convert sales revenue into cash collected from customers, and we use changes in inventory and accounts payable to convert cost of goods sold to cash paid to vendors. For the indirect method, if we adjust net income for every change in each current asset—with the exception of cash—and every change in each current liability, we will make every adjustment we need to convert net income into net cash from operating activities.

We will continue preparing the statement of cash flows using the indirect method with Tom's Wear for March. We start with net income of $1,020 and add back any noncash expenses. Depreciation of $100 is added back. Then, using Exhibit 9.4, we examine each current asset account and each current liability account for changes during the month.

Accounts receivable increased by $1,850. That increase represents sales for which we did not collect any cash yet. Thus, we need to subtract this increase in accounts receivable from net income to convert net income into a cash number.

The next change in a current asset is the increase in inventory of $200. This $200 represents purchases made that have not yet been reported as part of cost of goods sold on the income statement because the items have not been sold. Still, Tom's Wear did pay cash for them (we will assume cash was paid and make any adjustment when we examine accounts payable), so the amount needs to be deducted from net income because it was a cash outflow.

Prepaid insurance decreased from $125 to $75. This decrease of $50 was deducted as insurance expense on the income statement, but it was not a cash outflow this period. This amount must be added back to net income because it was not a cash outflow.

The last changes in current assets and current liabilities are the changes in payables. Tom's Wear started the month with $800 of accounts payable and $50 of other payables. Tom's Wear ended the month with a zero amount of each of these. That means $850 was the cash outflow related to these two amounts. The other current liability is interest payable. It started the month with no interest payable but ended the month with $30 of interest payable. That is $30 Tom's Wear did not pay out. So the total change in current liabilities is a net decrease of $820. This $820 amount was not included on the income statement— not deducted in the calculation of net income. Because the amount was a cash outflow, we

EXHIBIT 9.6

Cash from Operating Activities— Indirect Method

tom's wear

Tom's Wear, Inc.
Partial Statement of Cash Flows
For the Month Ended March 31, 2006

Net income	$ 1,020
+ Depreciation expense	100
– Increase in accounts receivable	(1,850)
– Increase in inventory	(200)
+ Decrease in prepaid insurance	50
– Decrease in payables	(820)*
Net cash from operating activities	$(1,700)

*This is comprised of the decrease in accounts payable of $800, the decrease in other payables for $50, and the increase in interest payable for $30.

need to deduct an additional $820 from net income to finish converting net income into cash from operating activities.

Look at the operating section of the statement of cash flows for Tom's Wear for March in Exhibit 9.6. The statement starts with net income and makes all the adjustments we discussed. Compare the cash from operating activities section of this statement of cash flows prepared using the indirect method with the same section using the direct method shown in Exhibit 9.5. The net cash flow from operating activities is the same no matter how we prepare it—when we prepare the statement by examining every cash transaction, as we did in Chapter 3; when we prepare it using the direct method, as we did earlier in this chapter; and when we prepare it using the indirect method, as we just did.

Which way is easier to understand? The presentation produced by the direct method—the presentation shown in Exhibit 9.5—gives details about cash that are easier to understand than the details provided by the indirect method. Still, over 90% of companies today use the indirect method. A change in this practice could be a real benefit to users of financial statements.

Your Turn 9-4
Your Turn
Your Turn

Suppose a company had net income of $50,000 for the year. Depreciation expense, the only noncash item on the income statement, was $7,000. The only current asset that changed during the year was accounts receivable, which began the year at $6,500 and ended the year at $8,500. The only current liability that changed was salaries payable, which began the year at $2,500 and ended the year at $3,000. Assume this is all the relevant information. Calculate net cash from operating activities using the indirect method.

L.O.6
Prepare the *cash flows from investing activities* section and the *cash flows from financing activities* section of the statement of cash flows.

Cash from Investing and Financing Activities

In addition to cash from operating activities, there are two other sections of the statement of cash flows: cash from investing activities and cash from financing activities. No matter which method you use to prepare the statement of cash flows, direct or indirect, the cash from investing activities and cash from financing activities sections are prepared the same way—by reviewing noncurrent balance sheet accounts. The primary amounts on the balance sheet to review are property, plant, and equipment; notes payable; bonds payable; common stock; and retained earnings.

For Tom's Wear during March, start in the noncurrent assets section of the balance sheet. The balance sheet at March 31 shows equipment with a cost of $4,000. The carrying value is $3,900 and the accumulated depreciation is $100, for a total cost of $4,000. The asset representing this equipment was not on the March 1 balance sheet, so Tom's Wear must have purchased $4,000 worth of equipment during March. The purchase of equipment is an investing cash flow.

When we see that a company purchased a noncurrent asset, we must investigate how the company paid for the asset. In this case, we find that Tom's Wear paid cash of $1,000 and signed a note for $3,000. We include only the $1,000 cash outflow in the statement of cash flows, but we must add a note disclosing the amount of the equipment purchase financed by the note payable. All investing and financing activities must be disclosed, even if there was no cash involved.

Next we review the liability section of the balance sheet for changes in non-operating liabilities. Notice that on the balance sheet at March 1, Tom's Wear shows no notes payable. On the balance sheet at March 31, notes payable shows a balance of $3,000. That means Tom's Wear borrowed $3,000 during March. Again, when we discover such a change, we must find out the details of the transaction before we can decide how the transaction affects the statement of cash flows. Generally, borrowing money using a note would result in a financing cash inflow. However, in this case, the note was given in exchange for equipment. Notice that the loan is disclosed, even though the amount is not included on the statement of cash flows. Whenever a company engages in a financing or investing activity, it must be disclosed on the statement of cash flows, even though the company never actually received or paid out any cash. The cash is considered implicit in the transaction. It is as if Tom's Wear received the cash from the loan and immediately turned around and purchased the equipment with it.

Other transactions we should look for when preparing the financing section of the statement of cash flows include any principal payments on loans and any new capital contributions—such as stock issued. We should also look for any dividends paid to the stockholders. For Tom's Wear for March 2001, none of these transactions took place.

When we put the information about investing activities and financing activities with the cash from operating activities we have already prepared, we have all the information we need to complete the statement of cash flows. Look at the two statements in Exhibit 9.7. We used different methods to prepare the statements, but they are similar in form and amounts.

Check it out. The balance sheets in Exhibit 9.4 show that cash went from $6,695 on March 1 to $3,995 on March 31. The difference is a $2,700 decrease in cash. Explaining that change in the cash balance is the purpose of the statement of cash flows.

Summary of Direct and Indirect Methods

There are two ways, both ways acceptable using GAAP, to prepare and present the statement of cash flows: the direct method and the indirect method. The direct method provides more detail about cash from operating activities. It shows the individual operating cash flows. When a company uses the direct method, GAAP requires that the company also show a reconciliation of net

EXHIBIT 9.7A

Statement of Cash Flows (Direct)

tom's wear

Tom's Wear, Inc.
Statement of Cash Flows
For the Month Ended March 31, 2006

Cash from operating activities
Cash collected from customers	$ 150	
Cash paid to vendors	(1,800)	
Cash paid for other expenses	(50)	
Net cash from operating activities		$(1,700)

Cash from investing activities
Purchase of equipment	$(1,000)ᵃ	
Net cash from investing activities		(1,000)

Cash from financing activities
		0
Net increase (decrease) in cash		$(2,700)
Beginning cash balance		6,995
Ending cash balance		$ 3,995

ᵃEquipment was purchased for $4,000. A note was signed for $3,000 and cash paid was $1,000.

EXHIBIT 9.7B

Statement of Cash Flows (Indirect)

Tom's Wear, Inc.
Statement of Cash Flows
For the Month Ended March 31, 2006

Cash from operating activities		
Net income	$ 1,020	
+ Depreciation expense	100	
– Increase in accounts receivable	(1,850)	
– Increase in inventory	(200)	
+ Decrease in prepaid insurance	50	
– Decrease in payables	(820)	
Net cash from operating activities		$(1,700)
Cash from investing activities		
Purchase of equipment	(1,000)[a]	
Net cash from investing activities		(1,000)
Cash from financing activities		0
Net increase (decrease) in cash		$(2,700)
Beginning cash balance		6,995
Ending cash balance		$ 3,995

[a]Equipment was purchased for $4,000. A note was signed for $3,000 and cash paid was $1,000.

income to net cash from operating activities in a supplemental schedule. That reconciliation looks exactly like the operating section of the statement of cash flows using the indirect method.

The indirect presentation of the statement of cash flow is easier to prepare from the income statement and the beginning and ending balance sheets for the period, but the presentation of the information is not easily understood. A company that uses the indirect method must make separate disclosures for cash paid for interest and cash paid for taxes somewhere in the financial statements. This is required by GAAP. Keep in mind that the investing activities and the financing activities sections for the two methods are identical; and the total net cash flow is the same for both methods.

L.O.7
Perform general analysis of the statement of cash flows and calculate free cash flow.

Applying Your Knowledge: Financial Statement Analysis

Look at the statement of cash flows for Auto Zone Inc., shown in Exhibit 9.8. First, notice the organization of the statement. The statement has the three required parts: (1) cash flows from operating activities, (2) cash flows from investing activities, and (3) cash flows from financing activities. Second, notice the first section—cash provided by operating activities—is prepared using the indirect method.

The statement starts with the amount for net income and makes several adjustments to that amount. Look at the adjustments and see if you understand what information they provide. For example, depreciation and amortization are added back to net income to work toward net cash from operating activities because the amounts for depreciation and amortization were subtracted in the original computation of net income but they were not cash expenditures. That subtraction is undone by adding the amounts back to net income. There are many other adjustments that are beyond the scope of an introductory accounting course, but you should understand why these adjustments are being made. They are "undoing" the noncash amounts that were included in the calculation of net income. Investors are looking for a positive net cash flow from operating activities. In the long run, this is crucial for the continuing success of any business.

The cash flows from investing activities section of the statement shows capital expenditures as the first entry. Those are items such as property, plant, and equipment. Recall the discussion in Chapter 4 about capital versus revenue expenditures—capitalizing a cost versus expensing a cost. These are costs that have been capitalized by Auto Zone. Other entries in the cash flows from investing activities section include cash inflows and outflows

<table>
<tr><td colspan="3" align="center">AutoZone
Statement of Cash Flows</td></tr>
</table>

EXHIBIT 9.8

AutoZone's Statement of Cash Flows

This statement of cash flows has been prepared using the indirect method.

	Year Ended	
(in thousands)	August 27, 2005 (52 Weeks)	August 28, 2004 (52 Weeks)
Cash flows from operating activities:		
Net income	$ 571,019	$ 566,202
Adjustments to reconcile net income to net cash provided by operating activities:		
Depreciation and amortization of property and equipment	135,597	106,891
Deferred rent liability adjustment	21,527	–
Amortization of debt origination fees	2,343	4,230
Income tax benefit realized from exercise of options	31,828	24,339
Gains from warranty negotiations	(1,736)	(42,094)
Changes in operating assets and liabilities:		
Deferred income taxes	(16,628)	44,498
Accounts receivable	(42,485)	3,759
Merchandise inventories	(124,566)	(119,539)
Accounts payable and accrued expenses	109,341	43,612
Income taxes payable	(67,343)	32,118
Other, net	29,186	(25,637)
Net cash provided by operating activities	648,083	638,379
Cash flows from investing activities:		
Capital expenditures	(283,478)	(184,870)
Acquisitions	(3,090)	(11,441)
Proceeds from disposal of capital assets	3,797	2,590
Net cash used in investing activities	(282,771)	(193,721)
Cash flows from financing activities:		
Net change in commercial paper	(304,700)	254,400
Proceeds from issuance of debt	300,000	500,000
Repayment of debt	–	(431,995)
Net proceeds from sale of common stock	64,547	33,552
Purchase of treasury stock	(426,852)	(848,102)
Settlement of interest rate hedge instruments	–	32,166
Other	(349)	(929)
Net cash used in financing activities	(367,354)	(460,908)
Net increase (decrease) in cash and cash equivalents	(2,042)	(16,250)
Cash and cash equivalents at beginning of year	76,852	93,102
Cash and cash equivalents at end of year	$ 74,810	$ 76,852
Supplemental cash flow information:		
Interest paid, net of interest cost capitalized	$ 98,937	$ 77,871
Income taxes paid	$ 339,245	$ 237,010

See Notes to Consolidated Financial Statements.

related to the purchase and sale of long-term assets not related to the normal operations of AutoZone. (When AutoZone buys the items that it resells in the normal course of business, the cash flows are included in the first section—cash provided from operating activities.)

The cash flows from investing activities section of the statement of cash flows gives information about the company's plans for the future. Investments in property, plant, and equipment may indicate an expansion or, at the very least, a concern about keeping the company's infrastructure up to date. Over time, a company's failure to invest in the infrastructure may indicate a problem.

The cash flows from financing activities section of the statement of cash flows shows the cash flows related to the way the company is financed. Some of the items should be recognizable—proceeds from issuance of debt and proceeds from the sale of common stock. All of the items in this section relate to AutoZone's financing. This information, when combined with the information on the balance sheet, gives the financial statement user a complete picture of the way the company is financing the business.

We should consider two more characteristics of the statement. First, following the calculation of the net increase or decrease in cash for the year, the reconciliation from the year's beginning cash balance to the year's ending cash balance is shown. Second, there is supplementary information disclosed concerning the cash paid for interest and the cash paid for taxes during the year. This is required by GAAP.

When analyzing the statement of cash flows, managers and analysts often calculate an amount called **free cash flow**. Free cash flow is defined as net cash from operating activities minus dividends and capital expenditures. This gives a measure of a firm's ability to engage in long-term investment opportunities. It is sometimes seen as a measure of a company's financial flexibility. AutoZone's free cash flow is quite adequate: $648 million − $283 million = $365 million. Looking over the capital expenditures for the past 2 years, you can see that $365 million should be enough for new investment opportunities.

> **Free cash flow** is equal to net cash from operating activities minus dividends and minus capital expenditures.

Your Turn 9-5

DRP Company reported net cash from operating activities of $45,600. Suppose the firm purchased $25,000 worth of new long-term assets for cash and did not pay any dividends during the year. The firm's average current liabilities for the year were $40,000. What was the firm's free cash flow during the year?

UNDERSTANDING **Business**

The Cash Conversion Cycle

You have heard the old adage that "cash is king," but there is a broader way of thinking about a firm's cash position than simply looking at its cash balance. As you learned in the second chapter of this book, liquidity refers to an asset's proximity to cash. According to Richard Loth ("The Working Capital Position," Investopedia.com, August 4, 2006), it is actually *liquidity* that is king. He says that

A liquidity squeeze is worse than a profit squeeze. A key management function is to make sure that a company's receivable and inventory positions are managed efficiently. This means ensuring an adequate level of product availability and providing appropriate credit terms, while at the same time making sure that working capital assets don't tie up undue amounts of cash. This is a balancing act for managers, but an important one. It is important because with high liquidity, a company can take advantage of price discounts on cash purchases,

reduce short-term borrowings, benefit from a top commercial credit rating and take advantage of market opportunities.

A firm's liquidity position can be measured by its cash conversion cycle. That is the length of time, in days, it takes for a firm to convert its resource inputs into cash. This measurement is the sum of 1 and 2 minus 3:

1. The average number of days inventory is outstanding, calculated from the inventory turnover ratio;
2. The average number of days accounts receivable are outstanding, calculated from the accounts receivable turnover ratio; and
3. The average number of days accounts payable are outstanding, calculated from the calculation of accounts payable turnover.

Next time you are analyzing a firm's financial statements, look up some information on the cash conversion cycle. It could help you uncover important information about how efficiently a firm is using its working capital.

The statement of cash flows is a crucial part of the financial reporting for any company. Often creditors and investors will look at this statement first when they are analyzing the financial condition of a firm. For the firm, however, the importance of the statement of cash flows is tied to the cash budget and how the actual sources and uses of cash compare to the budgeted amounts. This analysis is an important function of managerial accounting.

The statement of cash flows provides important information for managers, creditors, and investors. In corporate annual reports, the statement of cash flows is presented with the other three basic financial statements—the income statement, the balance sheet, and the statement of changes in shareholders' equity—to provide information needed to evaluate a company's performance and to provide a basis for predicting a company's future potential.

Business Risk, Control, and Ethics

In Chapter 6, you learned about the controls a company should have to minimize the risks associated with cash. Now we will talk about investors' risks associated with the statement of cash flows. The misleading financial statements that have been at the heart of such failures as Enron and WorldCom have been the income statement and the balance sheet. Managers can rarely falsify cash inflows and outflows, so few people think of this statement as a place where the ethics of a firm's management could be tested. However, managers can manipulate the classification of the cash flows. Because analysts are often looking for positive net cash flows from operating activities, especially in established companies, a firm's managers may feel some pressure to make sure that this part of the statement of cash flows is positive. There is an opportunity to engage in the same type of manipulation as WorldCom did when it classified expenses that belonged on the income statement as long-term assets on the balance sheet. Someone could misclassify cash outflows from operating activities as investing cash outflows. This changes the whole nature of such expenditures. Operating expenses are the costs of doing business, so investors want to see a low number. Investing cash outflows are often interpreted as a positive signal for future growth of the firm, so investors want to see a high number.

There is a great deal of information in the statement of cash flows, and it deserves careful consideration when you are analyzing a firm's financial statements. As with the information provided by the other financial statements, the statement of cash flows provides reliable information only when the firm's management is ethical.

L.O.8
Use the statement of cash flows and the related controls to evaluate the risk of investing in a firm.

News Flash

Cash from Operating Activities—Can It Be Manipulated?

The statement of cash flows is often cited as the one statement that cannot be manipulated. After all, cash is cash. However, there are ways a firm can increase its cash from operating activities on short notice if it needs a boost. It is called *securitization of accounts receivable*. It is when a company borrows against its receivables, classifying the cash inflow as an operating activity. It is allowed by GAAP, but it may be misleading. In many ways, it is more like a financing cash flow. Be sure to read the notes to the financial statements, even when you are analyzing something that should be as obvious as cash!

[Source: "Quick Cash via Receivables Deals Can Leave a Blurry Fiscal Picture," by Michael Rapoport, *The Wall Street Journal*, June 1, 2006, p. C3.]

Chapter Summary Points

- The statement of cash flows explains the change in cash from the beginning of the accounting period to the end of the accounting period—the amount on one balance sheet and the amount on the subsequent balance sheet.
- Cash flows can be categorized as cash from operating activities, cash from investing activities, and cash from financing activities. The statement of cash flows has a section for each of these categories.
- There are two methods—direct and indirect—for preparing and presenting the statement of cash flows. The direct method simply provides all operating cash inflows and outflows in a straightforward manner. The indirect method starts with net income and adjusts it for all noncash items—depreciation expense and gains or losses on the sale of long-term assets are typical noncash items. It also adjusts for changes in the current assets (excluding cash) and the current liabilities. These two methods describe the cash from the operating activities section of the statement. The other two sections—cash from investing activities and cash from financing activities—are the same on both types of statements of cash flows.
- Free cash flow is the amount of cash left after cash spent on investments in long-term assets and cash paid for dividends are subtracted from net cash from operating activities. It measures how much cash a firm has available for long-term investment opportunities.
- Before you invest in a firm, look at its statement of cash flows. A growing or established firm should be generating positive net cash flows from operating activities. Investing cash flows may provide insights into the firm's plans for the future. Be sure to look at the firm's cash situation over several years and also compare the firm's sources and uses of cash to those of the competitors.

Chapter Summary Problems

Suppose Attic Treasures, a retail store, provided you with the following comparative balance sheets and the related income statement. (Notice the most recent year is in the right column.) Assume the firm did not purchase any property, plant, and equipment (PP&E) during the year.

At	January 30, 2008	January 29, 2009
Assets		
Cash	$ 23,000	$ 39,200
Accounts receivable	12,000	23,450
Merchandise inventory	25,200	28,100
Prepaid rent	6,000	5,500
Property, plant, and equipment (PP&E)	79,500	70,000
Accumulated depreciation	(24,000)	(29,000)
Total assets	$121,700	$137,250
Liabilities and Shareholders' Equity		
Accounts payable	$ 12,300	$ 26,200
Income taxes payable	10,000	8,100
Long-term notes payable	39,700	25,800
Common stock and additional paid-in capital	18,500	20,000
Retained earnings	41,200	57,150
Total liabilities and shareholders' equity	$121,700	$137,250

+---+
| Attic Treasures |
| Income Statement |
| For the year ended January 29, 2009 |
+---+

Sales		$234,900
Cost of goods sold		178,850
Gross margin		56,050
Selling expenses	$24,000	
General expense*	8,500	32,500
Income from operations		23,550
Interest expense		1,200
Income before income taxes		22,350
Income tax expense		3,400
Net income		$ 18,950

* includes rent expense of $2,000 and depreciation expense of $6,000

Instructions

Prepare a statement of cash flows. Your instructor will tell you whether to use the indirect method or the direct method (or both). Solutions for each are provided.

Solution

Direct Method

To prepare the cash from operating activities section using the direct method, go down the income statement and convert the accrual amounts to cash amounts by referring to the related current asset or current liability account.

1. Convert *sales* to *cash collected from customers*.
   Sales = $234,900.
   Increase in accounts receivable (AR) from $12,000 to $23,450 = $11,450.
   The increase in AR is the amount of sales Attic Treasures did NOT collect in cash, so the cash collected from customers is $234,900 − $11,450 = **$223,450**.

2. Convert *cost of goods sold* to *cash paid to vendors*. This takes two steps. First, convert cost of goods sold to total purchases.
   Cost of goods sold = $178,850.
   Increase in inventory from $25,200 to $28,100 = $2,900 of additional purchases.
   The increase in inventory is added to the cost of goods sold to get total purchases = $178,850 + $2,900 = $181,750. Then, convert total purchases to cash paid to vendors.
   Total purchases = $181,750.
   Increase in accounts payable of $12,300 to $26,200 = $13,900 represent purchases that did not get paid for, so cash paid to vendors = $181,750 − $13,900 = **$167,850**.

3. Convert *selling expenses* to *cash paid for selling expenses*. Because there are no current assets or current liabilities related to selling expenses (such as accrued selling expenses), Attic Treasures must have paid cash for this entire amount. So cash paid for selling expenses = **$24,000**.

4. Convert *general expenses* to *cash paid for general expenses*.
   General expenses = $8,500. This includes $2,000 rent expense and $6,000 depreciation expense. So we could break down the general expenses as follows:

Rent expense	$2,000
Depreciation expenses	$6,000
Other expenses	$ 500

   First, rent expense is related to prepaid rent on the balance sheet. Prepaid rent decreased from $6,000 to $5,500. This means the company used rent it had already (last

year) paid for, so the decrease in prepaid rent reduces the rent expense by $500 to get cash paid for rent = $2,000 − $500 = **$1,500**.
Depreciation expense is a noncash expense, so there is no cash flow associated with it. Other expenses of $500 must have been all cash because there are no associated current assets or current liabilities on the balance sheet. So the total cash paid for general expenses = $1,500 + $500 = **$2,000**.

5. Change *interest expense* to *cash paid for interest*.
Interest expense = $1,200.
This must have been all cash because there were no current assets or current liabilities associated with it. Cash paid for interest = **$1,200**.

6. Change *income tax expense* to *cash paid for taxes*:
Income tax expense = $3,400.
Decrease in income taxes payable from $10,000 to $8,100 = $1,900, which represents additional taxes the company paid beyond the income tax expense on the income statement. Cash paid for income taxes = $3,400 + $1,900 = **$5,300**.
.You have now converted all the income statement items to cash inflows and outflows and are ready to prepare the first part of the statement of cash flows.

Cash from operating activities	
Cash collected from customers	$223,450
Cash paid to vendors	(167,850)
Cash paid for selling expenses	(24,000)
Cash paid for general expenses	(2,000)
Cash paid for interest	(1,200)
Cash paid for income taxes	(5,300)
Net cash provided by operating activities	$ 23,100

7. Next, calculate cash from investing activities. An analysis of long-term assets shows that property, plant, and equipment decreased by $9,500. A decrease is caused by disposing of assets. Because the income statement showed no gain or loss from disposal of long-term assets, the assets must have been sold for book value. The property, plant, and equipment account decreased by $9,500 (the cost of the PPE sold) and the accumulated depreciation account increased by $5,000. Recall from the income statement that depreciation expense for the year was $6,000. If accumulated depreciation only increased by $5,000, then $1,000 must have been subtracted. That means the PPE sold had a book value of $8,500 ($9,500 − $1,000). Because there was no gain or loss on the disposal, the company must have received proceeds equal to the book value. So the cash inflow—proceeds—from disposal of PPE was an investing cash inflow of **$8,500**.

8. To calculate the cash flows from financing activities, analyze what happened in the long-term liability accounts and the shareholders' equity accounts. Long-term notes payable decreased from $39,700 to $25,800. That must have been a cash outflow of $13,900. Common stock and additional paid-in capital increased by $1,500. That must have been a cash inflow from the issue of stock of $1,500. Lastly, see if the company paid any dividends during the year. Retained earnings increased from $41,200 to $57,150 = $15,950. How does that compare to net income? Net income was $18,950 but retained earnings only increased by $15,950, so **$3,000** must have been declared as dividends. The absence of dividends payable indicates that the dividends were paid.

You are now ready to put the whole statement together using the direct method.

Attic Treasures
Statement of Cash Flows—Direct Method
For the year ended January 29, 2009

Cash from operating activities	
Cash collected from customers	$223,450
Cash paid to vendors	(167,850)
Cash paid for selling expenses	(24,000)
Cash paid for general expenses	(2,000)
Cash paid for interest	(1,200)
Cash paid for income taxes	(5,300)
Net cash provided by operating activities	23,100
Cash from investing activities	
Cash proceeds from sale of property, plant and equipment	8,500
Cash from financing activities	
Cash paid on loan principal	(13,900)
Cash proceeds from stock issue	1,500
Cash paid for dividends	(3,000)
Net cash used for financing activities	(15,400)
Net increase in cash during the year	16,200
Cash balance, beginning of the year	23,000
Ending cash balance	$ 39,200

Indirect Method

To prepare the statement using the indirect method, start with net income. Adjust it for any noncash expenses and the change in every current asset (excluding cash) and every current liability. The other two sections—cash from investing activities and cash from financing activities—are the same as for the direct method.

Attic Treasures
Statement of Cash Flows—Indirect Method
For the year ended January 29, 2009

Cash from operating activities	
Net income	$ 18,950
Add depreciation expense	6,000
Deduct increase in accounts receivable	(11,450)
Deduct increase in inventory	(2,900)
Add decrease in prepaid rent	500
Add increase in accounts payable	13,900
Deduct decrease in income taxes payable	(1,900)
Net cash provided by operating activities	23,100
Cash from investing activities	
Cash proceeds from sale of property, plant and equipment	8,500
Cash from financing activities	
Cash paid on loan principal	(13,900)
Cash proceeds from stock issue	1,500
Cash paid for dividends	(3,000)
Net cash used for financing activities	(15,400)
Net increase in cash during the year	16,200
Cash balance, beginning of the year	23,000
Ending cash balance	$ 39,200

Key Terms for Chapter 9

Direct method (p. 429)   Free cash flow (p. 440)   Indirect method (p. 429)

Answers to YOUR TURN Questions

Chapter 9

Your Turn 9-1

The difference is in the cash flows from operating activities. The direct method identifies each cash flow, whereas the indirect method starts with net income and adjusts it to a cash amount. The net cash flow from operating activities is the same no matter which method is used. The other two sections—cash from investing activities and cash from financing activities—are identical with both methods.

Your Turn 9-2

$50,000 + ($25,000 − $15,000) = $60,000.

    This is a cash flow from operating activities.

Your Turn 9-3

$400 − ($350 − $250) = $300.

    This is a cash flow from operating activities.

Your Turn 9-4

Begin with net income and add back depreciation expense: $50,000 + $7,000 = $57,000. Then, subtract the $2,000 increase in accounts receivable. Sales on account were included in net income but should be deducted if the cash has not been collected. Next, add the $500 increase in salaries payable. Some of the salaries expense, which was deducted on the income statement, was not paid at the balance sheet date.

    $50,000 + $7,000 − $2,000 + $500 =
    $55,500 net cash from operating activities.

Your Turn 9-5

Free cash flow = Net cash from operations − Purchase of long-term assets − Dividends =
    $45,600 − $25,000 = $20,600.

Questions

1. What is the purpose of the statement of cash flows?
2. Which two financial statements are required to prepare the statement of cash flows?
3. Describe the three categories of cash flows that explain the total change in cash for the year.
4. Why is the statement of cash flows so important?
5. What are the two traditional approaches for preparing and presenting the statement of cash flows? What is the difference between these two approaches?
6. Which types of business transactions would result in cash from operating activities? Give three examples of transactions that would be classified as cash flows from operating activities.
7. Which types of business transactions would result in cash flows from investing activities? Give three examples of transactions that would be classified as cash flows from investing activities.
8. Which types of business transactions would result in cash flows from financing activities? Give three examples of transactions that would be classified as cash flows from financing activities.
9. How is depreciation expense treated when using the direct method of preparing the statement of cash flows? When using the indirect method?
10. Which account(s) must be analyzed to determine the cash collected from customers? How is this cash flow classified?
11. Which account(s) must be analyzed to determine the proceeds from the sale of a building? How is this cash flow classified?
12. Which account(s) must be analyzed to determine the cash paid to vendors? How is this cash flow classified?
13. Which account(s) must be analyzed to determine the cash paid for dividends? How is this cash flow classified?

14. How is interest collected or interest paid classified on the statement of cash flows?
15. Define free cash flow and explain what this amount indicates about a firm.
16. How might a firm misuse the statement of cash flows to give investors a better impression of the firm's operations?

Multiple-Choice Questions

Use the following information to answer Questions 1–3.
Quality Products engaged in the following **cash** transactions during May.

Purchase of inventory	$ 5,000
Cash proceeds from loan	$ 7,000
Cash paid for interest	$ 400
Cash collected from sales	$26,500
New stock issued	$25,000
Salaries paid to employees	$ 4,600
Purchase of new delivery van	$20,000

Note: Answers in parentheses indicate net cash outflows.
1. How much is net cash from financing activities?
   a. $ 7,000
   b. $25,000
   c. $31,600
   d. $32,000
2. How much is net cash from investing activities?
   a. $(20,000)
   b. $(25,000)
   c. $ 25,000
   d. $ 32,000
3. How much is net cash from operating activities?
   a. $26,500
   b. $ (3,500)
   c. $16,500
   d. $16,900
4. Cash from the sale of treasury stock
   a. Would not be included in the statement of cash flows
   b. Would be classified as a contra-equity cash flow
   c. Would be classified as an investing cash flow
   d. Would be classified as a financing cash flow
5. The cash proceeds fron the sale of a building will be
   a. The cost of the building
   b. The book value of the building
   c. The book value plus any gain or minus any loss
   d. Shown on the financing portion of the appropriate financial statement
6. If a firm has net investing cash inflows of $5,000, net financing cash inflows of $24,000, and a net increase in cash for the year of $12,000, how much is net cash from operating activities?
   a. Net cash inflow of $17,000
   b. Net cash inflow of $29,000
   c. Net cash outflow of $17,000
   d. Net cash outflow of $19,000
7. Depreciation for the year was $50,000 and net income was $139,500. If the company used cash for all transactions except those related to long-term assets, how much was net cash from operating activities?
   a. $139,500
   b. $189,500
   c. $ 89,500
   d. Cannot be determined from the given information

Use the following information to answer the next three questions.
The income statement and additional data for Frances Company for the year ended December 31, 2006, follows.

Sales revenue	$400,000
Cost of goods sold	$165,000
Salary expense	$ 70,000
Depreciation expense	$ 55,000
Insurance expense	$ 20,000
Interest expense	$ 10,000
Income tax expense	$ 18,000
Net income	$ 62,000

Accounts receivable decreased by $12,000. Inventories increased by $6,000 and accounts payable decreased by $2,000. Salaries payable increased by $8,000. Prepaid insurance increased by $4,000. Interest expense and income tax expense equal their cash amounts. Frances Company uses the direct method for its statement of cash flows.

8. How much cash did Frances Company collect from customers during 2006?
   a. $400,000
   b. $412,000
   c. $406,000
   d. $388,000

9. How much cash did Frances Company pay its vendors during 2006?
   a. $173,000
   b. $165,000
   c. $167,000
   d. $163,000

10. How much cash did Frances Company pay for insurance during the year?
   a. $20,000
   b. $24,000
   c. $16,000
   d. $48,000

Short Exercises

SE9-1. *Identify cash flows. (LO 1)*
Given the following cash transactions, classify each as a cash flow from: (a) operating activities, (b) investing activities, or (c) financing activities.
   a. Payment to employees for work done
   b. Dividends paid to shareholders
   c. Payment for new equipment
   d. Payment to supplier for inventory
   e. Interest payment to the bank related to a loan

SE9-2. *Identify cash flows. (LO 1)*
Given the following cash transactions, classify each as a cash flow from: (a) operating activities, (b) investing activities, or (c) financing activities.
   a. Principal payment to the bank for a loan
   b. Collection from customers to whom sales were previously made on account
   c. Collection from customers for cash sales
   d. Collection for sale of land that had been purchased as a possible factory site
   e. Petty cash used to pay for doughnuts for staff

SE9-3. *Calculate and identify cash flows. (LO 1, 3, 4)*
College Television Company had supplies on its balance sheet at December 31, 2006, of $20,000. The income statement for 2007 showed supplies expense of $50,000. The balance sheet at December 31, 2007, showed supplies of $25,000. If no supplies were purchased on account (all were cash purchases), how much cash did College Television Company spend on supplies during 2007? How would that cash outflow be classified on the statement of cash flows?

SE9-4. *Calculate and identify cash flows. (LO 1, 3, 4)*
Col Corporation reported credit sales of $150,000 for 2006. Col's accounts receivable from sales were $25,000 at the beginning of 2006 and $38,000 at the end of 2006. What was the amount of cash collected from sales in 2006? How would the cash from this transaction be classified on the statement of cash flows?

SE9-5. *Calculate and identify cash flows. (LO 6)*
A building cost $55,000 and had accumulated depreciation of $15,000 when it was sold for a gain of $5,000. It was a cash sale. How would the cash from this transaction be classified on the statement of cash flows?

SE9-6. *Calculate and identify cash flows. (LO 1, 3, 4)*
Sales for 2008 were $50,000; cost of goods sold was $35,000. If accounts receivable increased by $2,000, inventory decreased by $1,300, accounts payable decreased by $2,000, and other accrued liabilities decreased by $1,000, how much cash was paid to vendors and suppliers during the year? How would the cash from this transaction be classified on the statement of cash flows?

SE9-7. *Calculate and identify cash flow. (LO 1, 3, 4)*
During 2007, Cameron Company had $300,000 in cash sales and $3,500,000 in credit sales. The accounts receivable balances were $450,000 and $530,000 at December 31, 2006 and 2007, respectively. What was the total cash collected from all customers during 2007? How would the cash from this transaction be classified on the statement of cash flows?

SE9-8. *Evaluate adjustments to net income using the indirect method. (LO 5)*
The income statement for Lilly's Company for the year ended June 30, 2008, showed sales of $50,000. During the year, the balance in accounts receivable increased by $7,500. What adjustment to net income would be shown in the operating section of the statement of cash flows prepared using the indirect method related to this information? How much cash was collected from customers during the fiscal year ended June 30, 2008?

SE9-9. *Evaluate adjustments to net income using the indirect method. (LO 5)*
The income statement for Sharp Inc. for the month of May showed insurance expense of $250. The beginning and ending balance sheets for the month showed an increase of $50 in prepaid insurance. There were no payables related to insurance on the balance sheet. What adjustment to net income would be shown in the operating section of the statement of cash flows prepared using the indirect method related to this information? How much cash was paid for insurance during the month?

SE9-10. *Evaluate adjustments to net income using the indirect method. (LO 5)*
During 2007, Mail Direct Inc. incurred salary expense of $67,500, as shown on the income statement. The January 1, 2007, balance sheet showed salaries payable of $10,450; and the December 31, 2007, balance sheet showed salaries payable of $13,200. What adjustment to net income would be shown in the operating section of the statement of cash flows prepared using the indirect method related to this information? How much cash was paid to employees (for salary) during 2007?

SE9-11. *Evaluate adjustments to net income using the indirect method. (LO 5)*
Havelen's Road Paving Company had depreciation expense of $43,000 on the income statement for the year. How would this expense be shown on the statement of cash flows prepared using the indirect method? Why?

SE9-12. *Calculate and identify cash flows using the indirect method. (LO 5)*
Beta Company spent $40,000 for a new delivery truck during the year. Depreciation expense of $2,000 related to the truck was shown on the income statement. How are the purchase of the truck and the related depreciation reflected on the statement of cash flows prepared using the indirect method?

SE9-13. *Evaluate adjustments to net income under the indirect method. (LO 5)*
B&W Inc. reported net income of $1.2 million in 2006. Depreciation for the year was $120,000, accounts receivable increased $728,000, and accounts payable decreased $420,000. Compute net cash provided by operating activities using the indirect method.

SE9-14. *Evaluate adjustments to net income under the indirect method. (LO 1, 5)*
In 2007, Jewels Company had net income of $350,000. The depreciation on plant assets during 2007 was $73,000, and the company incurred a loss on the sale of plant assets of $20,000. Compute net cash provided by operating activities under the indirect method.

SE9-15. *Evaluate adjustments to net income under the indirect method. (LO 5)*
The comparative balance sheets for JayCee Company showed the following changes in current asset accounts: accounts receivable decreased by $50,000, prepaid expenses decreased by $23,000, and merchandise inventory increased by $17,000. These were all the changes in the current assets and current liability accounts (except cash). Net income for the year was $275,500. Compute net cash provided by or used by operating activities using the indirect method.

SE9-16. *Calculate and identify cash flows. (LO 5)*
C&S Supply Inc. had $125,000 of retained earnings at the beginning of the year and a balance of $150,000 at the end of the year. Net income for the year was $80,000. What transaction occurred to cause the decrease in retained earnings? How would this decrease be shown on the statement of cash flows?

SE9-17. *Use a statement of cash flows for decision making. (LO 7, 8)*
If you were interested in investing in a company, what item(s) on the statement of cash flows would be of most interest to you? Why?

SE9-18. *Identify risks and controls. (LO 8)*
If you were an investor, why would you look at the statement of cash flows? Which amounts would provide information about the risk to an investor?

SE9-19. *Identify risks and controls. (LO 8)*
If you believe there is a risk that a firm is not taking advantage of long-term investment opportunities, how would the statement of cash flows help you confirm or disconfirm this belief?

Exercises—Set A

E9-1A. *Identify cash flows. (LO 1)*
For each of the following items, tell whether it is a cash inflow or cash outflow and the section of the statement of cash flows in which the item would appear. (Assume the direct method is used.)

Item	Inflow or Outflow	Section of the Statement
a. Cash collected from customers		
b. Proceeds from issue of stock		
c. Interest payment on loan		
d. Principal repayment on loan		
e. Cash paid for advertising		
f. Proceeds from sale of treasury stock		
g. Money borrowed from the local bank		
h. Cash paid to employees (salaries)		
i. Purchase of equipment for cash		
j. Cash paid to vendors for inventory		
k. Taxes paid		

E9-2A. *Identify cash flows. (LO 1, 4, 6)*
For each transaction, indicate the amount of the cash flow, indicate whether each results in an inflow or outflow of cash, and give the section of the statement in which each cash flow would appear. Assume the statement of cash flows is prepared using the direct method.

Amount	Inflow or Outflow	Section of the Statement
a. Issued 100 shares of $2 par common stock for $12 per share		
b. Borrowed $7,000 from a local bank to expand the business		
c. Purchased $500 of supplies for $400 cash and the balance on account		
d. Hired a carpenter to build some bookcases for the office for $500 cash		
e. Earned revenue of $19,000, receiving $9,200 cash and the balance on account		
f. Hired a student to do some typing and paid him $250 cash		
g. Repaid $7,000 of the bank loan along with $250 interest.		
h. Paid dividends of $600		

E9-3A. *Prepare cash from operating activities section of statement of cash flows using the direct method. (LO 4)*

Use the income statement for Clark Corporation for past year and the information from the comparative balance sheets shown for the beginning and the end of the year to prepare the cash from operating activities section of the statement of cash flows using the direct method.

Excel Template
www.prenhall.com/reimers

Sales		$100,000
Cost of goods sold		35,000
Gross margin		65,000
Operating expenses		
Wages	$ 2,500	
Rent	1,200	
Utilities	980	
Insurance	320	5,000
Net income		$ 60,000

Account	Beginning of the Year	End of the Year
Accounts receivable	$ 10,000	$ 12,000
Inventory	21,000	18,500
Prepaid insurance	575	400
Accounts payable	9,000	10,400
Wages payable	850	600
Utilities payable	150	-0-

E9-4A. *Prepare cash from operating activities section of statement of cash flows using the indirect method. (LO 5)*

Use the information from E9-3A to prepare the cash from operating activities section of the statement of cash flows using the indirect method. Then, compare it with the statement you prepared for E9-3A. What are the similarities? What are the differences? Which statement do you find most informative?

Excel Template
www.prenhall.com/reimers

E9-5A. *Calculate change in cash. (LO 1, 4, 6)*

Given the following information, calculate the change in cash for the year.

Cash received from sale of equipment	$ 20,000
Cash paid for salaries	8,250
Depreciation expense for the year	12,450
Cash received from issue of stock	150,000
Cash collected from customers	87,900
Cash received from sale of land	14,500
Cash paid for operating expenses	2,000
Cash paid to vendor for inventory	32,480

E9-6A. *Calculate cash from operating activities. (LO 3, 4)*
Use the information given for Evans Company to calculate
  a. Cash paid for salaries
  b. Cash paid for income taxes
  c. Cash paid for inventory items
  d. Cash collected from customers
  e. Cash proceeds from stock issue

From the Financial Statements for Evans Company

	Income Statement Amount for the Year	Balance Sheet Beginning of the Year	End of the Year
Sales revenue	$ 85,600		
Accounts receivable		$ 8,700	$ 10,000
Salary expense	21,400		
Salaries payable		2,300	2,100
Cost of goods sold	24,300		
Inventory		4,800	8,000
Accounts payable		2,500	3,000
Income tax expense	28,500		
Income taxes payable		7,400	8,500
Common stock and additional paid-in capital	n/a	630,000	718,000

E9-7A. *Prepare the cash from operating activities section of the statement of cash flows and determine the method used. (LO 2, 4, 6)*
Use the information from E9-6A to calculate the cash flow from operations for Evans Company. Based on the information provided, which method of preparing the statement of cash flows does Evans use?

E9-8A. *Calculate cash flows from investing and financing activities. (LO 1, 6)*
The following events occurred at Gadgets Inc. during 2006.

January 15	Issued bonds for $250,000
March 8	Purchased new machinery for $80,000 cash
May 10	Sold old machinery for $30,000, resulting in a $10,000 loss
July 14	Paid interest of $20,000 on the bonds
September 25	Borrowed $5,000 from a local bank
October 30	Purchased a new computer for $3,000 cash
December 31	Paid cash dividends of $4,600

Compute Gadgets' net cash flow from (1) investing activities and from (2) financing activities for 2006.

E9-9A. *Calculate cash from operating activities using the direct method. (LO 1, 4)*
The following information applies to Computer Company.

Income Statement for the Year Ended December 31, 2007

Sales	$ 20,000
Cost of goods sold	(15,200)
Gross margin	4,800
Rent expense	(1,000)
Net income	$ 3,800

1. Accounts receivable started the year with a balance of $1,000 and ended the year with a balance of $3,300.

2. The beginning balance in accounts payable (to vendors) was $2,000, and the ending balance was zero. Inventory at the end of the year was the same as it was at the beginning of the year (i.e., there was no change in inventory).

3. The company started the year with $5,000 of prepaid rent and ended the year with $4,000 of prepaid rent.

Determine the following cash flows.
   a. Cash collected from customers for sales during the year
   b. Cash paid to vendors for inventory during the year
   c. Cash paid for rent during the year

E9-10A. *Calculate cash from operating activities using the indirect method. (LO 5, 6)*
Brass Company reported net income of $290,000 for 2007. The company also reported depreciation expense of $70,000 and a gain of $3,000 on the sale of equipment. The comparative balance sheet shows a decrease in accounts receivable of $8,000 for the year, a $5,000 decrease in accounts payable, and a $1,700 increase in prepaid expenses. Prepare the cash from operating activities section of the statement of cash flows for 2007 using the indirect method.

E9-11A. *Calculate cash from operating activities using the indirect method. (LO 5)*
The following information was taken from Tram Inc.'s balance sheets at December 31, 2005 and 2006. Prepare the net cash provided by operating activities section of the company's statement of cash flows for the year ended December 31, 2006, using the indirect method.

	2006	2005
Current assets		
Cash	$103,000	$ 99,000
Accounts receivable	90,000	79,000
Inventory	150,000	142,000
Prepaid expenses	47,000	50,000
Total current assets	$390,000	$370,000
Current liabilities		
Accrued expenses payable	$ 17,000	$ 15,000
Accounts payable	60,000	92,000
Total current liabilities	$ 77,000	$107,000

Net income for 2006 was $185,000. Depreciation expense was $25,000.

E9-12A. *Calculate cash from operating activities using the direct method. (LO 4)*
Compton Company completed its first year of operations on December 31, 2006. The firm's income statement for the year showed revenues of $175,000 and operating expenses of $84,000. Accounts receivable was $54,000 at year-end and payables related to operating expense were $21,000 at year-end. Compute net cash from operating activities using the direct method.

E9-13A. *Calculate cash from operating activities using the direct method. (LO 1, 4)*
During the fiscal year ended September 30, 2006, Napster Company engaged in the following transactions. Using the relevant transactions, prepare the cash from operating activities section of the statement of cash flows using the direct method.
   a. Paid interest of $7,000
   b. Collected $175,000 on accounts receivable
   c. Made cash sales of $128,000
   d. Paid salaries of $52,000
   e. Recorded depreciation expense of $27,000
   f. Paid income taxes of $32,000
   g. Sold equipment for cash of $152,000
   h. Purchased new equipment for cash of $41,000
   i. Made payments to vendors of $62,700
   j. Paid dividends of $20,000
   k. Purchased land for cash of $174,000
   l. Paid operating expenses of $32,500

E9-14A. *Prepare the statement of cash flows using the indirect method. (LO 5, 6)*
Use the following information for Just Nuts Company to prepare a statement of cash flows using the indirect method.

Just Nuts Company
Balance Sheet
June 30

	2007	2006
Assets		
Cash	$193,000	$120,500
Accounts receivable	64,000	60,000
Inventories	120,000	175,000
Land	95,000	120,000
Equipment	250,000	180,000
Accumulated depreciation	(75,000)	(45,000)
Total assets	$647,000	$610,500
Liabilities and Shareholders' Equity		
Accounts payable	$ 42,000	$ 50,000
Bonds payable	160,000	220,000
Common stock and additional paid-in capital	200,000	180,000
Retained earnings	245,000	160,500
Total liabilities and shareholders' equity	$647,000	$610,500

Additional information:
- a. Net income for the fiscal year ended June 30, 2007, was $95,000.
- b. The company declared and paid cash dividends.
- c. The company redeemed bonds payable amounting to $60,000 for cash of $60,000.
- d. The company issued common stock for $20,000 cash.

E9-15A. *Prepare the statement of cash flows using the direct method. (LO 4, 6)*
Using the information from E9-14A, prepare a statement of cash flows for Just Nuts Company using the direct method.

E9-16A. *Analyze a statement of cash flows. (LO 7)*
The following information has been taken from the most recent statement of cash flows of Expansion Company:

Net cash used by operating activities	$ (932,000)
Net cash provided by investing activities	$ 1,180,500
Net cash provided by financing activities	$ 2,107,000

- a. What information do these subtotals from the statement of cash flows tell you about Expansion Company?
- b. What additional information would you want to see before you analyze Expansion Company's ability to generate positive operating cash flows in the future?
- c. Did Expansion have a positive net income for the period? What information would you like to see to help you predict next year's net income?

E9-17A. *Compute free cash flow. (LO 7)*
Use the Pier 1 Imports Inc. consolidated statement of cash flows to compute the company's free cash flow for the 3 years shown. What does the trend in free cash flow tell you about Pier 1?

Pier 1 Imports, Inc.
Consolidated Statements of Cash Flows
(In thousands)

	2006	Year Ended 2005	2004
		(As restated, See Note 2)	(As restated, See Note 2)
Cash flow from operating activities:			
Net income (loss)	$(39,804)	$ 60,457	$ 118,001
Adjustments to reconcile to net cash (used in) provided by operating activities:			
Depreciation and amortization	78,781	75,624	64,606
Loss (gain) on disposal of fixed assets	1,781	315	(316)
Loss on impairment of fixed assets	6,024	741	459
Write-down of assets held for sale	7,441	–	–
Deferred compensation	11,402	7,710	6,573
Lease termination expense	4,176	2,243	3,258
Deferred income taxes	(14,496)	2,035	184
Sale of receivables in exchange for beneficial interest in securitized receivables	(74,550)	(91,071)	(83,931)
Tax benefits from options exercised by employees	760	3,668	4,897
Other	(524)	(222)	4,894
Change in cash from:			
Inventories	882	(6,860)	(40,520)
Other accounts receivable, prepaid expenses and other current assets	(22,778)	(11,302)	(16,927)
Income tax receivable	(18,011)	–	–
Accounts payable and accrued expenses	7,369	21,572	34,410
Income taxes payable	(6,966)	(14,116)	184
Other noncurrent assets	(2,558)	336	(2,027)
Other noncurrent liabilities	(3,226)	–	–
Net cash (used in) provided by operating activities	(64,297)	51,130	93,745
Cash flow from investing activities:			
Capital expenditures	(50,979)	(99,239)	(121,190)
Proceeds from disposition of properties	1,401	3,852	34,450
Proceeds from sale of restricted investments	3,226	–	–
Purchase of restricted investments	(3,500)	(10,807)	(8,752)
Collections of principal on beneficial interest in securitized receivables	60,240	99,712	78,788
Net cash provided by (used in) investing activities	10,388	(6,482)	(16,704)
Cash flow from financing activities:			
Cash dividends	(34,667)	(34,762)	(26,780)
Purchases of treasury stock	(4,047)	(58,210)	(76,009)
Proceeds from stock options exercised, stock purchase plan and other, net	7,641	12,473	15,709
Issuance of long-term debt	165,000	–	–
Notes payable borrowings	86,500	–	–
Repayment of notes payable	(86,500)	–	(6,390)
Debt issuance costs	(6,739)	(169)	(584)
Purchase of call option	(9,145)	–	–
Net cash provided by (used in) financing activities	118,043	(80,668)	(94,054)
Change in cash and cash equivalents	64,134	(36,020)	(17,013)
Cash and cash equivalents at beginning period (including cash held for sale of $3,359, $6,148 and $6,506, respectively)	189,081	225,101	242,114
Cash and cash equivalents at end of period (including cash held for sale of $7,100, $3,359 and $6,148, respectively)	$ 253,215	$ 189,081	$ 225,101
Supplemental cash flow information:			
Interest paid	$ 8,136	$ 868	$ 1,791
Income taxes paid	$ 21,342	$ 45,655	$ 63,788

The accompanying notes are an integral part of these financial statements

Source: www.pier1.com/investorrelations/annualReports.asp; fiscal year 2006 Annual Report.

E9-18A. *Identify risks and controls. (LO 8)*
Using the Pier 1 statement of cash flows shown in E9-17A, determine whether or not the firm appears to be taking advantage of new investment opportunities. Is the firm in a growth stage or a more mature stage of its business life? What evidence supports your opinion?

Exercises—Set B

E9-1B. *Identify cash flows. (LO 1)*
For each of the following items, tell whether it is a cash inflow or cash outflow and the section of the statement of cash flows in which the item would appear. (Assume the direct method is used.)

Item	Inflow or Outflow	Section of the Statement
a. Cash paid to vendor for supplies		
b. Purchase of treasury stock		
c. Principal repayment on bonds		
d. Interest payment on bonds		
e. Cash paid for salaries		
f. Cash from issuance of common stock		
g. Cash dividends paid		
h. Cash paid for rent and utilities		
i. Purchase of computer for cash		
j. Cash paid for company vehicle		
k. Income taxes paid		

E9-2B. *Identify cash flows. (LO 1, 4)*
For each transaction, indicate the amount of the cash flow, indicate whether each results in an inflow or outflow of cash, and give the section of the statement in which each cash flow would appear. Assume the statement of cash flows is prepared using the direct method.

Item	Inflow or Outflow	Section of the Statement
a. Issued 660 shares of $0.10 par common stock for $15 per share.		
b. Sold $2,500 of inventory, received $1,500 in cash and remaining $1,000 on account		
c. Purchased a $2,500 computer by paying cash of $1,000 and signing a short-term note for the other $1,500		
d. Paid $600 for routine maid service to clean office		
e. Paid rent and utility expenses totaling $2,250		
f. Hired a runner to carry correspondences between offices and paid her $175		
g. Repaid the $1,500 short-term note along with $100 interest		
h. Purchased $1,500 of treasury stock		

E9-3B. *Prepare cash from operating activities using the direct method. (LO 4)*
Use the income statement for Kristen Harrison's Cosmetics Inc. for the past year and the information from the comparative balance sheets shown for the beginning and the end of the year to prepare the operating section of the statement of cash flows using the direct method.

Sales		$ 150,000
Cost of goods sold		55,000
Gross margin		95,000
Operating expenses		
Wages	$ 3,750	
Rent	1,600	
Utilities	850	
Insurance	175	6,375
Net income		$ 88,625

Account	Beginning of the Year	End of the Year
Accounts receivable	$ 12,000	$ 10,000
Inventory	18,200	19,700
Prepaid insurance	600	200
Accounts payable	8,000	7,400
Wages payable	725	850
Utilities payable	0	-275-

E9-4B. *Prepare cash from operating activities using the indirect method. (LO 5)*
Use the information from E9-3B to prepare the cash from operating activities section of the statement of cash flows using the indirect method. Then, compare it with the statement you prepared for E9-3B. What are the similarities? What are the differences? Which statement do you find most informative?

E9-5B. *Calculate change in cash. (LO 1, 5)*
Given the following information, calculate the change in cash for the year.

Cash received from sale of company van	$ 15,000
Cash paid for utilities and rent	5,150
Cash paid for interest expense during the year	10,650
Cash paid for purchase of treasury stock	25,000
Cash collected from customers	68,250
Cash received from issuance of bonds	114,500
Cash paid for salaries	12,000
Cash paid to do a major repair of equipment to prolong its useful life for five more years	32,480

E9-6B. *Calculate cash from operating activities. (LO 2, 5)*
  a. Cash paid for utilities
  b. Cash paid for interest
  c. Cash paid for inventory items
  d. Cash collected from customers

From the Financial Statements for MF Company

	Income Statement Amount for the Year	Balance Sheet	
		Beginning of the Year	End of the Year
Sales revenue	$ 314,250		
Accounts receivable		$ 6,500	$ 1,200
Utilities expense	18,300		
Utilities payable		1,500	2,700
Cost of goods sold	25,600		
Inventory		7,800	6,000
Accounts payable		1,500	2,000
Interest expense	5,750		
Interest payable		2,400	2,300

E9-7B. *Prepare cash from operating activities section of statement of cash flows and determine the method used. (LO 2, 4)*
Use the information from E9-6B to calculate the cash flow from operating activities for MF Company. Based on the information provided, which method of preparing the statement of cash flows does MF use?

E9-8B. Calculate cash flows from investing and financing activities. *(LO 1, 6)*
The following events occurred at Garden & Home Store Inc. during 2009.

January 25	Issued common stock for $175,000
February 8	Purchased a delivery truck for $65,000 cash
April 15	Sold old delivery truck for $28,500, resulting in a $3,500 gain
July 24	Borrowed $7,500 from a local bank
September 20	Purchased new machinery for $18,000 cash
December 15	Paid interest of $150 on the loan
December 31	Paid cash dividends of $1,750

Compute Garden & Home Store Inc.'s net cash flow from (1) investing activities and from (2) financing activities for 2009.

E9-9B. *Calculate cash from operating activities using the direct method. (LO 1, 4)*
The following information applies to Electronics Plus Inc.:

Income Statement for the Year Ended June 30, 2010

Sales	$ 35,000
Cost of goods sold	(20,600)
Gross margin	14,400
Rent expense	(1,400)
Net income	$13,000

1. Accounts receivable started the year with a balance of $1,500 and ended the year with a balance of $500.
2. The beginning balance in accounts payable (to vendors) was $1,650, and the ending balance was $550. Inventory at the end of the year was the same as it was at the beginning of the year (i.e., there was no change in inventory).
3. The company started the year with $3,000 of prepaid rent and ended the year with $1,600 of prepaid rent.

Determine the following cash flows.
   a. Cash collected from customers for sales during the year
   b. Cash paid to vendors for inventory during the year
   c. Cash paid for rent during the year

E9-10B. *Calculate cash from operating activities using the indirect method. (LO 5)*
St. Augustine Steel Inc. reported net income of $320,000 for 2008. The company also reported depreciation expense of $65,000 and a loss of $5,000 on the sale of equipment. The comparative balance sheet shows a decrease in accounts receivable of $6,500 for the year, a $3,500 increase in accounts payable, and a $1,450 decrease in prepaid expenses. Prepare the cash from operating activities section of the statement of cash flows for 2008 using the indirect method.

E9-11B. *Calculate cash from operating activities using the indirect method. (LO 5)*
The following information was taken from Fix-It Company's balance sheets at June 30, 2007 and 2008. Prepare the net cash provided by operating activities section of the company's statement of cash flows for the year ended June 30, 2008, using the indirect method.

	2008	2007
Current assets		
Cash	$105,000	$ 95,000
Accounts receivable	80,000	89,000
Inventory	210,000	188,000
Prepaid expenses	53,000	45,000
Total current assets	$448,000	$417,000
Current liabilities		
Accrued expenses payable	$ 18,000	$ 22,000
Accounts payable	85,000	63,000
Total current liabilities	$103,000	$ 85,000

Net income for the year ended June 30, 2008 was $215,000. Depreciation expense was $30,500.

E9-12B. *Calculate cash from operating activities using the direct method. (LO 4)*
Capital Appliances Inc. completed its first year of operations on June 30, 2007. The firm's income statement for the year showed revenues of $180,000 and operating expenses of $62,000. Accounts receivable was $30,000 at year-end and payables related to operating expense were $18,500 at year-end. Compute net cash from operating activities using the direct method.

E9-13B. *Calculate cash from operating activities using the direct method. (LO 1, 4)*
During the fiscal year ended March 31, 2008, Radio Technology Inc. engaged in the following transactions. Using the relevant transactions, prepare the cash from operating activities section of the statement of cash flows using the direct method.
a. Paid $130,000 on accounts payable related to operating expenses
b. Collected $185,000 on accounts receivable
c. Made cash sales of $315,000
d. Paid salaries of $40,000
e. Recorded amortization expense of $15,000
f. Declared a 2-for-1 stock split
g. Paid interest on loan in the amount of $21,500
h. Repaid principal of loan for $275,000
i. Sold equipment for $295,000
j. Paid dividends of $15,000
k. Purchased a new building for cash of $215,000
l. Paid operating expenses of $65,500

E9-14B. *Prepare the statement of cash flows using the indirect method. (LO 2, 5)*
Use the following information for LAW Office Products and Supplies Inc. to prepare a statement of cash flows for the year ended December 31, 2007, using the indirect method.

LAW Office Products and Supplies Inc.
Balance Sheet

	At December 31,	
	2007	2006
Assets		
Cash	$ 55,000	$ 23,500
Accounts receivable	78,000	64,000
Inventories	180,000	169,000
Land	135,000	105,000
Equipment	350,000	260,000
Accumulated depreciation	(90,000)	(60,000)
Total assets	$ 708,000	$ 561,500

Liabilities and Shareholders' Equity

Accounts payable	$ 35,000	$ 40,000
Bonds payable	185,000	215,000
Common stock and additional paid-in capital	225,000	175,000
Retained earnings	263,000	131,500
Total liabilities and shareholders' equity	$708,000	$561,500

Additional information:
   a. Net income for the fiscal year ended December 31, 2007, was $145,000.
   b. The company declared and paid cash dividends.
   c. The company redeemed bonds payable amounting to $30,000 for cash of $30,000.
   d. The company issued common stock for $50,000 cash.

E9-15B. *Prepare the statement of cash flows using the direct method. (LO 4)*
Using the information from E9-14B, prepare a statement of cash flows for LAW Office Products and Supplies Inc. using the direct method.

E9-16B. *Analyze a statement of cash flows. (LO 7, 8)*
The following information was taken from the most recent statement of cash flows of Innovative Electronics Company.

Net cash provided by operating activities	$ 845,000
Net cash used by investing activities	$ (530,000)
Net cash provided by financing activities	$1,675,000

   a. What information do these subtotals from the statement of cash flows tell you about Innovative Electronics Company?
   b. What additional information would you want to see before you analyze Innovative Electronics Company's ability to generate positive operating cash flows in the future?
   c. Did Innovative Electronics have a positive net income for the period? What information would you like to see to help you predict next year's net income?

E9-17B. *Compute free cash flow. (LO 7)*
Use the Best Buy consolidated statement of cash flows to compute the company's free cash flow for 2005 and 2006. What does the free cash flow tell you about Best Buy?

Best Buy Company, Inc.
Consolidated Statements of Cash Flows
($ in millions)

	For the Fiscal Years Ended		
	February 25, 2006	February 26, 2005	February 28, 2004
Operating Activities			
Net earnings	$ 1,140	$ 984	$ 705
(Gain) loss from and disposal of discontinued operations, net of tax	–	(50)	95
Earnings from continuing operations	1,140	934	800
Adjustments to reconcile from continuing operations to total cash provided by operating activities from continuing operations:			
Depreciation	456	459	385
Asset impairment changes	4	22	22
Stock-based compensation	132	(1)	8
Deferred income taxes	(151)	(28)	(14)
Excess tax benefits from stock-based compensation	(33)	–	–
Other, net	(3)	24	8
Changes in operating assets and liabilities, net of acquired assets and liabilities:			
Receivables	(110)	(30)	(27)
Merchandise inventories	(457)	(240)	(507)
Other assets	(11)	(50)	(7)
Accounts payable	385	347	272
Other liabilities	165	243	250
Accrued income taxes	178	301	197
Total cash provided by operating activities from continuing operations	1,695	1,981	1,387
Investing Activities			
Additions to property and equipment, net of $75, $117 and $26 non-cash capital expenditures in fiscal 2006, 2005 and 2004, respectively	(648)	(502)	(545)
Purchases of available-for-sale securities	(4,319)	(8,517)	(2,989)
Sales of available-for-sale securities	4,187	7,730	2,175
Change in restricted assets	(20)	(140)	(18)
Other, net	46	7	1
Total cash used in investing activities from continuing operations	(754)	(1,422)	(1,376)
Financing Activities			
Repurchase of common stock	(772)	(200)	(100)
Issuance of common stock under employee stock purchase plan and for the exercise of stock options	292	256	114
Dividends paid	(151)	(137)	(130)
Long-term debt payments	(69)	(371)	(17)
Net proceeds from issuance of long-term debt	36	–	–
Excess tax benefits from stock-based compensation	33	–	–
Other, net	(10)	(7)	46
Total cash used in financing activities from continuing operations	(641)	(459)	(87)
Effect of Exchange Rate Changes on Cash	27	9	1
Cash Flows from Discontinued Operations (Revised - See Note 2)			
Operating cash flows	–	–	(52)
Investing cash flows	–	–	(1)
Net Cash Used in Discontinued Operations	–	–	(53)
Increase (Decrease) in Cash and Cash Equivalents	327	109	(128)
Cash and Cash Equivalents at Beginning of Year	354	245	373
Cash and Cash Equivalents at End of Year	$ 681	$ 354	$ 245
Supplemental Disclosure of Cash Flow Information			
Income tax paid	$ 547	$ 241	$ 306
Interest paid	16	35	22

See Notes to Consolidated Financial Statements.

E9-18B. *Identify risks and controls. (LO 8)*
Use the Best Buy consolidated statements of cash flows presented in E9-17B to determine whether or not the firm appears to be taking advantage of new investment opportunities. Is the firm in a growth stage or a more mature stage of its business life? What evidence supports your opinion?

Problems—Set A

Excel Template
www.prenhall.com/reimers

P9-1A. *Prepare the statement of cash flows (direct or indirect method). (LO 2, 3, 4, 5, 6, 7)*
The income statement for the year ending December 31, 2007, and the balance sheets at December 31, 2006, and December 31, 2007, for Samsula Service Company are presented here.

Samsula Service Company
Income Statement
For the Year Ended Dec. 31, 2007

(amounts in thousands, except earnings per share)		
Service revenue		$ 92,000
Expenses:		
Wages and salaries	$ 60,000	
Advertising	10,000	
Rent	4,800	
Depreciation	3,600	
Miscellaneous	5,200	
Total expenses		83,600
Income before taxes		$ 8,400
Income taxes		2,940
Net income		$ 5,460
Earnings per share		$ 0.55

Samsula Service Company
Comparative Balance Sheets
December 31, 2007

(amounts in thousands)		2007		2006
Assets:				
Current assets:				
Cash		$ 6,910		$ 3,500
Accounts receivable		12,000		14,000
Supplies		200		370
Prepaid advertising		800		660
Total current assets		$ 19,910		$ 18,530
Property, plant, and equipment				
Equipment	$ 44,000		$ 40,000	
Less: Accumulated depreciation	21,600		18,000	
Total property, plant, and equipment		22,400		22,000
Total assets		$ 42,310		$ 40,530

Liabilities and Stockholders' Equity:
  Current liabilities:

Wages and salaries payable	$ 2,700	$ 3,300
Taxes payable	1,900	1,780
Total current liabilities	$ 4,600	$ 5,080

Stockholders' equity:

Common stock	$ 30,000		$ 30,000
Retained earnings	7,710		5,450
		37,710	35,450
Total liabilities and stockholders' equity		$ 42,310	$ 40,530

Required

a. Prepare a statement of cash flows for the year ending December 31, 2007, using (a) the direct method and (b) the indirect method.
b. Why is the statement of cash flows important to the company and to parties external to the company?
c. As a user, which format would you prefer—direct or indirect—and why?
d. Evaluate the way in which the company spent its cash during the year. Do you think the company is in a sound cash position?
e. Calculate the firm's free cash flow for the 2 years shown.

P9-2A. *Calculate cash from operating activities-indirect method. (LO 5)*
The information shown is from the comparative balance sheets of M&S Record Company at December 31, 2007 and 2006.

(in thousands) At December 31	2007	2006
Current assets:		
Cash	$3,000	$2,490
Accounts receivable	2,325	1,700
Inventory	2,150	1,380
Prepaid rent	320	270
Total current assets	$7,795	$5,840
Current liabilities:		
Accounts payable	$1,890	$1,050
Salaries payable	2,500	3,800
Total current liabilities	$4,390	$4,850

Net income for 2007 was $356,000. Depreciation expense of $135,000 was included in the operating expenses for the year.

Required

Use the indirect method to prepare the *cash from operations* section of the statement of cash flows for M&S Record Company for the year ended December 31, 2007.

Excel Template
www.prenhall.com/reimers

P9-3A. *Calculate cash from operating activities using the indirect method. (LO 5)*
The information shown comes from the balance sheets of TCB Company at June 30, 2008
and 2007.

TCB Company
Balance Sheets (Adapted)
June 30, 2008, and June 30, 2007

(in thousands)	2008	2007
Current assets:		
Cash	$2,110	$2,650
Accounts receivable	1,254	977
Inventory	730	856
Prepaid insurance	127	114
Total current assets	$4,221	$4,597
Current liabilities:		
Accounts payable	$1,054	$1,330
Wages payable	2,100	1,750
Total current liabilities	$3,154	$3,080

Net income for the year ended June 30, 2008, was $86,900. Included in the operating ex-
penses for the year was depreciation expense of $102,000.

Required

Prepare the *cash from operating activities* section of TCB Company's statement of cash
flows for the year ended June 30, 2008. Use the indirect method.

P9-4A. *Calculate cash from operating activities using the indirect method. (LO 5)*
Rollins Land Corporation had the following information available for 2005.

	January 1	December 31
Accounts receivable	$178,000	$151,000
Prepaid insurance	38,000	16,000
Inventory	66,000	71,000

Rollins Land Corporation reported net income of $295,000 for the year. Depreciation ex-
pense, included on the income statement, was $26,500.

Required

Assume this is all the information relevant to the statement of cash flows. Use the indirect
method to prepare the *cash flows from operating activities* section of Rollins Corporation's
statement of cash flows for the year ended December 31, 2005.

P9-5A. *Calculate investing and financing cash flows. (LO 6)*
To prepare its statement of cash flows for the year ended December 31, 2008, Myers Company gathered the following information.

Loss on sale of machinery	$ 8,000
Proceeds from sale of machinery	50,000
Proceeds from bond issue (face value $100,000)	80,000
Amortization of bond discount	1,000
Dividends declared	25,000
Dividends paid	15,000
Purchase of treasury stock	30,000

Required

a. Prepare the *cash from investing* section of the statement of cash flows.
b. Prepare the *cash from financing* section of the statement of cash flows.

P9-6A. *Calculate investing and financing cash flows. (LO 6)*
To prepare its statement of cash flows for the year ended December 31, 2005, Martin Company gathered the following information.

Gain on sale of equipment	$ 4,000
Proceeds from sale of equipment	10,000
Purchase of equipment	80,000
Dividends declared	5,000
Dividends paid	2,000
Proceeds from sale of treasury stock	90,000
Repayment of loan principal	21,000
Payment of interest on loan	210

Required

a. Prepare the *cash from investing* section of the statement of cash flows.
b. Prepare the *cash from financing* section of the statement of cash flows.

P9-7A. *Calculate investing and financing cash flows. (LO 6)*
To prepare its statement of cash flows for the year ended December 31, 2008, Murray Company gathered the following information.

Dividends paid	$ 16,200
Purchase of treasury stock	40,000
Proceeds from bank loan	180,000
Gain on sale of equipment	9,000
Proceeds from sale of equipment	25,000
Proceeds from sale of common stock	250,000

Required

a. Prepare the *cash from investing* section of the statement of cash flows.
b. Prepare the *cash from financing* section of the statement of cash flows.

P9-8A. *Analyze a statement of cash flows. (LO 5, 6, 7)*
Use the statement of cash flows for the Matlock Company to answer the required questions.

Matlock Company
Statement of Cash Flows
For the Year Ended December 31, 2007

(in thousands)

Cash flows from operating activities:		
Net income		$1,500
Depreciation expense	$ 210	
Decrease in accounts receivable	320	
Increase in inventory	(70)	
Increase in prepaid rent	(10)	
Increase in accounts payable	150	600
Net cash provided by operating activities		$2,100
Cash flows from investing activities:		
Purchase of equipment	$(1,000)	
Proceeds from sale of old equipment	200	
Net cash used by investing activities		(800)
Cash flows from financing activities:		
Repayment of long-term mortgage	$(1,350)	
Proceeds from sale of common stock	500	
Payment of cash dividends	(200)	

Net cash used by financing activities	(1,050)	
Net increase in cash during 2007		$ 250
Cash balance, January 1, 2007		346
Cash balance, December 31, 2007		$ 596

Required

    a. How did Matlock Company use the majority of its cash during 2007?
    b. What information does this give you about Matlock Company?
    c. What was Matlock Company's major source of cash during 2007?
    d. Is this an appropriate source of cash for the long run? Explain.
    e. Calculate Matlock's free cash flow for 2007.

Problems—Set B

Excel Template
www.prenhall.com/reimers

P9-1B. *Prepare the statement of cash flows (direct or indirect method). (LO 2, 3, 4, 5, 6, 7)*
Given here are the income statement for Oviedo Oil Company for the year ending December 31, 2007, and the balance sheets at December 31, 2006, and December 31, 2007.

Oviedo Oil Company
Income Statement
For the Year Ended Dec. 31, 2007

Sales revenue		$ 150,000
Cost of goods sold		63,000
Gross margin		87,000
Other expenses:		
Wages and salaries	$ 32,000	
Depreciation	4,500	
Miscellaneous	12,400	
Total other expenses		48,900
Income before taxes		$ 38,100
Income taxes		8,200
Net income		$ 29,900

Oviedo Oil Company
Comparative Balance Sheets
December 31, 2007

($ in thousands)	2007	2006
Assets:		
Current assets:		
Cash	$ -0-	$ 6,400
Accounts receivable	2,900	2,700
Inventory	60,000	42,000
Total current assets	$ 62,900	$ 51,100
Property, plant, and equipment		
Equipment	$ 82,300	$ 39,000
Less: Accumulated depreciation	(20,100)	(15,600)
Total property, plant, and equipment	62,200	23,400
Total assets	$ 125,100	$ 74,500

Liabilities and shareholders' equity

Current liabilities:

Accounts payable	$ 6,400	$ 5,700
Salaries payable	1,500	1,300
Taxes payable	1,900	2,100
Total current liabilities	$ 9,800	$9,100
Notes payable	30,000	10,000
Total liabilities	$ 39,800	$19,100
Shareholders' equity:		
Common stock	$40,000	$40,000
Retained earnings	45,300	15,400
Total shareholders' equity	85,300	55,400
Total liabilities		
and shareholders' equity	$125,100	$74,500

Required

a. Prepare a statement of cash flows for the year ending December 31, 2007, using (1) the direct method and (2) the indirect method.

b. Why is the statement of cash flows important to the company and to parties external to the company?

c. As a user, which format—direct or indirect—would you prefer and why?

d. Evaluate the way in which the company spent its cash during the year. Do you think the company is in a sound cash position?

e. Compute the firm's free cash flow.

P9-2B. *Calculate cash from operating activities using the indirect method. (LO 5)*
The information shown is from the comparative balance sheets of Matt's Music Company at December 31, 2008 and 2007.

(in thousands) At December 31	2008	2007
Current assets:		
Cash	$3,500	$2,090
Accounts receivable	2,725	2,980
Inventory	1,050	1,300
Prepaid insurance	520	470
Total current assets	$7,795	$6,840
Current liabilities:		
Accounts payable	$2,890	$1,650
Salaries payable	1,500	3,200
Total current liabilities	$4,390	$4,850

Net income for 2008 was $211,000. Depreciation expense of $80,000 was included in the operating expenses for the year.

Required

Use the indirect method to prepare the *cash from operations* section of the statement of cash flows for Matt's Music Company for the year ended December 31, 2008.

P9-3B. *Calculate cash from operating activities using the indirect method. (LO 5)*
The information shown comes from the balance sheets of Walker Corporation at September 30, 2008 and 2007.

Excel Template
www.prenhall.com/reimers

Walker Corporation
Balance Sheets (Adapted)
September 30, 2008, and September 30, 2007

(in thousands)	2008	2007
Current assets:		
Cash	$2,110	$1,650
Accounts receivable	1,254	1,977
Inventory	700	656
Prepaid insurance	157	314
Total current assets	$4,221	$4,597
Current liabilities:		
Accounts payable	$2,000	$2,330
Wages payable	1,154	750
Total current liabilities	$3,154	$3,080

Net income for the year ended September 30, 2008, was $146,000. Included in the operating expenses for the year was depreciation expense of $112,000.

Required

Prepare the *cash from operating activities* section of Walker Corporation's statement of cash flows for the year ended September 30, 2008. Use the indirect method.

P9-4B. *Calculate cash from operating activities using the indirect method. (LO 5)*
Ace Corporation had the following information available for 2008.

	January 1	December 31
Accounts receivable	$80,000	$76,000
Prepaid insurance	48,000	26,000
Inventory	76,000	60,000

Ace Corporation reported net income of $130,000 for the year. Depreciation expense, included on the income statement, was $20,800.

Required

Assume this is all the information relevant to the statement of cash flows. Use the indirect method to prepare the cash flows from operating activities section of Ace Corporation's statement of cash flows for the year ended December 31, 2008.

P9-5B. *Calculate investing and financing cash flows. (LO 6)*
To prepare its statement of cash flows for the year ended December 31, 2007, Wright Company gathered the following information.

Proceeds from bond issue (face value $100,000)	$120,000
Amortization of bond premium	1,000
Dividends declared	15,000
Dividends paid	12,000
Purchase of treasury stock	50,000
Loss on sale of machinery	18,000
Proceeds from sale of machinery	30,000

Required

a. Prepare the *cash from investing* section of the statement of cash flows
b. Prepare the *cash from financing* section of the statement of cash flows.

P9-6B. *Calculate investing and financing cash flows. (LO 6)*
To prepare its statement of cash flows for the year ended December 31, 2008, Bowden Company gathered the following information.

Dividends declared	$15,000
Dividends paid	12,000
Proceeds from sale of treasury stock	70,000
Repayment of loan principal	32,000
Payment of interest on loan	320
Gain on sale of equipment	3,500
Proceeds from sale of equipment	11,000
Purchase of equipment	75,000

Required

a. Prepare the *cash from investing* section of the statement of cash flows.
b. Prepare the *cash from financing* section of the statement of cash flows.

P9-7B. *Calculate investing and financing cash flows. (LO 6)*
To prepare its statement of cash flows for the year ended December 31, 2007, Tango Company gathered the following information.

Proceeds from bank loan	157,000
Gain on sale of equipment	12,500
Proceeds from sale of equipment	35,000
Proceeds from sale of common stock	100,000
Dividends paid	12,400
Purchase of treasury stock	85,000

Required

a. Prepare the *cash from investing* section of the statement of cash flows.
b. Prepare the *cash from financing* section of the statement of cash flows.

P9-8B. *Analyze a statement of cash flows. (LO 5, 6, 7)*
Use the statement of cash flows for the SS&P Company to answer the required questions

SS&P Company
Statement of Cash Flows
For the Year Ended December 31, 2007

(in thousands)		
Cash from operating activities:		
Net income		$ 2,500
Depreciation expense	$ 510	
Decrease in accounts receivable	720	
Increase in inventory	(90)	
Increase in prepaid rent	(20)	
Decrease in accounts payable	(150)	970
Net cash provided by operating activities		$ 3,470
Cash from investing activities:		
Purchase of equipment	$(3,000)	
Proceeds from sale of old equipment	900	
Net cash used by investing activities		(2,100)
Cash from financing activities:		
Repayment of long-term mortgage	$(7,500)	
Proceeds from sale of common stock	2,100	
Payment of cash dividends	(1,200)	
Net cash used by financing activities		(6,600)
Net increase in cash during 2007		$ (5,230)
Cash balance, January 1, 2007		10,580
Cash balance, December 31, 2007		$ 5,350

Required

    a. How did SS&P Company use the majority of its cash during 2007?

    b. What information does this give you about SS&P Company?

    c. How did SS&P Company obtain the majority of its cash during 2007?

    d. Is this an appropriate source of cash in for the long run? Explain.

    e. Calculate SS&P's free cash flow for 2007.

Financial Statement Analysis

FSA9-1. *Analyze a statement of cash flows. (LO 7)*

Use Office Depot's financial statements on the book's website to answer the following questions.

    a. What were the major sources and uses of cash during the most recent fiscal year? What does this indicate about Office Depot's cash position?

    b. What evidence, if any, is there that Office Depot is expanding?

FSA9-2. *Analyze a statement of cash flows. (LO 7, 8)*

The statements of cash flow shown here are from Callaway Golf Company's 2005 annual report.

Answer the following questions:

    a. Did the company use the direct or the indirect method of preparing the statement of cash flows?

    b. Did accounts receivable increase or decrease from December 31, 2004, to December 31, 2005? Explain.

    c. Why is depreciation, a noncash expense, included on the statement of cash flows?

    d. On the most recent statement of cash flows, inventory is shown as a negative number (subtracted). However, the prior year's statement shows a positive number (added). Describe what happened to the balance in the inventory account during each of those years.

    e. Did the balance in accounts payable and accrued expenses increase or decrease during the most recent year? Explain.

    f. For every year of the 3-year period shown, Callaway Golf Company's net income has been significantly lower than its net cash from operating activities. How would you explain this to a friend who read somewhere that net income and net cash from operating activities should be quite close? Does this suggest added risk for investors?

Callaway Golf Company
Consolidated Statements of Cash Flows
(In thousands)

	Year Ended December 31,		
	2005	2004	2003
Cash flows from operating activities:			
Net income (loss)	$ 13,284	$(10,103)	$ 45,523
Adjustments to reconcile net income (loss) to net cash provided by operating activities:			
Depreciation and amortization	38,260	51,154	44,496
Loss on disposal of long-lived assets	4,031	7,669	24,163
Tax benefit (reversal of benefit) from exercise of stock options	2,408	2,161	(982)
Noncash compensation	6,527	1,741	15
Net noncash foreign currency hedging loss	–	1,811	2,619
Net loss from sale of marketable securities	–	–	98
Deferred taxes	(3,906)	7,707	(8,320)
Changes in assets and liabilities, net of effects from acquisitions:			
Accounts receivable, net	2,296	(1,048)	12,698
Inventories, net	(65,595)	10,299	4,897
Other assets	7,583	1,554	(4,743)
Accounts payable and accrued expenses	32,740	(16,945)	(2,561)
Accrued employee compensation and benefits	5,121	(5,895)	(3,898)
Accrued warranty expense	1,224	(584)	(838)
Income taxes receivable and payable	26,676	(40,711)	4,004
Deferred compensation	(351)	(273)	1,572
Net cash provided by operating activities	70,298	8,537	118,743
Cash flows from investing activities:			
Capital expenditures	(34,259)	(25,986)	(7,810)
Proceeds from sale of capital assets	1,363	431	178
Acquisitions, net of cash acquired	–	(9,204)	(160,321)
Proceeds from sale of marketable securities	–	–	24
Net cash used in investing activities	(32,896)	(34,759)	(167,929)
Cash flows from financing activities:			
Issuance of Common Stock	14,812	20,311	17,994
Acquisition of Treasury Stock	(39)	(6,298)	(4,755)
Proceeds from (payments on) Line of Credit, net	(13,000)	13,000	–
Dividends paid, net	(19,557)	(19,069)	(18,536)
Other financing activities	(44)	–	(8,117)
Net cash (used in) provided by financing activities	(17,828)	7,944	(13,414)
Effect of exchange rate changes on cash and cash equivalents	(1,750)	2,595	1,488
Net increase (decrease) in cash and cash equivalents	17,824	(15,683)	(61,112)
Cash and cash equivalents at beginning of year	31,657	47,340	108,452
Cash and cash equivalents at end of year	$ 49,481	$ 31,657	$ 47,340
Supplemental disclosures (See Note 3 for acquisitions-related disclosures):			
Cash paid for interest and fees	$ (2,096)	$ (1,384)	$ (835)
Cash paid for income taxes	$(24,837)	$(17,379)	$ (30,925)

The accompanying notes are an integral part of these financial statements.

FSA9-3. *Analyze a statement of cash flows. (LO 7, 8)*
The following is the statement of cash flows for Chico's FAS Inc. for the years ended January 28, 2006, January 29, 2005 and January 31, 2004.

Chico's FAS, Inc, and Subsidiaries
Consolidated Statements of Cash Flows
(In thousands)

	Fiscal Year Ended		
	January 28, 2006	January 29, 2005	January 31, 2004
Cash flows from operating activities			
Net income	$ 193,981	$ 141,206	$ 100,230
Adjustments to reconcile net income to net cash provided by operating activities—			
Depreciation and amortization, cost of goods sold	4,651	3,605	1,970
Depreciation and amortization, other	44,201	32,481	21,130
Deferred tax (benefit) expense	(8,411)	(2,986)	1,336
Stock-based compensation expense	1,615	–	–
Tax benefit of stock options exercised	21,461	27,297	15,126
Deferred rent expense, net	3,673	6,450	1,874
Loss on impairment and disposal of property and equipment	753	311	3,746
Decrease (increase) in assets, net of effects of acquisition—			
Receivables, net	(7,147)	1,069	(1,953)
Inventories	(22,198)	(18,280)	(4,658)
Prepaid expenses and other	(5,955)	(2,734)	(1,281)
Increase (decrease) in liabilities, net of effects of acquisition—			
Accounts payable	10,709	8,929	(3,175)
Accrued and other deferred liabilities	31,073	26,272	11,035
Total adjustments	74,425	82,414	45,150
Net cash provided by operating activities	268,406	223,620	145,380
Cash flows from investing activities:			
Purchases of marketable securities	(357,237)	(404,211)	(166,855)
Proceeds from sale of marketable securities	207,026	257,299	153,447
Acquisition of The White House, Inc., net of cash acquired	–	–	(87,636)
Acquisition of equity investment	(10,418)	–	–
Acquisition of franchise store	–	(1,307)	–
Purchases of property and equipment	(147,635)	(93,065)	(52,300)
Net cash used in investing activities	(308,264)	(241,284)	(153,344)
Cash flows from financing activities:			
Proceeds from issuance of common stock	28,467	22,684	15,231
Repurchase of common stock	–	(4,992)	–
Payments on capital leases	–	(1,278)	(344)
Net cash provided by financing activities	28,467	16,414	14,887
Net (decrease) increase in cash and cash equivalents	(11,391)	(1,250)	6,923
Cash and cash equivalents, beginning of period	14,426	15,676	8,753
Cash and cash equivalents, end of period	$ 3,035	$ 14,426	$ 15,676
Supplemental disclosures of cash flow information:			
Cash paid for interest	$ 360	$ 107	$ 142
Cash paid for income taxes, net	$ 106,091	$ 56,489	$ 47,855
Non-cash investing and financing activities			
Common stock issued in acquisition	$ –	$ –	$ 4,266

The accompanying notes are an integral part of these consolidated statements.

Answer the following questions:
   a. Does Chico's use the direct or the indirect method of preparing the statement of cash flows?
   b. Did receivables increase or decrease during the most recent fiscal year?
   c. Why is depreciation, a noncash expense, included on the statement of cash flows?
   d. On the three years' statements, inventory is shown as a negative number (subtracted). Describe what happened to the balance in the inventory account during each of those years.
   e. Did the balance in accounts payable increase or decrease during the most recent year? Explain.
   f. Do you think Chico's is expanding? Find some numbers to support your answer.
   g. Calculate Chico's free cash flow for all three years. What do these values indicate?
   h. Do you see any particular risks indicated by Chico's cash flow patterns?

Critical Thinking Problems

Risk and Control

To be successful, a company must anticipate its cash flows. What evidence can you find in the Staples' annual report in the back of the book that this company does adequate cash planning? Is there any information not available in the annual report that would help you make this evaluation?

Ethics

After 2 years of business, the Lucky Ladder Company decided to apply for a bank loan to finance a new store. Although the company had been very successful, it had never prepared a cash budget. The owner of Lucky Ladder Company used the information from the first 2 years of business to reconstruct cash forecasts, and he presented them with his financial statements as though they had been prepared as part of the company's planning. Do you think this behavior was ethical? What would you do in similar circumstances? Why?

Group Assignment

To prepare the class for a debate about the format of the statement of cash flows, assign the direct method to half of the groups in the class and the indirect method to the other half of the groups. Have each group prepare arguments about the superiority of their assigned method of presenting the operating section of the statement of cash flows. Think about both theoretical and practical aspects of the methods.

Internet Exercise: Carnival Corp.

Carnival Corp. prides itself on being "The Most Popular Cruise Line in the World®"—a distinction achieved by offering a wide array of quality cruise vacations.

IE 9-1. Go to www.carnival.com, select About Us.
   a. Select World's Leading Cruise Lines and list three of the seven cruise lines operated by the Carnival Corp. Close the World's Leading Cruise Lines window.
   b. Select News, Virtual Press Kit and then Carnival Cruise Lines' Fleet Information. Within the past 5 years, how many new ships has Carnival put into service?
   c. Are the payments for ships considered capital expenditures or revenue expenditures? On the statement of cash flows, which business activity category will report these payments?

IE 9-2. Go to www.carnival.com, select About Us and find Investor Relations. You will find a link to the annual report (pdf file). Find the annual cash flow statement (page 7 of the 2005 annual report) to answer the following questions.

a. Does Carnival use the direct or the indirect method to prepare the statement of cash flows? How can you tell? Which activity section is affected by this choice of method?

b. For the most recent year, list the amount of net cash inflow or outflow from each of the three major types of activities reported on the statement of cash flows. Which type of activity is providing the most cash? Is this considered favorable or unfavorable?

c. For the most recent year, what amount is reported for net income and net cash from operating activities? Are these amounts the same? Explain why or why not.

d. For the most recent year, did Carnival report cash inflows or outflows for capital expenditures? Is this considered favorable or unfavorable? Explain why. What do you think these capital expenditures are primarily for? What was the net amount of the capital expenditure? Which activity section reports this information?

e. For the most recent year, what amount of cash dividends did Carnival pay out? For the most recent year did Carnival issue or retire any common stock? What was the net amount issued or retired? For the most recent year did Carnival issue or retire any long-term debt? What was the net amount issued or retired? Which activity section reports this information?

f. Does this statement of cash flows indicate a strong or weak position with regard to cash and liquidity? Explain.

Using Financial Statement Analysis to Evaluate Firm Performance

Here's Where You've Been . . .

You learned to construct a statement of cash flows from an income statement and comparative balance sheets.

Here's Where You're Going . . .

You will learn to use vertical analysis, horizontal analysis, and ratio analysis.

Learning Objectives

When you are finished studying this chapter, you should be able to:

1. Recognize and explain the components of net income.

2. Perform and interpret a horizontal analysis and a vertical analysis of financial statement information.

3. Perform a basic ratio analysis of a set of financial statements and explain what the ratios mean.

4. Recognize the risks of investing in stock and explain how to control those risks.

Ethics Matters

Accounting information is an important part of the financial information investors use to evaluate a firm's performance. As an investor, you need to feel confident in a firm's reported earnings. When a firm has made an error, earnings may need to be restated. There were a record number of earnings restatements in 2005—around 1,200. The surprising thing about this high number of restatements is that only five were the result of an investor class-action lawsuit against accounting firms. This is a sharp decline from previous years.

According to Professor Joseph Grundfest of Stanford Law School, a former SEC commissioner, one reason is the improved corporate governance after the passage of the Sarbanes-Oxley Act. Even when a firm must restate its earnings, investors are beginning to realize that honest firms are doing their best to produce accurate financial statements.

[Source: "Legal Beat; Earnings Restated? Don't Blame a Lawsuit for It," by Stephen Labaton, *The New York Times*, February 3, 2006.]

L.O.1
Recognize and explain the components of net income.

A Closer Look at the Income Statement

You have learned a great deal about the basic financial statements and how accountants record, summarize, and report transactions. There is information you can easily see in the financial statement, but there is also information that is difficult to see. It is important to look beyond the size and source of the numbers to see what the numbers *mean*. We have been examining the individual parts of the financial statements. Now we will examine all the parts of the four financial statements together to answer the following questions: What information do financial statements provide? What does the information mean? How can we use it?

Before beginning the detailed analysis of the financial statements, we need to take a closer look at some of the characteristics of the income statement. Because earnings—net income—is the focus of financial reporting, companies worry about how current and potential investors will interpret the announcement of earnings each quarter. It is not uncommon for companies to be accused of manipulating their earnings to appear more profitable than they actually are. In an effort to make the components of earnings clear and to represent exactly what they should to financial statement users, the Financial Accounting Standards Board (FASB) requires that two items be separated from the regular earnings of a company. The major reason for segregating these items is that they should not be considered as part of the ongoing earnings of the firm. Reported earnings is an amount used to predict future earnings, but these two items are not expected to be repeated in the future.

1. Discontinued operations
2. Extraordinary items

Exhibit 10.1 shows the components of net income.

Discontinued Operations

If you pay attention to the financial news, you are bound to hear about a company selling off a division. In 2004, Motorola, one of the largest communications firms in the world, discontinued operating its semiconductor business segment so that the segment could form its own firm, Freescale Semiconductor. The gains or losses from these kinds of transactions are shown separately on the income statement. Firms are always evaluating the contribution that the various divisions make to the profits of the firm. If a division is not profitable or no longer fits the strategy of the firm, a firm may sell it to remain profitable or change the firm's focus. Parts of a company's operations that are eliminated are called **discontinued operations**.

Discontinued operations
Those parts of the firm that a company has eliminated by selling a division.

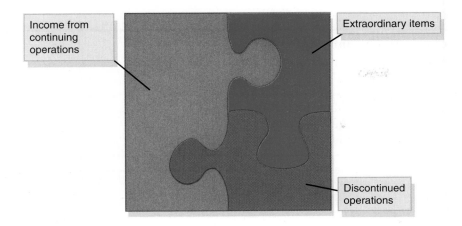

EXHIBIT 10.1

**Components
of Net Income**

It's important for investors to see
the individual pieces of earnings.

When a firm eliminates a division, the financial implications are shown separately
from the regular operations of the firm. Why would this separation be useful? Earnings is
an important number because it is used to evaluate the performance of a firm and to predict its future performance. To make these evaluations and predictions more meaningful,
it is important that one-time transactions be separated from recurring transactions. This
separation allows investors to see one-time transactions as exceptions to the normal operations of the firm. In addition to the gain or loss from the sale, the earnings or loss for the
accounting period for the discontinued operations must also be shown separately. We will
look at an example of a firm with discontinued operations. In 2007, Muzby Manufacturing sold off a major business segment, the crate-production division, because the firm
wanted to focus its operations on its core business, which did not include the crate division. Both the current year's income or loss from the crate-production division and the gain
or loss from the sale of those operations are shown separately on the income statement.
Suppose:

1. Muzby Manufacturing's income from continuing operations before taxes was $395,600.
2. Taxes related to that income were $155,000.
3. The discontinued segment contributed income of $12,000 during the year.
4. Taxes related to that contributed income were $1,900.
5. The discontinued segment was sold for a gain of $63,000.
6. The taxes related to the profit from that gain were $28,000.

Exhibit 10.2 shows how this information would be presented on the income statement for
Muzby Manufacturing.

Extraordinary Items

You have learned that discontinued operations are the first item that accountants disclose
separately on the income statement. The second item is the financial effect of any event that
is *unusual* in nature and *infrequent* in occurrence. The financial effects of such events are
called **extraordinary items**. To qualify as extraordinary, the events must be abnormal and
must *not* be reasonably expected to occur again in the foreseeable future. There is a great
deal of judgment required to decide if an event should be considered extraordinary. Examples of occurrences that have been considered extraordinary include eruptions of a volcano,
a takeover of foreign operations by the foreign government, and the effects of new laws or
regulations that result in a one-time cost to comply. Each situation is unique and must be
considered in light of the environment in which the business operates.

Extraordinary items Events
that are unusual in nature
and infrequent in occurrence.

Suppose Muzby Manufacturing has a factory in China, and the Chinese government
decides to take possession of all American businesses in the country. The value of the lost
factory is $200,000. U.S. tax law allows companies to write off this type of extraordinary
loss, which means the company receives a tax savings. Suppose the applicable tax savings
is $67,000. Exhibit 10.3 shows how Muzby Manufacturing would present the information
on its income statement for the year.

EXHIBIT 10.2

Showing Discontinued Operations on the Income Statement

The highlighted portion of the income statement shows how amounts related to discontinued operations are presented.

Muzby Manufacturing Income Statement For the year ended December 31, 2007		

Income from continuing operations before income taxes		$395,600
Income tax expense		155,000
Income from continuing operations		240,600
Discontinued operations		
Income from discontinued crate-production segment (net of taxes of $1,900)	$10,100	
Gain on disposal of crate-production segment (net of taxes of $28,000)	35,000	45,100
Net income		$285,700

EXHIBIT 10.3

Showing Extraordinary Items on the Income Statement

The highlighted portion of the income statement shows how amounts related to extraordinary items are presented.

Muzby Manufacturing Income Statement For the year ended December 31, 2007		

Income from continuing operations before income taxes		$395,600
Income tax expense		155,000
Income from continuing operations		240,600
Discontinued operations		
Income from discontinued crate-production segment (net of taxes of $1,900)	$10,100	
Gain on disposal of crate-production segment (net of taxes of $28,000)	35,000	45,100
Income before extraordinary item		$285,700
Loss on extraordinary item		
Expropriation of foreign operation (net of taxes of $67,000)		(133,000)
Net income		$152,700

News Flash

Was Huricane Katrina an extraordinary event?

Almost everyone would consider Hurricane Katrina an extraordinary event. That is, everyone except the Financial Accounting Standards Board. For firms that incurred losses from the hurricane, their financial statements did not treat the losses as extraordinary. However, if any of the firm's operating segments were lost or shut down, the losses were segregated as discontinued operations. Check out Ruth's Chris Steak House's income statement, which you can find on the firm's website, for the year ended December 31, 2005. Included in operating costs, hurricane and relocation costs amounted to $2,660,000.

Reporting Taxes

In general, firms report total revenues and expenses and then subtract the associated taxes. However, the financial effects of discontinued operations and extraordinary items are shown net of tax.

What does it mean for a company to show discontinued operations and extraordinary items *net of tax*? What is the alternative?

Your Turn 10-1
Your Turn
Your Turn

Horizontal and Vertical Analysis of Financial Information

L.O.2
Perform and interpret a horizontal analysis and a vertical analysis of financial statement information.

Now that you are prepared to recognize extraordinary items and discontinued operations that may appear on the income statement, you are ready to analyze an entire statement or set of statements.

There are three primary ways to analyze financial information: horizontal analysis, vertical analysis, and ratio analysis.

Horizontal Analysis

Horizontal analysis is a technique for evaluating a financial statement item over a period of time. The purpose of a horizontal analysis is to express the change in a financial statement item in percentages rather than in dollars. Financial statement users can spot trends more easily with horizontal analysis than by simply looking at the raw numbers. Consider the cash flows for Wal-Mart. According to its past six statements of cash flows, Wal-Mart made the following cash expenditures for property, plant, and equipment.

Horizontal analysis A technique for evaluating financial statement items across time.

Wal-Mart Capital Expenditures
For fiscal years ended on January 31, 2001–2006
(in millions of dollars)

2006	2005	2004	2003	2002	2001
$14,583	12,893	10,308	9,245	8,285	8,042

Often, the analyst selects one of the years as the reference point. It is called the base year, and the amounts reported for the other years are expressed as a percentage of the chosen base year. The difference between the amount of the financial statement item each year and the base year is expressed as a percentage of the base year. Suppose we choose 2001 as the base year. Then, we subtract the 2001 capital expenditures ($8,042) from 2002 capital expenditures ($8,285) and divide by the base year number ($8,042).

$$\frac{\$8,285 - \$8,042}{\$8,042} = \frac{\$243}{\$8,042} = 3.02\%$$

Our calculation shows that during the fiscal year ended January 31, 2002, Wal-Mart increased capital expenditures by just 3.02% of the base year's capital expenditures. The calculation is done the same way for each year. The percentage change from the base year to 2003 is calculated as follows:

$$\frac{\$9,245 - \$8,042}{\$8,042} = \frac{\$1,203}{\$8,042} = 15.0\%$$

Wal-Mart
Capital Expenditures Comparison—Base year 2001
(dollars in millions)

	2006	2005	2004	2003	2002	2001
Capital expenditures	$14,583	12,893	10,308	9,245	8,285	8,042
% change	81.3%	60.3%	28.2%	15.0%	3.0%	100%

There is more than one way to do a horizontal analysis. Frequently, the analysis is done by comparing one year with the next, rather than using a fixed base year.

It is usually difficult to understand the significance of a single item such as capital expenditures when viewing the raw numbers. To make trends more apparent, it may be useful to express the changes in spending in percentage form. A horizontal analysis makes it clear that Wal-Mart continues to make a significant investment in its property, plant, and equipment.

Vertical Analysis

Vertical analysis is similar to horizontal analysis, but the analysis involves items on a single year's financial statement. Each item on a financial statement is expressed as a percentage of a selected base amount. For example, a vertical analysis of an income statement almost always uses sales as the base amount because almost all of a firm's expenditures depend on the level of sales. Each amount on the statement is expressed as a percentage of sales. This type of analysis can point out areas in which the costs might be too large or growing without an obvious cause. For example, if managers at Wal-Mart see that employee salaries, as a percentage of sales, are increasing, they can investigate the increase and, if necessary, take action to reduce the firm's salaries expense. Vertical analysis also allows the meaningful comparison of companies of different sizes. Exhibit 10.4 shows a vertical analysis for Wal-Mart's income statements for the years ended January 31, 2006, and January 31, 2005.

Ratio Analysis

Throughout this book, you have learned that ratio analysis uses information in the financial statements to formulate specific values that determine some measure of a company's financial position. We will review all the ratios you have learned and then look at an additional category of ratios.

A Review of All Ratios

There are four general categories of ratios, named for what they attempt to measure:

- **Liquidity ratios**: These ratios measure a company's ability to pay its current bills and operating costs—obligations coming due in the next fiscal year.
- **Solvency ratios**: These ratios measure a company's ability to meet its long-term obligations, such as its long-term debt (bank loans), and to survive over a long period of time.
- **Profitability ratios**: These ratios measure the operating or income performance of a company. Remember the goal of a business is to make a profit, so this type of ratio examines how well a company is meeting that goal.
- **Market indicators**: These ratios relate the current market price of the company's stock to earnings or dividends.

The first part of Exhibit 10.5 reviews the three types of ratios you learned about in earlier chapters. Also, there are two new ratios provided.

Your Turn 10–2

Suppose Wal-Mart pays off a current liability with cash. What effect would this have on the company's current ratio? What effect would the pay off have on the company's working capital?

EXHIBIT 10.4

Vertical Analysis

The analysis for a single year provides some information, but the comparison of two years reveals more about what's going on with Wal-Mart. The percentages look very consistent across these two years. What item(s) stands out in the analysis? The notes to the financial statements are the first place to look for additional information whenever an analysis reveals something interesting or suspicious.

Wal-Mart Stores, Inc.
Consolidated Statements of Income
For the fiscal years ended

(in millions)

	January 31, 2006		January 31, 2005	
Net sales	$312,427	100.00%	$285,222	100.00%
Other income, net	3,227	1.03%	2,910	1.02%
	315,654		288,132	
Costs and expenses:				
Cost of sales	240,391	76.94%	219,793	77.06%
Selling, general, and adm. expenses	56,733	18.16%	51,248	17.97%
Operating profit	18,530	5.93%	17,091	5.99%
Interest expense (net)	1,172	0.38%	986	0.35%
Income from continuing operations before				
income taxes and minority interest	17,358	5.56%	16,105	5.65%
Provision for taxes (current and deferred)	5,803	1.86%	5,589	1.96%
Income from continuing operations before minority interest . . .	11,555	3.70%	10,516	3.69%
Minority interest	(324)	0.10%	(249)	0.09%
Net income	$ 11,231	3.60%	$ 10,267	3.60%

Company A has a gross profit ratio of 30%, and Company B has a gross profit ratio of 60%. Can you tell which company is more profitable? Why or why not?

Your Turn 10–3

Market Indicator Ratios

The market price of a share of stock is what an investor is willing to pay for the stock. There are two ratios that use the current market price of a share of stock to help potential investors predict what they might earn by purchasing that stock. One ratio is the **price–earnings (P/E) ratio**. This ratio is defined by its name: It is the price of a share of stock divided by the company's current earnings per share.

Price–earnings (P/E) ratio The market price of a share of stock divided by that stock's earnings per share.

$$\text{P/E ratio} = \frac{\text{Market price per share}}{\text{Earnings per share}}$$

Investors and financial analysts believe the P/E ratio indicates future earnings potential. A high P/E ratio indicates that the company has the potential for significant growth. When a new firm has no earnings, the P/E ratio has no meaning because the denominator is zero. For the first several years of business, Amazon.com had no earnings but a rising stock price. Analysts have varying opinions about the information contained in the P/E ratio.

The other market indicator ratio is the **dividend yield ratio**. This ratio is the dividend per share divided by the market price per share. You may find that the values for the dividend

Dividend yield ratio Dividend per share divided by the current market price per share.

EXHIBIT 10.5A

Common Ratios

*Turnover ratios are often considered efficiency ratios.

Ratio	Definition	How to use the ratio	Chapter where you studied the ratio
LIQUIDITY			
Current ratio	$\dfrac{\text{Total current assets}}{\text{Total current liabilities}}$	To measure a company's ability to pay current liabilities with current assets. This ratio helps creditors determine if a company can meet its short-term obligations.	2
Quick ratio (also known as the acid-test ratio)	$\dfrac{\text{Cash} + \text{short-term} + \text{net accounts}}{\text{investment} \quad \text{receivable}}$ $\overline{\text{Total current liabilities}}$	To measure a company's ability to meet its short-term obligations. This ratio is similar to the current ratio. However, by limiting the numerator to very liquid current assets, it is a stricter test.	3
Working capital	Current assets – current liabilities	To measure a company's ability to meet its short-term obligations. Although technically not a ratio, working capital is often measured as part of financial statement analysis.	3
Inventory turnover ratio	$\dfrac{\text{Cost of goods sold}}{\text{Average inventory}}$	To measure how quickly a company is selling its inventory.	5
Accounts receivable turnover ratio	$\dfrac{\text{Net credit sales}}{\text{Average net accounts receivable}}$	To measure how quickly a company collects the cash from its credit customers.	6
SOLVENCY			
Debt-to-equity ratio	$\dfrac{\text{Total liabilities}}{\text{Total shareholders' equity}}$	To compare the amount of debt a company has with the amount the owners have invested in the company.	7
Times-interest-earned ratio	$\dfrac{\text{Income from operations}}{\text{Interest expense}}$	To compare the amount of income that has been earned in an accounting period (before interest) to the interest obligation for the same period. If net income is used in the numerator, be sure to add back interest expense.	7

News Flash

When picking an investment, you might get the advice to look for a firm that offers good shareholder value. But what is good shareholder value? Richard Berstein of Merrill Lynch has suggested three qualities: a high dividend yield, strong dividend growth, and a solid history of returning profits to investors by purchasing treasury stock.

[Source: "Market Values; Picking the Cream of the Cream," by Conrad De Aenlle, *The New York Times*, March 4, 2006.]

EXHIBIT 10.5B

PROFITABILITY			
Return on assets	$\dfrac{\text{Net income} + \text{interest expense}}{\text{Average total assets}}$	To measure a company's success in using its assets to earn income for owners and creditors, those who are financing the business. Because interest is part of what has been earned to pay creditors, it is often added back to the numerator. Net income is the return to the owners and interest expense is the return to the creditors. Average total assets are the average of beginning assets and ending assets for the year.	4
Asset turnover ratio	$\dfrac{\text{Net sales}}{\text{Average total assets}}$	To measure how efficiently a company uses its assets.	4
Return on equity	$\dfrac{\text{Net income} - \text{preferred dividends}}{\text{Average common shareholders' equity}}$	To measure how much income is earned with the common shareholders' investment in the company.	8
Gross profit ratio	$\dfrac{\text{Gross profit}}{\text{Net sales}}$	To measure a company's profitability. It is one of the most carefully watched ratios by management because it describes the percentage of the sales price that is gross profit. A small shift usually indicates a big change in the profitability of the company's sales.	5
Earnings per share	$\dfrac{\text{Net income} - \text{preferred dividends}}{\text{Weighted average number of shares of common stock outstanding}}$	To calculate net income per share of common stock.	8
MARKET INDICATORS			
Price–earnings ratio	$\dfrac{\text{Market price per common share}}{\text{Earnings per share}}$	To calculate the market price for $1 of earnings.	10
Dividend yield ratio	$\dfrac{\text{Dividend per share}}{\text{Market price per share}}$	To calculate the percentage return on the investment in a share of stock via dividends.	10

yield ratio are quite low compared to the return an investor would expect on an investment. Investors are willing to accept a low dividend yield when they anticipate an increase in the price of the stock.

Stocks with low growth potential, however, may need to offer a higher dividend yield to attract investors.

$$\text{Dividend yield ratio} = \frac{\text{Dividend per share}}{\text{Market price per share}}$$

Exhibit 10.6 shows the earnings per share, the dividends per share, and the market price per share for Google Inc. and for General Mills. Which stock would be a better buy for long-term growth? Which would be best if you needed regular dividend income?

The types of stock that will appeal to an investor depend on the investors' preferences for income and growth. A young investor, for example, will not need dividends from retirement funds invested in stocks. These long-term investors would prefer to invest in companies with high growth potential, no matter what the dividend yield. Google might be more attractive, with its high P/E ratio of 64.05, than General Mills, with its lower P/E ratio of

EXHIBIT 10.6

Price/Earnings and Dividend Yield Ratios

For fiscal years ended	Google, Inc. December 31, 2005	General Mills May 28, 2006
Earnings per share	$ 0.77	$3.05
Dividends per share	$ 0.00	$1.34
Ending market price per share	$49.32	$51.79
Price/earnings ratio	64.05	16.98
Dividend yield ratio	n/a	2.59%

16.98. A retiree who needs a dividend income for living expenses will be more concerned with the size of the dividend yield of an investment and less concerned with the investment's long-term growth. General Mills would be better than Google for dividends.

These two market-related ratios are very important to management and to investors because analysts and investors use them in evaluating stocks. If you examine a company's annual report, you are likely to see these ratios reported, usually for the most recent 2 or 3 years.

Understanding Ratios

A ratio by itself does not give much information. To be useful, a ratio must be compared to the same ratios from previous periods, ratios of other companies in the industry, or industry averages. Keep in mind that, with the exception of earnings per share, the calculations to arrive at a specific ratio may vary from company to company. There are no standard or required formulas to calculate a ratio. One company may calculate a debt ratio as *debt* to *equity*, whereas another company may calculate a debt ratio as *debt* to *debt plus equity*. When interpreting and using any company's ratios, be sure you know how those ratios have been computed. When you are computing ratios, be sure to be consistent in your calculations so you can make meaningful comparisons among them.

Even though the only ratio that must be calculated and presented as part of the financial statements is EPS, managers typically include in their company's annual report many of the ratios we have discussed in this chapter. When these ratios are not shown as part of the financial statements, they may be included in other parts of the annual report, often in graphs depicting ratio trends over several years.

Any valuable financial statement analysis requires more than a cursory review of ratios. The analyst must look at trends, components of the values that are part of the ratios, and other information about the company that may not even be contained in the financial statements.

Using Ratio Analysis

We will compute some of the ratios shown in Exhibit 10.5 for J&J Snack Foods Corp. using the company's 2005 annual report. Exhibit 10.7 shows the income statements for 3 years, and Exhibit 10.8 shows the balance sheets for 2 years.

Other information needed for the analysis:

• Market price per share at the close of fiscal year: approximately $55 per share at September 24, 2005 and $42 per share at September 25, 2004.
• No dividends were paid by J&J Snack Foods Corp. during the fiscal year ended September 25, 2004. However, J&J Snack Foods Corp. paid dividends of $0.05 per share during the fiscal year ended September 24, 2005.

All the ratios shown in Exhibit 10.9 are calculated for J&J Snack Foods Corp. for the fiscal years ended September 24, 2005, and September 25, 2004. Even though 2 years of ratios do not give us enough information for making decisions, use this as an opportunity to practice how to calculate the ratios. Exhibit 10.9 shows the computations.

EXHIBIT 10.7

Income Statements for J&J Snack Foods Corp.

J&J Snack Foods Corporation
Consolidated Statement of Earnings
(in thousands, except per share data)

Fiscal year ended	September 24, 2005 (52 weeks)	September 25, 2004 (52 weeks)	September 27, 2003 (52 weeks)
Net sales	$457,112	$416,588	$364,567
Cost of goods sold	302,065	276,379	239,722
Gross profit	155,047	140,209	124,845
Selling, general and administrative expenses	114,798	105,017	93,998
Operating profit	40,249	35,192	30,847
Investment income	1,689	566	362
Interest expense and other	(136)	(113)	(113)
Earnings before taxes	41,802	35,645	31,096
Income taxes	15,759	12,935	11,194
Net earnings	$ 26,043	$ 22,710	$ 19,902
Weighted average number of basic shares	9,097	8,909	8,800
Earnings per basic share	$ 2.86	$ 2.55	$ 2.26
Weighted average number of diluted shares	9,300	9,143	9,051
Earnings per diluted share	$ 2.80	$ 2.48	$ 2.20

The accompanying notes are an integral part of these statements.

Financial Statement Analysis—More than Numbers

You have probably noticed the following sentence at the end of every actual financial statement you have ever seen, "The accompanying notes are an integral part of these financial
statements." Some analysts believe there is more real information about the financial health
of a company in the notes than in the statements themselves. Go to the back of the book where
you will find the financial statements for Staples and Office Depot. Look at the detailed and
extensive notes that accompany the statements. The more you learn about analyzing and evaluating a company's performance, whether in subsequent courses or in actual business experience, the more you will understand the information in the notes to the financial statements.
When you are comparing two or more firms, you need to know the accounting choices those
firms have made—such as depreciation and inventory methods—to make valid comparisons.
Often, analysts compute new amounts using a different method than the one the firm used so
that amounts can be meaningfully compared to those of another firm. For example, if one
company uses LIFO and another uses FIFO, an analyst would convert the LIFO values to
FIFO values using the disclosures required to be in the notes of firms that use LIFO.

   To better appreciate the role of accounting information in business, look at a business
plan. A business plan is a detailed analysis of what it would take to start and maintain the
operation of a successful business. Anyone writing a business plan includes a sales forecast,
expense estimates, and prospective financial statements. These are "what-if" financial
statements, forecasts that are part of the business plan. Banks often require these statements
before they will lend money to a new firm.

   Because accounting is such an integral part of business, accounting principles will
continue to change as business changes. Each year, the FASB and the SEC add and change
the rules for valuing items on the financial statements. FASB is also concerned with the
continued usefulness and reliability of the accounting data from electronic transactions,

EXHIBIT 10.8

Balance Sheets of J&J Snack Foods Corp.

J&J Snack Foods Corporation
Consolidated Balance Sheets
(in thousands, except share amounts)

	September 24, 2005	September 25, 2004
Assets		
Current Assets		
Cash and cash equivalents	$ 15,795	$ 19,600
Marketable securities available for sale	54,225	36,500
Receivables		
Trade, less allowances of $1,054 and $1,104, respectively	46,261	47,753
Other	660	233
Inventories	33,684	29,587
Prepaid expenses and other	1,215	1,354
Deferred income taxes	2,393	3,385
Total current assets	154,233	138,412
Property, plant and equipment, at cost	326,143	314,880
Less accumulated depreciation and amortization	237,098	225,406
	89,045	89,474
Other Assets		
Goodwill	53,622	46,477
Other intangible assets, net	7,043	1,804
Other	1,981	1,257
	62,646	49,538
	$305,924	$277,424
Liabilities and Stockholder's Equity		
Current Liabilities		
Accounts payable	$ 37,029	$ 34,497
Accrued liabilities	14,731	13,149
Dividends payable	1,142	–
Total current liabilities	52,902	47,646
Deferred income taxes	17,987	19,153
Other long-term liabilities	273	529
Stockholder's Equity		
Preferred stock, $1 par value; authorized, 5,000,000 shares; none issued	–	–
Common stock, no par value; authorized, 25,000,000 shares; issued and outstanding, 9,136,000 and 9,006,000 respectively	36,091	33,069
Accumulated other comprehensive loss	(1,918)	(2,061)
Retained earnings	200,589	179,088
	234,762	210,096
	$305,924	$277,424

EXHIBIT 10.9A

Ratio Analysis for J&J Snack Foods Corp.

As you evaluate the ratios, keep in mind that even two years' worth of ratios is rarely enough information to come to any conclusions. Most annual reports provide the data for ten years' worth of ratios. For J&J Snack Foods Corp., almost all of the ratios appear to be moving in the right direction. Often, ratio analysis is useful for identifying potential problem areas. None is obvious for J&J Snack Foods Corp. from this analysis.

Ratio	Definition	Computation	Computation	Interpretation
LIQUIDITY		For FYE Sept. 2005	For FYE Sept. 2004	
Current ratio	Total current assets / Total current liabilities	$\frac{154,233}{52,902} = 2.92$	$\frac{138,412}{47,646} = 2.91$	This is an excellent current ratio. A value over 2 is considered good. Industry average for this industry—processed and packaged goods—is 1.9.
Acid-test ratio (also known as the quick ratio)	Cash + short-term investments + net accounts receivable / Total current liabilities	$\frac{15,795 + 54,225 + 46,261}{52,902}$ $= 2.20$	$\frac{19,600 + 47,753 + 36,500}{47,646}$ $= 2.18$	This is a very high acid-test ratio. Industry average is 0.8.
Working capital (technically not a ratio, but still a measure of liquidity)	Total current assets – Total current liabilities	$154,233 - 52,902 = \$101,331$ (in thousands)	$138,412 - 47,646 = \$90,766$ (in thousands)	This amount supports the strong liquidity of the firm.
Inventory turnover ratio	Cost of goods sold / Average inventory	$\frac{302,065}{(29,587 + 33,684)/2} = 9.55$	$\frac{276,379}{(29,587 + 23,202^*)/2}$ $= 10.47$	The company is turning over its inventory 10 times each year. Industry average is 10.6.
Accounts receivable turnover ratio	Net sales / Average net accounts receivable	$\frac{457,112}{(47,753 + 46,261)/2} = 9.72$	$\frac{416,588}{(47,753 + 37,645^*)/2} = 9.76$	The company is turning over its receivables over 9 times each year. If you divide 365 days by 9.72, you'll see that it takes the company about 38 days to collect its recevables. The industry average is 34 days.
			* From the 2003 balance sheet not shown here	
SOLVENCY				
Debt to equity	Total liabilities / Total equity	$\frac{52,902 + 18,260}{234,762} = 0.30$	$\frac{47,646 + 19,682}{210,096} = 0.32$	The company does not have excessive debt. The industry average is 0.51.
Times interest earned	Net income + interest expense / Interest expense	$\frac{26,043 + 136}{136} = 192.5$	$\frac{22,710 + 113}{113} = 202$	This company has no problem meeting its interest obligation. The industry average is 6.4.

EXHIBIT 10.9B

PROFITABILITY				
Return on assets	$\dfrac{\text{Net income} + \text{interest expense}}{\text{Average total assets}}$	$\dfrac{26{,}043 + 136}{(305{,}924 + 277{,}424)/2}$ $= 8.98\%$	$\dfrac{22{,}710 + 113}{(277{,}424 + 239{,}478^*)/2}$ $= 8.83\%$ *From the 2003 balance sheet	This is a good return on assets. The industry average is 4.6%.
Return on equity	$\dfrac{\text{Net income} - \text{preferred dividends}}{\text{Average common shareholders' equity}}$	$\dfrac{26{,}043 - 0}{(234{,}762 + 210{,}096)/2}$ $= 11.7\%$	$\dfrac{22{,}710 - 0}{(210{,}096 + 182{,}564^*)/2}$ $= 11.57\%$ *From the 2003 balance sheet	Most investors would be happy to earn an 11% return on their investment. The industry average is 10%.
Gross profit ratio	$\dfrac{\text{Gross profit}}{\text{Sales}}$	$\dfrac{155{,}047}{457{,}112} = 34\%$	$\dfrac{140{,}209}{416{,}588} = 33.7\%$	The gross profit shows that for every dollar of product the company sells, approximately $0.66 is the cost of the item to J&J Snack Foods. The industry average gross profit percentage is 36.8%.
Earnings per share	$\dfrac{\text{Net income} - \text{preferred dividends}}{\text{Number of shares of common stock outstanding}}$	$\dfrac{26{,}043 - 0}{9{,}097^*} = \$2.86$ *Disclosed on the income statement.	$\dfrac{22{,}710 - 0}{8{,}909^*} = \$2.55$ *Disclosed on the income statement.	A two-year trend is not very informative. However, for the two years shown, the ratio is certainly moving in the right direction.
MARKET INDICATORS				
Price–earnings ratio	$\dfrac{\text{Market price per common share}}{\text{Earnings per share}}$	$\dfrac{\$55}{\$2.86} = 19.23$	$\dfrac{\$42}{\$2.55} = 16.47$	This PE ratio is a bit lower than the industry average of 19.8.
Dividend yield	$\dfrac{\text{Dividend per share}}{\text{Market price per share}}$	$\dfrac{\$0.50}{\$55.00} = 0.9\%$	$\dfrac{0}{\$42.00} = 0$	This firm did not pay dividends in 2004. In 2005, the firm paid $0.50, which is a little less than 1% of the stock price.

UNDERSTANDING **Business**

What is EBITDA?

If you read much about financial statements and earnings, you will eventually come across the expression "EBITDA" (pronounced ība duh). It is an acronym for *earning before interest, taxes, depreciation, and amortization*. EBITDA can be calculated from information on the income statement (earnings, taxes, and interest) and the statement of cash flows (depreciation and amortization—added back to net income when calculating cash from operating activities). Eliminating these items—because they involve management discretion and estimates—can make it easier to compare the financial health of various firms. Because it is a result of management's financing choices (debt rather than equity), eliminating interest takes away the effect of a firm's capital structure.

Even though EBITDA has became a popular measure of a firm's performance, it does not tell the whole story. According to Investopidia.com, there are at least four reasons to be wary of EBITDA.

1. There is no substitute for cash flows. No matter what EBITDA is, a firm can not operate without sufficient cash.
2. The items that are eliminated from earnings are not avoidable, so ignoring them can be misleading.
3. EBITDA ignores the quality of earnings. You will learn more about that in Chapter 11.
4. Using EBITDA to calculate a price–earnings ratio could make a firm look cheaper than it actually is.

The bottom line: EBITDA is useful, but it is only one of many measures of a firm's performance. Remember that EBITDA is NOT defined by GAAP, so firms may measure EBITDA different ways.

---

e-business, and real-time access to financial data. As competition takes on new dimensions, particularly due to new technology, the scrutiny of a firm's financial information will increase. Together with the influence of the financial scandals of the early 2000s, the financial information needed for good decision making will continue to grow in importance.

Business Risk, Control, and Ethics

L.O.4
Recognize the risks of investing in stock and explain how to control those risks.

We already discussed, in Chapter 1, the risks associated with starting a business. Now we will take the perspective of an investor. After all, you are very likely to buy stock in a publicly traded company sometime in your life. Many working people have money in retirement funds that are invested in the stock of publicly traded companies. Additionally, the movement of the stock market affects a large number of firms and individual investors. How should you, as an investor, minimize the risks associated with stock ownership? That risk, of course, is losing your money!

First, you should be diligent about finding a financial advisor or financial analyst to help you, or you should become an expert from your own study and analysis of available stocks. You also need to know and understand some financial accounting and financial statement analysis, which you have been exposed to in this course. However, being knowledgeable or consulting an expert does not give an investor complete protection against losses.

That leads to the second and most effective way to minimize the risks associated with stock ownership: Diversify. In everyday usage, to diversify means to vary or expand. In the language of investment, diversify means to vary the investments you make—to expand beyond a narrow set of investments. Diversification means not putting all of your eggs in one basket. A diversified set of investments allows an investor to earn a higher rate of return for a given amount of risk.

There is no way to eliminate all of the risks of stock ownership, but having many different types of investments will help you minimize your risk or, equivalently, increase your return for a given amount of risk. According to Bank One, "A diversified portfolio does not concentrate in one or two investment categories. Instead, it includes some investments whose returns zig while the returns of other investments zag."

Chapter Summary Points

- Components of net income include income from continuing operations, discontinued operations, and extraordinary items. Gains and losses from discontinued operations and from extraordinary items are segregated from other revenues and expenses so that an investor can easily separate these nonrecurring items from those expected to reoccur in the future.
- Horizontal analysis compares a specific financial statement item across time, often with reference to a chosen base year. A vertical analysis, also know as common size statements, shows every item on a single year's financial statement as a percentage of one of the other financial statement items. Most often, a vertical analysis of the income statement calculates all items as a percentage of sales.
- Ratio analysis is a tool used by anyone who wants to evaluate a firm's financial statements. Remember that a ratio is meaningful only when it is compared to another ratio.
- Investing in a firm as an owner, by purchasing a firm's stock, can create risks. The biggest risk is that the firm will not do well and its stock price will decrease. The best protection for an investor is to have a diversified portfolio. That is, buy a variety of stocks so that a decrease in the price of one stock may be offset by an increase in the price of another. Also, do not put all of your investment money in stock ownership. Invest in a variety of assets, such as stocks, bonds, and real estate.

Chapter Summary Problems

Instructions

Use the information in the annual report provided in the back of the textbook and the other from the textbook's website to perform a ratio analysis on the most recent fiscal years of both Office Depot and Staples. Use Exhibit 10.9 as a model. Comment on your results.

Solution

Ratio	Definition	Office Depot For FYE Dec. 31, 2005	Staples For FYE Jan. 28, 2006	Interpretation
LIQUIDITY				
Current ratio	$\dfrac{\text{Total current assets}}{\text{Total current liabilities}}$	$\dfrac{3,530,062}{2,468,751} = 1.43$	$\dfrac{4,144,544}{2,479,906} = 1.67$	Industry average for this industry—specialty retail, other—is 1.9.
Acid-test ratio (also known as the quick ratio)	$\dfrac{\text{Cash}+\text{short-term}+\text{net investments receivables}}{\text{Total current liabilities}}$	$\dfrac{703,197 + 200 + 1,232,107}{2,468,751}$ $= 0.78$	$\dfrac{977,822 + 593,082 + 576,672}{2,479,906}$ $= 0.87$	Industry average is 1.1.
Working capital (technically not a ratio, but still a measure of liquidity)	Total current assets − Total current liabilities	$3,530,062 - 2,468,751 =$ $1,061,311$ in thousands	$4,144,544 - 2,479,906 =$ $1,664,638$ in thousands	Both firms appear to have adequate working capital.
Inventory turnover ratio	$\dfrac{\text{Cost of goods sold}}{\text{Average inventory}}$	$\dfrac{9,886,921}{(1,360,274 + 1,408,778)/2}$ $= 7.14$	$\dfrac{11,493,310}{(1,706,372 + 1,602,530)/2}$ $= 6.95$	Both firms are turning over their inventory approximately 7 times each year. Industry average is 8.0.
Accounts receivable turnover ratio	$\dfrac{\text{Net sales}}{\text{Average net accounts receivable}}$	$\dfrac{14,278,994}{(1,232,107 + 1,303,888)/2}$ $= 11.26$	$\dfrac{16,078,852}{(576,672 + 485,126)/2}$ $= 30.29$	Staples is collecting its receivables at a much faster rate than Office Depot. Because these calculations are based on total sales (rather than credit sales), these values may not be comparable if Office Depot has significantly more credit sales than Staples.
SOLVENCY				
Debt to equity	$\dfrac{\text{Total liabilities}}{\text{Total equity}}$	$\dfrac{2,468,751 + 321,455 + 569,098}{2,739,221}$ $= 1.23$	$\dfrac{2,479,906 + 527,606 + 5,845 + 233,426 + 4,335}{4,425,471}$ $= 0.735$	Industry averages are often based on long-term debt only. In that case, Office Depot would have a debt-to-equity ratio of .117 and Staples' would be .119. Industry average is 0.40.
Times interest earned (interest coverage ratio)	$\dfrac{\text{Net income} + \text{interest expense}}{\text{Interest expense}}$	$\dfrac{273,792 + 32,380}{32,380}$ $= 9.46$	$\dfrac{834,409 + 56,773}{56,773} = 15.7$	The industry average is 19.8.

Ratio	Definition	Office Depot For FYE Dec. 31, 2005	Staples For FYE Jan. 28, 2006	Interpretation
PROFITABILITY				
Return on assets	$\dfrac{\text{Net income} + \text{interest expense}}{\text{Average total assets}}$	$\dfrac{273,792 + 32,380}{(6,098,525 + 6,794,338)/2}$ $= 4.75\%$	$\dfrac{834,409 + 56,773}{(7,676,589 + 7,071,448)/2}$ $= 12.09\%$	Staples' ROA significantly beats the industry average of 7.4%, but Office Depot has earned only 4.75% on total assets.
Return on equity	$\dfrac{\text{Net income} - \text{preferred dividends}}{\text{Average common stockholders' equity}}$	$\dfrac{273,792 - 0}{(2,739,221 + 3,223,048)/2}$ $= 9.18\%$	$\dfrac{834,409 - 0}{(4,425,471 + 4,115,196)/2}$ $= 19.5\%$	Staples is significantly outperforming Office Depot on ROE. The industry average is 15.1%.
Gross profit percentage	$\dfrac{\text{Gross profit}}{\text{Sales}}$	$\dfrac{4,392,023}{14,278,944} = 30.8\%$	$\dfrac{4,585,542}{16,078,852} = 28.5\%$	The gross profit shows that for a dollar of sales, these firms are between 28 and 31 cents. The industry average gross profit percentage is 27.8%.
Earnings per share	$\dfrac{\text{Net income} - \text{preferred dividends}}{\text{Number of shares of common stock outstanding}}$	$\$0.88^*$ *Provided on the income statement	$\$1.14^*$ *Provided on the income statement	Staples has outperformed Office Depot on the basis of EPS.
MARKET INDICATORS				
Price–earnings ratio	$\dfrac{\text{Market price per common share}}{\text{Earnings per share}}$	$\dfrac{31.40}{0.88} = 35.68$	$\dfrac{23.64}{1.14} = 20.74$	Office Depot has a PE ratio that is significantly higher than the industry average of 22.7. Staples' PE ratio is slightly lower than the industry average.
Dividend yield ratio	$\dfrac{\text{Dividends per share}}{\text{Market price per share}}$	$\dfrac{0}{31.40} = 0$	$\dfrac{0.17}{23.64} = 0.72\%$	Office Depot did not pay dividends in 2005. In 2005, Staples paid $0.17 per share.

Key Terms for Chapter 10

Discontinued operations
  (p. 476)
Dividend yield ratio (p. 481)
Extraordinary items (p. 477)
Horizontal analysis (p. 479)

Liquidity ratios (p. 480)
Market indicators (p. 480)
Price–earnings (PE) ratio
  (p. 481)

Profitability ratios (p. 480)
Solvency ratios (p. 480)
Vertical analysis (p. 480)

Answers to YOUR TURN Questions

Chapter 10
Your Turn 10-1

Those items must be shown after the tax consequences have been subtracted because this method of reporting the items net of taxes keeps the tax implications of these items separate from the company's regular tax expense. The alternative is to show the items before the tax implications and then to include the tax savings or tax increases in the company's regular tax expense.

Your Turn 10-2

This payoff would increase the current ratio. We can use a simple example to illustrate why: Suppose current assets were $500 million and current liabilities were $250 million. The current ratio would be 2. Now suppose $50 million worth of current liabilities were paid off with current assets. Then current assets would be $450 million, and current liabilities would be $200 million. The current ratio is now 2.25. When both the numerator and the denominator of a fraction are reduced by the same amount, the value of the fraction will increase. Working capital will remain unchanged. It started at $500 million minus $250 million in the example. After $50 million worth of liabilities is paid off with cash, the current assets will be $450 million and the current liabilities will be $200 million. The difference is still $250 million.

Your Turn 10-3

No, the gross profit ratio does not tell which company is more profitable because one company may have higher sales than the other. For example 30% of a large number is better than 60% of a small number. Also, the amount of costs the companies must cover beyond the cost of goods sold is unknown. The gross profit ratio is most useful for comparing companies in the same industry or evaluating performance of a single company across time.

Your Turn Appendix 10A

The FASB wants to make the changes to shareholders' equity that do not affect net income more apparent to financial statement users.

Your Turn Appendix 10B

1. The securities will be shown in the current asset section of the balance sheet at a value of $52,000. The write-up will be balanced with a $2,000 unrealized gain on the income statement.
2. The securities will be shown in either the current asset or the long-term asset section of the balance sheet (depending on a firm's intent) at a value of $52,000. The write-up will be balanced with a $2,000 unrealized gain that will go directly to equity, as part of accumulated other comprehensive income.
3. The securities will be shown at their cost of $50,000 in the long-term asset section of the balance sheet (unless the debt securities are maturing in the coming year, in which case they would be current assets).

Questions

1. Define the items that the Financial Accounting Standards Board requires a firm to report separately on the income statement. Why is this separation useful?
2. What criteria must be met for an event to be considered extraordinary? Give an examples of events that would be considered to be extraordinary.
3. What does it mean to show an item net of tax?
4. What is horizontal analysis? What is the purpose of this method of analysis?
5. What is vertical analysis? What is the purpose of this method of analysis?
6. What is liquidity? Which ratios are useful for measuring liquidity and what does each measure?
7. What is solvency? Which ratios are useful for measuring solvency and what does each measure?
8. What is profitability? Which ratios are useful for measuring profitability and what does each measure?
9. What are market indicators? Which ratios are market indicators and what does each measure?
10. How are financial ratios used to determine how successfully a company is operating?

Multiple-Choice Questions

1. Suppose a firm had an extraordinary loss of $300,000. If the firm's tax rate is 35%, how will the loss be shown in the financial statements?
   a. On the income statement, below income from operations, net of tax savings, for a net loss of $195,000
   b. On the income statement as part of the calculation of income from operations, before taxes, for a loss of $300,000
   c. As supplementary information in the notes to the financial statements
   d. As a cash outflow from financing on the statement of cash flows
2. Current assets for Kearney Company are $120,000 and total assets are $600,000. Current liabilities are $80,000 and total liabilities are $300,000. What is the current ratio?
   a. 2.00
   b. 2.50
   c. 1.90
   d. 1.50
3. Ritchie Company sold some fixed assets for a gain of $100,000. The firm's tax rate is 25%. How would Ritchie Company report this transaction on its financial statements?
   a. On the income statement as part of the calculation of income from continuing operations, net of tax, in the amount of $75,000
   b. As an extraordinary item, net of tax, in the amount of $75,000
   c. As discontinued operations, net of tax, in the amount of $75,000
   d. On the income statement as part of the calculation of income from continuing operations at the before tax amount of $100,000
4. Gerard Company reported sales of $300,000 for 2006, $330,000 for 2007, and $360,000 for 2008. If the company uses 2006 as the base year, what were the percentage increases for 2007 and 2008 compared to the base year?
   a. 10% for 2007 and 10% for 2008
   b. 120% for 2007 and 120% for 2008
   c. 110% for 2007 and 110% for 2008
   d. 10% for 2007 and 20% for 2008
5. On June 30, Star Radio reported total current assets of $45,000, total assets of $200,000, total current liabilities of $42,000, and total liabilities of $80,000. How much working capital did Star Radio have on this date?
   a. $87,000
   b. $200,000
   c. $3,000
   d. $123,000

6. Talking Puppet Company reported a P/E ratio of 50 on the last day of the fiscal year. If the company reported earnings of $2.50 per share, how much was a share of the company's stock trading for at that time?
   a. $20 per share
   b. $125 per share
   c. $50 per share
   d. $47.50 per share

7. Singleton Company had sales of $2,000,000, cost of sales of $1,200,000, and average inventory of $400,000. What was the company's inventory turnover ratio for the period?
   a. 3.00
   b. 4.00
   c. 5.00
   d. 0.33

8. Suppose a firm had an inventory turnover ratio of 20. Suppose the firm considers a year to be 360 days. How many days, on average, does an item remain in the inventory?
   a. 5.56 days
   b. 18 days
   c. 20 days
   d. 360 days

9. Suppose a new company is trying to decide whether to use LIFO or FIFO in a period of rising inventory costs. The CFO suggests using LIFO because it will give a higher inventory turnover ratio. Is he correct?
   a. Yes, the average inventory will be lower (the ratio's denominator) and the cost of goods sold (the ratio's numerator) will be higher than if FIFO were used.
   b. No, the average inventory would be the same because purchases are the same no matter which inventory method is chosen.
   c. The inventory method has no effect on the inventory turnover ratio.
   d. Without specific inventory amounts, it is not possible to predict the effect of the inventory method.

10. If a firm has $100,000 debt and $100,000 equity, then
   a. The return on equity ratio is 1.
   b. The debt-to-equity ratio is 1.
   c. The return on assets ratio is 0.5.
   d. The firm has too much debt.

Short Exercises

SE10-1. *Discontinued operations. (LO 1)*
In 2006, Earthscope Company decided to sell its satellite sales division, even though the division had been profitable during the year. During 2006, the satellite division earned $54,000 and the taxes on that income were $12,500. The division was sold for a gain of $750,000, and the taxes on the gain amounted to $36,700. How would these amounts be reported on the income statement for the year ended December 31, 2006?

SE10-2. *Discontinued operations. (LO 1)*
In 2007, Office Products decided to sell its furniture division because it had been losing money for several years. During 2007, the furniture division lost $140,000. The tax savings related to the loss amounted to $25,000. The division was sold at a loss of $350,000, and the tax savings related to the loss on the sale was $50,000. How would these amounts be reported on the income statement for the year ended December 31, 2007?

SE10-3. *Discontinued operations. (LO 1)*
After the terrorist attacks on the World Trade Center in 2001, Congress passed a law requiring new security devices in airports. One airport security firm had to get rid of an entire segment of the business that produced the old devices, and they suffered a significant loss on the disposal of the segment. The loss amounted to $320,000, with a related tax benefit of 10% of the loss. How would this be reported on the firm's income statement?

SE10-4. *Extraordinary item. (LO 1)*
Sew and Save Company suffered an extraordinary loss of $30,000 last year. The related tax savings amounted to $5,600. How would this tax savings be reported on the income statement?

SE10-5. *Horizontal analysis. (LO 2)*
Olin Copy Corporation reported the following amounts on its 2007 comparative income statement.

(in thousands)	2007	2006	2005
Revenues	$6,400	$4,575	$3,850
Cost of sales	3,900	2,650	2,050

Perform a horizontal analysis of revenues and cost of sales in both dollar amounts and in percentages for 2007 and 2006, using 2005 as the base year.

SE10-6. *Horizontal analysis. (LO 2)*
Use the following information about the capital expenditures of Andes Company to perform a horizontal analysis, with 2004 as the base year. What information does this provide about Andes Company?

(in millions)	2007	2006	2005	2004
Capital expenditures	$41,400	$45,575	$43,850	$50,600

SE10-7. *Vertical analysis. (LO 2)*
Bessie's Quilting Company reported the following amounts on its balance sheet at December 31, 2007.

Cash	$ 5,000
Accounts receivable, net	40,000
Inventory	35,000
Equipment, net	120,000
Total assets	$200,000

Perform a vertical analysis of the assets of Bessie's Quilting Company. Use total assets as the base. What information does the analysis provide?

SE10-8. *Vertical analysis. (LO 2)*
Perform a vertical analysis on the following income statement, with sales as the base amount. What other information would you need to make this analysis meaningful?

Sales	$35,000
Cost of goods sold	14,000
Gross margin	21,000
Other expenses	7,000
Net income	$14,000

SE10-9. *Ratio analysis. (LO 2)*
Fireworks reported current assets of $720,000 and a current ratio of 1.2. What were current liabilities? What was working capital?

SE10-10. *Ratio analysis. (LO 3)*
A 5-year comparative analysis of Low Light Company's current ratio and quick ratio follows.

	2004	2005	2006	2007	2008
Current ratio	1.19	1.85	2.50	3.40	4.02
Acid-test ratio	1.15	1.02	0.98	0.72	0.50

a. What has been happening to the liquidity of Low Light Company over the 5 years presented?

   b. Considering both ratios, what does the trend indicate about what has happened to the makeup of Low Light's current assets over the 5-year period?

SE10-11. *Ratio analysis. (LO 3)*
A company's debt-to-equity ratio has been increasing for the past 4 years. Give at least two company actions that might have caused this increase.

SE10-12. *Ratio analysis. (LO 3)*
The following is a 5-year comparative analysis of Accent Company's return on assets and return on equity.

	2005	2006	2007	2008	2009
Return on assets	8%	7.5%	7.12%	6.54%	6%
Return on equity	20%	21%	21.8%	22.2%	23%

   a. What does this analysis tell you about the overall profitability of Accent Company over the 5-year period?
   b. What does this analysis tell you about what has happened to Accent's amount of debt over the past 5 years?

SE10-13. *Ratio analysis. (LO 3)*
Earnings for Archibold Company have been fairly constant over the past 6 months, but the P/E ratio has been climbing steadily. How do you account for this climb? What does it tell you about the market's view of the company's future?

SE10-14. *Risk and control. (LO 4)*
Suppose you are the financial advisor to AHA Company, a local software development company. The CFO suggests the firm invest all of its extra cash in technology stocks. He thinks that will demonstrate the company's confidence in that sector of the market. What advice would you give him and why?

SE10-15. *Appendix 10A: Comprehensive income.*
Give an example of a gain or loss that would be excluded from the income statement and shown directly on the balance sheet as part of accumulated other comprehensive income.

SE10-16. *Appendix 10B: Investments.*
Convey Company had some extra cash and purchased the stock of various companies with the objective of making a profit in the short run. The cost of Convey's portfolio was $79,450 at December 31, 2008. On that date, the market value of the portfolio was $85,200. How would this increase in value be reflected in Convey's financial statements for the year ended December 31, 2008?

Exercises—Set A

E10-1A. *Discontinued operations. (LO 1)*
Use the following information to construct a partial income statement beginning with income from continuing operations.

Income from continuing operations	$230,000
Loss during the year from operating discontinued operations	50,000
Tax benefit of loss	8,500
Loss from sale of discontinued operations	138,500
Tax savings from loss on the sale	41,000

E10-2A. *Extraordinary item. (LO 1)*
Devon's Central Processing Agency suffered a $560,000 loss due to a disaster that qualifies as an extraordinary item for financial statement purposes. The tax benefit of the loss amounts to $123,000. If income from continuing operations (net of tax) amounted to $1,300,500, what is net income?

E10-3A. *Horizontal analysis. (LO 2)*

Jones Furniture reported the following amounts for its sales during the past 5 years. Using 2004 as the base year, perform a horizontal analysis. What information does the analysis provide that was not apparent from the raw numbers?

2008	2007	2006	2005	2004
$30,000	$28,400	$26,300	$24,200	$25,400

E10-4A. *Vertical analysis. (LO 2)*

Use the income statement from Color Copy to perform a vertical analysis with sales as the base.

Color Copy Inc.
Income Statement
For the year ended September 30, 2007

Sales revenue		$10,228
Cost of goods sold		5,751
Gross profit		$ 4,477
Operating expenses:		
Depreciation—buildings and equipment	$ 100	
Other selling and administrative	2,500	
Total expenses		2,600
Income before interest and taxes		$ 1,877
Interest expense		350
Income before taxes		$ 1,527
Income taxes		150
Net income		$ 1,377

E10-5A. *Current ratio and working capital. (LO 3)*

Calculate the current ratio and the amount of working capital for Albert's Hotels for the years given in the following comparative balance sheets. Although 2 years is not much of a trend, what is your opinion of the direction of these ratios?

Albert's Hotels Inc.
Balance Sheet
At December 31, 2008 and 2007

	2008	2007
Current assets:		
Cash	$ 98,000	$ 90,000
Accounts receivable, net	110,000	116,000
Inventory	170,000	160,000
Prepaid expenses	18,000	16,000
Total current assets	396,000	382,000
Equipment, net	184,000	160,000
Total assets	$580,000	$542,000
Total current liabilities	$206,000	$223,000
Long-term liabilities	119,000	117,000
Total liabilities	325,000	340,000
Common stockholders' equity	90,000	90,000
Retained earnings	165,000	112,000
Total liabilities and stockholders' equity	$580,000	$542,000

E10-6A. *Debt-to-equity ratio. (LO 3)*
Use the balance sheets from Albert's Hotels in E10-5A to compute the debt-to-equity ratio for 2008 and 2007. Suppose you calculated a debt ratio using debt plus equity as the denominator. Which ratio—debt to equity or debt to debt plus equity—seems easiest to interpret? As an investor, do you view the "trend" in the debt-to-equity ratio as favorable or unfavorable? Why?

E10-7A. *Ratio analysis. (LO 3)*
Zap Electronics reported the following for the fiscal years ended January 31, 2007, and January 31, 2006.

Excel Template
www.prenhall.com/reimers

January 31 (in thousands)	2007	2006
Accounts receivable	$ 36,184	$ 24,306
Inventory	106,754	113,875
Current assets	174,369	124,369
Current liabilities	71,616	68,001
Long-term liabilities	12,316	35,200
Shareholders' equity	121,851	198,935
Sales	712,855	580,223
Cost of goods sold	483,463	400,126
Interest expense	335	709
Net income	11,953	4,706

Assume all sales are on credit and the firm has no preferred stock outstanding. Calculate the following ratios.
   a. Current ratio (for both years)
   b. Accounts receivable turnover ratio (for 2007)
   c. Inventory turnover ratio (for 2007)
   d. Debt-to-equity ratio (for both years)
   e. Return on equity ratio (for 2007)

Do any of these ratios suggest problems for the company?

E10-8A. *Ratio analysis. (LO 3)*
Evans Family Grocers reported the following for the two most recent fiscal years.

December 31	2008	2007
Cash	$ 25,000	$ 20,000
Receivables (net)	60,000	70,000
Merchandise inventory	55,000	30,000
Plant assets	280,000	260,000
Total assets	$420,000	$380,000
Accounts payable	45,000	62,000
Long-term notes payable	75,000	100,000
Common stock	135,000	122,000
Retained earnings	165,000	96,000
Total Liabilities and Shareholders' Equity	$420,000	$380,000
Net income for the year ended 12/31/08	$ 75,000	
Sales (all sales were on account)	450,000	
Cost of goods sold	210,000	
Interest expense	1,500	

Calculate the following for the year ended December 31, 2008.
   a. Current ratio
   b. Working capital

   c. Accounts receivable turnover ratio
   d. Inventory turnover ratio
   e. Return on assets
   f. Return on equity

E10-9A. *Ratio analysis. (LO 3)*
Furniture Showcase reported the following for its fiscal year ended June 30, 2008.

Sales	$530,000
Cost of sales	300,000
Gross margin	230,000
Expenses*	113,000
Net income	$117,000

*Included in the expenses was
$12,000 of interest expense.
Assume no income tax expense.

At the beginning of the year, the company had 50,000 shares of common stock outstanding. At the end of the year, there were 40,000 shares outstanding. The market price of the company's stock at year-end was $20 per share. The company declared and paid $80,000 of dividends near year-end.

    Calculate earnings per share, the price–earnings ratio, and times-interest-earned ratio for Furniture Showcase.

Use the balance sheet and income statement for The Talbots Inc. for E10-10A through E10-13A.

E10-10A. *Horizontal analysis. (LO 2)*
Use the statement of earnings for Talbots to perform a horizontal analysis for each item reported for the year from January 29, 2005, to January 28, 2006. What does your analysis tell you about the operations of Talbots for the year?

E10-11A. *Vertical analysis. (LO 2)*
Use the statement of earnings for Talbots to perform a vertical analysis for each item reported for the last two fiscal years using net sales as the base. What does your analysis tell you about the operations for the years reported?

E10-12A. *Liquidity ratios. (LO 3)*
Use the financial statements for Talbots to calculate the following liquidity ratios for FYE January 28, 2006. What information does this provide about the firm's liquidity?
   a. Current ratio
   b. Acid-test ratio
   c. Working capital
   d. Inventory turnover ratio
   e. Accounts receivable turnover ratio (Assume all sales are credit sales.)

E10-13A. *Solvency and profitability ratios. (LO 3)*
Use the financial statements for Talbots to calculate the following solvency and profitability ratios for FYE January 28, 2006. What information does this provide about the firm's solvency and profitability?
   a. Debt-to-equity ratio
   b. Times-interest-earned ratio
   c. Return on assets
   d. Return on equity
   e. Gross margin percentage

The Talbots, Inc. and Subsidiaries
Consolidated Balance Sheets
(Amounts in thousands except share data)

	January 28, 2006	January 29, 2005
Assets		
Current Assets:		
Cash and cash equivalents	$ 103,020	$ 31,811
Customer accounts receivable–net	209,749	199,256
Merchandise inventories	246,707	238,544
Deferred catalog costs	6,021	5,118
Due from affiliates	7,892	9,073
Deferred income taxes	14,115	14,006
Prepaid and other current assets	33,157	29,589
Total current assets	620,661	527,397
Property and equipment–net	387,536	405,114
Deferred income taxes	6,407	–
Goodwill–net	35,513	35,513
Trademarks–net	75,884	75,884
Other assets	20,143	18,222
Total Assets	$1,146,144	$1,062,130
Liabilities and Stockholder's Equity		
Current Liabilities:		
Accounts payable	$ 85,343	$ 65,070
Accrued income taxes	37,909	27,196
Accrued liabilities	121,205	110,372
Total current liabilities	244,457	202,638
Long-term debt	100,000	100,000
Deferred rent under lease commitments	110,864	109,946
Deferred income taxes	–	5,670
Other liabilities	63,855	55,288
Commitments		
Stockholder's Equity:		
Common stock, $0.01 par value; 200,000,000 authorized; 77,861,128 shares and 76,940,134 shares issued, respectively, and 53,359,556 shares and 54,123,667 shares outstanding, respectively	779	769
Additional paid-in capital	455,221	432,912
Retained earnings	783,397	715,580
Accumulated other comprehensive loss	(16,682)	(17,142)
Deferred compensation	(13,403)	(11,821)
Treasury stock, at cost; 24,501,572 and 22,816,467 shares, respectively	(582,344)	(531,710)
Total stockholder's equity	626,968	588,588
Total Liabilities and Stockholder's Equity	$1,146,144	$1,062,130

See notes to consolidated financial statements.

The Talbots, Inc. and Subsidiaries
Consolidated Statements of Earnings
(Amounts in thousands except per share data)

	Year ended		
	January 28, 2006	January 29, 2005	January 31, 2004
Net sales	$1,808,606	$1,697,843	$1,594,790
Costs and Expenses			
Cost of sales, buying and occupancy	1,153,734	1,093,023	995,765
Selling, general and administrative	502,724	462,705	432,424
Operating Income	152,148	142,115	166,601
Interest			
Interest expense	4,480	2,616	2,402
Interest income	1,374	506	307
Interest expense–net	3,106	2,110	2,095
Income Before Taxes	149,042	140,005	164,506
Income taxes	55,891	44,639	61,615
Net income	$ 93,151	$ 95,366	$ 102,891
Net income per share			
Basic	$ 1.76	$ 1.73	$ 1.82
Diluted	$ 1.72	$ 1.70	$ 1.78
Weighted Average Number of Shares of Common Stock Outstanding			
Basic	52,882	54,969	56,531
Diluted	54,103	56,252	57,901

E10-14A. *Risk and control. (LO 4)*
Often a firm will contribute its own shares of stock to its pension fund rather than cash. What problem could this cause? How could it be avoided? Have you heard of any firm that did this and the result was a disaster?

E10-15A. *Appendix 10B: Investments.*
Omicron Corporation invested $125,000 of its extra cash in securities. Under each of the following independent scenarios, (a) calculate the amount at which the investments would be valued for the year-end balance sheet, and (b) indicate how the effect of these scenarios should be reported on the other financial statements, if at all.

1. All the securities were debt securities, with a maturity date in 2 years. Omicron will hold the securities until they mature. The market value of the securities at year-end was $123,000.
2. Omicron purchased the securities for trading, hoping to make a quick profit. At year-end the market value of the securities was $120,000.
3. Omicron is uncertain about how long it will hold the securities. At year-end the market value of the securities is $126,000.

E10-16A. *Appendix 10B: Investments.*
During 2007, Nike has invested $200,000 of extra cash in securities. Of the total amount invested, $75,000 was invested in bonds that Nike plans to hold until maturity (the bonds were issued at par value); $65,000 was invested in various equity securities that Nike plans to hold for an indefinite period of time; and $60,000 was invested in the stock of various com-

panies that Nike intends to trade to make a short-term profit. At the end of the year, the market value of the held-to-maturity securities was $80,000; the market value of the trading securities was $75,000; and the market value of the available-for-sale securities was $55,000. Use the accounting equation to record all adjustments required at year-end, and indicate how the effects of each group of securities will be reported on the financial statements.

Exercises—Set B

E10-1B. *Discontinued operations. (LO 1)*

Use the following information to construct a partial income statement beginning with income from continuing operations.

Income from continuing operations	$310,000
Loss during the year from operation of discontinued operations	75,000
Tax benefit of loss	19,400
Loss from sale of discontinued operations	105,750
Tax savings from loss on the sale	32,000

E10-2B. *Extraordinary items. (LO 1)*

Tropical Vacations suffered a $1,070,000 loss due to a tsunami, which qualifies as an extraordinary item for financial statement purposes. The tax benefit of the loss amounts to $155,000. If income from continuing operations (net of tax) amounted to $1,861,250, what is net income?

E10-3B. *Horizontal analysis. (LO 2)*

Making Every Day Sunny Umbrellas reported the following amounts for sales during the past 5 years. Using 2006 as the base year, perform a horizontal analysis. What information does the analysis provide that was not apparent from the raw numbers?

2010	2009	2008	2007	2006
$27,925	$30,400	$33,525	$26,250	$30,300

E10-4B. *Vertical analysis. (LO 2)*

Use the income statement from Designers Discount Inc. to perform a vertical analysis with sales as the base.

Designers Discount Inc.
Income Statement
For the year ended March 28, 2008

Sales revenue		$16,374
Cost of goods sold		7,985
Gross profit on sales		$ 8,389
Operating expenses:		
Depreciation—buildings and equipment	$ 265	
Other selling and administrative	3,750	
Total expenses		4,015
Income before interest and taxes		$ 4,374
Interest expense		254
Income before taxes		$ 4,120
Income taxes		1,236
Net income		$ 2,884

E10-5B. *Current ratio and working capital. (LO 3)*

Calculate the current ratio and the amount of working capital for Mike & Kat Racing Company for the years given in the following comparative balance sheets. Although 2 years will not show a significant trend, what is your opinion of the direction of these ratios?

Mike & Kat Racing Company
Balance Sheet
At December 31, 2008 and 2007

	2008	2007
Current assets:		
Cash	$186,000	$192,000
Accounts receivable, net	94,000	85,000
Inventory	185,000	170,500
Prepaid expenses	17,000	14,000
Total current assets	482,000	461,500
Equipment, net	215,000	195,000
Total assets	$697,000	$656,500
Total current liabilities	$267,000	$269,000
Long-term liabilities	185,000	190,000
Total liabilities	452,000	459,000
Shareholders' equity	163,750	148,250
Retained earnings	81,250	49,250
Total liabilities and shareholders' equity	$697,000	$656,500

E10-6B. *Debt-to-equity ratio. (LO 3)*
Use the balance sheets from Mike & Kat Racing Company in E10-5B to compute a debt-to-equity ratio for 2008 and 2007. Suppose you calculated a debt ratio using debt plus equity as the denominator. Which ratio—debt to equity or debt to debt plus equity— seems easiest to interpret? As an investor, do you view the "trend" in the debt to equity ratio as favorable or unfavorable? Why?

E10-7B. *Ratio analysis. (LO 3)*
Crystal Cromartie's Frozen Foods reported the following for the fiscal years ended September 30, 2008, and September 30, 2007.

September 30 (in millions)	2008	2007
Accounts receivable	$ 21,265	$ 13,802
Inventory	45,692	47,682
Current assets	185,716	155,716
Current liabilities	80,954	72,263
Long-term liabilities	15,251	17,852
Shareholders' equity	21,871	58,035
Sales	88,455	70,223
Cost of goods sold	60,463	52,750
Interest expense	21.5	43.2
Net income	1,842	1,006

Assume there is no outstanding preferred stock and all sales are credit sales. Calculate the following ratios.
a. Current ratio (for both years)
b. Accounts receivable turnover ratio (for 2008)
c. Inventory turnover ratio (for 2008)
d. Debt-to-equity ratio (for both years)
e. Return on equity (for 2008)

Do any of these ratios suggest problems for the company?

E10-8B. *Ratio analysis. (LO 3)*

Hutson Coffee Shops reported the following for the two most recent fiscal years.

December 31	2010	2009
Cash	$ 34,000	$ 17,000
Receivables (net)	85,000	80,000
Merchandise inventory	74,000	48,000
Fixed assets	365,000	324,000
Total assets	$558,000	$469,000
Accounts payable	65,000	83,000
Long-term notes payable	82,000	112,000
Common stock	176,000	144,000
Retained earnings	235,000	130,000
Total liabilities and shareholders' equity	$558,000	$469,000
Net income for the year ended 12/31/10	$115,000	
Sales (all sales were on account)	620,000	
Cost of goods sold	284,000	
Interest expense	3,000	

Calculate the following for the year ended December 31, 2010.
   a. Current ratio
   b. Working capital
   c. Accounts receivable turnover ratio
   d. Inventory turnover ratio
   e. Return on assets
   f. Return on equity

E10-9B. *Ratio analysis. (LO 3)*

International Imports Corporation reported the following for its fiscal year ended June 30, 2007.

Sales	$640,000
Cost of sales	470,000
Gross margin	170,000
Expenses*	94,000
Net income	$ 76,000

*Included in the expenses were $9,000
of interest expense and $14,000
of income tax expense.

At the beginning of the year, the company had 40,000 shares of common stock outstanding and no preferred stock. At the end of the year, there were 25,000 common shares outstanding and no preferred stock. The market price of the company's stock at year-end was $15 per share. The company declared and paid $46,000 of dividends near year-end.

Calculate earnings per share, the price–earnings ratio, and times-interest-earned ratio for International Imports.

E10-10B. *Horizontal analysis. (LO 2)*

Use the statement of income for Wendy's to perform a horizontal analysis for each item reported for the year from January 2, 2005, to January 1, 2006. What does your analysis tell you about the operations of Wendy's for the years reported?

E10-11B. *Vertical analysis. (LO 2)*

Use the statement of income for Wendy's to perform a vertical analysis for each item reported for 2005 and 2004 using sales and other operating revenues as the base. What does your analysis tell you about the operations of Wendy's for the years reported?

Wendy's International, Inc. and Subsidiaries— Consolidated Balance Sheets

(Dollars in thousands)	January 1, 2006 and January 2, 2005	
	2005	2004
Assets		
Current assets		
Cash and cash equivalents	$ 393,241	$ 176,749
Accounts receivable, net	138,999	127,158
Notes receivable, net	11,746	11,626
Deferred income taxes	29,043	27,280
Inventories and other	62,868	56,010
Advertising fund restricted assets	53,866	60,021
Assets held for disposition	66,803	0
Total current assets	756,566	458,844
Property and equipment, net	2,325,888	2,349,820
Notes receivable, net	14,796	12,652
Goodwill	128,808	166,998
Deferred income taxes	6,623	6,772
Intangible assets, net	41,757	41,787
Other assets	165,880	160,671
Total assets	$3,440,318	$3,197,544
Liabilities and Shareholder's Equity		
Current liabilities		
Accounts payable	$ 188,481	$ 197,247
Accrued expenses		
Salaries and wages	51,184	46,971
Taxes	116,920	108,025
Insurance	58,147	53,160
Other	90,263	92,838
Advertising fund restricted liabilities	68,929	60,021
Current portion of long-term obligations	9,428	130,125
Total current liabilities	583,352	688,387
Long-term obligations		
Term debt	559,097	538,055
Capital leases	56,736	55,552
Total long-term obligations	615,833	593,607
Deferred income taxes	78,206	109,674
Other long-term liabilities	104,338	90,187
Commitments and contingencies		
Shareholder's equity		
Preferred stock, Authorized: 250,000 shares		
Common stock, $.10 stated value per share, Authorized: 200,000,000 shares.		
Issued: 125,490,000 and 118,090,000 shares, respectively	12,549	11,809
Capital in excess of stated value	405,588	111,286
Retained earnings	1,858,743	1,700,813
Accumulated other comprehensive income (expense):		
Cumulative translation adjustments and other	115,252	102,950
Pension liability	(1,096)	(913)
	2,391,036	1,925,945
Treasury stock, at cost: 7,681,000 and 5,681,000 shares, respectively	(294,669)	(195,124)
Unearned compensation–restricted stock	(37,778)	(15,132)
Total shareholder's equity	2,058,589	1,715,689
Total liabilities and shareholder's equity	$3,440,318	$3,197,544

See accompanying Notes to the Consolidated Financial Statements.

Wendy's International, Inc. and Subsidiaries
Consolidated Statements of Income

(In thousands, except per share data)	Year Ended January 1, 2006 2005	Year Ended January 2, 2005 2004	Year Ended December 28, 2003 2003
Revenues			
Retail sales	$3,028,414	$2,935,899	$2,534,135
Franchise revenues	754,733	699,539	614,777
Total revenues	3,783,147	3,635,438	3,148,912
Costs and expenses			
Cost of sales	2,003,804	1,900,635	1,618,002
Company restaurant operating costs	682,505	668,948	550,643
Operating costs	171,919	168,492	135,332
Depreciation of property and equipment	199,680	178,394	163,481
General and administrative expenses	321,518	283,721	261,070
Goodwill impairment	36,141	190,000	0
Other (income) expense, net	(9,603)	18,644	1,942
Total costs and expenses	3,405,964	3,408,834	2,730,470
Operating income	377,183	226,604	418,442
Interest expense	(46,405)	(46,950)	(45,773)
Interest income	7,286	4,409	4,929
Income before income taxes	338,064	184,063	377,598
Income taxes	113,997	132,028	141,599
Net income	$ 224,067	$ 52,035	$ 235,999
Basic earnings per common share	$1.95	$0.46	$2.07
Diluted earnings per common share	$1.92	$0.45	$2.05
Dividends per common share	$0.58	$0.48	$0.24
Basic shares	114,945	113,832	113,866
Diluted shares	116,819	115,685	115,021

See accompanying Notes to the Consolidated Financial Statements.

E10-12B. *Liquidity ratios. (LO 3)*
Use the financial statements for Wendy's to calculate the following liquidity ratios for 2005. What do these ratios tell about the firm?
  a. Current ratio
  b. Acid-test ratio
  c. Working capital

E10-13B. *Solvency and profitability ratios. (LO 3)*
Use the financial statements for Wendy's to calculate the following solvency ratios and profitability for 2005 and provide an interpretation for each ratio.
  a. Debt-to-equity ratio
  b. Times-interest-earned ratio
  c. Return on assets
  d. Return on equity
  e. Gross margin percentage

E10-14B. *Risk and control. (LO 4)*
Describe the risks of investing your money in the stock market. How can you reduce those risks? Why are you willing to take risks like these?

E10-15B. *Appendix 10B: Investments.*
Kinsey Scales invested $164,000 of its extra cash in securities. Under each of the following independent scenarios, (a) calculate the amount at which the investments would be valued for

the year-end balance sheet, and (b) indicate how these scenarios should be reported on the other financial statements, if at all.

1. All the securities were debt securities, with a maturity date in 2 years. Kinsey will hold the securities until they mature. The market value of the securities at year-end was $158,000.
2. Kinsey purchased the securities for trading, hoping to make a quick profit. At year-end the market value of the securities was $162,000.
3. Kinsey is uncertain about how long it will hold the securities. At year-end the market value of the securities is $167,000.

E10-16B. *Appendix 10B: Investments.*
During 2009, Arctic Fans & Blowers has invested $245,000 of extra cash in securities. Of the total amount invested, $115,000 was invested in bonds that Arctic plans to hold until maturity (the bonds were issued at par); $55,000 was invested in various equity securities that Arctic plans to hold for an indefinite period of time; and $75,000 was invested in the stock of various companies that Arctic intends to trade to make a short-term profit. At the end of the year, the market value of the held-to-maturity securities was $108,000, the market value of the trading securities was $52,000, and the market value of the available-for-sale securities was $85,000. Use the accounting equation to record all adjustments required at year-end and indicate how the effects of each group of securities will be reported on the financial statements.

Problems—Set A

P10-1A. *Discontinued operations and extraordinary item. (LO 1)*
Each of the following items was found on the financial statements for Hartsfield Company for the year ended December 31, 2007.

Net income from continuing operations	$136,500
Gain on the sale of a discontinued segment, net of taxes of $42,000	140,000
Loss from operation of discontinued segment, net of taxes of $24,000	(80,000)
Gain on sale of land	65,000
Extraordinary loss, net of taxes of $6,000	(20,000)

Required

a. For the items listed, indicate the financial statement and appropriate section, where applicable, on which each would appear.
b. Provide a description of each item and give as many details of each item's financial statement presentation as possible.
c. Based on the data provided, what is Hartsfield Company's tax rate?

P10-2A. *Prepare an income statement. (LO 1)*
The Pops Corporation had the following for the year ended December 31, 2008.

Sales	$575,000
Cost of goods sold	230,000
Interest income	10,000
Gain on sale of equipment	8,000
Selling and administrative expenses	12,000
Interest expense	5,000
Extraordinary gain	15,000
Loss from discontinued segment operations	(10,500)
Gain on disposal of discontinued segment	28,000

Required

Assume the corporation is subject to a 30% tax rate. Prepare an income statement for the year ended December 31, 2008.

P10-3A. *Prepare an income statement. (LO 1)*
The following balances appeared in the general ledger for Hacky Sak Corporation at fiscal year end September 30, 2008:

Selling and administrative expenses	$ 25,000
Other revenues and gains	50,000
Operating expenses	75,000
Cost of goods sold	135,000
Net sales	375,000
Other expenses and losses	15,000

In addition, the following occurred throughout the year.

1. On April 10, a tornado destroyed one of the company's manufacturing plants resulting in an extraordinary loss of $55,000.
2. On July 31, the company discontinued one of its unprofitable segments. The loss from operations was $25,000. The assets of the segment were sold at a gain of $15,000.

Required

   a. Assume Hacky Sak's income tax rate is 40%; prepare the income statement for the year ended September 30, 2008.

   b. Calculate the earnings per share the company would report on the income statement assuming Hacky Sak had a weighted average of 200,000 shares of common stock outstanding during the year and paid preferred dividends of $5,000.

P10-4A. *Prepare horizontal and vertical analysis. (LO 2)*
Given the following income statements:

Excel Template
www.prenhall.com/reimers

Year ended December 31,
(in thousands)

	2009	2008	2007
Net sales	$5,003,837	$4,934,430	$4,881,103
Cost of goods sold	2,755,323	2,804,459	2,784,392
Gross profit	2,248,514	2,129,971	2,096,711
Selling, general, and administrative expenses	1,673,449	1,598,333	1,573,510
Operating income	575,065	531,638	523,201
Interest expense	61,168	71,971	80,837
Interest and net investment expense (income)	(5,761)	(6,482)	(8,278)
Other expense—net	29,540	26,046	23,365
Income before income taxes	490,118	440,103	427,277
Income taxes	186,258	167,239	166,663
Net income	$ 303,860	$ 272,864	$ 260,614

Required

   a. For each of the years shown, prepare a vertical analysis, using sales as the base. Write a paragraph explaining what the analysis shows.

   b. Using 2007 as the base year, prepare a horizontal analysis for sales and cost of goods sold. What information does this analysis give you?

P10-5A. *Calculate and analyze financial ratios. (LO 3)*
Given the information below from a firm's financial statement:

	Year ended December 31, (in thousands)		
	2009	2008	2007
Net sales (all on account)	$5,003,837	$4,934,430	
Cost of goods sold	2,755,323	2,804,459	
Gross profit	2,248,514	2,129,971	
Interest expense	61,168	71,971	
Income taxes	186,258	167,239	
Net income	$ 303,860	$ 272,864	
Cash and cash equivalents	$ 18,623	$ 19,133	$ 3,530
Accounts receivable, less allowance	606,046	604,516	546,314
Total current assets	1,597,377	1,547,290	1,532,253
Total assets	4,052,090	4,065,462	4,035,801
Total current liabilities	1,189,862	1,111,973	44,539
Long-term liabilities	1,163,696	1,237,549	
Total shareholders' equity*	1,698,532	1,715,940	1,592,180

*The firm has no preferred stock.

Required

a. Calculate the following ratios for 2009 and 2008:
   1. Current ratio
   2. Acid-test ratio (assume no short-term investments)
   3. Working capital
   4. Accounts receivable turnover ratio
   5. Debt-to-equity ratio
   6. Times-interest-earned ratio
   7. Return on equity
   8. Gross profit percentage
b. Suppose the changes from 2008 to 2009 in each of these ratios were consistent with the direction and size of the change for the past several years. For each ratio, explain what the trend in the ratio would indicate about the company.

P10-6A. *Calculate and analyze financial ratios. (LO 3)*

The following information was taken from the 2008 annual report of Presentations.

	At December 31, (in thousands)	
	2008	2007
ASSETS		
Current assets		
Cash	$ 1,617	$1,220
Accounts receivable	1,925	3,112
Merchandise inventory	2,070	966
Prepaid expenses	188	149
Total current assets	5,800	5,447
Plant and equipment:		
Buildings, net	$ 4,457	$2,992
Equipment, net	1,293	1,045
Total plant and equipment	$ 5,750	$4,037
Total assets	$11,550	$9,484
LIABILITIES		
Current liabilities		
Accounts payable	$ 1,817	$1,685
Notes payable	900	1,100
Total current liabilities	2,717	2,785
Long-term liabilities	3,500	2,000
Total liabilities	6,217	4,785
STOCKHOLDERS' EQUITY		
Common stock, no par value	3,390	3,042
Retained earnings	1,943	1,657
Total stockholders' equity	5,333	4,699
Total liabilities and stockholders' equity	$11,550	$9,484
Sales revenue	$12,228	
Cost of goods sold	8,751	
Gross profit on sales	3,477	
Operating expenses:		
Depreciation—buildings and equipment	102	
Other selling and administrative	2,667	
Total expenses	2,769	
Income before interest and taxes	708	
Interest expense	168	
Income before taxes	540	
Income taxes	114	
Net income	$ 426	

Required

a. Calculate the following ratios for 2008 and 2007 whenever possible.
   1. Debt-to-equity ratio
   2. Gross margin percentage
   3. Current ratio
   4. Acid-test ratio
   5. Times-interest-earned ratio
b. What do the ratios indicate about the success of Presentations? What additional information would help you analyze the overall performance of this company?

P10-7A. *Calculate and analyze financial ratios. (LO 3)*
The financial statements of For the Kitchen include the following items.

	At June 30, 2007	June 30, 2006	June 30, 2005
Balance sheet:			
Cash	$ 17,000	$ 12,000	$ 14,000
Investments (in trading securities)	10,000	16,000	20,000
Accounts receivable (net)	54,000	50,000	48,000
Inventory	75,000	70,000	73,000
Prepaid expenses	16,000	12,000	10,000
Total current assets	172,000	160,000	165,000
Total current liabilities	$140,000	$ 90,000	$ 75,000
Income statement for the year ended	June 30, 2007:	June 30 2006:	
Net credit sales	$420,000	$380,000	
Cost of goods sold	250,000	225,000	

Required

a. Compute the following ratios for the years ended June 30, 2007, and whenever possible for the year ended June 30, 2006. For each, indicate if the direction is favorable or unfavorable for the company.
   1. Current ratio
   2. Accounts receivable turnover
   3. Inventory turnover ratio
   4. Gross profit percentage
b. Suppose the industry average for similar retail stores for the current ratio is 1.7. Does this information help you evaluate For the Kitchen's liquidity?

P10-8A. *Calculate and analyze financial ratios. (LO 3)*
You are interested in investing in Reese Company, and you have obtained the balance sheets for the company for the past 2 years.

Reese Company
Balance Sheet
At June 30, 2007 and 2006

	2007	2006
Current assets:		
Cash	$198,000	$ 90,000
Accounts receivable, net	210,000	116,000
Inventory	270,000	160,000
Prepaid rent	15,000	16,000
Total current assets	693,000	382,000
Equipment, net	280,000	260,000
Total assets	$973,000	$642,000
Total current liabilities	$306,000	$223,000
Long-term liabilities	219,000	117,000
Total liabilities	525,000	340,000
Common stockholders' equity	150,000	90,000
Retained earnings	298,000	212,000
Total liabilities and stockholders' equity	$973,000	$642,000

The following amounts were reported on the income statement for the year ended June 30, 2007.

Sales	$450,000
Cost of goods sold	215,000
Interest expense	7,500
Net income	80,000

Required

a. Compute as many of the financial statement ratios you have studied as possible with the information provided for Reese Company. Some ratios can be computed for both years and others can be computed for only 1 year.
b. Would you invest in Reese Company? Why or why not? What additional information would be helpful in making this decision?

Problems—Set B

P10-1B. *Discontinued operations and extraordinary item. (LO 1)*
Each of the following items was found on the financial statements for Logan Company for the year ended December 31, 2008.

Income from continuing operations	85,000
Gain on the sale of discontinued segment, net of taxes $9,000	30,000
Loss from operation of discontinued segment, net of taxes of $9,750	(32,500)
Gain on sale of equipment	12,000
Extraordinary loss from earthquake, net of taxes $45,000	(150,000)

Required

a. For each item listed, indicate the financial statement and appropriate section, if applicable, on which each would appear.
b. Provide a description of each item and give as many details of each item's financial statement presentation as possible.
c. Based on the data provided, what is Logan Company's tax rate?

P10-2B. *Prepare an income statement. (LO 1)*
The Blues Corporation had the following for the year ended December 31, 2007.

Sales	$425,000
Cost of goods sold	185,000
Interest income	8,000
Gain on sale of equipment	4,000
Selling and administrative expenses	18,000
Interest expense	3,000
Extraordinary gain	25,000
Loss from discontinued segment operations	(9,500)
Gain on disposal of discontinued segment	36,000

Required

Assume the corporation is subject to a 40% tax rate. Prepare an income statement for the year ended December 31, 2007.

P10-3B. *Prepare an income statement. (LO 1)*
The following balances appeared in the general ledger for Ski Daddle Corporation at fiscal year-end December 31, 2007.

Selling and administrative expenses	$ 45,000
Other revenues and gains	80,000
Operating expenses	110,000
Cost of goods sold	185,000
Net sales	325,000
Other expenses and losses	8,000

In addition, the following occurred throughout the year.

1. On August 20, a fire destroyed one of the company's warehouses resulting in an extra-ordinary loss of $35,000.
2. On October 31, the company discontinued one of its unprofitable segments. The loss from operations was $35,000. The assets of the segment were sold at a gain of $19,000.

Required

a. Assume Ski Daddle Corporation's income tax rate is 30%; prepare the income statement for the year ended December 31, 2007.
b. Calculate the earnings per share the company would report on the income statement assuming Ski Daddle had 100,000 shares of common stock outstanding during the year and paid preferred dividends of $15,000.

Excel Template
www.prenhall.com/reimers

P10-4B. *Perform horizontal and vertical analysis. (LO 2)*
Here are the income statements from a firm's recent annual report.

	Year ended December 31, (in millions)		
	2008	2007	2006
Net revenue	$26,971	$25,112	$23,512
Cost of sales	12,379	11,497	10,750
Selling, general, and administrative expenses	9,460	8,958	8,574
Amortization of intangible assets	145	138	165
Other expenses	204	224	356
Operating profit	4,783	4,295	3,667
Income from investments	323	280	160
Interest expense	(163)	(178)	(219)
Interest income	51	36	67
Income before income taxes	4,994	4,433	3,675
Income taxes	1,424	1,433	1,244
Net income	$ 3,570	$ 3,000	$ 2,431

Required

a. For each of the years shown, perform a vertical analysis, using sales as the base. Write a paragraph explaining what the analysis shows.
b. Using 2006 as the base year, perform a horizontal analysis for net revenue and cost of sales. What information does this analysis give you?

Consolidated Statement of Income
RadioShack Corporation and Subsidiaries

Year Ended December 31,

(In millions, except per share amounts)	2005		2004	
	Dollars	% of Revenues	Dollars	% of Revenues
Net sales and operating revenues	$5,081.7	100.0%	$4,841.2	100.0%
Cost of products sold	2,706.3	53.3	2,406.7	49.7
Gross profit	2,375.4	46.7	2,434.5	50.3
Operating expenses:				
Selling, general and administrative	1,901.7	37.4	1,774.8	36.7
Depreciation and amortization	123.8	2.4	101.4	2.1
Total operating expenses	2,025.5	39.8	1,876.2	38.8
Operating income	349.9	6.9	558.3	11.5
Interest income	5.9	0.1	11.4	0.2
Interest expense	(44.5)	(0.8)	(29.6)	(0.5)
Other income, net	10.2	0.2	2.0	—
Income before income taxes	321.5	6.4	542.1	11.2
Provision for income taxes	51.6	1.0	204.9	4.2
Income before cumulative effect of change in accounting principle	269.9	5.4	337.2	7.0
Cumulative effect of change in accounting principle, net of $1.8 million tax benefit	(2.9)	(0.1)	—	—
Net income	$ 267.0	5.3%	$ 337.2	7.0%

Consolidated Balance Sheets
RadioShack Corporation and Subsidiaries
December 31,

(In millions, except for share amounts)	2005	2004
Assets		
Current assets:		
Cash and cash equivalents	$ 224.0	$ 437.9
Accounts and notes receivable, net	309.4	241.0
Inventories, net	964.9	1,003.7
Other current assets	129.0	92.5
Total current assets	1,627.3	1,775.1
Property, plant and equipment, net	476.2	652.0
Other assets, net	101.6	89.6
Total assets	$ 2,205.1	$ 2,516.7
Liabilities and Stockholders' Equity		
Current liabilities:		
Short-term debt, including current maturities of long-term debt	$ 40.9	$ 55.6
Accounts payable	490.9	442.2
Accrued expenses and other current liabilities	379.5	342.1
Income taxes payable	75.0	117.5
Total current liabilities	986.3	957.4
Long-term debt, excluding current maturities	494.9	506.9
Other non-current liabilities	135.1	130.3
Total liabilities	1,616.3	1,594.6
Commitments and contingent liabilities (see Notes 11 and 12)		
Stockholders' equity:		
Preferred stock, no par value, 1,000,000 shares authorized:		
Series A junior participating, 300,000 shares designated and none issued	—	—
Series B convertible, 100,000 shares authorized and non issued	—	—
Common stock, $1 par value, 650,000,000 shares authorized; 191,033,000 shares issued	191.0	191.0
Additional paid-in capital	88.2	82.7
Retained earnings	1,741.4	1,508.1
Treasury stock, at cost; 56,071,000 and 32,835,000 shares, respectively	(1,431.6)	(859.4)
Unearned compensation	(0.5)	—
Accumulated other comprehensive income (loss)	0.3	(0.3)
Total stockholders' equity	588.8	922.1
Total liabilities and stockholders' equity	$ 2,205.1	$ 2,516.7

The accompanying notes are an integral part of these consolidated financial statements.

P10-5B. *Calculate and analyze financial ratios. (LO 3)*
The information given in P10-4B was taken from Radio Shack's financial statements. Even though you did not study all of the items on the statements, you should recognize most of them.

Required

a. Calculate the following ratios for 2005.
   1. Current ratio
   2. Acid-test ratio
   3. Working capital
   4. Accounts receivable turnover ratio (Assume all sales are credit sales.)
   5. Debt-to-equity ratio
   6. Times-interest-earned ratio
   7. Return on equity
b. Notice that Radio Shack provides a vertical analysis of the income statement. Comment on the changes between the 2 years shown.

P10-6B. *Calculate and analyze financial ratios. (LO 3)*
The following information was taken from the annual report of ROM.

	At December 31, (in thousands) 2008
ASSETS:	
Current assets:	
Cash	$ 1,220
Accounts receivable	3,112
Merchandise inventory	966
Prepaid expenses	149
Total current assets	5,447
Plant and equipment:	
Buildings, net	2,992
Equipment, net	1,045
Total plant and equipment	4,037
Total assets	$ 9,484
LIABILITIES:	
Current liabilities:	
Accounts payable	$ 1,685
Notes payable	1,100
Total current liabilities	2,785
Long-term liabilities	2,000
Total liabilities	4,785
STOCKHOLDERS' EQUITY:	
Common stock, no par value	3,042
Retained earnings	1,657
Total stockholders' equity	4,699
Total liabilities and stockholders' equity	$ 9,484
Sales for the year	$10,200
Cost of goods sold	6,750
Total assets at Dec. 31, 2007	8,980
Total liabilities at Dec. 31, 2007	4,535
Total stockholders' equity at Dec. 31, 2007	4,445

Required

  a. Calculate the following ratios for 2008:
1. Debt-to-equity ratio
2. Gross profit percentage
3. Current ratio
4. Acid-test ratio

  b. What do the ratios indicate about the success of ROM? What additional information would be useful to help you analyze the overall performance of this company?

Excel Template
www.prenhall.com/reimers

P10-7B. *Calculate and analyze financial ratios. (LO 3)*
The financial statements of Builder Bob's include the following items.

At	Sept. 30, 2008	Sept. 30, 2007
Balance sheet:		
Cash	$ 27,000	$ 22,000
Investments (short-term)	15,000	12,000
Accounts receivable (net)	44,000	40,000
Inventory	85,000	75,000
Prepaid rent	6,000	2,000
Total current assets	$177,000	$151,000
Total current liabilities	$120,000	$ 80,000

Income statement for the year ended September 30, 2008:

Net credit sales	$320,000
Cost of goods sold	150,000

Required

  a. Compute the following ratios for the year ended September 30, 2008, and September 30, 2007. For each, indicate if the direction is favorable or unfavorable for the company.
1. Current ratio
2. Quick ratio
3. Accounts receivable turnover (2008 only)
4. Inventory turnover ratio (2008 only)
5. Gross margin percentage (2008 only)

  b. Which financial statement users would be most interested in these ratios?

  c. Suppose the industry average for similar retail stores for the current ratio is 1.2. Does this information help you evaluate Builder Bob's liquidity?

P10-8B. *Calculate and analyze financial ratios. (LO 5)*

You are interested in investing in Apples and Nuts Company, and you have obtained the balance sheets for the company for the past 2 years.

Apples and Nuts Company
Balance Sheet
At December 31, 2008 and 2007

	2008	2007
Current assets		
Cash	$ 98,000	$ 90,000
Accounts receivable, net	310,000	216,000
Inventory	275,000	170,000
Prepaid rent	10,000	6,000
Total current assets	693,000	482,000
Equipment, net	180,000	258,000
Total assets	$873,000	$740,000
Total current liabilities	$206,000	$223,000
Long-term liabilities	219,000	217,000
Total liabilities	425,000	440,000
Common stockholders' equity	250,000	190,000
Retained earnings	198,000	110,000
Total liabilities and stockholders' equity	$873,000	$740,000

Net income for the year ended December 31, 2008 was $100,000.

Required

a. Compute as many of the financial statement ratios you have studied as possible with the information from Apples and Nuts Company. (Compute 2008 ratios.)

b. Would you invest in this company? Why or why not? What additional information would be helpful in making this decision?

Critical Thinking Problems

Risk and Control

Think about the risks of investing in a company and about the information provided by the financial ratios you studied in this chapter. Which financial ratios do you believe might give you information about the risk of investing in a company? Comment on those ratios from Staples and Office Depot, which you calculated at the end of the chapter in the Chapter Summary Problem.

Ethics

Atlantis Company sells computer components and plans on borrowing some money to expand. After reading a lot about earnings management, Andy, the owner of Atlantis, has decided he should try to accelerate some sales to improve his financial statement ratios. He has called his best customers and asked them to make their usual January purchases by December 31. Andy told the customers he would allow them until the end of February to pay for the purchases, just as if they had made their purchases in January.

a. What do you think are the ethical implications of Andy's actions?

b. Which ratios will be improved by accelerating these sales?

Group Assignment

In groups, try to identify the type of company that is most likely indicated by the ratios shown below. The four types of companies represented are: retail grocery, heavy machinery, restaurant, and drug manufacturer. Make notes on the arguments to support your position so that you can share them in a class discussion.

	Gross Margin Ratio	(Long-term) Debt-to-Equity Ratio	Accounts Receivable Turnover Ratio	Inventory Turnover Ratio	Return on Equity
1	82.9%	25%	5.5 times	1.5 times	22.9%
2	33.7%	134%	49.3 times	11.2 times	3.6%
3	25.3%	147%	2.3 times	5.0 times	5.0%
4	37.4%	62%	34.9 times	32.9 times	15.7%

Internet Exercise: Papa John's International

Papa John's has surpassed Little Caesars to become the number three pizza chain, behind only number one Pizza Hut and number two Domino's Pizza. Papa John's 2,800 restaurants (about 75% are franchised) are scattered across the United States and 10 other countries. Examine how Papa John's compares with its competition.

IE 10-1. Go to www.papajohns.com and explore "Papa John's Story" and "Our Pizza Story." What differentiates Papa John's from its competition?

IE 10-2. Go to http://moneycentral.msn.com and get the stock quote for PZZA, Papa John's stock symbol. Identify the current price-to-earnings ratio and dividend yield ratio. What do these market indicators mean for Papa John's?

IE 10-3. Select "Financial Results" and then "Key Ratios."
   a. Select "Financial Condition." Calculate the current ratio and quick (acid-test) ratio for Papa John's and the industry. Who would find these ratios of primary interest? Identify the debt-to-equity ratio and interest coverage ratio (another name for times-interest-earned ratio) for Papa John's and the industry. Is Papa John's primarily financed by debt or equity? How can you tell? Does Papa John's have the ability to pay its interest obligations? Explain why or why not.
   b. Select "Investment Returns." Identify return on equity and return on assets for Papa John's and the industry. What do these ratios measure?
   c. Select "Ten-Year Summary." Review the information provided for return on equity and return on assets. What additional information is revealed about Papa John's financial position? Is this information helpful?

IE 10-4. Review the information recorded earlier. Does Papa John's compare favorably with industry averages? Support your judgment with at least two observations.

Please note: Internet Web sites are constantly being updated. Therefore, if the information is not found where indicated, please explore the Web site further to find information.

Appendix 10A

Comprehensive Income

In the chapter, you learned that the Financial Accounting Standards Board (FASB) has defined two items that companies need to separate from regular earnings on financial statements: discontinued operations and extraordinary items. There is a third item—**comprehensive income**.

Even though most transactions that affect shareholders' equity are found on the income statement—revenues and expenses—there are a small number of transactions that affect shareholders' equity that are excluded from the calculation of net income. We already know about two of them:

1. Owners making contributions (paid-in capital)
2. Owners receiving dividends

In addition to these two, there are several other transactions that affect equity without going through the income statement. The most common examples of these transactions are (1) unrealized gains and losses from foreign currency translations and (2) unrealized gains and losses on certain investments. Rather than including either of these kinds of gains and losses on the income statement, they are reported as a direct adjustment to equity. The reason is that these items do not really reflect a firm's performance, so firms have lobbied to have them kept out of the calculation of earnings. To keep these transactions from getting lost among all the financial statement numbers, the FASB requires the reporting of net income plus these other transactions that affect shareholders' equity in an amount called comprehensive income. Comprehensive income includes all changes in shareholders' equity during a period except those changes in equity resulting from contributions by shareholders and distributions to shareholders. There are two parts of comprehensive income: net income and *other comprehensive income*. We know what types of transactions are included in net income—revenues, expenses, discontinued operations, and extraordinary items. Items included in other comprehensive income include unrealized gains and losses from foreign currency translation and unrealized gains and losses on certain types of investments. Exhibit 10A.1 shows all of the items that affect shareholders' equity.

> **Comprehensive income** The total of all items that affect shareholders' equity except transactions with the owners; comprehensive income has two parts: net income and other comprehensive income.

What is the purpose of having a statement of comprehensive income rather than a simple income statement?

Your Turn
Your Turn
Your Turn

EXHIBIT 10.A1

Comprehensive Income

The items in the left column appear on the financial statements in the equity classifications shown in the right column.

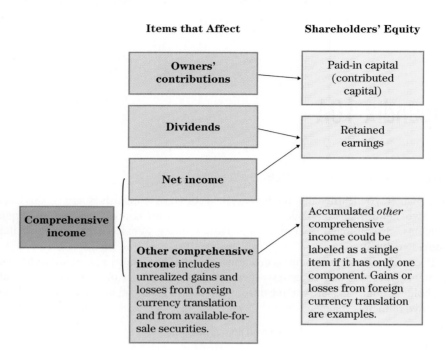

Appendix 10B

Investments in Securities

You have learned that certain gains and losses related to investments may be included in other comprehensive income. We will take a closer look at how a firm accounts for its investments in the securities of another firm. You will see how gains and losses on some of these investments are reported as part of comprehensive income.

When interest rates are low, a company's extra cash—cash not immediately needed—may earn more in the stock market or bond market than it would in a bank savings account or certificate of deposit. That is when a company buys stocks and bonds of other companies with its extra cash. For entities such as banks and insurance companies, investing cash in other companies is a crucial part of managing their assets. As you learned in previous chapters, stocks are equity securities and bonds are debt securities. Both may be purchased with a company's extra cash. When a company buys another company's debt securities or less than 20% of its equity securities, the accounting rules require firms to classify their investments in securities into one of three categories: held to maturity, trading, and available for sale.

Held-to-Maturity Securities

Sometimes a company purchases debt securities and intends to keep them until they mature. Recall that all bonds have a maturity date, but equity securities do not. If a company has the intention of keeping the securities until maturity and their financial condition indicates that they should be able to do this, the securities will be classified as **held-to-maturity securities**. Such investments are recorded at cost, and they are reported at that same amount on the balance sheet—plus or minus any unamortized discount or premium. No matter how much held-to-maturity investments are worth on the market, a company will always report them at amortized cost when preparing its balance sheet.

Held-to-maturity securities Investments in debt securities that the company plans to hold until they mature.

Trading Securities

If a company buys the securities solely to trade them and make a short-term profit, the company will classify them as **trading securities**. The balance sheet shows trading securities at their market value. A company obtains the current value of the investments from *The Wall Street Journal* or a similar source of market prices. Those values are then shown on the balance sheet. Updating the accounting records to show the securities at their market value is called *marking to market*. If the securities' cost is lower than market value, then the company will record the difference as an unrealized gain. If the securities' cost is higher than market value, then the company will record the difference as an unrealized loss. Remember, *realizing* means actually getting something. Any gain or loss on an investment the company is holding (holding means *not* selling) is something the company does not get (a gain) or does not give up (a loss) until the company sells the securities. **Unrealized gains or losses** are gains or losses on securities that have not been sold. Such a gain or loss may also be called a *holding gain* or *loss*. The unrealized gains and losses from trading securities are reported on the income statement.

Trading securities Investments in debt and equity securities that the company has purchased to make a short-term profit.

Unrealized gain or loss An increase or decrease in the market value of a company's investments in securities is recognized either on the income statement—for trading securities—or in other comprehensive income in the equity section of the balance sheet—for available-for-sale securities—when the financial statements are prepared, even though the securities have *not* been sold.

For example, suppose Avia Company has invested $130,000 of its extra cash in securities—stocks and bonds traded on the stock and bond markets. At the end of the year, the securities that cost Avia $130,000 have a market value of $125,000. On the income statement for the year, Avia will show an unrealized loss of $5,000. The loss is recorded in an adjustment made before the financial statements are prepared.

The securities' new value of $125,000 (originally $130,000 minus loss of $5,000) has replaced their original cost. Now, $125,000 will be the "cost" and will be compared to the market value on the date of the next balance sheet. Remember, the company purchased these trading securities as investments to trade in the short run, so the firm's investment portfolio is likely to look very different at the next balance sheet date.

Available-for-Sale Securities

Available-for-sale securities Investments the company may hold or sell; the company's intention is not clear enough to use one of the other categories—*held to maturity* or *trading*.

Sometimes a company is not sure how long it will keep the debt or equity securities it has purchased. If the company does not intend to sell the securities in the short term for a quick profit or does not intend to hold them until maturity, the company will classify the securities as **available for sale**. Every year, when it is time to prepare the annual balance sheet, the cost of this group of securities is compared to the market value at the balance sheet date. The book value of the securities is then adjusted to market value, and the corresponding gain or loss is reported in shareholders' equity. Such a gain or loss is called an *unrealized* or *holding* gain or loss, just as it is called for trading securities. But these gains and losses do not go on the income statement. Instead, they are included as part of accumulated other comprehensive income in the shareholders' equity section of the balance sheet.

Your Turn
Your Turn
Your Turn

A corporation has invested $50,000 in the securities of other companies. At the end of the year, that corporation's portfolio has a market value of $52,000. Describe where these securities would be shown on the annual financial statements and at what amount under each of the conditions described.

1. The investment is classified as trading securities.
2. The investment is classified as available for sale.
3. The investment is classified as held to maturity.

Suppose Avia Company classified its portfolio of securities that cost $130,000 as available for sale. If the market value of the securities is $125,000 at the date of the balance sheet, the securities must be shown on the balance sheet at the lower amount. In this case, the unrealized loss will *not* be shown on the income statement. Instead of going through net income to retained earnings, the loss will go through comprehensive income to accumulated other comprehensive income in the shareholders' equity section of the balance sheet. The loss will be shown after retained earnings, either alone—and labeled as an unrealized loss from investments in securities—or combined with other nonincome statement gains and losses—and labeled as accumulated other comprehensive income.

Selling the Securities

When a firm sells any of these securities—trading, available for sale, and held to maturity—the gain or loss on the sale is calculated like other accounting gains and losses. The book value of the security at the time of the sale is compared to the selling price. The selling price is often called the proceeds from the sale. If the book value is greater than the proceeds, the firm will record a loss on the sale. If the book value is less than the proceeds, the firm will record a gain on the sale. Gains and losses from the actual sale of the securities are both *realized*—the sale has actually happened—and *recognized*—the relevant amounts are shown on the income statement.

Quality of Earnings and Corporate Governance

Here's Where You've Been . . .

You learned to analyze a set of financial statements using vertical analysis, horizontal analysis, and ratio analysis.

Here's Where You're Going . . .

You will learn how to explain quality of earnings.
You will learn to identify the characteristics of high-quality earnings.
You will learn about the current issues related to corporate governance.

Learning Objectives

When you are finished studying this chapter, you should be able to:

1. Explain Wall Street's emphasis on earnings and the potential problems that result from this emphasis.

2. Define quality of earnings and explain how it is measured.

3. Recognize the common ways that firms can manipulate earnings.

4. Describe the corporate accounting failures of the early 2000s.

5. Explain the requirements of the Sarbanes-Oxley Act of 2002.

6. Evaluate a firm's corporate governance.

Ethics Matters

Would you blow the whistle on fraud? In 2002, Sherron Watkins of Enron, Cynthia Cooper of WorldCom, and Coleen Rowley of the FBI were *Time* magazine's "People of the Year 2002." These women were credited with blowing the whistle on fraud in their respective organizations. The Sarbanes-Oxley Act of 2002 requires that firms have a hotline to make it easier for whistle-blowers to anonymously report any suspicious actions or behavior going on in the company, particularly as it pertains to financial information. Having such a hotline has provided unintended benefits to many companies, including Fisher Communications. Fisher Communications is a Seattle-based broadcaster with radio and TV stations in Washington, Oregon, Idaho, and Montana. The company started using EthicsPoint, a firm that provides hotlines services, to check on a laundry list of potential problems: accounting, conflict of interest, discrimination, embezzlement, falsification of contracts, reports or records, sabotage or vandalism, securities violations, substance abuse, theft, violence, and threats. The broad scope helps keep executives in touch with problems throughout a company so they can stop problems before they harm employees or stockholders.

L.O.1

Explain Wall Street's emphasis on earnings and the potential problems that result from this emphasis.

Why Are Earnings Important?

You have learned about the four basic financial statements and the notes to the financial statements. To wrap up your introduction to financial accounting, we are going to step back and look at the big picture. What do investors focus on when they evaluate a firm's financial statements? How accurate is the information? Who, or what, stands behind the information to assure investors that it is truthful and reliable? These are just a few questions we will consider in this chapter. We start with the market's focus on earnings, which appears on the income statement.

How often have you read or heard about a firm's earnings? Managers estimate earnings and disclose those estimates to the public. Financial analysts study managements' earnings estimates and announce their own expected earnings for the firm. Among the hundreds of measurements shareholders consider—gross domestic product (GDP), housing starts, interest rates, unemployment figures, and budget deficits, to name a few—there is one number that Wall Street simply calls "the number." A firm's stock price moves up when earnings exceed analysts' forecasts and down when reported earnings do not meet the forecasts. According to Alex Berenson, a financial reporter for *The New York Times* and author of *The Number: How the Drive for Quarterly Earnings Corrupted Wall Street and Corporate America*, "Earnings per share is the number for which all other numbers are sacrificed. It is the distilled truth of a company's health. Earnings per share is the number that counts. Too bad it's a lie." Accountants define **earnings per share** as net income divided by the weighted average number of outstanding shares of (common) stock.

Earnings per share (EPS) Net income divided by the weighted average number of outstanding shares of (common) stock.

As Berenson points out, earnings alone cannot accurately reveal the state of a firm's financial performance. A narrow focus on a single number can result in serious miscommunication between the firm and its investors. However, reported earnings have a real effect on a firm's stock price.

Your Turn 11-1
Your Turn
Your Turn

Describe why earnings is such an important number.

The Quality of Earnings

As you have learned, investors typically use earnings per share to evaluate a firm's performance. How accurate and reliable is this number? **Quality of earnings** is a term accountants use to describe how well a reported earnings number communicates the firm's true performance. The quality of earnings is a subjective concept, and few people agree on the definition. Bernstein and Wild, two accounting authors,[1] identify three ways to evaluate the quality of earnings.

1. Firms that make more conservative choices of accounting principles often have a higher quality of earnings.
2. Firms that face fewer internal and external risks that threaten their survival and profitability often have a higher quality of earnings.
3. Firms that recognize revenue early or postpone recognition of expenses often have a lower quality of earnings.

Sometimes the accounting choices managers make are classified as conservative or aggressive. Conservative choices are those that reduce net income and assets or increase liabilities. Aggressive choices are those that increase net income and assets or decrease liabilities. Potentially understating income or assets is more conservative than potentially overstating income or assets. Can you see why this is true? If a firm overstates earnings, shareholders may sue the firm and its auditors; but if a firm understates earnings, shareholders are less likely to be disappointed. Higher-quality earnings are associated with more conservative accounting choices. Here are some examples.

Recall that a firm must estimate the useful life and salvage value of depreciable assets, make inventory cost flow assumptions such as LIFO or FIFO, and estimate bad debts expense. Each of these choices will affect the quality of the firm's reported earnings. Consider a capital-intensive company in the manufacturing sector. Firms such as General Motors and Dow Chemical have huge investments in property, plant, and equipment. The income statements for these firms will have a significant amount of depreciation expense for manufacturing facilities and equipment. The amount of that expense will depend on how management estimates the useful lives of the assets. What kind of choices would make earnings appear larger? The longer the estimated useful lives of property, plant, and equipment, the smaller the annual depreciation expense. The smaller the depreciation expense, the larger the reported earnings. In cases such as depreciation, the more discretion management has, the more potential there is for a lower quality of the related earnings. Having more depreciable assets means more estimates and potentially a lower quality of earnings because managers can make choices that increase or decrease earnings.

In other cases, a manager views a particular choice as producing higher-quality earnings than another. Consider inventory methods. When a company chooses FIFO, the older inventory costs are matched with the sales revenue on the income statement. When a company chooses LIFO, however, the more recent costs are shown on the income statement. Which method produces a higher quality of earnings number? Analysts generally believe that LIFO produces a better income statement number because the costs used are more current and, therefore, LIFO produces a higher quality of earnings number than FIFO produces.

Next, we will discuss three common ways that firms can manipulate earnings, reducing the quality of their earnings. Then, we will turn to the Sarbanes-Oxley Act, the goal of which is to increase the quality of earnings and make financial reporting more transparent.

L.O.2
Define quality of earnings and explain how it is measured.

Quality of earnings Refers to how well a reported earnings number communicates the firm's true performance.

What makes one firm's earnings higher in quality than another's?

Your Turn 11-2
Your Turn
Your Turn

---

[1] Leopold Bernstein and John Wild, *2000 Analysis of Financial Statements* (New York: McGraw-Hill, 2000).

L.O.3
Recognize the common
ways that firms can
manipulate earnings.

Common Ways to Manipulate Earnings

You have learned that investors are concerned about the quality of firms' earnings. *Business Week's* cover on October 4, 2004, showed a magician's hat with the title "Fuzzy Numbers." Here is how the article described how difficult it is to understand a firm's financial statements: "The problem with today's fuzzy earnings numbers is not accrual accounting itself. It's that investors, analysts, and money managers are having an increasingly hard time figuring out what judgments companies make to come up with those accruals, or estimates." To help you increase your understanding of the fuzzy numbers on the financial statements, we will look at three specific accounting procedures that often reduce the quality of earnings. Unfortunately, firms often use these procedures to "cook the books." **Cooking the books** is a slang term that means to manipulate or falsify the accounting records to make the company's financial performance look better than it actually is. Although there are numerous activities used to manage earnings, many of which can be very complicated, the Securities and Exchange Commission identifies three activities that deserve special attention when you are evaluating a company's financial performance.

Cooking the books A slang expression that means to manipulate or falsify the firm's accounting records to make the firm's financial performance or position look better than it actually is.

1. Big bath charges
2. Cookie jar reserves
3. Revenue recognition

Big Bath Charges

The expression "big bath charges" was made famous among accountants in a 1998 speech by then chairman of the SEC, Arthur Levitt, to the New York University Center for Law and Business. According to the big bath theory of corporate financial reporting, one way to manage earnings is to maximize a current loss by recording expenses that actually belong on future income statements.

When a firm is not going to meet its earnings expectations, the firm's managers "clean up" the balance sheet by writing off any expense that looks like it may need to be written off in the next few years. The reasoning goes something like this: As long as our firm is going to be punished by Wall Street for missing our earnings number, we might as well go ahead and miss it big. That will help us in the future by moving as many expenses as we can from future periods into the current period.

Accounting researchers have found evidence to support this practice by studying firms that either exceed or miss the analysts' forecasts. There are a significant number of firms that just make their earnings forecast by a very small margin. However, when a firm misses its earnings forecast, the amount by which it misses is larger, on average, than the margin for firms that make their forecasts. This is consistent with the idea of taking a *big* bath as long as you are getting in the tub.

How can you identify the big bath type of accounting practice? Read the following material.

- Several years of financial statements rather than just a single year, and look for unusual expenses and write-offs that appear out of step with previous years
- The notes to the financial statements
- Management's discussion and analysis about the company's performance in newspaper and business magazines

Cookie Jar Reserves

Another way to manage earnings is to use reserve accounts to record expenses early and make future earnings look good. Using reserve accounts is a way to stash away amounts that can help the firm increase earnings in the future if, and when, the earnings are needed to meet earnings forecasts. You learned about the allowance method for estimating bad debts. A firm with a significant amount of uncollectible accounts must estimate future bad debts related to current sales so that the bad debts expense can be recorded in the same period as the sales to which it relates. Because bad debts expense is an estimate, and the corresponding amount is recorded in a reserve called the allowance for uncollectible accounts, this accounting rule creates an opportunity for a firm to "manage" one of its expenses and, consequently, manipulate earnings.

Suppose a firm had credit sales of $1,000,000 in Year 1 and estimated that related bad debts would be 5% of sales, or $50,000. The firm would record the following.

Assets	=	Liabilities	+	Shareholder's equity	
				Contributed capital	+ Retained earnings
Allowance for uncollectible accounts (50,000)					Bad debts expense (50,000)

This would reduce income by $50,000 in Year 1. During Year 2, as the actual customers who will not pay are identified and written off, no bad debts expense is recorded. Instead, the accounts are written off against the allowance for uncollectible accounts. Suppose that during Year 2, $48,000 worth of accounts are written off, leaving a balance of $2,000 in the allowance for uncollectible accounts. Now, at the end of Year 2, the firm must estimate its future bad debts from credit sales in Year 2. Whatever the estimate, the bad debts expense recorded for Year 2 will be $2,000 less than the estimate because the reserve—the allowance for uncollectible accounts—still has $2,000 left over from Year 1. (This example assumes the firm uses the accounts receivable method of estimating bad debts expense.)

Now go back to Year 1 and suppose that the firm is having a very poor year and it will definitely miss the analysts' earnings forecasts for the year. When the firm's accountant is recording the bad debts expense for the year, there may be a temptation to record an amount that exceeds the actual estimate. Why? As long as Year 1 is a bad year, the firm might as well take as many expenses as possible to help the future. Suppose the firm recorded $60,000 worth of bad debts expense. The same amount will be recorded in the allowance for uncollectible accounts. Now if $48,000 worth of bad debts are actually written off in Year 2, the balance in the allowance for uncollectible accounts will be $12,000 rather than $2,000—if the allowance for uncollectible accounts had been recorded at the correct estimate of $50,000. The firm now has a cushion of $12,000 to reduce Year 2's bad debts expense if it needs it to increase earnings in Year 2. Using a reserve such as the allowance for uncollectible accounts to manipulate or to smooth earnings is a common way to use cookie jar reserves.

Cookie jar reserves and big bath charges are both ways for firms to allocate expenses to different accounting periods to provide the most benefit. Sometimes a firm has a goal of smoothing earnings, and other times a firm wants to shift expenses from the future to the present to improve future earnings.

How can you tell if a firm is using cookie jar reserves? Watch for trends in the reported amounts for these reserves. Often, the specific amounts are not shown in the statements but are given in the detailed notes to the financial statements. Analyzing changes in ratios related to the reserves may also be helpful.

Revenue Recognition

A third way to manage earnings is to use improper revenue recognition techniques. In the first few chapters, you learned that GAAP allows a firm to recognize revenue when (1) the firm has earned it and (2) collection is reasonably assured. This accounting principle leaves some room for interpretation and judgment. A firm might violate this principle by recognizing revenue prematurely or by creating totally fictitious revenue. These two possibilities represent two ends of a continuum—a continuum that is a "slippery slope." Improperly recognizing revenue can help a firm meet analysts' earnings forecasts and keep the firm's stock price rising. There are cases of executives making millions of dollars by selling their stock in the firm when the stock price was inflated due to fraudulent earnings.

Here are some examples of how firms have improperly recognized revenue.

- Recorded sales of merchandise at the end of the quarter, but the goods were not delivered to the customer until the beginning of the following quarter
- Routinely kept their books open after the end of the accounting period to continue recording sales until the sales goals for the period were met
- Recorded sales of merchandise shipped to customers who had not placed orders for the merchandise
- Shipped goods to salespeople in the field and recorded the sales even though the salespeople had not delivered the goods to customers
- Shipped goods off-site to locations they controlled and recorded those shipments as sales revenue
- Created fictitious documents for both the purchase of goods and the subsequent sale of those goods to fictitious customers

When you analyze a firm's financial statements, how can you identify these types of revenue recognition problems? First, firms disclose their revenue recognition policies in the first note of the notes to the financial statements. If a firm has recently changed its revenue recognition policy, you should study the reasons and review the prior years' revenue patterns. Analyzing the relationship between sales and accounts receivable is quite useful in identifying early or fictitious revenue recognition. If accounts receivable as a percentage of sales is increasing, you should be concerned. Every industry or business sector has its own type of revenue recognition problem. You need to understand the way revenue is recognized in your company's accounting system to know the potential for problems with early or late revenue recognition.

What We Learned from the Business Scandals of the Early 2000s

L.O.4
Describe the corporate accounting failures of the early 2000s.

Even with the concern over quality of earnings and managers' potential to manipulate earnings with a big bath, cookie jar reserves, or improper revenue recognition, Congress has rarely interfered with accounting standards. Until recently, the 1933 and 1934 Securities Acts were the governing laws for publicly traded firms and their auditors. However, the scandals and financial failures of the early 2000s prompted Congress to pass the Sarbanes-Oxley Act of 2002. Sponsored by Senator Paul Sarbanes of Maryland, now retired, and Congressman Michael Oxley of Ohio, the Act brought the topic of corporate governance into the headlines.

Corporate governance has many definitions. Simply stated, it is the way a firm governs itself, as executed by the board of directors. **Corporate governance** has been defined as a process carried out by the board of directors to provide direction and oversight on behalf of all the company's stakeholders—owners, suppliers, and customers. The term has also been defined as a set of relationships between the board of directors, management, shareholders, auditors, and any others with a stake in the company. Corporate governance is not a new concept—corporations have been governing themselves for years. However, recent scandals have brought the topic to the attention of the media, government officials, and general public.

Corporate governance The way a firm governs itself, as executed by the board of directors. Corporate governance is also described as the set of relationships between the board of directors, management, shareholders, auditors, and any others with a stake in the company.

Accounting scandals and the resulting business failures are not a modern-day phenomenon. One of the biggest business failures in history occurred in 1931, when Insull Utility Investment collapsed under the weight of a complex corporate structure held together by creative accounting. At the time, the press dubbed Insull the biggest business failure in the history of the world. Fast forward to 2001—the collapse of one of the world's largest energy companies, Enron—and to 2002—the bankruptcy of WorldCom. These failures are huge and have had an enormous impact on our economy and the employees of the companies, but failures are not new. However, there are lessons to be learned from them.

See if you can find a recent update on the scandals shown in Exhibit 1.18 in Chapter 1. One of the best ways you can be an intelligent investor, manager, or employee is to stay up to date. Read current financial publications and keep up with news events. One of the positive things to come out of these business failures and scandals is the increased attention the news media gives business issues.

News Flash

Ken Lay's death on July 5, 2006, saved him from prison. But did you know that it also saved him from being legally convicted of his Enron crimes? According to legal precedent, because a dead person has not had the chance to appeal a conviction, he is considered innocent. In legal terms, Lay was not indicted, tried, or convicted of any crime related to Enron.

[Source: "Lay Cheats Justice," by Christopher Helman, *Forbes.com*, July 5, 2006.]

What have we learned from the business failures of the past decade? Here is just a sampling.

1. Some corporate executives will do almost anything to meet earnings expectations and keep the firm's stock price stable or rising. Often, the goal is one of personal enrichment through the executives' exercise of options and the sale of company stock.
2. The ethical climate in a firm is set by top management. Chief executive officers and chief financial officers must establish and demand the integrity of the firm's disclosures—both financial and nonfinancial.
3. Auditors and their clients can get too close. An auditor's independence is a necessary condition for a meaningful audit, and auditing firms need to take a close look at the relationship(s) between a firm and its external auditors.
4. Application of GAAP is subject to significant management discretion, and firms must make their earnings more transparent.
5. No matter how good or how effective the accounting principles are, there is no way for accounting standards to stop fraud. Auditors and the SEC, however, may be able to make some progress in reducing fraud.
6. Financial statements are only part of the information investors and creditors need to evaluate a company's past, present, and future. Overreliance on a single amount—earnings per share—can be a disaster.

As they did in the 1930s with the passage of the Securities Acts of 1933 and 1934, Congress responded to the corporate failures that came to light in the early 2000s with a new law—the Sarbanes-Oxley Act of 2002. As you read about the law, think about the problems it is meant to address.

What do you think auditors have learned from the recent financial failures?

The Sarbanes-Oxley Act of 2002

No one will be able to navigate successfully in the business world without some knowledge of the Sarbanes-Oxley Act of 2002. All publicly traded companies and any international companies that trade on the U.S. stock exchanges must comply with this law. Exhibit 11.1 summarizes the key provisions of the law. We will look at the major groups affected by the Sarbanes-Oxley Act and discuss how the law affects them.

Key Players in Corporate Governance

The Sarbanes-Oxley (SOX) Act has significant implications for four groups.

1. Management
   • The CEO and CFO are responsible for the firm's internal controls. The SOX Act requires the company to include, with its annual report, a separate report on the

Your Turn 11-3
Your Turn
Your Turn

L.O.5
Explain the requirements of the Sarbanes-Oxley Act of 2002.

EXHIBIT 11.1

Key Provisions of the Sarbanes-Oxley Act of 2002

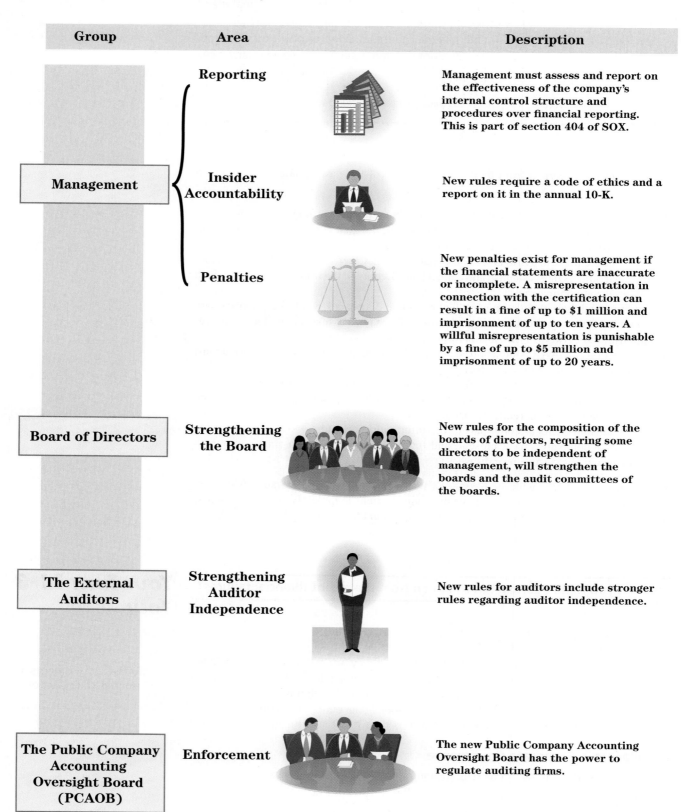

Group	Area		Description
Management	**Reporting**		Management must assess and report on the effectiveness of the company's internal control structure and procedures over financial reporting. This is part of section 404 of SOX.
	Insider Accountability		New rules require a code of ethics and a report on it in the annual 10-K.
	Penalties		New penalties exist for management if the financial statements are inaccurate or incomplete. A misrepresentation in connection with the certification can result in a fine of up to $1 million and imprisonment of up to ten years. A willful misrepresentation is punishable by a fine of up to $5 million and imprisonment of up to 20 years.
Board of Directors	**Strengthening the Board**		New rules for the composition of the boards of directors, requiring some directors to be independent of management, will strengthen the boards and the audit committees of the boards.
The External Auditors	**Strengthening Auditor Independence**		New rules for auditors include stronger rules regarding auditor independence.
The Public Company Accounting Oversight Board (PCAOB)	**Enforcement**		The new Public Company Accounting Oversight Board has the power to regulate auditing firms.

effectiveness of the company's internal controls. The firm's external auditors must attest to the accuracy of the internal control report.

- Management has the ultimate responsibility for the accuracy of the financial statements and the accompanying notes. In most firms, that responsibility is delegated to lower-level managers, but top management cannot escape ultimate legal responsibility. SOX requires the CEO and the CFO to certify the annual financial statements—they will swear that they have reviewed the statements and that, based on their knowledge, the report does not contain any false statements and does not omit any significant facts.

- Firms must provide a mechanism for the anonymous reporting of fraudulent activities in the company, including a hotline for the reporting. Whistle-blower protection is extended to company employees who lawfully disclose information that the employee reasonably believes constitutes a violation of securities laws or any law that deals with fraud against shareholders. According to SOX, no officer or agent of the company may "discharge, demote, suspend, threaten, harass, or in any other manner discriminate against an employee in the terms and conditions of employment because of any lawful act done by the employee." That means that the company cannot punish a person in any way for blowing the whistle—disclosing suspected fraud in the company.

2. The board of directors (BOD)

- These are the people who are elected by stockholders to establish general corporate policies and make decisions on major company issues, such as dividend policies. Members of the board are elected by the shareholders to represent the interests of shareholders.

- The part of the board of directors responsible for overseeing the financial matters of the firm is the audit committee. Members of this committee are concerned with the firm's controls over financial reporting and with overseeing the external auditors.

- SOX requires the audit committee to be made up of independent directors from the board of directors. Company managers cannot be on the committee. The audit committee is responsible for hiring, compensating, and overseeing the work of any public accounting firm hired by the company.

3. External auditors

- These are accountants specifically trained to examine the firm's financial statements and financial controls and report on the statements to the shareholders. External auditors give an opinion on whether or not the firm's financial statements fairly present the financial position and the results of operations in accordance with GAAP. As you know, the SEC requires all publicly traded firms to have an annual audit of the financial statements by external auditors.

- SOX requires that auditors remain independent of their clients to ensure objectivity. The SEC has always had rules about auditor independence, but the new law strengthens these rules. For example, auditors can no longer provide information processing or bookkeeping services to its audit clients.

- SOX also requires that the auditor report to the client's audit committee, which is part of the board of directors, rather than to the client's management team.

4. Public Company Accounting Oversight Board (PCAOB)

- This regulatory group was established by the SOX Act. Members are appointed by the SEC in consultation with the Chairman of the Board of Governors of the Federal Reserve System and the Secretary of the Treasury.

- The purpose of the PCAOB is to regulate the auditing profession.

- All accounting firms that audit publicly traded companies must register with the PCAOB and follow its rules.

- The SEC must approve any rules set by the PCAOB.

The purpose of the Sarbanes-Oxley Act is to strengthen financial reporting and the corporate governance of publicly traded companies. However, there are some potential disadvantages of the new requirements. Most of the arguments against the new law center on the high cost of implementing Section 404. Some people argue that the real problem in

News Flash

HCA, a large hospital operator, has announced a $21 billion plan to go from a publicly traded company to a private firm. Why? One reason given by the company's founder, Thomas First, is the "untenable cost of complying with Sarbanes-Oxley."

[Source: "Regulation, Yes. Strangulation, No.," by Maurice R. Greenberg, *The Wall Street Journal*, August 21, 2006, p. A10.]

corporate America is the lack of high moral and ethical values, which cannot be solved with this legislation.

Outlook for the Future

We are living in a time when the way companies do business is changing. The importance of accounting and financial reporting is unquestionable. All business managers—marketing managers, production managers, human resource managers, operations managers—must be able to understand financial information and the way it is gathered and reported. All business managers must identify risks for their specific areas and create internal controls to manage those risks. For example, a marketing manager must be aware of how the accounting is done for sales commissions in order to evaluate the accuracy of a salesperson's weekly sales report. Perhaps the accounting department pays the salespeople their commissions each Monday for sales submitted by noon on the previous Friday. There is a risk that the salesperson will include sales that are scheduled to be completed by the end of the day on Friday so that the Friday afternoon sales will be included in Monday's payment. A control for this would be to match the salesperson's report of sales to the shipping department's weekly shipments. Recall that, in general, revenue is not recognized until the goods are shipped. Commissions to the salespeople should be paid on amounts of revenue the firm has actually earned.

Firms spend a tremendous amount of money to comply with the Sarbanes-Oxley Act's rules and regulations. According to a July 28, 2006, article on CFO.com, the cost of compliance has declined slightly from 2005 to 2006—from $6.1 billion in 2005 to $6 billion in 2006. AMR Research Inc., who conducted the survey that produced this data, expects costs to start a gradual descent in 2007. Recent reports indicate that it is very difficult for a firm to calculate the total costs of implementing SOX.[2] Recognizing the high cost of compliance for smaller firms, current SEC chairman, Christopher Cox, announced (as this book goes to press) his support for a 1-year delay for certain small firms to comply with the internal control provisions of SOX.

The new climate and new laws have resulted in a surge in employment opportunities for accounting and auditing firms. According to The Federal Bureau of Labor Statistics, the number of accounting jobs is expected to increase by as much as 20% by 2012. Currently, business schools are straining to attract and graduate enough accountants to meet the demand. The American Institute of Certified Public Accountants projects double-digit growth in hiring by most of its member firms for the next 3 years. Filling those jobs will not be easy, due to a shortage of accounting majors.[3]

Your Turn 11-4
Your Turn
Your Turn

Explain why internal controls are so important to firms and their auditors.

---

[2] From Carl Bialik, "How Much Is It Really Costing to Comply with Sarbanes-Oxley?", *The Wall Street Journal*, June 16, 2005.
[3] From "Who's Counting?" CFO.com, May 1, 2005.

Evaluating Corporate Governance

L.O.6
Evaluate a firm's corporate governance.

The Sarbanes-Oxley Act of 2002 changed the way corporations govern themselves in the United States. In 2005, a study[4] of the corporate governance in the top 100 firms in the FORTUNE 500 revealed that many companies are voluntarily *exceeding* new requirements. For example, in 81 of the top 100 companies, 75% or more of the boards are made up of independent directors, whereas the NYSE and NASDAQ require only a simple majority of 51%. Although boards of directors are not generally meeting more frequently, the audit committees, compensation committees, and the nominating committees met, on average, more often in 2003 than they did in 2002. These are just a few examples of changes in corporate governance in the wake of Sarbanes-Oxley. As firms evaluate the changes they must make and also decide on voluntary changes in their corporate governance, every CEO, CFO, member of a board of directors, and investor would like to know the answer to this important question: What is *good* corporate governance?

Defining and Measuring Good Corporate Governance

Most experts—managers, the SEC, and academic researchers—agree that the most important factor in good corporate governance is an ethical climate, which top management sets. Steven Baum, chairman, president, and CEO of Sempra Energy (SRE), a San Diego-based natural gas and energy supplier with 2004 revenues of over $9 billion, gives the following as the top five most important elements for strong and effective corporate governance.[5]

1. Boards of directors [should be] independent from the executive management team and composed of highly qualified directors with diverse backgrounds.
2. The CEO must encourage board involvement for the review of major management and financial decisions.
3. Financial information for shareholders should be transparent—easily understandable, simple, and straightforward.
4. Incentive-based compensation plans should offer rewards to management for performance that creates increased shareholder value.
5. External auditors should be strong and independent from the firm.

Little research exists to confirm that these, or any other, elements of corporate governance actually prevent fraud. But even if you agree that these are desirable elements, can you see how difficult it might be to measure some of these elements?

Neither lack of supporting research nor measurement difficulty has stopped the development of corporate governance rating systems. Although not yet widespread, these rating systems are gaining exposure and popularity among investors. Some of the companies involved in developing rating systems for corporate governance are Institutional Shareholder Services, Governance-Metrics International, and Moody's.

How Can We Evaluate a Firm's Corporate Governance?

There are two key ways to find out about a firm's corporate governance.

1. Web sites
2. Annual reports or 10-Ks

Many large firms post their corporate governance policies on their Web sites, where you can find menus for corporate governance guidelines, code of ethics, and various committees of the board of directors. On some Web sites, you will find information about each member of the board and of the audit, compensation, and nominating committees.

---

[4] Shearman & Sterling LLP, *Trends in the Corporate Governance Practices of the 100 Largest U.S. Public Companies*, 2005. Copies are available on the firm's web site.
[5] From "Ask the CEO," *Business Week Online*, May 6, 2003.

EXHIBIT 11.2

Firm Report on Internal Control Weaknesses as Required by Section 404 of Sarbanes-Oxley.

SunTrust's Report on Internal Control Weaknesses as required by Section 404 of Sarbanes-Oxley

(Filed with the SEC in January 2005)

SunTrust Banks —   Jan. 20   MATERIAL WEAKNESS IDENTIFIED — The Company disclosed in its Form 10-Q for the
Superregional bank.   2004 third quarter that there was a material weakness in the Company's internal controls
                                     over financial reporting relating to the process of establishing the allowance for loan and
                                     lease losses and that the Company would likely not be able to fully remediate the weakness
2003 Sales: $7.0billion   in internal controls by December 31, 2004. Although significant remedial actions have been
Auditor: PricewaterhouseCoopers   taken, SunTrust was not able to fully remediate the material weakness in internal controls
                                     as of December 31, 2004. As a result, management will disclose this material weakness in
                                     internal controls in its report in the Company's Form 10-K and indicate that the Company's
                                     internal controls over financial reporting were not effective at such date. In addition, the
                                     Company expects that the material weakness will result in an adverse opinion by the
                                     Company's independent auditors on the effectiveness of the Company's internal controls.

Another useful input to evaluate a firm's corporate governance is management's report on internal controls. An example of a report is shown in Exhibit 11.2. Notice that SunTrust mentions a material weakness in its internal control system. Recall that the word *material* means significant in accounting language. When a firm reports a material weakness in its internal control system, the firm can minimize the adverse effects by informing investors that it has fixed the problem. Since this report in 2005, SunTrust has corrected this internal control weakness, and no material weaknesses were reported in the firm's most recent report.

You read earlier in the chapter that one of the requirements of SOX is that management must report on the effectiveness of the company's system of internal controls. Also, the external auditors must attest to and issue a report on management's assessment of internal controls.

Just as the financial statements alone are insufficient to come to a conclusion about the value of a company, the corporate governance information provided by a company is not sufficient to draw any definite conclusions about the integrity and honesty of the company and its management. However, as information about how a company's corporate governance policies are working becomes more readily available, it will be easier to evaluate this area of the company.

Your Turn 11-5
Your Turn
Your Turn

Name two characteristics of good corporate governance.

You Have Come a Long Way

As you finish your study of financial accounting, look back and see how far you have come. When you started Chapter 1, you probably did not know a balance sheet from an income statement. Now you know the elements of the four basic financial statements and the principles that accountants use to prepare these statements. You have learned that the statements alone do not provide sufficient information for investors. The accompanying notes that you often see referenced at the bottom of each statement are an integral part of the financial statements. You have learned that companies can "cook the books," but also remember that the vast majority of accountants, managers, and business executives are honest people who are doing their best, often in difficult situations.

Chapter Summary Points

- Analysts and investors use earnings per share (EPS) to evaluate a firm's performance, often putting excessive weight on this amount.
- Quality of earnings refers to how well a particular earnings number communicates a firm's true performance.
- Three common ways a firm can manipulate earnings are: (1) recognizing revenue too soon, (2) using cookie jar reserves to increase or decrease earnings as desired, and (3) using big baths charges—writing off as many expenses as possible in a bad year to minimize expenses in the future.
- The corporate accounting failures of the early 2000s were the result of accounting frauds. The result was new legislation—the Sarbanes-Oxley Act of 2002—to improve corporate governance.

Key Terms for Chapter 11

Cooking the books (p. 528)   Earnings per share (p. 526)   Quality of earnings (p. 527)
Corporate governance
  (p. 530)

Answers to YOUR TURN Questions

Chapter 11
Your Turn 11-1

Earnings are used by investors to evaluate a firm's performance. The price of a firm's stock often goes up if the firm meets earnings expectations and down if the firm doesn't meet earnings expectations.

Your Turn 11-2

Earnings are a function of the choices managers make in reporting earnings. Some choices—such as LIFO for inventory in a period of rising prices—lead to a higher quality of earnings than others.

Your Turn 11-3

There are several possible answers to this question. Two important ones are (1) independence, both actual and perceived, is crucial to doing an effective and credible job, and (2) high ethical values and personal integrity are essential—in auditing and life.

Your Turn 11-4

Managers must report on the firm's internal controls and their effectiveness. Some firms may need new ways to gather information about the effectiveness of the firm's controls. The auditors must attest to management's report, which means that the auditors must gather sufficient evidence to give their opinion on the truthfulness of management's report. These are added responsibilities for the firm's managers and the firm's auditors.

Your Turn 11-5

Here are a few: (1) a board of directors (BOD) with a majority of independent directors, (2) a BOD with a chairman who is not the firm's CEO, (3) a reputable and reliable internal audit function, (4) independent external auditors, (5) a strong code of ethics, with the top management setting the tone, (6) a compensation system that does not place too much reliance on the stock price but does reward increasing the firm's underlying value.

Questions

1. What determines the quality of earnings?
2. Why are earnings so important?
3. What events motivated Congress to pass the Sarbanes-Oxley Act of 2002?
4. What is the role of the newly created Public Company Accounting Oversight Board (PCAOB)?
5. Who is responsible for establishing auditing standards for audits of public companies? Who is responsible for establishing accounting standards for public companies? Explain these two sets of standards.
6. What provisions of Sarbanes-Oxley should increase auditor independence? Explain how.
7. What changes does Sarbanes-Oxley require for a company's board of directors?
8. What are internal controls and who is responsible for their effectiveness?
9. What is the responsibility of the audit committee of the board of directors?
10. Who is responsible for certifying the financial statements filed with the SEC?
11. What is a cookie jar reserve, and how is it used?
12. What is the big bath theory?
13. When should a company recognize revenue?

Multiple-Choice Questions

1. Which of the following is a problem resulting from the emphasis on earnings?
   a. Managers may ignore sales forecasts.
   b. Internal controls may deteriorate.
   c. Quality of earnings may suffer.
   d. Responsibilities of lower-level managers may increase.
2. A publicly traded firm must have
   a. A functioning board of directors
   b. A CFO with significant accounting experience
   c. A specific time each week to meet with employees regarding potential fraud
   d. An ethics committee
3. The audit committee is
   a. Part of the internal audit function
   b. A subset of directors who must be independent
   c. No longer part of corporate governance
   d. Chaired by a CPA
4. Who is responsible for selecting, hiring, and compensating the external auditors?
   a. CEO
   b. CFO
   c. Audit committee of the BOD
   d. All of the above
5. High-quality earnings are those that
   a. Fluctuate widely between periods
   b. Provide accurate and reliable information about a firm's earnings
   c. Exceed $1 per share
   d. Are found in the shareholders' equity section of the balance sheet

Short Exercises

SE11-1. *(LO 1)*
What is the most important number a firm reports in the opinion of Wall Street analysts? What problems has this created?

SE11-2. *(LO 2)*
How do you think analysts evaluate the quality of a firm's earnings? Do you think higher-quality earnings translate into higher stock prices?

SE11-3. *(LO 3)*

Describe the big bath theory and give some examples of items that could be written off early.

SE11-4. *(LO 3)*

What types of companies might have problems with revenue recognition? How can investors learn about the revenue recognition policies of a company?

SE11-5. *(LO 4)*

Some of the scandals of the early 2000s were the result of misapplying accounting principles, and others were the result of questionable accounting principles. Which do you think describes the WorldCom failure? Why? Do you think good accounting principles can eliminate financial failures like Enron and WorldCom? Explain.

SE11-6. *(LO 5)*

Discuss the costs and benefits of requiring managers to report on the company's internal controls. Do you think it is necessary for the external auditor to attest to management's report? Why or why not?

SE11-7. *(LO 5)*

One of the requirements of the new law is that the lead auditor or coordinating partner and the reviewing partner must rotate off the audit every 5 years. In your opinion, what is the purpose of this requirement? Do you think it will be achieved?

SE11-8. *(LO 5, 6)*

What is the advantage of having a financial expert on the board of directors? Are there any drawbacks?

SE11-9. *(LO 5, 6)*

Discuss the advantages and disadvantages of having the audit committee deal directly with the external auditors.

SE11-10. *(LO 6)*

Do you think that good corporate governance can be measured? Would you use it in a decision to invest in a specific company?

Internet Exercises

IE 11-1. *(LO 6)*

Go to Google and type in "corporate governance." How many hits did you get? Check out a few of the links to see what type of information is available on the topic of corporate governance.

IE 11-2. *(LO 5, 6)*

Go to the PCAOB Web site at www.pcaobus.org. According to its Web site, what is the mission of the PCAOB? So far, do you believe it is accomplishing this mission? Why or why not?

IE 11-3. *(LO 5, 6)*

Go to the Pixar Web site at www.pixar.com. Follow the link to Investor Relations and then to Corporate Governance. What information is available about the company's corporate governance? See if you can find out how many times the audit committee must meet each year. Do you think that is a sufficient number of meetings? Why or why not?

IE 11-4. *(LO 5, 6)*

Select a pair of companies in the same industry—such as Wal-Mart and Target, Hershey Foods and Tootsie Roll, The Home Depot and Lowe's. For the two companies you select, go to their Web sites and locate the information about corporate governance. Summarize the information you found. How does the information for the two companies compare? Did you find any surprising similarities or differences? Do you think investors are interested in this information?

IE 11-5. *(LO 5)*

Go to www.enron.com and see if you can find the annual report for 2000. See if you can locate *Management's Responsibility for Financial Reporting*. What does it say? Do you think that the new requirements of Sarbanes-Oxley will stop frauds like those that caused the Enron collapse? Why or why not?

IE 11-6. *(LO 5, 6)*

Prior to 2003, the Walt Disney Company was severely criticized for its corporate governance practices. Go to http://corporate.disney.go.com and read about the firm's corporate governance. Check out the members of the board of directors. Are the roles of CEO and chairman of the board held by the same person? How would you evaluate Disney's corporate governance?

Appendix A: Staples Financial Reports

ITEM 8   **APPENDIX C**

INDEX TO CONSOLIDATED FINANCIAL STATEMENTS

Report of Independent Registered Public Accounting Firm

Board of Directors and Shareholders
Staples, Inc.

We have audited the accompanying consolidated balance sheets of Staples, Inc. and subsidiaries as of January 28, 2006 and January 29, 2005, and the related consolidated statements of income, stockholders' equity, and cash flows for each of the three years in the period ended January 28, 2006. Our audits also included the financial statement schedule listed in the Index at Item 15(a). These financial statements and schedule are the responsibility of the Company's management. Our responsibility is to express an opinion on these financial statements and schedule based on our audits.

We conducted our audits in accordance with the standards of the Public Company Accounting Oversight Board (United States). Those standards require that we plan and perform the audit to obtain reasonable assurance about whether the financial statements are free of material misstatement. An audit includes examining, on a test basis, evidence supporting the amounts and disclosures in the financial statements. An audit also includes assessing the accounting principles used and significant estimates made by management, as well as evaluating the overall financial statement presentation. We believe that our audits provide a reasonable basis for our opinion.

In our opinion, the financial statements referred to above present fairly, in all material respects, the consolidated financial position of Staples, Inc. and subsidiaries at January 28, 2006 and January 29, 2005, and the consolidated results of their operations and their cash flows for each of the three years in the period ended January 28, 2006, in conformity with U.S. generally accepted accounting principles. Also, in our opinion, the related financial statement schedule, when considered in relation to the basic financial statements taken as a whole, presents fairly in all material respects the information set forth therein.

As discussed in Note B to the consolidated financial statements, in fiscal year 2003, the Company changed its method of accounting for cash consideration received from vendors to conform with Emerging Issues Task Force Issue No. 02-16, "Accounting by a Customer (Including a Reseller) for Certain Consideration Received from a Vendor."

We also have audited, in accordance with the standards of the Public Company Accounting Oversight Board (United States), the effectiveness of Staples, Inc.'s internal control over financial reporting as of January 28, 2006, based on criteria established in Internal Control—Integrated Framework issued by the Committee of Sponsoring Organizations of the Treadway Commission, and our report dated February 27, 2006 expressed an unqualified opinion thereon.

/s/ ERNST & YOUNG LLP
Ernst & Young LLP

Boston, Massachusetts
February 27, 2006

STAPLES, INC. AND SUBSIDIARIES
Consolidated Balance Sheets
(Dollar Amounts in Thousands, Except Share Data)

	January 28, 2006	January 29, 2005
ASSETS		
Current assets:		
Cash and cash equivalents	$ 977,822	$ 997,310
Short-term investments	593,082	472,231
Receivables, net	576,672	485,126
Merchandise inventories, net	1,706,372	1,602,530
Deferred income tax asset	149,257	86,041
Prepaid expenses and other current assets	141,339	138,374
Total current assets	4,144,544	3,781,612
Property and equipment:		
Land and buildings	705,978	649,175
Leasehold improvements	884,853	762,946
Equipment	1,330,181	1,140,234
Furniture and fixtures	672,931	597,293
Total property and equipment	3,593,943	3,149,648
Less accumulated depreciation and amortization	1,835,549	1,548,774
Net property and equipment	1,758,394	1,600,874
Lease acquisition costs, net of accumulated amortization	34,885	38,400
Intangible assets, net of accumulated amortization	240,395	222,520
Goodwill	1,378,752	1,321,464
Other assets	119,619	106,578
Total assets	$ 7,676,589	$ 7,071,448
LIABILITIES AND STOCKHOLDERS' EQUITY		
Current liabilities:		
Accounts payable	$ 1,435,815	$ 1,241,433
Accrued expenses and other current liabilities	1,041,200	954,184
Debt maturing within one year	2,891	1,244
Total current liabilities	2,479,906	2,196,861
Long-term debt	527,606	557,927
Deferred income tax liability	5,845	23,314
Other long-term obligations	233,426	178,150
Minority interest	4,335	—
Stockholders' Equity:		
Preferred stock, $.01 par value, 5,000,000 shares authorized; no shares issued	—	—
Common stock, $.0006 par value, 2,100,000,000 shares authorized; issued 829,695,100 shares at January 28, 2006 and 813,049,139 shares at January 29, 2005	498	488
Additional paid-in capital	2,544,692	2,254,947
Cumulative foreign currency translation adjustments	87,085	114,427
Retained earnings	3,529,170	2,818,163
Less: treasury stock at cost, 99,253,565 shares at January 28, 2006 and 68,547,587 shares at January 29, 2005	(1,735,974)	(1,072,829)
Total stockholders' equity	4,425,471	4,115,196
Total liabilities and stockholders' equity	$ 7,676,589	$ 7,071,448

See notes to consolidated financial statements.

STAPLES, INC. AND SUBSIDIARIES

Consolidated Statements of Income

(Dollar Amounts in Thousands, Except Share Data)

	Fiscal Year Ended		
	January 28, 2006	January 29, 2005	January 31, 2004
Sales..	$16,078,852	$14,448,378	$12,967,022
Cost of goods sold and occupancy costs	11,493,310	10,343,643	9,468,890
Gross profit	4,585,542	4,104,735	3,498,132
Operating and other expenses:			
Operating and selling......................................	2,617,958	2,359,551	2,167,764
General and administrative.................................	641,296	610,568	524,094
Amortization of intangibles.................................	13,008	8,743	7,986
Total operating expenses................................	3,272,262	2,978,862	2,699,844
Operating income	1,313,280	1,125,873	798,288
Other income (expense):			
Interest income	59,937	31,042	10,135
Interest expense...	(56,773)	(39,888)	(31,575)
Miscellaneous income (expense)	(1,945)	(1,455)	1,264
Income before income taxes and minority interest..............	1,314,499	1,115,572	778,112
Income tax expense..	479,792	407,184	287,901
Income before minority interests	834,707	708,388	490,211
Minority interest	298	—	—
Net Income..	$ 834,409	$ 708,388	$ 490,211
Earnings per common share			
Basic	$ 1.14	$ 0.95	$ 0.68
Diluted	$ 1.12	$ 0.93	$ 0.66

See notes to consolidated financial statements.

STAPLES, INC. AND SUBSIDIARIES

Consolidated Statements of Stockholders' Equity

(Dollar Amounts in Thousands)

For the Fiscal Years Ended January 28, 2006, January 29, 2005 and January 31, 2004

	Common Stock	Additional Paid-In Capital	Cumulative Translation Adjustments	Retained Earnings	Treasury Stock	Comprehensive Income
Balances at February 1, 2003	$ 299	$1,484,833	$ 11,481	$1,719,091	$ (556,812)	$484,710
Equity Offering	8	252,964	—	—	—	—
Issuance of common stock for stock options exercised	8	121,545	—	—	—	—
Tax benefit on exercise of options	—	30,613	—	—	—	—
Contribution of common stock to Employees' 401(K) Savings Plan	—	9,136	—	—	—	—
Sale of common stock under Employee Stock Purchase Plan	1	16,169	—	—	—	—
Issuance of Performance Accelerated Restricted Stock	—	18,389	—	—	—	—
Reissuance of Treasury Stock	—	97	—	—	28	—
Net income for the year	—	—	—	490,211	—	490,211
Foreign currency translation adjustments	—	—	96,075	—	—	96,075
Changes in the fair value of derivatives (net of taxes of $17,126)	—	—	(26,554)	—	—	(26,554)
Purchase of treasury shares	—	—	—	—	(4,315)	—
Other	—	(367)	—	—	—	—
Balances at January 31, 2004	$ 316	$1,933,379	$ 81,002	$2,209,302	$ (561,099)	$559,732
Issuance of common stock for stock options exercised	8	187,163	—	—	—	—
Tax benefit on exercise of options	—	69,257	—	—	—	—
Contribution of common stock to Employees' 401(K) Savings Plan	—	13,311	—	—	—	—
Sale of common stock under International Savings Plan	—	124	—	—	—	—
Sale of common stock under Employee Stock Purchase Plan	1	19,098	—	—	—	—
Issuance of Performance Accelerated Restricted Stock	—	32,778	—	—	—	—
Stock split	163	(163)	—	—	—	—
Net income for the year	—	—	—	708,388	—	708,388
Common stock dividend	—	—	—	(99,527)	—	—
Foreign currency translation adjustments	—	—	46,861	—	—	46,861
Changes in the fair value of derivatives (net of taxes of $9,729)	—	—	(13,436)	—	—	(13,436)
Purchase of treasury shares	—	—	—	—	(511,730)	—
Balances at January 29, 2005	$ 488	$2,254,947	$ 114,427	$2,818,163	$(1,072,829)	$741,813
Issuance of common stock for stock options exercised	9	159,726	—	—	—	—
Tax benefit on exercise of options	—	56,354	—	—	—	—
Contribution of common stock to Employees' 401(K) Savings Plan	—	15,426	—	—	—	—
Sale of common stock under Employee Stock Purchase Plan	1	23,181	—	—	—	—
Issuance of Performance Accelerated Restricted Stock	—	35,979	—	—	—	—
Stock split and cash paid in lieu of fractional shares	—	(921)	—	—	—	—
Net income for the year	—	—	—	834,409	—	834,409
Common stock dividend	—	—	—	(123,402)	—	—
Foreign currency translation adjustments	—	—	(15,837)	—	—	(15,837)
Changes in the fair value of derivatives (net of taxes of $8,332)	—	—	(11,505)	—	—	(11,505)
Purchase of treasury shares	—	—	—	—	(663,145)	—
Balances at January 28, 2006	$ 498	$2,544,692	$ 87,085	$3,529,170	$(1,735,974)	$807,067

See notes to consolidated financial statements.

STAPLES, INC. AND SUBSIDIARIES

Consolidated Statements of Cash Flows

(Dollar Amounts in Thousands)

	Fiscal Year Ended		
	January 28, 2006	January 29, 2005	January 31, 2004
Operating activities:			
Net income	$ 834,409	$ 708,388	$ 490,211
Adjustments to reconcile net income to net cash provided by operating activities:			
Depreciation and amortization	303,900	278,845	282,811
Deferred income tax (benefit) expense	(99,551)	1,595	(13,725)
Other	44,891	65,771	36,434
Change in assets and liabilities, net of companies acquired:			
Increase in receivables	(80,166)	(49,786)	(4,218)
(Increase) decrease in merchandise inventories	(97,538)	(63,747)	147,130
Increase in prepaid expenses and other assets	(15,646)	(8,736)	(34)
Increase (decrease) in accounts payable	187,402	82,355	(27,266)
Increase in accrued expenses and other current liabilities	136,746	107,608	95,549
Increase in other long-term obligations	20,922	56,915	12,840
Net cash provided by operating activities	1,235,369	1,179,208	1,019,732
Investing activities:			
Acquisition of property and equipment	(456,103)	(335,435)	(277,793)
Acquisition of businesses, net of cash acquired	(40,560)	(111,657)	(2,910)
Investment in joint venture, net of cash acquired	(16,636)	(29,330)	—
Proceeds from the sale of short-term investments	8,097,199	10,708,696	8,180,025
Purchase of short-term investments	(8,218,049)	(10,246,652)	(9,014,125)
Net cash used in investing activities	(634,149)	(14,378)	(1,114,803)
Financing activities:			
Proceeds from the sale of capital stock	—	—	252,972
Proceeds from the exercise of stock options and the sale of stock under employee stock purchase plans	181,997	206,394	136,821
Proceeds from borrowings	535	—	—
Payments on borrowings	(16,735)	(235,081)	(325,235)
Repayments under receivables securitization agreement	—	—	(25,000)
Cash dividends paid	(123,402)	(99,527)	—
Purchase of treasury stock, net	(663,145)	(511,730)	(4,287)
Net cash (used in) provided by financing activities	(620,750)	(639,944)	35,271
Effect of exchange rate changes on cash	42	14,959	21,376
Net (decrease) increase in cash and cash equivalents	(19,488)	539,845	(38,424)
Cash and cash equivalents at beginning of period	997,310	457,465	495,889
Cash and cash equivalents at end of period	$ 977,822	$ 997,310	$ 457,465

See notes to consolidated financial statements.

STAPLES, INC. AND SUBSIDIARIES
Notes To Consolidated Financial Statements

NOTE A Summary of Significant Accounting Policies

Nature of Operations: Staples, Inc. and subsidiaries ("Staples" or "the Company") pioneered the office products superstore concept and Staples is a leading office products company. Staples operates three business segments: North American Retail, North American Delivery and International Operations. The Company's North American Retail segment consists of the U.S. and Canadian business units that operate office products stores. The North American Delivery segment consists of the U.S. and Canadian business units that sell and deliver office products and services directly to customers, and includes Staples Business Delivery, Quill and the Company's Contract operations (Staples National Advantage and Staples Business Advantage). The International Operations segment consists of operating units that operate office products stores and that sell and deliver office products and services directly to customers in 19 countries in Europe, South America and Asia.

Basis of Presentation: The consolidated financial statements include the accounts of Staples, Inc. and its wholly and majority owned subsidiaries. All intercompany accounts and transactions are eliminated in consolidation.

All share and per share amounts reflect, or have been restated to reflect, the three-for-two common stock split that was effected in the form of a common stock dividend distributed on April 15, 2005.

Fiscal Year: Staples' fiscal year is the 52 or 53 weeks ending on the Saturday closest to January 31. Fiscal year 2005, 2004 and 2003 consisted of the 52 weeks ended January 28, 2006, January 29, 2005 and January 31, 2004, respectively.

Use of Estimates: The preparation of financial statements in conformity with generally accepted accounting principles requires management of Staples to make estimates and assumptions that affect the amounts reported in the financial statements and accompanying notes. Actual results could differ from those estimates.

Cash Equivalents: Staples considers all highly liquid investments with an original maturity of three months or less to be cash equivalents.

Short-term Investments: Short-term investments, which primarily consist of market auction rate preferred stock and debt securities and treasury securities, are classified as "available for sale" under the provisions of Statement of Financial Accounting Standards ("SFAS") No. 115, "Accounting for Certain Investments in Debt and Equity Securities." Accordingly, the short-term investments are reported at fair value, with any related unrealized gains and losses included as a separate component of stockholders' equity, net of applicable taxes. Realized gains and losses and interest and dividends are included in interest income or interest expense, as appropriate. At January 28, 2006, the available for sale investments consisted of $410.1 million of market auction rate preferred stock and debt securities, $100.0 million of treasury securities and $83.0 million of municipal securities, with contractual maturities ranging from February 2006 through September 2047.

Receivables: Receivables include trade receivables financed under regular commercial credit terms and other non-trade receivables. Gross trade receivables were $444.8 million at January 28, 2006 and $380.5 million at January 29, 2005. Concentrations of credit risk with respect to trade receivables are limited due to Staples' large number of customers and their dispersion across many industries and geographic regions.

An allowance for doubtful accounts has been recorded to reduce trade receivables to an amount expected to be collectible from customers based on specific evidence as well as historical trends. The allowance recorded at January 28, 2006 and January 29, 2005 was $16.4 million and $16.5 million, respectively.

Other non-trade receivables were $148.3 million at January 28, 2006 and $121.1 million at January 29, 2005 and consisted primarily of amounts due from vendors under various incentive and promotional programs.

In fiscal year 2000, Staples entered into a receivables securitization agreement, which was terminated on December 29, 2003, under which it sold participating interests in non-interest bearing accounts receivable of Quill and Staples' Contract business at a discount to an unrelated third party financier. The transfers qualified for sales treatment under SFAS No. 140 "Accounting for Transfers and Servicing of Financial Assets and Extinguishments of Liabilities". As a result of renegotiating the termination provision in this agreement, on December 29, 2003, the third party financier sold its interest in the outstanding receivables, which represented $25.0 million, back to the Company.

STAPLES, INC. AND SUBSIDIARIES
Notes To Consolidated Financial Statements (Continued)

NOTE A Summary of Significant Accounting Policies (Continued)

Merchandise Inventories: Merchandise inventories are valued at the lower of weighted-average cost or market value.

Private Label Credit Card: Staples offers a private label credit card which is managed by a financial services company. Under the terms of the agreement, Staples is obligated to pay fees which approximate the financial institution's cost of processing and collecting the receivables, which are non-recourse to Staples.

Property and Equipment: Property and equipment are recorded at cost. Expenditures for normal maintenance and repairs are charged to expense as incurred. Depreciation and amortization, which includes the amortization of assets recorded under capital lease obligations, are provided using the straight-line method over the following useful lives: 40 years for buildings; the lesser of 10-15 years or term of lease for leasehold improvements; 3-10 years for furniture and fixtures; and 3-10 years for equipment, which includes computer equipment and software with estimated useful lives of 3-5 years.

Lease Acquisition Costs: Lease acquisition costs are recorded at cost and amortized using the straight-line method over the respective lease terms, including option renewal periods if renewal of the lease is probable, which range from 5 to 40 years. Accumulated amortization at January 28, 2006 and January 29, 2005 totaled $61.5 million and $57.9 million, respectively.

Goodwill and Intangible Assets: SFAS No. 142, "Accounting for Goodwill and Other Intangible Assets" requires that goodwill and intangible assets that have indefinite lives not be amortized but, instead, tested at least annually for impairment. Management uses a discounted cash flow analysis, which requires that certain assumptions and estimates be made regarding industry economic factors and future profitability of acquired businesses to assess the need for an impairment charge. If actual results are not consistent with management's assumptions and judgments, the Company could be exposed to a material impairment charge. The Company has elected the fourth quarter to complete its annual goodwill impairment test. In addition, annual impairment tests for indefinite lived intangible assets are also performed in the fourth quarter. As a result of the fourth quarter impairment analyses, management has determined that no impairment charges are required.

The changes in the carrying amount of goodwill during the year ended January 28, 2006 are as follows (in thousands):

	Goodwill At January 29, 2005	2005 Net Additions	Goodwill At January 28, 2006
North American Retail	$ 37,109	$ —	$ 37,109
North American Delivery	395,035	36,336	431,371
International Operations	889,320	20,952	910,272
Consolidated	$1,321,464	$57,288	$1,378,752

Intangible assets not subject to amortization, which include registered trademarks and trade names, were $153.0 million at both January 28, 2006 and January 29, 2005; intangible assets subject to amortization, which include certain trademarks and trade names, customer related intangible assets and non-competition agreements, were $120.9 million and $90.3 million at January 28, 2006 and January 29, 2005, respectively. At January 28, 2006, intangible assets subject to amortization had a weighted average life of 11.8 years. Accumulated amortization for intangible assets subject to amortization was $33.5 million and $20.8 million at January 28, 2006 and January 29, 2005, respectively.

Impairment of Long-Lived Assets: SFAS No. 144, "Accounting for the Impairment or Disposal of Long-Lived Assets" ("SFAS No. 144") requires impairment losses to be recorded on long-lived assets used in operations when indicators of impairment are present and the undiscounted cash flows estimated to be generated by those assets are less than the assets' carrying amount. Staples' policy is to evaluate long-lived assets for impairment at a store level for retail operations and an operating unit level for Staples' other operations.

Fair Value of Financial Instruments: Pursuant to SFAS No. 107, "Disclosure About Fair Value of Financial Instruments" ("SFAS No. 107"), Staples has estimated the fair value of its financial instruments using the following methods and assumptions: the carrying amounts of cash and cash equivalents, short-term investments, receivables and

STAPLES, INC. AND SUBSIDIARIES
Notes To Consolidated Financial Statements (Continued)

NOTE A Summary of Significant Accounting Policies (Continued)

accounts payable approximate fair value because of their short-term nature, and the carrying amounts of Staples' debt approximates fair value because of the Company's use of derivative instruments that qualify for hedge accounting.

Revenue Recognition: Revenue is recognized at the point of sale for the Company's retail operations and at the time of shipment for its delivery sales. The Company offers its customers various coupons, discounts and rebates, which are treated as a reduction of revenue.

Sales of extended service plans are either administered by an unrelated third party or by the Company. The unrelated third party is the legal obligor in most of the areas they administer and accordingly bears all performance obligations and risk of loss related to the service plans sold in such areas. In these areas, Staples recognizes a net commission revenue at the time of sale for the service plans. In certain areas where Staples is the legal obligor, the revenues associated with the sale are deferred and recognized over the life of the service contract, which is typically one to five years.

Cost of Goods Sold and Occupancy Costs: Cost of goods sold and occupancy costs includes the costs of merchandise sold, inbound and outbound freight, receiving and distribution and store and distribution center occupancy (including real estate taxes and common area maintenance).

Shipping and Handling Costs: All shipping and handling costs are included as a component of cost of goods sold and occupancy costs.

Operating and Selling Expenses: Operating and selling expenses include payroll, advertising and other operating expenses for the Company's stores and delivery operations not included in cost of goods sold and occupancy costs.

Advertising: Staples expenses the production costs of advertising the first time the advertising takes place, except for the cost of direct-response advertising, primarily catalog production costs, which are capitalized and amortized over their expected period of future benefits (i.e., the life of the catalog). Direct catalog production costs included in prepaid and other assets totaled $28.4 million at January 28, 2006 and $30.8 million at January 29, 2005. Total advertising and marketing expense was $588.2 million, $526.0 million and $492.7 million for fiscal years 2005, 2004 and 2003, respectively.

Pre-opening Costs: Pre-opening costs, which consist primarily of salaries, supplies, marketing and distribution costs, are expensed as incurred.

Stock Option Plans: Staples accounts for its stock-based plans under Accounting Principles Board Opinion No. 25, "Accounting for Stock Issued to Employees" ("APB No. 25") and provides pro forma disclosures of the compensation expense determined under the fair value provisions of SFAS No. 123, "Accounting for Stock-Based Compensation" ("SFAS No. 123") as amended by SFAS No. 148 "Accounting for Stock-Based Compensation—Transition and Disclosure" ("SFAS No. 148"). Under APB No. 25, since the exercise price of Staples' employee stock options equals the market price of the underlying stock on the date of grant, no compensation expense is recognized.

Pro forma information regarding net income and earnings per share is required by SFAS No. 148, which also requires that the information be determined as if Staples had accounted for its employee stock options granted subsequent to January 28, 1995 under the fair value method of that Statement. For options granted prior to May 1, 2005, the fair value for these options was estimated at the date of grant using a Black-Scholes option-pricing model. For stock options granted on or after May 1, 2005, the fair value of each award is estimated on the date of grant using a binomial valuation model. The binomial model considers characteristics of fair value option pricing that are not available under the Black-Scholes model. Similar to the Black-Scholes model, the binomial model takes into account variables such as volatility, dividend yield rate, and risk free interest rate. However, in addition, the binomial model considers the contractual term of the option, the probability that the option will be exercised prior to the end of its contractual life, and the probability of termination or retirement of the option holder in computing the value of the option. For these reasons, the Company believes that the binomial model provides a fair value that is more representative of actual experience and future expected experience than that value calculated using the Black-Scholes model.

STAPLES, INC. AND SUBSIDIARIES
Notes To Consolidated Financial Statements (Continued)

NOTE A Summary of Significant Accounting Policies (Continued)

The fair value of options granted in each year was estimated at the date of grant using the following weighted average assumptions:

	2005	2004	2003
Risk free interest rate	3.8%	3.8%	2.6%
Expected dividend yield	0.8%	0.7%	0.0%
Expected stock volatility	33%	41%	43%
Expected life of options	5.0 years	5.0 years	5.0 years

For purposes of pro forma disclosures, the estimated fair value of the options is amortized to expense over the options' vesting period. For purposes of SFAS No. 148's disclosure requirements, the Company's employee stock purchase plans are considered compensatory plans. The expense was calculated based on the fair value of the employees' purchase rights. Staples' pro forma information follows (in thousands, except for per share information):

	Fiscal Year Ended January 28, 2006	Fiscal Year Ended January 29, 2005	Fiscal Year Ended January 31, 2004
Net income as reported	$834,409	$708,388	$490,211
Add: Stock based compensation, net of related tax effects, included in reported net income	32,134	29,122	17,584
Deduct: Stock based compensation determined under the fair value based method for all awards, net of related tax effects	(82,425)	(72,935)	(57,584)
Pro forma net income	$784,118	$664,575	$450,211
Basic earnings per common share			
As reported	$ 1.14	$ 0.95	$ 0.68
Pro forma	$ 1.07	$ 0.90	$ 0.62
Diluted earnings per common share			
As reported	$ 1.12	$ 0.93	$ 0.66
Pro forma	$ 1.05	$ 0.88	$ 0.61

The weighted-average fair values of options granted during fiscal years 2005, 2004 and 2003 were $6.32, $7.25, and $4.85, respectively.

Foreign Currency Translation: The assets and liabilities of Staples' foreign subsidiaries are translated into U.S. dollars at current exchange rates as of the balance sheet date, and revenues and expenses are translated at average monthly exchange rates. The resulting translation adjustments, and the net exchange gains and losses resulting from the translation of investments in Staples' foreign subsidiaries, are recorded as a separate component of stockholders' equity.

Derivative Instruments and Hedging Activities: The Company recognizes all derivative financial instruments in the consolidated financial statements at fair value. Changes in the fair value of derivative financial instruments that qualify for hedge accounting are recorded in stockholders' equity as a component of comprehensive income or as an adjustment to the carrying value of the hedged item. Changes in fair values of derivatives not qualifying for hedge accounting are reported in earnings.

New Accounting Pronouncements: On December 16, 2004, the Financial Accounting Standards Board ("FASB") issued Statement No. 123 (revised 2004), "Share Based Payment" ("SFAS No. 123R"), which is a revision SFAS No. 123. Statement No. 123R supersedes APB No. 25 and amends Statement No. 95, "Statement of Cash Flows". Under SFAS No. 123R, companies must calculate and record in the income statement the cost of equity instruments, such as stock options, awarded to employees for services received; pro forma disclosure is no longer permitted. The cost of the equity instruments is to be measured based on fair value of the instruments on the date they are granted (with certain exceptions) and is required to be recognized over the period during which the employees are required to provide services in exchange for the equity instruments.

STAPLES, INC. AND SUBSIDIARIES
Notes To Consolidated Financial Statements (Continued)

NOTE A Summary of Significant Accounting Policies (Continued)

SFAS No. 123R provides two alternatives for adoption: (1) a "modified prospective" method in which compensation cost is recognized for all awards granted subsequent to the effective date of this statement as well as for the unvested portion of awards outstanding as of the effective date; or (2) a "modified retrospective" method which follows the approach in the "modified prospective" method, but also permits entities to restate prior periods to record compensation cost calculated under SFAS No. 123 for the pro forma disclosure. The Company adopted SFAS No. 123R as of January 29, 2006 using the modified retrospective method. Since the Company currently accounts for stock options granted to employees and shares issued under the Company's employee stock purchase plans in accordance with the intrinsic value method permitted under APB No. 25, no compensation expense is recognized. The adoption of SFAS No. 123R is expected to have a significant impact on the Company's results of operations, although it will have no impact on its overall financial position. The impact of adopting SFAS No. 123R cannot be accurately estimated at this time, as it will depend on the market value and the amount of share based awards granted in future periods. However, had the Company adopted SFAS No. 123R in a prior period, the impact would approximate the impact of SFAS No. 123 as described in the disclosure of pro forma net income and earnings per share in Note A to the Consolidated Financial Statements. SFAS No. 123R also requires that tax benefits received in excess of compensation cost be reclassified from operating cash flows to financing cash flows in the Consolidated Statement of Cash Flows. This change in classification will reduce net operating cash flows and increase net financing cash flows in the periods after adoption. While the amount of this change cannot be estimated at this time, the amount of operating cash flows recognized in prior periods for such excess tax deductions were $36.6 million, $41.2 million and $16.8 million in fiscal 2005, 2004 and 2003, respectively.

On April 14, 2005, the Securities and Exchange Commission announced that it would delay the required implementation of SFAS No. 123R, allowing companies that are not small business issuers to adopt the Statement no later than the beginning of the first fiscal year beginning after June 15, 2005. As a result of this delay, the Company adopted SFAS No. 123R as of January 29, 2006.

Reclassifications: Certain previously reported amounts have been reclassified to conform with the current period presentation.

NOTE B Change in Accounting Principle

In November 2002, the Emerging Issues Task Force ("EITF") reached consensus on Issue No. 02-16, "Accounting by a Customer (Including a Reseller) for Certain Consideration Received from a Vendor" ("Issue 02-16"). Issue 02-16 addresses the accounting for vendor consideration received by a customer and is effective for new arrangements, or modifications of existing arrangements, entered into after December 31, 2002. Under this consensus, there is a presumption that amounts received from vendors should be considered a reduction of inventory cost unless certain restrictive conditions are met. Under previous accounting guidance, the Company accounted for all non-performance based volume rebates as a reduction of inventory cost and all cooperative advertising and other performance based rebates as a reduction of marketing expense or cost of goods sold, as appropriate, in the period the expense was incurred. Beginning with contracts entered into in January 2003, the Company adopted a policy to treat all vendor consideration as a reduction of inventory cost rather than as an offset to the related expense because the administrative cost of tracking the actual related expenses, to determine whether the Company meets the restrictive conditions required by Issue 02-16, would exceed the benefit.

To record the impact of including cooperative advertising and other performance based rebates in inventory at the end of the first quarter of 2003, the Company recorded an aggregate, non-cash adjustment of $98.0 million ($61.7 million net of taxes) as an increase to cost of goods sold and occupancy costs, or $0.09 per diluted share. This adjustment reflected all of the Company's outstanding vendor contracts, as substantially all contracts were either entered into or amended in the first quarter of 2003. In addition, the new accounting method resulted in reporting $246.6 million of the Company's cooperative advertising rebates earned in 2003 as cost of goods sold and occupancy costs, whereas these amounts would have been reported as a reduction of operating and selling expenses under previous accounting guidance. In accordance with this consensus, prior periods have not been restated to reclassify amounts recorded as a reduction of operating and selling expenses to cost of goods sold and occupancy costs.

STAPLES, INC. AND SUBSIDIARIES
Notes To Consolidated Financial Statements (Continued)

NOTE B Change in Accounting Principle (Continued)

In November 2003, the EITF reached consensus on Issue No. 03-10 "Application of Issue No. 02-16 by Resellers to Sales Incentives Offered to Consumers by Manufacturers" ("Issue 03-10"), which addresses the accounting for consideration received by a reseller from a vendor that is a reimbursement by the vendor for honoring the vendor's sales incentives offered directly to consumers (e.g., coupons). Beginning with the first quarter of fiscal 2004, vendor consideration received in the form of sales incentives is now recorded as a reduction of cost of goods sold when recognized, rather than as a component of sales. In addition, the Company has reclassified certain other coupons previously classified as operating and selling expenses to a reduction of sales. In accordance with Issue No. 03-10, the Company's fiscal 2003 results have been reclassified, however no change has been made to the fiscal 2002 results reported. These reclassifications had no impact on net income.

The following summarizes the as reported results for 2005 and 2004, with the as reported and pro-forma results for 2003, assuming the retroactive application of these accounting principles as of February 1, 2003 (in thousands, except per share data):

	As Reported 52 Weeks Ended		
	January 28, 2006	**January 29, 2005**	**January 31, 2004**
Sales	$16,078,852	$14,448,378	$12,967,022
Cost of goods sold and occupancy costs	11,493,310	10,343,643	9,468,890
Gross profit	4,585,542	4,104,735	3,498,132
Operating and other expenses:			
Operating and selling	2,617,958	2,359,551	2,167,764
Other expenses	653,085	629,612	552,256
Total operating and other expenses	3,271,043	2,989,163	2,720,020
Income before income taxes and minority interest	1,314,499	1,115,572	778,112
Income tax expense	479,792	407,184	287,901
Income before minority interest	834,707	708,388	490,211
Minority interest	298	—	—
Net income	$ 834,409	$ 708,388	$ 490,211
Earnings per common share:			
Basic	$ 1.14	$ 0.95	$ 0.68
Diluted	$ 1.12	$ 0.93	$ 0.66

	Pro Forma 52 Weeks Ended		
	January 28, 2006	**January 29, 2005**	**January 31, 2004**
Sales	$16,078,852	$14,448,378	$12,967,022
Cost of goods sold and occupancy costs	11,493,310	10,343,643	9,370,915
Gross profit	4,585,542	4,104,735	3,596,107
Operating and other expenses:			
Operating and selling	2,617,958	2,359,551	2,167,764
Other expenses	653,085	629,612	552,256
Total operating and other expenses	3,271,043	2,989,163	2,720,020
Income before income taxes and minority interest	1,314,499	1,115,572	876,087
Income tax expense	479,792	407,184	324,152
Pro forma income before minority interest	834,707	708,388	551,935
Minority interest	298	—	—
Pro forma net income	$ 834,409	$ 708,388	$ 551,935
Pro forma earnings per common share:			
Basic	$ 1.14	$ 0.95	$ 0.76
Diluted	$ 1.12	$ 0.93	$ 0.75

STAPLES, INC. AND SUBSIDIARIES
Notes To Consolidated Financial Statements (Continued)

NOTE C Business Acquisitions and Equity Method Investments

In accordance with SFAS No. 141 "Business Combinations," Staples records acquisitions under the purchase method of accounting. Accordingly, the purchase price is allocated to the tangible assets and liabilities and intangible assets acquired, based on their estimated fair values. The excess purchase price over the fair value is recorded as goodwill. Under SFAS No. 142, goodwill and purchased intangibles with indefinite lives are not amortized but are reviewed for impairment annually, or more frequently, if impairment indicators arise. Purchased intangibles with definite lives are amortized over their respective useful lives.

During 2004 and the first three quarters of 2005, the Company invested in a mail order and internet company in the People's Republic of China, Staples Commerce and Trade ("Staples China"). The Company has been the majority shareholder of Staples China since the first quarter of 2005 and has included the operating results of Staples China in the consolidated financial statements since then. The results of Staples China are reported as part of its International Operations segment for segment reporting.

As of January 28, 2006, the Company recorded $77.5 million of goodwill and $22.5 million of intangible assets for all acquisitions and investments completed in 2005. None of the goodwill recorded is expected to be deductible for tax purposes. The $22.5 million recorded for intangible assets was assigned to trade names and customer related intangible assets that will be amortized over a weighted average life of 13.0 years.

2004 Acquisitions:

On November 29, 2004, the Company acquired Officenet SA, a mail order and internet company operating in Argentina and Brazil, for $23.2 million. This acquisition represents Staples' entry into South America.

In September 2004, the Company acquired Pressel Versand International GmbH, a mail order company based in Austria and operating in nine European countries, for 25.0 million Euros (approximately $30.5 million) and Malling Beck A/S, a mail order company based in Denmark, for $4.0 million. These acquisitions expand Staples' delivery business into Eastern Europe and Denmark and strengthen the Company's business in western Europe through access to new customers and product categories.

On August 4, 2004, the Company acquired the United Kingdom office products company Globus Office World plc ("Office World") for 31.3 million British Pounds Sterling (approximately $57.0 million), strengthening Staples' retail presence in the United Kingdom. In connection with this acquisition, Staples accrued approximately $17.2 million for merger-related and integration costs, reflecting costs associated with planned Office World store closures, a distribution center closure, severance and transaction related costs. As of January 28, 2006, approximately $5.5 million has been charged against this accrual and $11.7 million remains accrued for these merger-related and integration costs.

The results of the businesses acquired have been included in the consolidated financial statements since the dates of acquisition and are reported as part of the Company's International Operations segment for segment reporting. As of January 28, 2006, the Company recorded $107.6 million of goodwill and $16.2 million of intangible assets for all acquisitions completed in 2004. $3.5 million of the goodwill recorded is expected to be deductible for tax purposes. Of the $16.2 million recorded for intangible assets, $8.4 million was assigned to a trade name that has an indefinite life and will not be subject to amortization, and $7.8 million was assigned to trade names and customer-related intangible assets that will be amortized over a weighted average life of 4.7 years.

STAPLES, INC. AND SUBSIDIARIES
Notes To Consolidated Financial Statements (Continued)

NOTE D Accrued Expenses and Other Current Liabilities

The major components of accrued liabilities are as follows (in thousands):

	January 28, 2006	January 29, 2005
Taxes	$ 318,971	$234,960
Employee related	253,828	254,954
Acquisition and store closure reserves	57,501	90,805
Advertising and marketing	71,005	53,417
Other	339,895	320,048
Total	$1,041,200	$954,184

NOTE E Debt and Credit Agreements

The major components of debt outstanding are as follows (in thousands):

	January 28, 2006	January 29, 2005
Notes due October 2012 (see below)	$325,000	$325,000
Senior Notes due August 2007 (see below)	200,000	200,000
Lines of credit (see "Credit Agreements" below)	184	—
Capital lease obligations and other notes payable in monthly installments with effective interest rates from 2% to 5%; collateralized by the related equipment	12,803	18,729
	537,987	543,729
Deferred gain on settlement of interest rate swap and fair value adjustments on hedged debt	(7,490)	15,442
Less current portion	(2,891)	(1,244)
Net long-term debt	$527,606	$557,927

Debt maturing within one year consists of the following (in thousands):

	January 28, 2006	January 29, 2005
Current portion of long-term debt	2,891	1,244
Total debt maturing within one year	$ 2,891	$ 1,244

Aggregate annual maturities of long-term debt and capital lease obligations are as follows (in thousands):

Fiscal Year:	Total
2006	2,891
2007	203,937
2008	2,157
2009	1,226
2010	1,935
Thereafter	325,841
	$537,987

Future minimum lease payments under capital leases of $9.6 million, excluding $1.0 million of interest, are included in aggregate annual maturities shown above. Staples entered into new capital lease agreements totaling $3.1 million, $0.5 million and $1.0 million during fiscal years 2005, 2004 and 2003, respectively.

Interest paid by Staples totaled $41.2 million, $22.5 million and $32.5 million for fiscal years 2005, 2004 and 2003, respectively. There was no capitalized interest in fiscal 2005 and 2004; capitalized interest totaled $0.1 million in fiscal 2003.

STAPLES, INC. AND SUBSIDIARIES
Notes To Consolidated Financial Statements (Continued)

NOTE E Debt and Credit Agreements (Continued)

Notes: On September 30, 2002, Staples issued $325 million principal amount of senior notes due October 1, 2012 (the "Notes"), with a fixed interest rate of 7.375% payable semi-annually on April 1 and October 1 of each year commencing on April 1, 2003. Staples has entered into an interest rate swap agreement to turn the Notes into variable rate obligations (see Note F).

Senior Notes: On August 12, 1997, Staples issued $200 million principal amount of senior notes due August 15, 2007 (the "Senior Notes"), with a fixed interest rate of 7.125% payable semi-annually on February 15 and August 15 of each year commencing on February 15, 1998. Staples has entered into interest rate swap agreements to turn the Senior Notes into variable rate obligations (see Note F).

Credit Agreements: On December 14, 2004, Staples entered into a revolving credit facility (the "Credit Facility") with a syndicate of banks, which provides for a maximum borrowing of $750 million. The Credit Facility terminates on December 14, 2009. The Credit Facility replaced a $600 million revolving credit facility (the "Prior Credit Facility") that had been entered into on June 21, 2002 and was scheduled to terminate in June 2006. On December 14, 2004, there were no borrowings outstanding under the Prior Credit Facility, and approximately $62.4 million of letters of credit issued under the Prior Credit Facility were transferred to the Credit Facility.

Borrowings made pursuant to the Credit Facility may be syndicated loans, competitive bid loans, or swing line loans. Syndicated loans bear interest, payable quarterly or, if earlier, at the end of any interest period, at either (a) the base rate, which is the higher of the annual rate of the lead bank's prime rate or the federal funds rate plus 0.50%, or (b) the Eurocurrency rate (a publicly published rate) plus a percentage spread based on the Company's credit rating and fixed charge coverage ratio; competitive bid loans bear the competitive bid rate as specified in the applicable competitive bid; and swing line loans bear interest that is the lesser of the base rate or the swing line rate. Under the Credit Facility, the Company pays a facility fee, payable quarterly, at rates that range from 0.090% to 0.250% depending on the Company's credit rating and fixed charge coverage ratio, and when applicable, a utilization fee.

Payments under the Credit Facility are guaranteed by the same subsidiaries that guarantee the Company's publicly issued notes. The Credit Facility contains customary affirmative and negative covenants for credit facilities of its type. The covenants require that in the event a Staples subsidiary that is not currently a guarantor under the Credit Facility becomes a guarantor of any of Staples' publicly issued notes or bonds, Staples shall cause such subsidiary to become a guarantor under the Credit Facility. The Credit Facility also contains financial covenants that require us to maintain a minimum fixed charge coverage ratio of 1.5 and a maximum adjusted funded debt to total capitalization ratio of 0.75. The Credit Facility provides for customary events of default with corresponding grace periods, including defaults relating to other indebtedness of at least $50,000,000 in the aggregate and failure to meet the requirement that Staples and its guarantor subsidiaries collectively have at least $355,000,000 of consolidated EBT (as defined in the Credit Facility). As of January 28, 2006, no borrowings were outstanding under the Credit Facility, however $68.1 million of letters of credit were issued under the facility.

Euro Notes: Staples issued notes in the aggregate principal amount of 150 million Euros on November 15, 1999 (the "Euro Notes"). These notes came due on November 15, 2004 and were repaid in full on this date. Prior to their repayment, these notes were designated as a foreign currency hedge on the Company's net investments in Euro denominated subsidiaries and gains or losses were recorded in the cumulative translation adjustment line in Stockholders' Equity.

On October 4, 2002, the Company entered into a $325 million 364-Day Term Loan Agreement with a group of commercial banks to finance a portion of the purchase price of the European mail order businesses that the Company acquired in October 2002. The Term Loan was repaid in its entirety on May 2, 2003.

Staples had $125.0 million available under lines of credit, which had an outstanding balance of $0.2 million at January 28, 2006, with $0.8 million of letters of credit issued under the facilities.

STAPLES, INC. AND SUBSIDIARIES
Notes To Consolidated Financial Statements (Continued)

NOTE F Derivative Instruments and Hedging Activities

Staples uses interest rate swaps to turn fixed rate debt into variable rate debt and currency swaps to fix the cash flows associated with debt denominated in a foreign currency and to hedge a portion of the value of Staples' net investment in Canadian dollar denominated subsidiaries. These derivatives qualify for hedge accounting treatment as the derivatives have been highly effective in achieving offsetting changes in fair value of the hedged items.

Interest Rate Swaps: During fiscal year 1999, Staples entered into interest rate swaps, for an aggregate notional amount of $200 million, to turn Staples' fixed rate Senior Notes into a variable rate obligation. On October 23, 2001, Staples terminated these interest rate swaps which were originally scheduled to terminate on August 15, 2007. Upon termination of the swaps, Staples realized a gain of $18.0 million, which is being amortized over the remaining term of the underlying hedged debt instrument, as an adjustment to interest expense. Simultaneous to the termination of these interest rate swaps, Staples entered into another $200 million of interest rate swaps whereby Staples is entitled to receive semi-annual interest payments at a fixed rate of 7.125% and is obligated to make semi-annual interest payments at a floating rate based on the LIBOR. These swap agreements, scheduled to terminate on August 15, 2007, are designated as fair value hedges of the Senior Notes and the differential to be paid or received on the interest rate swap agreement is accrued and recognized as an adjustment to interest expense over the life of the agreement. At January 28, 2006, the new interest rate swap agreements had a fair value gain of $0.6 million, which was included in other assets.

On January 10, 2003, Staples entered into an interest rate swap, for an aggregate notional amount of $325 million, designed to convert Staples' Notes into a variable rate obligation. The swap agreement, scheduled to terminate on October 1, 2012, is designated as a fair value hedge of the Notes. Under the interest rate swap agreement, Staples is entitled to receive semi-annual interest payments at a fixed rate of 7.375% and is required to make semi-annual interest payments at a floating rate equal to the 6 month LIBOR plus 3.088%. The interest rate swap agreement is being accounted for as a fair value hedge and the differential to be paid or received on the interest rate swap agreement is accrued and recognized as an adjustment to interest expense over the life of the agreements. At January 28, 2006, the interest rate swap agreement had a fair value loss of $12.9 million, which was included in other long-term obligations.

Foreign Currency Swaps: During fiscal year 2000, Staples entered into a currency swap, for an aggregate notional amount of $200 million. Upon maturity of the agreement, scheduled for August 15, 2007, or earlier termination thereof, Staples is entitled to receive $200 million and is obligated to pay 298 million in Canadian dollars. Staples is also entitled to receive semi-annual payments on $200 million at a fixed rate of 7.125% and is obligated to make semi-annual interest payments on 298 million Canadian dollars at a fixed rate of 6.445%. This swap has been designated as a foreign currency hedge on Staples' net investment in Canadian dollar denominated subsidiaries and gains or losses were recorded as cumulative translation adjustments in stockholders' equity. At January 28, 2006, the currency swap had a fair value loss of $62.3 million, which was included in other long-term obligations. During fiscal years 2005, 2004 and 2003, foreign currency losses, net of taxes of $11.5 million, $13.4 million and $23.1 million, respectively were recorded in the cumulative translation adjustment line.

NOTE G Commitments and Contingencies

Staples leases certain retail and support facilities under long-term non-cancelable lease agreements. Most lease agreements contain renewal options and rent escalation clauses and, in some cases, allow termination within a certain number of years with notice and a fixed payment. Certain agreements provide for contingent rental payments based on sales.

STAPLES, INC. AND SUBSIDIARIES
Notes To Consolidated Financial Statements (Continued)

NOTE G Commitments and Contingencies (Continued)

Other long-term obligations at January 28, 2006 include $101.9 million relating to future rent escalation clauses and lease incentives under certain existing store operating lease arrangements. These rent expenses are recognized on a straight-line basis over the respective terms of the leases. Future minimum lease commitments due for retail and support facilities (including lease commitments for 54 retail stores not yet opened at January 28, 2006) and equipment leases under non-cancelable operating leases are as follows (in thousands):

Fiscal Year:	Total
2006	$ 617,021
2007	593,176
2008	558,355
2009	526,981
2010	491,310
Thereafter	2,460,031
	$5,246,874

Future minimum lease commitments do not include $65.4 million of minimum rentals due under non-cancelable subleases.

Rent expense approximated $566.1 million, $524.0 million and $480.0 million for fiscal years 2005, 2004 and 2003, respectively.

As of January 28, 2006, Staples had purchase obligations of $468.8 million. Many of the Company's purchase commitments may be canceled by the Company without payment, and the Company has excluded such commitments, along with intercompany commitments. Contracts that may be terminated by the Company without cause or pernalty, but that require advance notice for termination are valued on the basis of an estimate of what the Company would owe under the contract upon providing notice of termination. Such purchase obligations will arise as follows (in thousands):

Fiscal Year:	Total
2006	$363,703
2007 through 2008	65,777
2009 through 2010	22,453
Thereafter	16,857
	$468,790

Import letters of credit are issued by Staples during the ordinary course of business through major financial institutions as required by certain vendor contracts. As of January 28, 2006, Staples had open letters of credit totaling $50.9 million.

The Company is involved from time to time in litigation arising from the operation of its business. Various class action lawsuits have been brought against Staples for alleged violations of what is known as California's "wage and hour" law. The plaintiffs have alleged that the Company improperly classified both general and assistant managers as exempt under the California wage and hour law, making such managers ineligible for overtime wages. The plaintiffs are seeking to require the Company to pay overtime wages to the putative class for the period October 21, 1995 to the present. The court has granted class certification to the plaintiffs. The court's ruling is procedural only and does not address the merits of the plaintiffs' allegations. The Company believes that the class was improperly certified. If the case goes to trial, the Company believes it has meritorious defenses in the litigation and expects to prevail. If, however, there is an adverse judgment from which there is no successful appeal, damages could range from $10 million to $150 million, excluding interest and attorneys' fees.

STAPLES, INC. AND SUBSIDIARIES
Notes To Consolidated Financial Statements (Continued)

NOTE H Income Taxes

Deferred income taxes reflect the net tax effects of temporary differences between the carrying amount of assets and liabilities for financial reporting purposes and the amounts used for income tax purposes. The approximate tax effect of the significant components of Staples' deferred tax assets and liabilities are as follows (in thousands):

	January 28, 2006	January 29, 2005
Deferred tax assets:		
Deferred rent	$ 39,062	$ 34,649
Capitalized vendor money	26,855	24,164
Foreign tax credit carryforwards	—	7,505
Net operating loss carryforwards	47,447	15,310
Insurance	7,274	5,560
Employee benefits	24,234	21,229
Merger related charges	11,008	18,595
Store closure charge	10,325	12,197
Capital losses and asset write-downs	17,535	19,874
Inventory	40,715	15,340
Unrealized loss on hedge instruments	26,156	17,825
Deferred revenue	18,291	11,022
Depreciation	28,152	(11,570)
Other—net	33,405	28,026
Total deferred tax assets	330,459	219,726
Total valuation allowance	(44,314)	(55,454)
Net deferred tax assets	$286,145	$164,272
Deferred tax liabilities:		
Intangibles	$ (90,205)	$ (77,985)
Other—net	(1,499)	(3,104)
Total deferred tax liabilities	(91,704)	(81,089)
Net deferred tax assets	$194,441	$ 83,183

The gross deferred tax asset from tax loss carryforwards of $47.4 million represents approximately $244.8 million of net operating loss carryforwards, $7.3 million of which will expire in 2007 and $0.5 million of which will expire in 2009 if not utilized. The remainder has an indefinite carryforward period. The deferred tax asset from capital losses and asset write-downs includes approximately $14.0 million, $8.6 million and $11.3 million of capital loss carryforwards that expire in 2006, 2008 and 2010, respectively. The deferred tax assets for these carryforwards have been partially reserved against due to the uncertainty of their realization. The valuation allowance decreased by $11.1 million during the year due primarily to the utilization of foreign tax credits and the expiration of capital loss carryforwards.

For financial reporting purposes, income before income taxes includes the following components (in thousands):

	Fiscal Year Ended		
	January 28, 2006	January 29, 2005	January 31, 2004
Pretax income:			
United States	$1,137,499	$ 931,228	$648,179
Foreign	177,000	184,344	129,933
	$1,314,499	$1,115,572	$778,112

STAPLES, INC. AND SUBSIDIARIES
Notes To Consolidated Financial Statements (Continued)

NOTE H Income Taxes (Continued)

The provision for income taxes consists of the following (in thousands):

| | Fiscal Year Ended | | |
	January 28, 2006	January 29, 2005	January 31, 2004
Current tax expense:			
Federal	$484,326	$315,989	$231,122
State	19,027	19,899	20,023
Foreign	75,990	69,701	50,481
Deferred tax (benefit) expense:			
Federal	(56,989)	13,213	(5,384)
State	(8,501)	1,441	(1,236)
Foreign	(34,061)	(13,059)	(7,105)
Total income tax expense	$479,792	$407,184	$287,901

A reconciliation of the federal statutory tax rate to Staples' effective tax rate on historical net income is as follows:

| | Fiscal Year Ended | | |
	January 28, 2006	January 29, 2005	January 31, 2004
Federal statutory rate	35.0%	35.0%	35.0%
State effective rate, net of federal benefit	1.7	2.3	3.7
Effect of foreign taxes	(0.6)	(0.4)	(0.3)
Tax credits	(0.5)	(0.6)	(0.4)
Other	0.9	0.2	(1.0)
Effective tax rate	36.5%	36.5%	37.0%

The effective tax rate in any year is impacted by the geographic mix of earnings.

The tax impact of the unrealized gain or loss on instruments designated as hedges of net investments in foreign subsidiaries is reported in the cumulative translation adjustment line in stockholders' equity.

The Company operates in multiple jurisdictions and could be subject to audit in these jurisdictions. These audits can involve complex issues that may require an extended period of time to resolve and may cover multiple years. In the Company's opinion, an adequate provision for income taxes has been made for all years subject to audit.

Income tax payments were $472 million, $322 million and $282 million during fiscal years ended January 28, 2006, January 29, 2005 and January 31, 2004, respectively.

Undistributed earnings of the Company's foreign subsidiaries amounted to approximately $408 million as of January 28, 2006. The Company has not provided any additional federal or state income taxes or foreign withholding taxes on the undistributed earnings as such earnings have been indefinitely reinvested in the business. The determination of the amount of the unrecognized deferred tax liability related to the undistributed earnings is not practicable because of the complexities associated with its hypothetical calculation.

NOTE I Employee Benefit Plans

Employee Stock Purchase Plans

The Amended and Restated 1998 Employee Stock Purchase Plan authorizes a total of up to 15.8 million shares of common stock to be sold to participating employees and the Amended and Restated International Employee Stock Purchase Plan authorizes a total of up to 1.3 million shares of common stock to be sold to participating employees of non-U.S. subsidiaries of the Company. Under both plans, participating employees may purchase shares of common stock at 85% of its fair market value at the beginning or end of an offering period, whichever is lower, through payroll deductions in an amount not to exceed 10% of an employee's annual base compensation.

STAPLES, INC. AND SUBSIDIARIES

Notes to Consolidated Financial Statements (Continued)

NOTE I Employee Benefit Plans (Continued)

Stock Award Plans

The Amended and Restated 2004 Stock Incentive Plan (the "2004 Plan") was implemented in July 2004 and replaces the amended and restated 1992 Equity Incentive Plan (the "1992 Plan") and the amended and restated 1990 Director Stock Option Plan (the "1990 Plan"). Unexercised options under both the 1992 Plan and the 1990 Plan remain outstanding. Under the 2004 Plan, Staples may issue up to 23 million shares of common stock to management and employees using various forms of awards, including nonqualified options and restricted stock, subject to certain restrictions. As of February 27, 1997, Staples' 1987 Stock Option Plan (the "1987 Plan") expired; however, unexercised options under this plan remain outstanding. Options outstanding under these plans have an exercise price equal to the fair market value of the common stock on the date of grant. Some options outstanding are exercisable at various percentages of the total shares subject to the option starting one year after the grant, while other options are exercisable in their entirety three to five years after the grant date. All options expire ten years after the grant date, subject to earlier termination in the event of employment termination.

Stock Options

Information with respect to stock options granted under the above plans is as follows:

	Number of Shares	Weighted Average Exercise Price Per Share
Outstanding at February 1, 2003	77,513,274	$10.80
Granted	14,824,936	10.57
Exercised	(13,915,038)	7.24
Canceled	(3,479,306)	11.93
Outstanding at January 31, 2004	74,943,866	$11.49
Granted	15,553,603	19.10
Exercised	(18,963,776)	9.82
Canceled	(2,645,105)	12.93
Outstanding at January 29, 2005	68,888,588	$13.61
Granted	16,757,946	21.34
Exercised	(13,605,421	11.78
Canceled	(3,568,121)	17.08
Outstanding at January 28, 2006	68,472,992	$15.68

STAPLES, INC. AND SUBSIDIARIES

Notes to Consolidated Financial Statements (Continued)

NOTE I Employee Benefit Plans (Continued)

The following table summarizes information concerning currently outstanding and exercisable options for common stock:

Range of Exercise Prices	Number Outstanding	Options Outstanding		Options Exercisable	
		Weighted Average Remaining Contractual Life (Years)	Weighted Average Exercise Price	Number Exercisable	Weighted Average Exercise Price
$ 0.00 - $ 9.00	2,533,741	2.33	$ 6.75	2,530,623	$ 6.75
$ 9.001 - $10.00	6,858,093	5.04	9.72	6,775,203	9.72
$10.001 - $11.00	8,206,203	5.87	10.51	6,925,044	10.49
$11.001 - $13.00	10,360,076	7.14	12.15	6,425,566	12.11
$13.001 - $14.00	5,459,937	3.27	13.38	5,274,668	13.38
$14.001 - $19.00	2,651,788	5.18	16.43	1,950,946	16.05
$19.001 - $20.00	12,747,760	8.28	19.16	3,349,219	19.17
$20.001 - $21.00	4,383,810	4.69	20.67	3,463,853	20.62
$21.001 - $22.00	14,366,431	9.41	21.31	59,857	21.90
$22.001 - $25.00	905,153	9.12	22.74	87,009	22.39
$ 0.00 - $25.00	68,472,992	6.77	$15.68	36,841,988	$12.87

The number of exercisable shares was 36.8 million shares of common stock at January 28, 2006, 40.3 million shares of common stock at January 29, 2005 and 46.7 million shares of common stock at January 31, 2004.

STAPLES, INC. AND SUBSIDIARIES

Notes to Consolidated Financial Statements (Continued)

NOTE I Employee Benefit Plans (Continued)

Restricted Stock

In 2003, the Company began granting restricted shares in lieu of special grants of stock options in order to better align management and shareholder interests. All shares underlying awards of restricted stock are restricted in that they are not transferable (i.e., they may not be sold) until they vest. Subject to limited exceptions, if the employees who received the restricted stock leave Staples prior to the vesting date for any reason, the shares of restricted stock will be forfeited and returned to Staples. The following table summarizes the Company's grants of restricted stock in fiscal 2005, 2004 and 2003:

Date of Award	Number of Shares Granted	Weighted Average Fair Market Value	Vesting Date
July 2003	90,000	$12.23	July 2007
December 2003	18,000	18.51	December 2006
December 2003	27,000	17.37	January 2008
January 2004	300,000	17.55	February 2006
January 2004	1,012,500	17.55	January 2007
June 2004	46,500	20.09	June 2009
June 2004 - July 2004	10,116	19.14	June 2007 - July 2007
September 2004 - October 2004	112,200	19.82	September 2007 - October 2007
November 2004 - December 2004	7,523	21.86	November 2007 - December 2007
December 2004	34,500	21.97	December 2009
December 2004	112,500	22.20	February 2006
January 2005	12,000	21.90	January 2008
February 2005	4,368	21.82	50% February 2007; 50% February 2008
March 2005	5,247	21.10	50% March 2007; 50% March 2008
March 2005 - April 2005	14,400	21.14	March 2008 - April 2008
June 2005 - August 2005	23,500	21.80	June 2008 - August 2008
September 2005	9,000	21.59	August 2006
September 2005	50,000	21.54	30% September 2008; 30%September 2009; 40% September 2010
September 2005	10,460	21.23	September 2008
December 2005	6,300	23.18	December 2008
December 2005	112,500	23.18	February 2006

In connection with the issuance of restricted stock, Staples included $15.1 million, $11.0 million and $0.9 million in compensation expense for fiscal year 2005, 2004 and 2003, respectively.

On February 3, 2002, the Company issued 450,000 shares of restricted stock with a weighted average fair market of $11.95 per share. 250,500 shares vested on March 1, 2004, and the remaining 199,500 shares vested on February 1, 2005. In connection with the issuance of the restricted stock, Staples included $2.7 million in compensation expense in fiscal year 2003.

Performance Accelerated Restricted Stock ("PARS")

PARS are shares of Staples common stock that may be issued to employees (including officers) of Staples. The shares, however, are restricted in that they are not transferable (i.e., they may not be sold) by the employee until they vest, generally after the end of five years. Such vesting date may accelerate if Staples achieves certain

STAPLES, INC. AND SUBSIDIARIES

Notes to Consolidated Financial Statements (Continued)

NOTE I Employee Benefit Plans (Continued)

compound annual earnings per share growth over a certain number of interim years. Subject to limited exceptions, if the employee leaves Staples prior to the vesting date for any reason, PARS will be forfeited by the employee and will be returned to Staples. Once PARS have vested, they become unrestricted and may be transferred and sold. Based on the terms of these awards, the Company accounts for PARS using fixed plan accounting and recognizes compensation expense over the expected life of the award on a straight-line basis.

As of January 28, 2006, Staples had 1,073,732 and 995,066 PARS that were issued during fiscal years 2005 and 2004, respectively. PARS issued in fiscal year 2005 have a weighted-average fair market value of $21.72 and initially vest in March 2010 or will accelerate in March 2007, 2008 or 2009. PARS issued in fiscal year 2004 have a weighted-average fair market value of $19.79 and will vest in March 2006 as a result of Staples achieving its target earnings per share growth for the fiscal year ended January 28, 2006. PARS issued in fiscal year 2003 have a weighted-average fair market value of $17.37 and vested on April 1, 2005. PARS issued in fiscal year 2000 have a weighted-average fair market value of $9.46 and vested on February 1, 2005.

In connection with the issuance of PARS, Staples included $20.9 million, $21.7 million and $15.1 million in compensation expense for fiscal years 2005, 2004 and 2003, respectively.

Employees' 401(k) Savings Plan

Staples' Employees' 401(k) Savings Plan (the "401(k) Plan") is available to all United States based employees of Staples who meet minimum age and length of service requirements. Company contributions are based upon a matching formula applied to employee contributions that are made in the form of Company common stock and vest ratably over a five year period. The Supplemental Executive Retirement Plan (the "SERP Plan"), which is similar in many respects to the 401(k) Plan, is available to certain Company executives and other highly compensated employees, whose contributions to the 401(k) Plan are limited, and allows such individuals to supplement their contributions to the 401(k) Plan by making pre-tax contributions to the SERP Plan. Company contributions to the SERP Plan are based on a similar matching formula and vesting period; however, beginning in October 2004, such contributions were made in cash rather than in Company common stock.

In connection with these plans, Staples included approximately $14.6 million, $13.4 million and $9.3 million in expense for fiscal years 2005, 2004 and 2003.

NOTE J Stockholders' Equity

In 2005, the Company repurchased 30.1 million shares of the Company's common stock for a total purchase price (including commissions) of $649.6 million under the Company's share repurchase program, which was announced in 2004 and amended in the third quarter of 2005. Under the original program, the Company was authorized to repurchase up to $1.0 billion of Staples common stock during fiscal years 2004 and 2005. Under the new program, the Board of Directors authorized the Company to repurchase up to an additional $1.5 billion of Staples common stock through February 2, 2008 following the completion of the Company's $1.0 billion repurchase program. In 2004, the Company repurchased 26.1 million shares of the Company's common stock for a total purchase price (including commissions) of $502.7 million.

On June 4, 2003, the Company issued and sold 20.7 million shares of its common stock in a public offering for a purchase price of $12.59 per share, including 2.7 million shares related to an over-allotment option that was granted to the underwriters. Upon closing, the Company received net proceeds of $253.0 million. The offering proceeds were used for working capital and general corporate purposes.

At January 28, 2006, 67.9 million shares of common stock were reserved for issuance under Staples' 2004 Plan, 401(k) Plan and employee stock purchase plans.

STAPLES, INC. AND SUBSIDIARIES

Notes to Consolidated Financial Statements (Continued)

NOTE K Computation of Earnings per Common Share

Earning per share has been presented below for Staples common stock for the fiscal years ended January 28, 2006, January 29, 2005 and January 31, 2004 (amounts in thousands, except per share data):

	Fiscal Year Ended January 28, 2006	Fiscal Year Ended January 29, 2005	Fiscal Year Ended January 31, 2004
Numerator:			
Net income	$834,409	$708,388	$490,211
Denominator:			
Weighted-average common shares outstanding	731,622	741,878	725,949
Effect of dilutive securities:			
Employee stock options and restricted stock	15,596	16,854	14,287
Weighted-average shares assuming dilution	747,218	758,732	740,236
Basic earnings per common share	$ 1.14	$ 0.95	$ 0.68
Diluted earnings per common share	$ 1.12	$ 0.93	$ 0.66

Options to purchase shares of common stock are excluded from the calculation of diluted earnings per share when their inclusion would have an anti-dilutive effect on the calculation. Options to purchase 0.2 million shares, 0.4 million shares and 5.5 million shares of Staples common stock were excluded from the calculation of diluted earnings per share for the fiscal years ended January 28, 2006, January 29, 2005 and January 31, 2004, respectively.

NOTE L Segment Reporting

Staples has three reportable segments: North American Retail, North American Delivery and International Operations. Staples' North American Retail segment consists of the U.S and Canadian business units that operate office supply stores. The North American Delivery segment consists of the U.S. and Canadian business units that sell and deliver office products and services directly to customers, and includes Staples Business Delivery, Quill and Staples' Contract operations (Staples National Advantage and Staples Business Advantage). The International Operations segment consists of operating units that operate office supply stores and that sell and deliver office products and services directly to customers in 19 countries in Europe, South America and Asia.

Staples evaluates performance and allocates resources based on profit or loss from operations before interest and income taxes, the impact of changes in accounting principles and non-recurring items ("business unit income"). The accounting policies of the reportable segments are the same as those described in the summary of significant accounting policies in Note A. Intersegment sales and transfers are recorded at Staples' cost; therefore, there is no intercompany profit or loss recognized on these transactions.

Staples' North American Retail and North American Delivery segments are managed separately because the way they market products is different, the classes of customers they service may be different, and the distribution methods used to deliver products to customers is different. The International Operations are considered a separate reportable segment because of the significant difference in the operating environment from the North American operations.

STAPLES, INC. AND SUBSIDIARIES

Notes to Consolidated Financial Statements (Continued)

NOTE L Segment Reporting (Continued)

The following is a summary of significant accounts and balances by reportable segment for fiscal years 2005, 2004 and 2003 (in thousands):

	Year Ended January 28, 2006	Year Ended January 29, 2005	Year Ended January 31, 2004
Sales:			
North American Retail	$ 9,037,513	$ 8,324,299	$ 7,665,804
North American Delivery	4,945,661	4,196,882	3,702,311
International Operations	2,095,678	1,927,197	1,598,907
Consolidated	$16,078,852	$14,448,378	$12,967,022
Business Unit Income:			
North American Retail	$ 816,512	$ 681,230	$ 523,612
North American Delivery	485,114	376,730	308,305
International Operations	11,654	67,913	64,346
Consolidated	$ 1,313,280	$ 1,125,873	$ 896,263
Depreciation & Amortization:			
North American Retail	$ 192,112	$ 181,307	$ 188,030
North American Delivery	60,103	51,909	54,631
International Operations	51,685	45,629	40,150
Consolidated	$ 303,900	$ 278,845	$ 282,811
Capital Expenditures:			
North American Retail	$ 284,173	$ 209,190	$ 149,500
North American Delivery	87,992	55,068	78,449
International Operations	83,938	71,177	49,844
Consolidated	$ 456,103	$ 335,435	$ 277,793

The following is a reconciliation of business unit income to income before income taxes and minority interest for fiscal years ended 2005, 2004 and 2003 (in thousands):

	Year Ended January 28, 2006	Year Ended January 29, 2005	Year Ended January 31, 2004
Total business unit income	$1,313,280	$1,125,873	$896,263
Interest and other expense, net	1,219	(10,301)	(20,176)
Impact of change in accounting principle	—	—	(97,975)
Income before income taxes and minority interest	$1,314,499	$1,115,572	$778,112

STAPLES, INC. AND SUBSIDIARIES

Notes to Consolidated Financial Statements (Continued)

NOTE L Segment Reporting (Continued)

Assets:	January 28, 2006	January 29, 2005
North American Retail	$3,022,370	$2,694,255
North American Delivery	1,706,468	1,449,880
International Operations	2,968,059	2,951,431
Total	7,696,897	7,095,566
Elimination of intercompany receivables	(20,308)	(24,118)
Total consolidated assets	$7,676,589	$7,071,448

Geographic Information:

Sales:	Year Ended January 28, 2006	Year Ended January 29, 2005	Year Ended January 31, 2004
United States	$11,967,718	$10,808,314	$ 9,859,899
Canada	2,015,456	1,712,867	1,508,216
International	2,095,678	1,927,197	1,598,907
Consolidated Total	$16,078,852	$14,448,378	$12,967,022

Long-lived Assets:	January 28, 2006	January 29, 2005
United States	$1,667,475	$1,539,219
Canada	275,672	238,027
International	1,469,279	1,436,585
Consolidated Total	$3,412,426	$3,213,831

STAPLES, INC. AND SUBSIDIARIES

Notes to Consolidated Financial Statements (Continued)

NOTE M Guarantor Subsidiaries

Under the terms of the Company's Notes and Senior Notes, certain subsidiaries guarantee repayment of the debt. The Notes and Senior Notes are fully and unconditionally guaranteed on an unsecured, joint and several basis by Staples the Office Superstore, LLC, Staples the Office Superstore East, Inc., Staples Contract & Commercial, Inc., and Staples the Office Superstore, Limited Partnership, all of which are wholly owned subsidiaries of Staples (the "Guarantor Subsidiaries"). The term of guarantees is equivalent to the term of the related debt. The following condensed consolidating financial data is presented for the holders of the Notes and Senior Notes and illustrates the composition of Staples, Inc. (the "Parent Company"), Guarantor Subsidiaries, and non-guarantor subsidiaries as of January 28, 2006 and January 29, 2005 and for the fiscal years ended January 28, 2006, January 29, 2005 and January 31, 2004. The non-guarantor subsidiaries represent more than an inconsequential portion of the consolidated assets and revenues of Staples.

Investments in subsidiaries are accounted for by the Parent Company on the equity method for purposes of the supplemental consolidating presentation. Earnings of subsidiaries are, therefore, reflected in the Parent Company's investment accounts and earnings. The principal elimination entries eliminate the Parent Company's investment in subsidiaries and intercompany balances and transactions.

Condensed Consolidating Balance Sheet
As of January 28, 2006
(in thousands)

	Staples, Inc. (Parent Co.)	Guarantor Subsidiaries	Non-Guarantor Subsidiaries	Eliminations	Consolidated
Cash and cash equivalents	$ 479,704	$ 49,390	$ 448,728	$ —	$ 977,822
Short-term investments	593,082	—	—	—	593,082
Merchandise inventories	—	1,048,654	657,718	—	1,706,372
Other current assets	138,792	325,075	403,401	—	867,268
Total current assets	1,211,578	1,423,119	1,509,847	—	4,144,544
Net property, equipment and other assets	297,144	989,490	866,659	—	2,153,293
Goodwill, net of amortization	173,029	96,737	1,108,986	—	1,378,752
Investment in affiliates and intercompany, net	(302,331)	2,553,321	1,516,819	(3,767,809)	—
Total assets	$1,379,420	$5,062,667	$5,002,311	$(3,767,809)	$7,676,589
Total current liabilities	$ 334,821	$1,222,145	$ 922,940	—	$2,479,906
Total long-term liabilities	30,781	608,371	127,725	—	766,877
Minority interest	—	—	4,335	—	4,335
Total stockholders' equity	1,013,818	3,232,151	3,947,311	(3,767,809)	4,425,471
Total liabilities and stockholders' equity	$1,379,420	$5,062,667	$5,002,311	$(3,767,809)	$7,676,589

STAPLES, INC. AND SUBSIDIARIES

Notes to Consolidated Financial Statements (Continued)

NOTE M Guarantor Subsidiaries (Continued)

Condensed Consolidating Balance Sheet
As of January 29, 2005
(in thousands)

	Staples, Inc. (Parent Co.)	Guarantor Subsidiaries	Non-Guarantor Subsidiaries	Eliminations	Consolidated
Cash and cash equivalents	$ 529,275	$ 44,300	$ 423,735	$ —	$ 997,310
Short-term investments	472,231	—	—	—	472,231
Merchandise inventories	—	1,004,819	597,711	—	1,602,530
Other current assets	80,358	255,319	373,864	—	709,541
Total current assets.....................	1,081,864	1,304,438	1,395,310	—	3,781,612
Net property, equipment and other assets	239,982	920,213	808,177	—	1,968,372
Goodwill, net of amortization	140,570	52,067	1,128,827	—	1,321,464
Investment in affiliates and intercompany, net ..	374,885	2,013,548	882,308	(3,270,741)	—
Total assets.............................	$ 1,837,301	$4,290,266	$4,214,622	$(3,270,741)	$ 7,071,448
Total current liabilities......................	$ 277,470	$1,045,733	$ 873,658	$ —	$ 2,196,861
Total long-term liabilities....................	26,208	600,554	132,629	—	759,391
Total stockholders' equity	1,533,623	2,643,979	3,208,335	(3,270,741)	4,115,196
Total liabilities and stockholders' equity....	$ 1,837,301	$4,290,266	$4,214,622	$(3,270,741)	$ 7,071,448

Condensed Consolidating Statement of Income
For the year ended January 28, 2006
(in thousands)

	Staples, Inc. (Parent Co.)	Guarantor Subsidiaries	Non-Guarantor Subsidiaries	Consolidated
Sales..	$ —	$10,649,559	$5,429,293	$16,078,852
Cost of goods sold and occupancy costs	(1,565)	7,648,788	3,846,087	11,493,310
Gross profit (loss)	1,565	3,000,771	1,583,206	4,585,542
Operating and other expenses..........................	3,167	2,053,316	1,214,560	3,271,043
Income (loss) before income taxes and minority interest.....	(1,602)	947,455	368,646	1,314,499
Income tax expense....................................	—	359,316	120,476	479,792
Income (loss) before minority interest....................	(1,602)	588,139	248,170	834,707
Minority interest	—	—	298	298
Net income (loss)......................................	$(1,602)	$ 588,139	$ 247,872	$ 834,409

STAPLES, INC. AND SUBSIDIARIES

Notes to Consolidated Financial Statements (Continued)

NOTE M Guarantor Subsidiaries (Continued)

Condensed Consolidating Statement of Income
For the year ended January 29, 2005
(in thousands)

	Staples, Inc. (Parent Co.)	Guarantor Subsidiaries	Non-Guarantor Subsidiaries	Consolidated
Sales...	$ —	$9,608,652	$4,839,726	$14,448,378
Cost of goods sold and occupancy costs	1,491	6,930,858	3,411,294	10,343,643
Gross profit (loss)	(1,491)	2,677,794	1,428,432	4,104,735
Operating and other expenses.............................	30,762	1,965,286	993,115	2,989,163
Income (loss) before income taxes........................	(32,253)	712,508	435,317	1,115,572
Income tax expense......................................	—	267,721	139,463	407,184
Net income (loss)..	$(32,253)	$ 444,787	$ 295,854	$ 708,388

Condensed Consolidating Statement of Income
For the year ended January 31, 2004
(in thousands)

	Staples, Inc. (Parent Co.)	Guarantor Subsidiaries	Non-Guarantor Subsidiaries	Consolidated
Sales...	$ —	$8,744,624	$4,222,398	$12,967,022
Cost of goods sold and occupancy costs	1,309	6,480,153	2,987,428	9,468,890
Gross profit (loss)	(1,309)	2,264,471	1,234,970	3,498,132
Operating and other expenses.............................	16,296	1,776,506	927,218	2,720,020
Income (loss) before income taxes........................	(17,605)	487,965	307,752	778,112
Income tax expense......................................	—	185,984	101,917	287,901
Net income (loss)..	$(17,605)	$ 301,981	$ 205,835	$ 490,211

STAPLES, INC. AND SUBSIDIARIES

Notes to Consolidated Financial Statements (Continued)

NOTE M Guarantor Subsidiaries (Continued)

Condensed Consolidating Statement of Cash Flows
For the year ended January 28, 2006
(in thousands)

	Staples, Inc. (Parent Co.)	Guarantor Subsidiaries	Non-Guarantor Subsidiaries	Consolidated
Net cash provided by operating activities	$ 803,976	$ 257,904	$ 173,489	$ 1,235,369
Investing activities:				
Acquisition of property, equipment and lease rights	(95,311)	(212,254)	(148,538)	(456,103)
Acquisition of businesses, net of cash acquired	—	(40,560)	—	(40,560)
Investment in joint venture	(16,636)	—	—	(16,636)
Purchase of short-term investments	(8,218,049)	—	—	(8,218,049)
Proceeds from the sale of short-term investments	8,097,199	—	—	8,097,199
Cash used in investing activities	(232,797)	(252,814)	(148,538)	(634,149)
Financing activities:				
Payments on borrowings	(16,735)	—	—	(16,735)
Purchase of treasury shares	(663,145)	—	—	(663,145)
Cash dividends paid	(123,402)	—	—	(123,402)
Other	182,532	—	—	182,532
Cash used in financing activities	(620,750)	—	—	(620,750)
Effect of exchange rate changes on cash	—	—	42	42
Net increase (decrease) in cash	(49,571)	5,090	24,993	(19,488)
Cash and cash equivalents at beginning of period	529,275	44,300	423,735	997,310
Cash and cash equivalents at end of period	$ 479,704	$ 49,390	$ 448,728	$ 977,822

STAPLES, INC. AND SUBSIDIARIES

Notes to Consolidated Financial Statements (Continued)

NOTE M Guarantor Subsidiaries (Continued)

Condensed Consolidating Statement of Cash Flows
For the year ended January 29, 2005
(in thousands)

	Staples, Inc. (Parent Co.)	Guarantor Subsidiaries	Non-Guarantor Subsidiaries	Consolidated
Net cash provided by operating activities	$ 697,878	$ 163,368	$ 317,962	$ 1,179,208
Investing activities:				
Acquisition of property, equipment and lease rights ...	(62,647)	(169,674)	(103,114)	(335,435)
Acquisition of businesses, net of cash acquired	—	(4,901)	(106,756)	(111,657)
Investment in joint venture	(29,330)	—	—	(29,330)
Purchase of short-term investments.................	(10,246,652)	—	—	(10,246,652)
Proceeds from the sale of short-term investments......	10,698,696	—	10,000	10,708,696
Cash provided by (used in) investing activities..........	360,067	(174,575)	(199,870)	(14,378)
Financing activities:				
Payments on borrowings	(235,081)	—	—	(235,081)
Purchase of treasury shares.......................	(511,730)	—	—	(511,730)
Cash dividends paid	(99,527)	—	—	(99,527)
Other..	206,394	—	—	206,394
Cash used in financing activities	(639,944)	—	—	(639,944)
Effect of exchange rate changes on cash	—	—	14,959	14,959
Net increase (decrease) in cash.......................	418,001	(11,207)	133,051	539,845
Cash and cash equivalents at beginning of period........	111,274	55,507	290,684	457,465
Cash and cash equivalents at end of period	$ 529,275	$ 44,300	$ 423,735	$ 997,310

STAPLES, INC. AND SUBSIDIARIES

Notes To Consolidated Financial Statements (Continued)

Note M Guarantor Subsidiaries (Continued)

Condensed Consolidating Statement of Cash Flows
For the year ended January 31, 2004
(in thousands)

	Staples, Inc. (Parent Co.)	Guarantor Subsidiaries	Non-Guarantor Subsidiaries	Consolidated
Net cash provided by operating activities	$ 601,508	$ 204,795	$213,429	$ 1,019,732
Investing activities:				
Acquisition of property, equipment and lease rights	(21,092)	(177,520)	(79,181)	(277,793)
Acquisition of businesses, net of cash acquired	—	—	(2,910)	(2,910)
Purchase of short-term investments.	(9,004,125)	—	(10,000)	(9,014,125)
Proceeds from the sale of short term investments.	8,180,025	—	—	8,180,025
Cash used in investing activities	(845,192)	(177,520)	(92,091)	(1,114,803)
Financing activities:				
Payments on borrowings	(325,235)	(25,000)	—	(350,235)
Proceeds from borrowings and other.	389,793	(4,287)	—	385,506
Cash provided by (used in) financing activities	64,558	(29,287)	—	35,271
Effect of exchange rate changes on cash	—	—	21,376	21,376
Net (decrease) increase in cash.	(179,126)	(2,012)	142,714	(38,424)
Cash and cash equivalents at beginning of period	290,400	57,519	147,970	495,889
Cash and cash equivalents at end of period	$ 111,274	$ 55,507	$290,684	$ 457,465

NOTE N Quarterly Summary (Unaudited)

	(In thousands, except per share amounts)			
	First Quarter	Second Quarter	Third Quarter	Fourth Quarter
Fiscal Year Ended January 28, 2006(1)				
Sales.	$3,899,052	$3,471,964	$4,245,519	$4,462,317
Gross profit	1,062,532	990,073	1,221,458	1,311,479
Net income.	159,426	147,178	237,824	289,981
Basic earnings per common share(2).	$ 0.22	$ 0.20	$ 0.33	$ 0.40
Diluted earnings per share(2)	$ 0.21	$ 0.20	$ 0.32	$ 0.39

	First Quarter	Second Quarter	Third Quarter	Fourth Quarter
Fiscal Year Ended January 29, 2005(1)				
Sales.	$3,452,155	$3,089,252	$3,830,466	$4,076,505
Gross profit	935,625	870,685	1,096,216	1,202,209
Net income.	125,731	122,466	208,866	251,324
Basic earnings per common share(2).	$ 0.17	$ 0.17	$ 0.28	$ 0.34
Diluted earnings per share(2)	$ 0.17	$ 0.16	$ 0.28	$ 0.33

(1) Results of operations for this period include the results of acquisitions since their acquisition dates (see Note C).

(2) All share and per share amounts reflect, or have been restated to reflect, the three-for-two common stock split that was effected in the form of a common stock dividend distributed on April 15, 2005.

Appendix B: The Mechanics of an Accounting System

Learning Objectives

When you are finished studying this appendix, you should be able to:

1. Define the general ledger system and explain how it works.

2. Explain and perform the steps in the accounting cycle.

3. Identify the adjustments needed before preparing financial statements and make those adjustments.

4. Describe the closing process and explain why it is necessary.

In the first three chapters of this book, you have been keeping track of Tom's Wear transactions using an accounting equation work sheet. We can do that in a simple world with a small number of transactions. In the real world, that wouldn't work very well. A company in the real world needs a better system to keep track of the large number of transactions represented in the four basic financial statements. A company may have an accounting system that gathers *only* accounting information—just recording the information that applies to the financial statements—and other information systems gathering information for marketing, production, and other parts of the company. Alternatively, a company may have a single, integrated information system in which all company information is recorded—data about suppliers, employees, operations; and the accounting information is simply a small part.

For years, the accountants have had their own separate record-keeping system called the **general ledger system**; and the other functional areas of the business—marketing, production, sales, etc.—have each had their own system for keeping track of the information they need. Since the development of computers and software programs that can manage large amounts of information, more and more companies are using a single, integrated information system. Thus, instead of keeping their data separately, accountants may get their information from the company's overall information system—often referred to as an **enterprise-wide resource planning system (ERP)**.

The accountants' traditional general ledger accounting system has been used for such a long time that it has become entrenched in the format and organization of the basic financial statements of every business. That's one reason we'll discuss the general ledger system in detail in this appendix, even though in many companies it is being absorbed into company-wide information systems. Another reason is that you must be able to understand the output of the general ledger accounting system because the new integrated information systems are designed to produce the financial records in the same format as the general ledger system. The same financial statements are produced with both the general ledger and the integrated types of information systems. We will use the general ledger system, which was designed as a manual system, to demonstrate how transactions are recorded, classified, and summarized for the financial statements.

> The **general ledger system** is the accountant's traditional way of keeping track of a company's financial transactions and then using those records to prepare the basic financial statements. The debits and credits used in this system are simply a mechanical way to keep track of financial transactions.

The General Ledger Accounting System

L.O.1

Define the general ledger system and explain how it works.

Keeping track of financial information with a traditional record-keeping system is often called *bookkeeping*. As transactions occur, they are recorded chronologically by a bookkeeper in a book called a **journal**. When we prepare an accounting equation work sheet—showing the effect of each transaction on the accounting equation—we are doing something similar to what we would record in a journal. The resources exchanged are shown with their dollar amounts. The journal contains a record of each transaction as it occurs. An example is shown in Exhibit B.1. Most companies use more than one journal; each department may have its own journal. Common journals are the (1) sales journal, (2) cash receipts journal, and (3) cash disbursements journal. For simplicity, we'll use a single, general journal for all our transactions.

> Business transactions are first recorded in a **journal**. Then they are transferred to accounts in the general ledger through a process called posting.

EXHIBIT B.1

An Example of the Journal

Page 4: General Journal

Ref.	Date	Journal entry	Debits	Credits
J-1	June 1	Cash	$65,000	
		Sales		$65,000
		To record the collection of cash for sales.		
J-2	June 4	Equipment	$20,600	
		Cash		$20,600
		To record the purchase of equipment for cash.		

The journal entries are recorded chronologically. Then, the individual items will be "regrouped" by account as they are posted to the General Ledger. Trace the cash amounts in the journal entries above to the General Ledger Cash account shown in Exhibit B–2. The amounts for Sales and Equipment will be posted to their own general ledger accounts.

Because a company may have thousands of transactions during an accounting period, it would be difficult, probably impossible, to try to gather and use the information from a chronological record such as the journal. To be useful, the information needs to be reorganized, grouping together transactions that involve the same resource. For example, when all the transactions that involve cash are grouped together, then the company's cash balance can be easily determined. As you can see from that example, it is useful for similar transactions to be grouped together. The transactions from the journal or journals are transferred to another book called the **general ledger**—a process called **posting** the transactions to the general ledger. Posting is done periodically; it could be daily, weekly, or monthly, depending on the size of the company.

The general ledger is the primary record of the financial information of the business. It is organized by what we have called up to this point a financial statement *item*. From here on, we will refer to the financial statement items as accounts. Like a financial statement item, an account is the basic classification unit of accounting information. Now we can think of each financial statement item as an account, and each account as a page in the general ledger. On the page for a particular account, we record all the additions to, and deductions from, that account.

For example, one account in the general ledger is cash. On the cash page in the general ledger, we find every cash collection and every cash disbursement made by the company. If there are more disbursements or collections than can fit on one page, they will be recorded on as many following pages as needed, all comprising the cash account. To make it easy to find the amount of cash on hand, the cash account has a running balance. That means a new balance is calculated after every entry. Think about your own checkbook—that's the record you keep of each check you write—a subtraction; each deposit you make—an addition; and the resulting total remaining in your checking account—that's your running balance. If you keep a running balance, it is much faster to find out how much cash you have in your account. (Have you discovered what happens when you fail to keep your checkbook balance current?)

Accounts in the general ledger include cash, accounts receivable, inventory, prepaid insurance, equipment, accumulated depreciation, accounts payable, notes payable, contributed capital, and retained earnings. (Notice, these are given in the order they appear on the balance sheet.) How many accounts does a company have? Every company is different, and the number of accounts depends on the detail the company wants in its financial records. For example, one company could have an account called utilities expenses in which many different utility-related expenses could be accumulated. Another company might prefer to have a separate account for each type of utility expense—a separate page in the general ledger for electricity expense, gas expense, water expense, etc. The number of accounts is determined by the amount of detail a company wants to be able to retrieve from its records. If a company uses very little gas or water, it would be a waste of time and space to keep a separate account for those expenses. A company that uses water in its production process, on the other hand, would definitely want to keep a separate account for water purchases.

Companies also have subsidiary ledgers. These are detailed records that support the balances in the general ledger. For example, the *accounts receivable subsidiary ledger* will have details about the customers—sales, receipts, and account balances for every customer. The total dollar amount of accounts receivable in the accounts receivable subsidiary ledger will be the total in the general ledger.

Most companies have a large number of accounts, and they combine the similar ones for the financial statements. When we look at the financial statements, we can't really tell how many individual accounts a company has in its general ledger. Many smaller accounts may be combined for financial statement presentation.

Anyone who wants to know the balance in any account at any time can find it by looking in the general ledger. A list of the balances in all the accounts of a company is called a **trial balance**.

Before the financial statements can be prepared, adjustments to the records must be made. We discussed those adjustments and how to make them in Chapter 3. Adjustments are needed because of the nature of accrual accounting. On the financial statements, we

A **trial balance** is a list of all the accounts of a company with the related debit or credit balance.

need to include revenues that have been earned and expenses that have been incurred, even if we have not yet received the cash earned or paid the cash for the expenses incurred during the accounting period. These adjustments are called accruals. The action has taken place, but the dollars have not been exchanged.

We also need to be sure to include on the income statement for the period any revenue we've earned or expenses we've incurred for which the dollars were exchanged at a previous time. These are called deferrals. The dollars were already exchanged, and we recorded the receipt of the cash when we received the cash. However, we did not recognize any revenue or expense at that time. At the end of the accounting period, we have to recognize any revenue we have earned and any expenses that we've incurred.

No matter what kind of accounting system a company uses, the information produced by that system must be adjusted before the financial statements can be prepared. After the adjustments are made, the financial statements are prepared. We have actually done all this—recording the transactions, making the adjustments, and preparing the financial statements—using the accounting equation work sheet. The general ledger system is simply a more feasible way to do it in an actual business.

Debit means left side of an account.

To use the general ledger system and to understand the information it makes available, we must learn a bit more accounting language. Don't panic over the terms **debit** and **credit**. You will find them easy to understand, but only if first you get rid of any notions of what you already think debit and credit mean. In accounting, each term has a very specific meaning that should not be confused with its more general meaning.

Credit means right side of an account.

Debits and Credits

In accounting, when we say *debit,* we mean the left side; when we say *credit,* we mean the right side. (This should be easy to remember.) Left is the only thing we can say about what *debit* means and right, about what *credit* means—unless we apply the terms to specific accounts.

A general ledger has been traditionally composed of a multi-column page, similar to the one shown in Exhibit B.2. The debit column on the right shows the running balance in the cash account. Notice there is never a credit balance in this account. Now it is often computerized in a similar format.

In the balance columns, the column on the left is called the debit (DR) column, and the column on the right is called the credit (CR) column. As a shortcut to using formal preprinted two-column paper, accountants often draw a T-account to represent a page in the general ledger. T-accounts shown in Exhibit B.3 are our representation of the general ledger shown in Exhibit B.2.

One T-account such as cash, shown next, represents a single page in the general ledger. The left side of a T-account is the debit side, and the right side of a T-account is the credit side.

Cash

Debit	Credit

Account: **Cash**

Account No. 1002

Date	Item	Jrnl. ref.	Debit	Credit	Balance Debit	Credit
2008						
June 1		J–1, p. 4	65,000		**65,000**	
June 4		J–2, p. 4		20,600	**44,400**	

This is the **Cash** account. The cash amounts from all the journal entries are posted here. Trace these amounts back to the journal entries shown in Exhibit B.1.

EXHIBIT B.3

Debits and Credits in T-Accounts

Asset		Liability		Shareholders' Equity	
Debit increases (normal balance)	Credit decreases	Debit decreases	Credit increases (normal balance)	Debit decreases	Credit increases (normal balance)

Revenue		Expense	
Debit decreases	Credit increases (normal balance)	Debit increases (normal balance)	Credit decreases

Numbers we put on the left side of the account are called debits, and *putting* a number in the left column is called *debiting* an account. *Debit* is a wonderful word that can be an adjective, a noun, or a verb. The same goes for the word *credit*. The right side of the account is called the credit side; the numbers we put on the right side are called credits; and putting a number in the right column is called *crediting* an account.

In the fifteenth century, a monk named Fra Luca Paccioli wrote about a system that uses debits and credits with the accounting equation. In his system, the accounting equation stays in balance with each transaction *and* the monetary amounts of debits and credits are equal for each transaction. Here's how it works:

1. For the balance sheet equation, the balance in the accounts on the left side of the equation (*assets*) will increase with debits; and the balance in the accounts on the right side of the equation (*liabilities* and *shareholders' equity*) will increase with credits. It follows that the balance in an asset account will decrease with credits. Liability and equity account balances decrease with debits. Putting that together,

- Asset accounts are increased with debits and decreased with credits.
- Liability and shareholders' equity accounts are increased with credits and decreased with debits.

This means that when we want to add an amount to our cash balance, we put the number of that amount on the left (in the left column of the two columns in the general ledger account for cash)—so that's a debit. When we disburse cash and want to subtract the amount disbursed from the cash account, we put the number of that amount on the right side—so that's a credit. The *increase* side of an account is called its "normal" balance. Cash has a normal debit balance. Because we put the cash we receive on the debit side and the cash we disburse on the credit side, it makes sense that our cash account will normally have a debit balance. (It's not normal to disburse more cash than you have—it's pretty unusual.)

In accounting, we do not literally *add* and *subtract* from an account balance—we debit and credit an account to accomplish the same thing. If we make an error, we do not erase the mistake and replace it with the correct answer. Instead, we debit or credit the account to correct the error and make the account balance correct. When accounting records are kept by hand, all entries are made in ink so that no entries can be erased or changed. This has been traditional in accounting to keep the records from being altered. Recording every increase to, and decrease from, an account balance gives a complete record of every change made to the account.

2. Because shareholders' equity is increased with credits, all accounts that increase shareholders' equity will increase with credits. Revenue accounts increase with credits and decrease with debits. When we make a sale, we *credit* the sales account.

3. Because shareholders' equity is *decreased* with debits, all accounts that decrease shareholders' equity work in the opposite way as revenue accounts work. For example, expense accounts—where a list of our expenses is kept—increase with debits. As we incur expenses, we put the amounts on the left side of expense accounts.

Your Turn B-1

Your Turn

Your Turn

Indicate whether each of the following accounts normally has a debit (DR) or credit (CR) balance and what type of account it is.

Account Title	Expense	Revenue	Asset	Liability	Shareholders' Equity
Accounts payable				CR	
Accounts receivable					
Advertising expense					
Cash					
Depreciation expense					
Furniture and fixtures					
Accumulated depreciation					
Unearned fees					
Salary expense					
Common stock					
Rent expense					
Dividends					
Retained earnings					
(Earned) fees					
Land					
Building					

A summary of the use of debits and credits is shown in Exhibit B.3. Remember, it's just a clever system to be sure that, when we record a transaction, the accounting equation is kept in balance and, at the same time, debits = credits with every transaction. This system is called double-entry bookkeeping.

L.O.2
Explain and perform the steps in the accounting cycle.

The **accounting cycle** begins with the transactions of a new accounting period. It includes recording and posting the transactions, adjusting the books, preparing financial statements, and closing the temporary accounts to get ready for the next accounting period.

The Accounting Cycle

The process that starts with recording individual transactions, produces the four basic financial statements, and gets our general ledger ready for the next accounting period is called the **accounting cycle**. Some of the steps in the accounting cycle won't make any sense to you yet, but this appendix examines each in detail. By the end of this appendix, you should be able to explain and perform each step. The steps in the accounting cycle follow:

1. Record transactions in the journal, the chronological record of all transactions. These are called journal entries.
2. Post the journal entries to the general ledger.
3. At the end of the accounting period, prepare an unadjusted trial balance.
4. Prepare adjusting journal entries and post them to the general ledger.
5. Prepare an adjusted trial balance.
6. Prepare the financial statements.
7. Close the temporary accounts.
8. Prepare a postclosing trial balance.

Let's look at each of these steps in detail.

Step 1: Recording Journal Entries

In the normal course of business, there are dozens of transactions that must be recorded in the accounting system. Let's look at how the transactions for a company's first year of business would be recorded in a journal. The transactions for the first year of Clint's Consulting Company, Inc. are shown in Exhibit B.4.

Date	Transaction
Jan. 2	Clint contributes $2,000 of his own money to the business in exchange for common stock
Jan. 10	Clint's Consulting, Inc. borrows $4,000 from a local bank to begin the business
Feb. 4	Clint's buys supplies for $400 cash
Apr. 10	Clint's hires a company to prepare and distribute a brochure for the company for $500 cash
July 12	Clint's provides consulting services and earns revenue of $9,000 cash
Aug. 15	Clint's pays someone to do some typing, which costs $350 cash
Oct. 21	Clint's repays the $4,000 note along with $150 interest
Dec. 10	Clint's Consulting, Inc. makes a distribution to Clint, the only shareholder, for $600

EXHIBIT B.4

Transactions for Clint's Consulting Company, Inc. during 2006

The first transaction in Clint's first year of business is his own contribution of $2,000 to the business in exchange for common stock. What a journal entry looks like on a journal page follows:

Date	Transaction	Debit	Credit
1/2/06	Cash	2,000	
	Common stock		2,000
	To record owner's cash contribution in exchange for common stock		1-1[a]

[a]This is a number we'll use to help us trace journal entries to the general ledger.

The cash account is increased by $2,000, so Clint would debit the cash account for $2,000. Shareholder's equity is increased, so Clint would credit common stock for $2,000. Notice, in this case two accounts are increased—one with a debit and one with a credit. In some transactions, both accounts are increased; in others, one account can be increased and one account can be decreased; or two accounts can be decreased. The only requirement for a journal entry is that the dollar amount of debits must equal the dollar amount of credits.

In the second transaction, Clint's Consulting Company borrows $4,000 from a local bank. Again, two different accounts are increased—one with a debit and one with a credit—in this transaction. Notice, debits ($4,000) = credits ($4,000).

Date	Transaction	Debit	Credit
1/10/06	Cash	4,000	
	Notes payable		4,000
	To record the loan from the bank		1-2

Debits are always listed first; credits are listed after all the debits—sometimes there is more than one account to debit or credit—and the accounts being credited are indented like the first sentence of a paragraph. Each page of the journal has a reference number that is used to trace journal entries to the general ledger. We'll see this number again when we post the journal entries to the general ledger.

The third transaction is the purchase of supplies for $400 cash. This is recorded with a debit to supplies and a credit to cash.

Date	Transaction	Debit	Credit
2/4/06	Supplies	400	
	Cash		400
	To record the purchase of supplies		1-3

Notice, this transaction increases one asset account—supplies—and decreases another asset account—cash. Because supplies is an asset, it is increased with a debit.

The fourth transaction is Clint's hiring a company to prepare and distribute a brochure for his new consulting business. He pays $500 for this service.

Date	Transaction	Debit	Credit
4/10/06	Advertising expense	500	
	Cash		500
To record the cost of the brochures			1-4

In this transaction, an expense account, advertising expense, is increased by $500. Because expense accounts are eventually deducted from shareholder's equity, they increase with debits, the opposite of the normal balance in shareholder's equity accounts. Cash, an asset account, is decreased with a credit of $500.

Next, the company provides consulting services for $9,000 cash.

Date	Transaction	Debit	Credit
7/12/06	Cash	9,000	
	Consulting fees		9,000
To record consulting revenue			1-5

In this transaction, cash is increased with a $9,000 debit. Consulting Fees, a revenue account that will eventually be added to shareholder's equity, is increased with a $9,000 credit.

Clint's Consulting Company has one employee who types for him occasionally, and he pays this person $350 for typing during his first year of business. This is an expense, which Clint categorizes as salary expense. Cash is reduced with a $350 credit, and salary expense is increased with a $350 debit.

Date	Transaction	Debit	Credit
8/15/06	Salary expense	350	
	Cash		350
To record the cost of an employee to type			1-6

Next, the company repays the loan to the bank, with interest. The principal of the loan—the amount borrowed—was $4,000; the interest—the cost of using someone else's money—was $150. The journal entry for this transaction is an example of an entry with more than one debit.

Date	Transaction	Debit	Credit
10/21/06	Notes payable	4,000	
	Interest expense	150	
	Cash		4,150
To record the repayment of a note plus interest			1-7

The debit to notes payable reduces the balance in that account. Before this transaction, it had a balance of $4,000. Now, when this debit is posted, the account will have a zero balance. The interest expense account will increase by $150 because expense accounts increase with debits. Cash is reduced by $4,150.

The final transaction of Clint's Consulting Company's first year of business is a $600 distribution to Clint, the only shareholder. In a sole proprietorship, a distribution is also called a **withdrawal**. Because Clint's Consulting Company is a corporation, the distribution is called a **dividend**. The dividends account has a debit balance and will eventually reduce retained earnings. Paying a dividend reduces the cash balance. Remember, a dividend payment is not an expense.

A distribution to the owner of a sole proprietorship is called a **withdrawal**; in a corporation, distributions to the shareholders are called **dividends**.

Date	Transaction	Debit	Credit
12/10/06	Dividends	600	
	Cash		600
To record a dividend payment			1–8

Step 2: Posting Journal Entries to the General Ledger

Each of the journal entries a company makes must be posted to the general ledger. How often this is done depends on the number of journal entries a company normally makes. Some computerized systems post every journal entry automatically when it is entered into the system. Other companies post transactions to the general ledger daily or weekly.

The accounts for Clint's Consulting Company, Inc. all begin with a zero balance, because this is Clint's first year of business. Each journal entry has the reference number from the journal with it when the entry is posted in the general ledger. This provides a way to trace every entry in the general ledger back to the original record of the transaction in the journal. After all the journal entries are posted, it is easy to calculate the balance in any account. The accounts, shown in Exhibit B.5 are listed in the following order: assets, liabilities, shareholder's equity, revenues, and expenses.

Step 3: Prepare an Unadjusted Trial Balance

A trial balance is a list of all the accounts in the general ledger, each with its debit or credit balance. The reasons for preparing a trial balance are to confirm that debits equal credits and to have a way to quickly review the accounts for needed adjustments. Exhibit B.6 shows the unadjusted trial balance for Clint's Consulting at December 31, 2006.

Step 4: Adjusting Journal Entries

Recording journal entries as transactions occur and posting them to the general ledger are routine accounting tasks. When a company gets ready to prepare financial statements at the end of the accounting period, there are more journal entries needed. These are not routine journal

> **L.O.3**
> Identify the adjustments needed before preparing financial statements and make those adjustments.

EXHIBIT B.5

Clint's Consulting Company, Inc. T-Accounts Cash (asset)

Cash (asset)					Supplies (asset)				Notes payable (liability)		
1-1	2,000	400	1-3		1-3	400			1-7	4,000	4,000 1-2
1-2	4,000	500	1-4								
1-5	9,000	350	1-6								
		4,150	1-7								
		600	1-8								

Common stock (shareholder's equity)			Consulting fees (revenue)			Advertising expense (expense)	
	2,000	1-1		9,000	1-5	1-4	500

Dividends (shareholder's equity temporary account)			Interest expense (expense)			Salary expense (expense)	
1-8	600		1-7	150		1-6	350

EXHIBIT B.6

Clint's Consulting Company, Inc. Unadjusted Trial Balance at December 31, 2006

Account	DR	CR
Cash	$ 9,000	
Supplies	400	
Notes payable		$ 0
Common stock		2,000
Dividends	600	
Consulting fees		9,000
Advertising expense	500	
Interest expense	150	
Salary expense	350	
	$11,000	$11,000

entries; they are called adjusting journal entries. As we discussed in Chapter 3, there are four situations that require adjustments before the financial statements are prepared. We need to adjust our records for *accrued revenues, accrued expenses, deferred revenues,* and *deferred expenses.* Let's look at an example of each of those adjustments in a general ledger system.

Accruals. Accrued Revenue. Suppose Clint's Consulting Company did some consulting for a fee of $3,000, but the company has not billed the client yet so the revenue has not been recognized—when it is recognized, it is put on the income statement. At December 31, Clint will adjust the company's records to recognize this revenue, even though he has not collected the cash. First, notice the effect of the adjustment on the accounting equation.

Assets	=	Liabilities +	Contributed capital (CC) +	Retained earnings
+3,000 Accounts receivable				+3,000 Consulting fees

The transaction increases assets—accounts receivable (AR). That means Clint would debit AR, because assets are increased with debits. Clint has also increased a revenue account, consulting fees. (The $3,000 is recorded in a revenue account, not directly into the retained earnings account. However, the revenue will end up increasing retained earnings on our balance sheet.) Revenue accounts increase with credits, so we would credit the revenue account consulting fees for $3,000. The accounting equation is in balance *and* debits = credits for our transaction. Here's what the journal entry would look like:

Date	Transaction	Debit	Credit
12/31/06	Accounts receivable	3,000	
	Consulting fees		3,000
To accrue revenue earned in 2006			A-1

Accrued Expenses Another situation that requires an adjustment is accrued expenses. If we have incurred an expense (the dollar amount that *will* be paid for an item or a service that has already been used to produce revenue), the matching principle requires us to put the expenses on the same income statement as the revenue it helped generate.

Sometimes matching an expense with a specific revenue is impossible to do. In that case, we record the expense in the time period when the expense item was used. For example, it is often impossible to match an employee's work with specific revenue the company earns. So the cost of the work done by an employee is put on the income statement as an expense in the accounting period when the work was done.

Let's look at an example of recording salary expense in the period in which the work was done. When companies pay their employees—on normal paydays during the year—they debit the account *salary expense* and credit the account *cash.* The salary expense account may have a significant balance at year-end because the company has been recording salary expense as the employees have been paid throughout the year. To make sure we've included *all* the salary expense for the year, we must examine the time our employees have worked near the end of the year. The purpose is to be sure to include the cost of *all* work done during a year in the salary expense on that year's income statement.

If we owe employees for work done in December 2006 but we will not pay them until January 2007, we have to accrue salary expense when we are adjusting our accounts at December 31, 2006. Suppose Clint's owes its employee $50 for work done in 2006, but the next payday is in 2007. To get this salary expense on the income statement for the year, Clint must debit salary expense for $50 and credit salaries payable for $50. The salary expense on the income statement for the year ended December 31, 2006 will now include this $50. Salaries payable on the balance sheet at December 31, 2006 will show the $50 obligation. Look at the adjustment in the accounting equation, and then look at the journal entry. Notice that in the adjusting entry, just like in a routine journal entry, debits = credits. The accounting equation remains in balance.

Assets	=	Liabilities	+	CC	+	Retained earnings
		+50 Salaries payable				(50) Salary expense

Date	Transaction	Debit	Credit
12/31/06	Salary expense	50	
	Salaries payable		50
To accrue salary expense at year-end			A-2

Your Turn B-2
Your Turn
Your Turn

Suppose a company owes employees $300 on December 31, 2007, the date of the financial statements; and the next payday is January 3, 2008. Give the adjusting journal entry necessary on December 31, 2007. How much salary expense will the company recognize when it actually pays the $300 to the employees on January 3, 2008? Give the journal entry for the payment on January 3, 2008.

Deferrals.   Deferred Revenue Deferred revenue is revenue that hasn't been earned yet, so it is recorded as a liability in a company's records—an obligation—when the cash is collected. Because cash has been collected, it must be recorded; but the goods or services have not yet been provided. The company must defer—put off—recognizing the revenue. When the cash is received, the company increases cash and increases a liability called unearned revenue. In a general ledger system, the amount of cash received is recorded in the cash account, where it is shown as a debit—that's an increase because assets are increased with debits. The journal entry is balanced with a credit to unearned revenue—that's an increase because liabilities are increased with credits.

Suppose Clint had received $4,000 on May 1 for consulting services to be provided over the next 16 months. This is how the receipt of the $4,000 cash for services to be provided in the future affects the accounting equation, followed by the journal entry for the receipt of the $4,000 cash.

Assets	=	Liabilities	+	CC	+	Retained earnings
+4,000 cash		+4,000 Unearned consulting fees				

Date	Transaction	Debit	Credit
5/1/06	Cash	4,000	
	Unearned consulting fees		4,000
To record the receipt of cash for services to be provided			1-9

Notice that this is *not* an adjusting entry; it's a regular journal entry—made when it occurs during the year—to record the receipt of cash. When we look at the T-accounts again, we'll see it posted with the transactions we posted previously.

Whenever a company has recorded unearned revenue during the year, an adjustment will be necessary at year-end to recognize the portion of the revenue that has been earned during the time between when the cash was received and year-end. If, on that basis, any of the unearned revenue becomes earned revenue by year-end, the unearned revenue account will be decreased and the revenue account will be increased with an adjustment. In terms of debits and credits, the unearned revenue account, which is a liability, will be decreased with a debit. In Clint's case, the credit corresponding to that debit will go to consulting fees, which means that the earned revenue will now show up on the income statement with the other consulting fees Clint has earned during the year. This adjustment is necessary to be sure all the earned revenue for the year is recognized—meaning, put on the income statement. Suppose Clint had earned half of the unearned revenue at year-end. The adjustment in the accounting equation and the corresponding journal entry for this adjustment follow:

Assets	=	Liabilities	+	CC	+	Retained earnings
		(2,000) Unearned consulting fees				+2,000 Consulting fees

Date	Transaction	Debit	Credit
12/31/06	Unearned consulting fees	2,000	
	Consulting fees		2,000
To record earned revenue at year-end			A-3

Deferred Expenses Deferred expenses may need to be adjusted before the financial statements are prepared. Recall, a deferred expense is something the company paid for in advance. One example is supplies, discussed in Chapter 3. Clint paid $400 for supplies during the year, and he recorded them as an asset. At the end of the year, he must determine how many supplies are left and how many he used. He counts the supplies on hand and then subtracts that amount from the amount he purchased. Suppose Clint finds that there is $75 worth of supplies left in the supply closet on December 31. Since he purchased $400 worth, that means he must have used $325 worth of supplies during the year. He wants to show supplies expense of $325 on the year's income statement; and he wants the asset supplies to show $75 on the balance sheet at year end. This is the adjustment to get the accounts to their correct year-end balances, first in the accounting equation and then as a journal entry:

Assets	=	Liabilities	+	CC	+	Retained earnings
(325) Supplies						(325) Supplies expense

Date	Transaction	Debit	Credit
12/31/06	Supplies Expense	325	
	Supplies		325
To record supplies expense for the year			A-4

The T-accounts with the adjusting entries posted to them are shown in Exhibit B.7.

Steps 5 and 6: Preparing the Adjusted Trial Balance and the Financial Statements

A trial balance is a list of all the accounts, each with its debit balance or its credit balance. An unadjusted trial balance is prepared before any adjustments have been made. An **adjusted trial balance** is prepared after adjustments have been made, and it can be used to prepare the financial statements.

After all the adjusting entries have been posted to the general ledger accounts and new balances have been computed in the general ledger, an **adjusted trial balance** is prepared. An adjusted trial balance is simply a list of all the general ledger accounts and their balances,

EXHIBIT B.7

Adjusted T-Accounts for Clint's Consulting Co., Inc.

Cash (asset)					Supplies (asset)				Notes payable (liability)	

Cash
(asset)

1-1	2,000	400	1-3
1-2	4,000	500	1-4
1-5	9,000	4,150	1-7
1-9	4,000	350	1-6
		600	1-8

Common stock
(shareholder's equity)

	2,000	1-1

Dividends

1-8	600	

Supplies expense
(expense)

A-4	325	

Supplies
(asset)

1-3	400	325	A-4

Accounts receivable
(asset)

A-1	3000	

Consulting fees
(revenue)

	9,000	1-5
	3,000	A-1
	2,000	A-3

Interest expense
(expense)

1-7	150	

Notes payable
(liability)

1-7	4,000	4,000	1-2

Salaries payable
(liability)

	50	A-2

Unearned consulting fees
(liability)

A-3	2,000	4,000	1-9

Advertising expense
(expense)

1-4	500	

Salary expense
(expense)

1-6	350	
A-2	50	

to verify that debits = credits for all the company's accounts after all the adjustments have been made. Preparing an adjusted trial balance—and making sure it actually balances—helps ensure the accuracy of the recording process. If the adjusted trial balance *is* in balance—debits = credits—it can be used to prepare the financial statements.

The adjusted trial balance is shown in Exhibit B.8, and the financial statements are shown in Exhibit B.9.

After the financial statements are prepared, we are *almost* ready to begin another accounting cycle. First, we must get our general ledger ready for a new fiscal year.

EXHIBIT B.8

Adjusted Trial Balance for Clint's Consulting Company, Inc. for the Year 2006

Account	DR	CR
Cash	$13,000	
Accounts receivable	3,000	
Supplies	75	
Notes payable		$ 0
Salaries payable		50
Unearned consulting fees		2,000
Common stock		2,000
Dividends	600	
Consulting fees		14,000
Advertising expense	500	
Interest expense	150	
Salary expenses	400	
Supplies expense	325	
	$18,050	$18,050

EXHIBIT B.9

Financial Statements for Clint's Consulting Company, Inc. for 2006

Clint's Consulting Company, Inc.
Income Statement
For the Year Ended December 31, 2006

Revenue		
Consulting fees		$14,000
Expenses		
Advertising	$500	
Salaries	400	
Supplies	325	
Interest	150	
Total expenses		1,375
Net income		$12,625

Clint's Consulting Company, Inc.
Statement of Changes in Shareholder's Equity
For the Year Ended December 31, 2006

Beginning common stock	$ 0	
Stock issued during the year	2,000	
Ending common stock		$ 2,000
Beginning retained earnings	$ 0	
Net income for the year	12,625	
Dividends	(600)	
Ending retained earnings		12,025
Total shareholder's equity		$14,025

Clint's Consulting Company, Inc.
Balance Sheet
At December 31, 2006

Assets		Liabilities and Shareholder's Equity	
Cash	$13,000	Salaries payable	$ 50
Accounts receivable	3,000	Unearned consulting fees	2,000
Supplies	75	Common stock	2,000
		Retained earnings	12,025
		Total liabilities and	
Total assets	$16,075	shareholder's equity	$16,075

Clint's Consulting Company, Inc.
Statement of Cash Flow
For the Year Ended December 31, 2006

Cash from operating activities		
Cash collected from customers	$13,000	
Cash paid for supplies	(400)	
Cash paid for interest	(150)	
Cash paid to employees	(350)	
Cash paid for advertising	(500)	
Net cash from operating activities	$11,600	
Cash from investing activities	0	
Cash from financing activities		
Cash from issue of stock	$ 2,000	
Proceeds from bank loan	4,000	
Repayment of bank loan	(4,000)	
Cash dividends paid	(600)	
Net cash from financing activities		1,400
Net increase in cash		$13,000

Step 7: Close the Revenue and Expense Accounts

Revenue accounts and expense accounts are **temporary accounts**. The balances in those accounts will be transferred to retained earnings at the end of each period; therefore, they will start each new period with a zero balance.

Think about the accounting equation and the work sheet we've been using to record transactions. We've been listing the revenues and expenses in the retained earnings column, because they increase and decrease the owner's claims to the assets of the business. The balance sheet will balance only when the revenue and expense amounts are incorporated into the retained earnings balance. The net amount of revenues minus expenses—net income—is incorporated into retained earnings when we prepare the statement of changes in shareholder's equity.

From a bookkeeping perspective, **closing the accounts** is done—meaning to bring their balances to zero—with journal entries. Each account receives a debit or a credit to close it. For example, if a revenue account has a balance of $300—which would be a credit balance—the account is closed with a debit for $300. The corresponding credit in that closing journal entry is to retained earnings. Thus, closing the revenue account increases retained earnings. On the other hand, closing an expense account will decrease retained earnings. For example, if an expense account has a balance of $100—which would be a debit balance—the account is closed with a credit for $100. The corresponding debit for that closing journal entry is to retained earnings. Closing the expense account decreases retained earnings.

Keep in mind the reason for having revenue accounts and expense accounts. For a single accounting period, usually a year, the revenues and expenses are recorded separately from retained earnings so that we can report them on the year's income statement. Then we want those amounts included in retained earnings, and we want the revenue and expense accounts to be "empty" so they can start over, ready for amounts that will come during the coming year. Remember, the income statement covers a single accounting period. We don't want to mix up last year's revenue with this year's revenue in our revenue accounts or last year's expenses with this year's expenses in our expense accounts. The process of bringing these accounts to a zero balance is called closing the accounts, and the journal entries are called closing entries. We cannot close the revenue accounts and expense accounts until we have prepared the financial statements.

Asset accounts, liability accounts, and shareholders' equity accounts are **permanent accounts**, or **real accounts**. A balance in any of these accounts is carried over from one period to the next. For example, the amount of cash shown in the cash account will never be zero (unless we spend our last cent). Think about your own personal records. If you keep track of your cash (like your checking account), you will have a continuous record of your cash balance. On the date of a personal balance sheet, you would see how much cash you have on that particular date. As the next year begins, you still have that cash. It doesn't go away because a new year begins.

To get a better idea of what we mean by the continuous record in a permanent account, let's consider a simple example of a *temporary* account. Suppose you were keeping a list of your grocery expenses for the year. At the end of the year, after you have reported the amount of those expenses on your annual income statement, you would want to start a new list for the next year. Because an income statement reports expenses for a period of time—a year, in this example—your grocery expenses for one year would be reported on *one* income statement, but those expenses would not apply to the following year. You would want the grocery expense account to be empty when you begin the next year. Expense amounts must apply to a specific time period for them to make sense.

Exhibit B.10 shows the closing journal entries for Clint's Consulting, which are recorded after the financial statements are prepared.

L.O.4
Describe the closing process and explain why it is necessary.

Temporary accounts are the revenue, expense, and dividends accounts. Their balances are brought to zero at the end of the accounting period, called **closing the accounts**.

Permanent accounts or **real accounts** are accounts that are never closed. They are the asset, liability, and shareholder's equity accounts.

Simple Company has one revenue account with a balance of $5,000 at year-end and one expense account with a balance of $3,000. Prepare the closing journal entries for Simple Company.

Your Turn B-3
Your Turn
Your Turn

EXHIBIT B.10

Closing Entries

Ref.	Date	Journal entry	DR	CR
c-1	12/31	Consulting fees	$14,000	
		Retained earnings..		$14,000
		To close revenue account		
c-2	12/31	Retained earnings..	1,375	
		Advertising expense...		500
		Salary expense		400
		Supplies expense		325
		Interest expense		150
		To close the expense accounts		
c-3	12/31	Retained earnings...	$ 600	
		Dividends...		$ 600
		To close dividends		

More About Closing Entries and the Relationship Between the Income Statement and the Balance Sheet. The formal way of making the balances zero in the revenue and expense accounts is called closing the accounts. Why do we bother with closing entries? They set the stage for the next accounting period by zeroing out the balances of all the temporary accounts. This is necessary because these accounts keep track of amounts that go to the income statement, which gives us the net income figure for *one specific period*. Without zeroing out the accounts, net income would include revenues or expenses for more than one period. Closing entries transfer the period's net income (or loss) to the retained earnings account (or to the owner's capital account in a sole proprietorship), so closing entries are the means by which net income flows downstream from the income statement through the statement of changes in shareholder's equity to the balance sheet.

Here's how the revenue amounts and expense amounts flow through the financial statements:

- *Income statement.* We present the details of net income—the revenues and expenses—on the income statement. The bottom line is net income.
- *Statement of changes in shareholder's equity.* We show net income as an addition to shareholder's equity on the statement of changes in shareholder's equity.
- *Balance sheet.* We present the total amount of shareholder's equity—which includes net income—on the balance sheet.

After we've used the revenue account balances and the expense account balances to prepare the income statement and after that information has flowed through to the balance sheet, we are ready to close the revenue accounts and expense accounts. That's the formal way of getting the correct balance in Retained Earnings. Here are the steps in detail to record closing entries:

1. Transfer all credit balances from the revenue accounts to retained earnings. This is done with a closing entry. The closing journal entry will have a debit to each of the revenue accounts for the entire balance of each—to bring them to a zero balance. The corresponding credit will be to Retained Earnings for the total amount of the period's revenue.

2. Transfer all debit balances from the expense accounts to retained earnings. This is done with a closing entry. The closing journal entry will have a debit to retained earnings and credits to all the expense accounts for their entire balances to bring them to a zero balance. The debit to retained earnings will be for the total amount of the period's expenses.

3. Transfer the dividends account balance to retained earnings. When a distribution is made to the shareholders of a corporation, a special account—dividends—is often used. This account is a temporary account that carries a debit balance. (When the dividends are declared and paid, dividends is debited and cash is credited.) The dividends account is closed directly to Retained Earnings. The amount of the dividends is not included on the income statement, but it is shown on the statement of changes in shareholders' equity. The journal entry to close this account will have a credit to dividends and a debit to retained earnings.

Look at the closing entries posted to Clint's T-accounts, shown in bold print in Exhibit B.11. Notice how the revenue and expense accounts have a zero balance.

EXHIBIT B.11

T-Accounts with Closing Entries for Clint's Consulting Company, Inc.

	Cash (asset)		
1-1	2,000	400	1-3
1-2	4,000	500	1-4
1-5	9,000	350	1-6
1-9	4,000	4,150	1-7
		600	1-8

	Common stock (shareholder's equity)	
	2,000	1-1

	Retained earnings (shareholder's equity)	
C-2	1,375	14,000 C-1
C-3	6006	

	Dividends (shareholder's equity)	
1-8	600	**600 C-3**

	Supplies expense (expense)	
A-4	325	**325 C-2**

	Supplies (asset)		
1-3	400	325	A-4

	Accounts receivable (asset)	
A-1	3000	

	Consulting fees (revenue)		
		9,000	1-5
		3,000	A-1
		2,000	A-3
C-1 14,000			

	Interest expense (expense)	
1-7	150	**150 C-2**

	Notes payable (liability)		
1-7	4,000	4,000	1-2

	Salaries payable (liability)	
		50 A-2

	Unearned consulting fees (liability)		
A-3	2,000	4,000	1-9

	Advertising expense (expense)	
1-4	500	**500 C-2**

	Salary expense (expense)	
1-6	350	**400 C-2**
A-2	50	

When closing is done, there is one step left to completing our record keeping for the year: That step is preparing a postclosing trial balance.

Step 8: Preparing a Postclosing Trial Balance

The final step in the accounting cycle is to prepare a **postclosing trial balance**. Remember, *post* means *after* (like *pre* means *before*). After the temporary accounts are closed, preparing a trial balance—a list of all the accounts with their debit or credit balances—accomplishes two things:

- It is a final check of the equality of debits and credits in the general ledger.
- It confirms that we are ready to start our next period with only real (permanent) accounts.

The postclosing trial balance for Clint's Consulting is shown in Exhibit B.12.

> A **postclosing trial balance** is a list of all the accounts and their debit balances or credit balances, prepared after the temporary accounts have been closed. Only balance sheet accounts will appear on the postclosing trial balance.

Review and Summary of the Accounting Cycle

To summarize, there are several steps in the process of preparing financial statements using a traditional general ledger system. Together, they are called the *accounting cycle.*

1. Record the transactions in the journal.
2. Post the journal entries to the ledger.
3. Prepare an unadjusted trial balance.

EXHIBIT B.12

Postclosing Trial Balance for Clint's Consulting Company, Inc. at December 31, 2006

Account	DR	CR
Cash	$13,000	
Accounts receivable	3,000	
Supplies	75	
Notes payable		$ 0
Salaries payable		50
Unearned consulting fees		2,000
Common stock		2,000
Retained earnings		12,025
Totals	$16,075	$16,075

4. Adjust the accounts at the end of the period—record the adjusting journal entries and post them to the general ledger.
5. Prepare an adjusted trial balance.
6. Prepare the financial statements.
7. Close the temporary accounts to get ready for the next accounting period.
8. Prepare a postclosing trial balance.

Tom's Wear Transactions for March 2006 in a General Ledger System

We've already analyzed the transactions for Tom's Wear for the third month of business, and prepared the financial statements for March in Chapter 3. Let's repeat the accounting cycle for the same month, this time using debits and credits. The transactions for March are shown in Exhibit B.13. Each transaction is recorded as an entry in the general journal, chronologically as it occurs during the company's business activity. Exhibit B.14 shows the transactions in the accounting equation worksheet. Then each transaction is posted to the general ledger (we'll use T-accounts). At March 31, we'll post the adjusting entries needed to prepare the four financial statements. After following along through the adjusted T-accounts, you will prepare the financial statements.

To use a general ledger system, we need to set up the accounts with their balances on March 1, 2006. Exhibit B.15 shows all the accounts with their beginning balances (indicated with BB). Those accounts, in the Tom's Wear general ledger, will remain with the beginning balances until we post journal entries from the month's transactions.

The first step in the accounting cycle is to record each transaction in chronological order in the journal—as each occurs in the business. Look at each transaction and its journal entry. Notice, for each journal entry there is:

- the date of the transaction
- the account names
- equality between the debits and credits—in every journal entry
- a brief explanation of the transaction

Study each journal entry to make sure you understand how the transaction was recorded.

EXHIBIT B.13

Transactions for March 2006 for Tom's Wear, Inc.

March 1	Purchased computer for $4,000 with $1,000 down and a 3-month, 12% note for $3,000. The computer is expected to last for 3 years and have a residual value of $400.
March 10	Paid the rest of last month's advertising bill, $50.
March 15	Collected accounts receivable of $150 from customers from February.
March 20	Paid for February purchases—paying off the accounts payable balance—of $800.
March 24	Purchased 250 shirts @ $4 each for cash, $1,000.
March 27	Sold 200 shirts for $10 each, all on account, for total sales of $2,000.

UNDERSTANDING Business

Enterprise Resource Planning Systems

Enterprise Resource Planning systems are changing the way businesses manage, process, and use information. ERP systems are computer-based software programs designed to process an organization's transactions and integrate information for planning, production, financial reporting, and customer service. These systems are designed for companies that have computer systems with enormous capabilities. It is estimated that the majority of companies with annual revenues exceeding $1 billion have implemented ERP systems.

Exactly how ERP systems operate varies from company to company, depending on the company's needs.

- ERP systems are packaged software designed for business environments, both traditional and Web based. *Packaged software* means that the software is commercially available—for purchase or lease—from a software vendor, as opposed to being developed in-house. ERP software packages incorporate what the vendors call "best practices." These are supposed to be the best way of doing certain business activities, such as the best practice for inventory management or production management.
- An ERP system is composed of modules relating to specific functions. There are modules for: *accounting,* including financial, managerial, and international accounting; *logistics,* including materials requirement planning, production, distribution, sales management, and customer management; and *human resources,* including payroll, benefits, and compensation management.
- All the modules work together with a common database. This creates an enterprise-wide system instead of separate, independent systems for each function of the business.
- ERP systems are integrated in terms of software, but not hardware. So, even though two companies may buy ERP packages from the same vendor, the way the system is used will likely be very different. A company may implement modules from more than one vendor in an attempt to customize its ERP system.
- Because of their popularity and growth, the large ERP vendors are familiar to many of us—SAP, Oracle, PeopleSoft, J.D. Edwards, and BAAN. Together these vendors hold a major share of the ERP market and provide their system packages along with training to their clients around the world.
- Because the ERP vendors have already sold their systems to most of the large international companies, the vendors are trying to expand their market to slightly smaller (i.e., middle-market) companies.

Companies implement ERP systems to:

- consolidate their systems and eliminate redundant data entry and data storage
- decrease their computer operating costs
- better manage their business processes
- accommodate international currencies and international languages
- standardize policies and procedures
- enhance and speed up financial reporting
- improve decision making
- improve productivity
- improve profitability

In spite of all the potential benefits of ERP systems, there are drawbacks. ERP systems are costly to implement, with total implementation costs running into the millions of dollars. The use of best practices embedded in the software usually requires companies to change the way they conduct their business processes to match the software. This is not always beneficial—especially when companies have business processes that may give them a competitive advantage. Finally, switching to a new system requires extensive and costly training for those who will use the system.

Given the widespread adoption of ERP systems, it is apparent that the market perceives the ERP system benefits to outweigh the costs. Therefore, whether you choose to go into accounting, information technology, finance, marketing, or management, it is likely that you will encounter an ERP system. However, given the speed with which technology changes, the ERP systems that you will encounter will be even more complex with greater capacities than the ones in existence today.

EXHIBIT B.14

Transactions for Tom's Wear for March in the Accounting Equation Worksheet before Adjustments

	Assets						=	Liabilities				+	Shareholder's Equity				
													Contributed Capital	Retained Earnings (RE)			
														Beginning RE 1,220			
	Cash	Accounts Receivable	Inventory	Prepaid Insurance	Computers	Accumulated Depreciation, Computers		Accounts Payable	Other Payables	Interest Payable	Notes Payable		Common Stock	Revenues	Expenses	Dividends	
Beginning Balances	$ 6,695	150	100	125	4,000			800	50				5,000				
March 1	(1,000)				4,000						3,000						
March 10	(50)								(50)								
March 15	150	(150)															
March 20	(800)							(800)									
March 24	(1,000)		1,000														
March 27		2,000	(800)											2,000	(800)		
Ending Balances	$ 3,995	2,000	300	125	4,000		=	0	0		3,000		5,000	2,000	(800)	0	1,220

Check for equality 10,420 = 10,420

— Income Statement — Statement of Changes in Shareholder's Equity — Balance Sheet — Statement of Cash Flows

594

EXHIBIT B.15

T-Accounts for Tom's Wear at the Beginning of March

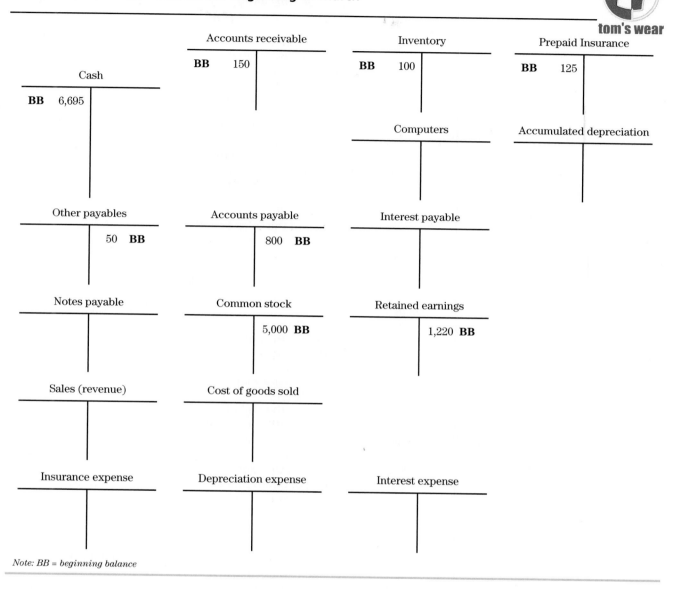

Note: BB = beginning balance

Journal Entries for March 2006

Ref.	Date	Journal entry	DR	CR
3-1	3/01/06	Equipment	4,000	
		Cash		1,000
		Notes payable		3,000
		To record the purchase of a computer with a cash payment of $1,000 and a note payable of $3,000		
3-2	3/10/06	Other payables	50	
		Cash		50
		To record the payment of a liability for last year's advertising expense		
3-3	3/15/06	Cash	150	
		Accounts receivable		150
		To record the collection of accounts receivable		
3-4	3/20/06	Accounts payable	800	
		Cash		800
		To record payment to vendor for last month's purchase		
3-5	3/24/06	Inventory	1,000	
		Cash		1,000
		To record the purchase of 250 T-shirts at $4 each, paid for in cash		
3-6a	3/27/06	Accounts receivable	2,000	
		Sales		2,000
		To record the sale of 200 T-shirts, on account		
3-6b	3/27/06	Cost of goods sold	800	
		Inventory		800
		To record the expense *cost of goods sold* and reduce the inventory by 200 × $4		

Required

1. Post the journal entries for March using the T-accounts shown in Exhibit B.15.
2. Then prepare an unadjusted trial balance at March 31.
3. Make the necessary adjusting journal entries at March 31 and post them to the T-accounts. For Tom's Wear, three adjustments need to be made before the financial statements can be prepared. The adjustments are:
   a. Depreciation expense for the computer: $100
   b. Insurance expense for the month: $50
   c. Interest payable on the note: $30
4. Prepare an *adjusted* trial balance at March 31, 2006.
5. Use the adjusted trial balance to prepare the four basic financial statements.

Solution

1. T-accounts are shown in the answer to part 3.

2.

Tom's Wear, Inc.
Unadjusted Trial Balance
March 31, 2006

Cash	$ 3,995	
Accounts receivable	2,000	
Inventory	300	
Prepaid insurance	125	
Equipment	4,000	
Notes payable		$ 3,000
Common stock		5,000
Retained earnings		1,220
Sales		2,000
Cost of goods sold	800	
Totals	*$11,220*	*$11,220*

3. Adjusting journal entries and explanations:

   a. The computer has been used for one full month, so you must record depreciation expense. The cost was $4,000, an estimated residual value of $400, and a 3-year useful life. Each year the equipment will be depreciated by $1,200 (= (4,000 − 400)/3 years). That makes the depreciation expense $100 per month.

Date	Transaction	Debit	Credit
3/31/06	Depreciation expense	100	
	Accumulated depreciation		100
	To record the depreciation expense for March		Adj-1

   b. Tom's Wear signed a $3,000 note on March 1 to purchase the computer. A month has passed, and Tom's Wear needs to accrue the interest expense on that note in the amount of $30 (= $3,000 × 0.12 × 1/12).

Date	Transaction	Debit	Credit
3/31/06	Interest expense	30	
	Interest payable		30
	To record the interest expense for March		Adj-2

c. In mid-February, Tom's Wear purchased 3 months of insurance for $150, which is $50 per month. On the March 1 balance sheet, there is a current asset called prepaid insurance in the amount of $125. A full month's worth of insurance expense needs to be recorded for the month of March. That amount will be deducted from prepaid insurance.

Date	Transaction	Debit	Credit
3/31/06	Insurance expense	50	
	Prepaid insurance		50
	To record the insurance expense for the year		Adj-3

T-accounts with adjustments for March 2006 posted (Balances in each account are shown with a double underline)

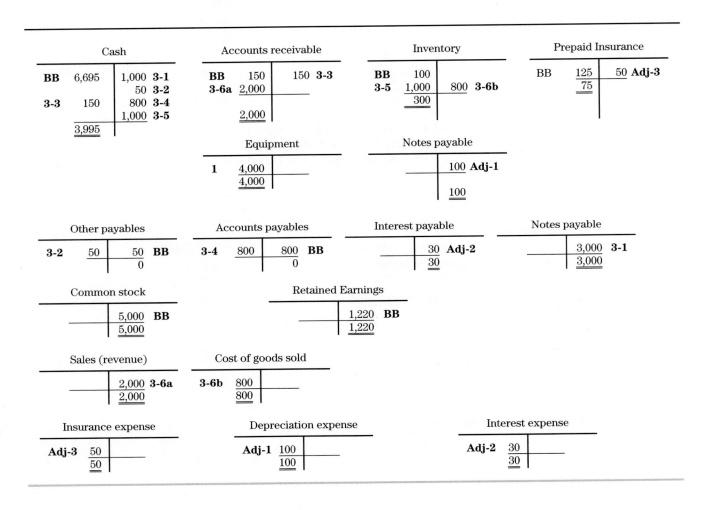

4.

Tom's Wear, Inc.
Adjusted Trial Balance
March 31, 2006

Cash	$ 3,995	
Accounts receivable	2,000	
Inventory	300	
Prepaid insurance	75	
Equipment	4,000	
Accumulated depreciation		$ 100
Interest payable		30
Notes payable		3,000
Common stock		5,000
Retained earnings		1,220
Sales		2,000
Cost of goods sold	800	
Insurance expense	50	
Depreciation expense	100	
Interest expense	30	
Totals	$11,350	$11,350

5. The financial statements:

Tom's Wear, Inc.
Income Statement
For the Month Ended March 31, 2006

Sales revenue			$ 2,000
Expenses			
Cost of goods sold	$ 800		
Depreciation expense	100		
Insurance expense	50		
Interest expense	30	980	
Net income		$ 1,020	

Tom's Wear, Inc.
Statement of Changes in Shareholder's Equity
For the Month Ended March 31, 2006

Beginning common stock	$ 5,000	
Common stock issued during the month	0	
Ending common stock		$ 5,000
Beginning retained earnings	$ 1,220	
Net income for the month	1,020	
Dividends declared	0	
Ending retained earnings		2,240
Total shareholder's equity		$ 7,240

Tom's Wear, Inc.
Balance Sheet
At March 31, 2006

Assets		Liabilities and Shareholder's equity	
Current assets		Current liabilities	
Cash	$ 3,995	Interest payable	$ 30
Accounts receivable	2,000	Notes payable	3,000
Inventory	300	Total current liabilities	3,030
Prepaid insurance	75	Shareholder's equity	
Total current assets	6,370	Common stock	5,000
Computer (net of $100		Retained earnings	2,240
accumulated depreciation)	3,900	Total shareholder's equity	7,240
		Total liabilities and	
Total assets	$10,270	shareholder's equity	$10,270

Tom's Wear, Inc.
Statement of Cash Flows
For the Month Ended March 31, 2006

Cash from operating activities:
Cash collected from customers	$ 150	
Cash paid to vendors	(1,800)	
Cash paid for operating expense	(50)	
Net cash from operating activities		$ (1,700)
Cash from investing activities:		
Purchase of asset*	$(1,000)	(1,000)
Cash from financing activities:		0
Net increase (decrease) in cash		$ (2,700)
Beginning cash balance		6,695
Ending cash balance		$ 3,995

You have seen these exact financial statements before. When we used the accounting equation to keep track of the transactions in Chapter 3, the results were the same as using the general ledger system here. No matter how we do the record keeping, the financial statements are the same. The mechanics of any accounting system—stand-alone or integrated with an enterprise resource planning system—must be designed to produce the information needed for the basic financial statements according to GAAP.

Key Terms

general ledger system (p. 576)
journal (p. 576)
trial balance (p. 577)
debit (p. 578)
credit (p. 578)

accounting cycle (p. 580)
withdrawal (p. 582)
dividend (p. 582)
adjusted trial balance (p. 586)
temporary accounts (p. 589)

closing the accounts (p. 589)
permanent accounts (p. 589)
real accounts (p. 589)
postclosing trial balance (p. 591)

Answers to YOUR TURN Questions

Your Turn B-1

Account title	Expense	Revenue	Asset	Liability	Shareholder's equity
Accounts payable				CR (Credit)	
Accounts receivable			DR		
Advertising expense	DR				
Cash			DR		
Depreciation expense	DR				
Furniture and fixtures			DR		
Accumulated depreciation			(Contra) CR		
Unearned fees				CR	
Salary expense	DR				
Common stock					CR
Rent expense	DR				
Dividends					DR
Retained earnings					CR
(Earned) Fees		CR			
Land			DR		
Building			DR		

Your Turn B-2

Date	Transaction	Debit	Credit
12/31/07	Salaries expense	300	
	Salaries payable		300
To accrue salary expense for December 2007			

No expense will be recognized in January 2008. It was recognized in December 2007, but will be paid in January 2008.

Date	Transaction	Debit	Credit
1/3/08	Salaries payable	300	
	Cash		300
To record the cash payment of salaries payable			

Your Turn B-3

Date	Transaction	Debit	Credit
12/31/07	Revenue account	5,000	
	Retained earnings		5,000
To close the revenue account to retained earnings			

Date	Transaction	Debit	Credit
12/31/07	Retained earnings	3,000	
	Expense account		3,000
To close the expense account to retained earnings			

Questions

1. What is the general ledger system and what are its advantages?
2. What is an account?
3. What is the trial balance?
4. Which accounts are permanent and which are temporary?
5. What is the normal balance in each of these accounts?

Accounts receivable	Cash
Accounts payable	Supplies expense
Common stock	Distributions (dividends)
Retained earnings	Inventory
Sales revenue	Bonds payable
Salary expense	Cost of goods sold

6. What are the basic steps in the accounting cycle?
7. Can accounting transactions be recorded directly into the general ledger accounts? What is the advantage of using a journal first?
8. Is a credit a good thing or a bad thing? Explain.
9. What are adjusting entries and why are they necessary?

Multiple-Choice Questions

1. Evans Company completes a service engagement and bills a customer $50,000 on June 19, 2006. Included in the journal entry to record this transaction will be a:
   a. Debit to cash, $50,000.
   b. Credit to cash, $50,000.
   c. Credit to accounts receivable, $50,000.
   d. Credit to service revenue, $50,000.
2. A trial balance is a:
   a. List of all the accounts with a six-digit account number used by a business.
   b. Place to record increases and decreases to a particular financial statement item's balance.
   c. Chronological list of all recorded transactions.
   d. List of all the accounts used by the business along with each account's debit or credit balance at a point in time.
3. Bob Frederick, the owner of a delivery business, wants to know the balance of cash, accounts receivable, and sales on April 15 of the current period. Bob should look at what part of his accounting system?
   a. The journal.
   b. The ledger.
   c. The balance sheet.
   d. The subsidiary journal.
4. What is accomplished by preparing a trial balance?
   a. A firm can make sure the debits equal the credits in the accounting system.
   b. A firm can make sure there are no errors in the accounting system.
   c. A firm can identify accruals and deferrals.
   d. All of the above.
5. The data needed to prepare a trial balance comes from the:
   a. Journal.
   b. Ledger.
   c. Balance sheet.
   d. Post-closing income statement.
6. If the income statement includes revenues earned even if the cash has not been collected from customers yet, it means that the:
   a. Closing entries have not been completed yet.
   b. Journal has errors in it.
   c. Accrual basis of accounting is being used.
   d. Adjusting entries have not been done yet.

7. Myers Company pays its employees every Friday for a 5-day workweek (Monday through Friday). The employees earn $3,000 per day of work. If the company pays the employees $15,000 on Friday, October 3, 2008, the entry into the journal would include:
   a. A debit to wages expense for $15,000.
   b. A debit to cash for $15,000.
   c. A credit to wages payable for $15,000.
   d. A debit to cash for $3,000.

8. Jules, Inc. had a June 1, 2007 balance of office supplies of $100. During June, the company purchased $900 more of the office supplies in exchange for cash. On June 30, 2007 the supplies were counted and it was determined that $200 worth of office supplies were left unused. The adjusting journal entry should include a:
   a. Debit to supplies expense of $800.
   b. Debit to office supplies of $900.
   c. Credit to cash for $200.
   d. Credit to supplies expense of $800.

9. Why should closing entries be completed at the end of each period?
   a. Because certain accounts are not needed in the future.
   b. Because it allows the trial balance and financial statements to be prepared.
   c. Because all accounts must begin the next period at zero.
   d. Because temporary accounts need to start the next period with a zero balance.

10. Which account below should NOT be closed?
    a. Accounts receivable.
    b. Interest revenue.
    c. Sales revenue.
    d. Wages expense.

Short Exercises

SEB-1. *Normal account balances.* Given the following accounts, tell whether the normal balance of each account is a debit (DR) or credit (CR). *(LO 1)*

  1. _____ Interest receivable
  2. _____ Accounts payable
  3. _____ Sonia Bostic, Capital account
  4. _____ Service revenue
  5. _____ Prepaid rent
  6. _____ Supplies inventory
  7. _____ Insurance expense
  8. _____ Income tax expense
  9. _____ Salaries payable
  10. _____ Retained earnings

SEB-2. *Recognize revenue and recording journal entries.* Indicate which of the following events would result in recognizing revenue for the year in which the described event takes place; indicate the amount and the account. Give the journal entry that would be made in each case. (Take the selling company's point of view.) *(LO 1, 2, 3)*

   a. DELL, Inc. sold a computer system worth $10,000; the customer financed the purchase because he didn't have any cash.
   b. Steel USA is producing 3 tons of steel for American Cans. It costs $4,500 per ton to produce, but American Cans has promised to pay $7,750 per ton when it receives the steel. Steel USA will probably ship it in the near future.
   c. Seminole Boosters has received $75,000 in advance ticket sales for next year's football games.
   d. Comcast Cable collected several accounts that were outstanding from last year. Usually accounts are collected in advance; but in this case, the customer received the cable services last year but didn't pay until this year.
   e. Customers paid over $6,500 in advance for services to be rendered next year.

SEB-3. *Recognize expenses and recording journal entries.* Indicate which of the following events would result in recognizing expenses for the year in which the described event takes place; give the journal entry. (Take the T-shirt company's point of view.) *(LO 1, 2, 3)*

    a. T-Shirts Plus, Inc. paid employees $6,000 for work performed during the prior year.

    b. T-Shirts Plus, Inc. purchased 15,000 T-shirts for their inventory for $30,000 on account.

    c. T-Shirts Plus, Inc. paid the factory cash for the 15,000 shirts purchased.

    d. T-Shirts Plus, Inc. sold 1,500 T-shirts to the FSU Bookstore for $16,500 cash.

    e. T-Shirts Plus, Inc. received a utility bill for the last month of the year in the amount of $575 but won't actually pay it until next year.

    f. T-Shirts Plus, Inc. paid $8,600 for a 2-year insurance policy—for the current year and for next year.

SEB-4. *Relate the accounting equation to debits and credits.* Below are selected transactions for Jenna & Yvonne Enterprises, Inc. that occurred during the month of December. For each transaction, tell how it affects the accounting equation. Then, tell which accounts will be affected and how. (Ignore adjustments that may be needed on December 31.) For example, Jenna & Yvonne purchased a new computer for $5,000 for cash. It is expected to last for 5 years. Solution: Assets are increased by $5,000 (equipment) and also reduced by $5,000 (cash): debit (increase) equipment, credit (decrease) cash. *(LO 1)*

    a. The company issued common stock to investors for $15,000 cash.

    b. The company rented a warehouse for $1,500 per month, and paid for 3 months rent on December 1.

    c. The company purchased inventory for $4,500 on account.

SEB-5. *Record journal entries.* The following selected transactions for Garret & Wilson's Consulting, Inc. occurred during the month of April. Give the journal entry for each. *(LO 1)*

    a. The firm provided services to customers for $10,000: Seventy percent were paid with cash and thirty percent were on account.

    b. Garret & Wilson's paid $1,000 for part of a $3,000 purchase made in March on account.

    c. The company incurred operating expenses for $800 cash.

    d. Garret & Wilson's purchased supplies for $500 cash, to be used during May.

SEB-6. *Effect of transactions on cash.* How do the following transactions affect Toys, Toys, Toys, Inc.'s cash account? (Tell if it would be a debit or a credit.) *(LO 1)*

    a. Toys, Toys, Toys purchased $6,000 of baby cribs for cash.

    b. The company sold one of their buildings, allowing the buyer to give them a short-term note for $135,000.

    c. The employees were paid $5,400 cash in sales commissions.

    d. The firm gave customers $1,500 cash for returned merchandise.

    e. Toys, Toys, Toys issued stock to investors for $7,750 cash.

SEB-7. *Effect of transactions on the liability and shareholders' equity accounts.* How do the following transactions affect the liability and shareholders' equity accounts for Fast Signs, Inc. during 2007? (Tell if it would be a debit or a credit.) *(LO 1)*

    a. Fast Signs paid the remainder of a $3,000 loan.

    b. The company obtained a loan for $10,000.

    c. Fast Signs earned $12,000 in sales for the year.

    d. An estimated $2,500 will be due for yearly income taxes, payable in 2008.

SEB-8. *Effect of transactions on accounts.* Determine how the accounts would be affected. (increase or decrease and debit or credit) for the following transactions occurring in January 2009 for Networking Solutions, Inc. *(LO 1)*

    a. Networking Solutions received $25,000 cash from the owner in exchange for common stock.

    b. The company purchased $10,000 of new office computers on account.

c. The company sold $2,500 of inventory for cash.
d. Networking Solutions paid $4,500 for next year's rent.
e. The company paid $2,000 of the amount owed for the computers.
f. The company declared and distributed $500 of dividends.

SEB-9. *Determine permanent or temporary accounts.* For each of the following accounts, tell whether it is a permanent account or a temporary account. *(LO 4)*

1. _____ Cash
2. _____ Accounts payable
3. _____ Common stock
4. _____ Sales revenue
5. _____ Prepaid rent
6. _____ Merchandise inventory
7. _____ Insurance expense
8. _____ Interest expense
9. _____ Income taxes payable
10. _____ Common stock

Exercises—Set A

EB-1A. *Record transactions to T-accounts.* Record the following transactions for Brazwells at Bradford, Inc. in T-accounts and tell how each affects assets, liabilities, or stockholder's equity. The year-end for Brazwells at Bradford, Inc. is June 30. *(LO 1, 2)*

a. On September 1, Brazwells issued a $6,000 note at 12%, both interest and principal due in 1 year.
b. On October 1, Brazwells rented a copy machine and paid 1 year of rent in advance at a rate of $200 per month.
c. On December 30, Brazwells purchased an insurance policy for a term of 1 year, beginning immediately. The cost was $800, paid in cash.
d. On March 1, Brazwells replenished the supply closet with the purchase of $700 worth of supplies for cash. The company started the year with $100 worth of supplies on hand.
e. Over the course of the year, Brazwells earned $45,000 of service revenue, collected in cash.

EB-2A. *Record adjustments to T-accounts.* Use the information from EB-1A, including your answers to a through e to make the necessary adjustments to Brazwells' accounts in preparation for the year-end financial statements. You may need to use the additional information that follows: *(LO 1, 2, 3)*

• On hand at year-end was $50 worth of supplies.

EB-3A. *Record transactions to T-accounts and prepare unadjusted trial balance.* Matt opened his Reading is Fun, Inc., "a bookstore" on April 1, 2008, selling new and used books. Matt contributed $4,000 in exchange for common stock to start the business. *(LO 1, 2)*

a. On April 1, the business buys $3,000 of new books from his supplier with cash.
b. On April 30, customers bring in used books and the business buys them for $750 cash.
c. On June 30, $1,200 of new books are sold for $3,000. Half of these sales are on account.
d. On June 30, the business sells all the used books for $1,500 cash.

Record the transactions into T-accounts for the new company. Calculate the account balances and prepare an unadjusted trial balance at June 30, 2008.

EB-4A. *Record transactions to T-accounts and prepare unadjusted trial balance.* The trial balance of Wisteria Lane Productions, Inc. on March 1, 2007, lists the company's assets, liabilities, and shareholders' equity on that date. *(LO 1, 2)*

BALANCE

Account Title	Debit	Credit
Cash	$15,000	
Accounts receivable	5,700	
Accounts payable		$ 3,200
Common stock		9,000
Retained earnings		8,500
Total	$20,700	$20,700

During March, Wisteria Lane completed the following transactions:
a. The company borrowed $6,000 from the bank with a short-term note payable.
b. Wisteria Lane paid cash of $12,000 to acquire land.
c. The company performed service for a customer and collected the cash of $3,500.
d. Wisteria Lane purchased supplies on credit, $225.
e. The company performed service for a customer on account, $1,800.

Set up T-accounts for the accounts given in the March 1 trial balance. Then post the preceding transactions to the accounts. Calculate the account balances and prepare an unadjusted trial balance at March 31.

EB-5A. *Recognize adjusting and closing entries.* Use the information from EB4-A to identify the accounts that will likely need to be adjusted before the monthly financial statements are prepared. What additional information would you need in each case to make the appropriate adjustment? Which accounts will need to be closed at the end of the accounting period and why? *(LO 3, 4)*

EB-6A. *Record closing entries and compute net income.* Given the following adjusted trial balance, record the appropriate closing entries. What is net income for the year? *(LO 4)*

BRETT'S BAIT & TACKLE, INC.
ADJUSTED TRIAL BALANCE
JUNE 30, 2009

	Debit	Credit
Cash	$ 13,000	
Accounts receivable	20,000	
Supplies	21,500	
Equipment	20,000	
Accumulated depreciation		$ 9,000
Property	64,000	
Prepaid rent	28,000	
Accounts payable		23,000
Notes payable		25,000
Interest payable		2,000
Common stock		51,000
Retained earnings		29,500[a]
Dividends	4,000	
Sales		94,000
Cost of goods sold	45,000	
Depreciation expense	3,000	
Salaries expense	15,000	
Totals	$233,500	$233,500

[a]Retained earnings at July 1, 2008. (No accounts have been closed.)

EB-7A. *Record journal entries, adjusting entries, and explain the accounting cycle.* The Problem Solvers Consulting Corporation began business in 2007. The following transactions took place during January: *(LO 1, 2, 3, 4)*

Jan. 1 Owners invested $65,000 in exchange for common stock.

1 The company borrowed $10,000 from a local bank with a 12% note and a 6-month term. Both the principal and interest will be repaid in 6 months.

1 The company purchased computer equipment for $9,360 cash. It should last 4 years, with no residual value.

6 Supplies were purchased on account for $550.

8 Office rent of $800 for January was paid in cash.

20 The company received $5,150 from a customer for services to be performed in February.

31 Consulting services performed during January on account totaled $14,000.

31 The company paid salaries of $8,500 to employees.

31 The company paid $400 to the supplies vendor as part of the $550 owed to the vendor from the purchase on January 6. The company only paid part of the invoice because it only used $400 worth of the supplies in January.

Required: Give the journal entry for each transaction. Provide the reason for each entry. Then, make the necessary adjusting entries at January 31, 2007. What else should be done to finish the accounting cycle for the month?

EB-8A. *Record journal entries, post to T-Accounts, and prepare unadjusted trial balance.* Ray & Hawthorne CPAs decided to open their own tax practice, Tax Specialists, Inc. The following transactions are the events which occurred during May 2007, the company's first month: *(LO 1, 2)*

May 1 Ray and Hawthorne each donated $20,000 cash in exchange for common stock. They also signed a note with National Bank for $25,000.

May 2 Tax Specialists paid $28,000 prepaid rent for the first year.

May 11 Office equipment was purchased on account for $17,500.

May 16 The company purchased insurance for 2 years with $6,500 cash. The policy was effective June 1.

May 18 A discolored piece of the office equipment arrived and the supplier agreed to remove $3,500 from Tax Specialists' account.

May 25 The company purchased some office furniture on sale worth $10,000 on account.

May 28 Tax Specialist paid off the balance owed on the equipment.

May 30 An office manager was hired at a rate of $110 a day. The start date is June 1.

Required: Give the journal entry for each transaction. Set up the required T-accounts and post the entries to these accounts. Prepare an unadjusted trial balance.

Exercises—Set B

EB-1B. *Record transactions to T-accounts.* Record the following transactions for Marilyn Ivory's Pianos & Music, Inc. in T-accounts and tell how each affects assets, liabilities, or shareholders' equity. The year-end for Pianos & Music, Inc. is December 31. *(LO 1, 2)*

a. On March 1, Pianos & Music issued a $15,120 note at 10%, both interest and principal due in 1 year.

b. On May 1, Pianos & Music rented a warehouse and paid $8,400 for 2 years of rent in advance.

c. Pianos & Music purchased an insurance policy for a term of 3 years on July 1, beginning immediately. The cost was $5,400, paid in cash.

    d. The company replenished the supply closet with the purchase of $575 worth of supplies for cash on November 1. The company started the year with $375 worth of supplies on hand.

    e. Over the course of the year, Pianos & Music earned $54,500 for cash sales of $15,000 worth of inventory, collected in cash. The company started the year with $20,000 in inventory.

EB-2B. *Record adjustments to T-accounts.* Use the information from EB-1B, including your answers to a through e to make the necessary adjustments to Pianos & Music's accounts in preparation for the year-end financial statements. You may need to use the additional information that follows: *(LO 1, 2, 3)*

- On hand at year-end was $375 worth of supplies.

EB-3B. *Record transactions to T-accounts and prepare unadjusted trial balance.* Flynt Freedman opened Flynt's Grindz & Brew, Inc. on March 1, 2007, selling gourmet coffees, teas, and desserts. Flynt contributed $5,500 in exchange for common stock to start the business. *(LO 1, 2)*

    a. On March 1, the business buys $2,750 of inventory from the supplier with cash.

    b. Flynt's purchases equipment for $350 cash on March 15.

    c. On March 30, Flynt's pays $500 for operating expenses.

    d. At the end of the month Flynt's has earned sales revenue of $5,500 by selling $2,000 of inventory. Cash sales are $5,000 and a local business who purchased items for a conference owes Flynt's $500.

Record the transactions into T-accounts for Flynt's. Calculate the account balances and prepare an unadjusted trial balance at March 31, 2007.

EB-4B. *Record transactions to T-accounts and prepare unadjusted trial balance.* The trial balance of Jewel's Diamond Dazzles, Inc. on November 1, 2008, lists the company's assets, liabilities, and shareholders' equity on that date. *(LO 1, 2)*

TRIAL BALANCE

Account title	Debit	Credit
Cash	$18,000	
Accounts receivable	6,500	
Inventory	7,500	
Accounts payable		$ 11,700
Common stock		8,800
Retained earnings		11,500
Total	$32,000	$32,000

During November, Diamond Dazzles completed the following transactions:

    a. The company borrowed $5,000 from the bank with a short-term note payable.

    b. Diamond Dazzles paid cash of $8,500 to acquire land.

    c. The company sold $5,000 of inventory to customers and collected the cash of $15,000.

    d. Diamond Dazzles purchased supplies on credit, $375.

    e. The company sold $1,000 of inventory to customers for $2,500 on account.

Set up T-accounts for the accounts given in the November 1 trial balance. Then post the preceding transactions to the accounts. Calculate the account balances and prepare an unadjusted trial balance at November 30.

EB-5B. *Recognize adjusting and closing entries.* Use the information from EB-4B to identify the accounts that will likely need to be adjusted before the monthly financial statements are prepared. What additional information would you need in each case to make the appropriate adjustment? Which accounts will need to be closed at the end of the accounting period and why? *(LO 3, 4)*

EB-6B. *Record closing entries and compute net income.* Given the following adjusted trial balance, record the appropriate closing entries. What is net income for the year? *(LO 4)*

LILLIAN SCURLOCK'S SKI SHOP, INC.
ADJUSTED TRIAL BALANCE
DECEMBER 31, 2008

	Debit	Credit
Cash	$ 15,000	
Accounts receivable	23,000	
Supplies	21,750	
Equipment	18,000	
Accumulated depreciation		$ 10,000
Property	72,000	
Prepaid rent	19,600	
Accounts payable		27,650
Notes payable		30,000
Interest payable		3,610
Common stock		45,500
Retained earnings		26,370[a]
Dividends	2,000	
Sales		69,220
Cost of goods sold	15,000	
Depreciation expense	5,000	
Salaries expense	21,000	
Totals	$212,350	$212,350

[a]Retained earnings at January 1, 2008. (No accounts have been closed.)

EB-7B. *Record journal entries, adjusting entries, and explain the accounting cycle.* Health & Nutrition Importance, Inc. began business July 1, 2007. The following transactions took place during July: *(LO 1, 2, 3, 4)*

July	1	Owners invested $75,000 in exchange for common stock.
	1	The company borrowed $15,000 from a local bank with a 10% note and a 6-month term. Both the principal and interest will be repaid in 6 months.
	1	The company purchased health equipment for $25,500 cash. It should last 5 years, with no residual value.
	5	Supplies were purchased on account for $750.
	15	Rent of $675 for July was paid in cash.
	23	The company received $3,500 in customer dues (service revenues) for the month of August.
	31	Health consulting services performed during July on account totaled $15,000.
	31	The company paid salaries of $6,000 to employees.
	31	The company paid $500 to the supplies vendor as part of the $750 owed to the vendor from the purchase on July 5. The company only paid part of the invoice because it only used $500 worth of the supplies in July.

Required: Give the journal entry for each transaction. Provide the reason for each entry. Then, make the necessary adjusting entries at July 31, 2007. What else should be done to finish the accounting cycle for the month?

EB-8B. *Record journal entries, post to T-Accounts, and prepare unadjusted trial balance.* Brunetta decided to open her own dry cleaning shop, Prestige Dry Cleaners, Inc. The following transactions are the events which occurred during April 2009, the company's first month: *(LO 1, 2)*

April	1	Brunetta donated $45,000 cash in exchange for common stock. She also signed a note with 1st Regional Bank for $30,000.
April	3	Prestige Dry Cleaners rented out a store at a shopping center and paid $14,400 prepaid rent for the first year.
April	10	Dry cleaning equipment was purchased on account for $21,250.
April	19	The company purchased insurance for 3 years with $5,400 cash. The policy was effective May 1.
April	21	A damaged iron (part of the dry cleaning equipment) arrived and the supplier agreed to remove $3,150 from Prestige Dry Cleaners' account.
April	24	The company purchased furniture for $6,000 for Brunetta's office on account.
April	27	Prestige Dry Cleaners paid off the balance owed on the equipment.
April	30	Three employees were hired at a rate of $56 a day each. Their start date is May 1.

Required: Give the journal entry for each transaction. Set up the required T-accounts and post the entries to these accounts. Prepare an unadjusted trial balance.

Problems—Set A

PB-1A. *Prepare a trial balance and financial statements.* The following is account information for Gifford's Ceramics Corporation as of June 30, 2007. *(LO 1, 2)*

Revenue	$20,000
Prepaid rent	2,000
Equipment	10,000
Accumulated depreciation, equipment	3,000
Common stock	5,000[a]
Accounts receivable	5,000
Accounts payable	2,000
Salaries expense	2,000
Depreciation expense	1,000
Cash	1,000
Inventory	8,000
Dividends	1,000

[a]Balance at July 1, 2006. (No additional common stock has been issued during the year.)

Required: Prepare a trial balance at June 30, 2007, income statement and statement of changes in shareholders' equity for the year ended June 30, 2007, and balance sheet at June 30, 2007.

PB-2A. *Record journal entries, post to T-Accounts, and prepare unadjusted trial balance.* Architectural Design and Associates, Inc. began business on May 1, 2009. The following transactions were entered into by the firm during its first two months of business, May and June: *(LO 1, 2)*

May	1	Common stock was issued to investors in the amount of $275,000.
	1	Architectural Design signed a long-term note with 1st Regional Bank for $65,000.
	9	The company purchased an office building with cash for $130,500.
	13	Equipment was purchased on account for $35,000.
	20	Supplies worth $3,500 were purchased with cash.
	27	Architectural Design paid for equipment that was purchased on May 13.
	30	The company purchased a 2-year insurance policy that began on June 1 with cash for $4,800.

30	The city utility bill for $675 was received by Architectural Design. The utility bill is always due the 15th of the following month and will be paid then.	
June 1	Architectural Design purchased some inventory on account for $50,000.	
3	The company purchased some advertising in a local newspaper and on a local radio station for $5,000 cash.	
15	May's utility bill for $675 was paid (note that the bill was recorded as a payable in May).	
30	June salaries of $12,500 were owed to employees who started during the month. Salaries are always paid the last day of the month earned.	
30	Architectural Design earned service revenues of $60,000 for the month, of which $15,000 were on account.	
30	The city utility bill for $625 was received by Architectural Design.	

Required:
1. Give the journal entry for each transaction.
2. Post each transaction to T-accounts.
3. Prepare an unadjusted trial balance.

PB-3A. *Prepare closing entries and financial statements.* Tia's Cotton Fabrics, Inc. has the following account information on its adjusted trial balance. *(LO 3, 4)*

TIA'S COTTON FABRICS, INC.
ADJUSTED TRIAL BALANCE
MARCH 31, 2008

	Debit	Credit
Cash	$ 24,000	
Accounts receivable	28,000	
Supplies	15,250	
Equipment	25,000	
Accumulated depreciation		$ 7,500
Property	44,000	
Prepaid rent	9,500	
Accounts payable		24,805
Notes payable		17,650
Interest payable		2,175
Common stock		23,650[a]
Retained earnings		35,000[b]
Dividends	4,000	
Sales		97,675
Gain on sale of equipment		7,450
Cost of goods sold	51,475	
Depreciation expense	2,500	
Salaries expense	12,180	
Totals	$215,905	$215,905

[a]Balance at April 1, 2007. (No common stock has been issued during the year.)
[b]Balance at April 1, 2007. (No closing entries have been made.)

Required: Prepare the necessary closing entries and the income statement, statement of changes in shareholders' equity for the year ended March 31, 2008, and balance sheet as of March 31, 2008.

PB-4A. *Record adjusting journal entries, post to T-Accounts, and prepare closing entries.* Gourmet Teas & Coffee, Inc. has the following account balances at the end of the year: *(LO 1, 2, 3, 4)*

Prepaid insurance	$ 4,000
Rental income	35,670
Unearned rental income	3,800
Accumulated depreciation	7,625
Salaries payable	5,550
Taxes expense	4,398
Depreciation expense	7,625
Salaries expense	10,400

The following information is available at the end of the year:
a. $1,000 worth of the prepaid insurance has not yet expired.
b. Of the unearned rental income only $1,500 remains unearned.
c. The business actually owes salaries of $5,500; the accountant recorded $50 extra by mistake.
d. The company owes an additional $4,700 in property taxes, not yet recorded.
e. Due to a clerical error, the depreciation expense amount is incorrect. It has been recalculated, and the total depreciation expense should be $8,750 for the year.

Required:
1. Prepare the journal entries necessary to adjust the accounts.
2. Use T-accounts to compute and present the balances in these accounts after the adjustments have been posted.
3. Prepare the closing entries.

PB-5A. *Record business transactions and prepare financial statements.* Salwa opened a tropical fish store as a corporation and called Exotic_Aquatics.com, selling only via the Internet. During 2009, Salwa's company had the following transactions: *(LO 1, 2, 3, 4)*
a. The business was started with Salwa's contribution of $16,500 in exchange for common stock on January 1.
b. The company borrowed $10,000 from First American Bank at 7.5% for 12 months on January 1.
c. The company purchased $6,000 in inventory for cash on February 15.
d. The company paid $3,600 of rent to a Webmaster on June 30 for use of a maintained website for two years starting July 1.
e. The company had cash sales of $11,100 for 2009 with cost of goods sold of $2,500.
f. The company paid $1,050 in advertising fees.

Required:
1. Post the above transactions to T-account to determine the balance of each account on December 31, 2009; include any adjusting transactions necessary.
2. Prepare the adjusted trial balance at December 31, 2009, the income statement, statement of changes in shareholder's equity, a statement of cash flows for the year ended December 31, 2009, and the balance sheet.
3. Prepare the closing entries and the postclosing trial balance at December 31, 2009.

PB-6A. *Record business transactions.* A partial list of transactions from Quality Auto Repair, Inc. during 2010 follows: *(LO 1, 2, 3, 4)*
a. Mark, Dave, & Glen each donated $6,500 in exchange for common stock to start the business.
b. On February 1, 2010, the shop paid $12,000 for 2 years rent in advance.
c. The shop purchased $8,000 of supplies for cash.
d. On March 15, 2010, the shop obtained necessary equipment for $12,000 cash. The equipment should last for 5 years. The company will take a full year of depreciation in 2010.
e. On April 1, 2010, the shop paid an annual insurance premium of $1,000, for coverage beginning April 1.
f. On June 1, 2010, to increase business, the company paid for a year of advertising for $1,020.
g. On November 1, 2010, the company obtained a 3-month loan for $30,000 at 12% from Three Rivers Bank payable on February 1, 2011.

h. As of December 31, 2010, cash revenues totaled $30,000.
i. At the close of business on December 31, the company entered into a contract with a local company to do all their auto repairs in 2011 for $8,000 payable in four installments (beginning on March 1, 2011).
j. On December 31, the company paid $1,000 in cash dividends.

[Note: at the end of the year, remaining supplies totaled $2,000.]

Required:
1. Give the journal entries for the transactions; include any adjusting entries.
2. Post the transactions to T-Accounts and prepare the adjusted trial balance at December 31, 2010.
3. Prepare the closing entries and post-closing trial balance for Quality Auto Repair, Inc. at December 31, 2010

PB-7A. *Analyze business transactions and prepare financial statements.* The accounting department for Fun in the Great Outdoors Resort, Inc. recorded the following journal entries for 2007, the first year of business. Fun in the Great Outdoors generates revenue by renting mountainside cottages to vacationers to the area. When a reservation is made in advance, Fun in the Great Outdoors collects half the week's rent to hold the reservation; however, Fun in the Great Outdoors does not require reservations, and sometimes customers will come in to rent a unit the same day. These types of transactions require that Fun in the Great Outdoors' accounting department record some cash receipts as unearned revenues and others as earned revenues. *(LO 1, 2, 3, 4)*

	DESCRIPTION	DEBIT	CREDIT
a.	Cash	50,000	
	Common stock		50,000
b.	Office supplies	300	
	Accounts payable		300
c.	Prepaid rent	12,000	
	Cash		12,000
d.	Building	225,000	
	Note payable		225,000
e.	Cash	5,000	
	Unearned rent revenue		5,000
f.	Utilities expense	225	
	Cash		225
g.	Accounts payable	300	
	Cash		300
h.	Cash	12,000	
	Rent revenue		12,000
i.	Unearned rent revenue	3,000	
	Rent revenue		3,000
j.	Supplies expense	130	
	Supplies		130
k.	Rent expense	6,000	
	Prepaid rent		6,000
l.	Interest expense	100	
	Interest payable		100
m.	Depreciation expense	1,500	
	Accumulated depreciation—building		1,500
n.	Dividends	5,000	
	Cash		5,000
o.	Salary expense	1,200	
	Salaries payable		1,200

Required:

    a. Explain the transaction or event that resulted in each journal entry.

    b. Post entries a through o to T-accounts and calculate the balance in each account.

    c. Did Fun in the Great Outdoors generate net income or net loss for the period ending December 31, 2007? How can you tell?

    d. Prepare the four financial statements required at year-end.

    e. Prepare the closing entries.

PB-8A. *Record business transactions and prepare financial statements* The accounting records for Shelby & Sammy Pet Boarders, Inc. contained the following balances as of December 31, 2010: *(LO 1, 2, 3, 4)*

	Assets		Liabilities and equity	
Cash	$40,000	Accounts payable	$17,000
Accounts receivable	16,500	Common stock	45,000
Land	20,000	Retained earnings	14,500
Totals	$76,500		$76,500

The following accounting events apply to Shelby & Sammy Pet Boarders, Inc.'s 2011 fiscal year:

Jan. 1   The company acquired an additional $20,000 cash from the owners by issuing common stock.

    1   Pet Boarders purchased a computer that cost $17,000 for cash. The computer had a $2,000 salvage value and a 3-year useful life.

Mar. 1   The company borrowed $10,000 by issuing a 1-year note at 12%.

May 1   The company paid $2,400 cash in advance for a 1-year lease for office space.

June 1   The company made a $5,000 cash distribution to the shareholders.

July 1   The company purchased land that cost $10,000 cash.

Aug. 1   Cash payments on accounts payable amounted to $6,000.

    1   Pet Boarders received $9,600 cash in advance for 12 months of service to be performed monthly for the next year, beginning on receipt of payment.

Sept. 1   Pet Boarders sold land for $13,000 cash. The land originally cost $13,000.

Oct. 1   Pet Boarders purchased $1,300 of supplies on account.

Nov. 1   Pet Boarders purchased a 1-year, $20,000 certificate of deposit at 6%.

Dec. 31   The company earned service revenue on account during the year that amounted to $40,000.

    31   Cash collections from accounts receivable amounted to $44,000.

    31   The company incurred other operating expenses on account during the year of $6,000.

    31   Salaries that had been earned by the sales staff but not yet paid amounted to $2,300.

    31   Supplies worth $200 were on hand at the end of the period.

    31   Based on the preceding transaction data, there are five additional adjustments that need to be made before the financial statements can be prepared.

Required: Post the journal entries to T-accounts, make the appropriate adjustments, prepare an adjusted trial balance, and prepare the financial statements (all four) for 2011. Then prepare the closing entries and the postclosing trial balance.

Problems—Set B

PB-1B. *Prepare a trial balance and financial statements.* The following account information pertains to Carrie & Runnels Bikes Plus, Inc. as of December 31, 2010.

Sales	$22,000	Other revenue	$13,000
Prepaid advertising	2,000	Equipment	10,000
Common stock	14,000ᵃ	Accounts receivable	5,000
Accounts payable	4,000	Cost of goods sold	11,000
Operating expense	3,000	Cash	2,000
Inventory	18,000	Dividends	2,000

ᵃBalance at January 1, 2010. (No additional common stock has been issued during the year.)

Required: Prepare a trial balance at December 31, 2010, income statement and statement of changes in shareholders' equity for the year ended December 31, 2010, and balance sheet as of December 31, 2010.

PB-2B. *Record journal entries, post to T-Accounts, and prepare unadjusted trial balance.* Cell Phones, Palm Pilots & More, Inc. began business on February 1, 2008. The following transactions were entered into by the firm during its first two months of business, February and March: *(LO 1, 2)*

Feb. 1 Common stock was issued to investors in the amount of $305,000.

1 Cell Phones, Palm Pilots & More signed a long-term note with National Bank for $70,000.

8 The company purchased a store front building with cash for $125,000.

12 Equipment was purchased on account for $45,000.

20 Supplies worth $4,300 were purchased with cash.

28 Cell Phones, Palm Pilots & More paid for equipment that was purchased on February 12.

29 The company purchased a 2-year insurance policy that began on March 1 with cash for $5,000.

29 The city utility bill for $475 was received by Cell Phones, Palm Pilots & More. The utility bill is always due the 12th of the following month and will be paid then.

Mar. 1 Cell Phones, Palm Pilots & More purchased some inventory on account for $65,000.

3 The company purchased some advertising in a local newspaper and on a local radio station for $3,500 cash.

12 February's utility bill for $475 was paid (note that the bill was recorded as a payable in Feb.).

31 March salaries of $14,150 were owed to employees who started during the month. Salaries are always paid on the last day of the month earned.

31. Cell Phones, Palm Pilots & More earned sales revenues of $125,000 for the month, of which $35,000 were on account. Cost of inventory sold was $31,250.

31. The city utility bill for $425 was received by Cell Phones, Palm Pilots & More.

Required: Give the journal entry for each transaction. Post each transaction to T-accounts. Prepare an unadjusted trial balance at March 31, 2008.

PB-3B. *Prepare closing entries and financial statements.* Here is an adjusted trial balance from Shamara's Lighting Solutions, Inc. *(LO 3, 4)*

SHAMARA'S LIGHTING SOLUTIONS, INC.
ADJUSTED TRIAL BALANCE
DECEMBER 31, 2007

	Debit	Credit
Cash	$ 32,655	
Accounts receivable	52,000	
Prepaid rent	11,250	
Equipment	40,000	
Accumulated depreciation		$ 10,000
Land	25,755	
Prepaid insurance	6,800	
Salaries payable		1,250
Notes payable		16,875
Interest payable		1,820
Common stock		25,000[a]
Retained earnings		48,000[b]
Dividends	3,500	
Sales		151,595
Cost of goods sold	46,880	
Rent expense	14,000	
Insurance expense	1,200	
Depreciation expense	5,000	
Salaries expense	15,500	
Totals	$254,540	$254,540

[a]Balance at December 31, 2006. (No common stock has been issued during the year.)

[b]Balance at December 31, 2006. (No closing entries have been made.)

Required: Prepare the necessary closing entries, the income statement, and the statement of changes in shareholders' equity for the year ended December 31, 2007, and balance sheet as of December 31, 2007.

PB-4B. *Record adjusting journal entries, post to T-Accounts, and prepare closing entries.* Indoor Sun Solutions, Inc. has the following account balances at the end of the year: *(LO 1, 2, 3, 4)*

Service revenue	$34,320
Insurance expense	$4,000
Unearned service revenue	3,200
Salaries payable	2,550
Accumulated depreciation	2,000
Taxes expense	3,650
Depreciation expense	2,000
Salaries expense	8,250

The following information is also available:
1. The company accountant forgot to depreciate the matrix tanning bed that was purchased at the beginning of the year. The matrix tanning bed cost $24,000, has a useful life of 6 years, and has no expected residual value.
2. The unearned service revenue consists of gift certificates sold during the year. Indoor Sun Solutions has lost track of customers redeeming certificates, but only $1,200 of the gift certificates have not been redeemed.

3. The company currently owes employees $200 of salaries in addition to those given here.
4. The company owes an additional $1,075 in real estate taxes.
5. Only $2,000 of insurance expenses were incurred; the other $2,000 should still be accounted for as prepaid.

Required:
   a. Prepare the adjusting journal entries necessary at year-end.
   b. Use T-accounts to compute and present the balances in these accounts after the adjustments have been posted.
   c. Prepare the closing journal entries.

PB-5B. *Record business transactions and prepare financial statements.* Darinda and Sue started Granny Apple Delicious, Inc. on July 1, 2007 to sell their famous applesauce. The following transactions occurred during the year. *(LO 1, 2, 3, 4)*
   a. Darinda and Sue started the business by contributing $15,000 each in exchange for common stock on July 1.
   b. Also on July the company borrowed $20,000 from Local Bank at 9.5%. The loan was for 1 year.
   c. The company purchased $10,000 worth of apples and other inventory during the year.
   d. The company grew and needed to rent a shop. They paid $27,000 for rent on the shop for 18 months, beginning January 1.
   e. Granny Apple Delicious, Inc. sold $36,000 worth of applesauce for cash during the first fiscal year and of the inventory purchased in c. only $1,000 remained.
   f. Granny Apple Delicious, Inc. paid $1,525 in operating expenses.

Required:
   1. Post the above transactions to T-accounts to determine the balance of each account on June 30, 2008; include any adjusting transactions necessary.
   2. Prepare the adjusted trial balance, the income statement, statement of changes in shareholder's equity, balance sheet, and a statement of cash flows.
   3. Prepare the closing entries and the postclosing trial balance.

PB-6B. *Record business transactions.* The following information is a partial list of transactions from Home Cleaning Service, Inc. *(LO 1, 2, 3, 4)*
   a. Brenda, Don, Michael, Trina, and McKenzie each donated $3,250 in exchange for common stock to start the business on January 1, 2009.
   b. On March 1, Home Cleaning paid $6,000 cash for a 2-year insurance policy that was effective immediately.
   c. On March 15, the company purchased $10,000 of supplies on account.
   d. On April 5, the company purchased some cleaning equipment for $8,000 cash. The equipment should last for 5 years with no residual value. Home Cleaning will take a full year of depreciation in 2009.
   e. On May 1, Home Cleaning purchased a year's worth of advertising in a local newspaper for $1,500 cash.
   f. On September 1, Home Cleaning obtained a 9-month loan for $15,000 at 12% from City National Bank, with interest and principal payable on June 1, 2010.
   g. On December 31 Home Cleaning paid $7,000 of what it owed on account for supplies from c.; the company had $3,000 of the supplies still on hand at the end of the year.
   h. For the year ending December 31, 2009, Home Cleaning had revenues of $26,225. The cash had been received for all but $3,000.
   i. Home Cleaning paid $1,170 in cash dividends on December 31, 2009.

Required:

1. Give the journal entries for the transactions; include any adjusting entries.
2. Post the transactions to T-Accounts and prepare the adjusted trial balance at December 31, 2009.
3. Prepare the closing entries and post-closing trial balance for Home Cleaning Service, Inc. at December 31, 2009.

PB-7B.   *Analyze business transactions and prepare financial statements.* The accounting department for Entertainment Activities, Inc. recorded the following journal entries for the fiscal year ended June 30, 2007. Entertainment Activities generates revenue by selling tickets for local events such as concerts, fights, and sporting events. Sometimes tickets are sold in advance and sometimes customers will purchase their tickets the same day as the event. These types of transactions require that Entertainment Activities accounting department record some cash receipts as unearned revenues and others as earned revenues. *(LO 2, 3, 4)*

	DESCRIPTION	DEBIT	CREDIT
a.	Cash	150,000	
	Common stock		150,000
b.	Office Supplies	475	
	Accounts payable		475
c.	Prepaid rent	18,000	
	Cash		18,000
d.	Building	375,000	
	Note payable		375,000
e.	Cash	16,000	
	Unearned ticket revenue		16,000
f.	Utilities expense	525	
	Cash		525
g.	Accounts payable	475	
	Cash		475
h.	Cash	50,000	
	Ticket revenue		50,000
i.	Unearned ticket revenue	10,000	
	Ticket revenue		10,000
j.	Supplies expense	300	
	Supplies		300
k.	Rent expense	7,000	
	Prepaid rent		7,000
l.	Interest expense	225	
	Interest payable		225
m.	Depreciation expense	2,000	
	Accumulated depreciation—building		2,000
n.	Dividends	7,500	
	Cash		7,500
o.	Salary expense	5,500	
	Salaries payable		5,500

Required:

1. Explain the transaction or event that resulted in each journal entry.
2. Post entries a. through o. to T-accounts and calculate the balance in each account.
3. Did Entertainment Activities generate net income or net loss for the fiscal year ending June 30, 2007? How can you tell?
4. Prepare the four financial statements required at year-end.
5. Prepare the closing entries.

PB-8B. *Record business transactions and prepare financial statements* The accounting records for Juan Electric & Communications Corporation contained the following balances as of December 31, 2008: *(LO 1, 2, 3, 4)*

	Assets	Liabilities and shareholders' equity	
Cash	$50,000	Accounts payable	$17,500
Accounts receivable	26,500	Common stock	48,600
Prepaid rent (through 04/30/2009)	3,600	Retained earnings	24,500
Land	10,500		
Totals	$90,600		$90,600

The following accounting events apply to Juan Electric & Communications Corporation's 2009 fiscal year:

Jan. 1   Juan Electric purchased a computer that cost $20,000 for cash. The computer had a $2,000 salvage value and a 3-year useful life.

Mar. 1   The company borrowed $20,000 by issuing a 2-year note at 12%.

May 1   The company paid $6,000 cash in advance for a 6-month lease for office space. The lease started immediately.

June 1   The company paid cash dividends of $2,000 to the shareholders.

July 1   The company purchased land that cost $15,000 cash.

Aug. 1   Cash payments on accounts payable amounted to $6,000.

1   Juan Electric received $6,000 cash in advance for 12 months of service to be performed monthly for the next year, beginning on receipt of payment.

Sept. 1   Juan Electric sold land for $13,000 cash. The land originally cost $15,000.

Oct. 1   Juan Electric purchased $1,300 of supplies on account.

Nov. 1   Juan Electric purchased a 1-year, $10,000 certificate of deposit at 5%.

Dec. 31   The company earned service revenue on account during the year that amounted to $50,000.

31   Cash collections from accounts receivable amounted to $46,000.

31   The company incurred other operating expenses on account during the year that amounted to $6,000.

Also: Salaries that had been earned by the sales staff but not yet paid amounted to $2,300.

There was $200 of supplies on hand at the end of the period.

Based on the preceding transaction data, there are some additional adjustments that need to be made before the financial statements can be prepared.

Required: Give the journal entries for the transactions; include any adjusting entries. Post the journal entries to T-accounts, prepare an adjusted trial balance, and prepare the financial statements (all four) for 2009. Then prepare the closing entries and the post-closing trial balance.

Issues for Discussion

Financial statement analysis
1. Use the annual report from Staples, Inc. to answer these questions:
   a. When you look at the financial statements for Staples, can you tell if the company uses a general ledger accounting system? Explain.
   b. Find at least four pieces of quantitative information contained in the Staples annual report that would not be found in a general ledger system.
2. Who are the auditors for Staples?
3. How does having an audit affect business risk?

Ethics

Companies often try to manage earnings by recognizing revenue before it is actually earned according to GAAP or deferring expenses that have been incurred. For example, to meet the targeted earnings for a specific period, a company may capitalize a cost that should be expensed. Read the following scenario and then decide how you would handle this opportunity to manage earnings.

You are a division manager of a large public company. Your bonus is calculated on your division's net income targets that you must meet. This year that target is $1.5 million. You are authorized to sign off on any decision made within your division. You are faced with the following situation:

On December 15, 2008, your division of the company ordered $150,000 worth of supplies in anticipation for the seasonal rush. Most of them will be used by year-end. These supplies were delivered on the evening of December 27. If you record this supplies expense this year, your net income will be $1.45 million and you will not meet the target and will therefore not receive your bonus of $25,000 that you have worked hard for. (Your company generally expenses supplies when purchased.) If you do record this expense this year for the year ended December 31, 2008, then you and some of your support employees will not receive a bonus.

What would you do and why?

Internet Exercise: Intuit Inc.

The accounting cycle illustrated in this chapter may be simplified with the aid of a computerized general ledger system. Intuit Inc. is a leader in e-finance and develops and supports Quicken®, the leading personal finance software; TurboTax®, the best-selling tax preparation software; and QuickBooks®, the most popular small business accounting software.

Please go to the www.prenhall.com/reimers Web site. Go to Appendix B and use the Internet Exercise company link.

IEB-1.
a. Briefly summarize the top story in Today's News.
b. In the "Get Quotes and Research" section type INTU, the stock symbol of Intuit Inc., and then click on Go. Review the information provided and comment on one item of interest.

IEB-2. *In the left-hand column click on Financial Statements.* For the most recent year list the amounts reported for cash, common stock, total revenues, and interest expense. Note that these amounts are reported in thousands.
a. Which financial statement reports each of these amounts?
b. What was the beginning balance for each of these accounts?
c. Which of these accounts is a real account?
d. Which of these accounts is closed at the end of the accounting period?
e. Which of these accounts has a normal debit balance?
f. Which of these accounts might be affected by an adjusting journal entry? Explain why the account might need to be adjusted.

IEA-3. What are the advantages of a computerized general ledger system such as QuickBooks® developed by Intuit? Is it important to understand the accounting cycle even though computerized general ledger systems are available? Explain why or why not.

Please note: Internet Web sites are constantly being updated. Therefore, if the information is not found where indicated, please explore the Web site further to find the information.

Glossary

A

Accelerated depreciation is a depreciation method in which more depreciation expense is taken in the early years of the asset's life and less in the later years.

Accounts payable are amounts that a company owes its vendors. They are liabilities and are shown on the balance sheet.

Accounts receivable is a current asset that arises from sales on credit; it is also the total amount customers owe the firm.

The **accounts receivable (AR) turnover ratio** is a ratio that measures how quickly a firm collects its accounts receivable. It is defined as credit sales divided by average accounts receivable.

An **accrual** is a transaction in which the revenue has been earned or the expense has been incurred but no cash has been exchanged.

Accrual accounting refers to the way we recognize revenues and expenses. Accountants do not rely on the exchange of cash to determine the timing of revenue recognition. Firms recognize revenue when it is earned and expenses when they are incurred no matter when the cash is received or disbursed. Accrual accounting follows the matching principle.

Accumulated depreciation is the reduction to the cost of the asset. Accumulated depreciation is a contra-asset, deducted from the cost of the asset for the balance sheet.

Activity method depreciation is the method of depreciation in which useful life is expressed in terms of the total units of activity or production expected from the asset, and the asset is written off in proportion to its activity during the accounting period.

Adjusting the books means to make changes in the accounting records, at the end of the period, just before the financial statements are prepared, to make sure the amounts reflect the financial condition of the company at that date.

An **aging schedule** is an analysis of the amounts owed to a firm by the length of time they have been outstanding.

Allowance for uncollectible accounts is a contra-asset account, the balance of which represents the total amount the firm believes it will not collect from its total accounts receivable.

Allowance method is a method of accounting for bad debts in which the amount of the uncollectible accounts is estimated at the end of each accounting period.

Amortization means to write off the cost of a long-term asset over more than one accounting period.

Annuity A series of equal cash receipts on cash payments oven equally space intervals of time.

Assets are the economic resources owned or controlled by a company, resulting from past transactions.

Authorized shares are shares of stock that are available for a firm to issue per its corporate charter.

Available-for-sale securities: Investments the company may hold or sell; the company's intention is not clear enough to use one of the other categories *held to maturity* or *trading*.

B

Bad debts expense is the expense to record uncollectible accounts receivable.

The **balance sheet** is one of the four major financial statements. It shows the amounts of a firm's assets, liabilities, and owners' equity at a specific point in time.

A **bank reconciliation** is a comparison between the cash balance in the firm's accounting records and the cash balance on the bank statement to identify the reasons for any differences.

A **bank statement** is a summary of the activity in a bank account sent each month to the account holder.

The **book value** of an asset is the cost minus the accumulated depreciation related to the asset.

The **books** are a company's accounting records.

A **bond** is an interest-bearing, long-term note payable issued by corporations, universities, and governmental agencies.

Bonds issued at a discount are bonds issued for an amount less than the face value of the bond. This happens when the market rate of interest is greater than the bond's stated rate of interest.

Bonds issued at par are bonds issued for the face value of the bond. This happens when the market rate of interest is equal to the bond's stated rate of interest.

Bonds issued at a premium are bonds issued for an amount more than the face value of the bond. This happens when the market rate of interest is less than the bond's stated rate of interest.

C

Capital, as shown on a balance sheet, is the combined contributed capital and earned capital retained earnings of a sole proprietorship or partnership.

Capital is a term often used to describe the resources used to start and run a business.

A **capital expenditure** is a cost that is recorded as an asset, not an expense, at the time it is incurred. This is also called *capitalizing* a cost.

Capital structure is the combination of debt and equity that a firm uses to finance its business.

To **capitalize** is to record a cost as an asset rather than to record it as an expense.

Carrying value is another expression for book value.

Cash basis accounting is a system based on the exchange of cash. In this system, revenue is recognized only when cash is collected, and an expense is recognized only when cash is disbursed. This is not an acceptable method of accounting under GAAP.

Cash equivalents are highly liquid investments with a maturity of 3 months or less that a firm can easily convert into a known amount of cash.

A **certified public accountant (CPA)** is someone who has met specific education and exam requirements set up by individual states to make sure that only individuals with the appropriate qualifications can perform audits. To sign an audit report, an accountant must be a CPA.

A **classified balance sheet** shows a subtotal for many items, including current assets and current liabilities.

Common stock is the most widespread form of ownership in a corporation; common shareholders have a vote in the election of the firm's board of directors.

Comparative balance sheets are the balance sheets from consecutive fiscal years for a single company.

Comprehensive income The total of all items that affect shareholders' equity except transactions with the owners; comprehensive income has two parts: net income and other comprehensive income.

Contingent liabilities are potential liabilities that depend on a future event related to some past action.

A **contra-asset** is an amount that is deducted from an asset.

A **contra-revenue** is an account that is an offset to a revenue account and therefore deducted from the revenue for the financial statements.

Contributed capital, sometimes called **paid-in capital**, is the amount the owners have put into the business.

Cooking the books A slang expression that means to manipulate or falsify the firm's accounting records to make the firm's financial performance or position look better than it actually is.

A **copyright** is a form of legal protection for authors of "original works of authorship," provided by U.S. law.

A **corporation** is a special legal form for a business in which the business is a legal entity separate from the owners. A corporation may have a single owner or a large number of owners.

Corporate governance The way a firm governs itself, as executed by the board of directors. Corporate governance is also described as the set of relationships between the board of directors, management, shareholders, auditors, and any others with a stake in the company.

Cost of goods available for sale is the total of beginning inventory plus the net purchases made during the period (plus any freight-in costs).

Current assets are the assets the company plans to turn into cash or use to generate revenue in the next fiscal year.

Current liabilities are liabilities the company will pay off in the next fiscal year.

Current ratio is a liquidity ratio that measures a firm's ability to meet its short-term obligations.

D

Declining balance depreciation is an accelerated depreciation method in which depreciation expense is based on the declining book value of the asset.

A **deferral** is a transaction in which the cash is exchanged before the revenue is earned or the expense is incurred.

Definitely determinable liabilities are obligations that can be measured exactly.

Depletion is the amortization of a natural resource.

A **deposit in transit** is a bank deposit the firm has made but is not included on the month's bank statement because the deposit did not reach the bank's record-keeping department in time to be included on the current bank statement.

Depreciating an asset means to recognize the cost of the asset as an expense over more than one period.

Depreciation is a systematic and rational allocation process to recognize the expense of long-term assets over the periods in which the assets are used.

The **direct method** shows every cash inflow and outflow to prepare the statement of cash flows.

The **direct write-off method** is a method of accounting for bad debts in which they are recorded as an expense in the period in which they are identified as uncollectible.

Discount on bonds payable is a contra-liability that is deducted from bonds payable on the balance sheet; it is the difference between the face value of the bond and its selling price, when the selling price is less than the face (par) value.

Discontinued operations Those parts of the firm that a company has eliminated by selling a division.

The **discount rate** is the interest rate used to compute the present value of future cash flows.

Discounting means to compute the present value of future cash flows.

Dividend yield ratio Dividend per share divided by the current market price per share.

Dividends are the distribution of a corporation's earnings to shareholders.

E

Earnings per share (EPS) Net income divided by the weighted average number of outstanding shares of (common) stock.

Estimated liabilities are obligations that have some uncertainty in the amount, such as the cost to honor a warranty.

Expenses are the costs incurred to generate revenue.

Extraordinary items Events that are unusual in nature and infrequent in occurrence.

F

The **Financial Accounting Standards Board (FASB)** is the group that sets accounting standards. It gets its authority from the SEC.

Financial leverage is the use of borrowed funds to increase earnings.

Financial services companies deal in services related to money.

First-in, first-out (FIFO) is the inventory cost flow method that assumes the first items purchased are the first items sold.

A **fiscal year** is a year in the life of a business. It may or may not coincide with the calendar year.

FOB (free on board) destination means that the vendor (selling firm) pays the shipping costs, so the buyer has no freight-in cost.

FOB (free on board) shipping point means the buying firm pays the shipping costs. The amount is called freight-in and is included in the cost of the inventory.

A **for-profit firm** has the goal of making a profit for its owners.

A **franchise** is an agreement that authorizes someone to sell or distribute a company's goods or services in a certain area.

Free cash flow is equal to cash from operating activities minus dividends and minus capital expenditures.

The **full-disclosure principle** means that the firm must disclose any circumstances and events that would make a difference to the users of the financial statements.

G

Generally accepted accounting principles (GAAP) are the guidelines for financial reporting.

The **going-concern assumption** means that, unless there is obvious evidence to the contrary, a firm is expected to continue operating in the foreseeable future.

Goodwill is the excess of cost over market value of the net assets when one company purchases another company.

Gross profit ratio is equal to the gross profit (sales minus cost of goods sold) divided by sales. It is a ratio for evaluating firm performance.

H

Held-to-maturity securities Investments in debt securities that the company plans to hold until they mature.

The **historical-cost principle** means that transactions are recorded at actual cost.

Horizontal analysis A technique for evaluating financial statement amounts across time.

I

The **income statement** shows all revenues minus all expenses for an accounting period a month, a quarter, or a year.

Impairment is a permanent decline in the fair market value of an asset such that its book value exceeds its fair market value.

The **indirect method** starts with net income and makes adjustments for items that are not cash to prepare the statement of cash flows.

Intangible assets are rights, privileges, or benefits that result from owning long-lived assets that do not have physical substance.

The **interest** is the cost of using someone else's money.

Interest payable is a liability. It is the amount a company owes for borrowing money (after the time period to which the interest applies has passed).

Internal controls are a company's policies and procedures to protect the assets of the firm and to ensure the accuracy and reliability of the accounting records.

The **Internal Revenue Service (IRS)** is the federal agency responsible for federal income tax collection.

The **inventory turnover ratio** is defined as cost of goods sold divided by average inventory. It is a measure of how quickly a firm sells its inventory.

Issued shares are shares of stock that have been offered and sold to shareholders.

L

Last-in, first-out (LIFO) is the inventory cost flow method that assumes the last items purchased are the first items sold.

Liabilities are obligations the company has incurred to obtain the assets it has acquired.

Liquidity is a measure of how easily an asset can be converted to cash. The more liquid an asset is, the more easily it can be turned into cash.

Liquidity ratios measure the company's ability to pay its current bills and operating costs.

The **lower-of-cost-or-market (LCM) rule** is the rule that requires firms to use the lower of either the cost or the market value (replacement cost) of its inventory on the date of the balance sheet.

M

The **maker** of a note is the person or firm making the promise to pay.

A **manufacturing** company makes the goods it sells.

Market indicators ratios relate the current market price of the company's stock to earnings or dividends.

The **market rate of interest** is the interest rate that an investor could earn in an equally risky investment.

The **matching principle** says that expenses should be recognized shown on the income statement in the same period as the revenue they helped generate.

A **merchandising** company sells a product to its customers.

The **monetary-unit assumption** means that the items on the financial statements are measured in monetary units (dollar in the U.S.).

A **multistep income statement** starts with sales and subtracts cost of goods sold to get a subtotal called gross profit on sales, also known as gross margin. Then, other operating revenues are added and other operating expenses are deducted. A subtotal for operating income is shown before deductions related to nonoperating items and taxes are deducted. Then, income taxes are subtracted, leaving net income.

N

Net income equals all revenues minus all expenses for a specific period of time.

Noncurrent assets, or **long-term assets,** are assets that will last for more than a year.

Noncurrent liabilities, or **long-term liabilities**, are liabilities that will take longer than a year to settle.

Notes to the financial statements are information provided with the four basic statements that describes the company's major accounting policies and provide other disclosures to help external users better understand the financial statements.

A **not-for-profit firm** has the goal of providing goods or services to its clients.

O

On account means *on credit*. The expression applies to either buying or selling on credit.

Ordinary annuities An annuity whose payments are made at the end of each interval or period.

An **outstanding check** is a check the firm has written but has not yet cleared the bank. That is, the check has not been presented to the bank for payment.

Outstanding shares are shares of stock that are owned by stockholders.

P

Paid-in capital is the amount of the owner's contributions to the firm; also known as **shareholders' equity** or **stockholders' equity.**

Par value is the monetary amount assigned to a share of stock in the corporate charter. It has little meaning in today's business environment.

A **partnership** is a company owned by two or more individuals.

A **patent** is a property right that the U.S. government grants to an inventor "to exclude others from making, using, offering for sale, or selling the invention throughout the United States or importing the invention into the United States for a specified period of time."

The **payee** of a note is the person or firm receiving the money.

The **periodic inventory system** is a method of record keeping that involves updating the accounting records only at the end of the accounting period.

The **perpetual inventory system** is a method of record keeping that involves updating the accounting records at the time of every purchase, sale, and return.

Preferred stock are shares of stock that represent a special kind of ownership in a corporation. Preferred shareholders do not get a vote but they do receive dividends before the common shareholders.

Premium on bonds payable is an adjunct-liability that is added to bonds payable on the balance sheet; it is the difference between the face value of the bond and its selling price, when the selling price is more than the face (par) value.

Prepaid insurance is the name for insurance a business has purchased but not yet used. It is an asset.

Prepaid rent is an asset. It represents amounts paid for rent not yet used. The rent expense is deferred until the rented asset has actually been used when the time related to the rent has passed.

The **present value** is the value today of a given amount of money to be invested or received in the future, assuming compound interest.

Price–earnings (P/E) ratio The market price of a share of stock divided by that stock's earnings per share.

The **principal** of a loan is the amount of money borrowed.

Profitability ratios measure the operating or income performance of a company.

A **promissory note** is a written promise to pay a specified amount of money at a specified time.

The **Public Company Accounting Oversight Board (PCAOB)** is a group formed to oversee the auditing profession and the audits of public companies. Its creation was mandated by the Sarbanes-Oxley Act of 2002.

A **purchase discount** is a reduction in the price of an inventory purchase for prompt payment according to terms specified by the vendor.

A **purchase order** is a record of the company's request to a vendor for goods or services. It may be referred to as a P.O.

Purchase returns and allowances are amounts that decrease the cost of inventory purchases due to returned or damaged merchandise.

Q

Quality of earnings Refers to how well a reported earnings number communicates the firm's true performance.

R

Realized means the cash is collected. Sometimes revenue is *recognized* before it is *realized*.

Recognized revenue is revenue that has been recorded so that it will show up on the income statement.

Relative fair market value method is a way to allocate the total cost for several assets purchased together to each of the individual assets. This method is based on the assets' individual market values.

Replacement cost is the cost to buy similar items in inventory from the supplier to replace the inventory.

Residual value, also known as *salvage value*, is the estimated value of an asset at the end of its useful life. With most depreciation methods, residual value is deducted before the calculation of depreciation expense.

Retained earnings is the total of all net income amounts minus all dividends paid in the life of the company. It is descriptively named it is the earnings that have been kept (retained) in the company. The amount of retained earnings represents the part of the owner's claims that the company has earned (i.e., not contributed). Retained earnings is *not* the same as cash.

Revenue is the amount the company has earned from providing goods or services to customers.

The **revenue-recognition principle** says that revenue should be recognized when it is earned and collection is reasonably assured.

A **risk** is a danger something that exposes a business to a potential injury or loss.

S

A **sales discount** is a reduction in the sales price of a product offered to customers for prompt payment.

Sales returns and allowances is an account that holds amounts that reduce sales due to customer returns or allowances for damaged merchandise.

Salvage value (also known as *residual value*) is the estimated value of an asset at the end of its useful life.

The **Securities and Exchange Commission (SEC)** is the governmental agency that monitors the stock market and the financial reporting of the firms that trade in the market.

Segregation of duties means that the person who has physical custody of an asset is not the same person who has record-keeping responsibilities for that asset.

The **separate-entity assumption** means that the firm's financial records and financial statements are completely separate from those of the firm's owners.

A **service company** does something for its customers;

Shareholders' equity is the name for owners' claims to the assets of the firm. It includes both contributed capital and retained earnings.

Shares of common stock are the units of ownership in a corporation.

A **single-step income statement** groups all revenues together and shows all expenses deducted from total revenue.

A **sole proprietorship** is a company with a single owner.

Solvency ratios measure the company's ability to meet its longterm obligations and to survive over a long period of time.

The **specific identification method** is the inventory cost flow method in which the actual cost of the specific goods sold is recorded as cost of goods sold.

The **statement of cash flows** shows all the cash collected and all the cash disbursed during the period. Each cash amount is classified as one of three types:

The **statement of changes in shareholder's equity** starts with the beginning amount of contributed capital and shows all changes during the accounting period. Then the statement shows the beginning balance in retained earnings with its changes. The usual changes to retained earnings are the increase from net income and the decrease from dividends paid to shareholders.

Stock dividends are new shares of stock that are distributed to the company's current shareholders.

A **stock exchange** also called the **stock market** is a marketplace where buyers and sellers exchange their shares of stock. Buying and selling shares of stock can also be done on the Internet.

A **stock split** is the division of the current shares of stock by a specific number to increase the number of shares.

Stockholders or **shareholders** are the owners of the corporation.

Straight-line depreciation is a depreciation method in which the depreciation expense is the same each period.

T

Tangible assets are assets with physical substance; they can be seen and touched.

The **time-period assumption** means that the life of a business can be divided into meaningful time periods for financial reporting.

Timing differences arise when revenues are earned and collected in different accounting periods. They also arise when expenses are incurred in one accounting period and paid for in another.

A **trademark** is a symbol, word, phrase, or logo that legally distinguishes one company's product from any others.

Trading securities Investments in debt and equity securities that the company has purchased to make a short-term profit.

Treasury stock are shares of stock that have been repurchased by the issuing firm.

U

Unearned revenue is a liability. It represents the amount of goods or services that a company owes its customers. The cash has been collected, but the action of *earning* the revenue has not taken place.

Unrealized gain or loss An increase or decrease in the market value of a company's investments in securities is recognized either on the income statement for trading securities or in other comprehensive income in the equity section of the balance sheet for available-for-sale securities when the financial statements are prepared, even though the securities have not been sold.

V

Vertical analysis A technique for comparing items on a financial statement in which all items are expressed as a percent of a common amount.

W

Working capital equals current assets minus current liabilities.

Weighted average cost is the inventory cost flow method in which the weighted average cost of the goods available for sale is used to calculate the cost of goods sold and the ending inventory.

Index